In the two hundred years from 1475 London was transformed from a medieval commune into a metropolis of half a million people, a capital city, and a major European trading centre. New possibilities emerged for cultural exchange and combination, social and political order, and literary expression. Integrating literary and historical analysis, and drawing on recent work in literary theory and cultural studies, *Literature and culture in early modern London* provides a comprehensive account of the changing image and influence of London in lyrics, ballads, jests, epics, satires, plays, pageants, chronicles, treatises, sermons, and official documents. Lawrence Manley shows how the literature and culture of London contributed to the new structures of capitalism, the process of "behavioral urbanization", and a paradoxical liberation of the individual through the city's concentrated power.

Literature and culture in early modern London

Literature and culture in early modern London

Lawrence Manley

Yale University

CAMBRIDGE UNIVERSITY PRESS
Cambridge, New York, Melbourne, Madrid, Cape Town, Singapore, São Paulo

Cambridge University Press
The Edinburgh Building, Cambridge CB2 2RU, UK

Published in the United States of America by Cambridge University Press, New York

www.cambridge.org
Information on this title: www.cambridge.org/9780521461610

First published 1995
Reprinted 1997
This digitally printed first paperback version 2005

The publishers and author gratefully acknowledge the generosity of the John
Simon Guggenheim Memorial Foundation in providing a subvention towards
the publication of this book.

A catalogue record for this publication is available from the British Library

Library of Congress Cataloguing in Publication data

Manley, Lawrence, 1949–
Literature and culture in early modern London/Lawrence Manley.
    p. cm.
Includes index.
ISBN 0 521 46161 8 (hardback)
1. English literature – Early modern, 1500–1700 – History and criticism.   2.
English literature – England – London – History and criticism.   3. Literature
and anthropology – England – London – History.   4. Literature and society –
England – London – History.   5. London (England) – History – 16th
century.   6. London (England) – History – 17th century.   7. London
(England) – In literature.   8. London (England) – Civilization.   I. Title.
PR421.M27   1995
820.9′32421–dc20   93-51069   CIP

ISBN-13 978-0-521-46161-0 hardback
ISBN-10 0-521-46161-8 hardback

ISBN-13 978-0-521-02197-5 paperback
ISBN-10 0-521-02197-9 paperback

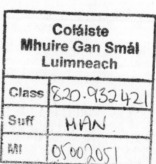

For Ruth

Contents

Illustrations

A note on conventions

Unless otherwise noted, the place of publication for early modern books is London. Spelling has not been modernized, but titles have been regularized to "maximum capitals" style. Citations of classical sources, unless otherwise indicated, are from editions in the Loeb Classical Library.

Abbreviations

BIHR	*Bulletin of the Institute of Historical Research*
CL	*Comparative Literature*
CSPD	*Calendar of State Papers, Domestic Series*
CSPV	*Calendar of State Papers, Venetian Series*
EconHR	*Economic History Review*
EETS	Early English Text Society
ELH	*English Literary History*
ELR	*English Literary Renaissance*
ES	*English Studies*
FS	*French Studies*
HLQ	*Huntington Library Quarterly*
JEGP	*Journal of English and Germanic Philology*
JWCI	*Journal of the Warburg and Courtauld Institutes*
MLN	*Modern Language Notes*
MLQ	*Modern Language Quarterly*
MLR	*Modern Language Review*
MP	*Modern Philology*
N&Q	*Notes and Queries*
PLL	*Papers on Language and Literature*
PMLA	*Publications of the Modern Language Association*
PQ	*Philological Quarterly*
RenD	*Renaissance Drama*
RenP	*Renaissance Papers*
RenQ	*Renaissance Quarterly*

RES	*Review of English Studies*
RORD	*Research Opportunities in Renaissance Drama*
SEL	*Studies in English Literature*
ShS	*Shakespeare Survey*
SP	*Studies in Philology*
SRen	*Studies in the Renaissance*
TRHS	*Transactions of the Royal Historical Society*
TSLL	*Texas Studies in Language and Literature*
UTQ	*University of Toronto Quarterly*

Acknowledgements

This book would not exist were it not for the generous assistance and good will of many individuals and institutions. Academic leaves were supported by a Morse Fellowship from Yale University and by fellowships from the American Council of Learned Societies and the John Simon Guggenheim Memorial Foundation. The Guggenheim Foundation also provided a generous subvention in support of publication.

The illustrations were obtained with support from the A. Whitney Griswold Research Fund of Yale University. For permission to publish them I am grateful to the British Museum, the Ashmolean Museum, the Royal Library in Stockholm, the Vienna Kunsthistorisches Museum, the Trier Landesmuseum, the Folger Shakespeare Library, the Society of Antiquaries, the Duke of Devonshire and the Chatsworth Trust, the Houghton Library of Harvard University, the Yale Center for British Art, the Museum of London, and the Beinecke Rare Book and Manuscript Library of Yale University.

The book contains material published previously as: "Spenser and the City: The Minor Poems," *Modern Language Quarterly* 43 (1982), 203–227; "Proverbs, Epigrams, and Urbanity in Renaissance London," *English Literary Renaissance*, 15 (1985), 247–276; "Fictions of Settlement: London, 1590," *Studies in Philology*, 88:2 (1991), 201–224; "From Matron to Monster: Tudor-Stuart London and the Languages of Urban Description," in *The Historical Renaissance: New Essays in Tudor and Stuart Literary Culture*, ed. Heather Dubrow and Richard Strier (© 1988 by The University of Chicago. All rights reserved); "Of Sites and Rites: Ceremony, Theater, and John Stow's *Survey of London*," in David Bevington, Richard Strier, and David Smith, eds., *London: The Theatrical City* (Cambridge University Press, 1995). I am grateful to these publishers for permission to incorporate that material here.

For their expertise and courtesy I wish to thank the staff at the Bishopsgate Institute, the Bodleian Library, the British Library, the

Corporation of London Records Office, the Guildhall Library, the Museum of London, the Public Records Office, the Folger Shakespeare Library, the Huntington Library, the New York Public Library, the Houghton and Widener Libraries at Harvard University, and the Beinecke and Sterling Libraries at Yale.

Among the many students, colleagues, and friends from whose learning this project has benefitted, I wish to single out George Fayen, John Hollander, Maija Jansson, Yoon Sun Lee, Rosemarie McGerr, David Quint, Joanna Handlin Smith, Eugene Waith, Suzanne Wofford, and the late Michael Cooke. For helpful comments and suggestions on various chapters of this book I am grateful to Stephen Barney, Richard Brodhead, Heather Dubrow, Kevin Dunn, Kevis Goodman, Richard Helgerson, Blair Hoxby, Shelagh Hunter, Thomas Hyde, Christina Malcolmson, Clarence Miller, James Shulman, Richard Strier, Leonard Tennenhouse, David Underdown, Lee Wandel, and Thomas Whitaker.

I owe a very special thanks to my colleagues Thomas M. Greene, G. K. Hunter, and Claude Rawson. Over a period of many years they have offered learning, counsel, and encouragement that have been indispensable to the completion of this book.

The dedicatee, knowing me as she does, will understand why her name does not appear here.

Introduction

In 1501, London was a late medieval commune of 35,000 souls, located on the cultural fringe of Northern Europe; its population stood just where it had in 1377, before the 1379 recurrence of the Black Death.[1] By 1670, London was a rapidly changing metropolis of nearly half a million, the engine of an evolving early modern society, a capital and *entrepôt* that would soon become the most populous in Europe. In cultural terms early modern London was the largest and most widely experienced human creation in Britain. Its growth helped to produce, in the words of a recent critic, "a community of arts and letters such as had not existed since the Athens of the fifth century."[2] Like the language, London was undergoing rapid growth and change, offering new possibilities for exchange and combination, producing signs, symbols, civic habits, and systems of order. These emerged in part from medieval traditions, humanist learning, and practical experiment, but they were shaped by many other novel factors – by the emergence of the absolutist state and a national consciousness; by transformations in the late medieval aristocracy and rural economy; by the development of new class functions, tied especially to commerce, bureaucracy, and law; by new types of religious and economic association; and by a host of problems – inflation, unemployment, shortages, poverty, crime, and disease – whose causes were poorly understood.

Literature and Culture in Early Modern London is a study of these and other developments in relation to the production of literary works, major and minor, from Thomas More to Milton. Set against the literature of classical antiquity and the continental Renaissance and against English history from the fifteenth to the early eighteenth century, these works include a great variety of lyrics, ballads, jests, epics, praises, satires, plays, narratives, pageants, descriptions, chronicles, political and

---

[1] C. S. L. Davies, *Peace, Print, and Protestantism, 1450–1558* (London: Hart-Davis, Macgibbon, 1976), p. 259.

[2] Angus Fletcher, *Colors of the Mind: Conjectures on Thinking in Literature* (Cambridge, Mass.: Harvard University Press, 1991), p. 59.

1

economic treatises, sermons, and official documents and speeches. The aim is to tell a large and complex story by clarifying the relations between a literature and its society and by eliciting from that literature its embodiment of a collective experience. That experience is not simply "reflected" in the works in question but inhabits their very forms; it comes to life most vividly where those forms exert productive force upon each other, within a body of work that constitutes a vast polemic space binding individuals and groups together in the creative elaboration of consciousness. As Thomas Adams, a famous preacher in Jacobean London put it, London might "not unfitly be compared to certain pictures that represent to divers beholders, at divers stations, divers forms."[3]

The way to understand the cultural significance of early modern London is not to isolate or reify the local urban community but to highlight its situation at the center of a complex network of changing relationships. It was these long-distance relationships between center and periphery that for Thomas Milles, writing in 1608, defined the true character of London:

Our trades do meet in Companies, our Companies at halls, and our halls become monopolies of freedom, tied to London: where all our Crafts and Mysteries are so laid up together, that outrunning all the wisdom and prudence of the land, men live by trades they never learned, nor seek to understand. By means whereof, all our creeks seek to join one river, all our rivers run to one port, all our ports join to one town, all our towns make but one city, and all our cities but suburbs to one vast, unwieldy and disorderly Babel of buildings, which the world calls London.[4]

The core of early modern London and the focal-point, if not in every case the cause, of the relationships Milles describes was the "City," a civic government and square-mile physical jurisdiction that owed its privileges and self-rule to a series of royal charters dating from the eleventh century.[5] A period of internal conflict in the late fourteenth century had established the basic form of civic government that would prevail into the nineteenth century. It established as well the domination

[3] "The City of Peace" (1612), in *Works*, ed. Joseph Angus (3 vols. Edinburgh: J. Nichol, 1861–2), 3: 331.
[4] Thomas Milles, *The Customer's Alphabet* (1608), sig. L1v, quoted in L. C. Knights, *Drama and Society in Early Modern London* (1937; rpt. New York: W. W. Norton, 1968), p. 138.
[5] Throughout this book the term "City," when capitalized, denotes the Court of Aldermen, the Court of Common Council, and their officers and legal jurisdiction. In lower case, according to context, "city" denotes London's generic status as an urban settlement, the physical extension of the City's twenty-six wards, or, like "London," this area plus the built-up areas of Westminster, Southwark, and the other suburbs.

of the city's crafts and retail trades by international merchants, a domination that was reinforced in the late fifteenth and early sixteenth centuries by the incorporation of the Merchants Adventurers (1497) and by the consolidation of the Twelve Great Livery Companies (1523–38), the major guilds from whose ranks London's leaders were almost invariably chosen.[6] The executive governing body of the City, the Lord Mayor and the Court of Aldermen, was supplemented by a legislative assembly of Common Council and by an electoral assembly called the Court of Common Hall. The City's largest assembly, the Court of Common Hall, consisting of guild liverymen (about 10 percent of freeman householders), annually nominated two candidates for Lord Mayor and confirmed the actual choice made by the aldermen. It assisted in the election of London's two sheriffs and chose the City's four Members of Parliament. The roughly two hundred members of London's Common Council (six or eight from each of the City's twenty-six wards) were elected by all freemen at the annual meeting of the wardmote, presided over by the ward alderman; under the control of the Court of Aldermen, which managed its agenda and possessed the power of veto, the Council assisted in legislating civic order and taxation. Each of the twenty-six aldermen was nominated in his ward but chosen by the Court of Aldermen, whose members, usually the wealthiest of Londoners, held office for life. Together with the mayor and sheriffs, usually chosen from their ranks, the aldermen formed an oligarchic, self-perpetuating executive and judicial body. The aldermen issued licenses, heard complaints, controlled the City's finances, markets, courts, and jails, and sat on or appointed the City's main commissions and administrative posts. London was thus a self-governing merchant community, with its own laws, police, courts, militia, and welfare system.[7]

Essential to the functioning of this independent commune were London's guilds. The freedom of the City, and thus the right to trade within its jurisdiction, could be inherited by birth or purchased by

---

[6] On the fourteenth-century crisis and its civic consequences, see Ruth Bird, *The Turbulent London of Richard II* (London, 1949), pp. 76–81; D. W. Robertson, *Chaucer's London* (New York: John Wiley and Sons, 1968), ch. 4; A. R. Myers, *London in the Age of Chaucer* (Norman: University of Oklahoma Press, 1972), pp. 91–109; George Unwin, *The Gilds and Companies of London* (1908; rpt. London: George Allen & Unwin, 1938), pp. 127–175. For a revisionist account, however, see Pamela Nightingale, "Capitalists, Crafts, and Constitutional Change in Late Fourteenth-Century London," *Past and Present*, 122 (1989), 3–35.

[7] The best summary of London's civic constitution is Valerie Pearl, *London and the Outbreak of the Puritan Revolution* (Oxford University Press, 1961), ch. 1; see also Frank Freeman Foster, *The Politics of Stability: A Portrait of the Rulers in Elizabethan London* (London: Royal Historical Society, 1977), chs. 2–3; Ian W. Archer, *The Pursuit of Stability: Social Relations in Elizabethan London* (Cambridge University Press, 1991), ch. 2; T. F. Reddaway, "London and the Court," *Shakespeare Survey*, 17 (1964), 3–12.

"redemption," but the principal means of enfranchisement was through seven years' guild apprenticeship. The guilds thus controlled citizenship, from which were excluded both "strangers," or immigrants from abroad, and "foreigners," or non-free Englishmen – the provincial craftsmen and migrants, the casual laborers and domestic servants, the disabled, criminal, and unemployed who made up a substantial portion of the city's population. From the upper echelons of those privileged to wear the company's livery came the masters, wardens, and courts of assistants (former masters and wardens) who managed the affairs of the guild and governed its lower echelons of bachelors, yeomen, journeymen, and apprentices. The opportunity of advancement, a degree of solidarity in common interests, and an elaborate system of deference and ceremony contributed to the cohesion within the guild hierarchy, as did a variety of religious, charitable, and fraternal functions. Financed by fines, enrollment fees, and quarterly dues, the guilds exercised tight control over their membership, approving candidates for enrollment and drawing up their indentures. The court of wardens oversaw production and merchandising, heard complaints, and settled disputes between members. The guilds also provided a channel through which orders and proclamations could be issued, and they were a source from which the Crown could extract both able-bodied men and money.[8]

The stabilizing effects of the guilds were supplemented by a system of more than two hundred local constabular precincts (averaging 120 yards to a side) and by more than a hundred parishes, whose vestries were a generating force in city politics. While churchwardens handled parish finances and the life-records of parishioners, several vestrymen, who often sat on the wardmote inquest and participated in the electoral nominating process, dealt with civic business that included taxation, poor relief, and policing. Recent studies by Valerie Pearl and Steven Rappaport have thus stressed the fundamentally stable conditions of a community that was open to advancement, minutely regulated, and overseen by the more than three thousand men who served annually in some civic capacity.[9] Frank Freeman Foster has maintained that through kinship, common interests, and a commitment to the orderly maintenance of the City's traditional institutions, London's oligarchic elite "fashioned and refined" a "politics of stability."[10] Ian Archer has most recently explained that stability was maintained by a delicate

[8] Steven Rappaport, *Worlds within Worlds: Structures of Life in Sixteenth-Century London* (Cambridge University Press, 1989), chs. 2, 7; Archer, *The Pursuit of Stability*, ch. 4; T. F. Reddaway, "The Livery Companies of Tudor London," *History*, 51 (1966), 287–299.
[9] Valerie Pearl, "Change and Stability in Early Modern London," *London Journal*, 5 (1979), 3–34; Rappaport, *Worlds within Worlds*, ch. 6.
[10] Foster, *The Politics of Stability*, p. 162.

balance of hierarchical authority with commensalism, by a solidarity among the elite, by a division of interests and plurality of sustaining subcommunities among the lower orders, and by a fundamental responsiveness on the part of City government toward grievances and social problems.[11]

The internal stability of London, however, is an inadequate measure of the impact of the city's growth on the traditional economy and social order of England. Economically, the hypertrophic growth of London brought with it both a solvent effect on the late feudal economic system and a fundamental transformation in the finance and government of the English state. Largely through the enterprise of the Merchants Adventurers, dominated by London's Mercers, the export of woolen cloths increased seventeen to eighteen times between 1350 and 1500, and another five-fold by 1550. Accounting for 43 percent of these exports at the beginning of the sixteenth century, London's share of the expanding trade had increased to 86 percent by the mid-1540s.[12] Changing patterns in the late feudal economy – the movement toward money rents, capitalist tenancy, agricultural innovation and production for the market – were thus intensified by the spectacular rise in the cloth trade, by the enhanced importance of exchange values and surplus accumulation, and by the diversification of petty crafts and services, all of which "caused the terms of trade between town and country to tip to the latter's disadvantage,"[13] accelerating the reciprocal processes of rural expropriation and urban growth. Three times as large as Bristol, its nearest domestic rival in the early fourteenth century, London was by 1520 ten times as large as Norwich, which had overtaken Bristol for second place. Already supplying 50 percent of England's customs revenue under Henry VII, London's share increased to 61 percent in 1559–60 and 86 percent by 1581–82.[14]

The growth of London and its markets contributed in important ways to the powers of the newly emergent English state. In addition to customs revenues and regular levies, official loans from the City to the Crown

---

[11] Archer, *The Pursuit of Stability*, pp. 17, 32, 62, 98.

[12] S. E. Rasmussen, *London: The Unique City* (1934; rev. edn. Cambridge: MIT Press, 1982). G. D. Ramsay, *The City of London in International Politics at the Accession of Elizabeth I* (Manchester University Press, 1975), p. 39. A. L. Beier and Roger Finlay, eds., Introduction, *London 1500–1700; The Making of the Metropolis* (London: Longman, 1986), p. 15; Robert Brenner, *Merchants and Revolution: Commercial Change, Political Conflict, and London's Overseas Traders, 1550–1653* (Princeton University Press, 1993), pp. 6–9; C. G. A. Clay, *Economic Expansion and Social Change: England 1500–1700* (2 vols. Cambridge University Press, 1984), 1: 111–112.

[13] Kohachiro Takahasi, "A Contribution to the Discussion," in Paul Sweezy, Maurice Dobb, et al., *The Transition from Feudalism to Capitalism* (London: New Left Books, 1976), p. 166.

[14] Ramsay, *The City of London in International Politics*, p. 50; Peter Ramsey, *Tudor Economic Problems* (London: Gollancz, 1963), p. 54.

totaled £120,000 in the years 1575–98, while unofficial loans from individual merchants and aldermen raised the total much higher. Foreign loans to the Crown were typically backed by City credit, and the national currency was shored up by Londoners' management of the exchange. In return, the Crown backed mercantile bills of credit and protected large lenders with both relief at law and the award of Crown offices, contracts, monopoly patents, licenses, and customs farms.[15]

The courtly concessionaires and merchant syndicates who operated the revenue system, furthermore, provided the "administrative machinery" by which a nascent state government could carry out an "ambitious programme of economic and social controls."[16] The mid-sixteenth-century recession in the textile trade, meanwhile, had encouraged the use of royal prerogative to enhance the exclusive charter privileges of the North-European oriented Merchant Adventurers and to establish a number of new import–export consortia trading to the Mediterranean and East, such as the Muscovy (1555), Spanish (1577), Turkey (1580–81), Venice (1583), Levant (1592), and East India (1599) Companies. Leading Privy Councillors, many of whom had family connections with the City, held stakes in companies floated in London. Frank Kermode, recently quoting J. M. Keynes, has noted that "with the profit on Drake's venture in the *Golden Hind*, Elizabeth 'paid off the whole of her foreign debt,' ... and had a nice sum left over to invest in the East India company, so preparing the way to the larger empire of the future."[17] Though the new mercantilist theories that emerged with a second crisis in the cloth trade in the 1620s did not have so immediate an effect, they gradually became reality with the First and Second Navigation Acts and with the development of an *entrepôt* colonial trade that made London a world metropolis.[18] These developments suggest that in England, at least, the Renaissance state and its princes rose to power on the back of urban commerce.[19]

These economic developments were accompanied by profound social changes. At the lower end of the spectrum, the role of London's markets in reterritorializing the feudal landscape and in recoding its displaced peasants as wage-laborers produced the hordes of vagabonds and migrants who thronged the highways and swelled the burgeoning

[15] Ramsey, *Tudor Economic Problems*, pp. 50–60; Foster, *The Politics of Stability*, ch. 8.
[16] Robert Ashton, *The City and the Court, 1603–1643* (Cambridge University Press, 1979), p. 17.
[17] "The High Cost of the New History," *New York Review of Books*, 39: 12 (1992), 45.
[18] See Ralph Davis, "A Commercial Revolution," and Charles Wilson, "'Mercantilism': The Changing Meaning of a Word," in K. H. D. Haley, ed., *The Historical Association Book of the Stuarts* (London: Sidgwick and Jackson, 1973), pp. 186–209, 156–185.
[19] See Hugh Trevor-Roper, "The General Crisis of the Seventeenth Century," in *The Crisis of the Seventeenth Century* (New York: Harper and Row, 1968), pp. 55–60.

London suburbs. A series of royal edicts, beginning in 1580, attempted to halt the growth of London by fiat, by reason that "such multitudes could hardly be governed by ordinary justice to serve God and obey her Majesty."[20] The growth of this displaced laboring population meant that the City of London jurisdiction, which had represented as much as 80 percent of the metropolitan population in 1560, represented less than half of it by 1630.[21] The events of 1640–42 and 1647–49 would demonstrate the cost of this changing balance. To the extent that the "really revolutionary path" to capitalism was not through the commercial capital of merchants applied to production but through the industrial capital of petty producers,[22] unregulated labor and manufacture was essential to the development of a home market and an economy in which half of London's mid-seventeenth-century population and three-fifths of its trades were involved in the production of goods.[23]

Toward the other end of the social spectrum, meanwhile, the growth of London had transformed the feudal order of the three estates into a six-part taxonomy in which the notable hot spot was the boundary between gentlemen and merchants. This boundary, which also distinguished status based on birth and landholding from status based on wealth and ability, was, as the social anatomists Sir Thomas Smith and William Harrison observed, becoming both fluid and permeable, as citizens changed estate "with gentlemen, as gentlemen doo with them, by a mutuall conversion of the one into the other."[24] Even before 1500 William Caxton had noted that "one name and lineage ... in this noble city of London ... rarely continue into the third heir, or scarcely to the second."[25] An anonymous apologist for London observed c. 1580 that the economic opportunities of London and the attractions of the court caused "the Gentlemen of all shires" to "flie and flock to this Citty."[26] Yet it could be plausibly maintained by Edmund Bolton that "all the parts of

[20] Proclamation of June 27, 1602, in Paul L. Hughes and James F. Larkin, eds., *Tudor Royal Proclamations* (3 vols. New Haven: Yale University Press, 1969), 3: 245.
[21] Roger Finlay and Beatrice Shearer, "Population Growth and Suburban Expansion," in Beier and Finlay, eds., *London 1500–1700*, p. 42.
[22] Marx, *Capital*, III.xx (3 vols. New York: International Publishers, 1967), 3: 323; cf. Maurice Dobb, *Studies in the Development of Capitalism* (London: George Routledge and Sons, 1946), ch. 4.
[23] Brian Dietz, "Overseas Trade and Metropolitan Growth," and A. L. Beier, "Engine of Manufacture: The Trades of London," in Beier and Finlay, eds., *London 1500–1700*, pp. 126, 129, 149–150; cf. Charles Wilson, *England's Apprenticeship* (2nd edn. London: Longman, 1984), pp. 59–62.
[24] Harrison, *The Description of England* (1587), ed. Georges Edelin (Ithaca: Cornell University Press, 1968), p. 115; cf. Sir Thomas Smith, *De Republica Anglorum*, ed. Mary Dewar (Cambridge University Press, 1982), pp. 64–77.
[25] *Prologues and Epilogues of William Caxton*, ed. W. J. B. Crotch (London: EETS, 1928), pp. 77–78.
[26] *An Apologie of the Cittie of London*, in John Stow, *A Survey of London* (1598; 1603), ed. C. L. Kingsford (2 vols. 1908; rpt. Oxford: Clarendon Press, 1971), 2: 212.

England are full of families, either originally raised to the dignity of Gentlemen out of this one most famous place: or so restored, and enriched as may well seeme to amount to an originall raising."[27] As a "rich and wealthy seedplot" from which "courtiers, lawyers, and merchants" were "continuously transplanted," the metropolis helped to interlegitimate capital and late feudal tenure; it created a new sort of "honour community" in which "valiant hearts, great spirits, ... exalting wisedome, and reposed experience" were as much "the badge of a Merchant, as cognisance of a true Gentleman."[28] Ernest Gellner argues that the formation of nation–states requires social mobility, lowered class barriers, rapid urbanization, diversified but relatively open markets, and "sustained, frequent ... communication between strangers."[29] London, with its facilities for exchange and recombination and its varied and mobile population, "by birth for the most part a mixture of all the countries" of the realm,[30] was not only the underpinning of the new Tudor state, but also the place where the possibilities of an English nation were most visible, "the spectacle of the whole realm whereof all other cities and places take example."[31]

In debate among historians about the preponderance of stability or disorder, stasis or change, in early modern London, the meaning of these terms is a function of the perspective being taken.[32] The present study does not limit itself to the citizen-class of London or to developments in which London played the exclusive, or even necessarily the central role; rather, it examines larger historic changes from the standpoint of London, in order that the city's role *within* the process of change may be more fully appreciated.

In the twentieth century, the name of Henri Pirenne is most closely connected with the view that the development of urban life in medieval

---

[27] *The Cities Advocate* (1629), sig. Kv.

[28] William Gainsford, *The Glory of England* (1618), p. 318; on the new "honour community," see Mervyn James, *Society, Politics and Culture: Studies in Early Modern England* (Cambridge University Press, 1986), p. 328.

[29] Ernest Gellner, *Nations and Nationalism* (Ithaca: Cornell University Press, 1983), pp. 25, 34, 40–42.   [30] *Apologie of the Cittie of London*, in Stow, *Survey*, 2: 207.

[31] Corporation of London Records Office, *Journals of the Common Council*, 20, fo. 65 (1572–73), cited in Michael Berlin, "Civic Ceremony in Early Modern London," *Urban History Yearbook* (1986), p. 23.

[32] For emphasis on the conditions of instability, see Peter Clark and Paul Slack, *English Towns in Transition* (Oxford University Press, 1976), pp. 69–70, 72–73; A. L. Beier, "Social Problems in Elizabethan London," in Jonathan Barry, ed., *The Tudor and Stuart Town: A Reader in English Urban History 1530–1688* (London: Longman, 1990), pp. 121–138; Peter Clark, "Devouring Capital," *TLS*, 4516 Oct. 20–26, (1989), p. 1162. For emphasis on stability, see the works of Pearl, Rappaport, and Foster, cited above, as well as M. J. Power, "A 'Crisis' Reconsidered: Social and Demographic Dislocation in London in the 1590s," *London Journal*, 12 (1986), 133–145. The evidence is judiciously weighed in Archer, *The Pursuit of Stability*, pp. 1–17.

Europe was the driving force in the movement from feudalism to capitalism, from agrarian subsistence to market structure, from servitude to freedom: *Stadtluft macht frei* is the proverb Pirenne cites.[33] As John Merrington points out, the view that the urban marketplace is progressive, that its extension erodes feudal patriarchalism, liberates producers, induces the rule of law, and supplants an ethic of gratification and stasis with one of creative labor and ingenuity, "was explicitly formulated in the earliest theories of the origins of capitalism – those of eighteenth-century political economy."[34] The Whiggishness of this view – in which history becomes the justification of the marketplace – is obvious enough; more interesting is Merrington's theoretical objection that in the Pirenne thesis and its variants, urbanization, instead of being a historical product and part of a historical process, becomes identified with the totality of history itself. In this treatment, Merrington notes, the city cannot be fully historicized, i.e., the development of urban life cannot be explained historically except by reference to external, fortuitous factors such as shifting trade routes. The teleological outcome of history, the development of the urban marketplace, is in this view the origin and driving force of history.

Without rejecting the valuable contribution of the Pirenne thesis in emphasizing the corrosive effects of urbanization on feudalism and its role in the development of capitalism, law, and liberty, recent work has helped to situate urbanization in a less continuous process, tracing its origins to developments within the late feudal economy, on the one hand,[35] and examining, on the other hand, its contribution to the overdetermined development of absolutist states, which extended the domination of the old nobility even while they provided and protected new legal rights for a nascent bourgeoisie.[36]

London in fact operated, through its charters and privileges, as a "collective seigneur" within the feudal system of parcellized sovereignty. Governed by exclusionary and highly stratified guilds, London depended heavily for its growing wealth on the trade in luxury goods, that is to say, "on the purchasing power of the aristocracy," and on a

[33] *Economic and Social History of Medieval Europe*, tr. I. E. Clegg (1936; rpt. New York: Harcourt, Brace, 1966), p. 51.
[34] "Town and Country in the Transition to Capitalism," in Paul Sweezy, Maurice Dobb, et al., *The Transition from Feudalism to Capitalism*, p. 170.
[35] The theory is associated especially with the work of Robert Brenner; see R. H. Hilton, "A Crisis of Feudalism," in T. H. Aston and C. H. E. Philbin, eds., *The Brenner Debate: Agrarian Class Structure and Economic Development in Pre-Industrial Europe* (Cambridge University Press, 1985), pp. 119–137.
[36] See Perry Anderson, *Lineages of the Absolutist State* (1974; rpt. London: Verso, 1979), pp. 22–24.

surplus whose principal form was still landed rent.[37] The city's solvent effects on feudalism, moreover, were balanced by its "involution towards *rentier* forms of economy," that is to say, by the flight of urban capital back to the land, still the primary means of production, and by the transformation of the "urban elite into a landed or *rentier* aristocracy, merged in turn with the nobility itself."[38]

When A. F. Pollard declared that "Tudor despotism consisted in London's domination over the rest of England,"[39] he had in mind the promulgation of the English Reformation and a state religion by an increasingly powerful monarchy and parliament. But the development of the absolutist state, and of London as its capital, is inseparable from the city's economic role in "fusing merchant capital and landed property."[40] The hypertrophic growth of London, and the diversifying services and population that went with it, reflect London's preeminence as the administrative center of the state and the main conduit for government revenues and landed wealth.

The absolutist state, Perry Anderson argues, was neither the arbiter between the aristocracy and the bourgeoisie nor an instrument of the latter against the former, but a "new political carapace of the threatened nobility"; but at the same time, the emergence of the state's politico-juridical apparatus was overdetermined by the influence of the new urban class, which blocked any return to the old ways of feudalism and determined the new shape the aristocracy was to take.[41] This power of London's socio-economic mixture to resist the feudal past and to bring on the state is celebrated by the anonymous apologist who declared around 1580 that "Cities and great townes are a continuall bridle against tyranny ... not onely in the Aristocritie, but also in the lawfull kingdome or iust royalty."[42] The unitary development of the landowning class and merchant capital meant that the aristocracy, earlier in England than elsewhere on the continent, turned to the commerce and mercantilism resulting from London's creation of a national market.[43] And this market, in turn, was connected to new types of industrial organization and to new classes of capitalists and artisans whose innovations help to explain why, despite its role as a *rentier* capital and parasitic consumer within the neofeudal state, London was not – like other such European

[37] Hilton, "A Crisis of Feudalism," in Aston and Philbin, eds., *The Brenner Debate*, p. 128.
[38] Merrington, "Town and Country in the Transition to Capitalism," p. 183.
[39] "Local History," *TLS*, 19 (1920), 161.
[40] Merrington, "Town and Country in the Transition to Capitalism," p. 184.
[41] *Lineages of the Absolutist State*, pp. 22–24.
[42] In John Stow, *A Survey of London*, 2: 206, 198–199.
[43] Anderson, *Lineages of the Absolutist State*, pp. 125, 135, 138; Brenner, *Merchants and Revolution*, pp. 649–651.

capitals as Naples, Madrid, and Constantinople – merely a "spectator ... present at the forthcoming industrial revolution,"[44] but an engine of growth that continued to lead the nation in manufacturing output (if not in the innovation of the factory system) into the mid-Victorian period.[45] In simultaneously helping to change the mode of agricultural production and to reassimilate peasants as laborers and petty producers, the growth of London created markets, industries, credit and transport systems that averted demographic crisis and economic collapse even while they mobilized values and social status.[46]

In examining the literary and cultural dimensions of these changes, this book proceeds from (and aims to substantiate) the assumption, derived from structural linguistics and literary formalism, that the history of literary expression, like other historical developments, involves a complex of changing structures, so that while structure is always undergoing evolution, "evolution is inescapably of a systemic nature."[47] Shaped by a system of historically dominant forms, practices, and beliefs, but containing both residual elements, "effectively formed in the past, but ... still active in the cultural practice," and by emergent elements that make for innovation, literary and cultural creations form a behaviorally meaningful response to the changing historical environment; they engage that environment in a process of mutual destructuration and restructuration, assimilating the environment to consciousness and action even while consciousness and action are accommodated to environment.[48]

In keeping with the formal and collective nature of such structuration, the focus of this book falls heavily upon the systemic relationships of literary genres and on the myths, motifs, and mental structures that sustain these genres and change with them. Elaborated by individuals from within collective situations, these forms and genres, constituent elements rather than reflections of social consciousness, invite a systematic exploration of creative responses to a changing objective

---

[44] Fernand Braudel, *Capitalism and Material Life*, tr. Miriam Kochan (New York: Harper and Row, 1973), p. 440.

[45] Francis Sheppard, *London 1808–1870: The Infernal Wen* (Berkeley: University of California Press, 1971), p. 158.

[46] E. A. Wrigley, "A Simple Model of London's Importance in Changing English Society and Economy 1650–1750," in P. Abrams and E. A. Wrigley, eds., *Towns in Societies* (Cambridge University Press, 1978), pp. 237–239.

[47] R. Jakobson and J. Tynianov, "Problems in the Study of Language and Literature" (1928), in Roman Jakobson, *Selected Writings* (8 vols. The Hague: Mouton, 1981), 3: 4.

[48] Raymond Williams, *Marxism and Literature* (Oxford University Press, 1971), pp. 122–124; Lucien Goldmann, "The Genetic-Structuralist Method in the History of Literature," in *Towards a Sociology of the Novel*, tr. Alan Sheridan (London: Tavistock Publications, 1975), pp. 156–157; and *The Hidden God*, tr. Philip Thody (London: Routledge and Kegan Paul, 1964), p. 15.

environment. The social groups that perform significant cultural work[49] include first of all those literary communities that participate (often homologously with social groupings) in the common endeavor of adapting and modifying particular forms and genres. The verse satirists of the Inns of Court, the seriocomic prose pamphleteers, and the popular dramatists, for example, all of whom formed contemporary literary responses to Elizabethan–Jacobean London, can often be distinguished not only in terms of literary form, but also in terms of social background, bias, and outlook; even individuals who wrote in all of these forms adapted, in each case, to the very different mediating institutions (coterie manuscript circulation, commercial publication, public and private performance), audience expectations, and linguistic strata that these forms involved.

At the same time, the obvious inter-orientation of these genres (and their practitioners) reveals the extent to which the elaboration of consciousness through form is traversed and inflected by a process of historic change that marks writers as members as well of different generations and discursive phases. The practices of Londoners writing after 1560, in the shadow of the post-1550 reorientation of London's markets and within the neofeudal symbiosis of the Elizabethan political and religious settlement, differed systemically from those who wrote earlier, in the first phases of London's disruptive emergence from the late medieval landscape, and from those who, after the second trade crisis of the 1620s, wrote from within the framework of a nascent mercantilism, an emerging metropolitanism, and a declining political and religious consensus.

Responding to structural changes in the environment, the Tudor–Stuart literary system was thus dominated, at different points in time, by configurations of inter-oriented forms and practices, each incorporating, modifying, and excluding aspects of the others. It is finally this inter-orientation that makes the city itself – with its many strata, mentalities, and discursive possibilities – a significant site and engine of cultural creation. As a common environment and object of consciousness, the city enabled its constituent communities to "participate ... in the common culture formed by their relationships to one another."[50] London was for Thomas Adams a picture that represented "to divers beholders, at divers stations, divers forms." But it was a picture nonetheless.

The status of London as a site of social negotiation and a threshold of historic change links its literary culture with the social and material processes of elaborating "specific and different 'ways of life.'"[51] The

---

[49] Goldmann, "The Genetic-Structuralist Method," pp. 160–161.
[50] David Harris Sacks, "Searching for 'Culture' in the English Renaissance," *Shakespeare Quarterly*, 39: 4 (1988), 480.   [51] Williams, *Marxism and Literature*, p. 19.

work of anthropologists on the structural changes effected by cultural practices sheds useful light on these processes.[52] Historical change differs from ritual practice, of course, in that the differences and transformations effected by historical change are not foreseen and dictated as they are by ceremonial tradition.[53] But Victor Turner has shown how even within the liminary logic of ritual and ceremony, the enactment of communal solidarity and stasis can produce novelty, as common values and symbols "fractionate into sets and arrays of cultural values" that motivate historical change. As a model of cultural transformation, the anthropological logic of liminality correlates cultural with literary and socio-political change; it integrates the mechanisms of cultural transition both with the residuation-dominance-emergence of literary forms and with the systemically *overdetermined* nature of the historical process.

All of these models emphasize "the structured negotiation and exchange," by which "collective beliefs and experiences were shaped, moved from one medium to another, concentrated in manageable aesthetic form, offered for consumption."[54] But this process of negotiation was not a zero-sum game. The New Historicism, with its anecdotal manner and its dialectic of subversion and containment, has usefully estranged the culture of the early modern period, but at the cost of failing to account for the long-term changes that cultural activity effects. Without inaugurating a new formalism, it is the aim here, by widening a focus too often narrowly concentrated on the *bizarreries* and political culture of the court, and by attempting a "social history of literary forms in their full particularity and variety,"[55] to produce a mode of historical inquiry more fully theorized – from the socio-economic and the literary standpoint – than has commonly been the case in the New Historicism. Though concentrated on the literature and culture of London, the focus here is neither, in the historical sense, "local," nor, in the literary-historical sense, "topical." Facts are adduced insofar as they are elements of structure and symptoms of change.

Three conceptual frameworks govern the shape of this book. The first is the transition from feudalism to capitalism. This framework situates London in the context of changing socio-economic relationships – beginning with the fifteenth-century emergence of London as a major

---

[52] See, for example, Victor Turner, *The Ritual Process: Structure and Anti-Structure* (Ithaca: Cornell University Press, 1969), p. 94.
[53] For the view that ceremonial rites "mediate the discontinuities that they themselves create," see Louis Adrian Montrose, "The Purpose of Playing: Reflections on a Shakespearian Anthropology," *Helios*, 7 (1980), 63.
[54] Stephen Greenblatt, *Shakespearean Negotiations: The Circulation of Social Energy in Renaissance England* (Berkeley: University of California Press, 1988), pp. 5–6.
[55] Williams, Introduction to *Racine* (Cambridge, Mass.: Rivers Press, 1972), p. xv.

force in the nation's socio-economic life and ending with its late seventeenth-century establishment as the metropolitan center of an urbanizing nation and maritime empire. In this period, even while the growth of London helped to secure the development of an absolutist state that extended the power of the feudal aristocracy in new form, it also facilitated political, economic, and legal arrangements that secured the power, practices, and mentality of a nascent bourgeoisie. The paradoxes of this historically *overdetermined* situation are embodied in the literature of London as fruitful interchanges between courtly and urban modes, traditional and innovative approaches to representing the social order. The peculiar richness of the literature of the English Renaissance – a richness we associate with the linguistic and imaginative integration between popular and elite, lewd and learned elements – is thus a function of the role of literature in the process of historical change.

Secondly, the book traces a pattern of *behavioral urbanization*. The history of urbanization in the West has as one of its dimensions the process of adaptation whereby evolving moral technologies – along with demographic and infrastructural developments – have helped to organize and discipline populations for cohabitation and cooperation in settlements of massive scale.[56] As the American urban sociologist Robert Park observed, urbanization is "accompanied by corresponding changes in the habits, sentiments, and character of the urban population."[57] During some phases of urbanization, such changes become exponentially related to urban growth; this is why, according to Jan de Vries, "the cultural impact of cities ... grew more than proportionally with their size."[58] This quantitative disproportion is perhaps better put in terms of qualitative change: "the mobility of a population is unquestionably a very large factor in its intellectual development."[59] Such intellectual development includes the moral techniques – the modes of identity-formation, systems of belief, habits of deportment and civility, means of aggression and defense – that facilitate cohabitation, making urban life endurable, viable, desirable.

Aided by these technologies, but also by the rationalizations of post-Enlightenment social science and by the hindsight that has come with

---

[56] See, for example, the two classic accounts of these technologies by Max Weber, *The City*, tr. Don Martindale and Gertrud Neuwirth (Glencoe: Free Press, 1958) and Georg Simmel, "The Metropolis and Mental Life," tr. H. H. Gerth, in Richard Sennett, ed., *Classic Essays on the Culture of Cities* (Englewood Cliffs: Prentice-Hall, 1969), pp. 47–60). A three-part terminology that links "behavioral urbanization" with demographic and structural urbanization is the basis for Jan de Vries' recent study of *European Urbanization, 1500–1800* (Cambridge, Mass.: Harvard University Press, 1984), pp. 10–13.

[57] "The City: Suggestions for the Investigation of Human Behavior in the Urban Environment" (1916), in Sennett, ed., *Classic Essays on the Culture of Cities*, p. 110.

[58] *European Urbanization*, p. 154.   [59] Park, "The City," p. 106.

centuries of urban development, we are far more readily inclined than Tudor-Stuart Londoners to equate the process of urbanization with the advance of civilization. Aristotle's confidence in this equation not-withstanding, a more persuasive case to Renaissance Londoners might have been that of the fourteenth-century Tunisian philosopher Ibn Khaldun, who defined urban settlement as a feature of "sedentary culture," in the fullest sense a secondary culture which "come(s) after the Bedouin life and the features that go with it." "Cities and towns," he declared, "are not among the things that are necessary matters of general concern to human beings, in the sense that all human beings desire them or feel compelled to have them. As a matter of fact, [human beings] must be forced and driven [to build cities]."[60] That Elizabethan and Jacobean Londoners were being forbidden by their monarchs to build any further is not a point that makes against Ibn Khaldun.

Early modern England was an *urbanizing* society lacking indigenous traditions of *urbanism*.[61] Countless factors worked against any sup-position that London's was a settled or sedentary culture. That a city should grow at the rate and to the extent that Elizabethan and Jacobean London did was a new and disturbing thing. Even while London grew, the city's most important institution, the court, remained peripatetic. Still vulnerable to the older agricultural rhythms of dearth and plenty, and also tied to the newer economic rhythms by the cycles of the law terms and marriage season, London was subject to mass emigration by those of its inhabitants who were not carried off by plague or locked within their houses when it descended. Prior to the sudden growth of London, and the transformations it wrought on the social system, English society, rooted in the lands of the countryside, had been slow to receive the civic philosophy and mores of the ancient world and contemporary Italy. The very ancient ruins that led many humanists to identify with the glory of ancient cities told just as much against their perdurability, and in Biblical typology the ruined cities of the Old Testament combined with Pauline and Augustinian theology to suggest that there could be no abiding city in the realm of human history. Destabilizing traditional social structures and mores even while it proliferated in new forms of life, the massive scale of settlement in London was a profoundly unsettling experience.

To be sure, Reformation theology produced new strategies – such as the doctrines of election, vocation, and stewardship – which, like the

---

[60] *The Muqaddimah* , tr. Franz Rosenthal (3 vols. New York: Pantheon Books, 1958), 2: 235.
[61] For this distinction, see Paul Wheatley, *The City as Symbol* (London: H. K. Lewis, 1969), p. 4, and *The Pivot of the Four Quarters: A Preliminary Enquiry into the Origins and Character of the Ancient Chinese City* (Edinburgh University Press, 1971), p. xviii.

older doctrine of good works, helped to rationalize the process of urban settlement. And London itself abounded in civic institutions – government, guilds, and parishes – whose longstanding traditions symbolized and sustained stability. Yet London's government and jurisdiction, which represented 80 percent of the greater metropolitan population in 1560, represented less than half of it by 1630.[62] The unregulated suburbs, with their population of casual laborers and unassimilated artisans, immigrants and paupers, were outstripping the City of London in growth. Traditional civic and economic institutions were being undermined by tax farms and other forms of royal intervention, by new forms of speculation and commercial organization, including joint-stock ventures and trading syndicates, and by new modes of social and religious affiliation. The ravages of poverty, dearth, and disease meant that the city's expansion could only be fueled by a massive immigration that in 1590 made one in every eight Englishmen Londoners at some point in their lives.[63]

The literature of early modern London was part of a cultural response to the challenges of this unsettling experience, a response whose effect was to articulate urbane mentalities of settlement. Just as it was, in a sense, the function of London's growth to deterritorialize peasants from the land and reterritorialize them as wage-laborers, so it was a function of literature to inculcate new forms of sedentarism, ways of perceiving the self and society that encouraged settlement and civility, allayed anxieties, and encouraged innovation. This literary contribution to the process of behavioral urbanization demonstrates the extent to which literature, according to Hans Robert Jauss, "not only preserves actual experiences, but also anticipates unrealized possibility, broadens the limited space of social behavior for new desires, claims, and goals, and thereby opens paths to future experience."[64]

The four parts into which the chapters of this book are organized trace the theme of sedentarism from the emergence of London as a mental fact in the national consciousness (Part 1), through the development of new social visions, styles, and modes of association both within (Part 2) and in opposition to (Part 3) the neofeudal framework of the Tudor-Stuart state, to their dissemination through the transformation of human character by the new patterns of metropolitan life (Part 4). By naturalizing the mobility of markets, classes, and individuals as the

[62] Roger Finlay and Beatrice Shearer, "Population Growth and Suburban Expansion," p. 42.
[63] Roger Finlay, *Population and Metropolis: The Demography of London 1580–1650* (Cambridge University Press, 1981), p. 9.
[64] Hans Robert Jauss, *Toward an Aesthetic of Reception*, tr. Timothy Bahti (Minneapolis: University of Minnesota Press, 1982), p. 41.

ultimate form of sedentarism, the literary culture of London reinforced the codependent trends toward capitalism and demographic and structural urbanization, trends which transformed the 2.3 percent of mid-sixteenth-century Englishmen who were Londoners and the 6 percent who were town dwellers into the 11.4 percent and 19 percent, respectively, who were by 1700 linked together by an elaborate physical and economic infrastructure.[65] This is why the book does not concentrate exclusively on the burgher community of London, why it begins with the story of a few prominent London families but ends with images of people roaming the English landscape and the earth.

A third framework is the conceptual conflict between order and reform, between the radical concentration of power and the radical distribution of justice. This conflict originates in classical philosophy, but it correlates both with the paradoxical tendency of cities to enslave *and* liberate their populations (indeed to liberate by means of hyper-organization) and with the evaluative terms within which cities are typically the subject of blame or praise. The sense of conflict was strongest during the periods represented by the first and fourth parts of the book, i.e., first of all in the period when, coinciding with the upheaval of the Reformation, the medieval socio-economic order was seriously challenged by the coming of the Tudor state and by the new forms of socio-economic order evolving in response to the first rapid growth of London; and secondly in the period when, coinciding with the Revolution, the neofeudal symbiosis between feudal and bourgeois interests within the absolutist state was tipped in favor of the latter. The book begins and ends, in other words, with studies of the discursive formations which accompanied two transitional phases in the history of London and the development of capitalism – the transformation of the medieval social order by the urban beginnings of capitalistic accumulation, and the transformation of this initially paternalistic, neofeudal, court-sponsored system into a more widespread bourgeois ethic and praxis. These two liminal situations are marked by a utopianism that sharply divides the literature of London into alternative languages and viewpoints, a language of novel myths and forms (in Part 1, humanism; in Part 4, cosmopolitanism) whose defense of concentrated urban power conflicts with an older language of justice (in Part 1, that of native complaint and

---

[65] London percentages are from Jeremy Boulton, *Neighbourhood and Society : A London Suburb in the Seventeenth Century* (Cambridge University Press, 1987), p. 3. The earlier town-dweller estimate is based on towns of over 4,000; Peter Clark and Paul Slack, *English Towns in Transition*, p. 11. The later estimate is based on towns of over 2,500; Peter Borsay, *The English Urban Renaissance : Culture and Society in the Provincial Town 1660–1770* (Oxford: Clarendon Press, 1989), pp. 19–20.

homiletic; in Part 4, that of individual liberty), even while these languages of justice are transfigured by the new forms of power from which they dissent (producing, in Part 1, the concept of the city, and in Part 4, the introjected habits of civility and bourgeois accumulation).

The pair of chapters which form Part 1 thus trace "the invention of London," i.e., the emergence of London as a major force in mental life and in literature. The first chapter, dealing with More's *Utopia* and the advent of humanism, demonstrates why, despite the urban outlook and bias of classical and continental humanism, the idea of an urbanized order of reform was still unthinkable in view of the prevailing models of social justice; and why, at the same time, by appearing to legislate radical justice, More's Utopia actually instituted the radical concentration of wealth and power through the model of surplus extraction. The second chapter, dealing with various "native" forms of complaint, protest, and satire in the early Tudor period, explains why, despite its unthinkability within traditional social thought, the idea of the city had to be invented, and thus how traditional models like that of the "three estates" modulated into that of "country, court, and city."

The pair of chapters in Part 4, with which the book ends, trace the "dissemination" of new forms of urbanity and bourgeois thought through the contrasting utopian visions of a radical metropolitan power in the "august" forms of the Caroline and Restoration periods, and of a radical republican and spiritual liberty – and hence of bourgeois subjectivity – in the works of Milton, Lilburne, Hartlib, Harrington, and other writers of the Revolutionary period. Thus, while Part 1 analyzes the emergence of London as a mental fact, Part 4 deals with that stage in the urbanizing process when quantity translates into quality, when the metropolis well and truly makes its impact felt beyond its borders by transforming human character, creating new patterns of mobility, and transforming the relationship between countryside and city, self and society.

The two long middle sections of the book treat the converse of this pattern of sharpened conflict, namely, a period of particularly fruitful "neofeudal" symbiosis, when the increasing growth and power of London, by securing the advent of the absolutist state, extended the life of medieval tradition even while it evolved new ideas, modes of association, and forms of order in tension with it.[66] It is in this period that

---

[66] I use the term "neofeudal" throughout this book to characterize a number of overlapping phenomena: first, an economic system in which production was still primarily agrarian and in which the primary form of wealth was land but in which economic practices were substantially transformed by urban commerce and finance, which were themselves still governed in many respects by quasi-feudal arrangements in which royal charters and privileges were exchanged for tribute and military support;

the most genuinely innovative techniques of sedentarism were developed. This process of development accounts for the extraordinarily rich body of urban literature produced between 1580 and 1620, the height of the English literary Renaissance. Part 3 deals with (primarily courtly) forms of praise – description, encomium, epic, and pageantry. Part 4 deals with (primarily popular) forms of blame – seriocomic prose pamphleteering, verse satire, epigram, and stage comedy.

As applied to Parts 2 and 3, the terms "fictions" and "techniques" of settlement indicate a difference in kind which (like the generic difference between praise and blame) arises from differences of degree and emphasis. The inter-orientation of the two parts embodies, in literary terms, the socio-economic symbiosis described above, "a continuous cross-fertilization between courtly and urban forms."[67] The encomiastic works examined in Part 3 treat London primarily as the capital and symbol of a state that providentially extends a noble feudal past into a harmonious present and destined imperial future. In these works, the novel impact of London is accommodated to a traditional chivalric decor, but often in ways that modify or seriously challenge it. Chapter 3 examines the personification of the city as a neofeudal technique of description and encomium, and it traces its decay under the impact of such new developments as the rise of individualism and manufactures. Chapter 4 explores the tensions between aristocratic and bourgeois, courtly and urban interests in the historical vision of Spenser's *Faerie Queene* and its contemporary analogues. Chapter 5 traces similar tensions as they shaped the two main forms of London pageantry, the royal entry and the Lord Mayor's inaugural show.

Part 3 examines the same symbiosis, but from the perspective of works which, while participating in the same neofeudal synthesis, represent in degree a more radically innovative urbanity rooted in popular culture, geared to the rhythms of the marketplace, and designed to exploit the new industries of publishing, public theater, and popular entertainment.

second, a political system and society in which the emerging state, supported and shaped by urban commerce, helped to maintain the power and status of the traditional ruling class of landholders; third, a neo-chivalric decorum that Frances Yates has associated with "an imaginative refeudalization of culture ... going on all over Europe," "Elizabethan Chivalry: The Romance of the Accession Day Tilts," *JWCI*, 20 (1957), 4–25. "Through its conventions of feudal loyalty and romantic devotion," Richard McCoy observes, "Elizabethan chivalry confirmed Tudor sovereignty," *The Rites of Knighthood: The Literature and Politics of Elizabethan Chivalry* (Berkeley: University of California Press, 1989), p. 3. Like the other dimensions of the "neofeudal" framework, however, this decorum was *overdetermined* by the influence of the urban classes, producing what Malcolm Smuts has called "a continuous cross-fertilization between courtly and urban forms," *Court Culture and the Origins of a Royalist Tradition in Early Stuart England* (Philadelphia: University of Pennsylvania Press, 1987), p. 64.

[67] Smuts, *Court Culture and the Origins of a Royalist Tradition*, p. 64.

Chapter 6 analyzes in the seriocomic prose pamphleteering of Greene, Nashe, and Dekker, the development of ethical alternatives to the morality and social vision of the established authorities. Among these alternatives are an endorsement of mobility, a cultivation of bohemianism and aggressive individuality, a new sense of "crisis" and temporality geared to the rhythms of economic exchange, and a tendency to naturalize the frightening sense of change associated with London. Chapter 7 takes up the similar attempt, on the part of the more socially privileged Inns of Court wits, to constitute an urbane morality on the basis of the imitation of classical verse satire; it demonstrates how and why this attempt was frustrated by the perception of social change, and it points forward to the more successful development of the techniques of cosmopolitanism by Jonson and his coterie successors, who are the subject of chapter 9. Chapter 8 concludes the discussion of popular "heteroglot" genres with an examination of the comic theater; it demonstrates how the interdependence of comic modes – especially the interplay between city comedy and romance – elaborates, in a "romance of the theater," a social consciousness of provisionality and tolerance. The decline of this dialogue or "romance" is traced into the Caroline period, again in preparation for matters of sharpened conflict discussed in chapters 9 and 10.

Devoted, respectively, to the lyric cultivation of urbane pleasures and gentility and the visionary defense of liberty in the puritan Revolution, these final two chapters demonstrate how the social and political conflicts of the mid-seventeenth century were conditioned by the forces of radical power and radical justice that attended metropolitan growth. Taken together, however, they also suggest how, despite considerable divergences, these two conflicting forms of utopianism converged in a cosmopolitan sense of autonomy that finally outstripped the limits of the very local community in which it originated, completing a metropolitan pattern of diversification, specialization, individuation, and mobility – a pattern by which the sedentary, civilizing process was carried from within the commune that had nurtured it to the furthest corners of the realm and the globe.

Part I

The invention of London

1   The city and humanism

The city, the state, and the advent of humanism

By a provision in the will of Judge John More, the father of Sir Thomas, student priests at Oxford and Cambridge were left a maintenance to pray for the long-departed soul of King Edward IV, the monarch in whose reign the judge, a descendant of two established London families, had embarked on his career of public service and received his coat of arms.[1] It was in the same King's reign that Henry Colet, a third son from rural Buckinghamshire who had come to London to learn the art and mystery of a Mercer, was elected alderman (Farringdon Ward Without, 1476) and sheriff (1477), thus beginning his rise to the mayoralty in 1486 and 1495. From this mayor's patrimony his son, the Dean of St. Paul's, re-endowed St. Paul's School as the first English grammar school to reflect the new curriculum of humanism.

Edward had come to the throne with the support of London's wealthier merchants.[2] His support of the traders in London's merchant community and his bellicose foreign policy, highly appealing to xenophobic Londoners, helped, along with the development of money rents and markets within the fluid conditions of the late feudal economy, to usher in a new period of prosperity for London's merchant community. One chronicler noted with alarm that "this same king in person ... like a man living by

---

[1] James McConica, "The Patrimony of Thomas More," in *History and Imagination: Essays in Honour of Hugh Trevor-Roper*, ed. Hugh Lloyd-Jones, Valerie Pearl, and Blair Worden (London: Duckworth, 1981), p. 57.

[2] S. B. Chrimes points out that in the final decade of his reign Edward raised £40,000 from London's merchant community, more than four times what his Lancastrian predecessor raised over a considerably longer period, "The Reign of Edward IV," in S. B. Chrimes, et al., eds., *Fifteenth-Century England, 1399–1485: Studies in Politics and Society* (New York: Barnes & Noble, 1972), p. 51; cf. C. L. Kingsford, "London in the Fifteenth Century," in *Prejudice and Promise in Fifteenth-Century England* (1925; rpt. London: Frank Cass & Co., 1962), p. 120; for a recent re-examination of the City's support of Edward IV, see C. M. Barron, "London and the Crown, 1451–61," in J. R. L. Highfield and Robin Jeffs, eds., *The Crown and Local Communities in England and France in the Fifteenth Century* (Gloucester: Alan Sutton, 1981), pp. 88–109.

merchandise, exchanged goods for goods."[3] The eighteen London citizens knighted between 1461 and 1471 (only eleven had been knighted before, the last in 1439) would probably have agreed with the chronicler who claimed that Edward's bounty was "a great worship unto all the city."[4]

By the beginning of the fifteenth century, well before Edward's reign, two centuries of internal turmoil and strife with English kings had endowed London with the basic set of civic institutions which would carry it into the eighteenth century. After the tumultuous crisis of the late fourteenth century, when the City magistracy finally established its control over London's fractious community of feudal guilds, the quarrel between the victuallers, who favored the strict control of markets, and the traders, who favored commerce and imports, was resolved in favor of the latter.[5] With control in the hands of the major trading companies (i.e. the Mercers, Grocers and Drapers), but restricted by charter arrangements and a well-defined magistracy, London's course as an independent, oligarchic, trading community was set. As a result, London had begun by the time of Edward's reign to experience the economic consolidation and growth that would eventually elevate it to the status of a world capital. This growth did not at first extend through the realm as a whole; indeed, the rise of London may have exacerbated the depopulation of England's countryside and the decay of its lesser towns and outports. The post-1450 recovery of the wool trade produced a wave of enclosures in the 1480s, thereby inaugurating the process of expropriation that followed the growth of the markets.[6]

But for London itself, which was already handling 70 percent of the export trade in raw wool and cloth, the more than three-fold increase in exports between 1465 and 1500 brought with it not only prosperity – a

[3] *Croyland Chronicle*, quoted in Charles Ross, *Edward IV* (Berkeley: University of California Press, 1974), p. 352; cf. More, *The History of Richard III*, ed. Richard S. Sylvester, in *The Complete Works of St. Thomas More* (New Haven: Yale University Press, 1963–), 2: 5. With the exception of *Utopia*, subsequent references to the Yale edition in the text will be noted by the abbreviation *CW*, followed by volume and page numbers. References to page and line numbers of *Utopia*, volume 4 of the Yale edition, are given in parentheses in the text.

[4] *Gregory's Chronicle*, in *Historical Collections of a Citizen of London*, ed. V. Gairdner (London: Camden Society, 1876), p. 228.

[5] On the later-fourteenth-century crisis in London, see R. Bird, *The Turbulent London of Richard II* (London: Longmans, Green, 1949); P. Nightingale, "Capitalists, Crafts and Constitutional Change in Late Fourteenth-Century London," *Past and Present*, 124 (1989), 3–35; D. W. Robertson, *Chaucer's London* (New York: John Wiley & Sons, 1968), ch. 4; A. R. Myers, *London in the Age of Chaucer* (Norman: University of Oklahoma Press, 1972), pp. 91–109; and George Unwin, *The Gilds and Companies of London* (1908; rpt. London: George Allen & Unwin, 1938), pp. 127–176.

[6] See below pp. 46–48, 68–70.

woolen cloth export boom that would last until the mid-sixteenth century – but also a flowering of the City's medieval civic and intellectual heritage.[7] By the end of the fifteenth century, the most powerful of London's guilds had been chartered to form most of the Twelve Great Livery Companies, and countless lesser guilds had received the official charters which enabled them to hold property in perpetuity.[8] Before 1400, only the Merchant Taylors and the Goldsmiths had halls of their own, but by 1500 the number stood at twenty-six.[9] The Guildhall, begun in 1411, received elaborate decorations and expansions throughout the next century; between 1447 and 1458, citizens endowed another five grammar schools in addition to the four already existing. In a step especially beneficial to trade, the Merchant Adventurers, always dominated by Londoners, were consolidated with the London Mercers by an act of Common Council in 1486. Though the settlement of the royal administration and law courts in Westminster in the fourteenth century ensured that London was already becoming a national capital, the City of London still retained the character of a late medieval commune, enjoying the independent status upheld through its hard-earned liberties. It was not yet the engine of the Tudor state, swollen with overpopulation and divided by religious faction and an ever-widening gap between rich and poor.[10]

Fifteenth-century Londoners thus enjoyed not only relative stability and prosperity but local traditions of civic consciousness and pride. After the City had won its great charter following the *Iter* of 1321, Andrew Horn, the City Chamberlain, expounded its terms for his fellow citizens. In so doing he carefully copied into his *Liber Custumarum* the *Livres dou Trésor*, a treatise on town government by Dante's teacher, Brunetto Latini; he thoughtfully inserted the title *mayor*, unknown to the original,[11] and included Latini's claim that eloquence was the essential

[7] Robert Brenner, *Merchants and Revolution: Commercial Change, Political Conflict, and London's Overseas Traders 1550–1653* (Princeton University Press, 1993), pp. 6–10; J. R. Lander, *Government and Community* (Cambridge Mass.: Harvard University Press, 1980), p. 25; D. C. Coleman, *The Economy of England, 1450–1750* (New York: Oxford University Press, 1977), pp. 49–50; S. E. Rasmussen, *London: The Unique City* (New York: Macmillan, 1937), p. 55.

[8] Unwin, *The Gilds and Companies of London*, pp. 157–172.

[9] Mary Cathcart Borer, *The City of London: A History* (London: Constable, 1977), p. 101.

[10] Paul Murray Kendall, *The Yorkist Age* (New York: Norton, 1962), p. 151.

[11] Gwyn A. Williams, *Medieval London: From Commune to Capital* (London: Athlone, 1963), pp. 312–313; cf. J. Catto, "Andrew Horn: Law and History in Fourteenth-Century England," in *The Writing of History in the Middle Ages: Essays Presented to Richard William Southern*, ed. R. H. C. Davis and J. M. Wallace-Hadrill (Oxford: Clarendon Press, 1981), pp. 367–391.

expression of civic wisdom.[12] In 1419 John Carpenter, Town Clerk of London, added official sanction to the City's foundation-myth by including it in a City custumal, the *Liber Albus* (1419). From William Fitzstephen, the twelfth-century biographer of Thomas à Becket, Carpenter took via Horn the ancient claim that "London was founded by Brut, in imitation of great Troy, before the foundation of Rome by Remus and Romulus; whence it is that even to this day it possesses the liberties, rights, and customs of the ancient city Troy. For it has its own senatorial rank as well as its minor magistracies." From this ancient myth Carpenter drew the legal conclusion that "all persons too that come here, of whatever condition they may be, whether freemen or serfs, obtain a refuge here, as well as protection and liberty."[13]

As a London officeholder, Carpenter exemplified the links that had been forged between civic service and intellectual pursuits. Carpenter's circle included such London intellectuals as Sir John Neele (founder of the Mercers' school), Reginald Pecock, and William Lichfield, the author, Stow said, of "many books both moral and divine in prose and verse."[14] Carpenter's combination of study and service was imitated in the late fifteenth century by the many London officeholders and merchants who compiled the greater London chronicles, thereby tailoring English history to a point of view dominated by the city – Notary Robert Bale (c. 1460), Mayor William Gregory (1470), Sheriff Robert Fabyan (1504), Grocer Richard Hill (1536), the Haberdasher Richard Arnold (1503), who, according to Stow, "being inflamed with the fervent loue of good learninge ... noted the charters, liberties, lawes, constitucions, and customes, of the Citie of London."[15] By the early sixteenth century, London's intellectual community had expanded

---

[12] *Liber Custumarum*, in *Munimenta Gildhallae Londoniensis*, ed. H. T. Riley (2 vols. London: Longman, Green, Logan, and Roberts, 1860), 2: 18, 20.

[13] *De Concordia Inter Regem Ric. II. et Civitatem London*, ed. Thomas Wright (London: Camden Society, 1838), pp. 31–59. John Carpenter, *Liber Albus*, ed. H. T. Riley (London: John Russell Smith, 1862), p. 54; cf. p. 427. Chaucer's associate, Mayor Nicholas Brembre, was accused of planning to change London's name to "Parva Troia"; see John P. McCall and George Rudisill, "The Parliament of 1386 and Chaucer's Trojan Parliament," *JEGP*, 58 (1959), 276–288 and esp. n. 25.

[14] John Stow, *A Survey of London* (1598; 1603), ed. C. L. Kingsford (2 vols. 1908; rpt. Oxford: Clarendon Press, 1971), 1: 235. See Thomas Brewer, *Memoir of the Life and Times of John Carpenter* (London: Arthur Taylor, 1856), pp. 62ff.; William Kellaway, "John Carpenter's *Liber Albus*," *Guildhall Studies in London History*, 3: 2 (1978), 67–84.

[15] *The Customs of London, Otherwise Called 'Arnold's Chronicle'* (London, 1811), p. 2. On the chronicle tradition, see C. L. Kingsford, *English Historical Literature in the Fifteenth Century* (1913; rpt. New York: Burt Franklin, 1962), ch. 4; Antonia Gransden, *Historical Writing in England, Volume 2 : c. 1307 to the Early Sixteenth Century* (Ithaca: Cornell University Press, 1982), pp. 230–233.

further still. *The Great Chronicle of London*, probably compiled "for the honour of this Citie" (Stow, 1 : 111) by Robert Fabyan, linked the names of several younger contemporaries – Skelton, William Cornish, and Thomas More – with those of Ralph Strode, Gower, Chaucer, and Usk, in order to claim for London an illustrious succession of "poettis of... fame."[16] William Caxton, meanwhile, had become Governor of the Merchant Adventurers in Bruges in the same year that Edward had ascended the throne, and he set up his new press at the Red Pale in Westminster in 1476. Along with his *Caton* (1485), dedicated to the City of London, "my moder of whom I haue receyued my nourture & lyuying,"[17] Caxton's titles already included several other practical and edifying works that were commissioned by or dedicated to such aspiring London merchants and officials as the mercers Hugh Bryce and William Pratt.[18] Well before Caxton had set up his press, John Shirley, a substantial London landowner, was operating a profitable scriptorium purveying works to such major London collectors as the Mercer Roger Thorney.[19] Against a background of baronial warfare, the stability and prosperity of London's merchant community had produced a substantial intellectual and literary culture.

That culture, however, was expanded, enriched, and ultimately transformed by the new generation of writers and officials – most of them Londoners by birth or career – who grew up in the traditional urban milieu but brought the novel influence of continental humanism to bear on many areas of English life, including the perception of London itself. The central figures in this movement, Thomas More and John Colet, were the sons of established Londoners, held citizenship, and belonged to the powerful Company of Mercers. Like More and Colet, many of the outstanding early humanists were active in the public life of London, William Grocyn as rector of St. Lawrence Jewry, Thomas Linacre as a practicing physician and founder of the Linacre Lectures and the College of Physicians, William Lily as first master of the re-endowed St. Paul's School.[20] Thomas Lupset, an early humanist protégé and one of the first pupils at the new St. Paul's, was the son of a London goldsmith. It is not surprising, then, that the first English translations of Erasmus' *Praise of Folly* and More's *Utopia* "were made by two citizens of London – a

---

[16] *The Great Chronicle of London*, ed. A. H. Thomas and I. D. Thornley (London, 1938), p. 361.
[17] Prologue to *Caton*, in *Prologues and Epilogues of William Caxton*, ed. W. J. B. Crotch (London: EETS, 1928), p. 77.
[18] See N. F. Blake, *Caxton and his World* (London: André Deutsch, 1969).
[19] Derek Pearsall, *John Lydgate* (London: Routledge and Kegan Paul, 1970), p. 73.
[20] Maria Dowling, *Humanism in the Age of Henry VIII* (London: Croom Helm, 1986), pp. 8–9.

mercer and a goldsmith – at the request of London entrepreneurs."[21] Thanks in part to the relative openness of London's merchant class to the novel influence of humanism, and in part to the opportunities London provided for exercising the active roles promoted by humanism, "the brightest and the best of the English humanist community were gathered in London on the eve of the Reformation."[22] Erasmus could claim after his second visit to England that "there is no land on earth which, even over its whole extent, has brought me so many friends, or such true, scholarly, helpful, and distinguished ones, graced by every kind of good quality, as the single city of London."[23]

By thus identifying England's renascent culture with the urban sphere of London, Erasmus was implicitly reinforcing the common connection between the literary and pedagogical ideals of humanism and its civic aims and bias – a connection underlined in his recollection of the Socratic dictum that "it is not the fields and trees which can teach me, but men who live in towns."[24] It is virtually a commonplace that in the development of humanist learning in the Renaissance the reception of ancient prudence was attached to the rise of "civic" humanism; to the spread of intellectual debate, secularism, republicanism, and regular government; to the elevation of talent and learning over birth, individuality over feudal structure, mobility (vertical and horizontal) over status; and to the active use of virtue, ingenuity and risk-taking in the creative shaping of the human environment.[25] But in fact the humanist republic of letters was not wholly congruent with anything like a steady vector of civic and political development. Rather, the new learning followed a number of tortuous paths from the urban, civic contexts of

---

[21] Margo Todd, *Christian Humanism and the Puritan Social Order* (Cambridge University Press, 1987), p. 41.
[22] Susan Brigden, *London and the Reformation* (Oxford: Clarendon Press, 1989), p.71.
[23] Ep. 195, in *The Correspondence of Erasmus*, tr. R. A. B. Mynors and D. F. S. Thomson, in *The Collected Works of Erasmus* (Toronto University Press, 1974-), 2: 199; cf. Ep. 118, in 1: 235–236. For the appeal of humanism to the merchant class, see Brigden, *London and the Reformation*, pp.68–86 and Fritz Caspari, *Humanism and the Social Order in Tudor England* (University of Chicago Press, 1954), p. 3.
[24] *The Antibarbarians*, tr. Margaret Mann Phillips, in *The Collected Works of Erasmus*, 23: 119.
[25] The classic statement of this view is in Hans Baron, *The Crisis of the Early Italian Renaissance: Civic Humanism and Republican Liberty in an Age of Classicism and Tyranny* (Princeton University Press, 1966), pp. 191–272. An important critique of the Baron thesis is Jerrold Siegel, "Civic Humanism or Ciceronian Rhetoric?: The Culture of Petrarch and Bruni," *Past and Present*, 34 (1966). For a recent survey of debate on the subject, see Albert Rabil, Jr., "The Significance of 'Civic Humanism' in the Interpretation of the Italian Renaissance," in Rabil, ed., *Renaissance Humanism: Foundations, Forms, and Legacy* (3 vols. Philadelphia: University of Pennsylvania Press, 1988), 1: 141–174.

republicanism to the contexts of courtiership, diplomacy, poetry, aestheticism, and service to absolutism.[26]

When humanism finally took root in the London of Thomas More's generation, the movement arrived at a time and in a place that were historically transitional. While in many respects an insular commune that had developed its local rights and privileges in a late-feudal setting, London was also in the process of becoming the economic engine and administrative center of the new Tudor state. The traditional culture of London, as yet largely untouched by humanism, had been essentially local and inward-looking. The principal literary works were, in the tradition of Horn and Carpenter, local custumals and annals written by (and largely for) local officeholders. Even the poet Lydgate's works for the City were either public ceremonials like his royal entry for Henry VI and his Corpus Christi procession text,[27] or, perhaps more tellingly, private indoor mummings for London's leading officeholders and companies.[28] The London chronicle tradition, still being followed by Stow in the later sixteenth century, was localist in perspective and highly insular in its ritualized practice of organizing history around the annual elections of London's mayor and sheriffs. Thomas Nashe would later mock the narrow citizen mentality of "good maister Stow" and "lay Chronographers, that write of nothing but of Mayors and Sheriefs."[29] But as the course of events in the fifteenth century had demonstrated, the highly regular and cohesive government of the municipality provided an important counterbalance to the unpredictabilities of baronial rivalry, dynastic succession, and changing royal policies. Upon the death of a monarch, the Lord Mayor of London became the highest-ranking officer in the kingdom, and English monarchs had learned – some to their cost – that "London is a mighty arme and instrument to bring any great desire to effect, if it may be woon to a mans deuotion" (Stow, 2: 206). London's stable merchant community provided the Crown with a dependable source of revenue and credit, and its elaborate and effective

---

[26] See especially the accounts of Eugene Garin, *Italian Humanism: Philosophy and Civic Life in the Renaissance*, tr. Peter Munz (Oxford: Blackwell, 1965), and G. K. Hunter, *John Lyly: The Humanist as Courtier* (Cambridge, Mass.: Harvard University Press, 1962), ch. 1.

[27] *Ordenaunces ffor the Kyng Made in the Cite off London* (1432), in H. N. MacCracken, ed., *The Minor Poems of John Lydgate* (2 vols. 1934; rpt. London: EETS, 1961), 2: 630; *An Ordenaunce of a Precessyoun of þe Feste of Corpus Cristi Made in London*, ibid., 1: 35.

[28] *A Balade by Lydegate, Sent by a Poursyvant to þe Shirreves of London, Minor Poems*, 2: 668; *A Lettre Made in Wyse of Balade ... fore þe Mayre of London, Eestfeld*, 2: 695; *A Mommynge, whiche þe Goldesmithes of þe Cite of London Mommed ... to þeyre Mayre Eestfeld*, 2: 698.

[29] *Works*, ed. R. B. McKerrow (5 vols. Oxford: Blackwell, 1958), 1: 317, 294.

administrative machinery became a means by which the nascent Tudor state could carry out its programs and policies.[30]

The contribution of the traditional urban community to the emerging state is perhaps epitomized in the London chronicle tradition itself, which culminated in Fabyan's *New Chronicles* (1504), where the celebration of the providential advent of the Tudors set the precedent for Hall, Holinshed, and other encomiasts of the new nation–state. This moment of the civic community's outward turn, the moment of the humanistic reception, was simultaneously the moment of Thomas More and of the advent of the Tudor state, with its new nobility and its new community of honor. From this moment the practice of letters moved from the notarial, manuscript culture of London officeholders to the polemical, print culture of humanists like More, who set the new pattern whereby intellectual talent and eloquence – like other assets of the local London community – were recruited or appropriated by the emerging state apparatus. As civic officials virtually ceased to write for themselves, a new place and perspective for letters was created, an external space in which traditional visions of the city were shaped by new and wider concerns. Like the other members of his generation who were nurtured in the older civic heritage but went on to serve the promise of the new order, More occupied perspectives both within and without the traditional civic community and its ways of thinking, so that the city appeared to him at once as a solid, visible body and a fluid force.

No Londoner before More's time had subjected the city – or himself as citizen – to such penetrating scrutiny. His *Utopia*, focused on Amaurotum, the capital and urban centerpiece of an ideally constituted realm, is the first work in the English-speaking world to reflect that totalizing social vision whereby Renaissance thinkers, according to Michel de Certeau, transformed "the urban fact into the concept of a city." Bringing the influence of Renaissance civic humanism to bear on the concerns of the emerging Tudor state, More exemplifies a new form of "utopian" thinking that attributes to the city "all the functions and predicates that were previously scattered and assigned to many different real subjects – groups, associations, and individuals." While More's *Utopia* surveys a host of problems besetting the contemporary world, it imagines their solution within a conceptual framework whose material counterpart is a perfectly ordered urbanistic space. Between history and utopian ideation there is thus what de Certeau calls a "progressive symbiosis: to plan a city is both to *think the very plurality* of the real and

---

[30] Robert Ashton, *The City and the Court, 1603–1643* (Cambridge University Press, 1979), p. 17.

to make that way of thinking the plural effective" through the command-and-control rigor of geometry. Yet in More's pioneering work, this symbiosis is never a simple identity, because for More the complex, plural realities of contemporary historical experience give rise to "contradictory movements that counterbalance and combine themselves outside the reach" of the geometrically perfected, urbanistic ideal.[31]

More's peculiar situation – experientially liminal (divided between City and court) and historically transitional (moving from medieval commune to Renaissance capital) – perhaps accounts for his creation of the literary genre of the utopia, in Louis Marin's view the literary genre most sensitive to contradiction. According to Marin, the utopian genre functions as a critique of ideology precisely insofar as it does not smooth over or conceal contradictions but gives them figurative expression.[32] Yet, paradoxically, insofar as the utopian genre cannot historicize itself or provide the scientific theory of its own production, it can only designate "the [empty] place for the scientific theory of society" (p. 198). Unlike myth, a positive which resolves or harmonizes contradictions or opposites,[33] utopia takes place in a neutral space where contradictions, represented or figured without being scientifically historicized, are characterized by mobility, heterogeneity, and noncongruence.

Writing when a number of historic developments converged on London, and influenced by the conflicting elements of a new evangelical humanism, More embodied in his *Utopia* an intellectual impasse, in which it was possible neither to isolate the city as a local community from its larger historical setting nor to integrate it with this setting in anything like a scientific manner. If More's vision of the city and citizenship exhibits a tendency toward what Stephen Greenblatt calls "self-cancellation,"[34] this is precisely because the city was for More the focus for the contradictory possibilities of his moment – for the hope that radical reform might reshape a declining feudal kingdom as a community of citizens, for the fear that this reform would require a dangerously new and radical concentration of power. As the center of More's reformed Utopian social order, the capital city of Amaurotum aspires to be the mythical positive that resolves the contradictions of contemporary England; but it is also an anti-mythic negative that figuratively highlights

[31] Michel de Certeau, *The Practice of Everyday Life*, tr. Steven F. Rendall (Berkeley: University of California Press, 1984), pp. 94–95.

[32] Louis Marin, *Utopics: Spatial Play*, tr. Robert Vollrath (London: Macmillan, 1984), pp. 195, 201.

[33] See Fredric Jameson, "Of Islands and Trenches: Naturalization and the Production of Utopian Discourse," *Diacritics*, 7: 2 (1977), 4–5.

[34] *Renaissance Self-Fashioning, From More to Shakespeare* (University of Chicago Press, 1980), p. 45.

those contradictions and the lack of a means of resolving them. The representational noncongruences of Amaurotum, heart of the Utopian order, thus converge figuratively to yield a complex, three-dimensional picture with many affinities – if only in negative form – to the perspectival art of Renaissance humanism. Several different – even contradictory – aspects or meanings of urban life and social order are held ironically in mutual configuration, lending depth and substance to More's image of civic man. Starting from within both the ideology and the geometrical techniques of humanism, which promote the city as the perfected center of human achievement and the norm from which humans derive their identity and being, More came to articulate the city's deepest paradox, the tension between concentration and decentralization, between the radical convergence of power and the radical distribution of justice, between the power of civic order to liberate its creators and its power to enslave them. Though in part a function of More's humanism – of the tensions between More's civic impulses and his evangelical spirituality – the paradox was more deeply conditioned by More's historical standpoint at a crucial moment of transition, as London's contribution to the emerging concentration of power in the Tudor state created possibilities of reform and social change which were nevertheless at odds with the traditional ideals of the urban commune. The sense of depth and complexity in the *Utopia*, then, is achieved, by playing points of view and conflicting historical possibilities against each other, allowing them, by mutual configuration (and even cancellation), to represent the contradictions of More's historical moment. Essential to the *Utopia*, the work in which More comes closest to plotting out in an imagined space the paradoxes of the urban life of his time, these techniques originate in the very identities More fabricated for himself.

Representing the city and the self

In the biographical portraits composed by More himself and by his contemporaries, the posture of detachment from the world is so pervasive as to seem iconic. In the famous portrait of More sketched for Ulrich von Hutten, Erasmus declared that

One might say he was another Democritus – or better, that Pythagorean philosopher who strolls around the market place, completely detached, and observes all the hubbub among the buyers and the sellers. Nobody is less influenced by the judgement of the masses but on the other hand nobody is closer to the feeling of the common man.[35]

[35] Ep. 999, in *Erasmus and His Age*, ed. Hans J. Hillerbrand, tr. M. A. Haworth (New York: Harper and Row, 1968), pp. 142–143.

This posture of detachment was widely disseminated in the humanist circles of which More was a member. Erasmus had claimed in the dedication of *The Praise of Folly* (1511) that More habitually played the role of Democritus, and Richard Pace, extolling More's character as *urbanus*, went on to label him "the son or successor of Democritus."[36] The adjective *urbanus*, however, actually highlights the mutual implication between More and his social surroundings, linking the urbane pose he strikes to the urban world – the hubbub of buyers and sellers – that helps to shape it. The city is the background that brings the persona into life, just as the detachment of the bemused persona gives the city its contrastingly feverish cast. The same principles apply to an early self-portrait, part of a letter to John Colet, in which More adopts a pose remarkably similar to the ones delineated by his friends:

> For in the city what is there to move one to live well? but rather, when a man is straining in his own power to climb the steep path of virtue, it turns him back by a thousand devices and sucks him back by its thousand enticements. Wherever you betake yourself, on one side nothing but feigned love and the honeyed poisons of smooth flatterers resound; on the other, fierce hatreds, quarrels, the din of the forum murmur against you. Wherever you turn your eyes, what else will you see but confectioners, fishmongers, butchers, cooks, poulterers, fishermen, fowlers, who supply the materials for gluttony and the world and the world's lord, the devil? Nay even houses block out from us I know not how large a measure of light, and do not permit us to see the heavens. And the round horizon does not limit the air but lofty roofs.[37]

In this darker portrait, the depicted self negotiates a more treacherous terrain, a whirlpool of devices and enticements, with less self-possession than the Erasmian Democritus. But beneath the tonal variation lies a roughly similar mixture of detachment and proximity toward the "din of the Forum," and an even more strikingly familiar symbiosis of self and world, persona and scene. More's detachment from the noisy forum is inseparable from his representing it as such; he escapes implication in the busy world of urban life only by affirming its alien reality.

This tactic of playing his urbane persona against the scene of urban folly is common in More's writing. Folly, More once wrote, "is really a large metropolis," thereby referring to the claim of Erasmus' Folly that she so pervades civic life and forms that "one Democritus would not be

---

[36] *The Praise of Folly*, tr. Clarence Miller (New Haven: Yale University Press, 1979), p. 2; Richard Pace, *De Fructu*, tr. Frank Manley and R. S. Sylvester (New York: Unger, 1967), pp. 104–105. Colet invokes the laughing Democritus in his *Exposition of St. Paul's First Epistle to the Corinthians*, tr. J. H. Lupton (London: George Bell, 1874), pp. 45–46.

[37] *Selected Letters*, tr. Elizabeth F. Rogers (New Haven: Yale University Press, 1961), pp. 4–5; hereafter cited in the text as "Rogers."

enough to make fun of them."[38] In More's work even more than in Erasmus', the city is the favored scene for entertainments staged by Folly. The urbane, saturnine persona of More's epigrams, for example, is witness to a scene populated by "merchants, lawyers, courtiers, harlots, cuckolds, worldly priests, stepmothers, actors, sailors, peasants, physicians, drunkards, illiterate bishops, and wives of various unsavoury sorts."[39] More frequently adopts the withdrawn stance of those philosophers who in *Utopia* "observe the people rushing out into the streets and being soaked by constant showers and cannot induce them to go indoors and escape the rain. Therefore... they keep at home, since they cannot remedy the folly of others" (102/15–20).

If this configuration of urbanity with urban folly was predominantly Lucianic in tone and derivation, its underlying motives also included the late medieval spirituality and habits of expression typical of More's earliest works. In the *Rueful Lamentacion* and the *Nine Pageants*, for example, More's vision of "Worldly vanitee" owed more to Christian asceticism than to Lucianic irony.[40] Yet More's Christianity finally rendered earthly life more complex and opaque without leading to its repudiation.[41] Rarely does More invoke the move that would terminate the game, the ultimate renunciation that would cancel the world, and with it, the self. More's Menippus, for example, arrives at an uneasy peace with the city, endorsing the advice of Teiresias that "The life of the common sort is best... Make it always your sole object to put the present to good use and hasten on your way, laughing a great deal and taking nothing seriously."[42] The Democritean More who habitually ridicules the lives of ordinary mortals in Erasmus' dedication to the *Folly* is also the remarkably sweet and gentle man for all seasons with all men (p. 2).

The human sympathy beneath More's posture of detachment reflects the means by which the pose had been derived, a necessary dependency on community, without which a definition of the self would have been, for humanists like Erasmus and More, unthinkable. Another of More's favored personae thus affirmed his deep commitment to the common life. Like his urbane persona, More's posture as citizen was a collective artifact, perpetrated by his admirers as well as by himself. Erasmus noted that "to be born and educated in that most famous of all cities is regarded as bestowing some nobility on a person."[43] But the city also provided the sphere for noble and distinguished acts. The official records of London

---

[38] Rogers, p. 119; *The Praise of Folly*, p. 41.
[39] Alistair Fox, *Thomas More: History and Providence* (Oxford: Basil Blackwell, 1982), p. 45.
[40] *The Workes of Sir Thomas More, Knyght...in the Englysh Tonge* (1557), sig. cv.
[41] Greenblatt, *Renaissance Self-Fashioning*, pp. 14–15.   [42] *Menippus, CW*, 3: 179.
[43] Ep. 2750, in Hillerbrand, ed., *Erasmus and His Age*, p. 272.

extolled More as a "specyall lover and ffrende in the busynesses and Causes of this Citie."[44] "As he was borne in London," an early biographer reported, so was More "of the saide Citie dearly beloued" for conducting himself "sincerely and uprightly" as Under-Sheriff and in other roles.[45] In *The Book of Sir Thomas More*, a late sixteenth-century play by several hands, More had become a legendary citizen who "set a glosse on Londons fame," and was "the best freend that the poore ere had."[46]

In this portrait-type, as in its seeming opposite, city and self are shaped by mutual configuration. The image of citizen More is a reciprocal function of the image of London, "the chiefe and notable principall Citie of this our noble Realme."[47] Four times in the 1518 Basle edition of *Utopia*, beginning with the title-page, imposing Roman capitals ceremoniously announced the author as INCLYTAE CIVITATIS LONDINENSIS CIVIS & VICECOMITIS – Citizen and Sheriff of the famous City of London.[48] The authorship of this inscriptional apparatus is problematic, but More's self-composed epitaph also identified him as *urbe Londinensi familia non celebri sed honesta natus*.[49] More's commissioned orations on behalf of London were presumably the tributes of a loyal citizen rather than the barbs of a Lucianic ironist; if the case were otherwise, the City would hardly have recorded its thanks for the "labour and payn that he toke for the Citie" on welcoming Charles V in 1522.[50]

Yet it is finally the interplay between detachment and involvement, distaste and dedication that accounts for the peculiar density of More's

[44] John R. O'Connell, "Saint Thomas More as Citizen," *Dublin Review*, 197 (1935), 47. The full title of the first English translation of *Utopia* reveals More's traditional appeal to Londoners: *A Fruteful and Pleasaunt Worke of the Beste State of a Publyque Weale, and of the Newe Yle Called Utopia: Written in Latine by Syr Thomas More, Knyght, and translated into Englyshe by Raphe Robynson Citizein and Goldsmithe of London, at the Procurement, and Earnest Request of George Tadlowe Citizein & Haberdassher of the Same Cittie*, 1551. Robinson was also, significantly, the translator of Patrizzi's *Moral Methode of Ciuile Policie*, 1576; see p. 55n below.

[45] Nicholas Harpsfield, *The Life and Death of Sir Thomas Moore, Knight*, ed. E. V. Hitchcock (London: EETS, 1932), pp. 19–20.

[46] *The Book of Sir Thomas More*, ed. W. W. Greg (London: Malone Society, 1911), ll. 965–966, 1647–1648.

[47] Harpsfield, *The Life and Death of Sir Thomas Moore, Knight*, p. 9.

[48] Variations from the title-page (*CW* 4: cxcv), quoted here, are slight. At the beginning of Book I, More is INCLYTAE BRITTANIARUM VRBIS LONDINI ET CIVEM, ET CIVITATEM (46/6–7), and at both the beginning and the end of Book II he is CIVEM ET VICECOMITEM LONDINENSEM (110/6; 246/9).

[49] The epitaph is printed in *The Workes of Sir Thomas More, Knyght ... in the Englysh Tonge*, p. 1419 ff. and reproduced as an appendix in E. V. Hitchcock's edition of Harpsfield, *The Life and Death of Sir Thomas Moore, Knight*, pp. 279–281. See also McConica, "The Patrimony of Thomas More," p. 57.

[50] O'Connell, "Saint Thomas More as Citizen," pp. 47–48; More also welcomed the Venetian ambassadors in 1517, 1525, and 1526.

self-image. More's most famous depiction of his civic dedication, in the *Utopia*, is thus shot through with a sense of unreality and ambivalence:

I am constantly engaged in legal business, either pleading or hearing, either giving an award as arbiter or deciding a case as judge. I pay a visit of courtesy to one man and go on business to another. I devote almost the whole day in public to other men's affairs and the remainder to my own. I leave to myself, that is to learning, nothing at all. (p. 39)

Here, in effect, the identities of philosopher and citizen simultaneously converge and conflict, as the active citizen and lover of the common life perceives with Democritean clarity the pointlessness of it all. Such conflicted moments show More's historical situation introjecting itself into both the career and the mind. Only six months before his involvement in quelling London's 1517 Evil May Day Riots, More wrote to Erasmus of his desire to withdraw from active life and especially from the drudgery of administering the law. The alternative he proposed was the famous wish to rule forever in Utopia:

in my daydreams I have been marked out by my Utopians to be their king forever; I can see myself now marching along, crowned with a diadem of wheat, very striking in my Franciscan frock, carrying a handful of wheat as my sceptre, thronged by a distinguished retinue of Amaurotians, and, with this huge entourage, giving audience to foreign ambassadors and sovreigns. (Rogers, p. 85)

Ironically, the effect of the daydream is not to clarify More's relation to the world but to complicate it, to compound paradoxes rather than resolve them. To emerge into authentic and independent selfhood in the guise of a king – even the philosopher–king Utopus – is, in keeping with its Platonic paradigm, a paradoxically political way of expressing a desire to withdraw from politics. But furthermore, the trappings of this king, especially the Franciscan robe which threatens to negate his power the moment it is asserted, point to even deeper contradictions. The Franciscan robe is a version of the cloak (*chlamyda*) of natural color worn by all Utopian citizens (p. 132), and the wheaten diadem and sceptre evoke the handful of wheat which is not, in fact, the *signum* of the king (which Utopia, in any case, does not have) but the symbol bestowed on each of the elected governors of Utopia's fifty-four city–states (p. 194). These contradictions are further underlined by the entourage of the would-be king, which consists of Amaurotians, not Utopians, the members of a city republic, not a national court. Taking up the role of a monarch in a realm that does not have one, More surrounds himself with a retinue of citizens from a free metropolis and wears the trappings by which Utopians symbolically repudiate the pomp of kings and honor their leading citizens. As King of Utopia More achieves the ultimate individuation, an autonomy that, free of implication in the world, endows him with the power to shape that world to his will. As Governor of Amaurotum he achieves the utmost integration with the commensal ways of civic life; first among equals, he accepts the responsibilities defined by the community of which he is a member.

More's daydream thus supplants one conflict with another, replaces the choice between public involvement and intellectual withdrawal with a series of self-cancelling possibilities: a king as against a republican governor, the centralized rule of a nation as against the shared administration of a city, an autonomous self endowed with power over the world as against a corporate identity that implicates More with it. The product of this mutual cancellation is a self at once detached from and involved in a dominion represented neither by a royal court nor by an egalitarian city. This creative play of possibilities is a function of More's historical moment, the moment of the weakening of feudalism and the economic emergence of the urban merchant community, but also the moment of the advent of the monarchical state, which that community helped to consolidate. There is thus a powerful reason for More's admission in the letter that this version of the self and world exists in Utopia, that is, nowhere, as a stable and coherent order. Nowhere is also, of course, the neutral space of Utopian letters.

The strategy of the daydream is essentially the strategy of a conflicted citizen who stands in problematic relation to the potentially divergent interests of London, a civic oligarchy, and the court, the center of the new monarchy's power. On the one hand, More's identification with the citizen community of London is undercut by an awareness of the isolated and privileged place of London in the kingdom and thus of the need for a higher authority to curb its power for the good of the common weal. Such was London's growing domination of the country at the time of the Reformation Parliament (1529) that it was being argued that while Londoners were at liberty to govern themselves, they might not "stretch to govern or to correct any other of the King's subjects being no such citizens."[51] At his trial More himself argued by analogy to London's place in England that a national church could no more usurp the universal laws of Christendom "than the City of London, being but one poor member in respect of the whole realm, might make a law against an act of Parliament to bind the whole realm."[52] More's position – the

---

[51] *A Dyalogue Betwene ... Clement a Clerke ... and Bernarde a Burges*, sig. B7, quoted in Brigden, *London and the Reformation*, p. 176.

[52] William Roper, *The Life of Sir Thomas More*, in *Two Early Tudor Lives*, ed. Richard S. Sylvester and Davis P. Harding (New Haven: Yale University Press, 1962), p. 248.

correct one in English law – was that in cases of conflict the power of the lesser entity must not take precedence over the interests of the greater whole.[53] To belong to "the chiefe and notable principall Citie" of London could, as Erasmus had said, bestow "some nobility upon a person." But with the privileges of London, and with all they entailed in the way of acquisitive self-interest, came a threat – at the national level – to the very ideals of common interest London citizenship theoretically implied. More's effort to imagine the larger and harmonious whole of the nation, however, founders on the necessary asymmetries and possible corruptions of the radical power – centered in the monarchy – on which the rule of that nation seemed increasingly to depend. The subjects of kings, More wrote to Erasmus in 1516, "are really worse off than slaves; ... it is a much higher honor to rule over a free people" (Rogers, p. 80). Harpsfield's claim that More initially resisted royal appointment lest his fellow-citizens think "he would not beare himselfe vprightly and sincerely" has a solid foundation in More's self-portraiture. In a letter to Erasmus, More expressed his hesitation to take a position at court because

its acceptance would mean that either I would have to leave my present post in London, which I do prefer even to a higher one, or, what is not at all to my liking, I would have to retain it and thereby occasion resentment among the townsfolk ... they would be skeptical about my sincerity and loyalty to them and consider me under obligation to the king as his pensioner. (Rogers, p. 70)

The conflict More sensed between the City and the court is embedded in the dilemma of *Utopia*'s Dialogue of Counsel, the contradiction between the desire for radical reform, based on the establishment of institutions that embody justice, and the necessity of a radical politics, which concentrates the massive power by which reform is brought about.[54] There is a commonsense perception of the conflict in Hythloday's warnings that the reformer who approaches the center of power risks the integrity of his reform and of his being.[55] But the philosophical basis of the dilemma is embodied in the contradictory approaches to politics in Plato's *Republic* and *Laws*. In *The Republic*, the realization and main-tenance of perfect justice cannot be entrusted to the feeble power of institutions but requires the radical potency of a philosopher–king; but

---

[53] See Duncan M. Derrett, "Thomas More and the Legislation of the Corporation of London," in *Essential Articles for the Study of Thomas More*, ed. Richard S. Sylvester and G. P. Marc'hadour (Hamden, Conn.: Archon Books, 1977), pp. 49–54.

[54] See Martin Fleisher, *Radical Reform and Political Persuasion in the Life and Writings of Thomas More* (Geneva: Librairie Droz, 1973), pp. 137–139.

[55] See Hexter's Introduction to *Utopia*, *CW* 4, p. xc.

when Plato endorses the ideal of rule through *recta instituta* in *The Laws*, the radically potent philosopher–king must disappear.

In the debate between More and Hythloday, as well as in More's daydream, the moral and philosophic conflicts between public life and the private pursuit of letters only thinly disguise a more weighty historical conflict between alternative modes of public service – between a reformer's dedication to a common life ruled by norms of civic commensality, and a reformer's need for radical power, epitomized in the rising state. The conflict is writ large in More's career: two prefatory pieces in the *Utopia* (by Geldenhauer and Grapheus) identify More as the glory of London, while two others (by Desmarais and Busleiden) extoll him as a Briton.[56]

It is important not to exaggerate the actual conflict between More's services to the Crown and his services to London. The interests of the two often coincided, and More's specialty was in diplomatic and commercial negotiations which were advantageous to both. As early as 1511 More was reported to be meeting frequently with the Chancellor and was speaking for the guilds before the House of Lords and the Bishop of Norwich; his petition for salary in arrears shortly after entering the Council in 1517 is an indication of royal employment well before this date.[57] Equally important, More's involvement in City affairs continued into his later career.[58] But the dramatic way in which More construed these activities as alternatives points to an underlying contradiction in the social fabric and in the choices available to an early Tudor humanist. While More might take up active roles in the City or the court, the friction between these roles would have told him that he was neither a typical citizen nor a typical courtier. It was, paradoxically, precisely his difference from the typical citizen or courtier that made it possible for him to "represent," both as statesman and artist, the interests and ideals of both the citizen community and the emerging nation–state. It is also

[56] *CW* 4, pp. 30/1–16, 28/14–25, 36/28–29.

[57] See Russell Ames, *Citizen Thomas More and His Utopia* (Princeton University Press, 1949), pp. 45, 51; O'Connell, "Saint Thomas More as Citizen," p. 38; J. A. Guy, *The Public Career of Sir Thomas More* (New Haven: Yale University Press, 1980), p. 8; and G. R. Elton, "Thomas More, Councillor," in *St. Thomas More: Action and Contemplation*, ed. Richard S. Sylvester (New Haven: Yale University Press, 1972), pp. 85–121.

[58] See William Nelson, "Thomas More, Grammarian and Orator," in Sylvester and Marc'hadour (eds.), *Essential Articles*, pp. 150–160, for an account of More's oratory on behalf of the City. O'Connell notes that More was assigned to explain the execution of Buckingham to the Aldermen in 1521, "Saint Thomas More as Citizen," p. 46. Ames takes note of More's negotiation between the Merchant Adventurers and the Lord Admiral in 1521 and his arbitration in a Chancery suit involving a London draper and a merchant of Toulouse in 1531, *Citizen Thomas More and His Utopia*, pp. 56–58.

what made him finally an intellectual citizen whose most important innovations and reforms took shape within the realm of letters.

The plotting of *Utopia*

As in the shaping of More's identity, so in the *Utopia*, the city plays a central role, even while it is set in a larger scheme of things. Hythloday's description of Utopia begins with a sweeping survey of the island's urban resources: the vast inland harbor crossed by ships in all directions, the vital ports that ring the island's outer shore, and the fifty-four magnificent and spacious city–states which are the heart of Utopian life.[59] The centerpiece of the description is the capital city of Amaurotum, the place visited by Hythloday and thus both the standpoint occupied by the narrator and the exemplary part that represents the whole in the narrative.[60] The entire account ends with More's reflection on what may be expected *in nostris ciuitatibus* (246/2).

What brings the urban bias and inspiration of *Utopia* most fully into focus, however, is the contrastive technique of the work itself, its power of keeping the known, familiar world so much in view while exploring the furthest reaches of a fictional realm. That realm, to adopt a title used by a later imitator of More, is a *mundus alter et idem*, a world different and yet the same.[61] Just as the island of Utopia resembles England in several geographical details,[62] so its chief and capital city, Amaurotum the foggy city, is in many respects the negative image of London. Sited on a low rising hill at the edge of a tidal river navigable for trade and spanned by a magnificent bridge, the city is twice as long as it is broad, surrounded by walls on three sides, and bisected by a second, smaller stream which provides its drinking water. These well-known resemblances, however, are only one basis for More's "lovingly idealized image of his native city";[63] another is the strong resemblance of Amaurotum's civic government to that of London. Like London, Amaurotum is governed by two bodies, an upper *senatus* and a lower assembly (*comitia*, 124/1), which resemble London's Aldermanic Court and Common Council, respectively. The upper *senatus* of twenty annually elected tranibors, like London's twenty-five aldermen, who met with the mayor on Tuesdays and Thursdays, "enter into consultation with the governor (*principus*)

[59] Ames, *Citizen Thomas More and His Utopia*, pp. 86, 99.
[60] Marin, *Utopics*, p. 120.
[61] Joseph Hall, *Mundus Alter et Idem* (1606), tr. John Millor Wands (New Haven: Yale University Press, 1981).
[62] See, for example, the notes in *CW* 4 on 110/7 (p. 384) and 116/21 (p. 392).
[63] Richard S. Sylvester, "Images of the City in Thomas More's *Utopia*," in *Les Cités au Temps de la Renaissance*, ed. M. T. Jones-Davies (Université de Paris–Sorbonne: Centre de Recherches sur la Renaissance, 1977), pp. 193–194.

every other day.''[64] Each tranibor represents a district of ten syphogrants, who are in many respects equivalent to the members of London's lower elective body, the Common Council. Each London ward popularly elected at the wardmote as many as eight councilmen; in a year when each of the twenty-five London wards elected eight, the number on the Council would be identical to the 200 syphogrants who serve in Amaurotum; the 187 who are known to have served in Edward VI's reign are roughly equivalent.[65] The business of the upper *senatus* is often laid before the assembly (*comitia*) of syphogrants (126/4–7), just as London's aldermen often brought their business before the Common Council.[66]

But if the 200 syphogrants are roughly equivalent to London's Common Council, they also consolidate the functions of those smaller units, the precinct and the parish. The number of syphogrants is roughly equivalent to the number of precincts (jurisdictions of the constable) in early sixteenth-century London.[67] Each syphograncy, comprising thirty households, forms one side of a square enclosing a common green. The paternalistic and familial nature of the syphograncy, as well as the etymology of these phylarchs or syphogrants, who preside in them as "heads of tribes" or "wise elders," strongly suggest the sort of personal ties and solidarity to be found in parish and precinct life.

The simplified consolidation of London parish, precinct, and ward offices in Utopia's syphograncies goes hand-in-hand with the geometrical and numerical integration of Amaurotum's parts into a perfect whole. The foursquare shape of Amaurotum, with its four quarters and its grid

[64] *Utopia* 122/23–25; in the *Confutation of Tyndale's Answer*, More explains that an Englishman who comes upon the Latin phrase *senatus Londinensis* "shold not translate yt in to this worde senate / but ... into mayre and aldermen" (*CW* 8: 187).

[65] The constitution of London and its civic practice were in fact somewhat ambiguous and fluid, and it is difficult to sketch a model that would be valid for every year between 1500 and 1640. See the very useful overview in Valerie Pearl, *London and the Outbreak of the Puritan Revolution* (Oxford University Press, 1961), pp. 45–68; cf. Frank Freeman Foster, *The Politics of Stability : A Portrait of the Rulers in Elizabethan London* (London: Royal Historical Society, 1977), pp. 30–41.

[66] Pearl, *London and the Outbreak of the Puritan Revolution*, pp. 57–58. There are further resemblances: in the election of a governor (*principus*), the equivalent of London's mayor, the syphograncy combines the function of the Common Council with the function of London's electoral assembly, the Common Hall, which at More's time was only beginning to be distinguished from the Common Council. The Common Hall sent up two nominations to the aldermen, who then signified their choice to the Common Hall for its approval (Pearl, p. 51). In Amaurotum, one of the four nominees from the popular assemblies in each of the city's four quarters – which thus perform the function of the Common Hall – is elected governor by the syphograncy and recommended to the Senate (122/13–19). In London aldermanic elections, four nominees were presented by the ward to the aldermen for their choice.

[67] In later Tudor London, there were 242 precincts; Foster, *The Politics of Stability*, p. 29; Pearl, "Social Policy in Early Modern London," in *History and Imagination*, ed. Lloyd-Jones, Pearl, and Worden, p. 116.

of enclosed squares, transforms social and political life into a coherent architectural space, giving articulate expression to a potential that remained confused and inarticulate in London, where "half of the City parishes stretched across ward boundaries, and nine-tenths of them were in more than one precinct."[68] This articulation of potential is of course also a revision.[69] But the undeniable presence of London behind the civic institutions as well as the landscape of Amaurotum suggests that in the urban centerpiece of *Utopia* there lies compelling reason to agree with Peter Giles, that "in all the five years which Raphael spent on the island, he did not see as much as one may perceive in More's description" (22/4–7).

The image of Amaurotum thus draws on contrastive principles that ramify in opposing perspectives throughout the work. The dramatic, dialogical nature of *Utopia*, its two-book structure, and the history of its composition all ensure that the old and new worlds, Europe and Utopia, are interdependent and mutually clarifying images. Europeans believe they inhabit an older world and possess, in name at least, the treasure of an ancient classical and Christian heritage, but they immediately forget the wisdom borne by visitors from the new world (p. 108). The Utopians, who believe there were cities among them before there were men in Europe, cherish the "new" influences brought by Egyptian, Roman, and Christian voyagers, thereby preserving and implementing, through their greater application (*studium*) and industry (*industrium*), a heritage common to both worlds (p. 106).[70] By recording for posterity Hythloday's recollection of this new world, More performs an act of memory for his own culture: Utopia serves not simply as a reminder of what Europe has forgotten, of the potential it has failed to realize, but also as a damning measure of the mean and bitter harvest Europe has actually reaped.

As the central expression of Utopia's achievement, Amaurotum implies that the city must also lie in some way at the heart of Europe's woes. Just as the tacit presence of London in Amaurotum helps to clarify the achievements of Book II, so in turn the portrait of Amaurotum implicitly evokes the city – and perhaps more specifically London – as the central but undepicted presence in the sick world of Book I. Hythloday does not mention London, nor does it figure conspicuously in

[68] Pearl, *London and the Outbreak of the Puritan Revolution*, p. 55, n. 37.
[69] Amaurotum is slightly more populous than More's London, much healthier and cleaner, and there is a slightly greater concentration of power at the top (twenty tranibors for twenty-five aldermen, a lifelong governor as against an annually elected mayor) and a somewhat broader representation at the bottom (two hundred syphogrants as against a possible minimum of one hundred Common Councilors in London).
[70] Fleisher, *Radical Reform and Political Persuasion*, pp. 46–47; on the reversal of the old/new worlds in Europe/Utopia, see Marin, *Utopics*, p. 75.

his analysis of Europe's ills, for which there is no want of possible causes. "From the monarch, as from a never-failing spring," Peter Giles asserts, "flows a stream of all that is good or evil over a whole nation" (56/14–16); and human pride, Hythloday concludes, is "the chief and progenitor of all plagues" (242/25–26). But More pointedly declines the gambit of writing a platitudinous mirror for princes,[71] and he concentrates his powers not on the spiritual sources of pride but on a secular analysis of the economic and political laws through which pride manifests itself. Utopia is the positive counterpart to this analysis, and Amaurotum, which lies, paradoxically, at the center of Hythloday's description precisely because it does not play a domineering, hegemonous, monopolistic role in Utopian life, provides in retrospect an analytic focus for the proliferating injustices of Book I. Before More had written Book I's Dialogue of Counsel, he must have believed that the "solutions" of Book II also figuratively analyzed the problems they solved.

The violent imbalances, disproportions, and inequalities of Book I everywhere express the assymmetrical domination of a part over the whole. They radiate as forces from and toward a point of disruption in the social fabric, around which wealth, power, violence, false ideals accumulate; this point is "where all the best things flow into the hands of the worst citizens ... where all is divided among very few, while the rest are downright wretched" (102/24–26). Amaurotum thus contributes not only to the equipollent logic of the work, to its basic figures of antithesis and paradox, but also to a structure of metonymy, helping to trace the ill effects depicted in Book I even closer to their cause.

The miseries surveyed by Hythloday in Book I tend to cluster around two main problems, war and economic injustice. In each of these problems, as the counter-example of Utopia suggests, the city is very much involved. The harvest of impoverished vagabonds and thieves that opens Hythloday's analysis is produced by war and by the rumors of war; the first sends men home aged or crippled and thus "prevents them from exercising their own crafts" (60/27–62/1); the second leads to the costly maintenance of a large and idle class of military retainers, which in turn causes nations to seek a pretext for war (64/5–7) or results in domestic ruin: "cities have been more than once destroyed by their own standing armies" (64/12–13). In both cases, the violent ambitions of feudal aristocrats and warrior–kings are seen to victimize common citizens and their communities. "The common folk," Hythloday proclaims, "do not go to war of their own accord but are driven to it by the madness of kings" (204/25–26). This is borne out in Hythloday's account of the

---

[71] See Hexter's Introduction to *Utopia, CW* 4, pp. cxvii–cxviii and Surtz's Introduction in the same volume, p. clxvii.

Achorians, who bear the heavy burden of a war undertaken to defend a questionable birthright of their king. "They were being plundered, their money was taken out of the country, they were shedding their blood for the little glory (*alienae gloriae*) of someone else" (90/3–4). In another example, Hythloday enters the council of an imaginary king to find him devising "a make-believe war under pretext of which he could raise money and then ... throw dust in his simple people's eyes" (90/28–92/2); in yet another case Hythloday discovers the French King plotting to beleaguer Europe: the great centers of urban culture and burgherly freedoms – Venice, Flanders, Brabant, and Burgundy – figure prominently as the planned victims (86). The poignant evocation of the costs of war in Busleiden's prefatory letter is a dismal fulfillment of the French King's threat; it is a scene of communities destroyed, "great cities laid waste, ... states (*ciuitates*) destroyed, ... commonwealths (*Respublicae*) overthrown, ... villages fired and consumed" (36/11–12). Written just after the French invasions which challenged the civic humanism of Italy, and delivered just as the great new powers of Europe – the Papacy, the empire, England and France – were squaring off for a half-century of war, Hythloday's indictment of war seems to follow the line of irenistic humanism that took the part of progressive and constructive urban culture against the dynastic ambitions and chivalric delusions of Europe's nobility.

According to Erasmus, for example, cities play the task of culture-building, a progressive task opposed by the intransigence of a backward and ruthless warrior-class: "Fine cities are built by the people, subverted by princes ... good laws are born by popular magistrates, violated by princes; the people desire peace, while princes stir up war."[72] In keeping with this view, the enlightened Macarians of *Utopia* curtail the war-making power of their monarchs in order "to forestall any shortage of the money needed in daily business transactions among the citizens" (96/24–26). By highlighting this consideration Hythloday identifies the reasons – the disruption of trade and the diversion of resources – that made urban citizens and officials so reluctant to finance dynastic wars. John Colet, the son of a London mercer, had for example aroused the King's deep concern with his Good Friday Sermon of 1513 in which he preached against war on the eve of the departure of the King's troops for war in France. More's role as Speaker in the subsidy debate of the 1521 Parliament reflected the same mercantile attitudes, which posed an obstacle to Henry's efforts to raise subsidies throughout his reign. The costs of war in Henry's reign – after the Forced Loan of 1522, Skelton

---

[72] Quoted in James D. Tracy, *The Politics of Erasmus: A Pacifist in His Intellectual Milieu* (Toronto University Press, 1978), p. 39.

jibed that London was but a "cupborde for lordys"-amounted to £2,000,000 in all, and this helps to explain why the interests of Crown and City could be so sharply divided: a London alderman who refused to pay his share of the so-called Benevolence of 1545 was summarily sent to the Scottish front, where he perished.[73]

Despite their own reluctance to make war, however, the Utopians fight more fiercely than against tyrants "when the merchants among their friends undergo unjust persecution under the color of justice in any other country" (201/17-19). Their willingness to avenge economic wrongs done to others, but not those to themselves, is a double standard necessitated, as Hythloday points out,[74] by the Utopians' recognition that "their friends' merchants suffer severely by the loss as it falls on their private property" (202/2-3 cf. 238/3-6). In this double standard, as elsewhere, *Utopia* registers the countervailing tendencies that made for contradiction in the early Tudor polity. Not simply opposed to the warmongering exactions of the new state, but eager for the trading advantages to be gained from a bellicose foreign policy, London was not simply an independent commune, but, as Skelton's *Why Come Ye Not to Courte* suggests, already complicit with the new state and its imperial ambitions. Utopia's intervention on behalf of exterior neighboring states is both economically necessary and morally questionable. At precisely this point of disjunction between two ways of defining the interests of community, the problem of war meshes with the problem of economic injustice. Common citizens may be driven to war by tyrannical barons and kings, but they may also be driven to it by the acquisitive lusts which they have themselves institutionalized. Thus Hythloday ends his description of Utopia by extolling its success in uprooting ambition and factionalism, the causes of "domestic discord, which has been the only cause of ruin to the well-established prosperity of many cities" (244/7-10). Paradoxically, the causes of war lie as much in mercantile pusuits as in the "madness of kings," but they are projected almost exclusively onto the feudal recrudescence of the latter in order to occult the novel influence of the former.

The same is true of economic ills. Hythloday's examples come almost exclusively from England; they fit together in an analysis even more brilliant and closely argued than the account of war. Hythloday's systematic analysis is ostensibly offered as an explicit alternative to the lawyer's view that England is overrun with thieves and vagabonds because they "voluntarily prefer to be rascals" (60/27). In the ever-

[73] W. G. Hoskins, *The Age of Plunder: King Henry's England 1500-1547* (London: Longmans, 1976), pp. 209-210, 215; Skelton, *Collyn Cloute*, l. 914.
[74] See J. C. Davis, *Utopia and the Ideal Society* (Cambridge University Press, 1981), p. 57.

expanding series of effects he traces from enclosures Hythloday apparently never loses the thread of connection; every imbalance or displacement is the function of another. As acquisitive landlords join house to house and field to field, the development of a whole civilization is reversed: displaced farmers become wandering vagabonds, towns and villages fall to ruin, cultivated fields grow wild. Outcast farmers find no work because towns decline in their absence, thus eliminating the work of crafts, and because the efficiency of shepherding reduces the need for labor. Yet in this cruel situation, the costs of food and clothing soar. The price of wool rises because the enlarged herds of sheep are subject to sudden onslaughts of disease, because the oligopoly of enclosers conspires to keep prices artificially high, and because the export of raw wool reduces the domestic supply and sends local cloth-working into decline. As the land is taken up by sheep, food supplies decline. The few remaining farmers fail to profit from this situation because the same oligopoly imports a competing supply of livestock from abroad, which is sold at artificially high prices. Once the remaining farmers are driven out of business and the foreign supply declines, food prices will rise yet further. Another drain on domestic resources is the lucrative import trade in luxury goods, which in turn fuels ostentation and thus leads to the further bleeding of the poor. Along with these luxuries come the dives, brothels, taverns, wineshops, alehouses, and gambling dens which rob rich and poor alike and send their clientele away more eager than ever to rob someone else.

As Hythloday's analysis moves toward its concluding image of brothels, taverns, and dens of vice, it comes closest to identifying London's newly resurgent economy as the hidden cause of the imbalances which pervade every level of the commonwealth. As More well knew, London did not simply cater to venal appetites; as the center of the lucrative wool trade it created the economic circumstances in which these tastes could thrive. By tracing the decay of the commonwealth to the expanding trade in wool, Hythloday outlines a series of developments that went hand-in-hand with London's increasing domination of the economic order.[75] Though the enclosing and engrossing of land was not

---

[75] The issue of enclosures has been a subject of great controversy among historians of the Tudor agrarian economy, a terrain "so dangerous that a non-specialist is almost certain to come to grief if he dares to trespass," J. J. Scarisbrick, "Cardinal Wolsey and the Common Weal," in *Wealth and Power in Tudor England: Essays Presented to S. T. Bindoff*, ed. E. W. Ives, R. J. Knecht, and J. J. Scarisbrick (London: Athlone, 1978), p. 46. To the qualifications that much of the enclosure had taken place prior to 1500 and that most of it was restricted to the Midlands, others must be added. First, unlike the enclosure and engrossing of the later sixteenth century, which was often for the purpose of growing food, and in which both the peasantry and London's merchants participated,

a new phenomenon – much of it had been done even before 1485 – it reached a climax just prior to 1510, during a period which coincided with the highest percentage increase in the expanding woolen trade.[76] The impact of this growth on England's agrarian order is reflected in legislation to halt enclosures in 1488, 1489, and 1515, and in the formation of Wolsey's investigative commission on enclosures in 1517. The decay of England's towns, which was sometimes attendant on enclosure, was also a cause of alarm; the town policies of Henry VII and Henry VIII attempted to stem the tide of decline by exempting some towns from subsidies, by defending local monopolies, and by imposing penalties on landlords who allowed buildings to decay.[77] But such measures were seldom effective, especially in view of the enormous profits to be made in textiles. Wolsey's commission noted that it was 40 percent more profitable to raise sheep for wool than to grow food, and the doubling of the price of wool between 1500 and 1550 amply justifies this conclusion.[78] Most of the enclosing was concentrated in the Midlands

enclosure in the early Tudor period does not appear to have been the work of merchants. Hoskins, for example, notes that in Leicestershire between 1485 and 1500, 2.1 percent of the enclosures were the work of the Crown, with the monasteries contributing 17.6 percent, the nobility 12.1 percent, and the squirearchy 67.5 percent. Furthermore, other factors, such as several bad harvests and a rising population, contributed at least to the inflation of food prices if not to unemployment and vagabondage. And finally, it must be acknowledged that the advent of printing contributed to contemporary perceptions of the problem. Nevertheless, it is clear that while the *amount* of enclosure in the early Tudor period was not significantly higher than in the fifteenth century, the *pace* of enclosure increased rapidly. It is clear, too, that while merchants themselves did not become landlords and enclosers until later in the century, most of the enclosing was done for the wool trade, of which London was the center. Though enclosure involved less than 3 percent of the land in the counties affected, it involved a much higher percentage of the *arable* land; by 1607, one of every three villages in Leicestershire had been affected by enclosures. Finally, even undramatic economic developments can have a dramatic impact when combined with social developments: the greatest mobility in Tudor society was concentrated at the very top and the bottom, among the richest and poorest people in England; the yeomen and small farmers who lay nearer the middle range and were closely rooted to their farms were perhaps those least adaptable. What is more, the areas most affected by enclosures were those where the potential uses of land and the potential for expansion were least flexible. See Peter Ramsey, *Tudor Economic Problems* (London: Gollancz, 1963), pp. 20–40; Hoskins, *The Age of Plunder*, pp. 64–72, 98; D. C. Coleman, *The Economy of England, 1450–1750*, pp. 34–36, 39–41.

[76] Ramsey, *Tudor Economic Problems*, p. 26; Ross, *Edward IV*, p. 364.

[77] See Robert Tittler, "The Emergence of Urban Policy, 1536–58," in *The Mid-Tudor Polity*, ed. Jennifer Loach and Robert Tittler (London: Macmillan, 1980), pp. 74–93; P. B. Dobson, "Urban Decline in Late Medieval England," *TRHS*, 27 (1977), 1–22; C. Pythian-Adams, "Urban Decay in Late Medieval England," in *Towns in Societies*, ed. P. Abrams and E. A. Wrigley (Cambridge University Press, 1978), pp. 159–188; Paul Clark and Peter Slack, *English Towns in Transition 1500–1700* (New York: Oxford University Press, 1976), pp. 31–32, 101–102.

[78] Ramsey, *Tudor Economic Problems*, p. 24. Without citing evidence, Coleman argues that "the divergence between wool and grain prices was not large," (*The Economy of England, 1450–1750*), p. 35.

and was done not by merchants but by the local gentry, and Hythloday's indictment of "noblemen, gentlemen, and abbots" (66/3) accurately lays blame on the local culprits. But in its larger dimensions, the problem was decisively influenced by London's role in the export trade. In the period 1510–15, London was already handling 70 percent of the nation's woolen trade; by the end of Henry VIII's reign, this figure had risen to 88 percent.[79] Though in the early fourteenth century London had been only three times as wealthy as Bristol, the next largest English town, by 1520 it was ten times as wealthy as Norwich, which had taken second place from Bristol. In the Loan Book of 1520, London was assessed at £20,000, or one-eighth of the whole for England, though it held only 3 percent of the population; its assessment was nearly twice that of Kent, the wealthiest county. The Loan Book listed forty-five London merchants who were worth £1,000 or more; only seven people in the rest of England could claim as much.[80]

As these figures suggest, the rapid growth and relative prosperity of London were coming at the short-term expense of the commonwealth as a whole. Behind the wandering vagabonds and displaced families of Hythloday's sketch, behind the ruined fields and dilapidated villages, behind the enclosers themselves, lies a concentrated force of commerce and venture capital throwing the entire order into imbalance. London, as More noted elsewhere, was a place of "greate resorte & confluence, not onely from other partes of this realme, but also from other landes" (*CW* 9: 116), and when Hythloday closes the whole dismal scene of England's economy with the vicious world of brothels, dens and taverns he approaches the unnamed center of the whole. The solution he proposes indicts not simply the enclosers themselves but "these rich individuals" who "buy up everything and ... exercise this monopoly for themselves" (70/1–2). Hythloday's peroration resonates with indignation at the conspiracy of the new economic order:

When I consider and turn over in my mind the state of all commonwealths flourishing anywhere today, so help me God, I can see nothing but a kind of conspiracy of the rich, who are aiming at their own interests under the name of the commonwealth. They invent and devise all ways and means by which, first, they may keep without fear of loss all that they have amassed by evil practices and, secondly, they may then purchase as cheaply as possible and abuse the toil and labor of the poor ... Now is not this an unjust and ungrateful commonwealth? It lavishes great rewards on so-called gentlefolk and banking-goldsmiths and the rest of that kind, who are either idle or mere parasites and purveyors of empty pleasures. On the contrary, it makes no provision for farmers, colliers, common laborers, carters, and carpenters without whom there would be no commonwealth

---

[79] Ramsey, *Tudor Economic Problems*, p. 54; cf. Hoskins, *The Age of Plunder*, p. 178.
[80] Hoskins, *The Age of Plunder*, pp. 14–21, 38–39.

at all. After it has misused the labor of their prime and after they are weighed down with age and disease and are in utter want, it forgets all their sleepless nights and all the great benefits received at their hands and ungratefully requites them with a most miserable death. (240/18–28, 6–14)

At the very moment that Hythloday's fiery peroration comes closest to indicting the economically systemic basis of England's social ills, however, it suddenly veers off its systemic tracks in order to reinstate a primary language of morality. The world would long ago have adopted

the laws of the Utopian commonwealth, had not one single monster, the chief and progenitor of all plagues, striven against it – I mean Pride.

Pride measures prosperity not by her own advantages but by others' disadvantages. Pride would not consent to be made even a goddess if no poor wretches were left for her to domineer over and scoff at, if her good fortune might not dazzle by comparison with her miseries, if the display of her riches did not torment and intensify their poverty. (243/30–38)

Far from closing in on the economic issue of surplus and deficiency, Hythloday's peroration finally returns the dialogue to the terms in which it began – to the lawyer's puzzlement over the perversity of human will that drives thieves to steal even under penalty of death. As Richard Halpern suggests, the peroration "only pushes the mystery" of human perversity "one step back," tracing England's problems not to impoverished thieves but to the lavish and prideful excess of feudal *dépense*.[81] As with the analysis of war, so here with economics, the systemic ills of urbanization are misrecognized as the results of feudal recrudescence even while expropriation is instated as a natural human norm. In Utopia itself, it will finally be the systemic eradication of feudal pride through the juridico-political enforcement of an ethic of "natural" need that will justify the permanent institutionalization of modern surplus extraction.

Like Hythloday's final withering blast in Book I, the whole of Book II appears to shed systemic light in retrospect upon his analysis of the contemporary world. The tacit presence of London in Book I is sharply clarified in the perspective provided by the urban centerpiece of Book II, a city which is not central, except as an equal to every other part in the whole, a city which is not a drain upon the whole, which knows no monopolies and uses no money, which does not make beggars of its farmers but farmers of its citizens, which lacks the corrupting influence of luxuries, which has no exclusive guilds and thus deprives no one of work, and which provides no opportunity – no consortia, mysteries or cabals – for special interests to conspire; it has "no wine shop, no alehouse, no brothel anywhere, no opportunity for corruption, no lurking

[81] *The Poetics of Primitive Accumulation: English Renaissance Culture and the Genealogy of Capital* (Ithaca: Cornell University Press, 1991), p. 160.

hole, no secret meeting-place (*conciliabulum*)" (146/16–19). With the emergence of physical differences between Amaurotum and the London-like landscape it overlays comes a recognition of the many institutional differences that exclude London from the Utopia of Book II and place it squarely in the center of the England of Book I. As a result of its role in the double vision of *Utopia*, Amaurotum contributes to a structure of metonymy: it helps to identify the network of causes and effects traced out in Book I as the figure for an occulted source. At the same time, however, that source – urban capitalism – is finally legitimized in very striking ways.

By contrast with the asymmetries of Book I, Amaurotum emerges as an equal and reciprocating element in a symmetrical and uniform distribution of wealth and power. It is not a swollen and diseased organ sapping the strength of the whole, but an independent and self-contained organism, the very model for each of the cellular parts which make the whole. But as the implied contrast with the dominating powers – the courts, conspiracies, and monopolies – of Book I suggests, the very centrality of Amaurotum is founded on contradiction. Amaurotum occupies the center of Utopia as the result of geographical accident; its position is more a function of geography than of wealth or power. Yet paradoxically, because it occupies "the very center (*umbilicus*) of the country" (112/26), it is considered "the chief as well as the capital city" (*prima princepsque*), (112/27). As Louis Marin has pointed out, the same mixture of functional and accidental causes that places Amaurotum at the center of Utopia also places it at the center of Hythloday's description: "but which should I describe rather than Amaurotum? First none is worthier (*dignior*), the rest referring to it as the meeting place of the national senate; and secondly, none is better known to me, as being the one in which I had lived for five whole years" (116/23–28). Like Amaurotum itself, Hythloday's description is purposefully shaped by the dynamics of power; Amaurotum, the place where the power of all is represented, is also the part which represents the whole in the discourse. Yet this purposeful concentration, in which Amaurotum epitomizes the Utopian forces of order, law, and regulation, is also a matter of chance: Amaurotum just happens to lie at the center of Utopia and just happened to be the place visited by Hythloday.[82]

When Hythloday insists that Amaurotum is at once different and not different from the other parts in the whole, he expresses a basic contradiction underlying Utopia's centralized geometry. On the one hand, the Utopians stress the importance of their common life by

[82] Marin, *Utopics*, p. 120.

arranging their political and social life, their institutions and their architecture, in symmetrical fashion around geographically central points; but on the other hand, at every step they suppress the functional differences in which such central points must perforce consist. This, at any rate, is what Hythloday's description implies, for as it moves inward toward the key central points of Utopian life it also hesitates to represent the concentration of power associated with them, a concentration which enables Utopia to exist. As a result, Utopia seems at once remarkably concrete and weirdly intangible. In its radiocentric design, it seems to incorporate the earthly aspirations of a Renaissance *città ideale*, but the suppression of functional difference or heterogeneity at its central points gives the whole design a ghostly, disembodied aura.

Each of the fifty-four city-states of Utopia, claims Hythloday, is identical to the others in language, customs, and laws; they are similar in layout and even in appearance where the terrain permits (112/15–19). Anyone who knows one of these cities will know them all, since they are exactly alike (*omnino similes*) (116/22–23). Nevertheless, these equal parts are ordered in a centralized geometry that makes Amaurotum a distillation of Utopian life. Each of Utopia's city-states lies no less than 24 miles from its nearest neighbor (112/19–20), and therefore roughly at the center of its own *vicina* or territory, which extends for at least 12 miles in every direction (112/27–30). Each city centralizes the functions of its territory, supplying the outlying farms with labor, absorbing their products, and providing for festivities on holy days (114/7–19, 116/10–14). The concentric principle which organizes Utopia also organizes the order of Hythloday's narrative. The narrative begins by noting that the two ends of Utopia converge to form a circle 500 miles in circumference. After taking in the harbors that ring the outer shores and the central inland lake, the narrative recounts the perfecting of this circular shape by the excavation of Utopus. In tracing out the circle of his realm, Utopus repeats a ritual performed by such founder-figures as Romulus, who traced the walls of Rome with his plough, and Trojan Brute, who "went round the whole circuit" of England before choosing the site of London.[83]

Having subdivided this circle into fifty-four parts and placed Amaurotum in its very center (*in umbilico*), Hythloday then turns this ichnographic groundplan on its side and approaches its center laterally, passing through several concentric layers as he moves in perspectival

[83] For Romulus and ancient foundation-rituals, see Fustel de Coulanges, *The Ancient City* (Garden City: Doubleday, 1956), pp. 134–143. For Brute's circular route and the founding of London, see Geoffrey of Monmouth, *History of the Kings of Britain*, tr. Charles W. Dunn (New York: E. P. Dutton, 1958), p. 27.

fashion from the countryside toward the center of the city. An account of the rural households and economy thus forms a prelude to the discussion of Amaurotum proper. The description of the city begins with remarks on its site, which stress the harmonious reciprocities of culture with nature; it then moves through the successive layers of artifice in the city itself – its surrounding walls, its streets, and finally its uniform squares, with their enclosed gardens and the happy citizens who till them. Both the shape of Amaurotum and the order of Hythloday's narrative follow the outlines laid down in Aristotle's plan for a city in the *Politics* (7.11.1ff.) and in the similar instructions in Vitruvius' *Ten Books of Architecture* (i.4–7). But these bare outlines are embellished with the aesthetic, political, and moral significance which the rhetoric of Italian humanism had attached to urban design. Unlike so many of his friends – Erasmus, Colet, Grocyn, Linacre, Pace, and Latimer – More had no direct experience of Italian civic life; but Hythloday's description of Amaurotum embodies the type of radiocentric conceit found in Leonardo Bruni's *Laudatio Florentinae Urbis* (c. 1402), the most brilliant praise of a city in the history of the Italian Renaissance.[84]

Bruni's depiction of Florence as the central boss of a shield or as the moon surrounded by stars draws first of all on Aristotle's dictum that a city ought to be "a common centre ... equally linked to the whole of the territory."[85] But it borrows, too, from the rhetorical embellishment of this dictum in Bruni's immediate model, the *Panathenaieos* of the Greek orator Aristides. Athens, Aristides claims, is to its surrounding territory as its territory is to Greece and the world: it "lies in the center of a central land" (p. 11). Bruni transforms this bird's eye view into a panoramic perspective as he approaches Florence: "thus the villas are more beautiful than the distant panorama, the suburbs are more handsome than the villas, and the city itself more beautiful than its suburbs"

---

[84] More may have encountered the influence of Bruni's unpublished *Laudatio* through Thomas Chaundler's *Libellus de Laudibus Duarum Civitatem*, a praise of the cities of Bath and Wells. Chaundler, who had been a Fellow of New College, Oxford since 1435, served as Warden of the College from 1454 to 1475, overlapping in his tenure with William Grocyn, who was Fellow of New College from 1467 to 1481; *Libellus de Laudibus Duorum Divitatum et Seddium Episcopalium, Welliae Silicet et Bathoniae*, Trinity Coll. MS R. 14. 5, ed. Rev. George Williams, *Somersetshire Archaeological and Natural History Society Proceedings*, XIX (1873), 98–121. There need not, in any case, be a direct link between Bruni and Chaundler; though Bruni's *Laudatio* was not printed, manuscripts were widely circulated in the 1430s, as Bruni sought to persuade the Church Council at Basle to locate the Council in Florence; see Hans Baron, *From Petrarch to Leonardo Bruni: Studies in Humanistic and Political Literature* (University of Chicago Press, 1968), pp. 152–253.

[85] Tr. B. G. Kohl, in *The Earthly Republic: Italian Humanists on Government and Society*, p. 145. Quotations from Aristotle's *Politics* are drawn from the translation by Sir Ernest Barker (1946; rpt. London: Oxford University Press, 1958).

(p. 142). Bruni begins his description with a discussion of Florence's site, which lies midway between extremes, neither too high nor too low (p. 233), and he orients the surrounding landscape to the points of the compass (p. 234) before turning to the city itself, a crown of walls enclosing an even more splendid interior (pp. 237, 234). As he passes through concentric layers toward the heart of Amaurotum, then, Hythloday follows a rhetorical path which Italian humanism had laid over Aristotle's philosophic terrain. The centralized design of Utopia invests the city of Amaurotum with a special privilege, the geometric vision of culture.

The layers aligned within the concentric space of Utopia, moreover, form a matrix rich in symbolic overtones. "Almost foursquare in outline (*figure fere quadrata*)," Amaurotum is "divided into four equal districts (*in quatuor aequales partes*)" by "two perpendicular streets or imagined lines which intersect at its center" (116/29, 136/26). With its four corners and central point Amaurotum is thus a version of the ideal fivesquare city, a form which is at once quadratic and radiocentric. Inscribed within the circular shape of the island and of Amaurotum's own territory, the foursquare walls stand as a measure of human achievement. As in the mandala, where circles alternate concentrically with polygons, circles and squares combine in Utopia to symbolize the harmonies of nature and culture, divine and mortal power, spiritual and material well-being.[86] One of the earliest figures of the city, the Egyptian hieroglyph *niwt*, consists of a cross within a circle; the walls and central crossroads of Amaurotum likewise form an image of exchange within enclosure, reciprocity within community, activity within stasis.[87] Like the Athens of Aristides' *Panathenaic Oration*, which lies "at the crossways of all points" (p. 25), Amaurotum forms the center of a civilized order.

Paradoxically, however, both Hythloday's narrative and Utopia itself tend in every way to suppress the importance implicitly attached to the central point of the crossroads. In other versions of the ideal city, that central point is almost always privileged with special power or sanctity. In Prudentius' *Psychomachia*, the virtues celebrate their victorious recovery of the holy city from the vices by building a centralized temple,

---

[86] Mircea Eliade, *Patterns in Comparative Religion*, tr. Rosemary Sheed (Cleveland: Meridian Books, 1958), ch. 10; Carl Jung, *Psychology and Alchemy*, tr. R. F. C. Hull, in *The Collected Works of C. G. Jung* (20 vols. Princeton University Press, 1968), 12: 124–126, 183. Here and in much that follows on the symbolic geometry of cities I am indebted to the immensely suggestive synthesis of James Dougherty, *The Fivesquare City* (Notre Dame, Ind.: University of Notre Dame Press, 1980), pp. 1–66.

[87] Robert S. Lopez, "The Crossroads Within the Wall," in *The Historian and the City*, ed. Oscar Handlin and John Burchard (Cambridge, Mass.: The MIT Press and Harvard University Press, 1963), p. 27.

in the innermost chamber of which Wisdom sits enthroned.[88] The Acropolis forms the center of Aristides' Athens, and in Bruni's adaptation, the Palazzo Vecchio looms over the center of Florence as a flagship over its fleet. Immediately after taking in the points of the compass around Wells, Thomas Chaundler, through whose work More may have encountered Bruni's, zeroes in on the most glorious and ornate temple of the city's patron, the Apostle Andrew.

But in contrast to these visions, Hythloday's narrative turns aside just as it approaches the center toward which it has moved. Its final focus is not the central point of the city's four districts, but the enclosed squares and gardens, of which Hythloday immediately notes there are many – there is "keen competition between blocks as to which will have the best kept garden" (120/17–19). Ultimately focused on a plurality of green spaces rather than a single edifice, Hythloday's description conspicuously resists the teleology of centralized design.

There are, of course, a number of candidates that might have filled this central space. It might have housed the national assembly, which is presumably located somewhere in Amaurotum; it might have housed the Ademus or governor of the city, or, on the models of London's Guildhall, the *senatus* and *comitia*, the city's two assemblies. Alternatively, it might have been the site of a temple; the city's thirteen temples would divide neatly among the four quarters and the central point. Yet the center itself remains a mysterious blank in the narrative, conspicuously so because at the moment Hythloday turns his gaze to the multitude of gardens he notes that "their founder attached the greatest importance to these gardens" and that "the whole plan of the city had been sketched at the very beginning by Utopus himself" (120/21–24). By invoking at this crucial point the name of the founder whose will is expressed in the design, Hythloday touches on the conception of artistic and political power which gave the designed city, and especially the radiocentric plan, its profound hold over the Renaissance imagination. The design of Amaurotum incorporates Aristotle's dictum that the shape of a city should be *eusynoptos*, easily taken in at a glance so that the citizens feel they are comprised in one body (*Politics*, 7.4.13–14, 7.5.3); but Amaurotum eschews the more sinister implications of the *eusynopsis* achieved in the Renaissance radiocentric plan, in which the all-encompassing view can be taken in only from one central point, the seat of power.[89]

---

[88] *Psychomachia*, ll. 804–887, cited in Dougherty, *The Fivesquare City*, pp. 20–21.
[89] In his discussion of what should form the central feature of a city, Francesco Patrizzi recommends a cathedral and notes that castles and towers have no place within a free city, for as "Aristotle affirmeth ... a castle is vnto a good common wealth, vnprofitable

Amaurotum in fact, lacks *any* centralizing edifice or function. In keeping with Aristotle's recommendation that markets occupy the periphery rather than the center of a city, Amaurotum disperses its markets to the centers of each of the city's four quarters. But the single central point emphasized by this quadratic arrangement makes even more obvious Amaurotum's failure to observe the Aristotelian corollary that the central square ought to be reserved as public space for the elders and magistrates and for recreation (*Politics*, 7.12.2–6). The empty center of Amaurotum goes hand-in-hand with the absence of any physical location for, or any actual depiction of, the political functions provided for in the amply detailed Utopian constitution (Marin, p. 130). Not only the highest political functions – the national assembly as well as the governor, *senatus*, and *comitia* – but even the lesser remain shadowy and incompletely depicted. The four syphograncies which compose the four sides of each enclosed common constitute a social and economic, rather than political unit; indeed, it is impossible for the ten syphograncies which form the constituency of each tranibor to be consolidated physically, since syphograncies are arranged in units of four. Furthermore, though each of the four quarters of the city nominates a candidate for governor, neither the process of nomination nor the site where it takes place are provided for; like the central gardens formed by blocks of four syphograncies, the central market of each quarter physically embodies an economic function while remaining void of political activity. The central halls of each syphograncy, the central gardens of each block, the central markets of each quarter give physical substance to a network of consumption, production, and exchange (Marin, p. 129). But just as contaminating influences – money, slaughter-houses, and hospitals – are excluded from the city (Marin, p. 141), so the political units of the ten syphogrants or the tranibor, the city's *senatus* and *comitia*, its governor and the national senate lack physical embodiment within the walls of Amaurotum. While the geometry of Utopia provides for a radically reformed society in which labor and the fruits of labor are evenly distributed, it seemingly suppresses any radical concentration of power, emphasizing not the focal points implicit in its political constitution but a multitude of green spaces and households, each of which is identical to the others.

On the one hand, this arrangement corrects the disruptions of Book I, where the concentration of wealth and power produces gross asymmetries, imbalances, and inequalities throughout the whole. The in-

and daungerous: &...yt geueth oportunitie vnto tyranny." (Francesco Patrizzi, *A Morall Methode of Ciuile Policie*, tr. Rycharde Robinson (1576), sigs. Tiv, siiii; cf. Aristotle, *Politics*, 7.9.5.

tegration of agrarian with urban life is a measure at once nostalgic and progressive, symbolic of the reforms that would restore old institutions to a new and healthy life, though paradoxically by accelerating and rationalizing the domination of the countryside by the urban economy. But on the other hand, by diffusing the concentrations implied in Utopia's geometry, the multitude of gardens threatens to cancel the dynamics of power that would give the realm reality and being.

The gardens are symptomatic of the tendency everywhere in Utopia for social and economic units – the family, the garden, the farm and common table – to seem more "natural" than political units and to take precedence over them. They are symptomatic, too, of the parallel tendency of the Utopians to derive their *mores* from conscience rather than from legal obligation. Those *mores* not only repudiate the false and artificial pleasures of Europe; they affirm precisely the natural, human bonds and the common life which Utopia's gardens foster. Admonished by reason of their "natural" fellowship (*naturae societate*), the Utopians hold it praiseworthy "to relieve the misery of others and ... restore them to enjoyment" (162/27–35). Just as they substitute homogeneity for heterogeneity, gardens and dining halls for edifices of power, so finally the Utopians place the community and society over the *polis*. Magistrates and citizens are linked not so much by political structures as by the loving bonds of fathers and children (194/2): "the whole island is like a single family" (148/2–3). Utopia is not the *dominium politicum et regale* of Fortescue,[90] but, as Hythloday puts it, an order of "mutual love and charity (*mutuus amor, charitasque*)" (224/8).

What is the function of this "natural," ethical order? One explanation is that it performs one of the central tasks of Christian humanism, restoring to modern Europe the forgotten meaning of active Christian charity in its own "cheerful and active" life (226/6–7). Yet for both Erasmus and Colet, as for most other humanists, the charitable communism of the disciples was less a desirable socio-economic institution than the expression of that Christian charity without which no community can cohere.[91] The community which expressed this charity most fully was for them much closer to St. Augustine's pilgrim city of God on earth, the universal Christian Church, which transcends the

---

[90] *The Governance of England*, ed. Charles Plummer (Oxford University Press, 1885), p. 109.
[91] For the limits Erasmus placed on communism, see *De Concordia*, in *The Essential Erasmus*, pp. 386–387. Compare More's remarks in *Dialogue of Comfort*, *CW* 12: 180, and for Colet's conservatism, see H. C. Porter, "The Gloomy Dean and the Law: John Colet, 1466–1519," in *Essays in Modern Church History in Memory of Norman Sykes*, ed. G. V. Bennett and J. D. Walsh (New York: Oxford University Press, 1966), pp. 18–43.

political and institutional order of contractual states.[92] Colet and Erasmus draw heavily on St. Augustine for their social teachings, as More's *Utopia* does for its image of social life; and in every case the social ideal is hedged by the limits that Augustine, like St. Paul, places on it. Insofar as earthly life is "common to both cities, so there is," according to Augustine, "a harmony between them in regard to what belongs to it."[93] But there remains at bottom an incompatibility between them. In the earthly city, "the princes and the nations it subdues are ruled by the love of ruling (*libido dominandi*)," while "in the other, the princes and subjects serve one another in love" (XIV.28). The mutual service inspired by love is inhospitable to the heterogeneities, the hierarchies and differences, of political dominion. The order of mutual love and charity (*mutuus amor charitasque*) on which Utopia is founded is thus a realization of Christian ideals; but the suppression of concentered political life that it entails carries with it a conviction that the truest basis for human community is a knowledge that – in the Pauline phrase More was fond of quoting – "we haue here no cyte nor dwellyng countrey at all / but seke for one that we shall come to / And in what countrey so euer we walke in this world, we be but as pilgryms & wayfaryng men" (*CW* 12/251).

Nothing is known of the lectures More read on St. Augustine *De Civitate Dei* in Grocyn's Church of St. Lawrence Jewry c. 1501, except that they were attended by "all the chiefe and best learned men of the Citie of London."[94] But some inkling of the political implications More saw in St. Augustine may be gathered from the occulted geometry of Utopia, its subordination of politics to "natural" ethics and Christian community. The whole outline of Utopia's political institutions consists of two short paragraphs,[95] and only the ethical consensus of the Utopians themselves, along with the laws left by King Utopus, is left to fill the vacuum.

If the ethical consensus of the Utopians cannot fully be imagined as an institutionally incarnate political good on earth, the reason is that the "natural" ethic is itself derivative from the political and economic concentration of power. In a recent reading of *Utopia* that meets and surpasses the challenges of Marin's, Richard Halpern argues that *Utopia*

---

[92] *Dulce Bellum Inexpertis*, in M. M. Phillips, *Erasmus on His Times*, p. 137.

[93] *The City of God*, XIX.17, tr. Marcus Dods (New York: The Modern Library, 1950), p. 696.

[94] Harpsfield, *The Life and Death of Sir Thomas Moore, Knight*, p. 14; Roper, *The Life of Sir Thomas More*, p. 198; Thomas Stapleton, *The Life and Illustrious Martyrdom of Sir Thomas More*, from *Tres Thomae*, tr. P. E. Hallett (New York: Benziger, 1928), pp. 7–8. Stapleton's phrase may only signify that More was speaking not as a cleric but as a lawyer and layman; see Martin N. Raitiere, "More's *Utopia* and *The City of God*," *SRen*, 20 (1973), p. 144.   [95] Fleisher, *Radical Reform and Political Persuasion*, p. 64.

does not essentially change the underlying conditions that produce the extremes of wealth and poverty, excess and deficiency; rather, it redirects production and expropriation into the accumulation of a massive surplus, from which, in turn, it derives its natural, ethical norm of what is "requisite for either the necessity (*necessitatem*) or convenience (*commoditatem*) of living" (128/32), i.e., what is "required by necessity (*necessitatis*) or comfort (*commoditatis*) or even pleasure, provided it be genuine and natural (*naturalis*)" (130/23–24). Far from dictating the Utopian economy, the norm of natural needs is actually dictated or produced *by* an economy which, rationalizing the integration of countryside and urban market and strictly enforcing labor on all ("exception from work is granted to hardly five hundred of the total of men and women whose age and strength make them fit for work," 130/26–27) is geared to overproduction:

Though they are more than sure how much food the city with its adjacent territory consumes, they produce far more grain and cattle than they require for their own use: they distribute the surplus (*reliquum*) among their neighbors [i.e. the other city-states of Utopia] ... To designated market buildings the products of each family are conveyed. Each kind of goods is arranged separately in storehouses. From the latter any head of a household seeks what he and his require and, without money or any kind of compensation, carries off what he seeks. Why should anything be refused? First, there is a plentiful supply of all things and, secondly, there is no underlying fear that anyone will demand more than he needs. Why should there be any suspicion that someone may demand an excessive amount when he is certain of never being in want? No doubt about it, avarice and greed are aroused in every kind of living creature by the fear of want, but only in man are they motivated by pride alone – pride which counts it as a personal glory to excel others in the superfluous display of possessions. The latter vice can have no place at all in the Utopian scheme of things. (116/6–10; 136/27–138/9)

What guarantees the economic surplus of Utopia, in other words, is the circuitous logic of "natural" need: no one takes more than he "needs" because there is always certain to be a surplus; there is always certain to be a surplus because no one takes more than he "needs." As Halpern points out, "natural" need is not here a term with positive content, but rather a function of surplus extraction. And surplus extraction is in its turn justified by its support of the politico-juridical function of suppressing immoral excess. In other words, even as it emerges in this description from the Utopian wager of the surplus, the ethic of "natural" need also continues to be defined, as a morally loaded term, against the background of deviational excess – pride. "Excess," as Halpern observes, "is the primary that founds need." Dedicated to the extirpation of the excesses of pride and greed, Utopia deploys a massive state apparatus that establishes "natural" needs of its subjects and, in so doing, guarantees the production of a surplus. In place of the dysfunctional overconsumption by a few in Europe, Utopia simply stresses an overproduction by the many ("this universal behavior must of necessity lead to an abundance of all commodities," 146/21–22). That surplus is not socialized and distributed, but, accumulated in the detestable forms (slaves for chains and chamber-pots) that reinforce the ethic of calculated need; it becomes the basis for the concentration of a tremendous national power:

> But when they have made sufficient provision for themselves ... , then they export into other countries ... By this trade they bring into their country not only such articles as they lack themselves – and practically the only thing lacking is iron – but also a great quantity of silver and gold. This exchange has gone on so long that now they have everywhere an abundance of these metals – In consequence, they now care little whether they sell for ready cash or appoint a future day for payment, and in fact have by far the greatest amount out on credit – But if circumstances require that they should lend some part of it to another nation, then they call in their debts – or when they must wage war. It is for that single purpose that they keep all the treasure they possess at home ... They use it above all to hire at sky-high rates of pay foreign mercenaries ... (148/3–32)

Thus, while appearing to reverse contemporary economic practices to produce that radical justice where "with equality of distribution, all men have abundance of all things" (102/30), Utopia in fact rationalizes and accelerates those processes in such a way as to bring on the radically innovative power of the state. By appearing to adopt "policies founded upon justice, compassion, and charity, the Utopians acquire," as Alistair Fox observes, "the very things [a vast treasury to serve the conquest and subversion of their adversaries] that the injustice and callousness of European practices are designed to procure."[96] *O artificem* – "O Artful Rogue!" – is the phatic gasp at this point in the otherwise pedestrian marginal gloss of Erasmus and Giles (150/6–7).

It is thus perhaps as much the derivation of the Utopian ethic from a rudimentary and as yet inarticulable political economy as it is an Augustinian religious suspicion that leaves that ethic not only without a focused embodiment but with a readiness to dissolve itself in the face of higher and better truths to come. Utopia in fact incorporates as conditions of its being ideals which continue to provide for the negation of its own radical concentration of power. With the Utopians' readiness, reflected in their prayers, to abandon the incarnate good of their own dominion in favor of some better, the *Utopia*'s inarticulateness about its own progressive impulse coincides with a "deeper" scepticism and

---

[96] *Politics and Literature in the Reigns of Henry VII and Henry VIII*, p. 97.

spirituality that tempers its humanism. In the *Dialogue of Comfort* More notes that the world's mad and feverish activity is propelled by "*Negocium*...a deuill that is euer full of besynes in temptyng folke to mich euill besynes"; and those who follow this devil

neyther wote which way they go nor wyther he goth / For verely they walke round as it were in a round mase / whan they wene them selfe at an end of theyr besynes they be but at the begynnyng agayne... The center or mydle place of this mase is hell. (*CW* 12: 167)

In the letter to Giles that concludes the 1518 edition, More glosses the facetious name of Amaurotum not simply as "foggy city," but as *vrbem euanidem* (250/13), "ghostly" or "phantom" city. This gloss suggests again that Raphael "did not see as much as one may perceive in More's description," but that Cornelius Schrijver may have seen with More's eyes when he claimed in his prefatory verses that *Utopia* revealed "the great emptiness lying concealed at the heart of things (*quantum rebus inane latet*)" (30/14).[97] In More's wider perspective, the absent center of Amaurotum is a response both to the dense and negative core of Book I's moral void and to the equally dense but inchoate emergence of state-sponsored surplus extraction in Book II. The shadow at Amaurotum's center is created by an apparent amelioration that paradoxically perpetuates and intensifies, in occulted form, the moral conditions which underlie the Psalmist's desolate vision of the city:

> I can see how Violence
>   and Discord fill the city;
> day and night they stalk together
>   along the city walls.
>
> Sorrow and Misery live inside,
>   Ruin is an inmate;
> Tyranny and Treachery are never absent
>   from its central square.   (Ps. 55: 9–11)[98]

By excluding the central square from Amaurotum, More prepares the city for a righteous peace, but simultaneously condemns it to a perpetually shadowy existence. Several of the prefatory letters and poems hint that More's work surpasses Plato's *Republic*, but only the

---

[97] The Yale editors believe this phrase refers to the emptiness of money and earthly goods. But a more sweeping interpretation is perhaps justified by Hythloday's description of the immense inland lake – which occupies the center of Utopia – as an *ingens inane* (110/14). The phrase, which perhaps echoes Lucretius' *vacuum quod inane vocamus* (*De Rerum Natura*, line 439), is translated as "a wide expanse" in the Yale edition, but it might be rendered "a great void," or "an enormous emptiness." See Alan F. Nagel, "Lies and the Limitable Inane: Contradiction in More's *Utopia*," *Ren Q*, 26 (1973), 173–180.   [98] I quote from the New Jerusalem translation.

foolish poet laureate Anemolius (Windbag) hazards the further claim that Utopia's greater achievement consists of embodying its ideals in real resources and laws. So, too, is he the only one to risk the further speculation that the name of Utopia (no place) signifies that it is Eutopia (nice place) (20/4–9). Oriented around its central, phantom city, yet uncommitted to – unable even fully to articulate – much of what this central focus implies, Utopia seemingly confirms what More proclaims elsewhere that "our own experience proveth"; we "haue not...our dwellyng citie here" (*CW* 12/41). As in More's self-portraits, so in Utopia, contrasting versions of the city reciprocate, each eliciting the limits and contradictions of the other, and pointing to the transitional nature of the city he represented in both life and art.

Budé's prefatory letter also remarks that Utopia is a "model of the happy life (*beatae vitae exemplar*)" (12/15–16), and it is in the way this model cuts so deeply against the grain of contemporary thinking that *Utopia* is not merely an anti-Utopian satire but a productive contribution to a new mentality of settlement. There is no more "proud, ridiculous, and obstinate prejudice," Hythloday remarks, than blind adherence to the accepted wisdom of our forefathers (58/5–14). The work of reform begins, however, not with institutions but with the reinscription of the human soul. Budé's first wish is not to see Utopia's institutions on earth but to see its principles "fixed in the minds of all mortals by the beam-spikes of a strong and settled conviction" (10/11–12). Utopia is an ideal (*ideam*), a pattern (*formulam*), a perfect model (*absolutissimumque simulacrum*), as Busleiden puts it, of morality (32/30). By observing that Utopia is "divided into many cities, but they all unite and harmonize in one state, named Hagnopolis"(12/5–6), Budé indicates that the fullest realization of Utopia lies outside of earthly experience, in a timeless, ideal realm akin to Augustine's city of God. Like the Jerusalem of Israel in exile, or like the city of God, Utopia is displaced from the here and now; but this very displacement, in all these cases, dialectically provokes an effort to imagine the way to the desired realm. In Colet's Oxford lectures on Paul's Epistle to the Romans, the City of the New Jerusalem, set high on a hill, provides the point of orientation for an uncompleted journey.[99] It is the function of *Utopia* to point out, in its own idiom, the path for such a journey, not by providing a map, but by serving as a "model of the happy life," a "rule of living" (12/12–13). That rule of living, the free and unrestricted satisfaction of "natural" wants that will produce "a calm and harmonious state of the body" (172/24–25), and "a state of

---

[99] Colet, *Exposition of...Romans*, pp. 101–102; cf. *Exposition of...Corinthians*, pp. 124–125.

stable and tranquil health" (174/4–5) provides for an internalized, self-induced discipline that prepares the way for future settlement.

The opening quatrains written in the Utopian alphabet – an alphabet that identifies Utopia as first of all a republic of letters – proclaim that "without the aid of abstract philosophy" Utopia has "represented for mortals the philosophical city" (18/24–25). By literary means and without the aid of that political economy which it cannot fully theorize, More sows the seeds for that city which, like Plato's Republic, is a pattern for the individual to contemplate "and beholding, to constitute himself its citizen" (*Republic*, 592 B). As citizens in the republic of letters, humanists like More and Erasmus transformed the political dominion of princes into a discursive domain. "The medium of the press," one historian explains, enabled the political process "to work in a way that had not been possible except in small city republics, and ... made possible and necessary the form of dialogue about public affairs typical of those republics."[100] In More's *Utopia* letters are not invertebrate but potent, an impetus for change. As Budé declares, *Utopia* is "a nursery of correct and useful institutions," a *seminarium* or seed-bed, a beginning-point for human growth, from which each man may "adapt (*importent*) trans-planted customs to his own city" (14/20–22).[101] Hythloday, he adds, has "brought home (*importarit*) to us the pattern of the good life" as grain is imported to sustain the life of a city (12/14–16). The complexity of that pattern, however, is finally a function of its overdetermination. The *Utopia* poses its resistances to the radical concentration of power precisely because its vision of reform anticipates a concept and a future – a political economy – it cannot articulate. That articulation would begin to come with the reformers who followed More.

---

[100] R. W. Scribner, "The Social Thought of Erasmus," *Journal of Religious History*, 6 (1970–71), 24–25; cf. W. M. Southgate, "Erasmus: Christian Humanism and Political Theory," *History*, 40 (1955), 240–254.

[101] See R. J. Schoeck, "A Nursery of Correct and Useful Institutions," in Sylvester and Marc'hadour (eds.) *Essential Articles*, pp. 281–289.

2 London and the languages of Tudor complaint

Social change and the structures of complaint

In the first half of the sixteenth century, the rapid expansion of London's economic power and social influence coincided with the development of printing. Next to doctrinal, devotional, and educational matters, one of the most common concerns in early printed works was the condition of England, the nation's social and economic problems and their possible solution. In part because the mechanisms of social control were slow in responding to the new print technology, this social criticism came in many forms and represented a variety of interests. A common feature in much of this work on England's condition, however, was the attempt to establish new priorities of communal life, to refashion the corporate identity of what was coming to be called the "common weal" or "commonwealth." Within limits that were often strict, it was in theory the duty of enlightened members of the commonwealth to identify and propose reforms for the emerging state to implement. As John Bale put it, "he that delighteth not to behold the condition of his own city is thereunto no loving citizen."[1]

Some of this new material, following the lead of More's *Utopia*, represented the most advanced trends of humanism; it was written largely by scholars and statesmen, sometimes, though not always, in direct connection with the making of Tudor policy. Other works, however, expressed popular dissent and were sometimes written to influence the reforming parliaments which, after 1529, sat so frequently on the King's business. The spirit of protestant reform, moreover, reinvigorated a long tradition of anticlerical complaint and prompted preachers to apply the social teachings of the gospels with new zeal to the life of the nation. "The cause of Protestantism and the cause of the poor were soon associated," as numerous reformers underlined connections

---

[1] *The Image of Both Churches*, in *Select Works*, ed. Henry Christmas (Cambridge: Parker Society, 1849), p. 252.

63

between "religious persecution and social oppression."[2] As religious reformers looked more and more to the Crown and Council for support, both courtly entertainments and popular drama concerned themselves increasingly with social and economic matters. Moral treatises and educational handbooks laid new stress on the duties of the just citizen in an unjust world, while an unprecedented volume of ballads, satires, and sub-literary complaints inveighed against the abuses of the age. By the mid-sixteenth century, as worsening economic conditions reached a crisis, and as religious reform gained both official sanction and widespread popular support, social criticism and polemic fed a printing trade that doubled in output between 1547 and 1548.[3]

The volume of printed works, moreover, was only part of a much wider field of discourse and debate. The large number of manuscript complaints suggests that the genre circulated widely, as memos at the top of the pyramid, as clandestine protest at the bottom. The true extent of social criticism is perhaps reflected in the number of sermons, ballads, dramas, and crude dialogues that drew heavily on conservative oral formulas and long-established popular motifs. To a remarkable extent, the "articulate citizen"[4] of the early Tudor age spoke in these traditional languages of complaint.

To judge from this large body of complaint, England was a nation in distress, uprooted from its past and reeling along a wayward path toward certain destruction. It was a nation of decaying towns and deserted farms and villages, a nation swarming with vagabonds, masterless men, and starving wretches. Traditional rights and relationships were cast aside and trampled by a new species of rapacious tyrants: landlords and merchants who laid house to house and field to field, sending England's raw wealth abroad or squandering it at home on luxuries. England's peasant laborers and small leaseholders were reaping the old, mean harvest of dearth, homelessness, and disease, but on a scale so unprecedented as to mark a momentous historical change. Bad harvests worsened the shortages, while debasement of the coinage added seriously to inflation at mid-century. The uncertainties of the Tudor succession, and the religious changes that came with them, added to instability. Vagabondage and outbreaks of rebellion dramatized the failure of local authority in the face of crisis, while the decline of long-established towns and guilds showed that the traditional forms of communal security were crumbling before the new economic freedoms. Despite the traditional

---

[2] Susan Brigden, *London and the Reformation* (Oxford: Clarendon Press, 1989), p. 408.
[3] Ibid., p. 438.
[4] Arthur B. Ferguson, *The Articulate Citizen and the English Renaissance* (Durham: Duke University Press, 1965).

hyperbole and the timeless sense of moral decline to which even the most dispassionate writers at times appealed, the urgency that runs through all the varieties of Tudor complaint bespeaks a genuine crisis.

Various theories have been advanced to explain the long-term causes behind this late-medieval economic crisis. At one extreme, an older "commercialization" theory associated with the names of Max Weber and Henri Pirenne asserts that the European feudal economy was from a very early stage (i.e., the eleventh century) under a process of dissolution from without by the novel capitalistic influences of long-distance trade, the development of urban markets and freedoms, and a shift from "natural" to "money" economy, from "use" to "exchange" values. According to this theory, "the essential character of the European bourgeoisie" was formed in the crucible of medieval town liberties.[5] Developing, in this theory, "as autonomous worlds according to their own propensities," towns were a source of commercial and industrial innovation; "the rigid confines of the desmenial system, which up to now hemmed in all economic activity, were broken down and the whole social order was patterned along more flexible, more active and more varied lines."[6] "Capitalism and towns," Fernand Braudel writes in support of this view, "were basically the same things in the West."[7]

At the opposite extreme, a neo-Malthusian theory, based in the relation of demographics to the market forces of supply and demand, has maintained that for some eight centuries between 1000 and 1800 an essentially static feudal economy remained in the grip of a *motion biséculaire* – a two-phase cycle of boom and bust, governed by the reciprocal influence of population and prices – that was like "the immense respiration of a social structure."[8] According to this theory,

---

[5] Henri Pirenne, *Economic and Social History of Medieval Europe*, tr. I. E. Clegg (1936; rpt. New York: Harcourt Brace, n.d.), p. 55.

[6] Max Weber, *The City*, tr. and ed. Don Martindale and Gertrud Neuwirth (New York: The Free Press, 1958), pp. 104–107; Henri Pirenne, *Medieval Cities*, tr. Frank D. Halsey (1925; rpt. New York: Anchor Books, 1956), p. 72.

[7] Fernand Braudel, *Capitalism and Material Life, 1400–1800*, tr. Miriam Kochan (New York: Harper and Row, 1973), p. 400.

[8] See Emmanuel Le Roy Ladurie, *The Peasants of Languedoc*, tr. John Day (Urbana: University of Illinois Press, 1974), p. 4. For the term "neo-Malthusian," see Ladurie, "A Reply to Robert Brenner," in T. H. Aston and C. H. E. Philbin *The Brenner Debate: Agrarian Class Structure and Economic Development in Pre-Industrial Europe* (Cambridge University Press, 1985), p. 103. see also M. M. Postan and John Hatcher, "Population and Class Relations in Feudal Society," in ibid., pp. 64–78. There is, corresponding to this theory of an economic *longue durée*, a theory of urbanization, opposed to that of Pirenne, which argues that no substantial innovations intervene between the static "traditional" city of the ancient, medieval and early-modern worlds and the "modern" industrial city of the nineteenth and twentieth centuries. See Gideon Sjöberg, *The Pre-Industrial City* (New York: The Free Press, 1960), esp. pp. 5–15.

rising population, tied to rising food prices, increasing rural rents, and declining per capita wages and production, resulted in self-correcting population declines followed by corresponding improvements in economic conditions. This latter theory has been especially appealing in the light of the particular conditions described in early Tudor complaint – inflation (a minimum 75 percent increase in food prices, for example, between 1542 and 1551),[9] dearth, mass displacement of peasant populations,[10] and chronic and severe unemployment.[11] However, uneven developments in response to changing demographics throughout the European economy, as well as the more specific failure of England to follow other nations in the cyclical pattern of decline during the seventeenth-century economic crisis, suggest that such self-correcting cycles were but symptoms of deeper contradictions within the feudal system of production, contradictions that led to substantial changes within the economy of late-feudal England. The displaced hordes and masterless men of Tudor complaint, especially insofar as they are associated with changing patterns of land-tenure, point to such major infrastructural changes.

A theory integrating some features of the conflicting "commercialization" and "population" theories traces the economic crisis of feudalism instead to conflicts and changes within the class structure that defined the feudal mode of production. According to this theory, elaborated most fully by Robert Brenner, the feudal system was both an economy and a polity where, in the absence of wages and labor power as such, a ruling class of landlords extracted from the direct peasant producers, by extra-economic means of force and law, a surplus above their level of subsistence, whether in the form of labor on the desmesne,

---

[9] This is the most recent estimate by Steven Rappaport, *Worlds within Worlds: Structures of Life in Sixteenth-Century London* (Cambridge University Press, 1989), p. 130. For a much higher estimate, see Francis A. Abernathy, "Popular Literature and Social Protest, 1485–1558," in *Studies in English Renaissance Literature*, ed. Waldo F. McNeir (Baton Rouge: Louisiana State University Press, 1962), p. 12.

[10] On enclosures and depopulation, see W. G. Hoskins, *The Age of Plunder: King Henry's England 1500–1547* (London: Longmans, 1976). On the decline of provincial towns, see also Charles Pythian-Adams, "Urban Decay in Late Medieval England," in Philip Abrams and E. A. Wrigley, eds., *Towns in Societies: Essays in Economic History and Historical Sociology* (Cambridge University Press, 1978), pp. 159–186.

[11] For the economy generally see John Guy, *Tudor England* (Oxford University Press, 1988), ch. 2; Peter Ramsey, *Tudor Economic Problems* (London: Gollancz, 1963), and D. C. Coleman, *The Economy of England 1450–1750* (New York: Oxford University Press, 1977), pp. 1–31; for studies of the crucial issues of demography and prices, see Y. S. Brenner, "The Inflation of Prices in Early Sixteenth-Century England," *EconHR*, 2nd series 14 (1961), 225–239, and E. H. Phelps Brown and S. V. Hopkins, "Wage-rates and Prices: Evidence for Population Pressure in the Sixteenth Century," *Economica*, n.s. 24 (1957), 289–306.

payment in kind, or money rent.[12] During the economic upsurge of feudalism, 1000–1350, a rising population, coupled with a growing demand for food and land, created favorable terms for landlords, who could extract "growing rents, *without* resort to extra-economic pressures or controls."[13] In this system, however, where the peasant population was sedentary and fixed to the limited resource of land, and where noble landlords were economically mobile, the possibilities of expansion were limited. In the absence of technical innovation, and under the pressure of rising population, the subdivision of holding and intensification of cultivation decreased per capita productivity. Removed from the direct production process, and able, under conditions of rising population and prices, to increase their surplus simply by raising rents and squeezing peasants harder, landlords were in no position to introduce technological or managerial innovations. Neither were peasants, who lived – once the landlords extracted their surplus – at a subsistence level, even when they operated as petty producers within the system of money rents and market exchange. Expansion of the economy could therefore only come through increasing the supply of land, either by moving onto less productive land or by colonizing new territory through warfare and political alliances. These latter politico-military alternatives brought immense new expenses to bear upon the feudal ruling class, whose members came to depend increasingly on money rents for the cash surplus with which to trade in the marketplace for the equipment and luxury goods to maintain their growing body of retainers and their increasingly lavish style of consumption and display. Meanwhile, the willingness of the landlords, under the favorable conditions of rising rents and population, to commute to money rents (the "dissolving form"[14] of feudal extraction) had several long-term effects, all of them contributing to important changes in the feudal structure: the encouragement of petty peasant production for the marketplace, the development of the marketplace and its freedoms, the loosening of serfdom by mobility and economic diversification and specialization, the weakening of the landlord surplus by the tendency of money rents, especially when fixed, to lag behind inflation.

Under pressure from the inherent limits of productivity, the feudal economy was then further weakened by the catastrophic population

[12] Robert Brenner, "The Agrarian Roots of European Capitalism," in *The Brenner Debate*, pp. 214, 227, 247, and "Agrarian Class Structure and Economic Development," in ibid., p. 36; cf. R. H. Hilton, "A Crisis of Feudalism," in ibid., p. 124.
[13] Brenner, "The Agrarian Roots," p. 230.
[14] Maurice Dobb, "From Feudalism to Capitalism," in Paul Sweezy, Maurice Dobb, et al., *The Transition from Feudalism to Capitalism* (London: New Left Books, 1976), p. 166; this volume hereafter cited as "*Transition*."

decline of the mid-fourteenth century. Peasants were the short-term beneficiaries of a new demand for labor and rents that led landlords to fix money rents at low rates and to extend the privileges of petty producers in markets, common lands, forests, and fisheries.[15] Improving peasant conditions were short-circuited,[16] however, because the short-term ability of the direct peasant producers to retain a portion of the surplus on the holding led to a population increase in the fifteenth century and thus to rising prices and rents. Feudal landlords, squeezed between low rents and the high costs of their military–aristocratic political accumulation, were "obliged to use their remaining feudal powers to further what in the end turned out to be capitalist development."[17] The chief form of this development was the more productive landlord–capitalist: tenant–wage-laborer structure.[18] Small holdings were consolidated by expelling the least productive peasants and renting at higher rates to yeoman–capitalists, who had emerged as the most successful producers from the favorable conditions of the market and money–rent system. Producing for profit on the market, drawing on a pool of wage-labor fed by rising population and the expropriation of smallholders, and accumulating the capital necessary for profitable large-scale sheep farming, the new entrepreneurial tenants introduced technological innovations in enclosure, convertible husbandry, and land reclamation.[19] The result was an economy that extended the life of the feudal aristocracy and produced a class of capitalist entrepreneurs by physically separating peasants from the land and putting them into the sphere of circulation as wage-laborers. The displaced, wandering hordes of More's *Utopia* and Tudor complaint thus mark the advent of a major transition in the socio-economic order.

In this transition, the urban market, and especially the growth of London, played an important role. The long-distance luxury trade that Pirenne saw as the solvent of feudalism may in fact have contributed to aristocratic consumption patterns; but insofar as this trade was mainly in high-finish textiles and luxury goods, and therefore "dependent on the purchasing power" of the aristocracy and feudal production, it could not by itself "provide the foundations for continuing growth" or for a structural change in productive relationships.[20] Through their charters and privileges, towns operated as "collective seigneurs" within the

[15] Hilton, "A Crisis of Feudalism," p. 133; Brenner, "The Agrarian Roots," p. 231.
[16] Brenner, "Agrarian Class Structure," p. 30.
[17] Brenner, "The Agrarian Roots," p. 293.
[18] Kohachiro Takahashi, "A Contribution to the Discussion," in *Transition*, p. 77.
[19] Brenner, "Agrarian Class Structure," p. 49; "The Agrarian Roots," p. 309.
[20] Hilton, "A Crisis of Feudalism," p. 128; Brenner, "The Agrarian Roots," p. 324.

feudal system of parcellized sovereignty,[21] and long-distance merchants, who extracted surplus at the point of alienation rather than production, thrived on feudal underdevelopment and price differentials in deprived areas.[22] Like the capital of usurers, which also accumulated from aristocratic extravagance and the bankruptcy of peasants, merchant capital remained in the sphere of exchange. Tending, moreover, "to be allies of the feudal aristocracy," urban patricians often merged with it; they were frequently "themselves landowners and, as such, opponents of the peasants in the same nexus of rural class relations as the nobility."[23] Nevertheless, the new merchant class was bound up especially with the new patterns of land tenure, enclosure, and capitalist farming. It may, in fact, have been the spectacular rise in the English cloth trade – increasingly centered in London – that "*set off* the overall process of English economic development in the early modern period" and "provided the *initial* pressure of demand which set in motion the highly responsive agricultural system."[24] By this means, "the weight of the urban society" upon feudalism "continued to grow, inviting serious disruption."[25]

Finally, however, it was less as a cause than as a result of changes within feudalism that urbanization came to have its solvent effects on the traditional social order.[26] With the movement toward money rents and markets, "peasants were in the position of commodity producers who simply had to put themselves in contact with the market, and whose position as commodity producers brought about the social differentiation of that condition, the petty mode of production."[27] While the market itself enhanced the importance of exchange values – and thus surplus accumulation – the growth of petty production provided for urbanization and for the increasing specialization of crafts and services, all of them being filled by a newly created proletariat, a body of displaced wage-laborers generated by changes in the countryside. The output of the burgeoning urban trades "caused the terms of trade between town and

---

[21] John Merrington, "Town and Country in the Transition to Capitalism," in *Transition*, p. 178.

[22] R. H. Hilton, "Capitalism – What's in a Name?" in *Transition*, p. 149.

[23] Dobb, "From Feudalism to Capitalism," in *Transition*, p. 166; Brenner, "Agrarian Class Structure," p. 39.

[24] Brenner "The Agrarian Roots," p. 324; Brenner says of this process, beginning in the "third quarter of the fifteenth century, and accelerating rapidly from the 1520s," that "ultimately, the growing shift of population into industrial employments, supplemented by a powerful demographic upturn, determined a long-term increase in the demand for agricultural products, leading to a rise of food prices, which called forth the growth of agricultural production and productivity," pp. 296–297.

[25] Brenner, "The Agrarian Roots," p. 241.

[26] See Maurice Dobb, "A Reply" (to Paul Sweezy), in *Transition*, p. 61.

[27] Takahashi, "A Contribution," in *Transition*, p. 82.

country to tip to the latter's disadvantage," further accelerating the process of rural expropriation and urban growth.

It is perhaps the long-term significance of this last process that accounts for the peculiar structures and concerns of Tudor complaint. The process coincided, at the turn of the fifteenth century, with the advent of the Tudor state, a new politico-juridical apparatus that extended the power of the feudal aristocracy – increasingly merged with a patrician merchant class – to extract a surplus by legal means.[28] As it went forward under the regime, however, the trend toward rural capitalism and urban trade and industry wrought major changes on the social order from within. Quite apart from the potential divergences between merchant and aristocratic interests within the neofeudal state, the growth of agrarian capital and urban craft and industry contributed to an *overdetermined* situation that proved not cyclical but evolutionary. The bottom had fallen out of the cloth boom by the mid-sixteenth century, and much of seventeenth-century Europe fell into deep economic crisis; but the proliferation of crafts and industries in England, fueled by the creation of wage-labor, and by the prosperity and productivity of agrarian capitalists, helped to sustain an economy – one of the most advanced in Europe – that was based increasingly on the production of "consumer" goods for a home market. Such was the agrarian productivity and industrial growth resulting from peasant expropriation that by the end of the seventeenth century as much as half of the English population was engaged in non-agricultural pursuits. If, according to Marx, the "really revolutionising path" to capitalism was not through the commercial capital of merchants applied to production but through the industrial capital of petty producers,[29] then the burgeoning labor pool of sixteenth- and seventeenth-century London, exemplified in the growth of journeymen's guilds and of unregulated labor and manufacture in the suburbs, was essential to what recent work has shown to be the development of a redistributional trade for a home market based in London[30] and an economy in which half of London's

---

[28] Dobb, "A Reply" (to Paul Sweezy), in *Transition*, p. 63; Christopher Hill, "A Comment," in *Transition*, p. 121; Takahashi, "A Contribution to the Discussion," in *Transition*, p. 87; R. H. Hilton, "Capitalism – What's in a Name?" in *Transition*, p. 153; Perry Anderson, *Lineages of the Absolutist State* (1974; rpt. London: Verso, 1979), p. 22.

[29] *Capital*, III.xx (3 vols. New York: International Publishers, 1967), 3: 323. See also Maurice Dobb, *Studies in the Development of Capitalism* (London: George Routledge & Sons, 1946), ch. 4; Takahashi, "A Contribution to the Discussion," in *Transition*, pp. 90–91; Giuliano Procacci, "A Survey of the Debate," ibid., pp. 136–140.

[30] Brian Dietz, "Overseas Trade and Metropolitan Growth," in A. L. Beier and Roger Finlay, eds., *London 1500–1700: The Making of the Metropolis* (London: Longman, 1986), p. 126.

mid-seventeenth-century laboring population and three-fifths of its trades were engaged in the production of goods.[31] This transformation in the socio-economic order – and with it the rise of new industries like silk-weaving, glass-, pin-, and paper-manufacture, and sugar-refining – helps to explain the rise of the mercantilist policies (formulated in the early seventeenth century by Thomas Mun, Lewis Roberts, and Henry Robinson) that, by tipping trade toward the import of raw material and the export of finished goods, enhanced England's standing as an imperialist power.[32] It also helps to explain the differences that during the Civil Wars led many of London's leading chartered merchants to join with court-sponsored monopolists, speculators, and industrial concessionaires in support of the Royalist cause, while London's journeymen, artisans, petty-producers and laborers joined with capitalist farmers of the middling rank in support of Parliament and the Army.[33] Finally, in the much longer run, the overdetermined role of London in the transformation of the feudal order helps to explain why the city, despite its function as a *rentier* capital and parasitic consumer within the neofeudal absolutist state, was not – like such other European capitals as Naples, Madrid, and Constantinople – merely a "spectator ... present at the forthcoming industrial revolution,"[34] but an engine of growth that continued to lead the nation in manufacturing output (if not in the industrial innovation of the factory system) into the mid-Victorian period. In simultaneously helping to change the mode of agricultural production and to reassimilate peasants as laborers and petty producers, the growth of London eventually created innovative markets, industries, credit and transport systems that averted demographic crisis and economic collapse even while they mobilized values and social status.[35]

This, however, is to leap far ahead of the early Tudor period, when the mass disruptions attendant on socio-economic change, coinciding with the advent of a centralizing state, registered verbally in Tudor complaint as a decomposition and realignment of social myths and taxonomic structures and a recomposition of the effects of voice and address. These structural transformations, linked to shifts with the traditional socio-

[31] A. L. Beier, "Engine of Manufacture: The Trades of London," in Beier and Finlay, eds., *London 1500–1700*, pp. 149–150.

[32] Dietz, "Overseas Trade and Metropolitan Growth," p. 129; Charles Wilson, *England's Apprenticeship* (2nd edn. London: Longman, 1984), pp. 59–62.

[33] See Robert Brenner, *Merchants and Revolution: Commercial Change, Political Conflict, and London's Overseas Traders, 1550–1653* (Princeton University Press, 1993), *passim*.

[34] Braudel, *Capitalism and Material Life*, p. 440.

[35] E. A. Wrigley, "A Simple Model of London's Importance in Changing English Society and Economy 1650–1750," in Abrams and Wrigley, eds., *Towns in Societies*, pp. 237–239.

economic order, demonstrate the paradox by which Gilles Deleuze and Felix Guattari link the process of expropriation to the process of sedentarism:

The earth is above all else the matter upon which the dynamic of lineages is inscribed ... Everything changes with state societies: it is often said that the territorial principle becomes dominant. One could also speak of deterritorialization, since the earth becomes an object, instead of being an active material element in combination with lineage. Property is precisely the deterritorialized relation between the human being and the earth.[36]

Though both historians and literary scholars have long concerned themselves with Tudor social criticism, the emphasis has fallen not so much on its structure as on content and development. At the most general extreme, Arthur B. Ferguson has described the broad areas of agreement around which the articulate citizenship of the earlier Tudor period was formed, while J. K. McConica has argued that this consensus was Erasmian.[37] At a nearly opposite extreme, Whitney Jones has traced several genetic strands of social comment to the different groups of intellectuals and reformers that formed at different times in the period.[38] G. R. Elton has concentrated on the group around Thomas Cromwell,[39] while Jennifer Loach has explored the dynamics of surreptitious criticism in the reign of Mary.[40] There is, however, a remarkable continuity in the social criticism of the various opposition groups that tended to emerge in tandem with the shifting factions and coalitions of the mid-Tudor years.

Historians have focused, too, on the conditions addressed in complaint. Despite the tendency of Tudor writers to exaggerate the importance of enclosures and middlemen and to overlook the more essential impact of rising population on inflation, dearth, and unemployment, there is now some agreement, as Jones explains, that "many commentators of the mid-Tudor period showed far more percipience and accuracy than are often allowed them ... To an extraordinary degree, specific contributions of contemporary observers are being validated by the conclusions of detailed research."[41] As with the historical study of ideas and authorship,

---

[36] *A Thousand Plateaus: Capitalism and Schizophrenia*, tr. Brian Massumi (Minneapolis: University of Minnesota Press), 1988, p. 388.

[37] Ferguson, *The Articulate Citizen and the English Renaissance*; McConica, *English Humanists and Reformation Politics* (Oxford: Clarendon Press, 1965). See also W. Gordon Zeeveld, *Foundations of Tudor Policy* (Cambridge, Mass.: Harvard University Press, 1948), and Fritz Caspari, *Humanism and the Social Order in Tudor England* (University of Chicago Press, 1954).

[38] *The Tudor Commonwealth, 1529–1559* (London: The Athlone Press, 1970).

[39] See especially *Reform and Renewal: Thomas Cromwell and the Common Weal* (Cambridge University Press, 1973).

[40] "Pamphlets and Politics, 1553–58," *BIHR*, 48 (1975), 31–44.

[41] *The Tudor Commonwealth*, p. 3.

there have been works on the separate issues addressed in complaint – agricultural crisis, poverty, social disorder, commercial policy, and so forth.[42] But whether the link of historical explanation has been between the ideas of social criticism and changes in the circumstances of its composition or between the topics of complaint and actual conditions, the effect of most historical analysis has been either to overparticularize this body of material or to overgeneralize it, without in either case disclosing the discursively systemic nature of its prevailing structures.

One reason for this is that in trying to ground written testimony against historical fact, historians have been reluctant to consider the larger body of literature and literary traditions of which Tudor social criticism is a part. G. R. Elton, for example, distinguishes between "the succession of men who thought coolly, secularly, and constructively about the problems of the commonweal and who faced the practical tasks involved in turning aspiration into action" and "the laudators of a glorious past that had never been and the lamenters over man's fallen nature."[43] To be sure, there are variations in precisely where this line of distinction is drawn, but its general persistence has meant that historians have failed to see any historical significance in the literary myths and structures by which the discourse of Tudor social criticism was mediated. As part of a larger literary tradition that included poetry and drama, complaint was shaped by an inherited system of structures, practices, myths, and motifs that transcended the specific circumstances of individual authors, issues, events. Yet insofar as this system itself was changing, as old structures were modified and new ones were generated, it has a genetic dimension, consisting not so much of the causalities of authorship and group dynamics, of changing events and responses to them, as of fundamental realignments in the myths and motifs themselves.

[42] See, for example, R. H. Tawney, *The Agrarian Problem in the Sixteenth Century* (London, 1912), Joan Thirsk, ed., *The Agrarian History of England and Wales, Volume 4: 1500–1640* (Cambridge University Press, 1967), and E. Kerridge, *The Agricultural Revolution* (London, 1967); John F. Pound, ed., *Poverty and Vagrancy in Tudor England* (Harlow: Longmans, 1971); Anthony Fletcher, ed., *Tudor Rebellions* (London: Longmans, 1968), Barret L. Beer, *Rebellion and Riot: Popular Disorder in England During the Reign of Edward VI* (Kent, Ohio: Kent State University Press, 1982), and Paul Slack, ed., *Rebellion, Popular Protest, and the Social Order in Early Modern England* (New York: Cambridge University Press, 1984); F. J. Fisher, "Commercial Trends and Policy in Sixteenth-Century England," *EconHR*, 2nd series 20 (1967), 441–466, and Joan Thirsk, *Economic Policy and Projects* (Oxford: Clarendon Press, 1978).

[43] "Reform and the 'Commonwealth Men' of Edward VI's reign," in *Studies in Tudor and Stuart Politics and Government* (3 vols. Cambridge University Press, 1974–1983), 3: 253; see also in the same series "State Planning in early-Tudor England," 1: 285–293, and "Reform by Statute: Thomas Starkey's *Dialogue* and Thomas Cromwell's Policy," 2: 236–258.

These realignments are highlighted by the historical situation of Tudor complaint between two relatively stable literary formations, two languages of social comment and analysis. On the one hand, most complaints were conservative in their appeal to the long-established models and values of medieval social commentary.[44] Compassion for the poor and oppressed were indigenous to both medieval Christian piety and chivalry, and litany and invective were hoary devices of rhetorical elaboration.[45] Even as the quietest traditions of the Middle Ages were being transformed by Erasmian humanism into an active reckoning with the material world, that reckoning continued to draw upon highly "ceremonial polemics against wealth"; allegory, anatomy, personification, and pageant continued to provide the central tropes in a common North European vocabulary of social criticism.[46] As it was deployed by Tudor writers, this vocabulary was used to portray the ills of England as a social and economic anomaly, as transgressions and violations against a just and ancient order. Feudal myths like the order of the three estates, agrarian motifs like the virtuous plowman, religious tropes like the heavenly and earthly cities were part of a heritage invoked by the writers of complaint to identify, clarify, and criticize the novel and unfamiliar developments of a changing world. In its use of tradition, Tudor complaint thus functioned metonymically, dramatizing in the collapse of an ancient and well-defined order the disruptive influence of forces as yet too new and obscure to be named.[47]

On the other hand, this traditional vocabulary was transformed by the circumstance of its application. In contrast to the sources from which it had emerged, the social commentary of late Elizabethan and early Jacobean literature was structured by very different social models, myths, and assumptions, most of which took as a basic norm a functional division between country and city that had been only half-articulate and considered altogether anomalous in earlier complaint. The common medieval model of the three estates, for example, was supplanted by the

---

[44] This is well established in the major literary studies of complaint, Helen C. White's *Social Criticism in the Popular Religious Literature of the Sixteenth Century* (New York: Macmillan, 1944), and John Peter's *Complaint and Satire in Early English Literature* (Oxford: Clarendon Press, 1956). Both writers, however, fail to show how this conservatism is a vital response to contemporary experience.

[45] See J. Huizinga, *The Waning of the Middle Ages* (1949; rpt. New York: Anchor Doubleday, 1954), pp. 63, 295.

[46] Simon Schama, *The Embarrassment of Riches: An Interpretation of Dutch Culture in the Golden Age* (New York: Knopf, 1987), ch. 5 and esp. pp. 327–332, 364.

[47] In a recent book which approaches the structures of complaint much as I do here, Barry Taylor argues that the new economic forms and practices transformed the social order into a "form which is uncontainable in its conceptual topography," *Vagrant Writing: Social and Semiotic Disorder in the English Renaissance* (New York: Harvester Wheatsheaf, 1991), p. 84.

division of English society into court, city, and country; as the formerly traditional functions of fighting, praying, and working were replaced by the functions of consumption, commerce, and production. The medieval plowman who had in early Tudor complaint still represented the virtue of all members of a unitary estate of commoners was replaced – in tandem with the humanist reception of classical genres, itself a phenomenon of urbanization – by the pastoral shepherd, whose very being was defined by a new opposition within the commoners' estate between rural husbandmen and urban merchants. The theology of the two cities, once used to invalidate earthly pursuits, was increasingly adapted to a protestant doctrine of vocation that legitimized pursuits that were within the earth without being of it. The urbane outlook of late Elizabethan satire and early Jacobean drama took the division of country from city as definitive of human relationship, and in the ballad lore of these later periods prolific lists and catalogues, which in earlier complaint had signified the collapse of all distinctions, were "normalized" as harmless traits of an urban sphere whose boundary was now itself a distinction productive of order. In short, the prominence of the city as a basic structure in the literature of the later Renaissance reveals in retrospect that the dynamics of Tudor complaint were not simply backward-looking in their appeal to long-established social myths and models but, in their response to social crisis, generative of new ones. In the changing languages of Tudor complaint, a whole system of tropes was realigned to accommodate the emergence of London as a basic fact in the nation's mental life.

The issue is the emergence of an explanatory framework by means of which all manner of previously obscure, anomalous, and seemingly destructive developments could be clearly represented and, in a sense, contained. London was often a major target in Tudor complaint, sometimes for directly causing England's ills, sometimes for its association with ruthlessly anti-social and amoral commerce. But far more interesting is the relative inarticulateness of the image of the city in these works. They seem at times unable, in their adherence to older, feudal ideals, to accommodate the structures of urban life to their vision of order, unable to accept the city as an organizing category in the English society and economy. The inability to encompass London with a fully defined ideology, the inability fully to separate country from city, may not have been so much a blind conservatism as a tacit percipience about the links that bound country and city together. The very absence of a sharp structural division between country and city may have enabled the writers of complaint to make connections that many late Elizabethan writers saw less clearly. Indeed, the more sharply the lines were drawn around London in the later period, the more obscured were the economic ties that made it inseparable from agricultural and landed interests. Even as the city was defined with increasing clarity as the source of all that was anomalous, it was becoming the accepted basis for new models of social structure, such as the myth in which courtiers and shepherds, gentlemen and their dependents, were joined in a circle of rural virtue, from which the common, acquisitive pursuits of the city were excluded, or the neofeudal myth in which social and economic mobility were legitimized in loyalty and service to the old order by morally "gentle" urbanites. The popularity of the first myth among courtiers, court poets, and gentlemen, as against the popularity of the second among the merchants and craftsmen, is a symptom of the emergence of that social boundary that was to be essential for the early modern age, the boundary between the rulers and the ruled. But insofar as each of these myths served to render imperceptible the connections between power and status on the one hand and commerce on the other – thereby strengthening the ties between them – both of them contributed to an urbanizing process in which both merchants and gentry actually participated. It is this process – a con-centering of wealth and power – that is the focus of Tudor complaint.

By approaching the city as the perfected center of human achievement, as the norm from which men derive their identity and being, Thomas More had been able to articulate the city's deepest paradox, the contradiction between the radical concentration of urban power and the radical distribution of justice. It seems ironic, then, that the body of Tudor complaint should have done the reverse, in effect discovering or inventing a vocabulary that "naturalized" or normalized the urbanizing process as a result of attacking, from a traditional, non-urban point of view, the maldistributions resulting from the urban concentration of wealth and power. Only half-successfully tracing the disruptions of their age to London, which could only seem anomalous from the standpoint of the older social models on which they relied, Tudor writers effectively transformed these models in such a way as to articulate the inarticulate, generating new structures in which the city was fully institutionalized. In leading to the seat of radical power, the quest for radical justice effectively reversed the poles of traditional social critique. The idea of an agrarian order, rooted in a sedentary feudal life, underwent a process of mobilization and displacement, while the anomalous mobility of urban life became a quasi-permanent or settled condition, around which new movements and displacements were constellated.

The world turned upside-down

When early Tudor writers sought to portray the problems of the changing social order, they typically resorted to tropes of inversion. In doing so, they adapted the traditionally ritual functions of carnival to the purposes of representation; from the aggressive and potentially subversive ensemble of carnivalian symbols, they selected elements for the purpose of counter-subversive social and moral commentary.[48] To be sure, the grotesque inversions practiced in carnival unflatteringly exposed the ills and deformities of the everyday social norm, but this exposure was decently confined to ritual occasions, allowing for a controlled, cathartic release of resentment and anxiety and a magical "cure" of the ills themselves. Tropes of inversion, furthermore, had long been used by writers to generalize about the world, to characterize the paradoxes of Christian humility, for example, or to dramatize the sudden reversals of fortune.[49] But the writers of Tudor complaint applied these motifs with increased specificity, in order to characterize a particular set of socio-economic developments. In order to imply that "the world was perverted or reversed, the times radically out of joint,"[50] they used the exceptional misrule of carnival to figure the overturning of traditional order, representing the body politic through the mock societies of ships, cartloads, and roll-calls of fools. On the one hand, their carnivalian images of the social order underlined the bewildering profusion of social roles, classes, species, and distinctions that were linked to socio-economic change and, especially, to the increasingly mobile environment of London. On the other hand, this anarchic profusion was dialectically linked to a drift toward regimentation, so that the representation of disorder and mobility was typically a function of the quest for stasis, and the terror of deterritorialization was implicitly a step toward the reterritorialization of the social landscape by the emerging state regime. The enumerative social schemes, lists, and prolific categories of Tudor complaint were thus directly related to the more sober anatomies of the age, which was preoccupied with naming and numbering, with the creation of commissions and panels of inquiry, of ecclesiastical and

---

[48] Samuel Kinser, "Presentation and Representation: Carnival at Nuremberg, 1450–1550," *Representations*, 13 (1986), 1–41; for the view that carnival motifs are always circumscribed by an implied moral commentary, see Umberto Eco, "The Frames of Comic Freedom," in *Carnival!*, ed. Thomas A. Sebeok (Berlin: Mouton, 1984), pp. 1–9.
[49] R. W. Scribner, *For the Sake of Simple Folk: Popular Propaganda for the German Reformation* (Cambridge University Press, 1981), pp. 164–165; E. R. Curtius, *European Literature and the Latin Middle Ages*, tr. Willard R. Trask (1953; rpt. New York: Harper and Row, 1963), pp. 94–98.   [50] Scribner, *For the Sake of Simple Folk*, p. 166.

heraldic visitations, of parish registers and sumptuary regulation, of measures to label and control the minuter species of the poor and disabled. All of these efforts were part of a reorganizing of the social terrain under the influence of the Tudor state.

Derived from rituals and social practices which were traditionally used to effect transitions from one set of rules or expectations to another, the carnivalian motifs of complaint were used to address a disturbing process of transition. They were applied in response to perceived conditions of anomaly – of mass displacement and deterritorialization – but in such a way as to lay these threats to rest. Their prominence in the work of social analysts reflects the extent to which native and popular influences still dominated the first half-century of England's print culture, when the civic and statist traditions of classical and continental humanism were only gradually taking hold. But the adaptation of these influences was also a selective and reflexive act on the part of literate social thinkers; it coincided with and was an early non-classicizing means of representing and rendering intelligible the disturbing effects of social and economic change. This is why there developed, in the literature of complaint, an inverse relationship between the prominence of London and the nightmare of social taxonomy gone mad: as London was increasingly portrayed as the center and epitome of the inverted world depicted in these works, the threat of proliferating categories and distinctions was more and more narrowly confined, until – in literature, if not in life – this threat of the socially strange and anomalous was reduced to a harmless form of recreation – a comic spectacle of urban folly in something like the form Bakhtin calls "alcove realism," a voyeuristic mode in which all things are safely and discretely confined to their "proper" place.[51] Subdividing, specialization, and the multiplication of categories and distinctions were not, then, simply anomalous from the point of view of traditional order; they were essential to the creation of a new regime. Early Tudor social critics succeeded in drawing a conceptual circle of containment around London even as the social segmentations, striations, and displacements continued to multiply within it; precisely because of its carnivalian, cornucopian capaciousness – the number of socio-economic specialties and innovations it could be made to contain – this circle in fact became the crucial structural boundary around which many later Tudor myths of the city were elaborated. The division between country

[51] *Rabelais and His World*, tr. Hélène Iswolsky (1968; rpt. Bloomington: Indiana University Press, 1984), p. 106. Once the category of the "urban" had been invented, of course, it was not fated to become merely the domain of the picturesque or of bourgeois realism, though this was one of its uses, even by the late sixteenth century (see ch. 9); it could also be mobilized or dialogized so as to form a moral order as durable and resilient as more traditional ones (see ch. 6).

and city, a virtually meaningless distinction within the traditional social order, became an essential feature of a society increasingly shaped by the forces of capitalism.

The ship of fools was one of the most common familiar means by which the carnivalian motif of the inverted world was applied to the social order. In *The Ship of Fools*, Alexander Barclay's English adaptation of Sebastian Brant's *Narrenschiff*, the traditional motif of the voyage to a fool's paradise is situated concretely in the changing social landscape of England, transforming an encyclopedia of human virtues and vices into a mirror of society and its common endeavors. In Barclay's version, the voyage is literally circular and metaphorically tautological; its purpose is to "sayle to that londe where folys abounde and flowe."[52] The ship's circulation is through the realm in general, the number of fools being infinite, but London occupies a special place in the voyage; as the greatest source in the kingdom of the sort of fools who overload the ship, it is simultaneously both the principal port of embarkation and the ultimate, paradisal haven where "folys abounde and flowe." As such, it is also paradoxically the narrative *terminus* that would bring to a coherent end the very *pointless* circulation of energy and motion, striving and turmoil, that make human folly incoherent and unnarratable:

> From London Rockes almyghty god vs saue
> For if we there anker, outher bote or barge,
> There be so many that they vs will ouercharge.
> Ye London Galantes, arere, ye shal nat enter,
> We kepe the streme, and touche nat the shore
> In Cyte nor in Court we dare nat well auenter
> Lyst perchaunce we sholde displeasure haue therefore. (1: 13–14)

Through the protective disclaimer that avoiding London provides him, Barclay implies that London is such a perfect point of departure, harboring enough fools to sink the ship, that it is also the ultimate destination. The topsy-turvy world of fools originates and ends in – while altogether avoiding – the fool's paradise of London. Along the way, the voyage touches every part of England with its influence, turning the whole nation upside-down: "eche seruant wolde a master be." Barclay's *Ship of Fools* brings together two key motifs of traditional complaint: "the sins triumph in a world upside down; and they triumph not only in the whole world but also in particular places."[53] London, its

---

[52] *The Ship of Fools*, ed. T. H. Jamieson (2 vols. Edinburgh, 1874), 2: 308.
[53] Joseph K. Keller, "The Triumph of Vice: A Formal Approach to the Medieval Complaint Against the Times," in Wolfgang Weiss, ed., *Die Englische Satire* (Darmstadt: Wissenschaftliche Buchgesellschaft, 1982), p. 11; see also in the same volume, Wolfgang Weiss, "'Land of Cockaigne' – Utopie, Parodie, oder Satire?" pp. 124–134.

liberties, and the proliferating crafts and cabals whose conflicting interests and ambitions create the turmoil that drives the ship, lie behind a swarming, mobile horde that ranges the English countryside.

The key to London's role in Barclay's poem is an analogy between physical and social mobility. Rooted to the land by an agricultural economy, the idea of social order is inseparable from topography: the stability of vertical social ranks depends upon the spatial fixity of subjects in the landscape.[54] Thomas Harman, an early Tudor anatomist of vagrancy who traced the problem to the failure of local authority, called on "justices and shrieves... in their circuits" to "be more vigilant to punish these malefactors" and on "the constables, bailiffs, and borsholders" to "be more circumspect in executing charge given over them by the aforesaid Justices. Then will no more this rascal rabblement range about the country."[55] It was clearly the aim of early Tudor statutes and proclamations against vagabonds to re-establish connections between social and topographical order by commanding "all beggars and vagabondes being within the city of London and the suburbs of the same" to "depart from the same city into their countries where they were born, or else where they last dwelled by the space of three years."[56] In view of the mobility associated with Barclay's Ship of Fools, it is not surprising that Harman claimed in his anatomy of rogues to "have repaired and rigged the ship of knowledge... that she may safely pass about and through all parts of this noble realm."[57]

In *Cock Lorell's Bote* (c. 1510), illicit forms of mobility and surreptitious enterprises are more explicitly associated both with London's urban "liberties" and with the city's anarchic inversion of the traditional social order. The extant fragment of the poem begins just where Cock Lorell's boat begins to define itself as an inverted social order, with a roll of membership that comprises a whole hierarchy of officers, provisioners, and police:

> Here is fyrst, Cocke Lorell the knyght,
> And symkyn emery, myntenaunce agayne ryght;
> And slyngethryfte fleshmonger...
> With adam auerus flayle swenger;
> And fraunces flaperoche, of stewys captayne late,
> With gylys vnyeste mayer of newgate,
> And lewes vnlusty the lesynge monger...

[54] See Taylor, *Vagrant Writing*, pp. 9–10.
[55] Thomas Harman, *A Caveat or Warning for Common Cursitors* (1566), in A. V. Judges, ed., *The Elizabethan Underworld* (London: George Routledge and Sons, 1930), p. 62.
[56] Proclamation Enforcing Statutes against Beggars and Vagabonds (1531), in Paul L. Hughes and James F. Larkin, eds., *Tudor Royal Proclamations* (3 vols. New Haven: Yale University Press, 1964–69), 1: 198.   [57] Harman, *Caveat*, p. 62.

... mathew merchaunte of shoters hyll;
Christopher catchepoll a crystes course gaderer,
And wat welbelyne of ludgate Iayler,
With laurence lorell of clerken well.
Here is gylys Iogeler of ayebery,
And hym sougelder of lothe bery ...
Also mathew tothe drawer of London
And sybly sole mylke wife of Islington ...
Here is george of podynge lane, carpenter,
And patryck peuysshe a conynge dyrte dauber,
Worshypfull wardayn of slouens In.[58]

Applying the in-law honorific titles of officialdom ("captayne ... mayer ... catchepoll ... Iayler") to a vast, mobile, outlaw population of thieves, touts, slovens, and jugglers, the catalogue plays fast and loose with the boundaries between the City of London jurisdiction and the extra-territorial liberties and suburbs, between burgherly sobriety and crime. In its blurred distinctions, it establishes a profound connection between the in-law freedoms of the municipality and the outlaw license of the suburban underworld, between the freedom of a swarming horde of displaced persons and the coming of a disciplinary order prolific in distinctions.

Horde and disciplined community are thus mutually defining in this carnivalian work, as a deterritorialized social landscape is subjected to a process of reterritorialization. The corrosive marketplace freedoms and mobility that the poem associates with London's unregulated suburban liberties are represented as essential to the creation of a new social order in which London dominates an emerging state. The poem establishes a dialectical relationship between the equality of men in an inverted festive world – where restlessness, mobility, and ambition break down order and degree – and the tendency of this social breakdown to proliferate in an endless series of new social categories and invidious distinctions. This proliferation signals the coming of a new order of more specialized and diverse economic and social relationships. The multiplication of fools and folly carries with it the double spectre of a social system collapsing, but collapsing into a multitude of disturbingly re-ordered species, potentially as numerous as its component atoms – i.e., as its newly individuated human subjects. The poem's *tour de force* is thus a gargantuan inventory of 214 trades and occupations and another 41 types of rogue, a mere tenth of which includes

taylers, tauerners, and drapers,
Potycaryes, ale brewers, and bakers,

[58] In *Early English Poetry* (30 vols. London: Percy Society, 1840–1851), 4: 4–5.

Mercers, fletchers, and sporyers.
Boke printers, peynters, bowers,
Myllers, carters, and botyll makers,
Waxechaundelers, clothers, and grocers,
Wolle men, vynteners, and flesshemongers,
Salters, Iowleres, and habardashers,
    Drouers, cokes, and pulters;
    Fruyters, chese mongers, and mynstrelles.   (p.9)

The poem's cornucopian prolixity goes hand in hand with its other festive motifs, but the sheer magnitude of the boat's swollen population adds an aggressive edge to the poem's topsy-turvy. What gives this threat real social point is the circumstance of the voyage – an ingathering and dispersal through the gates of London. Departing from a London whose streets are "all ouersprede" with crime and folly, Cock Lorell's voyage affects all "England thorowe and thorowe, / Vyllage, towne, cyte, and borowe" (p. 14).

Ships like Cock Lorell's sailed onto the stage, where they focused the new preoccupation of social interludes with the overturning of the social order. In *Hick Scorner* (c. 1515–16), "oppressors of people" descended in hordes on England from the hold of the *Envy*, a ship "of London, a great vessel and a mighty," while in *The Tyde Taryeth No Man* (1576) the riotous voyage of a vast crew of "false dealers" epitomized a whole society beset by feverish mobility,

With catching and snatching,
Waking and watching,
Running and ryding:
... ebbing and flowing,
Coming and going,
It doth never rest.[59]

Thomas Cromwell had asserted that "London is the common country from which is derived to all parts of the realm all good and ill occurent there."[60] Behind the mobility and contagious influence of these ships of fools, as behind the cartloads of rogues and fools assembled in *The xxv. Ordres of Fooles* and in John Hall's Cart of Avarice, lay a similar assumption that "the Citie is fyrst the Author of Ill." Its inversion of the social order unleashed on society "a packe of people sekyng gayne":

A hell wythout all order is
That realme where such do wonne,

[59] *Hick Scorner*, ed. Ian Lancashire (Baltimore: Johns Hopkins University Press, 1980), ll. 366–378; George Wapull, *The Tyde Taryeth no Man*, ed. Ernst Ruhl, *Jahrbuch der Deutschen Shakespeare-Gesellschaft*, 43 (1907), lines 57–158.
[60] Quoted in Brigden, *London and the Reformation*, p. 129.

A flocke of folke vngodly bent,
In synfull pathes to ronne.
    A packe of people sekyng gayne,
And priuate welthe prefer:
And common wealth doth none seke for,
But eche doth it hynder.
    Eche man is for hym selfe,
The dyuell is for all.[61]

In their attempt to reckon with prolific confusion, such catalogues announce the advent of a new social order. In Robert Copland's *Hye Way to the Spyttle House*, for example, the compelling image of highways thronged with beggars and rogues making their way to London magnifies the terror of a social order inverted and collapsed into chaos; but it also precipitates new taxonomies and versions of social order. On a cold November night, the poet seeks shelter with a porter under the porch of a City spital:

And as we talked there gathered at the gate
    People, as me thought, of very poore estate,
With bag and staf, both croked, lame and blynde,
    Scabby and scuruy, pocke eaten flesh and rynde,
Lousy and scalde, and pylled lyke as apes,
    With scantly a rag to couer their shapes,
Brechles, barefoted, all stynking with dyrt,
    With M. of tatters drabblyng to the skyrt,
Boyes, gyrles, and luskysh strong knaues.[62]

These displaced subjects, who "in the winter...draw to the town," are a new kind of liminaries. They are found everywhere in the City's physical interstices, "under the stalls, in porches, and in doors / ...And in many corners"; they loiter "in every way and street / ...In lanes and paths, and at each crossway." "In the highways" they "lie / At Westminster and Saint Paul's, / And in all these streets they sit as desolate souls" (p. 8).

The poet's dialogue with the knowledgeable hospital-porter seeks to confine the anomalies of vagabondage within decent limits by distinguishing, in almost digital fashion, between those "which ye leave" and those "which ye do succour," in other words, between the virtuous poor (the aged, sick, impotent, wounded in war) and the burgeoning varieties of losels, sturdy beggars, michers, hedgecreepers, fyllocks, lusks,

---

[61] *The Court of Virtue*, ed. Russell A. Fraser (New Brunswick: Rutgers University Press, 1961), pp. 309, 310.
[62] *The Hye Way to the Spyttle House*, in A. V. Judges, ed., *The Elizabethan Underworld*, pp. 4–5.

Newgate nightriders, rogers (bogus scholars), clewners (bogus priests), and mountebanks (p.4). To the category of sturdy beggars whom he rejects as undeserving the porter attributes a willful malice and pugnaciousness (later to become the phenomenon of "roaring"), in keeping with the observation of Deleuze and Guattari that the principal mobilized resistances to the state are catatonia (withdrawal) and affect, "the active discharge of emotion, the counterattack" (p. 400). The poem abounds in unruly, perverse figures who "run from all grace," who "keep no condition," who "traverse and conject," and "fall at anger and debate" (p. 2). These masterless hordes will

> abide no laborious subjection
> With honest persons, under correction;
> For, when they be weary, they will run away,
> And perchance carry with them what they may.   (p.7)

In ascribing their mobility to perverse willfulness, the poem provides the horde with a subjectivity which can then become the object of domesticating discipline.

The task of domestication is facilitated by a dialectical, agonistic relationship between frightening non-languages and reassuring languages of order. On the one hand, the porter offers such ordering schemes as simple binaries:

> Of these two estates there be four degrees:
> A rich rich, a poor poor, a rich poor also,
> A poor rich in all necessities.
> The two can agree, but the other, no.   (p. 2)

On the other hand, powerful resistances to such linguistic assimilation arise from the chaotic word-hoard of the poor:

> Enow, enow. With bousy cove maund nase,
>   Tour the patrico in the darkman case,
> Docked the dell for a copper make:
>   Cyarum, by Solomon, and thou shalt peck my jere
> In thy gan; for my watch it is nace gear;
>   or the bene bouse my watch hath a wyn.   (p. 24)

It is impossible to say which of these languages takes causal priority within the *Hye Way*, since the two are bound in mutually creative relationship. In the same way, the bodies for which these languages speak – the mobile swarm and the regiment – are also interdependent: if the displaced masses are created by the emergence of a new regime, with its new standards of property, propriety, and status, the regime is itself dependent upon the displaced, upon the process of expropriation and dispossession that calls the juridical function into being. As a liminary work inhabiting this transitional process, the *Hye Way* thus includes in its survey of mobility not just rogues and displaced peasants but also the proliferating functionaries of the new order,

> people so full of covetise,
> That all the world's good cannot them suffice,
> But by usury, rapine, and extortion,
> Do poll the poor folk of their portion. (p. 20)

The attempt to classify "all folke in generall, / That come the hye way to the hospytall" thus breaks down when the knowledgeable porter confesses that

> as for ordre,
> I promyse none to kepe,
> For they do come as they were scattered shepe,
> Wandryng without reason, rule, or guide. (p. 13)

The poem embraces a bewildering profusion of novel in-law and outlaw categories – unthrift heirs and wastrels, small renters spread too thin, crooked bailiffs, stewards, paymasters, creditors and receivers, slum landlords, stubborn plaintiffs, speculating merchants and cheating craftsmen, dishonest bakers and brewers, *as well as* taverners, gamesters, harlots, bawds, bolsterers, applesquires, and masterless men and vagabonds of all kinds. For this swarming population London is no longer the scene of joyous departure or the promised fool's paradise, but the last stop on the dismal shuffle from all the corners of England. The city has become a focus of inversion without festivity, of a profusion without abundance, of a society broken into its component atoms even as it is in the process of being reconstituted.

In attempting to order these social atoms, Copland's poem resorts to devices that are peremptory, arbitrary, and rigid, but at the same time conspicuously ineffectual. Copland refers in his prologue to the quaternion of fools, a numerical device also used in the ballad of *The xxv. Ordres of Fooles*, in Awdeley's *Fraternity of Vagabonds*, and in another poem by Copland, *Jyl of Brentford's Testament*. He resorts, too, to the alphabetical decoding of the varieties of vagabonds: "P. a Pardoner: Clewner a C. / R. a Roger; A. an Aurium, and a Sapyent S." (p. 50). Perhaps derived, like other carnivalian features of social commentary, from traditions of urban festivity, such schemes of social inventory became a staple in social interludes.[63] In Robert Wilson's *Three Ladies*

---

[63] On the 3NN of *Mankind*, the 4CC of Skelton's *Magnificence*, and the *Four PP* of Heywood, see also Lois Potter, "The Plays and the Playwrights," in *The Revels History of the Drama in English, Volume II: 1500–1576*, ed. N. Sanders, R. Southern, T. W.

of London (c. 1584), whimsical rhyme and alliteration organized the cornucopian list of roguish Londoners invited to a wedding with Dissimulation that transformed Love into Lust:

> There is, first and foremost, Master Forgery and Master
>   Flattery, Master Perjury and Master Injury:
> Master Cruelty and Master Pickery, Master Bribery and
>   Master Treachery;
> Master Wink-at-Wrong and Master Headstrong, Mistress
>   Privy-theft
> And Master Deep-deceit, Master Abomination and Mistress
>   Fornication his wife, Ferdinando False-weight and
>   Frisset False-measure his wife.[64]

A lost interlude by William Baldwin assembled sixty-two unsavory characters whose names all began with the letter L.[65] In *The Longer Thou Livest the More Fool Thou Art* (1569?), William Wager indicted as enemies to the commonweal an entire alphabet of double-dealing middlemen, corrupt administrators, and idle rogues:

> Sir Anthony Arrogant, auditor,
> Bartholomew Briber, bailie,
> Clament Catchpole, cofferer,
> Division Double-faced Davy,
> Edmund Envious, chief of the ewery,
> Fabian Falsehood, his head farmer,
> Gregory Gorbelly, the gouty,
> Governeth the grain in the garner,
> Hans Hazarder the housekeeper is,
> James the Just is the chief judge,
> Leonard Lecherous is man of law, Iwis,
> Kenolm the knave is in cookery no drudge,
> Martin the murderer, master of music,
> Nicol Never-thrift, the notary,
> Owen Overthwart, master in physic,
> Quintine the quaffer, for nothing necessary,
> Rafe Ruffian, the rude railer,
> Steven Sturdy, master surveyor,
> Thomas the thief, his chief tailor,
> William Witless, the great warrior,

Craik, and L. Potter (London: Methuen, 1980), p. 175; cf. F. P. Wilson, *The English Drama 1485–1585* (Oxford University Press, 1969), p. 28.

[64] *The Three Ladies of London*, in *Dodsley's Old English Plays*, ed. W. C. Hazlitt (12 vols. London, 1874), 6: 341.

[65] *Documents Relating to the Revels at Court in the Time of Edward VI and Queen Mary*, ed. Albert Feuillerat (Louvain: Materialien zur Kunde des alteren Englischen Dramas 44, 1914), p. 215.

With these and such like many moe,
We... be oppressed.[66]

In lists and schemes like these, social anomalies are dramatized by a paradigmatic principle of unity or likeness whose basis is its total speciousness and incoherence. They demonstrate the extent to which the levelling of traditional social distinctions was perceived as prolific of social division and subdivision. As one of the most patently physical forms of mobility, vagrancy, Barry Taylor explains, "opens up a dangerous topography of writing... in which the supposedly natural economy of the sign is replaced by an ungrounded, 'unlawful' vagrancy of the signifier."[67] Only a code as capacious and adaptable as the alphabet could serve as an effective taxonomic principle in the face of the terrifying number and apparent randomness of multiplying social categories.

By the end of the Tudor period, however, as the hyperbolic strains of social complaint modulated into the more articulate vocabulary of a specifically urban literature, such lists and categories became so clearly associated with the London environment as to be stabilized and contained by social and literary limits that were increasingly familiar. Samuel Rowlands' *Martin Mark-All, Beadle of Bridewell*, for example, announced on its title page the debt of its catalogue of knaves to Cock Lorell's precedent, but the catalogue itself decently confined Cock's domain, which had once been "England thorowe and thorowe," to a subterranean cavern beneath the northern part of London, "at first by estimation halfe a mile in compasse."[68] The size of this underworld cavern embodies a residual potency not entirely under the satirist's control. But in general, the mobility of antisocial rogues, and hence their power to spread contagion, was increasingly circumscribed. More and more, the contaminating mobile swarm of early Tudor complaint was confined within identifiable urban limits and even driven "underground." Ben Jonson's epigram *Upon the Famous Voyage*, for example, confined its fools' journey to the quite literal underworld of London's sewers. An even more circumscribed voyage, the popular metaphoric pun of sailing in the Fleet prison, reassured late Tudor Englishmen that London's rogues were going nowhere.[69] In Richard Tarlton's puppet-show-cum-jig, *A Horseload of Fools*, a cartload of social misfits paraded

---

[66] *The Longer Thou Livest the More Fool Thou Art*, ed. R. Mark Benbow (Lincoln: University of Nebraska Press, 1967), lines 1715–1736.

[67] *Vagrant Writing*, p. 10.

[68] *Complete Works*, ed. E. Gosse and S. J. H. Herrtage (3 vols. Glasgow, 1886), 2: 5.

[69] For the journey voyage to Tyburn, see, for example, *A new Ballad against Vnthrifts*, in Henry Huth, ed., *A Collection of Seventy-Nine Black-Letter Ballads and Broadsides* (London, 1870), p. 156.

harmlessly through Fleet Street.[70] The ability to render the swarm harmless by means of taxonomic inventory was inseparable from locating and confining the sources of disorder to the environment of London.

Just as ships and carts of fools gravitated more and more exclusively toward London as a conceptual barrier was erected around the city's underworld, so numerical, alphabetical, and serial schemes enjoyed a lengthy afterlife in jocular London lore which assured its audience that such profusion was characteristic of the city alone, where the condition of unsettlement became a quasi-permanent sedentary norm. In many popular ballad-types – medleys of street cries, church bells, taverns and tavern signs – unifying schemes of the most frivolous kind provided the occasion for delightfully swollen lists of individuals and species. In such ballads, abundance lost its terrifying edge; the spectre of variety was accommodated to a kind of alcove realism, in which the city became "naturally" bustling, teeming, and even, in some of the most fearless and innovative writers, productive of new social possibilities. But such qualities were restricted to the city and *only* the city – beyond whose limits other rules applied and such lists were rendered unthinkable.

In the earlier Tudor period, however, such lists portended the destruction of limits, a release into anarchy, just as arrival in London, through the "freedom" it offered, signified an empowering liberation from peasant servitude. Particularly revealing in this regard are the jests, fabliaux, and merry tales – in works like *Colin Blowbol's Testament* (1510), *Mayd Emylyn* (1520), *Doctor Dubble-Ale, The Wyll of the Deuyll and Last Testament* (1548), and *Pasquil's Merriments* – in which rogues and fools follow their dubious pursuits by exploiting the liberties of London, in ways that parody the civic privileges and freedoms through which London was in fact making inroads on the socio-economic order.[71] London thus became in the social imagination a kind of Cockaigne, a fool's paradise that, in suspending the traditional rules, turned England upside-down. In Robert Crowley's *Philargyrie of Greate Britayne* (1551), the giant Philargyrie advised his adoring subjects to get all "thingis in your hande" while his henchman Hypocrisy built

> A greate Citie
> Nodnoll he did it name
> It was allone

[70] In J. O. Halliwell, ed., *Tarlton's Jests and News out of Purgatory* (London: Shakespeare Society, 1844), pp. xx–xxvi.

[71] See *The Boke of Mayd Emylyn* (c. 1520), in W. C. Hazlitt, ed., *Early Popular Poetry of England* (4 vols. 1855; rpt. New York: AMS Press, 1966), 4: 96; *Colin Blowbol's Testament* (c. 1510), in Hazlitt, 1: ll. 85ff.; *The Wyll of the Deuyll*, ed. F. J. Furnivall (London, 1871).

With Babylon
If it were not the same.[72]

The occasion for the satiric dialogue of Philip Stubbes' *Anatomie of Abuses* (1583) was a journey toward the inverted city of Munidnol (Londinum), just as inversion was the informing structural principle of Thomas Lupton's *Sivqila* (1580), with its perverted domains of Ailgna (Anglia) and Munidnol (Londinum). At its worst, the topsy-turvydom of London was rendered in theriomorphism. In the inverted realm of London–Nodnol, according to one complaint, men were less careful for their brethren than "for their dogges... The Citie of London can of the Chambres cost prouyde a house to kepe .xx. or .xxx. dogges in and to gyue x. pounde by the yere for one to kepe them: but they wyll not allow .x. pens by yere of the Chambre, towardes the feeding of the poore."[73] London's poor were said to be suffered to die in the streets like dogs,[74] while its corrupt clergy were said to fawn on their rich masters with canine docility.[75] The theriomorphic extreme was cannibalism. More had written in *Utopia* of man-devouring sheep, but in William Baldwin's *Beware the Cat*, hordes of cats howl at midnight outside a window in Aldersgate for the dismembered flesh of executed criminals that hangs on the city's gates. Picking up on such motifs of inversion, Bernard Gilpin delivered a blistering sermon on

a people called Anthropophagi, eaters of men, which all mens hearts abhor to hear of; and yet, alas, by St. Paul's rule, England is full of such man-eaters. Every man envieth another, every man biteth and gnaweth upon another with venomous adder tongues, far more noisome than any teeth. And whereof cometh it? Covetousness is the root of all; every man scratcheth and pilleth from other; every man would suck the blood of other; every man encroacheth upon other.[76]

The aberrant economic relationships indicted by Gilpin were perceived by others as reversing the proper economic priorities, rewarding the idle rich and depriving the poor of the fruits of their labor. "In euery parysshe of London," John Gough observed, citizens had "gotten hepes of money and plate" while "pore people perysshe for faulte of a lytell thereof."[77] According to another complaint,

[72] *Philargyrie of Greate Britayne*, ed. John N. King, *English Literary Renaissance*, 10 (1980), lines 175, 155–157, 510–514.
[73] *The Prayse and Commendacion of Such as Sought Comenwelthes* (1548), sig. A4v.
[74] Philip Stubbes, *The Anatomie of Abuses* (1582), ed. William Turnbull (London, 1823), pp. 50–51.
[75] Henry Brinkelow, *The Lamentacyon of a Christian Agaynst the Cytye of London Made by Roderigo Mors* (1545), ed. J. M. Cowper (London: EETS, 1874), p. 91.
[76] *A Sermon Preached in the Court of Greenwich before King Edward VI, 1552*, in William Gilpin, *The Life of Bernard Gilpin* (London, 1753), p. 301.
[77] *The Mirrour or Lokynge Glasse* (1632), sigs. Iiii–Iiiiv.

the poore man mote gone to his labour in colde & in hete / in wete and drye / & spende his fleish & blode in the ryche mans workes vpon goddes grounde to fynde the rych man in ease & in lykynge ... Here is a great yeft of the poore man; for he yeueth his owne body. But what yeveth the ryche man him agenward? ... all men studdyeth on euery syde howe they may waxe ryche. And euerych man almest is ashamed to ben holden to a poore man ... But lorde the worlde is turned vpso downe.[78]

In countless early Tudor poems, antithesis became the rhetorical equivalent of social inversion. Skelton's *Speke Parott*, for example, lamented a world inverted by

> So many complayntes, and so small redresse;
> So myche callyng on, and so smalle takyng hede;
> So myche losse of merchandyse, and so remedyles;
> So lytell care for the comyn weall, and so much nede;
> So myche dowghtfull daunger, and so lytell drede.

(lines 470–474)

The *Treatise of a Galaunt* traced the realm's decay to similar disparities:

> So many barefote people / & so fewe good lyuers
> Hath no man sene / syth the worlde began...
> So moche rychesse in araye / and so moche nede...
> So moche fastynge for hungre / and so lytell mede...
> So many purfled garmentes / furred with non sequitur
> With so many penyles purses / hath no man sawe...
> We all go backwarde / from hyghe to the lowe.[79]

These imbalances and antitheses were associated in countless works with the rise of a new urban economy, dominated by the rule of money: "Full many a strong cyte and towne hath been wonne / By the meanes of money without ony gonne."[80] "Money," said a character in one of William Wager's interludes, "winneth both cities and towns." Through its new power to reproduce itself, money usurped the naturally created order, according to which money should not "beget or bring forth money, which was ordained to be a pledge or right betweixt man and

[78] *The Prayer and Complaynt of the Ploweman vnto Christ* (1531?), sig. E2.
[79] *A Treatise of a Galaunt*, in Hazlitt, ed., *Early Popular Poetry of England*, vol. 3, lines 120–121, 127, 129, 141–142, 144. Cf. the fifteenth-century *Now is Englond Perisshed*, lines 1–8, in Rossell Hope Robbins, ed., *Historical Poems of the XIVth and XVth Centuries* (New York: Columbia University Press, 1959), p. 159; and Dunbar's General Satire (c. 1510) in James Paterson, *The Life and Poems of William Dunbar* (Edinburgh: W. Nimmo, 1860), pp. 294–295. See also A. R. Heiserman, *Skelton and Satire* (University of Chicago Press, 1961), p. 185; E. V. Scattergood, *Politics and Poetry in the Fifteenth Century* (1971; rpt. New York: Barnes and Noble, 1972), pp. 298–306.
[80] Skelton, *Magnyfycence*, in *The Complete English Poems*, ed. John Scattergood (New Haven: Yale University Press, 1983), lines 1576–1578.

man, in contracts or bargayning, and not to increase itself, as a woman dothe, that bringeth foorth a childe, clean contrarye to the first institution of money."[81] The pattern of usurpation was completed as men were reduced to animals and chattels, and Money learned to talk. In Thomas Lupton's *All for Money* (1578), Money boasted that all degrees were levelled by his tyrannical influence:

> I dwell with euery degree
> The doctor, the draper, the plowman, the carter...
> The Smith and the Shoemaker, the minstrell,
>   the daunser...
> The Servingman, the spender, the usurer and the lender.
> No sooner come I to town, but manie bowe downe
> And comes if I hold vp the rodd.[82]

In the *Dialoge Betwene Man and Money*, man was finally struck dumb by Money's taunting jibe,

> Who builded London that named was newe Troye
> But I puisant peny, that eche man cloth and fede?   (sig. A3)

Markets, exchange, and the erosion of difference

In many Tudor complaints, the rule of "puisant peny" over the topsy-turvy world of Nodnol was merely a traditional way of describing a timeless moral tyranny – *Radix malorum est cupiditas*.[83] According to this enduring moral perspective, London was not a novel social problem, but, as William Wharton put it, an archetypal embodiment of evil:

like as the disease that lyeth ranckling and festering in the heart, ransacking euerie lym and ioynt of the body, and by that meanes makes all the members of the same subiect to his infirmitie. So the couetousnesse of London, the pride of London, the wantonnes of London, the ryotousnes of London, doth poyson the whole Realme of Englande, and maketh it apte to all wickednesse.[84]

Both the Bible and vernacular preaching associated the city with the sinful corruptions of wealth and power. Bishop John Longland, for example, claimed in a sermon before the King that "in the myddes of this citye, reygneth wrong doynges, iniuryes, with afflictyons & oppressyon

---

[81] Thomas Wilson, *A Discourse upon Usury* (1572), ed. R. H. Tawney (London: G. Bell and Sons, 1925), p. 286.

[82] *All for Money*, ed. J. S. Farmer (London: Tudor Facsimile Texts, 1910).

[83] See, e.g., John Barker, *A Balade Declaryng How Neybourhed, Loue, and trew Dealyng is Gone*, in Huth, *A Collection of ... Black-Letter Ballads*, p. 137; cf. *I Playne Piers*, sig. D, and *Aeger Diues habet nummos, sed non habet ipsum*, in *The Gorgious Gallery of Gallant Inuentions* (1578), ed. Hyder Rollins (Cambridge: Harvard University Press, 1926), pp. 96–97.   [84] *Whartons Dreame* (1578), sig. A3v.

of poore people. In the stretes of this Citye reyneth usurye and guyle, falsehoode and disceyte in all maner of kyndes."[85] As London's ruling elite attempted to steer the City on a cautious course amid the shifting tides of Tudor religious policy, London's wealth and privilege were assailed by fervid partisans on both sides. On one side, for example, Latimer asserted that there was "not reigning in London as much pride, as much covetousness, as much cruelty, as much oppression, and as much superstition, as was in Nebo"; on the other side, Bonner maintained that the faith and charity of Londoners had waxed so cold as to invite all the disasters that might befall a city, "first pleasure, then security, then violence, and at last ruin, destruction and desolation."[86] Above all, however, it was the rule of avarice, typified by urban pursuits, that turned the just and ancient order upside-down:

> now-a-days, the little thieves are hanged that steal of necessity, but the great Barabbases have free liberty to rob and spoil without all measure in the midst of the city ... And whence cometh it? Covetousness is the root of all; every man scratcheth and pilleth from other; every man would suck the blood of other.[87]

Yet for many writers the emphasis fell not so much on the timeless causes of acquisitive behavior as on its more immediate social manifestations and effects. None was so threatening as the destruction of seemingly fixed relationships. John Hooper, for example, complained that the social result of avarice was the replacement of traditional, natural values with arbitrary, transactional standards of the marketplace:

> Of this avarice cometh usury, fraud, false contracts, breaking of faith and promises, contempt of all truth and honesty, forestallings and engrossings of markets, compacts and agreements between the rich, that things may not be sold as they be worth, *but as their avarice hath agreed upon.*[88]

According to Thomas Wilson, "the value of moneye" should "be perpetual and unchangeable, according to a knowne standard." In his view, the avaricious new speculators who "geeue and sell moneye for moneye" were violating the natural principle that money should not "price it selfe by it selfe, or bee valued and esteemed by way of marchaundise, but that and other thinges shoulde receiue their prices and value of it."[89] The arbitrary mutations of markets and money were

---

[85] *A Sermond Spoken before the Kynge His Maiestye at Grenwiche, vpon Good Fryday* (1538), sig. F2. Cf. Latimer, *Third Sermon before Edward VI ... March 22, 1549,* in *Sermons,* ed. George Elwes Corrie (Cambridge: Parker Society, 1844), p. 137.

[86] Latimer, *Sermons,* p. 65; Bonner quoted in Brigden, *London and the Reformation,* p. 449.

[87] Gilpin, *The Life of Bernard Gilpin,* pp. 286, 301.

[88] *A Declaration of the Ten Commandments,* in *Early Works,* ed. Samuel Carr (Cambridge: Parker Society, 1844), p. 392.   [89] *A Discourse of Usury,* p. 307.

thought to destabilize the social order as well. It was because of the new financial power of "the Townes estate," Barnaby Googe declared, that "Nobylitie begyns to fade / and Carters vp do sprynge."[90] Such complaints were legion during the mid-Tudor crisis, and the traditional attitudes toward upstart aspiration or slippery fortune do not conceal a deeper anxiety that the whole order – not just the behavior of individuals but their whole system of relationship – was crumbling.[91] The challenge to the social order was not simply the rise of upstarts, or even of particular classes, but the emergence of anomalous relationships which undermined traditional social terms and structures.

The traditional order of the three estates had combined two binary distinctions to produce a ternary structure of knights, clergy, and commons. Distinguishing first between those who lead and the *servi* or serfs who follow, and then between things earthly and things spiritual, these oppositions generated the functions of those who fight, who pray, and who labor.[92] These functions had a hierarchical significance, as centuries of competition between temporal and Church leaders attests; but more important, they were not interchangeable and "non-negotiable facts; change them and the world is turned upside down."[93] The structure, in other words, depended on fixed binary distinctions – on the inalterable differences between "the lay man and the prest, / the poore man and the lorde," as a sixteenth-century poem put it.[94] Within each estate there was, of course, a separate hierarchy and hence a degree of mobility. A man might rise within his order or estate, according to such standards as the respect of his peers, but in principle each order or function was non-negotiable with the others.

According to the writers of Tudor complaint, this system was in danger of collapse, as all three estates began to function according to a single set of rules geared to the marketplace. Merchants, of course, had always been difficult to place among the three estates; earlier than the fourteenth century a preacher had declared that "God made the clergy,

---

[90] *Eglogs, Epytaphes, and Sonettes*, sig. A7v.

[91] See, e.g., the manuscript prophecy of the 1530s in *Ballads from Manuscripts*, ed. F. J. Furnivall (2 vols. London: Ballad Society, 1868–72), 1: 317.

[92] See Georges Duby, *The Three Orders: Feudal Society Imagined*, tr. Arthur Goldhammer (University of Chicago Press, 1980), pp. 72–100; Ruth Mohl, *The Three Estates in Medieval and Renaissance Literature* (New York: Ungar, 1962), pp. 13–31, 100. On ternary order, see also Claude Lévi-Strauss, *Structural Anthropolgy*, tr. Claire Jacobson and Brooke Grundfest Schoepf (New York: Basic Books, 1963), pp. 135, 140–141, 161.

[93] Michael Mendle, *Dangerous Positions: Mixed Government, the Estates of the Realm, and the Making of the "Answer to the xix Propositions"* (University of Alabama Press, 1985), p. 21.

[94] *The Image of Hypocrisy* (1533?), in *Ballads from Manuscripts*, 1: 239. Cf. Caxton, *The Mirrour of the World*, ed. C. H. Prior (London: EETS, 1973), p. 29.

knights, and commons, but the devil made burghers and usurers."[95]
Even in the early Tudor period, however, Edmund Dudley could still
follow the traditional practice of lumping "marchauntes, craftesmen,
artificers" together with "francklens, graciers, tyllours, and other
generally the people of this realme,"[96] and as late as 1550 Bishop Hooper
could hold together under the category of the "common people" a
dichotomy that would soon become one of the basic structural contrasts
in English society, the contrast between "the rustics, or people of the
country" and "citizens."[97] An incipient version of this contrast was
already evident in Clement Armstrong's *Treatise Concerning the Staple*
(c. 1519–35), which complained that "por mens sons natural born to
labour for their living" were leaving the land to become apprentices.
According to Armstrong, this "bredyng of so many marchants in
London, risen owt of pore mens sonnes, hath bene a mervelous
distruction to the holl realme."[98] By the 1570s, when Sir Thomas Smith
and William Harrison were creating new social anatomies for the nation,
the three estates had given way to a six-part scheme of monarch, nobles,
gentlemen, burgesses, yeomen, and the lowest sort of commoners. In this
scheme, prosperous urbanites had a more distinctive and consequential
role. One binary distinction, preserving one of the two that formed the
three estates, identified all but the last as fit for bearing office; but a
second boundary, drawn between gentlemen and burgesses marked not
so much a functional distinction as the point at which the crisis of social
mobility was most intense. Gentlemen had been made good cheap in
England, Harrison observed, adding that merchants and burgesses
"often change estate with gentlemen, as gentlemen do with them, by a
mutual conversion of the one into the other."[99] Propelling this "mutual
conversion" was the engine that so disturbed mid-Tudor writers – the
London marketplace, which enabled wealthier merchants to influence
agrarian developments and purchase landed estates, just as it provided
the younger sons of gentry with an entrée to trade and the legal and court
bureaucracies.

Like the later sixteenth-century mythology of the London underworld,
which confined the mobile rogues of earlier Tudor literature to an

---

[95] Harley MS. 268, fol. 29, quoted in G. R. Owst, *Literature and the Pulpit in Medieval England* (London: Cambridge University Press, 1933), p. 554.

[96] *The Tree of Commonwealth* (1509), ed. D. M. Brodie (Cambridge University Press, 1948), p. 45.   [97] Hooper, *Early Works*, pp. 467–468.

[98] *A Treatise Concerning the Staple*, in R. H. Tawney and Eileen Power, eds., *Tudor Economic Documents* (3 vols. London: Longmans Green, 1924), 3: 126.

[99] Harrison, *The Description of England* (1587), ed. Georges Edelin (Ithaca: Cornell University Press, 1968), p. 115; cf. Sir Thomas Smith, *De Republica Anglorum*, ed. Mary Dewar (Cambridge University Press, 1982), pp. 64–77.

increasingly narrow compass, the new schemes of Smith and Harrison helped to pinpoint the process of social change both taxonomically and topographically. Indeed, by the end of the sixteenth century, the problem of social change had for the most part been reassuringly confined to the mythical war between gentleman and citizen, country and city. What George Whetstone, in 1584, called the "mortall envie betweene these two woorthie estates" became a staple of the late Elizabethan satirists, and by the early Jacobean period, the war between gentlemen and merchants was being waged cathartically on London's stages in the plays of Middleton and Jonson.[100]

For the earlier writers who laid the groundwork for this myth, however, the sense of mobility was harder to confine; each of the three older estates seemed to be dissolving under the pressure of a new commercial life. The old nobility, said the author of "The Ruyn of a Ream" (1524), were abandoning their estates for the town, leaving their dependents to fend for themselves.[101] They were, Hooper charged, "degenerate" in their pursuit of wealth, while the newer upstart branch of the nobility "thinketh it enough to have the name, without effect."[102] William Turner claimed that "some gentlemen, yea some knightes and lordes, do nowe in Englande be not ashamed to sell oxen, shepe, bere, corne, mele, malt, coles & thynges muche vyler than these be," while Thomas Becon complained that they were "encroachers of farms, notable sheepmongers, graziers, butchers, clothiers, weavers, brewers, &c... O unworthy act! O unseemly sight! O abomination!"[103] On the other hand, another writer pointed out that common merchants usurped the place of gentlemen: "the politike deuices of the marchaunte ioyneth wyth the simplicitie of the gentleman, & neuer leaueth acquayntaunce nor familiaritie with hym vnto suche tyme as the marchauntes moneye hathe boughte the gentilman's land."[104] Under these strains, nobility and common merchants, it was claimed, were becoming indistinguishable: "As for buyldyng of costlye houses, and trimmynge of them wyth costly hangynges and fayre waynscot, manye marchauntes vse to do those

---

[100] "A Touchstone for the Time: Conteining many perillous Mischiefes, vsed in the Bowels of the Citie of London," in *A Mirour for Magestrates of Cyties* (1584), sig. IV. For more on the gentry/citizen distinction, see below pp. 308–309, 313–314, 336.

[101] *Ballads from Manuscripts*, 1: 15–21.   [102] *Early Works*, pp. 363, 392.

[103] William Turner, *A New Booke of Spirituall Physik for Dyuerse Diseases of the Nobilities and Gentlemen of Englande* (1555), sig. H4; Thomas Becon, *The Fortress of the Faithful*, in *The Early Works of Thomas Becon*, ed. John Ayre (Cambridge: Parker Society, 1844), 3: 601.

[104] *The Institucion of a Gentleman* (1568), unpaginated; cf. *Vox Populi, Vox Dei*: "For the statte of all youre marchantmen / Vndo most parte of youre gentyllmen, / And wrape them in such bandes / That they haue halle ther landes," in Hazlitt, ed., *Early Popular Poetry*, 3: 277.

thynges, better then many gentlemen do.''[105] The boundaries that distinguished clergy, knights, and commons were effectively dissolved by a common acquisitiveness – by "Prelatis negligence lordis rauyn & marchauntis deceytes.''[106] "All people in England," said Clement Armstrong in a memo, "lyuith comon euyn as they lyste with workes of synne and myschif to gete singler richis one frome an other.''[107]

The erosion of social order thus supplanted insulating differences with a system of open circulation. Like the land of Cockaigne, but without its ease, England had become a realm forgetful of hierarchy and distinction:

> Gods feare is gone, and each man for him selfe,
> To purchase pelfe the worldling toyles his head.
> The Childe forgets his Father being dead.[108]

For Robert Crowley, as for most of his contemporaries, the problem was epitomized by London,

> a Citye
> in name, but, in dede,
> It is a packe of people
> that seke after meede;
> For officers & al
> so seke their owne gaine.
> But for the wealth of the commons
> not one taketh paine.
> An hell with out order
> I maye it well call,
> Where euerye man is for him selfe,
> And no man for all.[109]

Under these conditions, generic roles and distinctions give way to endless varieties of atomistic species.[110] A certain speechlessness beset many writers when they undertook to name and number the causes of disorder. In *The Way to Wealth*, Crowley attacked

the great fermares, the grasiers, the riche buchares, the men of lawe, the merchauntes, the gentlemen, the knightes, the lordes, and I can not tel who; men that haue no name because they are doares in al thynges that ani gaine hangeth vpon. O good maisters, what shuld I cal you? You that haue no name, you that

---

[105] Turner, *A New Booke of Spirituall Physik*, sig. Cv.

[106] *A Treatise of a Galaunt*, ll. 165–166.

[107] *Howe to Reforme the Realme in Settynge them to Werke and to Restore Tillage*, in Tawney and Power, eds., *Tudor Economic Documents*, 3: 121.

[108] Richard Robinson, *The Rewarde of Wickednesse* (1574), sig. Fv.

[109] "Of Allayes," *One and Thyrtye Epigrammes*, in *Select Works*, ed. J. M. Cowper (London: EETS, 1872), lines 183–188.

[110] See *The Institucion of a Gentleman*, unpaginated; cf. Latimer, *Sermons*, p. 279.

haue so many occupacions & trads that there is no name meet for you! You vngentle gentlemen! You churles chickens, I say![111]

The esoterica of early Tudor economic coinages – the graziers, engrossers, enclosers, possessioners, forestallers, regrators, rack-renters, and leasemongers who remained the staple of economic analysis for another century – was amply matched by an exotica of invective tropes. Some of these – the insatiable beasts, greedy wolves, and quick-smelling hounds of complaint lore – played variations on the theriomorphic theme that rich men are "insatiable raueners and eaters of the poor," that "ryche men, eate poore men, euen as beastes eate grasse."[112] In many tropes, however, social disruption was portrayed as the work of parasites, insects, or vermin – of cumbrous cormorants, carrion birds, moles, greedy locusts, butterflies, and caterpillars of the commonweal.[113] Mary Douglas has noted that in primitive societies anomalous groups or individuals are likened to beetles, spiders, and vermin, who inhabit the cracks and joints of the social fabric.[114] The parasites and vermin of Tudor invective, middlemen who came between the bark and the tree, inhabited an expanding margin – the place of the market – that developed between and against existing status boundaries.

The invective gestures of complaint, virtually devoid of irony, often approached the incantatory rhythm of the purgative rituals with which satire has been compared.[115] In the traditonal ballad forms favored by early Tudor writers, additive, serial structures and a residue of other oral devices produced charm-like incantatory lists of deviant commercial middlemen and usurpers of social boundaries:

> The lawyere and the landelorde,
> The great reave and the recorde...
> Lorde chauncellor and chauncellours,
> Master of myntes and monyers,
> Secondaryes and surveyours,
> Auditors and receivours,
> Customers and comptrollers,
> Purveyours and prollers,

---

[111] *Select Works*, p. 132; cf. Becon, *The Fortress of the Faithful*, in *Works*, 3: 590.

[112] Hooper, *Early Writings*, p. 392; John Mardeley, *A Necessarie Instruction of All Couetous Ryche Men* (1548), sig. B7.

[113] Becon, *Works*, 3: 432; Crowley, *Select Works*, p. 171; William Conway, *An Exhortation to Charity* (1552), sig. B4; Bernard Gilpin, *A Sermon Preached in the Court at Greenwich before King Edward VI* (1552), in *The Life of Bernard Gilpin*, p. 285; Latimer, *Sermons*, p. 64.

[114] *Purity and Danger: An Analysis of Concepts of Pollution and Taboo* (New York, 1966), p. 102.

[115] See esp. Robert Elliott, *The Power of Satire: Magic, Ritual, and Art* (Princeton University Press, 1960), pp. 3–66.

Marchauntes of great sailes,
With the master of woodsales,
With graysers and regraters,
With Master Williams of shepe masters,
And suche lyke comonwelthe wasters.[116]

The effort to contain the social disarray was shored up, at mid-century and after, by a number of works restating social obligations and the proper uses of wealth.[117] Remarkably, some of these attempted to reconstruct, in the manner of a 2 x 2 table, binary systems like the one that had once organized the three estates. Copland's *Hye Way* begins with what the author calls a "quaternion," which is based, first, on one binary distinction between the rich and poor, to which a second is then added: "Of these two estates there be four degrees; / A ryche ryche, a poore poore, a ryche poore also, / A poore ryche in all necessytes" (lines 71–73). *The Institucion of a Gentleman* erects a system on the distinctions between gentle gentle, ungentle gentle, gentle ungentle, and ungentle ungentle. Thomas Lupton's *All for Money* (1578) depicts a set of social possibilities comprising Money without Learning, Money with Learning, Learning with Money, Learning without Money and Neither Learning nor Money. It may be that in such works the reform tradition of outlining Christian duties, descended from Erasmus' *Enchiridion*, suffered some narrowing in being adapted to simple handbooks and popular interludes. But it is not surprising that these crude and rigid schemes emerged precisely from that murky area that later became the battleground in the mythical war between gentlemen and merchants – from the point within the social order where traditional status and new money clashed head-on.

The displaced plowman

The dimensions of social and economic crisis were traced by Tudor analysts across a thousand English towns and villages. While these writers were perhaps ignorant of some of the causes of dearth, inflation, poverty, and displacement, they rightly saw that many problems of the age were agrarian in nature. But the tendency to attribute even agrarian

---

[116] *Vox Populi, Vox Dei*, in Hazlitt, ed., *Early Popular Poetry*, 3: 292–293.

[117] Francis Seagar, *The Schoole of Vertue, and Book of Good Noureture* (1557); anon., *The Institucion of a Gentleman* (1555); Thomas Lupset, *A Treatise of Charitie* (1533); John Mardeley, *A Necessarie Instruction* (1548); Turner, *A New Booke of Spirituall Physik* (1555); William Conway, *An Exhortation to Charity* (1552); Robert Crowley, *The Voice of the Last Trumpet* (1550); Thomas Lupton, *A Dreame of the Diuell and Diues* (1589); Roger Bieston, *The Bayte and Snare of Fortune*; *Spare Your Good* (1555); John Carr, *The Ruinous Fal of Prodigalitie* (1573).

problems to the transactions of mythical middlemen, and hence to London, was reinforced by a transformation of the wholly traditional contrast between virtuous past and corrupt present into an emergent contrast between country and city. For the author of *Vox Populi, Vox Dei*, the difference between past and present was marked by the transfer of wealth from country to city, "From the fermour and the poore / To the towne and the towre" (lines 9–14). Robert Copland similarly targeted the new commercial transactions that made merchants rural landowners and farmers urban vagabonds:

> Marchant men trauell the countree,
> Ploughmen dwell in the citie,
> Which will destroy us all shortlie,
> As will be seene in hast.[118]

As Thomas Lever put it in the *Sermon in the Shrouds* (1550), "the merchauntes of London ... be not content with the prosperous welth of that vocacion to satissfye theym selues, and to helpe other, but their riches muste abrode in the countrey to bie fermes out of the handes of worshypfull gentlemen, honeste yeomen, and pore laborynge husbandes."[119] Wolsey himself had complained that Londoners "use not yourselves like merchants but like graziers and artificers," and Bernard Gilpin asserted that the great Nimrods of the age could "lie at London and turn men out of their farms and tenements an hundred, some two hundred miles off."[120]

The obverse to the mobile fools' paradise, embarking through the gates of London for the shires of England, was the barefoot shuffle of the displaced toward London, represented in works like Copland's *Hye Way to the Spyttle House*. Many complaints of the period were written from the fictional standpoint or in the voice of the poor displaced commons.[121] By far the most important representative of the complaining commons was the figure of the sturdy plowman displaced from the land. Ironically, however, the conservative effects of the plowman's voice, emanating from a long tradition and invoking the old-world model of the three estates, were balanced by a picture of the world and a structure of address that deprived that voice of power. Typically lamenting their exile from a

---

[118] *The New Guyse Nowe a Dayes*, in J. Payne Collier, ed., *Broadsides and Black-letter Ballads* (1868; rpt. New York: Burt Franklin, 1968), p. 15. Cf. *A Pleasaunt Poesye of Princelie Practise* (1548), in Sidney J. Herrtage, ed., *England in the Reign of King Henry VIII* (London: EETS, 1878), p. xcv.

[119] *Sermons*, ed. E. Arber (London, 1870), p. 29.

[120] Brigden, *London and the Reformation*, p. 170; Gilpin, *The Life of Bernard Gilpin*, pp. 289–290.

[121] See, e.g., Thomas Thynne, *The Debate Between Pride and Lowliness*, ed. J. Payne Collier (London: Shakespeare Society, 1841), p. 56.

countryside bought up by merchants and enclosers, and bearing their complaints to a source of power now centered in London, the plowmen of early Tudor writers paradoxically contributed to a set of mythical contrasts – between country and city, provinces and capital, powerlessness and power – that negated the feudal, agrarian myth of the three orders, the myth that validated the plowman's symbolic power. The plowmen of Tudor complaint thus bear witness to the power of the marketplace to extend its reach from London to the remote corners of the realm and to reconstellate the countryside and its population around the new magnetism of the capital. In this reconstellation, the ancient rural gentry were "fallinge from the use of thir Auncestors...leav[ing] to dwell in their Country houses, inhabitinge Citties, and great townes"; new commercial and patronage arrangements were forcing them to "give over oure household, and to kepe either a chamber in London, or to wait on the court uncalled, with a man and a lackey after him."[122] With the decay of feudal structures that accompanied this change came the displacement of the virtuous husbandman.

The figure of the virtuous plowman left his mark on a variety of works, from *God Spede the Plough* (temp. Henry VIII) and *The Prayer and Complaynt of the Ploweman vnto Christ* (1531?), to *I Playne Piers Which Can Not Flatter* (1550?) and *Pyers Plowmans Exhortation vnto the Lordes Knyghtes and Burgaysses of the Parlyament House* (1550?). Helping to legitimate the plowman's stance was the circulation of the pseudo-Chaucerian *Plowman's Tale* (1542), and the publication of such medieval works as *Jack Upland* (1536, 1570), *Piers the Ploughmans Crede* (1553, 1561), and Langland's *The Vision of Piers Plowman*, first published by Robert Crowley in 1550.[123] Thomas Churchyard's plainspoken Davy Dicar was described by the author as "broug[ht] vp in pieres scole," and Gascoigne's studied recapitulation of the complaint tradition, *The Steel Glas* (1576), summoned up the authority of "good Pearce, thou plowman

---

[122] *Cyvile and Uncyvile Life* (1579), sigs. B2v–B3; *A Discourse of the Common Weal of this Realm of England*, ed. Elizabeth Lamond (1893; rpt. Cambridge University Press, 1926), p. 19. On the concern over the decline of hospitality among early protestant reformers, see Felicity Heal, *Hospitality in Early Modern England* (Oxford: Clarendon Press, 1990), pp. 122–127. On the relation between social mobility and a regressive emphasis on social hierarchy, see Anderson, *Lineages of the Absolutist State*, pp. 23, 39, 125; Lawrence Stone, *The Crisis of the Aristocracy* (Oxford: Clarendon Press, 1965), pp. 8–11, 16–21, 37, 71, 75, 97, 117, 131.

[123] An excellent account of the plowman tradition is in John N. King, *English Reformation Literature: The Tudor Origins of the Protestant Tradition* (Princeton University Press, 1982), esp. pp. 51–52. See also Owst, *Literature and the Pulpit in Medieval England*, ch. 9; Helen C. White, *Social Criticism in the Popular Religious Literature of the Sixteenth Century*, ch. 1; Alvin Kernan, *The Cankered Muse: Satire of the English Renaissance* (New Haven: Yale University Press, 1959), pp. 42–50.

by thy name. "[124] Even where the specific example of Piers Plowman was not invoked, a variety of works adopted the posture and persona of the exiled rural supplicant.[125]

The fundamental appeal of the plowman persona was its power to accommodate the ideals of honest labor and obedience to a model of ordered society, a model epitomized in Langland's sixth *passus*, where Piers plows his half-acre and all work together, each in his own way. Equally important were the anti-clerical elements in Langland that led Tudor writers to regard him as a prophet of the Reformation. But in addition to these factors, Tudor writers were attracted to the nascent satiric contrast between country and city intrinsic to Langland and the plowman tradition. In Langland's poem, for example, London is the scene of the Corruptions, of Lady Meed, Envy, Fals, and Favel, and merchants are denied all but a small codicil "in the margin" of Truth's pardon.[126] In keeping with this anti-urban bias, the pseudo-Chaucerian *Plowman's Tale* complained that the rapacious clergy "builde as brode as a cite," while *Jack Upland* charged that they lay land to land in violation of the Pauline dictum *non habemus hic manentem ciuitatem.*[127] *Piers the Ploughmans Crede* alleged that mendicants were so proud as to dress like aldermen and seek "greetings in the markets," while the plowman of *God Spede the Plough* lamented that there was no justice in the high places:

> At london Also yf we woll plete,
> We shal not be spared, good chepe nor dere;
> Our man of lawe may not be forgete,
> But he moste haue money euery quart.[128]

Of all the features of the medieval plowman motif, none so profoundly affected the structure of voice and address in Tudor complaint as this distinction between city and country, wealth and dearth, power and powerlessness. In the typical Tudor complaint, a displaced and peripatetic countryman prepares an indictment by gathering testimony along

---

[124] *Dauy Dicars Dreame*, in *The Contention Betwyxte Churchyeard and Camell* (1560), sig. c3v; *The Steel Glas*, in *Works*, ed. J. W. Cunliffe (2 vols. 1907; rpt. New York: Greenwood Press, 1969), 2: 169.

[125] Brinkelow's *Complaynt of Roderyck Mors* (1542) exemplifies the posture taken in *A Supplication of the Poore Commons* (1546) or Robert Crowley's *Informacion and Petition Agaynst the Oppressours of the Pore Commons of this Realme* (1549).

[126] 7.18–36; cf. 2.135; 2.155–60; 3.10–12; 3.87–92; 4.28; 5.128; 5.251.

[127] *Chaucerian and Other Pieces*, in *The Complete Works of Geoffrey Chaucer* , ed. W. W. Skeat (7 vols. 1897; rpt. London: Oxford University Press, 1935), 7: 171; *Jack Upland, Friar Daw's Reply, and Upland's Rejoinder*, ed. P. L. Heyworth (London: Oxford University Press, 1968), p. 108.

[128] *Piers the Ploughmans Crede*, ed. W. W. Skeat (London: EETS, 1867), lines 691, 566; *God Spede the Plough*, also in this edition, lines 81–84.

the highways, and he lays it at the feet of those in power in London. Skelton's honest Colin Clout, for example, reports what "wandrynge as I walke, / I here the people talke."[129] The speaker in Churchyard's *Myrrour for Man* similarly reports what he has seen and heard on the highways (sig. Av), and Churchyard's W. Waterman has "traueld here and theare, / I sought this worlde wide: / To fynde a resting quyet place" (sig. G3). Crowley adopts the posture of a "pore man of the country" in order "to playe the parte of a true Englishman" in delivering his testimony. The very titles of Tudor "complaints," "supplications," "informations," and "petitions" identify them as the speech-acts of poor countrymen approaching the seat of power.

Latimer's blistering *Sermon of the Plow* demonstrates how the persona could allow for putting the naked truth in rude words, as *Pyers Plowmans Exhortation* describes its task. Yet even as it evoked the Christian values of poverty and humility and made the depiction of economic misery more vivid and compelling, the posture of the rural supplicant also dramatized the central subject of complaint, the fact of London's growing domination of the countryside. By the early sixteenth century, the court, Council, Parliament, and legal apparatus settled permanently in London. Even when legal matters could be settled locally, commoners often preferred the expense and hardship of journeying to London in hope of a more neutral hearing or appeal.[130]

Approaching a seat of power that was both mighty and corrupt, both a haven of redress and a source of ills, the personae of complaint embodied in the very structure of voice and address the problem that was their central concern – the growing domination of the countryside by the city. To enact the paradox of the simple feudal commoner or plowman approaching the modern capital was to dramatize the devastating effects of change. It was to acknowledge that the very structure of relationships that had given this commoner his place and being – the model of the three estates – had been supplanted by a structure that divided city from countryside, wealth from dearth, power from impotence. In calling for radical reform, Tudor complaint called upon precisely the radical concentration of power that created the need for reform.

Many complaints thus underlined the paradoxical futility of seeking for redress in the places where social problems were created or most

---

[129] *Collyn Clout*, in Skelton, *The Complete English Poems*, ed. John Scattergood (New Haven: Yale University Press, 1983), p. 254. C. S. Lewis observes that the *on dit* convention derives its "strange and disquieting potency" by producing the effect of "a vast muttering and growling of rumours," *English Literature of the Sixteenth Century* (Oxford University Press, 1954), p. 139.

[130] See, for example, Harrison, *The Description of England*, p. 175; cf. Becon, *Works*, 3: 602.

prevalent. "Poor people," declared Gilpin, "are driven to seek their right among the lawyers; and there, as the prophet Joel saith, look what the caterpillars had left in their robbery and oppression at home, all that doth the greedy locusts, the lawyers, devour at London."[131] Life in the countryside, Crowley explained, had become unliveable, "and to go to the cities we haue no hope, for there we heare that these vnsaciable beastes haue all in theyr handes."[132] An early Elizabethan writer complained that "there cold neuer be wonne any good lawe or order that towched the lybertie and state of the merchaunte, but that they stayed it, either in the common house, or higher house of parliament, or ells by the prince him self."[133]

It was not lost on Tudor writers that London's four Members of Parliament were accorded seats of honor beside the Privy Councillors on the front bench. And so the more intense the paradox of radical power, the more radical the appeal to power. Clement Armstrong addressed his proposals for mercantile reform to King and Council, "so as the king and his lordes shall not nede to troble theymself to make no acts of parliament, which cane neuer preuayle, seeing how no acte for the common weale can passe these sortes in the common howse which gettith their riches from the commonaltie to their owne singularite."[134] But from the dilemma of the appeal to radical power there could be no escape, unless it be the higher appeal represented in *The Prayer and Complaynt of the Ploweman vnto Christ* (1531?).

Production and consumption

The perception of widening differences between country and city brought with it an awareness of growing divisions within the old estate of commoners. Rural husbandmen and urban merchants were theoretically bound together as commons in the model of the three estates, but, as the author of *Pyers Plowmans Exhortation* complained, they were becoming increasingly divided: "at this daye there be many fatte marchauntes which wold haue no reformation in the comen welth affirming that therein all thinges be wel"; but "thousandes of the poore comens can not get so muche as one ferme nor scant any litell house to put their head in"

---

[131] Gilpin, *The Life of Bernard Gilpin*, p. 285.
[132] *The Way to Wealth*, in *Select Works*, p. 133; cf. the *Dyaloge Betwene a Gentillman and a Husbandman* (1529–30), p. 9.
[133] Hatfield House, Cecil Papers, 152, fos. 96–99, quoted in Helen Miller, "London and Parliament in the Reign of Henry VIII," *BIHR*, 35 (1962), 128; cf. Crowley, *An Informacion and Petition*, in *Four Supplications, 1529–1553 AD*, ed. J. M. Cowper (London: EETS, 1871), p. 167.
[134] *Howe to Reforme the Realme*, in Tawney and Power, eds., *Tudor Economic Documents*, 3: 126.

(sig. A2). This growing bifurcation of the commons into urban rich and rural poor was reinforced by a second development, a nascent pastoralism in which the basic model of social structure was the contrast between urban and rural life. The context for the European revival of pastoralism was of course not feudalism but the culture of the Italian city–states, where both the basic structure of pastoral myth and its classical ambience were suited to a fundamentally urbanistic society. While the primary modes and motifs of early Tudor complaint were, by contrast, drawn from native and traditional sources, folk material and late-feudal ideals, by the mid-Tudor period writers were beginning to speak, as it were, in classical languages, adopting from classical and continental models the basic contrast between urban *negotium* and rural *otium*, and with it, an implicitly urban-centered point of view. Barnaby Googe's Menalcas, for example, having seen "the Towne's estate," explained that

> I, synce I sawe suche synfull syghts,
>   dyd neuer lyke the Towne,
> But thought it best to take my shepe
>   and dwell vpon the doune.
> Wheras I lyue, a plesant lyfe,
>   and free from cruell handes,
> I wolde not leaue, the plesaunt fyelde
>   for all the Townysh landes.[135]

More significant for the purpose of complaint, however, was the potential opposition between commerce and labor, an opposition which, by implicitly dividing the estate of commoners, helped to make the contrast between city and country a fundamental division of society. A particularly revealing instance of the revision is the account in Barclay's fifth eclogue of how "God first disposed and made diuersitie / Betwene rude plowmen and men of the citie."[136] Announcing that he has come "to promote each in his degree" (line 302), God appoints the eldest son of Eve an emperor, the next a king, and so on through what appears to be the first of the three orders: "Some made he Earles, some lordes, some barons, / Some squires, some knightes, some hardy champions" (lines 321–322). But then, leaving this group to govern chivalry, he creates a class of bureaucrats and merchants,

> iudges, maiors and gouernours,
> Marchauntes, shiriffes and other protectours,
> Aldermen, burgesses and other in degree,
> After the custome of court and citie.   (lines 329–332)

---

[135] *Egloga tertia*, ll. 53–65, in *Eclogues, Epitaphs, and Sonnets*, ed. Judith M. Kennedy (University of Toronto Press, 1989), p. 53.

[136] *Eclogues*, ed. Beatrice White (London: EETS, 1928), lines 183–184.

Once this basically urban power structure is laid down, God becomes offended with the baser urchins whom Eve drags forward for promotion:

> Ye smell all smoky, of stubble and of chaffe,
> Ye smell of the grounde, of weedes and of draffe ...
> Ye shall be plowmen and tillers of the grounde,
> To payn and labour shall ye alway be bounde ...
> To dig and delue, to hedge and to dike,
> Take this for your lot and other labour like, ...
> Yet shall towne dwellers oft laugh you vnto scorne.   (lines 355–374)

"Thus," ends the story, "began honour and thus began bondage, / And diuersitie of citie and village" (lines 391–392).[137]

In contrasting the "honour" of the "citie" with the "bondage" of the "village," Barclay interpreted the difference between commerce and labor in terms of consumption and production:

> Without our labour truely they haue nothing ...
> They clip vs, they poule vs, they pill vs to the skin,
> And what they may get that thinke they well to win ...
> The Citie is the well and grounde originall,
> Both first and last of deadly euils all: ...
> I trowe when the world with fire wasted shall be,
> The cause shall proceede and come of some Citie.
>   (lines 642, 953–954, 997–998, 1007–1008)

While the structure of pastoral myth explicitly developed many aspects of the country–city opposition inherent in complaint, it was not in fact widely adopted by social analysts. The shepherd's estate could not be idealized so long as there remained a perceived connection between enclosing shepherds, the woolen industry, and nascent urban commerce. To accept the myth of pastoral would be to accept the division between urban and rural commons that made the model of the three estates obsolete, to accept as a model of society a myth in which the anomalies of commercial life had become a kind of norm. And yet, ironically, only with the acceptance of this life as a basic and irreversible social fact could the sinister, disruptive ties between city and countryside be broken; only then could the city be contained by pastoral myth – a myth both classical and urbanistic in its tenor.

In a gambit offered but conscientiously declined, Barclay suggests how this was eventually to be done. In response to Amintas' tale of the

---

[137] George Gascoigne notes even more explicitly that by peasant "I do not meane, alonely husbandmen – / But he that labors any kind of way, / To gather gaines, and to enrich himselfe – / Al men of arte, which get goodes greedily / Must be content, to take a Peasants rome," *The Steel Glas*, in *Works*, 2: 160.

relationship between countryside and city, production and consumption, Faustus offers a more comforting myth about the origin and life of shepherds – a fratricidal foundation story of the sort that characterizes urban civilizations that have arrived at an advanced stage of necessary forgetfulness. The myth begins with the obstinate, mean-spirited Cain and the meek and gentle shepherd Abel, who offered pleasing sacrifice to God. As a result of this good office, ever after "God hath had fauour to people pastorall" (line 458). Abraham, Jacob, Lot, Isaac, Joseph, and Job all were shepherds, as were Paris, Pan, Silenus, Orpheus, Moses, Apollo, and the "ioly harper," David (lines 469–505). Highest and lowest, lord and swain, are joined together in a circle of virtue, while those who would divide them, the once shadowy and potent figures who pervaded the whole social order, have now receded into the hardened, well-defined mold of middlemen, the descendants of Cain, confined to the city and its mean pursuits. With the establishment of the distinction between true gentry and grasping merchants, it was only gentlemen who were nostalgically exhorted to return to their estates "to relieue their neighbours with meate and drinke, to fede many and be themselues fed of fewe, to seke London seldom, and at their houses often to be sought."[138]

This was advice only partly heeded in the later Elizabethan period, but this new mythical distinction between country and city, gentlemen and merchants, became the line of development followed by the later Elizabethan court poets. Like the increasingly narrow definition of the London underworld, like the war between gentlemen and merchants, and like the myth of the middleman, the pastoral contrast between country and city, which gradually hardened into clear-cut form in the later sixteenth century, first emerged in response to the mid-Tudor crisis. If, with the consolidation of the myth, there was some diminishment in the perception of anomaly and crisis, there was a corresponding gain in the power to reassure.

Projectors

The urban factors in the mid-Tudor crisis were most clearly identified not in the social commentary of preachers and popular writers but in the relatively more secular and "scientific" works of figures who, through humanistic education or commercial experience, were more accustomed to thinking of urban life as an established norm. What was most

---

[138]   *The Institucion of a Gentleman*, unpaginated.

remarkable in the works of court humanists like Thomas Starkey and Sir Thomas Smith or merchants like Clement Armstrong and William Cholmeley, however, was not their tendency to trace Tudor economic problems to London but their tendency to disavow myths in favor of analysis, or perhaps more properly, their tendency to substitute for the prevailing myths the very structure of production and consumption those myths resisted. Starkey's *Dialogue Between Cardinal Pole and Thomas Lupset*, for example, advanced an urbane and humanistic vision of "a polytyke ordur of men conspyryng togyddur in vertue and honesty."[139] Starkey's body politic was drawn not so much along the typical lines of subordination and mutual purpose, however, as along economic lines which had a planning aspect. Just as there must be fair proportion in the body, so, Starkey concluded, there must be economic balance in the commonwealth, "as craftysmen and plowmen in dew nombur and proportyon wyth other partys, accordyng to the place, cyty, or towne" (p. 49). Not surprisingly, given the importance of the city as his model of the commonwealth, Starkey characterized the malproportion between city and countryside in Tudor England by emphasizing the effect of agrarian problems on declining provincial towns: "yf you loke to the cytes and townys throughout the realme, you schal fynd that in tyme past they haue byn much bettur inhabyted, and much more replenyschyd wyth pepul then they be now" (p. 72). The chief cause of this decline, he maintained, was the disproportionate growth of London. Starkey singled out the removal of causes by writ to London (p. 117), the residence of the growing bureaucracy and court (pp. 133, 159), and commercial changes that were leading men to cross vocational boundaries (pp. 158–159). Nothing, however, so epitomized the malproportion between the city and the countryside as the imbalance between goods exported and imported through the Port of London. On the one hand, the bulk export of raw goods, especially unfinished woolen cloth, contributed to the agricultural practices that displaced husbandmen and raised the price of essential commodities; on the other hand, the import of finished luxury goods deprived native craftsmen of work and expended England's wealth on frivolities (pp. 93–94). "Yf we had fewar thyngys brought in from other partys, and les caryd out," Starkey argued, "we schold haue more commodyte and veray true plesure, much more then we haue now" (p. 95).

Starkey followed tradition in condemning the ostentation and waste associated with luxury trades, but his proposals took a different turn

---

[139] In *England in the Reign of King Henry the Eighth*, ed. J. M. Cowper (London: EETS, 1878), p. 19. Page references in the text are to this edition.

when he argued for import restrictions on luxuries which "we myght wel lake, *or els, at the lest,* our owne pepul myght be occupyed wyth the workyng therof" (p. 94). The novelty of Starkey's approach was not only his acceptance of the market for those luxuries that "by the dylygence of our owne men, can not be made," but also his claim that some luxuries *should* "be made by the arte, labur, and dylygence of our owne pepul" (p. 94). To a degree untypical of Tudor writers, Starkey tacitly accepted the functional division between the London market and the countryside, a division bridged by the transactions of production and consumption.

This note was lightly touched by Starkey, as it was by the author of *A Discourse of the Common Weal of This Realm of England* (1549/1581), who, like Starkey, stressed the decay of "all the townes of England, London excepted."[140] Like Starkey's *Dialogue*, the *Discourse* attacked ostentation, but it singled out the disruptive markets of "london, the head of this empire, wheare such excesses, by reason of the wealthe that of all this Realme is heaped vp, as the corne of the field into a barne, be most vsed" (p. 83). The author's solution to the imbalance between country and city, agriculture and trade, was to regulate the flow of wealth through London, to "take hede that we bie no moe of strangers than we sell them" (p. 63). The point of this embargo, however, was not to restrict the consumption of luxury goods, but to encourage production of them "with in oure owne Realme" (p. 63). Most remarkable was the recognition that profits were to be made on "thinges of no valew of them selues, but onelie for the labors of the workers of the same" (p. 64). Production and consumption were to be geared more or less to the new standard, Hooper lamented, "that thinges may not be sold as they be worth." Although disruptive of the national economy, the London marketplace was not to be abolished but to be made an engine of change, the basis for a projected future of prosperity.

In such analyses, not only did the structure of production and consumption legitimate the status of the city; it also gave rise to the new figure of the projector, the innovative speculator who was to become the hero of the Elizabethan age and the temporary villain of the Jacobean.[141] As early as 1553, an obscure clothmaker who signed himself "William Cholmeley, Londyner" was advancing projects for the domestic dyeing and finishing of cloth. The projects were to be advanced by placing curbs on the metropolis, stipulating that "no cloth dyed beyonde the seas be

---

140 *A Discourse of the Common Weal of This Realm of England,* p. 16. The accepted attribution is now to Sir Thomas Smith; see Mary Dewar, *Sir Thomas Smith : A Tudor Intellectual in Office* (London: Athlone, 1964), pp. 53–55.

141 See Joan Thirsk, *Economic Policy and Projects : The Development of a Consumer Society in Early Modern England* (Oxford: Clarendon Press, 1978), pp. 14–15.

suffered to be solde within the Citie of London."[142] Thus, along with
Cholmeley's indictment of London came the certainty that, turned
aright, London's economic power could lead the nation forward:

> if the merchauntis of London ... woulde take as great trauell and byde as great
> aduenture to profyte theyre contrey, *by maynteyning theyr contreymen in worke*
> [italics mine], and utteringe thyngis wrought by them, as they doe in carying
> away the thingis that shoulde be wrought by them, and in bryngynge tryfelynge
> thynges nothynge profitable to theyr contreymen ... then should we see that they
> could fynde the means to compasse not only this smalle matter, but manye other.
> (p. 144)

The full measure of London's resilience, its capacity to transform the
darkness of complaint into the glory of projection, emerged not in the
ebullient Cholmeley but in the cantankerous works of Clement
Armstrong, grocer and roof garnisher, friend of Rastell and protégé of
Cromwell.[143] No Tudor analyst wrote so frequently, at such length, and
in such detail about the economic complexities that made London a
target of complaint. No writer, either, quite so pointedly laid blame at
London's gates: "the rote of most myschief hath euer bredd in
London."[144] "London to this day," he complained, "hath lyvid at suche
a libertie without any good order of comen weale, by whose occupieng all
England is brought into nede and necessities."[145] As Armstrong saw it,
London's luxury trades were the source of inflation; there were in
London "ware housis full of trifell sold and bought for a hundred
pounde." Furthermore, the foreign demand for wool marketed through
London caused so much rural enclosure that "Oon stapler in London
will occupie as moche wolle as is encreasid owt of the distruction of 4 or
5 villages, where a 1400 or 1500 peple hathe hadde labours and levynge"
(p. 104). Monopolistic behavior meant that " if any English man wold
stody to devise and invent any new artificiall thynges, Londoners
incontynent is ever redy to destroy it" (p. 105). Finally, "the cause of all
grasiers and regraters of corne and cattales and of all maulte men hath
been onely for that London hath not made prouycion to vitall it self."[146]

---

[142] *The Request and Suite of a True-Hearted Englishman* (1553), in Tawney and Power,
eds., *Tudor Economic Documents*, 3: 147.

[143] See S. T. Bindoff, "Clement Armstrong and His Treatises of the Common Weal,"
EconHR, 14 (1944), 64–73.

[144] *A Treatise Concerninge the Staple*, in Tawney and Power, eds., *Tudor Economic
Documents*, 3: 96.

[145] Ibid. 3: 110. The strongest and most old-fashioned of Armstrong's attacks on London
is in "Clement Armstrong's Sermons and Declaracions agaynst Popish Ceremonies,"
in Reinhold Pauli, ed., *Drei Volkwirthschaftliche Denkschriften aus der Zeit Heinrichs
VIII. von England* (Gottingen, 1878), pp. 43–46.

[146] *Howe to Reforme the Realme*, in Tawney and Power, eds., *Tudor Economic Documents*,
3: 125.

For this seemingly endless list of ills Armstrong proposed a radical redistribution of power that would restore proper proportion to the body of the commonwealth. Because it was wrong for "one citie to distroy the common weale of a holl realme, the king hath nede to take the fredome of the citie into his handes, unto his grace hath reformed diuerse causes for the common weale of the holl realme. The salue must worke the remedy in London, where the sore is furste."[147] The radical remedy to be enacted by the king, however, was to develop native industry and to attract the international market from the Low Countries to London – in other words, to institutionalize London's markets on a massive national scale:[148]

A staple of wollen clothe in London shal be the moste noble thing for the honor and profite of Englande that euer was, ... which shall cause all strangers to bring plentie of gold and siluer into Englande yerly to bye moche better chepe at the kinges Staple in London, then cane be made in other contreys.[149]

Armstrong's glorious vision of a realm rebuilt around London demonstrates that the more clearly commonwealth analyses traced disruptive forces to London, the more clearly London emerged as the logically inevitable engine of reform. The very structure of this reform, built upon a widening differentiation between production, commerce, and consumption, effectively provided London a unique and essential place in the kingdom. The more radical the reform projected, the more radical the concentration of power in London.

New triangulations: country, court, and city

The tendency of most writers to approach this paradox as a terrible impasse did not prevent their endorsing it by a kind of *via negativa*. Implicit in the structure of complaint were the seeds of myths that only confirmed the irreversibility of unwanted changes. In a progeny of ballad complaints descended from the fifteenth-century "London Lickpenny," the journey of the rural plaintiff to London only reconfirmed the power of the system that brought him there. "London Lickpenny" may itself have descended from poems like "The World Upside Down"(Bodl. MS Eng. poet. b. 4), in which the vicious inversion of a once-moral world finds "Consciens Romyng in eueri path & strete."[150] Crucially for later

147 Ibid., 3: 125.
148 See, e.g., "How the Comen People may be set to worke an Order of the Comen welth," in Pauli, *Drei Volkwirthschaftliche Denkschriften*, p. 57.
149 *Howe to Reforme the Realme*, in Tawney and Power, eds., *Tudor Economic Documents*, 3: 118–119.
150 In Robbins, ed., *Historical Poems of the XIVth and XVth Centuries*, pp. 150–152.

writers, however, the conscience-figure of "London Lickpenny" was a Kentish husbandman who came to London seeking justice, only to be expelled, much the poorer, from the city's streets. Behind the poem's powerful appeal was a new ternary model of the realm of England, a model that juxtaposed not knights, clergy, and commons but court, countryside, and city.

The Kentish visitor's repeatedly rejected appeals for justice take him from the different judges, lawyers, and clerks of the King's Bench, Common Pleas, and Chancery to a variety of city hucksters and hawkers – cooks and crying costard-mongers, Cheapside clothiers, Candlewick drapers and fishmongers, Eastcheap taverners and minstrels, Cornhill pawnbrokers, and Billingsgate bargemen. This prolific serial construction, however, is adapted to a larger three-part structure, which traces the countryman's journey from Westminster to London (court to city) and then from Billingsgate to Kent (city to country). A three-part model of the social order thus emerges from the swirling tumult of the poem. The countryman's hood, lost in Westminster, turns up in a stall in Cornhill, so that court and city form barely distinguishable parts of a conspiratorial power structure in which the virtuous countryman, "for lack of mony,...myght not spede."

In *Conscience* (c. 1540), a slightly later example of this ballad type, written during the height of the mid-Tudor crisis, the emergence of the same three-part structure of court, city, and country is the more remarkable for pointedly displacing the ternary model of the three estates, vestiges of which are still discernible in the poem.[151] Conscience, once a peer of the King's Council, and now a "silly poore creature ragged & rent" (line 4), recounts the story of his exile, which takes him from court to city to country. As in "London Lickpenny," a prolific variety of avaricious urbanites – gallants, porters, spital-keepers, merchants, lawyers, cobblers and clerks – lends substance to a three-part structure in which the power of court and city is inflicted on the country, where gentlemen are destroyed by their leases and where landlords so plague husbandmen "that they were not able to keepe open doore" (lines 104–105). Only when Conscience has ended his tale does the interlocutor suggest he seek the clergy, who have, Conscience answers, nothing to give (lines 115–121). In other words, the potential model of knights, clergy, and commons is offered only as an afterthought, and it is mooted by the newer three-part model that forms the basis and the bulk of the poem. The city has intruded on the old model, forever sundering the

---

[151] *Bishop Percy's Folio Manuscript*, ed. John W. Hales and F. J. Furnivall (3 vols. London, 1868), 2: 174–189. Furnivall notes only that the poem must postdate 1497 and antedate 1560, but the allusion to the marriage of clergy must place it in the 1540s.

relationship of lord to serf to priest, dividing urban from rural commons and tainting both court and country with the smell of commerce.

Like other myths and structures that emerged from complaint, the model of court, city, and country became a staple of later writers. A ghostly survival of the three estates in Robert Greene's *Quip for an Vpstart Courtier*, for example, traces the clergy, knights, and commons to their roots in the three sons of Noah; but a new degree of mobility elevates topographical over social "place," so that the pamphlet actually demonstrates how Pride has "infected the Court with aspiring Enuie, the Citie with griping Couetousnesse, and the Countrye with contempte and disdaine." The erasure of the three estates by the three domains coincides in Greene's pamphlet with the exile of the conscience-figure, as "Neybourhood was exiled, Conscience was skoft at, and charitie lay frosen in the streets."[152] By 1600, in Anthony Munday's "The Woodemans walke," the path of the exiled conscience-figure from Westminster to London to countryside could be reduced to the terse observation that he had no place in "Citty, Court, nor Country too."[153] Even King James adopted the new taxonomy, noting that "as every fish lives in his own place, some in the fresh, some in the salt, some in the mud: so let everyone live in his own place, some at Court, some in the Citie, some in the Countrey."[154] A host of later ballads adopted the formula, from Martin Parker's "Robin Conscience" (1635) to "The Sorrowful Complaint of Conscience and Plain-Dealing" (1684–85) and "Robin Conscience ... his Progress through Court, City, and Country" (1683).[155] The last of these, devoting four stanzas each to court and country and forty-four to the city, carried to a logical extreme of malproportion the functional centrality of the city in giving rise to a new ternary system.

Based on geographical rather than social "place," this new ternary model assumed – indeed required – mobility in order to function. From Grimald and Puttenham to Bacon, Wotton, and Donne, the model of country, court, and city came to signal the privileges and challenges opened up by urban mobility.[156] By contrast with the rural perspective of earlier Tudor complaint, the popular ballads, jestbooks, and comedies of the Elizabethan period attributed to the rural pilgrim a mind so naive and narrow as almost to justify the city in casually destroying him. Had seventeenth-century readers and writers been able to recall, as did

---

[152] *The Life and Works of Robert Greene*, ed. A. B. Grosart (15 vols. London, 1881–86), 11: 209–225.

[153] *England's Helicon* (1600), ed, Hugh MacDonald (Cambridge, Mass.: Harvard University Press, 1962), p. 197.

[154] Quoted in Heal, *Hospitality in Early Modern England*, p. 119.

[155] See *The Bagford Ballads* (3 vols. Hertford, 1878), 3: 429–433.

[156] See below pp. 394–396, 444, 516.

the author of the 1540 *Conscience*, that Sir Conscience had once been a knight in Langland, they might have regarded less complacently the city–country power-structure represented in such works.

The two cities: vocation

The religious bias of much complaint was no less influential in bestowing special distinction on London. Biblical indictments of the city, for example, defined the righteous man's existence as an opposition to corruption in the high places, including the urban seat of power. Latimer charged that God was "more displeased with London than ever he was with Nebo. Repent, therefore, repent, London, and remember that the same God liveth now that punished Nebo, even the same God, and none other."[157] Brinkelow judged that Londoners "haue deserued a thousand tymes more plages then euer dede Tyre and Sidon, or Sodoma and Gomorra ... Yea, no doubt the vices committed in the, oh London, are as euell as euer ware in any of the foure cyties afore named."[158]

With the national consolidation of religion with political regime in the Reformation, however, London became less and less an alien Babylon or Nineveh and more and more a likeness of Jerusalem, the accepted if not unambiguous symbol of the nation's identity.[159] "The city of Jerusalem had never so many prophets crying at once in her streets," Henry Smith told his London parishioners, "as this city wherein we dwell ... Here is the college of the prophets, here is the voice of the crier, here dwells the seer."[160] As one preacher declared in 1571, "when I came out of the country hither to the city, methinks I came into another world, even out of darkness into light; for here the word of God is plentifully preached." As a result of its dominant role in the Reformation, London became a modern version of Jerusalem, "a regall citye, a metropolyke citie, a citye of magnifycencye, a famouse and populouse cytie: to whiche Citie was the comen course and haunte of all the worlde."[161]

Even the distinction between the old Jerusalem and the new had the paradoxical effect, in post-Calvinist theology, of legitimizing the city as the basic framework for life on earth. Early Tudor preachers had invoked

---

[157] *Sermons*, p. 64.

[158] *The Lamentacyon of a Christian Agaynst the Cytye of London*, in *Four Supplications*, pp. 96–97.

[159] Patrick Collinson, *The Birthpangs of Protestant England* (London: Macmillan, 1988), pp. 28–32.

[160] *The Art of Hearing*, in *Works* (2 vols. Edinburgh: James Nichol, 1866), 1: 319.

[161] *A Sermond Spoken Before the Kynge His Maiestie at Grenewiche* (1536), sig. F4; cf. Francis White, *Londons Warning, By Jerusalem* (1619), John Jones, *Londons Looking Back to Jerusalem* (1633), and Nashe's *Christes Teares over Jerusalem*; cf. below pp. 170, 306–307, 310, 336–337.

the two cities to attack worldliness from a higher perspective. In 1536, Thomas Berthelet was still printing the popular *Dives and Pauper*, in which the heavenly city was a spiritual place without rich or poor, high or low: "In this cite alle men and wymen be fre ... In this cyte shalle euerye man and woman haue so grete lordshyp that al they shalle haue place ynough with outen enuy."[162] The message of the New Jerusalem, as Thomas Becon put it, conflating Isaiah and St. Paul, was that there was no true dwelling place where men built gorgeously upon the backs of the poor.[163] The New Jerusalem remained for Henry Brinkelow a distant prospect: "We remayne also, and contynue styl, in a perpetual bondage and spiritual captiuyte."[164] But while the theology of the two cities condemned the ways of Babylon, it simultaneously required that men continue to walk its streets. It was the task of the oppressed commons, said Robert Crowley, to "learne thy duetie in captiuite ... Do thy laboure truly, cal vpon God continually."[165]

Implicit in the theology of the two cities were several corollaries that further normalized the anomalies of the changing order. For the two cities there were two memberships, so that the sublimely simple distinction between the reprobate and the elect actually enabled the elect to mingle with the reprobate, to be in a bewildering world without being of it. It was in the work of early Tudor reformers, too, that the idea of calling or vocation was developed as a means of consolidating the changing social order. "Every man," said Hooper, "is bound to do the works of the vocation he beareth the name of; and not to meddle with other men's labours."[166] As it was developed in early Tudor theology, however, the providential aspect of vocation actually provided for social mobility.[167] Tyndale, for example, advised ambiguously that if a man "be of low degree let him patiently therein abide, till God promote him, and exalt him higher."[168] Becon, going further, thought the vocational pursuit of wealth, though fraught with dangers, could be justified on the providential grounds that "whatsoever God hath given thee, he hath given thee for the profit of thy neighbour also."[169]

As Becon's logic indicates, a further corollary to the vocational pursuit of wealth was the doctrine of stewardship, which, as it was developed by

[162] *Dives and Pauper*, ed. Priscilla H. Barnum (2 vols. Oxford: EETS, 1980), 2: 319.
[163] *Works*, 3: 434.   [164] *The Complaynt of Roderyck Mors*, pp. 52–53.
[165] *Select Works*, pp. 139, 142.   [166] *Early Writings*, p. 506.
[167] As argued, for example, by Max Weber, *The Sociology of Religion*, tr. M. Fischoff (Boston: Beacon Press, 1964), pp. 246–261; R. H. Tawney, *Religion and the Rise of Capitalism* (1926; rpt. Harmondsworth: Penguin, 1980), pp. 227–251; Christopher Hill, *The Century of Revolution, 1603–1714* (1961; rpt. New York: Norton, 1966), pp. 92–94.   [168] *Doctrinal Treatises* (Cambridge: Parker Society, 1848), p. 137.
[169] *A Pleasant Nosegay*, in *Early Writings*, ed. John Ayre (Cambridge: Parker Society, 1843), p. 225.

several Tudor writers, allowed that wealth might be held by righteous men for righteous purposes.[170] Despite the Christian doctrine that "love maketh all things common," the doctrine of stewardship held in trust maintained that every man could "supply his neighbour's lack, of that wherewith God hath endowed him."[171] By this means, the doctrine justified the pursuit of wealth by those "which useth... their craft to profit many."[172] Sir Thomas Elyot hardly needed to belabor the point that the Latin term *res publica* meant "publike weal" rather than "common weal" when a divine like Thomas Becon could declare that every citizen of the commonwealth should "do his endeavour daily more and more to conserve and keep together his goods that he hath gotten, yea, to augment, increase and enlarge them, that he may be the more able both to live himself, and also to give unto other that have need."[173] As Henry Brinkelow put it, the commonwealth ideal of having "euery neyhbor lyue by other" was merely to have "the lordys and gentylmen [live] by their londys; the merchant man only by his marchandyse, the clothyer by making his cloth; the fermer by tylling his land and bredyng, & cete."[174]

Intended to reinforce collapsing social boundaries, the vocations described by Tudor writers were often not so much the clear social distinctions of an older age as the diversifying economic categories of a world being born. The summaries of vocational duties in Tudor complaint often merely reinstated the diversifying categories they were meant to stabilize. Thomas Becon, for example, noted that men were

bound by the commandment of God to live in their vocation. The lawyer in pleading and defending poor men's causes; the shoemaker in making shoes; the tailor in making garments; the merchant in occupying merchandise faithfully and truly; the schoolmaster in bringing up his scholars godly and virtuously ... and so forth in all other persons, in whatsoever state God hath called them.[175]

The vocational doctrine of Tudor writers thus often left intact and normalized the prolific lists of trades and categories that had seemed so threatening at the beginning of the period. In *The Steel Glas*, for example, Gascoigne's vision of a return to traditional order and social justice was not a retreat from diversification but merely a correction of it:

> I tell thee (priest) when shoomakers make shoes,
> That are wel sowed, with neuer a stitch amisse,

---

[170] See, e.g., Becon, *Works*, 3: 558; Crowley, in *Four Supplications*, p. 168; Turner, *A New Booke of Spirituall Physik*, sig. b4v; Tyndale, *The Parable of the Wicked Mammon*, in *Doctrinal Treatises*, passim; see also Richard Greaves, *Society and Religion in Elizabethan England* (Minneapolis: University of Minnesota Press, 1981), pp. 548–554.
[171] Tyndale, *Doctrinal Treatises*, p. 95.   [172] Hooper, *Early Writings*, p. 391.
[173] *Early Works*, p. 434.   [174] *The Complaynt of Roderyck Mors*, p. 52.
[175] *The Early Writings*, p. 253.

> And use no crafte, in uttring of the same,
> When Taylours steale, no stuffe from gentlemen,
> When Tanners are, with Corriers wel agreede,
> And both so dresse their hydes, that we go dry:
> When Cutters leaue, to sel olde rustie blades,
> And hide no crackes, with soder nor deceit;
> When Tinkers make, no more holes than they founde,
> When Thatchers thinke, their wages worth their worke,
> When colliers put, no dust into their sacks,
> When maltemen make, us drinke no firmentie,
> When Dauie Diker diggs, and dallies not,
> When smithes shoo horses, as they would be shod,
> When millers toll not with a golden thumbe,
> When bakers make, not barme beare price of wheat,
> When brewers put, no bagage in their beere
> When butchers blowe, not ouer al their flesche,
> When horsecorsers, beguile no friends with Jades,
> When weauers weight, is found in huswifes web,
> (But why dwel I, so long among these louts?)
> When mercers make, more bones to swere and lye,
> When vinters mix, no water with their wine,
> When printers passe, none errours in their bookes,
> When hatters use, to bye none olde cast robes,
> When goldsmithes get, no gains by sodred crownes,
> When upholsters, sel feathers without dust,
> When pewterers, infect no Tin with leade,
> When drapers draw, no gaines by giuing day,
> When perchmentiers, put in no ferret silke,
> When Surgeons heale, al wounds without delay ...
> When purveyors, provide not for themselves,
> When Takers, take no brybes, nor use no brags,
> When customes, conceal no covine usede,
> When Searchers see, al corners in a shippe, ...
> When al these things, are ordred as they ought,
> And see themselues within my glasse of steele,
> Even then (my priests) may you go make holyday,
> And pray no more but ordinarie prayers.[176]

Like many other motifs that emerged from Tudor complaint, the motif of the world reformed finally institutionalized and endorsed the very anomalies it had set out to oppose. Utopian dreaming did not banish waking nightmares, but made those nightmares seem so routine and familiar as to impoverish dreaming. The ballad "O maruelous tyd-ynges," for example, culminated with a visionary restoration of the golden age of England, yet that golden age had become remarkably mundane:

[176] *The Steel Glas*, in *Works*, 2: 171–172.

the golden world, I trust, wyll com agayn,
That folk may lyue easyly without any great payn;
Many egges for a peny at London I wolde se fayn,
    Flesche and fische better chepe, I trust it will be true.[177]

Mundane utopias

By approaching the city as the perfection of human achievement, as the ideal order from which men derive their identity and being, Thomas More had been able to articulate the city's deepest paradox, the contradiction between the radical concentration of urban power and the radical distribution of justice. He imagined a world so radically reformed that its very geometry cancelled the concentration its economy enforced, making Utopia's cities so contradictory that they could not logically exist in space. It seems ironic then that, taken as a whole, the structure of Tudor complaint should have done the reverse. Attempting to trace the disruptions of their age to the uprooting of traditional order and the corresponding concentration of power in London – which could only seem abnormal in the traditional social models on which they relied – Tudor writers effectively transformed these models in such a way as to articulate the hitherto inarticulate, thereby generating new languages and structures in which the power of the city was institutionalized. The language of complaint thus helped to bring on the new mentality that dissolved the old. The later history of motifs and structures developed in the early Tudor period clarifies this genetic process in retrospect. Initially disturbing changes connected with the growth of London were gradually given a shape and structure that made them seem "natural" in the framework of a new mental order.

The utopias of late-Tudor writers were consequently but shadows or projections cast by a power structure which had come to seem ineradicably real. Thomas Lupton's *Sivqila. Too Good, to be True* (1580), for example, is an account of the utopian realm of *Mauqsun* (nusquam), which reverses the topsy-turvy of *Ailgna* (Anglia): private profit, which in Ailgna "vndoeth many to make a few riche," is in Mauqsun turned into "a common comodities, that enricheth man and impouerisheth none" – but only because in the latter merchants are many and profits are vigorously pursued,[178] even while poor men are pious and humble, never "murmuring, impacient, vngodly," as in England. Ample charity is provided for widows, prisoners, beggars, poor apprentices and servants,

---

[177] In Huth, ed., *A Collection of... Black Letter Ballads*, pp. 208–213.
[178] Part I (1580), p. 8; Part II (1581), sigs. A2v, L2v, ZSC* 4v.

maimed soldiers, debtors, impoverished husbandmen, poor scholars, decayed gentlemen, decayed cities, decayed artificers – in short, for all the souls who must, perforce, exist in the stabilized *Mauqsun* as in its unstable counterpart, *Ailgna*. What had been for earlier writers a social order almost impossible to think has become for Lupton impossible not to think.

No Tudor utopia, however, more clearly illuminates the paradoxes of economic transition and their relation to London than William Bullein's *Dialogue of the Fever Pestilence* (1564), an extremely clever and undeservedly neglected work written in response to the devastating plague of 1563. In its survey of the contemporary social world, the work registers in literary terms a mobility and multidirectionality that powerfully oppose the regimentation which the work nevertheless attempts to impose. Bullein's *Dialogue* is a ferociously heterogeneous work, combining the features of narrative, colloquy, farce, and morality play. It contains a rhetorical treatise, a cosmology, an ethical handbook, a devotional manual, medical recipes, and a utopian tract. Combining letter, number, abbreviation and chemical symbolism, the dialogue speaks in prose and verse, English and Latin. The presence of these inventory-treatise forms is a symptom of the *Dialogue*'s subject – the plague, whose disorder calls into being lists, bills of mortality, and other organizational measures.[179]

As a transitional work, the *Dialogue* cites as its muses "old Morall Goore," "wittie Chaucer," "Lamenting Lidgate," "Dauie Linse," and "Bartlet" (i.e., Barclay), whose "pleasaunt Pipes" abhorred "the life of Courtiers, Citizens, Usurers, and Bankruptes, &c." (pp. 16–18). In the rhythmic but unmeasured "sharpe Distichons" of Skelton, it chooses a native, insular form of complaint opposed to the fashionable "French and Romaine" Renaissance models of "the continent" (p. 18), just as it also resists the "newe hongrie Flies" that "vexe the bodie of the common wealth" in the new Renaissance state. In these preferences lies the basis for its "rhizomatic" rather than centralized "arborescent" organization.[180] The "diuersitie or varietie of pleasaunte colours" in its rhetoric (p. 1) is, like the apothecary's "choise of sondri kindes of straunge flowers" at once "clensyng, healyng, losyng, bindyng, and restoryng" (p. 14).

[179] *A Dialogue Bothe Pleasaunte and Pietefull, Wherein is a Goodly Regimente Against the Feuer Pestilence* (1564), ed. Mark W. Bullen and A. H. Bullen (London: EETS, 1888), pp. 25, 31, 33; the relation between plague and disciplinary measures and conceptual inventories (what Bullein's title calls "regimente against the feuer") is explained in Michel Foucault, *Discipline and Punish: The Birth of the Prison*, tr. Alan Sheridan (New York: Vintage, 1979), pp. 197, 195.

[180] Deleuze and Guattari, *A Thousand Plateaus*, p. 21.

In the multiple filiations of its arguments, the *Dialogue* makes a number of surprising connections. A Northumberland beggar turns up at the door of a London citizen, for example, in order to dramatize and explain how the traditional English landscape is mobilized by a process of expropriation and displacement:

> In the countrie strife, ... much reisyng of rentes and gresomyng of men, causyng greate dearth, muche pouertie. God helpe, God helpe, the warld is sare chaunged; extortioners, couetous men, and hypocrites doe much preuaile. God cutte them shorter, for thei doe make a blacke warlde, euen hell vpon yearth. (pp.7–8)

The *Dialogue*'s preoccupation with the portentous changes wrought by plague is thus inseparable from its preoccupation with mobility and changes of estate, with deterritorialization and reterritorialization: its total purview is "Pestilence, yearthquake, hunger, and marueilous changes in commonwealthes" (p. 77). As London itself is mobilized and expelled into the countryside by the fluid contagion of the plague, so is the population of the countryside mobilized, expropriated, and displaced by the fluid, plague-like influence of the new order at London. As the beggar makes his way to London he passes Londoners coming in the opposite direction:

> I met with wagones, Cartes, & Horses full loden with yong barnes, for feare of the black Pestilence, ... O God, how fast did thei run by hundredes, and were afraid of eche other for feare of smityng. (p. 8)

Such is the nature of this urban-oriented cyclical exchange that the City's Lent and plague are the country beggar's carnival and feast. "Such plague," Mendicus observes,

> is no great losse. For ... it shall ... cutte of many couetous vsurers, – whiche neuer doe pleasure vnto the Lande or grounde vntill their heapes are cast abroade to the profites of many ... And in sike plagues we pure people haue muccle gud. Their losse is our lucke; when thei dooe become naked, we then are clethed againste their willes; with their dooles and almose we are reliued; their sickness is our health, their death our life. Besides vs pakers, many mo men haue gud lucke, as the Vicre, Parishe Clarke, and the Belle man; often tymes the Executours bee no losers by this game ... We beggers recke nought of the carcas of the dead body, but doe defie it; we looke for aude caste coates, Jackettes, Hose, Cappes, Beltes, and Shoes by their deathes, which in their liues thei waude not departe from, and this is our happe. God sende me of them. (p. 9)

Like London's merchants in time of health, beggars in time of plague enjoy the fruits of a carnivalian inversion; neither cares "which ende doe goe forwarde, so that thy tourne may be serued" (p. 10).

As a transitional work resistant to the new economic order and state regime, the *Dialogue* sides with the power of plague to level hierarchy and to produce "great heapes of rotten bones, whom ye knowe not of what degree thei were, rich or poore" (p. 50). Against the stratified space of the new order it poses the unassimilable "holey space" of the degraded worm-eaten body, the "stinking carrion for wormes delite" (p. 119). The plague is thus a projective and invasive force that opens doors and graves, gives rise to ringing, singing, comings-in, blazings-forth, and all manner of unseemly communications and interpenetrations. From St. Augustine Bullein borrows a charnell-house vision of distinctions levelled: "take vp the bones, marke well if thou canst knowe the master from the seruant, the faire from the foule, the rich from the poore, the wise from the foole, &c." (p. 132).

On the other hand, as a transitional work, the *Dialogue* also responds to the anomalies of social change by intensifying the regimentation that brings on the new order. Its quest for a cure for plague is a quest for the discipline and order that isolate and close off individual bodies within an ordered space. The causes of the plague are promiscuous mixing and opening: "repletion, Venus, Bathyng, or opening the poures ... many people [dwelling] on heapes together ... many people lying together in one bedde" (pp. 37, 44). Plague is a hydraulic disease, spread by fluid elements, by "the inspiration of the ayre" (p. 37), by the projective fumes of "Garlike and newe Ale, ... Onions, Leekes, Rocket, Radishe" (p. 43) and by projective and disorderly affects, "anger or perturbations, ... care, anger, wrath, &c." (pp. 43–44). Its cures, accordingly, are prophylactic withdrawal, separation, and drying: people should "auoide out of the euill ayre, ... drawe from the bodie superfluous moysture, ... vse the regiment of diet to driyng" (p. 39). Clothes, beds, houses should not be shared; everything should be individualized, marked off, and self-contained.

The coincidence of these cures with the creation of political subjects inscribed by the new order is reflected in the utopian dimensions of the work. In the hangings of a country inn, "very netly and trimely apparlled, London like" (p. 80), a number of emblems prepare the way to utopia. A fool sawing off the limb on which he sits emblematizes "all traitors against princes, children against Parentes, seruantes against Maisters, poore against rich, tenauntes against their lordes, &c." (p. 89). "A house, builded of stone, with many strong doores and windowes, barred and railed with strong yron barres" (and glossed in the margin as "Ludgate") demonstrates the proverb that "truthe seeketh no corners, as ... euill disposed vile Theeues do" (p. 89).

These disciplinary emblems form a fitting prelude to Mendax's account of the transequatorial utopia of Terra Florida. The realm contains "one old famous Citie of great antiquitie, the best reformed

Citie of this worlde; the like hath not been hard of, nether red of, nor seen"; it is called Ecnatneper (Repentance) of Nodnol (London):

This Citie is great, well walled, and strongly fortified; warlike, with great gates, verie beautifull, as euer Hierusalem was. These gates are locked faste vppon the Sabboth ... to this ende, that the Citizens doe not goe, neither ride forth of the Citie duryng the daie, except it be after the euenyng praier; then to walke honestlie into the sweet fieldes. (pp. 105–106)

In this Sabbatarian paradise, where "the gates are locked faste" and the citizens "doe not goe, neither ride forth," all "are Protestants." Taverns are closed and servants are allowed to attend early morning services that allow them to prepare dinner for their masters. Small economic concessions are made: "There is not one Usurer: not one," and strict oversight ensures that merchants do "no wronge one to an other, neither by extortion, vsuries, euill ware sold by vntruth for good &c. With collections of money for the poore in deede; the idle are set to worke or punished for slothe" (p. 108). Bearwards are whipped for staging shows on Sunday; ruffians are chained and whipped by beadles; double-dealing lawyers are imprisoned; papists are burned; servants and labourers are given fair wages (pp. 109–110). Nodnol, in short, eradicates venal abuses only to reinforce the social order and power structure of a highly regimented state, a striated order of rich and poor, masters and servants, employed and unemployed. The process of change is rationalized and rendered complete by the emergence of a totally reliable politico-juridical apparatus. "There are iudges and worthie Lawiers in euerie Citie which haue great stipendes of the prince," and "Euery manne doeth knowe his owne" (p. 110).

The tendency of the Utopian journey to mirror the *status quo* in perfected form is taken one step further when the Citizen and his wife pass beyond the inn into the fair fields that promise to be the end of pilgrimage. With their arrival at the safe haven of a splendid manor, the Citizen's wife learns that her husband is "a greate landed man" with "much cattell in store:"

Maistres, do you not knowe it? It is my Maisters; I am the Bailie there. All yonder towne is his; he hath raised the rent one hundred markes a yere more then it was. There were good lyuing in the plague tyme, for there are large pastures, and the houses are downe, sauynge the Maner place, for the carles haue forfected their leases, and are gone a beggyng like villains, and many of them are dedde for honger. (p. 112)

Following this shock of recognition, the Citizen comes to "knowe his owne" in a truer sense, as Death descends upon him and he penitently resolves "to bee a Citizen of eternall glorie" (p. 135). But this personal repentance does not reverse the socio-economic process the *Dialogue* has both resisted and endorsed. Released from his servitude, the Citizen's servant Roger vows once again to "goe to London and lurke in some bawdie Lane" (p. 122). The irreversible power of the urban magnet is exalted in Roger's last wish: "Oh, that I had as muche moneye as my Maister, and were a free man in London, then would I ..." A long list of potential selves – and potential scams, schemes, and abuses – for Roger follows: the topsy-turvy order of the new regime remains. Like More's *Utopia*, which reacts to the concentration of urban wealth and power by institutionalizing the novel process of surplus extraction, Bullein's *Dialogue* responds to changes in the English social body with solutions that consolidate and rationalize the forces of change. Both works typify the early Tudor establishment of discursive conditions favoring the development of a vision and vocabulary suited to a growing metropolis and capital of an emerging national regime. The elaboration of this new vision and vocabulary, and their contribution to a mentality of settlement, are the subject of the following chapters.

Part II

Fictions of settlement

3   From matron to monster: London and the languages of description

Fictions of settlement

London came into focus gradually in early Tudor literature. By the end of the sixteenth century, however, it had become the center of an innovative constellation of descriptions and praises, sermons and moral pamphlets, ballads and satires, chronicles, plays, and pageants. The decades between 1580 and 1620, which witnessed the emergence of a great courtly literature in the works of Sidney, Spenser, and others, also saw the birth of a major new urban literature. The literature of London comprised many developments – the emergence of a large public theater system, with its varied repertory, including more than a hundred comedies set in London,[1] the creation of the annual Lord Mayor's Show, the development of urban verse satire based on classical models, and the rise of a whole new class of literary professionals, many of them degraded urbanites, writing for the new heteroglot audience that was being drawn to the metropolis. All of these developments were the result of a greatly intensified process of urban settlement.

Between the death of Thomas More and the death of Milton, the population of London increased from 50,000 souls to half a million, transforming a late medieval commune into a metropolis that would soon become the largest capital and *entrepôt* in Europe. The later sixteenth century was a crucial phase in this process, as during the lifetimes of Sidney and Spenser the population increased by 50 percent and for the first time in history a monarch attempted to halt the growth of London by fiat. These decades were marked by important changes in the city's demography and economy. The increased pace and scale of urbanization brought with it an increasing degree of "social polarization, as society filled out at the bottom, particularly in the rapidly expanding extramural

---

[1] Anne Barton, "London Comedy and the Ethos of the City," *The London Journal*, 4: 2 (1978), 160.

parishes."[2] As a result of growth and diversification, the increasing stratification of urban society was marked by a widening barrier between journeyman status and the achievement of livery membership. The loosening control of the guilds over the economy was reflected at the top by the highly diversifying investments and activities of the elite, at the bottom by massive unemployment and an increase in wage labor. The traditional practices of the civic elite were transformed by the creation of international joint-stock trading consortia and court-sponsored syndicates, while those of ordinary Londoners were altered by the growth of artisanal manufactures, especially in the unregulated suburbs, for a developing home market, and by a large increase in the service sector, reflecting London's development as a capital, marriage market, and center for conspicuous consumption.

London's government and jurisdiction, which represented 80 percent of the greater metropolitan population in 1560, represented less than half of it by 1630.[3] The suburbs, with their population of casual laborers and unassimilated artisans, immigrants and paupers, were outstripping the City of London in growth. Traditional civic and economic institutions were being undermined by tax farms and other forms of royal intervention, by new forms of speculation and commercial organization, and by new modes of social and religious affiliation. The ravages of poverty, dearth, and disease meant that the city's expansion could only be fueled by a massive immigration that in 1590 made one in every eight Englishmen Londoners at some point in their lives.[4] Physically the largest human creation in Britain, London was also becoming the most commonly experienced.

Concerning itself with such new and unsettling aspects of urbanization as these, the literature of London was an important cultural innovation – a *representation of* the expanding urban settlement, but also a product and *instrument of* that very process of urbanization. In noting that contemporary images of London were like "certain pictures, that represent to divers beholders, at divers stations, divers forms,"[5] the preacher Thomas Adams underlined the extent to which, by constellating divergent perspectives around a common focus, such images served as

[2] Ian W. Archer, *The Pursuit of Stability: Social Relations in Elizabethan London* (Cambridge University Press, 1991), p. 92.
[3] Roger Finlay and Beatrice Shearer, "Population Growth and Suburban Expansion," in A. L. Beier and Roger Finlay, eds., *London 1500–1700: The Making of the Metropolis* (London: Longman, 1986), p. 42.
[4] Roger Finlay, *Population and Metropolis: The Demography of London 1580–1650* (Cambridge University Press, 1981), p. 9.
[5] "The City of Peace," in *Works*, ed. J. Angus (3 vols. Edinburgh: J. Nichol, 1861–1862), 3: 331.

"fictions of settlement." The literary representation of London was not merely mimetic, but socially functional, tied to the task of producing and reproducing the socio-economic relationships essential to urbanization. London's "fictions of settlement" were not just images, but actions or practices, modes of ideological innovation that actually contributed to the process of sedentarism. Their effect was to articulate urbane mentalities of settlement.

The context and background for this articulation was the neofeudal fusion of "merchant capital and landed property."[6] The hypertrophic growth of the capital, and the diversifying services and population that went with it, resulted from London's preeminence as the administrative center of the new absolutist state and the main conduit for government revenues and landed wealth. Both roles were celebrated in the first surviving published mayoral pageant of 1585, where London "ever more bequeathes / Service of Honour and Loyalty" to the "Royall Armes," while "The honest Franklin and the Husband-man / Layess downe his sackes of Corne at London's feet, / And bringes such presents as the Countrie yeeldes."[7]

The absolutist state, Perry Anderson argues, was neither the arbiter between the aristocracy and the bourgeoisie nor an instrument of the latter against the former, but a "new political carapace of the threatened nobility"; the state continued to uphold, through new forms of patronage, officeholding, and finance, the traditional status, power, and interests of landholding aristocrats and gentry. But at the same time, the emergence of the state's politico-juridical apparatus was overdetermined by the influence of the new urban class, which increasingly helped to finance the state and to carry out its programs through highly organized mechanisms of local government. This new influence blocked any return to the old ways of feudalism and determined the new shape the aristocracy was to take.[8] The power of London's socio-economic mixture to resist the feudal past and to bring on the state was celebrated by the anonymous apologist who declared around 1580 that "Cities and great townes are a continuall bridle against tyranny ... not onely in the Aristocritie, but also in the lawfull kingdome or iust royalty."[9] The unitary development of the landowning class and merchant capital meant that the aristocracy,

[6] John Merrington, "Town and Country in the Transition to Capitalism," in Paul Sweezy, Maurice Dobb, et al., *The Transition from Feudalism to Capitalism* , p. 184.
[7] George Peele, *The Device of the Pageant borne before Wolstane Dixie* (1585), in *Life and Minor Works*, ed. Charles T. Prouty (3 vols. New Haven: Yale University Press, 1952), 1: 209.
[8] *Lineages of the Absolutist State* (1974; rpt. London: Verso, 1979), pp. 22–24.
[9] In John Stow, *A Survey of London*, ed. C. L. Kingsford (2 vols. 1908; rpt. Oxford: Clarendon Press, 1971), 2: 206, 198–199.

earlier in England than elsewhere on the continent, turned to the commerce and mercantilism that made London the center of an expanding national market.[10] And this market, in turn, was connected to new types of industrial organization and to new classes of capitalists and artisans whose interests – in the Civil Wars and after – often formed a powerful counterweight to those of the ruling class.

Thus, though contained by the framework of neofeudalism, London exercised a profound "action at a distance" on the shape this framework took.[11] By the mid-Tudor period, the symbolic crownings, mysterious spousals, and heavenly visions that traditionally brought coronation pageants to a climax at the head of Cheapside had been supplemented by gift exchanges and harangues with the City's chief officials, underlining Sidney's observation in *Astrophil and Stella* that "No kings be crown'd, but they some covenants make."[12] London, said the anonymous apologist of 1580, was "a mighty arme and instrument to bring any great desire to effect, if it may be woon to a mans deuotion."[13] Through the mutually advantageous exchange of privileges and trade concessions for revenue and political support, London and the emergent state were bound in symbiosis. According to Thomas Headley, a leading seventeenth-century parliamentary opponent of impositions and monopolies, the merchants of London were "so compounded with or dealt with, that they will not, or dare not, bring any action against the King or his officers."[14]

The chivalric decor of the late Elizabethan period, elaborated *both* at court *and* as the preferred civic style of Londoners, was an essential feature of this neofeudal order. It reinforced the conceptual contract that defined a new national "community of honour"[15] by adapting London's socio-economic dynamism to the needs of the state. As it flourished "under the lengthening shadow of the state," the chivalric revival diluted the traditions of feudal service "to suit the taste of a relatively broad and to a large extent nonaristocratic public." For urban craftsmen and merchants, who "had not yet developed a consciousness of class in the sense that they had a set of values peculiarly their own," the values and conventions of aristocratic honor were a principal means of self-

---

[10] Anderson, *Lineages of the Absolutist State*, pp. 125, 135, 138.

[11] Ibid., pp. 39–40.

[12] *Astrophil and Stella*, line 69, quoted in Martin Raitiere, *Faire Bitts: Sir Philip Sidney and Renaissance Political Theory* (Pittsburgh: Duquesne University Press, 1984), p. 38.

[13] Stow, *Survey*, 2: 206.

[14] Quoted in Robert Brenner, *Merchants and Revolution: Commercial Change, Political Conflict, and London's Overseas Traders, 1550–1653* (Princeton University Press, 1993), p. 208.

[15] See Mervyn James, "English Politics and the Concept of Honour, 1485–1642," in *Society, Politics, and Culture: Studies in Early Modern England* (Cambridge University Press, 1986), esp. pp. 375–379.

definition.[16] Above all, the social and artistic decorum of chivalry encouraged the loyalty of Londoners toward a regime still being imagined in quasi-feudal terms, according to which service and tribute were exchanged for liberty, privilege, and honor. In London itself, the pursuit of status, honor, and authority by citizens was sustained by an elaborate *cursus honorum*, in which ceremonies, feasts, regalia, and oathtakings distinguished each degree and achievement in guild and civic life. The solidarity and privilege of the elite was enhanced, even as the expanding mass of artisans and laborers was indoctrinated, when the exemplary benefactions of prosperous Londoners were celebrated in ballads, sermons, and epitaphs, or when the dignity of the City's leaders was publicized in works like William Jaggard's *View of all the Right Honourable Lord Mayors of this Honorable City of London* (1601).

The neofeudal tenor of the civic ethos achieved particularly widespread appeal through popular myths extolling London's merchant–heroes. The pageant staged by the Fishmongers at the mayoral inauguration of 1590 celebrated the stabbing of the rebel Jack Straw by an earlier Fishmonger mayor in 1381, an act that was said to have gained the City the dagger in its coat of arms and the knighthoods awarded to all subsequent mayors.[17] Along with *The Life and Death of Iack Strawe*, published in 1593 but probably staged in connection with the 1590 mayoralty,[18] the Fishmongers' pageant helped establish what soon became a whole corpus of works devoted to the magnanimity, virtue, and chivalric elan of worthy Londoners. In plays like *The Book of Sir Thomas More*, Dekker's *Shoemaker's Holiday*, and Heywood's *Edward IV*, there emerged a whole company of urban luminaries whose natural nobility, moral virtue, and feudal loyalty rivalled those of any peer of the realm. In a two-part play celebrating the achievements of both Elizabeth I and the London magnate Sir Thomas Gresham, Thomas Heywood took his audience through a whole anthology of worthy Londoners whose works were commemorated in the civic portrait-gallery of Alexander Nowell, Dean of St. Paul's, while in *The Nine Worthies of London* (1592) Richard Johnson gathered "from our London gardens" the "flowers of chivalry" who had "reached to the aspiring top of arms."[19]

[16] Arthur B. Ferguson, *The Chivalric Tradition in Renaissance England* (Washington: Folger Shakespeare Library, 1986), pp. 107, 78.

[17] T. Nelson, *The Deuice of the Pageant: Set Forth by the Worshipfull Companie of Fishmongers for the Right Honourable John Allott, Established Lord Maior of London* (1590).

[18] See Robert Withington, "The Lord Mayor's Show for 1590," *PMLA*, 30 (1915), 110–115, and David M. Bergeron, "Jack Straw in Drama and Pageant," *The Guildhall Miscellany*, 2: 1 (1968), 459–463.

[19] *If You Know Not Me, You Know Nobody* (1605), in *The Nine Worthies of London*, sig. A2.

On at least one occasion, John Stow took exception to the new mythology, assailing the Fishmongers' pageant as the work of "men ignorant of their Antiquities" (2: 215). As a learned antiquary, Stow preferred veracity; but just as importantly, as an aged citizen who remembered the "incorporative rituals of the past," he was suspicious of the invidious and inflated claims promulgated by the new mythology and pageantry.[20] Yet it was not Stow, but popular writers like Anthony Munday and Thomas Middleton who, by ransacking Stow's scholarship in search of propaganda, received patronage through the newly created office of City Chronologer. As London came to play an increasingly important role in the national economy and polity, communal identification developed side-by-side with social differentiation, so that "community in the sense of people of different status doing things together was ... eroded" even while mythology and pageantry became more prominent.[21]

The *ethos* of loyalty, service, and solidarity developed in myth and pageantry sought to normalize the socially disruptive effects of the new urban order, accommodating the ambitious and acquisitive practices of citizens to traditional aristocratic values, even while it masked the mobility of entrepreneurs as a manifestation of nobility. Englishmen could now demonstrate their nobility and honor "by the seruice of our prince and countrey, *either* martially *or* ciuilly."[22] It was not merely nostalgia that led to such later sixteenth-century phenomena as the creation of a "friendly and franke fellowship of prince *Arthurs* knightes in and about the citie of London"; in staging "a costly showe of Prince Arthur" for Elizabeth around 1587, London's Leathersellers extracted in return the monarch's promise that "she would love, maintain, and advance, her Citizens of the City of London."[23]

It was within and through the context of this complex neofeudal situation that the new fictions of urban settlement were elaborated. In the encomiastic genres of description, epic, and pageant most closely associated with the power and official views of the court and the City of London government, a neofeudal framework of interpretation accom-

---

[20] See Ian W. Archer, "John Stow's *A Survey of London*," and Lawrence Manley, "Of Sites and Rites: Ceremony, Theater, and John Stow's *Survey of London*," in David Bevington, Richard Strier, and David Smith, eds., *London: The Theatrical City* (Cambridge University Press, 1995).

[21] Archer, *The Pursuit of Stability*, pp. 93, 99.

[22] *Cyvile and Uncyvile Life* (1579), p. 42, quoted in James, "English Politics and the Concept of Honour," p. 379.

[23] Richard Mulcaster, *Positions* (1581), pp. 101–102; John Nichols, ed., *Progresses and Public Processions of Queen Elizabeth I* (3 vols. 1823; rpt. New York: Burt Franklin, 1966), 2: 529–530; both cited in C. Bowie Millican, *Spenser and the Table Round* (Cambridge, Mass.: Harvard University Press, 1932), pp. 56, 60–61.

modated the growth of London – and the potentially divergent interests of its inhabitants – both to the aristocratic status- and value-systems of late feudalism and to the centralizing power of the emerging nation–state. Increasingly, the new "honor community" was represented not in local but in supra-individual and transhistorical terms, as a providentially ordained nation and destined empire. As a capital and epitome of Britain, "the head of our English flourishing commonwealth,"[24] London became a crucial symbol in a new process of national self-definition.

That definition tended to subordinate justice to power, mobility to stability, heterogeneity to unity, and history to providence, though, as in the society at large, tensions, resistances, and contradictions made for an often powerfully dialectical relationship. The most radically alternative forms of urban morality and values emerged in the more innovative genres of critique and vituperation, which, though written within the same neofeudal framework, were distanced from official sponsorship and in closer touch with popular culture and the new commercial audience. Nevertheless, while praise and blame, in the differing degree to which they emphasized stability and change respectively, amounted to differences in kind, these two bodies of contemporary material exercised a considerable reciprocal influence and created a broad, fluid consensus during the long transitional period between the crises of the Reformation and the Civil Wars. On the one hand, the novelties and innovations of seriocomic prose, verse satire, epigram, and stage comedy – with their emphasis on fluidity, change, discontinuity and subjective empowerment – contributed to progressive attitudes and practices that stabilized and enhanced the urbanizing process. Conversely, the stability, order, and degree celebrated in the more official and encomiastic genres embodied a sense of historic dynamism and evolving destiny.

London's entry into the national consciousness – indeed the powerful relationship between the two – was reflected in the most obvious and most official way by its appearance in topographical description and praise. As early as 1549, Sir John Coke had staked his claims for the international status of the new Tudor state on a description of the might and splendor of "the auncyent and famous Cytie of London."[25] Description of London became an essential feature of the new topographical genres which, as part of an expression of emerging national consciousness, flourished in the hands of such innovative Elizabethan and Jacobean writers as William Camden, John Norden, John Speed,

---

[24] Johnson, *The Nine Worthies of London*, sig. A2.
[25] *The Debate between the Heralds of England and France* (1550), in R. H. Tawney and Eileen Power, eds., *Tudor Economic Documents* (3 vols. London: Longmans, Green, 1924), 3: 7.

and John Stow. The aims of such writers were both intellectual and patriotic, scientific and encomiastic. While putting the English landscape and its history at the fingertips of English readers, they also framed them in ideological terms that justified the English way of life. Camden, for example, explained in the preface to his *Britannia* (1586/1610) that his motives were both "a firme settled study of the truth, and sincere antique faithfulnesse to the glory of my God and my countrie."[26] He evidently saw no difficulty, later in his survey of the nation, with settling the same title of "my deere natiue country" upon London, perhaps because it was for him "the Epitome and Breviary of all Britain" (pp. 437, 421). Stow was the only major topographer to publish a work devoted exclusively to "the chiefe and principall citie of the land,"[27] but London's overwhelming domination of England's economic, political, and intellectual life made it an especially pregnant crux in almost every reading of the landscape. Norden, for example, thought it "not vnfit to begin" his *Speculum Britanniae* (1593) with a volume on "MYDDLESEX, which aboue all other Shyres is graced, with that chiefe and head Citie LONDON: which as an adamant draweth vnto it all the other parts of the land."[28]

London was not, however, merely a microcosm of the national body but also one among its many subject members, and thus to the extent that London's achievements might underwrite the sovereign power they might also, potentially, usurp it. Speed's *Theatre of the Empire of Great Britaine* (1611), which had originally been dedicated to James I, was rededicated by its 1676 editor to the City of London; after all, Edward Phillips asked, to whom was it more proper to dedicate "The Description of our own Countrey, than to the Powers of that Supreme City, whose prosperous Trade distributes Wealth and Honour to the whole Nation"?[29] Precisely because they were symbolizing the nation's life, topographers drew the lineaments of London with special care.

Many of the leading descriptive works of the Tudor–Stuart age were based on innovative historical and topographical research, on techniques borrowed both from major continental writers like Ortelius and from such pioneering English antiquaries as John Leland, Matthew Parker, Alexander Neville, and William Lambarde.[30] But the often massive

---

[26] *Britain*, tr. Philemon Holland (1610), unpaginated preface.
[27] *A Survey of London*, 1 : xcviii.
[28] *Speculum Britanniae. The Firste Parte* (1593), p. 9.
[29] *The Theatre of the Empire of Great Britaine* (1676), sig. A4.
[30] See, for example, F. J. Levy, "The Making of Camden's *Britannia*," *Bibliothèque d'humanisme et renaissance*, 26 (1964), 70–79; Levy, *Tudor Historical Thought* (San Marino: The Huntington Library, 1967), pp. 132–136; Stuart Piggott, "William Camden and the *Britannia*," in *Ruins in a Landscape* (Edinburgh University Press, 1976), pp. 33–54; T. S. Dorsch, "Two English Antiquaries: John Leland and John Stow," *Essays and Studies*, n.s. 12 (1959), 18–35.

learning of the topographers was matched by an equally innovative concern with expository method, by an effort to shape the facts of topography – especially of urban life – into a coherent vision. For this reason, topography was neither a figure of speech (as in rhetoric) nor a science, but a mode of invention, with its own generic rules and assumptions. In fact, a fundamental feature of the new descriptions of Tudor–Stuart London was their use of inventive models or paradigms to guide the selection and arrangement of material. Through such models, the city's life was not simply organized, but justified.

Although the models for description came from different sources – from Aristotelian ideas adapted to the needs of statecraft, from Ramist dialectic, and from ancient rhetoric – they reinforced each other in their tendency to harmonize the facts of urban culture with the laws of nature. This naturalization of cultural fact contributed, furthermore, to the procedure of personifying the city as feminine, as a symbolically submissive intermediary between nature and the higher claims of political culture, between the bourgeois community and the neofeudal state.

This gender-based procedure, which dominated many of the major descriptions of Tudor–Stuart London, effectively suppressed the more dynamic aspects of urban life – especially the power of the metropolitan economy both to enfranchise and to enslave individual subjects without regard to the sovereign's intent. On the one hand, the freedom of London, though subject to its own rules and restrictions, posed a challenge to the hierarchical principles of feudal domination:

such was the Custome of London, that a villen having remained there the space of one whole yeare and a day, could not be fetched or removed from thence. For so great is the prerogatives of that place, that it giveth protection to the villen or bondman against his lord while the said bondman shall be resiant there.[31]

The socio-economic corollary of the political freedom was the spectacular opportunity for mobility. But on the other hand, these liberties and the rapid growth they spawned also made London an engine potentially dangerous to the national regime. "With time," James I declared in 1616, "England will onely be London, and the whole countrey be left waste."[32] One important reason for the monarchs' repeated attempts to halt London's growth by fiat was the city's economic domination of "the other good Townes and Borrowes of this Kingdome," which "by reason

---

[31] *A Breefe Discourse, Declaring and Approuing the Necessarie and Inuiolable Maintenance of Certain Laudable Custemes of London* (1584), pp. 16–17.

[32] Speech in Star Chamber, June 20, 1616, in C. H. McIlwain, ed., *The Political Works of James I* (Cambridge, Mass.: Harvard University Press, 1918), p. 343.

of so great receit for people in and about the said City, are much unpeopled, and in their trading, and otherwise, decayed. "[33] But another concern, according to an Elizabethan proclamation, was that "such multitudes could hardly be governed by ordinary justice to serve God and obey her Majesty. "[34] Hobbes, for example, argued in his history of the great rebellion that "there can hardly arise a long or dangerous rebellion that has not some such overgrown city with an army or two in its belly to foment it... great capital cities, when rebellion is upon pretence of grievances, must needs be of the rebel party. "[35] The royalist Peter Heylyn, commenting during the Commonwealth on the over-mightiness of the burgeoning metropolis, similarly noted that

London is... increased so much in wealth and honour from one Age to another, that it is grown at last too big for the Kingdom; which whether it may be profitable for the State, or not, may be made a question. And towns in the bodie of a State, are like the Spleen or Melt in the bodie naturall: the monstrous growth of which impoverisheth all the rest of the members, by drawing to it all the animal and vital spirits... And certainly the overgrowth of great Cities is a dangerous consequence... in respect of the irreparable danger of Insurrections, if once those multitudes, sensible of their own strength... should gather into a head and break out into action.[36]

Especially troubling from the political point of view were the ruptures, stretches, folds, and loosened threads of the social fabric, the potentially divergent powers and interests which were geographically epitomized by the subdivision of the city into a discontinuous terrain of holdings and jurisdictions, hidden tenements, alleys, byways, straight rooms and cellars. The attribution of a feminine persona to the city diminished these concerns ideologically, providing not only a gender-based model of obedient submission but also a transhistorical identity which absorbed and suppressed the spatial divisions and discontinuities which manifested the city's true historic dynamism. The inherently spatial bias of topography had the disturbing capacity for rendering change and for delineating sharply divided or discontinuous political domains[37] – a capacity apparent in James Boswell's somewhat later remark that "one end of London was like a different country from the other in look and

---

[33] Proclamation of October 12, 1607, in Paul L. Hughes and James F. Larkin, eds., *Stuart Royal Proclamations* (2 vols. New Haven: Yale University Press, 1973), 1: 171.

[34] Proclamation of June 27, 1602, in Paul L. Hughes and James F. Larkin, eds., *Tudor Royal Proclamations, Volume 3: The Later Tudors, 1588–1603* (New Haven: Yale University Press, 1969), 3: 245; cf. 2: 466.

[35] *Behemoth*, ed. William Molesworth (New York: Burt Franklin, 1963), pp. 130, 158.

[36] *Cosmographie* (1652), p. 270.

[37] See Michel Foucault, "Questions on Geography," in *Power/Knowledge*, ed. Colin Gordon (New York: Pantheon Books, 1980), pp. 69–70.

manners."[38] By subordinating to a transhistorical, transindividual identity the viewpoint of observers historically situated in space and time, and by stretching this identity over millennia, the personification of London unified in one body the city's discontinous spaces and naturalized the erratic development of its culture.

The dynamic contradictions in London's cultural development did not go unnoticed in other literary genres, but their incorporation into topographical writing, which was geared more heavily toward preserving the official interests of the neofeudal state, required the dismantling of the whole framework that supported this genre, the substitution, for the city's figurative humanity, of the humanity of the individual observer situated in historic time and space. This substitution occurred gradually, during the seventeenth century, as the cultural facts of urban life began to be conceptually opposed to nature, and as the human status once claimed by the city began to be appropriated to individual observers situated in an unnaturally changeful, even monstrous, landscape. That landscape was increasingly understood as having a dramatic and tumultuous history, as being formed and deformed by divergent interests, parties, groups, and populations. To trace the dominant models for describing cities, and to examine their use, meaning, and eventual demise in descriptions of London, is thus to trace not only changing perceptions, but the waning force of a neofeudal political framework in the face of an urbanizing process it had long contained.

Paradigms and personification

For Renaissance writers, the pleasures of geography were frequently the pleasures of intellectual power. Sir Thomas Elyot, for example, explained that in geography a reader was able "in one houre, to beholde those realmes, cities, sees, ryuers, and mountaynes, that uneth in an olde mans life can nat be iournaide and pursued ... I can nat tell what more pleasure shulde happen to a gentil witte than to beholde in his owne house euery thynge that with in all the worlde is contained."[39] This pleasurable sense of power – of appropriating a vast public space to the private recess of the study and the mind – was greatly enhanced by the typographical revolution and its treatment of the printed book as a container of knowledge readily mastered and possessed. Through the psychogeometric apparatus of print, the world was plotted and contained in the great cosmographies and atlases of Munster, Franck, Ortelius and

---

[38] Quoted in G. E. Mingay, *Georgian London* (London: B. T. Batsford, 1975), p. 20.
[39] *The Boke Named the Gouernour*, ed. H. H. S. Croft (2 vols. 1883; rpt. New York: Burt Franklin, 1967), 1: 76, 77–78.

Mercator.[40] It was not lost on topographers like Jodocus Hondius that the powers being claimed for the genre of the printed Atlas had once been those of a Titan.

The cities of Europe, regarded as wonders of the world even in the much older chronicle tradition,[41] quickly became a special concern of the new topography. The world atlases of Ortelius and Mercator were splendidly matched by the urban atlases of Georg Braun and Franz Hogenberg (1573ff.), of Matthias Merian (1633), and of Joan Blaeu (1663). The earliest of these, Braun and Hogenberg's *Civitates Orbis Terrarum*, grew to six folio volumes over several decades and inspired a host of surveys of the world's cities, including those by Adriano Romano (1585), Giovanni Botero (1588), and Hippolytus Collibus (1600). Together with the routiers and roadbooks that began to appear at the same time, these works reflect a widespread tendency to organize the world as a transnational grid of urban communities. The settled world, James Howell explained in 1657, might be compared "to a giant piece of embroidery, enchas'd up and down, whereof the most bossie, and richest compactest parts are Towns and Cities."[42] The formal apparatus of works devoted to this network is one of their most striking features; their tendency to epitomize, list, enumerate, and tabulate forms an urbane language of description by which large things are contained and written small.

What such a language must perforce assume is the conceptual means for simplifying the complex, for reducing the abundant, disparate, and changing facts of urban life to telling and economical schemes. Indeed, just as important as actual descriptions of cities were the metalanguages, the models or paradigms, which helped to structure the art of description. Behind the image of London in the works of the major Tudor and Stuart topographers lie a number of interrelated paradigms, which were available to these writers both directly and through the earlier descriptions from which they borrowed. Three of the most influential come from the fields of Renaissance statecraft, Ramist dialectic, and classical rhetoric. These paradigms demonstrate the exercise of powers which were not merely intellectual but ideological. Implicit in the intellectual shapes inscribed upon the cultural facts of urban life were a series of assumptions by which these facts were naturalized and subjected to the

---

[40] See, e.g., Svetlana Alpers, *The Art of Describing: Dutch Art in the Seventeenth Century* (University of Chicago Press, 1983), p. 133; Walter Ong, "System, Space, and Intellect in Renaissance Symbolism," in *The Barbarian Within* (New York: Macmillan, 1962), pp. 77–78.

[41] See J. K. Hyde, "Medieval Descriptions of Cities," *Bulletin of the John Rylands Library*, 48 (1966), 310; Antonia Gransden, "Realistic Observation in Twelfth-Century England," *Speculum*, 47 (1972), 29–51.   [42] *Londonoplis* (1657), p. 382.

interests of economic and political power. To describe a city through such paradigms was not only to know it but, implicitly, to control it.

The first of these paradigms emerged not from the intellectual needs of the printed book but from the practical needs of Renaissance diplomacy. Many descriptions of Tudor London as well as a basic scheme for describing cities in general may be traced to the Venetian senate, which around 1500 began to require detailed reports, or *relazioni*, on foreign states from the ambassadors it sent abroad. So essential was this intelligence that the Venetian authorities issued a four-part rubric for generating a relation:

i. These things are required for making a relation. First to describe the situation of the province ... and in how many lesser regions and provinces it is divided, not omitting to name the principal cities.

ii. It is necessary to treat of the quality of that province, that is to say the temperature and value of the air, likewise of the value of the waters, of the fertility or sterility of the crops

iii. It is customary to discuss the inhabitants, showing their customs, and ways, colour, stature, and character...

iv. It is necessary to come to particulars of the prince... his person, life, and customs, ... his revenues and expenses.[43]

In most of the surviving ambassadorial reports from England, information about the prince and politics at court dominates the other categories, yet it is rare to find a report that does not cover all four categories, usually in the specified order. London figured heavily, almost exclusively, in the part of the reports where cities should be mentioned, and quite remarkably most of the ambassadors appear simply to have applied the same four-fold scheme to the city itself, discussing first the natural features and resources of the site, second the artificial fabric, third the population, and fourth, the city government.[44] Robert Dallington's tabular arrangement of a similar scheme in *A Method for Travell* (1598, 1605) suggests that these four main categories may have been produced by crossing Aristotle's distinction between *res* and *homines* (the two essential considerations in Aristotle's sketch of an ideal *polis*) with the distinction between matter and form.[45] This is confirmed by the

---

[43] Pietro Donazzolo, *I Viaggiatori Veneti Minori* (1927), pp. 6–7, quoted in Clare Williams, tr., *Thomas Platter's Travels in England, 1599* (London: Jonathan Cape, 1937), p. 73. Cf. Marco Foscarini, *Della Letteratura Veneziana* (Venice, 1854), pp. 488–491; E. Aberi, ed., *Relazioni degli ambasciatori Veneti al Senato*, serie 1a, vol. 1, p. xx.

[44] For examples, see Francesco Capello, *Relatione ... dell' Isola d' Inghilterra*, ed. Charlotte A. Sneyd (London: Camden Society, 1847), pp. 42–46; Andreas Franciscus, *Itinerarium Britanniae*, in *Two Italian Accounts of Tudor England*, tr. C. V. Malfatti (Barcelona, 1953), pp. 32–38; and the reports in the *Calendar of State Papers, Venetian Series* by Mario Savorgnano (1533) (vol. 4, no. 682); Giacomo Sorano (1554) (vol. 5, no. 934); and Giovanni Michiel (1557), (vol. 6, pt. 2, no. 884). [45] *Politics* 1.5, 7.4.

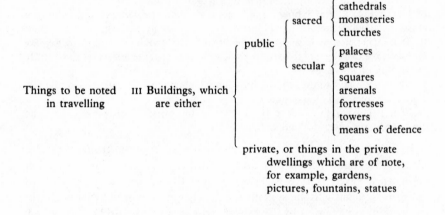

ɪ The name of the city, and the reason for the name,
    if extant
    Item: the founder, augmenter (enlarger), or
    renewer of the place

ɪɪ {
1 Rivers, each of them,
    their course, length, source
2 The seaside or harbor
3 Mountains
4 Woods, groves, or other things of note

Things to be noted   ɪɪɪ Buildings, which
in travelling   are either

public {
    sacred {
        cathedrals
        monasteries
        churches
    }
    secular {
        palaces
        gates
        squares
        arsenals
        fortresses
        towers
        means of defence
    }
}

private, or things in the private
    dwellings which are of note,
    for example, gardens,
    pictures, fountains, statues

ɪᴠ Method of Government,
    and things pertaining
    to it
{
1 The assembly, its members, and
    honest servants of the city
2 Schools, method of educating and
    training youth
    Item: learned men and libraries
3 Vulgar customs. Food and drink.
    Item, workshops
}

Fig. 1 Diagram from Nathan Chytraeus, *Variorum
in Europa Itinerum Deliciae* (1594)

encyclopedia of J. H. Alsted, who noted in tabular form that things in
cities are to be analyzed according to *locus* and *structurae*, and that men
in cities are to be analyzed according to a scale of offices that run from
agricolae and *artifices* to *senatores* and *judices*.[46] By implication, cities
convert natural resources into cultural forms just as rulers shape inchoate
political circumstance into order.

[46] *Cursus philosophici encyclopedia* (Herborn, 1620), p. 1657; Alsted elsewhere invokes the
four-part model of *res naturales, res artificiales, populus,* and *magistratus*, p. 23.

This four-part rubric, which justified the city as the cultural perfection of nature and its rulers as the perfectors of its people, found its way into both manuscript and printed descriptions of London by such Latin humanists as Domenico Mancini (c. 1487), John Major (1521), Polydore Vergil (1523), and Paolo Giovio (1548). In turn, these descriptions made their way – often verbatim – into compilers like Bale, Munster, Ortelius, and Braun, who influenced Camden and his contemporaries.

In addition to such embodiments in prose descriptions, however, the four-part Aristotelian model also found a reincarnation in another metalanguage – a metalanguage worked out primarily in the travel manuals and Ramist treatises of Germany. The *artes peregrinandi*, manuals designed for the aid of travellers, contained much practical and moralizing advice, but they also offered specific suggestions for what things should be observed in travelling. These guidelines were essential not only for writing the requisite journal, but also for reducing the bewildering variety of urban details to a manageable shape. The emphasis fell on method, with which, Albrecht Meier promised, "the thicke mistes of ignorance, and hard conception will soone be scattered, and the same converted into a quicke sight, and illumination of the senses."[47] The concept of "method" in these manuals owes a great deal to the influence of Ramus. German Ramism, however, was most fruitful in the hybrid practitioners known by their contemporaries as "Mixts," who were "followers in part of Ramus and in part of Aristotle."[48] Not surprisingly, then, the four-part Aristotelian model dominates a scheme proposed by the Ramist Hilary Pyrckmair. "When the names of the city and their derivation have been examined," Pyrckmair explains, the first of the external things to be examined are the site, and then the walls, fortifications, gates, and such things; next come the streets, markets, fountains, and gardens; then the buildings, "which are either public or private. The public can best be seen divided into two parts," the sacred and the profane. Finally come the internal considerations, the people and the civic and ecclesiastical government.[49]

The power of such schemes to codify the landscape is most apparent, however, when they take their most rigidly Ramist form as dichotomous diagrams. In these diagrams, the mastery of culture over nature, and of rulers over citizens, is enshrined as the visual mastery of space over time, eternal laws over history. Identical versions of one such diagram were

---

[47] *Certaine Briefe, and Speciall Instructions for Gentlemen, Merchants, Students, Souldiers, Mariners, &c. Employed in Seruices Abrode*, tr. Philip Jones (1589), sig. A3.

[48] See Walter J. Ong, *Ramus, Method, and the Decay of Dialogue* (Cambridge, Mass.: Harvard University Press, 1958), p. 299.

[49] *De Arte Apodemica*, pp. 21–33; cf. *The Traueiler of Ierome Turler* (1575), pp. 51–58.

published by Nathan Chytraeus in 1594 and Paul Hentzner in 1627.[50]
Both Chytraeus and Hentzner had in fact written descriptions of London
based on their visits, and their paradigm is perhaps closest in shape to the
descriptions of London by the major English topographers and antiquaries. Their scheme divides the standard topics into four basic
categories: 1) the city's name, founder, and augmenters, 2) site, 3)
buildings, 4) government, education, and social life. The last three of
these cover the topics in the four-part Venetian rubric as it was applied
to cities (site, fabric, governed, governors) while the first repeats a feature
– the city's name and founders – found throughout the German travel
guides and Ramist schemes.[51] There is thus a striking persistence of both
a basic set of topics and a basic order or arrangement. There seems to
have been not only a core of features regarded as essential to a city, but
also an overall conception of their relationship.

One such conception certainly remains the old Venetian–Aristotelian
paradigm. But the preoccupation with names, founders, and augmenters
comes from a third framework for description – the framework of ancient
rhetoric. There are in fact relatively few examples of urban description in
classical literature and relatively few instructions to be found in the
rhetorical treatises of Aristotle and Cicero. Quintilian, however, contains
the very useful hint that "Cities are praised after the same fashion as
men. The founder takes the place of the parent, and antiquity carries
great authority... The virtues and vices revealed by their deeds are the
same as in private individuals... Their citizens enhance their fame just as
children bring honour to their parents" (3.7.26). The *Rhetor* of
Menander similarly explains that the praise of cities draws on both the
rules for praising countries and "those which relate to individuals. Thus
we should select 'position' [i.e. site] from topics relating to countries,
and origins, actions, accomplishments from those relating to individuals."[52]

The bearing of this on the rubric of urban encomia is perhaps clarified
by the schemes devised for the praise of persons by Menander's
predecessors and contemporaries. For example, Aphthonius, a major
influence on Renaissance rhetoric, advises that the principal topics in
praising a person are ancestors and parents; upbringing and the attributes
which are its result; the beauties and exploits of body and mind;

---

[50] Chytraeus, *Variorum in Europa Itinerum Deliciae* (1594); Hentzner, *Itinerarium...
Angliae* (Breslau, 1627), unpaginated front-matter.

[51] As, for example, in the most massive of all tabular analyses of cities in Theodor
Zwinger's *Methodus Apodemica* (Basle, 1577), pp. 187–188.

[52] *Menander Rhetor*, ed. D. A. Russell and N. G. Wilson (Oxford; Clarendon Press, 1981),
pp. 32–33.

and finally a comparison that proves the case.[53] Significantly, when Aphthonius' scheme was translated by Richard Rainold in *The Foundacion of Rhetorike*, it was offered as a model for "the praise of all the Britaines: or of all the citezeins of London."[54] Rainold's hint for converting praise into prosopopoeia was no idle suggestion, for in the descriptive rubrics of figures like Pyrckmair, Chytraeus, and Hentzner, the topics are disposed in just the way a person is to be praised, beginning with the city's name, its founders, and augmenters. The advantages of birth and circumstance are embodied in discussion of the city's site, and the beauties and accomplishments of the person find their counterparts in the city's fabric, its government, and its worthy offspring. The personified London of Dekker's *The Dead Tearme* (1608) thus glosses the structure of her self-portrait by explaining that

because al Cities were bound in common ciuility, in pollicies, and in honour to maintaine their Names, their Callings, their Priuilidges, and those Ancient houses that Spring out of them, I wil ... Annatomize my selfe; euen from head to foot, thou shalt know euery limbe of me, and with how many parts my bodie is deuided. My birth, my bringing vp, and my rising shall bee ... manifest.[55]

The personification of the city is a very old tradition which originates in the myths of the Cretan and Asian goddess Cybele (see Fig. 4). In *The Aeneid*, Virgil claims that in Crete, the cradle of Trojan civilization, the ancient mother–goddess first took the form of Cybele (3.104–113); Anchises later likens Rome's surrounding wall to *Berecynthia mater ... turrita*, the great goddess Berecynthia tower-crowned (6.784–785). Both in Virgil's narrative and in general, Cybele is "characterized by her steady movement westward and her extraordinary assimilation into other, invariably more austere, versions of the Great Mother."[56]

What is essential to the strategy of personification is not simply that it bestows upon the city the familiar lineaments of human nature, extended into a lifespan that lasts for centuries, but that it subjects the city to the ideology of gender. Cities are personified as feminine because culture "recognizes that women are active participants in its special processes, but at the same time sees them as rooted in, as having more direct affinity

---

[53] Introduction to *Menander Rhetor*, pp. xxiv–xxix. The comparison of cities is not only a topic in the procedure of personification but a procedure of description in its own right. The history of this procedure extends from John Coke's *Debate Between the Heralds of England and France* (1550), to James Howell's *Parallel by Way of Corollary Betwixt London and Other Great Cities of the World* (1657) to Sir William Petty's statistical *Observations upon the Cities of London and Rome* (1687).

[54] *The Foundacion of Rhetorike* (1563), sig. κ4.

[55] *Non-Dramatic Works*, ed. A. B. Grosart (5 vols. London, 1884), 4: 71.

[56] Peter S. Hawkins, "From Mythography to Myth-making: Spenser and the *Magna Mater* Cybele," *Sixteenth Century Journal*, 12 (1981), 52.

with, nature."[57] Given this situation of female identity midway between nature and culture, it is not surprising to find so much overlap between the Aristotelian frameworks, which naturalize the facts of culture, and the rhetorical schemes for personifying cities; nor is it surprising to find this overlap inscribed authoritatively in the tables of Ramists. On the one hand, the biological role of women in the process of reproduction provided an analogy by which to rationalize the generation of wealth. At the same time, the domestic role of women in child-rearing and family life, understood to rest upon an affection "indifferent to sex, age, or other possible affiliations,"[58] provided a psychic model for social communion, and thus for the conversion of nature into culture. On the other hand, the subjection of feminine to masculine in family life could justify the subordination of domestic loyalties to the higher claims of public life. In the case of England, the feminine gender of London (see Figs. 3 and 5) placed implicit limits on the power of the city in relation to other groups and communities in the kingdom. By analogy to the rule of exogamous marriage, the subordination of the London commune to the neofeudal state prevented it from being seen as a self-sufficient, closed community and stressed its bonds of alliance – and thus loyalties – to the whole kingdom.

Insofar as it is a history of gender-typing, the history of personification is also a history of sexual ambivalence, as the Book of Revelation's contrast between Jerusalem, the bride of Christ, and Rome, the whore of Babylon, attests.[59] Thomas Dekker demonstrates this ambivalence when he observes that London "hast all things in thee to make thee fairest, and all things in thee to make thee foulest: for thou art attir'de like a Bride, ... but there is much harlot in thine eyes."[60] Such images drew upon traditional antifeminist archetypes, and in many respects they formed but the ideological obverse to the heroic matron of encomiastic description. The more potent sense of monstrosity lay not, however, in the devouring ogress of satire – who was an *alter-ego* of the civilizing

[57] Sherry B. Ortner, "Is Female to Male as Nature is to Culture?" in *Women, Culture, and Society*, ed. Michelle Zimbalist Rosaldo and Louise Lamphere (Stanford University Press, 1974), p. 73.   [58] Ibid., p. 83.

[59] See William S. Heckscher, "Goethe and Weimar," in *Art and Literature: Studies in Relationship*, ed. Egon Verheyen (Durham: Duke University Press, 1985), pp. 208–209, cited in Gail Kern Paster, *The Idea of the City in the Age of Shakespeare* (Athens: University of Georgia Press, 1985), pp. 5–6, 20–21.

[60] *The Seuen Deadly Sinnes of London* (1606), in *Non-Dramatic Works*, 4: 10–11. Cf. Nashe, *Pierce Penniless His Supplication to the Devil, The Unfortunate Traveller and Other Works*, ed. J. B. Steane (Harmondsworth: Penguin, 1972), p. 78; Thomas Middleton, *The Black Booke* (1604), in *Works*, ed. A. H. Bullen (8 vols. rpt. New York: AMS Press, 1964), 8: 22; Donald Lupton, *London and the Country Carbonadoed* (1632), in *Aungerville Society Reprints* (Edinburgh, 1881–82), p. 59.

mother – but in the completely dehumanized metropolis, the poly-morphic and discontinuous domain that began to be understood as a secondary creation threatening its human creators. Whether satiric or encomiastic, the personified city depended instead upon a temporal framework that extended the city's life over centuries, subjecting the experiential incoherencies of urban life to a unified, supra-personal identity.

The better to examine the separate incarnations and eventual demise of this identity in the works of Tudor–Stuart London's major topographers, it will be useful first to demonstrate, with reference to these writers and their contemporaries, how the Aristotelian harmonies of nature with culture and the rhetorical uses of gender coalesced as ideologies with each of the topics outlined in the idealized space of the Ramist diagram. The discussion is based on the influential table printed in Chytraeus and Hentzner (see Fig. 1).

The first categories in the table – name, founder, and augmenters – establish the venerable age of the city's persona. Just as the name of Rome could be traced to Romulus, or backward through the etymology of the Greek ῥώμη from Rome to army to bodily strength, so countless topographers traced the name of *Trinobantia* (by false etymology) to Trojan Brute, London's mythical founder. By the logic of personifica-tion, the changes in the city's name reflected her loyal submission to a series of royal masters. Dekker's London, for example, explains that she changed her name from *Trinobantia* to London when "Lud challenging me as his owne, tooke away none of my dignities, but as women married to great persons, loose their old names, so did I mine being wedded to that king."[61] The macaronic history of London's many different names, William Lambarde argued, was "no light Argument that [London] hath bene of great price these many Yeares,"[62] but Dekker's London was quick to add that she had "bin loued of our kings, because euer since haue [I] to our kinges bin loyall"(4: 75). Just as important as London's names were her epithets and honorifics – the "titles, Stiles, and Honours of our Metropolis," as Dekker called them. John Speed, for example, styled London "the cedar among all trees, the model of the land, the mart of the world, the lady of the sea." Dekker graced her as "the Queene of Cities & Queene-mother ouer her owne: her Kings royall chamber, his Golden Key, his store-house ... the Mistris of the Sciences, a Nurse to all the shiers in England."

The table ties the name together with the founder, and there is more involved here than the sanction of antiquity, for the notion of a founder

<hr>

[61] *Non-Dramatic Works*, 4: 74–75.
[62] *Dictionarium Anglicae Topographicum & Historicum* (c. 1570), p. 168.

implied that a city was not the product of organic growth but the result of a single decisive act performed on one day.[63] Through the foundation ritual, in theory, a sacred geometry was laid out at the moment of the city's foundation and fixed its identity for all time.

The augmenters and renewers who are linked in the table with the founder further emphasize the idea of a fixed and unalterable beginning. Augmentation is tied to a fundamental authority, to a unique, unrepeatable event.[64] Augmentation can extend but not begin and must always be submitted to the authority of the foundation. Linguistically, augmentation permanently excludes the idea of any new beginning; it asserts the sacredness of the foundation and declares it true for all generations. The sacral nature of the foundation is indicated in Fabyan's assertion in his verse encomium of London that "Christ is the very stone / That the city is set upon."[65] In countless descriptions the mythical King Lud renews London's walls and gates and gives the renewed city his name, but does not alter the fundamental act of his ancestor. It was perhaps not only practicality that led the series of royal proclamations opposing the chaos of "continuall new Buildings, and addition and increase of Buildings," repeatedly to stress that any new building was to be "upon the foundation of a former dwelling."[66]

Through their sacralizing of space, naming, founding, and augmenting are thus associated with the recurrent topics of walls, shape, and gates. These appear later in a separate category, but in most of the paradigms they represent the first of the city's physical aspects to be discussed. It is here that the potentially disturbing topographical emphasis on spatial divisions and partitions was subjected to ideologies of unified order. Anthony Munday observed that "the walles of any Citty, were termed of the Grecians... the cloathing or Garments of the Cittie." In the description of Tudor–Stuart London there are many poignant attempts to extract an ideal, symbolic figure from a misshappen reality. Nathan Chytraeus, for example, likens the city's shape to a half moon,[67] while Richard Zouche compares it to a rainbow.[68] John Stow, waxing uncharacteristically idealistic, but retaining his typical eye for mundane detail, likens the city to the "forme of a bow, except that denting in betwixt Criplegate, and Aldersgate" (1:9). James Howell's *Londonopolis*,

[63] Varro, *De Lingua Latina*, v.144; Plutarch, *Parallel Lives*, Romulus, ix–xii. See Fustel de Coulanges, *The Ancient City* (Garden City: Doubleday, 1966), pp. 134–143.

[64] John Guillory, *Poetic Authority: Spenser, Milton, and Literary History* (New York: Columbia University Press, 1983), pp. 262–267.

[65] *Concordance of Histories* (1516), sig. AA.

[66] *Stuart Royal Proclamations*, 1:193, 267–268.

[67] *Hodoeporica* (Frankfurt, 1575), p. 170.

[68] *The Doue, or, Passages of Cosmography* (1613), ed. Richard Walker (Oxford, 1839), p. 47.

based on Stow, proposes nobly that London is shaped like a laurel leaf, but then goes on to add, in view of the sprawling suburbs which by 1657 had grown larger than the walled City itself, that "the Suburbs of London are larger then the Body of the City, which make some compare her to a Jesuites Hat, whose brims are far larger than the Block."[69] As for the internal geometry of London, writers remarked that London Bridge made London the crossroads of England, though they differed in where they placed the crossroads.

Suppressed by an idealizing geometry, the cultural processes of growth and change were harmonized with nature in the second of the major topics, the discussion of the city's site and natural resources. In the case of London, such discussion commonly stressed the interplay between economic and aesthetic considerations, as in Camden's claim that London is "sweetly situate in a rich and fertile soil ... on the gentle ascent and rising of a hill, hard by the *Thamis* side, the most milde Merchant, as one would say, of all things that the world doth yield: ... A man would say that seeth the shipping there, that it is, as it were, a very wood of trees disbranched to make glades and let in light: So shaded it is with masts and sailes" (p. 422). If the city's names and handsome shape were graces it inherited from its ancestral founders, its resources were the rightful fortune at its disposal. Nearly all the London panoramas of the period make this point by foregrounding the Thames and its shipping, thus emphasizing a fundamental reciprocity between the powers of nature and culture (see Fig. 6). River and city, fluid and fabric, brought together a natural timelessness with human history. As John Speed put it, "the wealth of this Citie (as Isai once spake of Nilus) growes from the Reuenewes and Haruest of her south-bounding Thames: whose traffique for marchandising, is like that of Tyrus, whereof Ezekiel speakes... Upon this Thamesis the ships of Tharsis seeme to ride."

To the realm of culture and artifice belong the buildings of the table's third major category, including the walls and gates already mentioned. In Chytraeus' table, as in most such schemes, the distinctions between public and private, sacred and profane space articulate a kind of social order.[70] Not apparent from the table, however, is the extent to which, for antiquarians like Camden and Stow, London's buildings were also a means by which time was rendered visible, by which past generations left their mark on the civic heritage. This is true not only for the description

---

[69] *Londonopolis* (1657), p. 404.

[70] Most of the great descriptions of London embody some version of this three-part model, beginning with one of the earlier antiquarians, Lambarde, who passes from "the Bodye of the Citie," "the walls and gates," to "the Residue of the publicque Buildinges," and from these "publicque Ornamentes" to "Ecclesiastical Workes" and finally to "Private Buildinges" (pp. 171, 174, 178).

Fig. 2 Personifications of Rome (*left*) and Constantinople (*right*).
Ivory consular diptych, sixth century AD

Fig. 3 Personifications of Rome (*left*) and London (*right*). Edmund Bolton, *Nero Caesar* (1623)

Fig. 4 Berecynthia. Vincenzo Cartari, *Le imagini de i dei de gli antiche* (Venice, 1571)

Fig. 5 Personifications of Westminster and London. Michael
Drayton, *Poly-Olbion* (1622)

Fig. 6 Long view of London. Matthieu Merian (after J. C. Visscher, 1616), *Arcontologia cosmica* (1638)

Fig. 7 View of London. John Norden, *Civitas Londini* (c. 1600

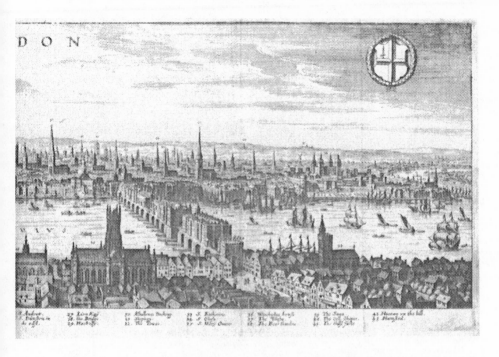

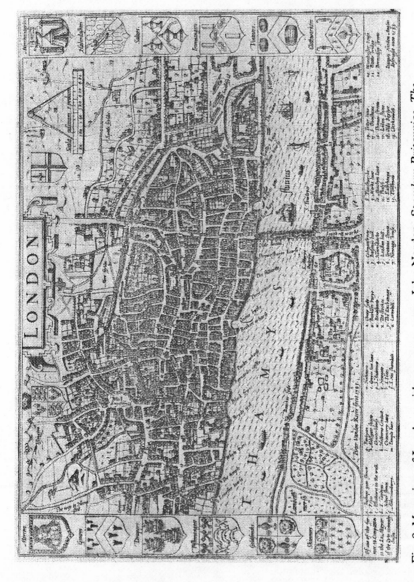

Fig. 8 Map-view of London, with company arms. John Norden, *Speculum Britanniae. The Firste Parte* (1593)

The
High and mighty
Prince, IAMES
KING of great
Britane Fraunce
and Ireland &c

Francisc Delaram
sculpsit.

Behold the shadow of great Britains KING
Whose Fame throughout the World the Muses sing
Heavens graunt Thy happy dayes may never end
Since on Thy life millions of lives depend

Comptor Holland
Excudit London.

Fig. 9 King James I on horseback. Francis Delaram (c. 1610)

of individual buildings but also for the temporal sequence or historical priority assigned to sacred, civic, and private construction.

The division of the city into public and private, sacred and profane space comes ultimately from Aristotle's *Politics* (7. 8–9). In terms of the actual economy and social life of Renaissance cities, however, the three-part model was narrow and exclusive, focused solely on the civic elite and the essential spaces which are defined as theirs. Among formal descriptions of Elizabethan London there are few signs of the small retailers, craftsmen, and casual laborers, the aliens, transients, vagabonds, and paupers who likely made up more than half of greater London's population.[71] The social model implied by the division of space is not, of course, without a certain dynamism; it articulates the many types of association that form a citizen, from the diocese, the parish, and its vestry, to the wards, precincts, guilds, schools, and militia, to the family, the household, and the business. This dynamism is limited, however, to the citizen elite; it does not account for dislocations and asymmetries, and it moves in a general direction away from the female, domestic sphere of social communion toward a hierarchical, patriarchal political culture.

The meaning of this movement comes out most fully in the final topic of the table, the discussion of people and government. Insofar as human resources come last in a scheme dominated by the idea of personification, citizens and leaders are not so much the makers of the city as its legacy, the "famous Patriots, and Worthies, which she hath produc'd and bred."[72] In many descriptions the treatment of the city's offspring extends the role of gender to include the nurturing of an elite whose loyalties ultimately reach out beyond the city. As one verse encomium put it,

> This Queene of citties, Lady of this Ile,
> … Upon her lap did nourse those sonnes of Fame,
> Whose deeds do now nobilitate her name.[73]

A special stress falls upon the transition into fame and power in a 1588 manuscript description by William Smith. Smith begins with eleven pages on the site and monuments of London, but the next ninety pages are given over to a discourse "Of the State and Pollicie of London," which centers on a lengthy account of the protocols of the Lord Mayor's

---

[71] On the proportion of freemen in London, see Valerie Pearl, "Change and Stability in Seventeenth-Century London," *The London Journal*, 5 (1970), 13; Steven Rappaport, "Social Structure and Mobility in Sixteenth-Century London: Part I," *The London Journal*, 9 (1983), 112; Roger Finlay and Beatrice Shearer, "Population Growth and Suburban Expansion," in *London 1500–1700*, p. 44; A. L. Beier, "Social Problems in Elizabethan London," *The Journal of Interdisciplinary History*, 9 (1978), 211–213.

[72] James Howell, *Londonopolis*, p. 1.

[73] Richard Niccols, *Londons Artillerie* (1616), p. 60.

procession.[74] As Robert Darnton has explained, to use a procession for the purposes of description is to construct a model of society which is not so much divided into classes as segmented in graduated degrees.[75] These degrees form a syntagmatic chain that leads upward toward the elite patriarchal leadership which holds the city to obedience. Norden emphasized these circumscribing limits when he bordered the *Speculum Britanniae* map with the arms of London's Twelve Great Livery Companies, or when he depicted a triumphal procession of the city's aldermen across the bottom of his *Civitas Londini* view (see Figs. 7 and 8).

The boundary of neofeudal political culture placed around the city was permeable in both directions. First of all the city effected a transition which took its leading sons, if not its daughters, outside the domestic urban field and into the fields of opportunity – the court and landed aristocracy – where great prestige and power lay. It was a great tribute to London, Edmund Bolton wrote, that "all the partes of England are full of families, either originally raised to the dignity of gentlemen out of this one most famous place, or so restored and enriched as to seem to amount to an original raising."[76] Not only did attention to London's over-achieving sons conceal from sight the more spectacular failures; it also implied that London was the garden where nature was nurtured. Thus William Harrison traced the rise of a new rural gentry to London, "from which (as it were from a seedplot) courtiers, lawyers, and merchants be continuously transplanted."[77]

Yet as Harrison's garden image suggests, the very metaphorical means by which London contributed to the court and monarchy provided for its cultivation by those higher powers. Placed midway between nature and culture, London's status was reinforced by a gender ideology that made it the "nymph of Britain, graced with the seat of Kings."[78] Thomas Churchyard wrote that London was

> the Maiden toune, that keepes her selfe so cleane,
> That none can touche, nor staine in trothe, by any cause or meane.
> ... Here is the soil and seat of Kyngs, and place of precious price.
> Here worthies makes their mansions still, & buildeth stately towres,
> Here sitts the Nobles of the realme, in golden halles and bowers.[79]

The visual counterpart here is not the bird's-eye views of Norden, framed by the city's leaders or their coats of arms (see Figs. 7 and 8), but

[74] *A Brieff Description of the Famous Cittie of London*, BM Harley MS 6363.
[75] "A Bourgeois Puts His World in Order: The City as a Text," in *The Great Cat Massacre and Other Episodes in French Cultural History* (1984; rpt. New York: Vintage Books, 1985), pp. 122–123.   [76] *The Cities Advocate* (1629), sig. Kv.
[77] Quoted in Raymond Williams, *The Country and the City* (New York: Oxford University Press, 1973), p. 49.   [78] Jan Sictor, *Panegyricon inaugurale* (1637), sig. B2v.
[79] *A Light Bondell of Liuly Discourses Calld Churchyardes Charge* (1580), sig. D4v.

the long view of Francis Delaram (c. 1610), where the city appears between the legs of a rearing horse bearing James I (see Fig. 9).

Changing identities

If in some respects the topical scheme of urban description resembles a mold into which any city might be fit, the overriding trope of personification was managed by such major topographers as Camden, Norden, Speed, and Stow to elicit quite different personae or identities, and to signal a fundamental overdetermination or instability within the neofeudal lineaments of the personification trope. Camden, for example, begins with a list of epithets and names, and with a discussion of the site, but then he takes the innovative step of combining the city's topography with a narrative history. After discussing the fabulous foundation myths on which London "fathereth her originalls," he turns to the firmer ground of recorded history and surviving monuments. He lays heaviest stress, however, on the glorious Norman period, when "the windes were laid, the clowds disparted and golden daies indeed shone upon" London, "since when it neuer susteined any great calamity to speak of." Following the Conquest, London, "through the speciall favour and indulgence of Princes obteined verie large and great Immunities, beganne to be called *The Kings Chamber*, and so flourished anew with fresh trade and traffique of merchants" (p. 427).

Topographically, this period of growth and prosperity takes Camden outside the City proper to the new suburbs, which "stretched forth from the gates a great length on every side but westward especially which are the greatest, and best peopled" (p. 427). By moving topographically westward, and by stressing the establishment of Westminster as the seat of Norman kings, Camden implicitly traces the greatness of modern London not to the City government, not to merchant life or trade, but to the royal power that makes it the capital of *Britannia*. In other words, London's civic and mercantile achievements are merely the by-product of its role as capital. Its powers and privileges are held at the pleasure of England's monarchs, and after London's "forme of common wealth" has been "established" by royal charters it becomes "incredible to tell how much London grew, and groweth still" (p. 435). Only when this is established does Camden turn finally to the fabric within the walls, to the civic and commercial buildings of the city and to the "forward service and loyalty" of London's citizens to their prince.

Unlike Camden before him, and Speed after him, Norden does not explicitly invoke an ideology of gender, and this perhaps reflects his relatively greater emphasis on London's independent civic life. After an account of London's names and mythical history, Norden turns, like Camden, to a three-part narrative which recounts the city's early history from Roman to Saxon times and then to the Norman Conquest. Norman history culminates, however, not with the royal settlement of Westminster but with the evolution of London's government. After a series of struggles with the City, King John "granted vnto the Citie by his letters pattents, that they should yeerely choose vnto themselues, a Mayor," and "in the time of H.3. also the Aldermen of the Citie were ordeined" (p. 28). There follows a list of the City's twenty-five aldermanic wards, to which the parishes in each are subordinated. Only after this sketch of London's civic evolution does Norden turn to the city's fabric and charitable institutions. The shape of Norden's London is no doubt a function of his segregation of Westminster for separate treatment elsewhere, yet this exclusion is itself a function of the connection he draws between the growth of London and the evolution of the constitutional mechanisms of the state.

Norden's position was adopted by Anthony Munday in his *Briefe Chronicle, of the Successe of Times, from the Creation of the World to This Instant* (1611). For Munday, all of history, beginning with the creation, was meant to lead to his final chapters on the "Originall, Antiquity and modern estate of London." Essentially a synopsis of Stow's *Survey*, these chapters were nevertheless colored by Norden's view of civic evolution. In Munday's account, London's history was a story of empowerment, as the City "cast off the yoke of strange confusion" and "came to haue command within it selfe, under the awe and gracious fauor of the worthie Kinges and Potentates, who made choyse of Magistrates, to be their Deputies" (sigs. B2–B2v). Political enfranchisement and urbanization went hand-in-hand, "as this worthy Citty grew to encrease, not onely in large extenture and beautie of buildings, but also in election of Companies and Corporations, for better supply of the Magistracy, and conveniency of all the aptest meanes thereto belonging" (sig. A2v).

In the hands of John Speed, the traditional topics are aligned to produce neither a royal nor an independent London, but a providentially ordained world *entrepôt*. In his opening discussion of the names and myths of London, Speed singles out the geographical advantage that makes her "the mart of the world: for thither are brought the silk of Asia, the spices from Africa, the balmes from Grecia, & the riches of both the Indies East & West" (p. 29). As if expanding outward from a religious seed to its civic fruits, Speed then makes Westminster a consequence, not a cause, of London's providential increase: "This London (as it were) disdaining bondage, hath set her selfe on each side, far without the wals, & hath left her West-Gate in the midst, from whence with continuall buildings (still affecting greatnesse) she hath continued her streets vnto a kings Palace and ioined a second Citie to her self." Following this auspicious union, the final movement in Speed's portrait carries the providential expansion outward from two sacred hills astride a river to an economic power that rules the globe:

The wealth of this Citie (as Isai once spoke of Nilus) grows from the Reuenewes and Haruest of her south-bounding Thames; whose traffique for merchandizing, is like that of Tyrus, whereof Ezekiel speaks ... Upon this Thamesis the Ships of Tharsis seeme to ride, and the Nauy, that rightly is termed the Lady of the Sea, spreds her saile. Whence twice with lucky successe hath bin accomplished, the compassing of the vniuersal Globe (p. 29).

Even John Stow's monumental *Survey of London*, which ran to more than five hundred pages in the first edition of 1598, came under the influence of such idealizing schemes. In his earlier chronicles, Stow had been essentially an old-fashioned annalist, and his original research in the City's archives might have produced a misshapen catalogue were it not for the well-established languages of description. For all its bulk, Stow's *Survey* was in structure an orderly account of London's antiquity, site, fabric, government, and worthies. Implicitly organic and prosopopoeic in nature, this structure was nevertheless deeply riven, in Stow's *Survey*, by a striking contrast between temporal continuity and spatial disjunction.

The most original aspect of Stow's achievement was the middle third of the *Survey*, the district-by-district perambulation of the boundaries and monuments of the wards, liberties, and suburbs of London. This innovative topographical center of the *Survey* was preceded and followed, however, by sections more exclusively concerned with the traditional practices and values of the citizen class. At the beginning of the *Survey*, Stow followed his main source, William Fitzstephen's twelfth-century *Descriptio nobilissimae ciuitatis Londoniae*, in a discussion of London's origins, walls, gates, conduits, and bridges, together with a canvass of "the orders and customs, sports and pastimes, watchinges, and martial exercises, and ... the honor and worthines of the Cittizens" (1: 117). At the conclusion of the *Survey*, Stow once again returned to the question of civic honor and ritual with an account of "the pollicie and gouernment, both Ecclesiasticall and ciuill, of London ... maintained by the customes thereof, most laudably vsed before all the time of memory" (2: 124).

Built into the three-part structure of the *Survey*, then, was a distinction between physical fabric and populace, between "sites" and "rites," that was in line with current humanist theory – both with the Aristotelian-Ramist notion that cities could be analyzed according to *res* and *homines*, and with the Aphthonian rhetorical scheme for the laudatory personification of cities. Furthermore, Stow's account of the "honour of citizens, and worthinesse of men" in London (1: 104–117) would have been supported by a wealth of ancient testimony, fashionable among humanists, to the effect that "the men, not the walls, ... make the city."[80] Yet the more likely source for Stow's distinction was Fitzstephen, whose declared aim in his *Descriptio* was to depict "*situm, et rem publicam Londoniae.*"[81] Stow underlined Fitzstephen's distinction by quoting John Bale's assertion that Fitzstephen had written concerning "the site and rites" (*de situ et ritibus*) of London.[82] For Stow, as for Fitzstephen, the topography of the city was ordered and sanctified by civic ritual and ceremonial observance: "I doe not thinke that there is any Citie, wherein are better customs, in frequenting the Churches, in serving God, in keeping holy dayes, in giuing almes, in entertaining straungers, in solemnizing Marriages, in furnishing banquets, celebrating funerals, and burying dead bodies" (1: 80).

In his expansive commentary on Fitzstephen's account of the "Orders and Customes" of London, Stow elaborated on the ceremonial patterns and ritual regulations – from market customs and military musters to mummings, triumphs, and rites of almsgiving – that governed virtually all aspects of urban life. Alongside an elaborate round of seasonal recreations – springtime cockfights and football matches, summertime water-sports, martial games, and dancing, wintertime ice sports and venery – communal custom had prescribed a ritual calendar of religious and civic observances: the Lords of Misrule who presided at Christmas and throughout the festal season between All Hallows' Eve and the Feast of the Purification, the Lenten ridings and Eastertide fetching-in of greenery, the Corpus Christi processions and plays, the Midsummer Watch and shrieval elections, the summertime fairs on saints' feasts. Attended by nobility and clergy as well as citizens, the cycle of traditional events proved, Stow concluded, "that in those dayes, the inhabitants & repayrers to this Citie of what estate soeuer, spirituall or temporal, hauing houses there, liued together in good amity with the citizens, euery man obseruing the customes and orders of the Citty" (1: 84–85).

In Stow's accounts of such ceremonies as the Midsummer marching watch, the processions to the Eastertide Spital sermons, the Lord Mayor's "going to Paules" on religious feasts, and various tourneys, jousts, and royal entries, the city became a sacral space, a physical

---

[80] Thucydides, *History of the Peloponnesian War*, 7.77, tr. Thomas Hobbes (1629), *Hobbes's Thucydides*, ed. Richard Schlatter (New Brunswick: Rutgers University Press, 1975), p. 501. Cf. Alcaeus, frags. 112 line 10, 426; *Coriolanus* 3.1.198.

[81] *Materials for the History of Thomas Becket*, ed. J. C. Robertson and J. B. Sheppard (7 vols. London: Rolls Series, 1875–85), 3: 2.

[82] *Illustrium maioris Britanniae scriptorum summarium* (1548), sig. siiv.

embodiment of ceremonial tradition and community spirit, as men literally trod in the "steps of the forefathers."[83] Walled and gated against invaders, this space was hallowed by local saints – by Becket and Erkenwald, whose cults had until recently been observed by Londoners (1: 333), by the martyred King Edmund, whose body wrought miraculous cures when it was brought into the City through Cripplegate (1: 33), and by Edward the Confessor, whose decision "to make his Sepulcher" on the former site of "a Temple of Apollo" at Westminster lay at the root of London's status as a capital (2: 105). Saints Peter and Paul, whose twin effigies were "of olde ... rudely engrauen" on the City seal (1: 221), gave their names to the City's two main temples – St. Peter's, founded as the first "Archbishops see or Metropolitane" when "Bishops were placed where *Flammines* before had bin" (2: 125), and St. Paul's, built on the site of "a Temple of Iupiter" during the second Christianization of Britain, "wherein Melitus began to bee Bishop in the yeere 619" (2: 127).

In keeping with Fitzstephen's claim that Londoners were ceremonially assiduous in "burying dead bodies," and with Lewis Mumford's theory that the earliest form of the city was the burial ground, the physical space of Stow's London was furthermore hallowed by the dead, not simply by the 1,775 worthy persons whose monuments Stow identified by name, but also by the "innumerable bodies of the dead" interred, in times of plague, in the mass graves of the suburbs – in East Smithfield, at the Charterhouse (containing "aboue 100000. bodies of Christian people"), and in the grounds of Bethlehem hospital, where in 1569 Mayor Thomas Roe buried his wife and countless other Londoners for "the ease of such parrishes... as wanted ground conuenient" (1: 124, 165, 2: 81–82). Indeed, Stow's archaeological impulse was inseparable from his spiritual membership in a community where the past was in a more-or-less continuous state of disinterral. Stow had seen what he believed were the remains of Romans, Britons, and Saxons unearthed in the Spitalfield brick-works. Though he was skeptical about the remains of giants found in London (1: 275, 389), Stow was in little doubt that the civic space was also a domain of spirits. He had himself seen the claw-marks, "three or foure inches deepe" (1: 196) and dating from his father's time, that had been left by the Devil on a midnight visit to St. Michael in Cornhill.

In his allegiance to an explicitly integrated urban order, where the articulations of custom, hierarchy, order and degree were visibly and ritually inscribed on the cityscape – as "the inhabitants and repayrers to this Citie of what state soeuer, ... liued together in good amity, euery man

---

[83] William Fleetwood, *The Effect of the Declaration Made in the Guildhall by M. Recorder of London* (1571), sig. A2.

obseruing the customes & orders of the Citty" – Stow registered his dismay at the decoding and recoding of the landscape by the privatization, commercialization, and theatricalization of public life that he associated with the coming of the Reformation, acquisitive individualism, and the secular bureaucratic state. According to Stow, the gospelling curate who incited a London mob to destroy the great maypole of St. Andrew Undershaft had struck a blow against the whole order of things, maintaining that "the names of the dayes of the week might be changed, the fish dayes to be kept any dayes, ... and the Lent any time, saue only betwixt Shrouetide and Easter" (1 : 144). The corollary to such assaults on the fixed temporal order and its collective, ritual observances was for Stow the transformation of familiar public symbolism into a manipulative theatricality marked by hypocrisy, ostentation, and divisive individualism. The "open pastimes in my youth, being now suppressed" in the post-Reformation climate of religious surveillance and state control, Stow sourly speculated that "worser practices within doores are to be feared" (1 : 95). The pattern of introversion was reinforced by "purpresture" – the feverish encroachment of formerly common space, which encouraged the replacement of outdoor, public recreation into indoor, commercialized leisure. "By the meane of closing in the common grounds," Stow noted, "our Archers for want of roome to shoote abroad, creepe into Bowling Allies, and ordinarie dicing houses, nearer home, where they haue roome enough to hazard money at vnlawfull games" (1: 104). Once restricted to the precincts of Northumberland House, London's "ancient and onely patron of misrule," such dubious establishments now honeycombed the city, "in al places ... increased, and too much frequented" (2: 79); "common to all commers for their money"(1: 149), their commercial nature eroded traditional distinctions while creating new ones between wealth and poverty, fashionable expense and prudent thrift.

The new distinctions were nowhere more apparent than in the public ostentation that Stow associated with the individualized withdrawal from community. Commenting on congestion caused by the newly fashionable coach, Stow observed that "the riding in Wherlicoates and chariots" was formerly "forsaken, except at Coronations and such like spectacles," but "now of late yeares ... there is neither distinction of time, nor difference of persons obserued: for the world runs on wheeles with many, whose parents were glad to goe on foote" (1 : 84). In the spectacle of the public making a spectacle of itself, Stow saw a ceremonial and civic heritage transformed. The common grounds north of the city, once fiercely defended against the saying that "no Londoner ought to goe out of the City, but in the high Waies," were now lost to public use by meanes of inclosure for Gardens, wherein are builded many fayre summer houses, and other such places of the Suburbes, some of them like Midsommer Pageantes, with Towers, Turrets, and Chimney tops, not so much for vse or profite, as for shewe and pleasure, bewraying the vanity of mens mindes, much vnlike the ancient Cittizens, who delighted in the building of Hospitals, and Almes houses for the poore, and therein both imployed their wits, and spent their wealthes in preferment of the common commoditie of this our Citie. (2: 78)

It is primarily in the topographical center of the *Survey*, the perambulation of the wards, that Stow canvasses the many developments that, in transforming the city's sites had also transformed its rites and social fabric – the conversion of religious houses into biscuit bakeries, gun foundries, glass manufactories, and storehouses; the subdivision into mazes of tenements of the houses of the old nobility, whose successors were abandoning the City to take up residence, sometimes in former bishops' properties, in the burgeoning West End; the pestering of the suburbs and liberties with a swollen population of strangers; the expansion of the state bureaucracy in Westminster; the pillage of monuments and charitable bequests by "bold and greedy men of spoyle" (1: 208). In the sharp disjunctures, sudden expansions, and disruptive realignments of the contemporary urban space – the subject of the middle third of the *Survey* – Stow confronted a register of change at odds with the temporal continuities stressed at the beginning of the *Survey* in his account of the ceremonial practices of the citizen class, and at the end of the *Survey* in his chronology of leaders and procession-like lists of the city's holidays, officers, and companies.

Much of Stow's appeal lies in his crusty, unadorned style and his interjection of personal memory and comment; but these stylistic aspects of Stow's persona are merely functions of a more profoundly innovative point of view. By perambulating the city street by street, he transformed what was, in the personifying rubrics, essentially a blazon or at best a triumphal procession of the city's attributes into an extended *voie* or exploration of the landscape. This not only allowed for more intimate detail, but also introduced a historically situated observer into the landscape. In Camden, Norden, or Speed the city might have a history of growth like any life-form, but by stretching over several millennia the span between London's ancestors and her recent achievements and progeny, the personifying rubric paradoxically suppressed the temporal dimension of urban life. The city's life was for them organic without being dynamic. The first and final thirds of Stow's *Survey*, devoted to civic tradition and government, have the same effect; but his perambulation introduced an entirely different measure of urban temporality – the life-span of the observer.

Stow was more than sixty years old when he began his work on the city in which he had been born and raised.[84] In childhood Stow had inhabited a pre-Reformation city where the old guilds still held sway and the new maritime consortia had yet to be formed. He could recall London's religious houses and their destruction, but he had also lived to see the city's new wealth and the suburban squalor brought on by a four-fold increase in population. He remembered, for example, that near the nunnery of St. Clare, now converted to "diverse fair and large storehouses," there had been a farm from which "I my selfe in my youth haue fetched many a halfe pennie worth of Milke ... alwayes hote from the Kine" (1: 126). He remembered too that part of his father's garden had been built upon without payment by Thomas Cromwell, noting "that the suddaine rising of some men, causeth them to forget themselues" (1: 179). In the dedication of the *Survey* to the City of London, Stow explained that "what London hath beene of auncient time men may here see, as what it is now euery man doth beholde" (1: xcviii). The novelty of Stow's work was to have traversed the ground between these two points in time. Unlike the travelogues of tourists, who observed the sights of London for the first time, Stow's *Survey* turned on the idea of revisiting sites to find them changed, of remarking how once "sweete and fresh waters" were "since decaied," and how the now squalid suburbs were "pestered with small tenements and homely cottages, having inhabitants, English and strangers, more in number than some cities in England" (2: 70).

By focusing on London's recent history, and especially on the changes in his own lifetime, Stow appropriated to himself the privileged human status that had once belonged to the personified city, and the result was to defamiliarize, depersonalize the latter. To take the measure of the city from the individual human perspective was implicitly to violate the rubric of personification, where the metaphoric scale of time was the millennial life-span of the city. The individual perspective, as James Howell slightly later pointed out, will gravitate toward novelty: "one's own ocular view, and personal conversation will strive to find out something new."[85] Despite his extremely conservative outlook, and in part because of it, Stow was no longer strictly augmenting according to a long-established outline for description. He was in effect supplanting the paradigm, sketching out a new foundation, showing that by the measure of human experience London itself had broken from its

---

[84] On the role of personal memory in Stow's method, see Kingsford's Introduction to the *Survey*, pp. xxix–xxx, and Arthur B. Ferguson, *Clio Unbound: Perception of the Social and Cultural Past in Renaissance England* (Durham: Duke University Press, 1979), pp. 99–104.   [85] *Instructions for Forrein Trauell* (1642), pp. 2, 5.

foundations and was losing its familiar human character. As they came to seem less natural, the cultural facts affecting London's growth stood out more clearly for "*every man* [to] beholde."

While topographers like Camden and Speed were quoted and epitomized throughout the seventeenth century, it was Stow who was repeatedly updated and expanded to reflect changes in London's life. It was Stow, too, who was the stimulus to later innovations that changed the image of London.[86] Much that was innovative was concerned with method,[87] a persistent concern since the Venetian rubrics, but made more urgent by the increasingly perceived fact of rapid change in London. One factor adding to this sense was a breakdown of the political consensus that had defined the nature and limits of the city's power. By changing one word in a passage from Speed, Samuel Clarke, writing in the Protectorate, established all the difference in the world: "It *was* the seat of the British Kings, and is the Model of the Land, the Mart of the World."[88] James Howell, remarking in his *Londonopolis* (1657) that "populous Cities are alwaies subject to bring forth turbulent spirits," attempted in vain to establish a line of political continuity in Westminster when he explained that "in regard of the Royal Court once was, so the residence of the Sovereign Magistrate is still there" (pp. 40, 346). With the breakdown of political consensus there had also developed a distinction between what Howell called the City of London's "Members and homogeneal parts" and "her heterogeneal, or Suburban parts." For John Evelyn, writing during the Commonwealth, regicide, faction, and sectarianism, "the natural effects of parity, popular libertinism," were closely associated with the chaotic landscape of the city itself:

there is nothing more deformed and unlike than the prospect of it at a distance, and its asymmetrie within the walls ... the magistrate has either no power, or no care to make them build with any uniformity, which render it [sic], though a large, yet a very ugly town, pestred with hackney-coaches and insolent carre-men, shops and taverns, noyse, and such a cloud of sea-coal, as if there be a resemblance of hell upon earth, it is in this volcano on a foggy day.[89]

As is suggested by this new concern with foul air – associated with the development of national brewing, sugar-refining, and leather industries

[86] Stow's *Survey* was expanded by Anthony Munday in 1618 and 1633, and by John Strype in 1720.
[87] Peter Heylyn, for example, boasted that while he took the matter for his *Microcosmographie* from others, "the wordes for the most part are mine owne, the method totallie." James Howell acknowledged his debt to Stow in *Londonopolis* (1657), but claimed "the trace, and form of the Structure be mine own," sig. bv.
[88] *A Mirror or Looking-Glass ... Whereunto is Added a Geographical Description ... of the Chiefest Citys Both Antient and Modern* (1656), p. 92.
[89] *A Character of England* (1651, 1659), rpt. in *The Miscellaneous Writings of John Evelyn*, ed. William Upcott (London: Henry Colburn, 1825), pp. 150, 156–157.

at London – the changing political climate entailed a stronger emphasis on the economic roots of urban life. Even as devoted a Royalist as Peter Heylyn was compelled to revise a seven-part scheme on urban wealth he had earlier borrowed from Giovanni Botero; having in 1621 put "The Pallace of the Prince" second only to the importance of maritime resources, he replaced this second resource in 1652 with the development of "some Staple-Manufactures or Commodities," which balanced out commercialism by enabling cities to "draw the like resort of Merchants, though the Conveniencies of Sea or Rivers invite them not."[90] The description prefaced to Bishop Fuller's account of London's Worthies (1662) consists simply of a two-part rubric – "Manufactures" and "The Buildings." Fuller's discourse on "the Needle and the Engine," the smallest and the largest of London's manufactures, establishes the point that London is not a natural but a cultural fact, a "field of art." It suffices as a mere synecdoche for a "labyrinth" too large to enter and stands as a striking measure of a major transformation in the tropological climate.[91] The transformation is reflected, too, in the first great statistical account of London by the virtuoso Gregory King in 1696, or in William Petty's use of statistics to transform the old mode of personified comparison in his *Observations upon the Cities of London and Rome* (1687).

Whether they stress industry or statistics, the new descriptions follow the path laid down by Stow in their focus on recent development. In 1681, for example, Thomas DeLaune published a discourse called *The Present State of London*, in which two hundred pages were devoted to London's "Increase, Magnitude, Publick Structures and number of Inhabitants." As its title suggests, DeLaune's survey lays heavy stress on London's new, post-fire beginnings and on changes of even more recent memory.[92] After a brief section on government, DeLaune concludes, not with an account of the city's worthy offspring, but with discourse "Of the Trade of London, its Merchants, the Original of Money": the discourse ends with prolific lists of London's exports.

Perhaps the strongest measure of Stow's influence, however, is a work written in protest against it, Daniel Defoe's description of London in the fifth letter of the *Tour Through the Whole Island of Great Britain*. Approaching the "great centre of England" as he nears the center of his work, Defoe is torn between a traditional ideal geometry and the asymmetries of London's recent growth. Viewed traditionally through

---

[90] *Cosmographie* (1652), p. 5; cf. *Microcosmus* (1621), pp. 7–8.
[91] *The History of the Worthies of England*, ed. P. A. Nuttall (2 vols. 1840), 1: 333–335.
[92] "In our Memory, we have seen London multiply exceedingly in beautiful Structures and numbers of Inhabitants. So that it is at present of a vast extent," *The Present State of London* (1681), p. 5.

the outline of its walls and liberties, the city might be described "in narrow compass," yet "in the modern acception" London is a "vast mass of buildings" extending "from Blackwall in the East to Tot-Hill fields in the West."[93] London's extent approaches the 50-mile compass of ancient Rome, yet even "Rome, though a monster for its greatness... was, in a manner, round, with very few irregularities in its shape" (p. 287). As for London, sprawling irregularly in all directions, "Whither will this monstrous city then extend, and where must a circumvallation or communication line of it be placed?" (p. 288). London's outline cannot be made a pleasing figure, but only measured, and so for several pages Defoe calculates the distances from one outlying point to the next, ending with the tidy circumference of 36 miles 2 furlongs and 39 rods.

Although he claims to be innovating, and pointedly eschews the antiquarian method of Stow's continuators, Defoe clearly adopts one of Stow's techniques by writing "in the person of an itinerant and giv[ing] a cursory view of [London's] present state" (p. 295). This street-level perspective tends to stress the dehumanizing scale of the environment, the jolting ruptures, discontinuities, and variegations which no urban perambulator can anticipate from the connected symmetries of a street-map. It is the perspective adopted in Ned Ward's *London Spy* (1698), where the narrator enters London laterally, "thro' Aldgate, like a Ball thro' the Port of a Billiard Table."[94] Defoe's focus on recent changes, moreover, is justified by what he explains is "a particular and remarkable crisis, singular to those who write in this age, and very much to our advantage in writing, that the great and more eminent increase of buildings... has been generally made in our time, not only within our memory, but even within a few years, and the description of these oddities, cannot be improper to a description of the whole" (p. 295). The description that follows is devoted to "the new Buildings created... since the Year 1666" (p. 296). Yet even this proves too long a view, for Defoe's letter on London actually concludes with "an account of new edifices and public buildings erected or erecting in and about London, since the writing the foregoing account."

Defoe links the expanding physical asymmetries of London, moreover, to the dynamic asymmetries of London's changing society and economy. The dynamism that deforms London into a monstrous shape also accounts for the growing disparity between the new post-fire fabric of the booming City and the decrepitude of Westminster, whose fabric, like the Westminster Hall, is "but the corpse of the old English grandeur laid in state" (p. 323). Thus are the former circumscribing powers laid to rest.

[93] *A Tour through the Whole Island of Great Britain*, ed. Pat Rogers (Harmondsworth: Penguin, 1971), p. 286.   [94] *The London Spy* (Nov., 1698), p. 4.

Overshadowed by the great financial institutions of the City, the royal apartments have become "but little offices for clerks, rooms for coffee-houses, auctions of pictures, pamphlet and toy-shops" (p. 324).

Finally, while searching for those asymmetries that propel the city's growth, Defoe takes note of the extreme polarities of wealth and poverty, privilege and privation, this growth entails. The lower orders, once unmentionable, are brought not only into Defoe's description but into close proximity to the wealth they help to generate. On London's bustling docks, for example, there are "porters, and poor working men, who, though themselves not worth, perhaps, twenty pounds in the world, are trusted with great quantities of valuable goods, sometimes to the value of several thousand pounds" (p. 313). Even more striking is Defoe's perception that "there are in London, notwithstanding we are a nation of liberty, more public and private prisons, and houses of confinement, than any city in Europe, perhaps as many as in all the capital cities of Europe put together." To have thus taken one measure of London's greatness through its toll on human lives was implicitly to have put the urban process in a different light. As Defoe wrote elsewhere, "Trade is almost universally founded upon Crime."[95] It was through the personal experience of an outlaw woman, however, that Defoe reflected most acidly on the means by which the cultural (or subcultural) norm becomes the "natural." Returned in later life to the prison in which she was born, Moll Flanders describes Newgate in terms that cast it as a microcosm of London: "how Hell should become by degrees so natural, and not only tollerable, but even agreeable, is a thing Unintelligible, but by those who have Experienc'd it, as I have."[96]

The experience of London's monstrosity had long been a powerful current in such Tudor–Stuart genres as satire and city comedy. But the exclusion of this perspective for so long from prose description is testimony both to the power of generic distinctions and to the ideological force of conceptual models through which – perhaps well past its proper prime – London retained a compelling and familiar humanized identity. The city lost this identity only as its portraitists discovered theirs.

[95] *The Complete English Tradesman* (2 vols. 1727), 2.ii: 108; quoted in Max Byrd, *London Transformed: Images of the City in the Eighteenth Century* (New Haven: Yale University Press, 1978), p. 19.

[96] *The Fortunes and Misfortunes of the Famous Moll Flanders, &c.*, ed. G. A. Starr (London: Oxford University Press, 1971), p. 276.

4 The emergence of a Tudor capital: Spenser's epic vision

The river and the city: epic, time, and culture

The life of Renaissance cities was shaped not only by evolving economic forces and civic forms, but also by a growth in civic awareness and by consciously novel efforts to frame an ideology suited to new urban opportunities. According to the Ciceronian myth fostered by civic humanists, the arts of speech lay at the heart of civic order. "The highest science with which to govern the city," Brunetto Latini explained, "is the science of language; without language there would be no cities, nor could we establish justice and human community."[1]

Latini's observation was duly recorded in 1327 by the City Chamberlain Andrew Horn in the civic custumal that became the *Liber Horn*, but it did not in London find the sort of living proof that it did, for example, in the Florentine chancellory, in thinkers like Salutati, Bruni, and Machiavelli. Though humanism took root in England in the early sixteenth-century London circle of Thomas More, most English humanists, like More, Vives, Elyot, Ascham, and Smith, tended to gravitate towards the court. London was not an independent power but a late feudal dependency of the Crown. Through its extensive patronage, the Crown monopolized the talents of learned humanists and writers, including Londoners. London could not claim, among the members of its citizen class and ruling elite a Salutati, Bruni, or Pirckheimer who combined office with eloquence in such a way as to transform the City's ideals into inspired literary monuments.[2]

Moreover, as English contemporaries observed, it was "the use and auncient custome of this Realme" for "all Noble men and Gentlemen" to "continually inhabite the countryes," and not to "inhabite the Citties

---

[1] *Li Livres dou Trésor*, ed. Francis J. Carmody (1948; rpt. Geneva: Slatkine Reprints, 1975), p. 317.

[2] See Frank Freeman Foster, *The Politics of Stability: A Portrait of the Rulers in Elizabethan London* (London: Royal Historical Society, 1977), p. 5.

and cheefe townes, as in some forraine nations is the custome."[3] Unlike Italy, where "the very princes disdain not to be merchants," Fynes Moryson remarked, England was ruled by a nobility and gentry who, tied to the land, "disdain traffic, thinking it to abase gentry."[4] Though members of the gentry were drawn in increasing numbers to London, it was primarily by the attractions of the newly powerful court. At its very advent in sixteenth-century England, then, the humanistic movement was greeted by the developments it encountered elsewhere in Europe: the rise of the princely dynasty, with its political absolutism, aristocratic court, and neochivalric tastes. In the political context of England, it was never possible, as William Harrison observed, "to frame a whole monarchy after the pattern of one town or city."[5]

Nonetheless, the new power of the English monarchy, even while it perpetuated the traditionally dominant interests of the landholding aristocracy and gentry, was also heavily dependent upon the growth of London, not just for its financial resources but for the administrative, financial, and cultural apparatus that enabled it to dominate the countryside. As the court, which in former days "was wonte to bee contented to remaine with a small companie, sometimes at an Abbey or Priorie," became accustomed to "abiding at London,"[6] the urban setting and resources of the capital transformed the nature of the monarchy and its regime. According to Sir Thomas Smith, the official policy of the new Tudor state in Ireland should be "to augment our tongue, our laws, and our religion in that Isle, which three be the true bands of the commonwealth whereby the Romans conquered and kept long time a great part of the world."[7] These were certainly the developments that enabled the Tudor state to maintain its hold in England. While an efficient and far-flung local administration was essential to maintaining something like Smith's three-pronged *imperium*, its standards and ideals were formed and exemplified by the culture of the capital. As the center of the licensed printing trade and the principal residence of "Poets, excelling in all kinde of Poesie (to wit) Dramaticke, Liricke, Heroicall, or Epicke, ... Pastorall, & Satyricall," the culture of the capital gave definitive shape to an emerging modern language, whose ideal type Puttenham declared was represented by "the vsuall speach of

---

[3] *Cyvile and Uncyvile Life* (1579), sig. A4v.

[4] *An Itinerary Written by F. Moryson, Gent.* (1617), sig. Rrr2.

[5] *The Description of England* (1587), ed. Georges Edelin (Ithaca: Cornell University Press, 1968), p. 98.

[6] *An Apologie of the Cittie of London* (c. 1580), in John Stow, *A Survey of London* (1603), ed. C. L. Kingsford (2 vols. 1908; rpt. Oxford: Clarendon Press, 1971), 2: 211–212.

[7] M. Dewar, *Sir Thomas Smith: A Tudor Intellectual in Office* (London: Athlone, 1964), p. 157.

the Court, and that of London and the shires lying about London within lx. myles, and not much aboue."[8] The seat of Parliament and the court, London was also, by virtue of its elaborate regular government, reliable treasury, and manpower pool, the chief guarantor of the emerging political order. As Richard Morison explained in the aftermath of the Pilgrimage of Grace, the "rude countries" of the remoter provinces would have to learn "as well as the noble and faithful city of London and other civil places of England do how much they be bound to love and truly serve King Henry VIII."[9] Finally, with the preaching cross at St. Paul's serving the first pulpit of the realm, and having "(beside her owne Ordinary with store)... her solemne Assemblies furnished with the choise of Vniuersitie and Countrie, to speak unto her," London was "the very Arke of the presence of God, aboue all other places of this Land."[10] As "the Representative body of the general state," the monarch's "Chamber-royall," "Golden-Key," and "Store-house,"[11] London was not, then, simply a symbol of the nationalist aspirations of the monarchy, but an embodiment of the overdetermined conditions in which that monarchy achieved and maintained its power. As John Speed observed in 1611, the expanding city of London, "disdaining bondage, hath set her selfe on each side, far without the wals, & hath left her West-Gate in the midst, from whence with continuall buildings (still affecting greatnesse) she hath continued her streets vnto a kings Palace and ioyned a second citie to her self."[12] It was not, however, simply financial dependency or the physical process of expansion and consolidation that, mingling court and commune, established London as the permanent capital seat of British monarchs; rather, as Thomas Dekker indicated, it was a social and political process of reciprocity and inter-legitimation, leading to a convergence of vision and interests (see Fig. 5), that made London and Westminster "euerie day... more and more so resemble

[8] Edmund Howes, "A Discourse, or Treatise of the third Universitie of England," *The Annales, or Generall Chronicles of England, Begun First by Maister Iohn Stow, and After Him Continued... by Edmund Howes* (1615), p. 984; Puttenham, *The Arte of English Poesie,* ed. Gladys Doidge Willcock and Alice Walker (Cambridge University Press, 1936), p. 145. Cf. Nashe's boast that "there are extant about London many most able men to reuiue Poetry," Preface to Greene's *Menaphon,* in *Works,* ed. R. B. McKerrow (5 vols. 1904; rpt. Oxford: Basil Blackwell, 1966), 3: 323.

[9] *A Lamentation in Which is Showed What Ruin and Destruction Cometh of Seditious Rebellion* (1536), in David Berkowitz, ed., *Humanist Scholarship and Public Order* (Washington: Folger Shakespeare Library, 1984), p. 97.

[10] Susan Brigden, *London and the Reformation* (Oxford: Clarendon Press, 1989), p. 7; Thomas Jackson, *The Converts Happines* (1609), p. 30.

[11] Thomas Dekker, *Britannia's Honor* (1628), *The Dramatic Works,* ed. Fredson Bowers (4 vols. Cambridge University Press, 1961), 4: 81.

[12] *The Theatre of the Empire of Great Britaine* (1676), p. 28.

each other that many who neuer knew vs before, woulde sweare that we were all one."[13]

By the early seventeenth century, as the final chapters of this book will show, court culture came under the direct influence of styles and tastes formulated in the expanding metropolis.[14] But there were few immediate signs of such influence in the literary Renaissance associated with the late Tudor court. Puttenham's definition of poets as "cunning Princepleasers" devoted to "Maiesties seruice, in that place of great honour and magnificence to geue enterteinment to Princes, Ladies of honour, Gentlewomen and Gentlemen" (p. 158) is a fair measure of the bias of Elizabethan courtly literature. William Webbe observed that "the rare deuices of Poetry" were primarily the amateur accomplishments of "many honourable and noble Lordes and Gentlemen in her Maiesties Courte."[15] In their entertainments, narratives, and lyrics, the chief writers of the Elizabethan Renaissance were largely the "encomiasts of tournaments, of hunting, and of amorous dalliance."[16] In keeping with this bias, Sidney's *Apologie for Poetrie* (1595) contrasts the true, amateur poetry of the court both with the inartistic "sullen gravity" of learned humanism (in the "definitions, divisions, and distinctions" of philosophers and the "old mouse-eaten records" of the historians) and with the "base servile wits" of popular professionals.[17] It was chiefly in these latter humanistic and popular veins, rather than in courtly literature, that the most compelling images of city life were elaborated.

Nevertheless, within the body of courtly literature, whose linguistic norm Puttenham located in "the vsuall speach of the Court, and that of London," there remained both a humanistic outlook, carried over from ancient and continental sources, and a pressure from bourgeois myth and

---

[13] *The Dead Terme* (1608), in *Non-Dramatic Works*, ed. A. B. Grosart (5 vols. London, 1884), 4: 70.

[14] Malcolm Smuts, for example, observes that in the Stuart period "court culture was still sometimes displayed in the country, but it was now usually created in or near the capital, or at least by men who nominally resided there ... The new styles and tastes which most influenced the court tended to originate in London or in foreign cities," "The Court and London as a Cultural Environment," in *Court Culture and the Origins of a Royalist Tradition in Early Stuart England* (Philadelphia: University of Pennsylvania Press, 1987), p. 54.

[15] *A Discourse of English Poetrie* (1586), in G. Gregory Smith, ed., *Elizabethan Critical Essays* (2 vols. 1904; rpt. London: Oxford University Press, 1959), 1: 243.

[16] G. K. Hunter, *John Lyly: The Humanist as Courtier* (Cambridge, Mass.: Harvard University Press, 1962), p. 31; see also Daniel Javitch, *Poetry and Courtliness in Renaissance England* (Princeton University Press, 1978); and Richard Helgerson, *Self-Crowned Laureates: Spenser, Jonson, Milton and the Literary System* (Berkeley: University of California Press, 1983), ch. 1.

[17] *An Apologie for Poetrie* (1595), ed. Geoffrey Shepherd (London: Thomas Nelson and Sons, 1965), pp. 113, 104, 105, 132.

popular piety that, while serving to reinforce the courtly image of the absolutist state, also spoke for the influence and contribution of urban life in shaping that state. Even courtly writers recognized the civic and rhetorical traditions that made cities the ideal symbols of the civilizing achievements of eloquence, law, and religion. No less a courtier, for example, than John Bourchier, Lord Berners, a translator of Arthurian and chivalric romance and of the chivalric chronicles of Froissart, observed that "through the monumentes of writynge, ... many men have ben moved, some to bylde cytes, some to devyse and establisshe lawes right profitable, necessarie, and behovefull for the humane lyfe."[18] Mythographic commonplace had given this favorite humanist theme a symbolic embodiment in the figures of Orpheus and Amphion, who exemplified the originary nexus of poetry and civil life.[19] Orpheus and Amphion figured frequently in civic pageantry throughout Renaissance Europe,[20] but perhaps more strikingly, they were prominent as well in the courtly treatises of the Elizabethan defenders of poetry. Citing "Amphion and Orpheus, two Poets of the first ages," Puttenham observed that the former "builded vp cities" and that the latter brought "sauage people to a more ciuill and orderly life" (p. 6). In support of the vatic function of poetry Sidney remarked that "Amphion was said to move stones with his poetry to build Thebes, and Orpheus to be listened by beasts" (p. 96). Webbe's reminder that Orpheus made men "keepe company, make houses, and keep fellowshippe together" and that Amphion "caused Citties to be builded" (1: 234) was put more flatly in Thomas Lodge's declaration that "Poetes were the first raysors of cities."[21]

In most of these formulations, the originary civic eloquence is distanced from the courtly present by a sharp distinction between the "graue ... wise men or eloquent men ... meant by *Vates*; and the rest which sange of ... lighter deuices alluring vnto pleasure and delight ... called *Poetae* or makers."[22] If, in its glorification of imaginative fiction-making, Sidney's distinction between "the first and most noble sort ... termed *vates*" and the "right poets" who "borrow nothing of what is,

---

[18] *The Chronicle of Froissart*, ed. William Paton Ker (2 vols. London: David Nutt, 1901), 1: 4.

[19] See, for example, the mythographical interpretations of Boccaccio, *Genealogia deorum gentilium libri*, ed. Vincenzo Romano (2 vols. Bari: G. Laterza & Figli, 1951), 1: 274; and Natalis Comes, *Mythologiae* (Venice, 1568), fol. 228r.

[20] See, e.g., David M. Bergeron, *English Civic Pageantry, 1558–1642* (Columbia: University of South Carolina Press, 1971), pp. 127–128; Estienne Jodelle, *Le Recueil des inscriptions* (1558), ed. Victor E. Graham and W. McAllister Johnson (University of Toronto Press, 1972), pp. 57, 103.

[21] *A Defence of Poetry, Music, and Stage Plays* (1579), in Smith, ed., *Elizabethan Critical Essays*, 1: 75.   [22] Webbe, in ibid., 1: 231.

hath been, or shall be," suggests a certain tension between civilizing eloquence and courtly entertainment, that tension is itself a function of the overdetermination of the courtly literary system, its tendency to host within itself a capacity for conflicted civic vision.[23]

Spenser's *Faerie Queene* is in Sidney's terms a vatic, visionary national epic as well as the greatest of Elizabethan courtly artifacts. While, in its dedicatee and titular heroine, it celebrated the Tudor supremacy, in its visionary deployment of the Virgilian theme of cultural *translatio*, it created a national identity and imperial destiny that merged bourgeois and aristocratic interests in a neofeudal synthesis. The chivalric decor of the poem adapts Elizabethan courtliness to the bourgeois ethos and practices of London's mercantile elite; its epic thesis of *translatio* is indebted both to learned, Latin humanism and to the amplitudinous temporality of the "mouse-eaten records" of popular chronicle; its local moral allegory often embraces the concerns of popular London moralists and preachers – excess and deficiency, profit and loss, marriage, concord, family, inheritance, and property.

The focus of the poem's prophetic vision of *translatio* is Troynovant, the capital seat of Britain, which carries on from Troy, by way of Virgil's Rome, the destined westering of civilization. If London, with its burgeoning power and varied population, its facilities for exchange and recombination, was not only the underpinning of the new Tudor state, but also the place where the possibilities of an English nation were most visible – "the principal Cittie and spectacle of the whole realm whereof all other cities and places take example"[24] – then the labyrinthine romance structure of *The Faerie Queene* is, like the contemporary multi-plot drama, an ideal form in which such possibilities might be represented. As part of a more general Elizabethan revival of romance forms,[25] *The Faerie Queene* participates in a romance figural logic that, according to Fredric Jameson, typically appears "in a transitional moment when two distinct modes of production, or moments of

---

[23] On the "continuous cross-fertilization between courtly and urban forms," see Smuts, *Court Culture and the Origins of a Royalist Tradition*, p. 64. For a reading of Sidney's courtly *Arcadia* in the light of urbanization, see my "Fictions of Settlement: London 1590," *SP* 88: 2 (1991), 201–224.

[24] Corporation of London Records Office, *Journals of the Common Council*, 20, fol. 65 (1572–73), quoted in Michael Berlin, "Civic Ceremony in Early Modern London," *Urban History Yearbook* (Leicester University Press, 1986), p. 23.

[25] The 1590 publication of the three-book *Faerie Queene* also saw the publication of *The Countess of Pembroke's Arcadia*. Longus and Heliodorus were both translated in 1587, while Robert Greene's Greek-inspired romances, *Pandosto* and *Menaphon*, were published in 1588 and 1589 respectively. 1588–90 also brought to the stage *The Rare Triumphs of Love and Fortune, Fair Em, the Miller's Daughter*, and Greene's historical romances, *James IV* and *Friar Bacon and Friar Bungay*. Shakespeare's *Comedy of Errors* appeared in 1593.

socioeconomic development, coexist."²⁶ The key to this logic is a simultaneity and suspension of closure that maintain a widened horizon of social and historical vision. In its vision, this work of a London journeyman's son not only "translates" culture over time and space, but effects the emergence of the English state by negotiating the liminary relations between bourgeois and aristocratic tendencies within the neofeudal synthesis. The poem both marks and narrates a transitional and overdetermined moment in the life of England.

It has been said of Spenser that "no poet has less to say about great cities" and that even in his nationalist epic poem "there is a surprising absence of cities."²⁷ The "Brittayne *Orpheus*," as one encomiast called him,²⁸ was also the courtly pastoral poet "whose Muse whilome did maske, / As time her taught, in lowly Shepheards weeds."²⁹ Yet in Spenser's understanding, the Virgilian model of poetic career, which begins with pastoral, includes within its later, epic culmination, the Orphic role of "raising cities." In this respect Spenser differs from many authors of Renaissance pastoral, who commonly resolved the sharp paradoxes of Virgil's first eclogue by conflating the return of Tityrus from Rome with the exile of Meliboeus,³⁰ thereby reducing pastoral to a genre of belatedness, exile, and urban disillusionment. To begin in this way as a Virgilian pastoralist was to begin late, not early, in the history of culture, with a sophisticated pose of disillusionment and flight, a gesture embodied in Cuddie's lament in *The Shepheardes Calender* that "walled townes do worke my greater woe"³¹ and in Calidore's pastoral quest, when

> from the citties to the townes him prest,
> And from the townes into the countries forst,
> And from the country back to priuate farmes he scorsed.
>
> From thence into the open fields he fled ...   (6.9.3–4)

²⁶ *The Political Unconscious: Narrative as a Socially Symbolic Act* (Ithaca: Cornell University Press, 1981), p. 148.
²⁷ M. Pauline Parker, *The Allegory of "The Faerie Queene"* (Oxford: Clarendon Press, 1960), p. 270; John Erskine Hankins, *Source and Meaning in Spenser's Allegory: A Study of "The Faerie Queene"* (Oxford: Clarendon Press, 1971), p. 55.
²⁸ In the commendatory poem to *The Faerie Queene* signed "R. S."; see Spenser, *Poetical Works*, ed. J. C. Smith and E. de Selincourt (1912; rpt. London: Oxford University Press, 1975), p. 409.
²⁹ *The Faerie Queene*, 1 Proem 1, ed. A. C. Hamilton (London: Longman, 1977), p. 27. All subsequent references to *The Faerie Queene* are to this edition.
³⁰ A point developed by Julia Reinhard Lupton, "Home-Making in Ireland: Virgil's Eclogue I and Book VI of *The Faerie Queene*," *Spenser Studies*, 8 (1990), p. 123.
³¹ *The Shepheardes Calender* (1579), "August," lines 157–158, in William A. Oram et al., eds., *The Yale Edition of the Shorter Poems of Edmund Spenser* (New Haven: Yale University Press, 1989), p. 144. References to all Spenserian poems other than *The Faerie Queene* are to this edition.

But in Spenser's poetry, the sense of pastoral as a flight or exile is played against the priority of the city – not just the historical priority that defines the pastoral flight, but the cultural priority that marks pastoral as the potential beginning of a re-civilizing process whose end is urban and imperial. For Spenser, as originally for Virgil, Meliboeus' exile is distinct, if not finally separable, from the new and hopeful beginning of Tityrus, a beginning which, made possible by his Roman patron, will point forward in Virgil's fourth eclogue to an epic vision of Roman grandeur. Spenser's epic vision – and the place of the city in it – will in fact always depend upon the conjunction of these distinct possibilities: every bridge or new beginning in the civilizing process of epic *translatio* will also be a breach or disjunction, a process of exclusion and domination that produces pastoral exile and belatedness. Having modelled himself on an English "Tityrus" and sung through Colin Clout his own messianic eclogue in praise of the new English empress, Immerito will emerge from the chrysalis of *The Shepheardes Calender* as Edmund Spenser, the author of the great neofeudal epic of the emergent English nation. Yet near the end of that epic, he will encounter both the disillusioned exile Meliboe, and the pastoral Colin Clout, who knew better than Immerito to leave the sheepfold and follow Tityrus.

In his approach to the city, then, Spenser finally adopts and expands the Virgilian capacity for paradox. The epic celebrant of a renascent civilization, he is simultaneously its chief poet of mutability, and in his poetry the symbolic glory of the city is rarely separable from a sense of its corruptible mortality. For these ultimately timeless alternatives there were both imposing classical precedents in Virgil and elsewhere and many reinforcements in the peculiarities of English Renaissance culture – in the humanist's perspective on the fall of ancient civilization and his sense of cultural belatedness, in the protestant's Augustinian perspective on the vanities of earthly life. Yet to these must be added the unsettled and uncertain state of urban life itself, its transitional and overdetermined nature within the emergence of a modern English nation.

For Spenser, the possible restoration of ancient grandeur to the present involves both urban and imperial vision, an assimilation of the Orphic to the Virgilian mode:[32]

> O that I had the *Thracian* Poets harpe,
> For to awake out of th'infernall shade
> Those antique *Caesars*, sleeping long in darke,

[32] For further discussion of how Spenser "lays claim to the role of the English Virgil, the English inheritor of the role of Orpheus," see Thomas H. Cain, "Spenser and the Renaissance Orpheus," *UTQ*, 41 (1971), p. 30.

> The which this auncient Citie whilome made:
>   Or that I had *Amphions* instrument,
> To quicken with his vitall notes accord,
> The stonie ioynts of these old walls now rent,
> By which th'*Ausonian* light might be restor'd:
>   Or that at least I could with pencill fine,
> Fashion the pourtraicts of these Palacis,
> By paterne of great *Virgils* spirit diuine ...   (*Ruines of Rome*, 25.337–47)

In many of Spenser's complaints, the urban ruins of antiquity form the poetic foundation for a larger fabric of reflection on the city and on the possible renewal of urban splendor in his time. In the "Sonets" Spenser translated for the English edition of Jan Van der Noot's *Theatre for Voluptuous Worldlings* (1569), eleven "Sonets" from Du Bellay's *Songe*[33] on the passing of Roman glory are followed by four apocalyptic sonnets by the Calvinist Van der Noot, establishing that "Now for a truth great Babylon is fallen" (13.14). In contrast to this apocalyptic culmination, however, the central poem in the sequence, taken from DuBellay, is occupied by a wailing nymph, "Hard by a riuers side" (8.1).[34] While the lament of this figure, a genius of Rome, owes much to Biblical models,[35] her evocation of the noble civic conscience of Rome in her attacks upon the "ciuile bate" that "Made me the spoile and bootie of the world" and the "Neroes and Caligulaes," the rapacious prelates, she has since brought forth (8.9–10, 14), lend poignance to her ultimate doom. The humanist foundations of the sequence are finally overshadowed by Van der Noot's Calvinist superstructure. The contrast in the eighth sonnet of nymph with river, Rome with Tiber, places the city in a temporal context that in turn gives way to an eternal parallel in the New Jerusalem, where

[33] On Van der Noot's rearrangement of the *Songe* and on the question of whether Spenser translated the Revelation sonnets, see *The Minor Poems, Volume Two*, ed. Charles Grosvenor Osgood and Henry Gibbons Lotspeich, in *The Works of Edmund Spenser: A Variorum Edition* (10 vols. Baltimore: Johns Hopkins Press, 1947), app. 6 (pp. 611–627); Harold Stein, *Studies in Spenser's Complaints* (New York: Oxford University Press, 1934), pp. 67–71; and Alfred W. Satterthwaite, *Spenser, Ronsard, and Du Bellay: A Renaissance Comparison* (Princeton University Press, 1960), app. 1 (pp. 255–263).

[34] Henri Chamard notes the exceptional nature of this sonnet in *Joachim du Bellay, 1522–1560* (Lille, 1900), p. 196, n. 9. On Du Bellay as a ruins poet, see Wayne A. Rebhorn, "Du Bellay's Imperial Mistress: *Les Antiquitez de Rome* as Petrarchist Sonnet Sequence." *RenQ*, 33 (1980), 609–622; and Margaret Brady Wells, "Du Bellay's Sonnet Sequence *Songe*," *FS*, 26 (1972), 1–8.

[35] She evokes the Biblical image of the Psalmist when "By the riuers of Babel we sate, and there we wept, when we remembred Zion" (Ps. 137: 1) or the desolate Jerusalem of Lamentations: "How doeth the citie remaine solitarie that was ful of people? She is as a widdow: she that was great among the nacions and princesse among the prouinces, is made tributarie. She wepeth continually in the night, & her teares *runne downe* by her chekes" (Lam. 1: 1–2). The analogy with Psalms is suggested by Gordon Braden, "riverrun: An Epic Catalogue in *The Faerie Queene*," *ELR*, 5 (1975), 27.

"A liuely streame, more cleere than Christall is, / Ranne through the mid" (15.12–13). Yet taken together the two visions point forward to the way in which the protestant New Jerusalem will finally legitimate Spenser's epic vision: the city that is not swept away before the flow of time may stand in triumph as the eternal order through which time flows. Polarized in the *Theatre* by an impassable gulf between the temporal and the eternal, these alternatives recur in shifting patterns throughout the Spenserian *œuvre*.

In the *Ruines of Rome*, a translation of the *Antiquitez de Rome* to which Du Bellay had appended the *Songe*, only "*Tyber* hastning to his fall / Remaines of all" (3.39–40). Having become "her selfe the matter of her fires" (23.313, 315–16), the city, now a ghost, has fallen to the river running through her heart and become warning of the apocalyptic point that "all this whole shall one day come to nought" (9.126). Similarly, in *The Ruines of Time*, the poet, walking "beside the shore / Of siluer streaming *Thamesis*" (lines 1–2), beholds at the site of Verulam "A Woman sitting sorrowfullie wailing" (line 9); she is "th'auncient *Genius* of that Citie brent" (line 19). In her ruin she has become the symbol of the "vaine worlds glorie" (line 43), or, in the fifth of the emblematic visions that conclude the poem, of the inability of cultural *translatio* to bridge the oceanic chasm of time:

> Then did I see a Bridge, all made of golde,
> Over the Sea from one to other side,
> Withouten prop or pillour it t'upholde,
> But like the coloured Rainbowe arched wide:...
> ... But (ah) what bootes it to see earthlie thing
> In glorie, or in greatnes to excell,
> Sith time doth greatest things to ruine bring?
> This goodlie bridge, one foote not fastned well,
> Gan faile, and all the rest downe shortlie fell,
> Ne of so brave a building ought remained,
> That griefe thereof my spirite greatlie pained.   (lines 547–550,554–560)

At once a recollection of Xerxes' bridge over the Hellespont and of the covenant promise of renewal after destruction, the collapsing bridge, its "foote not fastned well," is also a figure of the poet's own desolation in a world where no Orphic renewal or Virgilian *translatio* seems possible. Yet just as the poem's final consoling visions associated with the stellified Sidney include "The Harpe on which *Dan Orpheus* was seene / Wylde beasts and forrests after him to lead" (lines 607–608), so the configuration of city and river prefigures the shape in which Spenser will effect his own Orphic reconstruction of the city. Recalling that the Rome to which she once belonged "in the necke of all the world did ride" (line 74), the genius of Verulamium anticipates Britomart's description in *The Faerie Queene* of Troynovant,

> that with the waues
> Of wealthy *Thamis* washed is along,
> Vpon whose stubborne neck, whereat he raues
> With roring rage, and sore him selfe does throng,
> That all men feare to tempt his billowes strong,
> She fastned hath her foot, which standes so hy,
> That it a wonder of the world is song...   (3.9.45)

This avatar reverses the earlier configurations of city and river and presents the city as a symbol of the human triumph over time. Britomart offers the vision as an implicit criticism of Paridell's view of history, which, in focusing on the "idle name" of "*Priams* Citie sackt" (3.9.33, 38), overlooks the consolation of Troynovant, the power of the city to regenerate itself. Obsessed with the ruin of their city, Paridell's ancestors "Gathred the *Troian* reliques sau'd from flame" (3.9.36) and from them built the idle civilization of Paros, which, like Buthrotum and the other false cities of Virgil's *Aeneid*, is merely a regressive simulacrum of a lost past. As Britomart points out, the true successor of Troy is not reconstructed around relics but "built of old *Troyes* ashes cold" (3.9.38); like a giant tree, it grows organically "out of her dust" and from the seed of her "scattered of-spring" (3.9.44).

In contrast to Verulamium or the Rome Spenser translated from DuBellay, the *Faerie Queene*'s Troynovant substitutes for the poetic idolatry of visible desolation a prophetic sense of history as potentially renewable. The many sieges of Verulamium and its utter destruction by the Saxons, summarized in *The Ruines of Time* (lines 104–114), accord almost perfectly with Merlin's prophecy to Britomart, in which he says that the Saxons "all thy Cities... shall sacke and race" (3.3.34). Yet Merlin and *The Faerie Queene* also declare that history shall preserve "The royall seed, the antique *Troian* blood" (3.3.42). Britomart's description of Troynovant is a perfect symbol of this preservation; standing with its foot fastened on the neck of the Thames, the city emblematically adopts a posture once held by Verulamium's mistress, Rome. The pattern of endurance is carried forward into the fourth Book of *The Faerie Queene*, where, at the marriage of the Thames and Medway, the city emerges as the crowning expression of a humanized, historic time. Troynovant arises on the flowing, princely Thames

> like to a Coronet
> He wore, that seemed strange to common vew,
> In which were many towres and castels set,
> That it encompast round as with a golden fret.

> Like as the mother of the Gods, they say,
>   In her great iron charet wonts to ride,
>   When to *Ioues* pallace she doth take her way:
>   Old *Cybele*, arayd with pompous pride,
>   Wearing a Diademe embattild wide
>   With hundred turrets, like a Turribant.
>   With such an one was Thamis beautifide;
> In which her kingdomes throne is chiefly resiant.   (4.11.27–28)

"Like as the mother of the Gods ... Old *Cybele*": like, indeed, to the Rome once thought to lie in irreparable ruin:

> Such as the *Berecynthian* Goddesse bright
> In her swift charret with high turrets crownde,
> Proud that so manie Gods she brought to light;
> Such was this Citie in her good daies fownd:
>   This Citie, more than that great *Phrygian* mother
> Renowm'd for fruite of famous progenie,
> Whose greatnes by the greatnes of none other,
> But by her selfe her equall match could see:
>   *Rome* onely might to *Rome* compared bee ... (*Ruines of Rome*, 6.71–79)

The emergence of Troynovant in the guise of Cybele is thus a true *renovatio*, a triumph over history. It fulfills the promise of the *Ruines of Rome*, recovering the Orphic power by the circuitous Virgilian process of *translatio*: the westward progress of the Phrygian mother, arrested for a time in ruins, is carried on in epic movement toward Troynovant. As the major focus of this epic movement, the city symbolically embodies historic destiny; it extends the life of civilization and forms the basis of human culture. This is reflected in Spenser's use of Cybele, mother of civilization, for her mural crown (see Figs. 2–4) exalts the city as the crowning expression of earthly life:

her stately sitting [in her chariot] betokeneth the firme ground wheron is builded Cityes and townes: by her Crown so signified ...

On her head ... she weareth a stately crowne, made in the forme of many towers and castles, in that the circuit and compasse of the earth is round, like the shape of a crowne, and is replenished and filled with Citties, Castles, and Villages ...[36]

---

[36] For the first quotation, see Stephan Batman, *The Golden Booke of the Leaden Goddes* (London, 1577), sig. c4r; for the second, Richard Lynche, *The Fountaine of Ancient Fiction* (London, 1599), sig. M3v. There is a further resonance in Spenser's use of Cybele, for when her appearance in *The Faerie Queene* announces the fulfillment of a challenge laid down in the *Ruines of Rome*, it also acknowledges the Virgilian means by which – as had been promised there – that challenge would be fulfilled. When Anchises traces the succession of power in Italy from Lavinium, the first city to be founded by Aeneas, to Alba Longa, and thence to Rome, he likens Rome's enclosing wall to "Berecyntia mater ... turrita" (*Aeneid* 6.784–785). In so doing, he recapitulates in small

Troynovant and the translation of culture

As the mural crown of an emerging English civilization, London is the focal point of a pattern of epic *translatio* that was shaped most decisively by Virgil's *Aeneid*. Though, like the *Faerie Queene*, the *Aeneid* celebrates the establishment of *imperium sine fine* (1.279), the poem's opening lines portray Aeneas as the Orphic founder of a city, a man whose sufferings "brought a city into being" (*dum conderet urbem*, 1.5) and whose deeds resulted in "the ramparts of high Rome" (*altae moenia Romae*, 1.7).[37] This thesis, centered on the city, is indeed central to Jupiter's promise of empire, which is founded on the solace of "city walls and a way of life" (Fitzgerald, 1.357). Aeneas is driven by an Orphic, city-building instinct that scatters the early books with false starts and premature settlements, and the poem's prophetic ekphrases continually adumbrate a political order in which the *urbs* is a microcosm of the imperial *orb*.[38] When Aeneas plunges his sword into the breast of Turnus (*sub pectore condit*, 12.950) he thus symbolically fulfills the epic thesis that declared he would bring a city into being (*conderet urbem*).[39]

The violence of this foundational act, however, is but one means by which Virgil subjects the pattern of *translatio* to irony and doubt, to a sceptical appreciation of the entropic and "unholy madness" (1.293–296) that impedes and vitiates historic process. In the future history of Rome Anchises unfolds "a tale of madness and inhumanity,"[40] and the political dominion of Rome will spell the loss of many finer graces (6.847). When Aeneas returns to the upper light through the gates of ivory, "Virgil seems to be not quite free from doubts and uncertainties ... to wonder whether the pageant of Roman history has not the insubstantiality of a dream."[41]

his earlier recollection of a cultural *translatio* on a vaster scale: from hundred-citied Crete, the cradle of the Trojan people, the ancient mother–goddess came to take the form of Cybele (*Aeneid* 3.104–113). In his echo of this Virgilian motif, Spenser identifies the epic means by which he gets from ruined Rome to Troynovant.

[37] Unless otherwise noted, I quote from the English translation of Allen Mandelbaum (1971; rpt. New York: Bantam Books, 1972). References to "Fitzgerald" are to the translation of Robert Fitzgerald (New York: Random House, 1983).

[38] On connections between the shield and Hades, see Brooks Otis, *Virgil: A Study in Civilized Poetry* (Oxford: Clarendon Press, 1963), p. 218, and Michael Putnam, *The Poetry of the Aeneid* (Cambridge, Mass.: Harvard University Press, 1966), pp. 128–129, 150; for the relation between the poem and civil strife, see Kenneth Quinn, *Virgil's "Aeneid": A Critical Description* (Ann Arbor: University of Michigan Press, 1968), pp. 36, 105–106.

[39] Mario A. DiCesare, *The Altar and the City* (New York: Columbia University Press, 1974), pp. 236–237.

[40] Ibid., pp. 117–118; see also Quinn, *Virgil's "Aeneid"*, p. 105.

[41] C. M. Bowra, *From Virgil to Milton* (London: Macmillan, 1957), p. 83.

For Spenser, as for other epic poets of the Renaissance, these doubts were magnified by the experience of a profound cultural discontinuity. Thomas Greene suggests that for Renaissance humanists,

each imitation embodies a passage of history, builds it into the poetic experience as a constitutive element ... It is through a diachronic structure, an acting out of passage, that the humanist poem demonstrates its own conscientiousness and creative memory.[42]

The prolonged rite of passage that constituted epic *translatio* for Renaissance poets continued to orient itself to the city as to a point of destination. Ariosto's version leads to Ercole d'Este's enlargement of Ferrara *con muro e fossa* just as Ronsard's leads to the founding of *les grands murs de Paris*.[43] Yet the humanistic sense of loss and diminishment that haunts such poems was magnified by an awareness of the political disparity between the ancient cultural heritage and its modern descendants. As the chivalric decor of these poems suggests, the *translatio* of classical epic was adapted to a neofeudalism which, by comparison to the ancient political vision, was at once despotic and escapist. For Ariosto the ultimate achievement of Ercole d'Este is

> Not that the toune with wall enuiron round
> And store with things behoofull to their use ...
>
> But that he shall more and above all these
> Leave them behind him such a worthy race.   (3.48)

And Tasso's Estense Ferrara is finally

> the fair and noble toune
> Where they of Este should by succession long
> Command.[44]

Ariosto's version of the Este dynasty, however, concludes with *li dua si tristi* (3.60), the ill-fated Giulio and Ferrante, just as Tasso's version places Alphonso II in an age of decline, "When this frail world grows old, / Corrupted, poor, and bare of men of fame" (*quando corrotto e vegli / povero fia d'uomini illustri il mondo*)" (17.90). The discontinuity between cultural *translatio* and dynastic heredity, ancient political culture and modern court, perhaps accounts in part for Tasso's sense that celebration of "the origin of cities and illustrious families, the beginnings

[42] *The Light in Troy: Imitation and Discovery in Renaissance Poetry* (New Haven: Yale University Press, 1982), pp. 40–41.
[43] Ariosto, *Orlando Furioso*, tr. Sir John Harington (1591), ed. Robert McNulty (Oxford: Clarendon Press, 1972), 3.48; Ronsard, *Les Quatres premiers livres de la franciade*, in *Œuvres complètes*, ed. Gustave Cohen (2 vols. Paris: Gallimard, 1950), 1: 652.
[44] *Godfrey of Bulloigne*, tr. Edward Fairfax (1599–1600), ed. J. C. Nelson (New York: Capricorn Books, 1963), 17.71.

of kingdoms and empire" are but the "ornaments" of epic poems.[45] If the city remains a symbolic vessel of cultural *translatio* in Renaissance epic, the process of translation is itself doubly determined, and thus sometimes deflected, by potential divergences between "the origin of cities and illustrious families."

This creative tension lies at the heart of Spenser's *Faerie Queene*, in which the image of the "most royall Queene or Empresse" jostles with a vision of "The fairest City ... that might be seene" (1.10.58). By way of double determination, the chivalric milieu of the poem simultaneously links the sphere of epic action to its royal Tudor patron and the epic theme of *translatio* to bourgeois aspirations of London's citizen class. The proliferation of Arthurian myth and manner in sixteenth-century England was, on the one hand, an ideological corollary of absolutism; it contributed to the legitimization of Tudor claims and policies. King Arthur provided both a valid pedigree for the Welsh-descended Tudors and a valid precedent for their imperial ambitions. In 1533 Henry VIII had proclaimed "this realm of England is an empire,"[46] and apologists from Polydore Vergil to John Foxe attempted to substantiate this claim by recurring sometimes to the deeds of Arthur himself, and sometimes to his alleged descent from the Emperor Constantine.[47]

Yet behind these efforts lay the myth of Trojan origins, of the translation of empire through Aeneas' descendant, Brute, an exile who carried the translation of empire forward by founding the British nation and its capital, Troynovant. According to Geoffrey of Monmouth, from whose *History of the Kings of Britain* (c. 1139) later versions of the myth derived, Brute, the exiled son of Silvius, "was minded to build him a chief city," chose a site upon the Thames, "founded his city there and called it New Troy, and by this name was it known for many ages thereafter, until at last, by corruption of the word, it came to be called Trinovantum."[48] In Layamon's *Brut*, which formed the basis for countless later chronicles, Brute

> ... found a pleasant place   upon a water stream;
> There did he raise up   a very rich borough,
> With bowers and with halls,   and with high stone walls.

[45] *Discourses on the Heroic Poem*, tr. Mariella Cavalchini and Irene Samuel (Oxford: Clarendon Press, 1973), p. 51.
[46] The Act in Restraint of Appeals (1533) in G. R. Elton, ed., *The Tudor Constitution* (1960; rpt. Cambridge University Press, 1972), p. 344; see Arthur B. Ferguson, *The Indian Summer of English Chivalry* (Durham: Duke University Press, 1960), p. 100.
[47] See, for example, John Coke, *The Debate Between the Heralds of England and France* (1550), quoted in C. Bowie Millican, *Spenser and the Table Round* (Cambridge, Mass.: Harvard University Press, 1932), p. 34.
[48] *Historia Regum Britanniae*, tr. Sebastian Evans (New York: Dutton, 1958).

> When that city was made,   it was most glorious.
> The city was very well built,   and he set a name on her
> He gave her a glorious name,   Troy the new,
> To remind his kindred   when they were come.[49]

Passed on through the chroniclers, the story enabled propagandists to trace the Tudor descent back through Arthur to Trojan origins. The first commemoration of Henry VII's victory at Bosworth epitomized the new king as "the tall pillar from Brutus," from "the line of Dardan ... the line of Troy"; soon after his accession a commission appointed to report upon his genealogy claimed that from "Brutus which first inherited this land ... King Henry the Seventh is lineally descended by Issue-Male ... in five-score degrees."[50] The myth prevailed into the reign of Elizabeth, when Gabriel Harvey's brother Richard could assert "we are not Brittons, we are Brutans," and the monarch could be praised as the "beauteous Queene of second Troy."[51]

But because Brute founded London as well as the British line, the genealogical implications of the myth were seldom divorced from a cultural thesis in which the city occupied center stage. Jasper Fisher's *Fuimus Troes*, for example, recorded how

> Ancient Bards haue sung ...
> How Brute did gyants tame,
> And by Isis current,
> A second Troy did frame,
> A center of Delights.[52]

In William Warner's *Albion's England* (1586), the edification and etymological descent of London proceeds in tandem with the royal acts of Brute and Lud:

> for cities store
> Affords no little ayde,

---

[49] Translation from Lois H. Fisher, *A Literary Gazetteer of England* (New York: McGraw-Hill, 1980), p. 322.

[50] See Millican, *Spenser and the Table Round*, pp. 14, 16.

[51] Harvey quoted in S. K. Heninger, "The Tudor Myth of Troynovant," *South Atlantic Quarterly*, 61 (1962), 384; Thomas Watson, "Nimphes meeting their May Queene," in *England's Helicon*, ed. Hyder Rollins (2 vols. Cambridge, Mass.: Harvard University Press, 1935), 1:46. On the myth of Troynovant, see also George Gordon, "The Trojans in Britain," *Essays and Studies by Members of the English Association*, 9 (1924), 9–30; A. E. Parsons, "The Trojan Legend in England," *MLR*, 24 (1929), 253–264; J. W. Bennett, "Britain among the Fortunate Isles," *SP*, 53 (1956), 114–121; and Edwin Greenlaw, *Studies in Spenser's Historical Allegory* (Baltimore: Johns Hopkins University Press, 1932), pp. 11–12.

[52] *Fuimus Troes. The True Troianes ... Publikely represented by the Gentlemen Students of Magdalen Colledge in Oxford* (1633), sig. D3.

> Did Brute build vp his Troy-nouant,
>   Jnclosing it with wall;
> Which Lud did after beautifie,
>   And Luds-towne it did call
>
> That now is London; euermore
>   To rightfull princes trewe,
> Yea prince and people still to it
>   As to their storehouse drewe,
> For plenty and for populous
>   The like we no wheare vewe.[53]

In one respect the faithful servant of princes ("to princes trewe"), London is in another respect for Warner a common resource (or "storehouse") that binds "prince and people" in a common national destiny.

The prevailing vision of that destiny, in keeping with London's role as a catalyst of absolutism, was framed by the language of feudal loyalty and chivalric honor. Lydgate, for example, had reconfigured the epic *translatio* by asserting that "knighthood in Greece and Troy the City / Took his principles, and next in Rome toun,"[54] and the implications of this view were followed out in a poem "In Honour of the City of London" (c. 1501), attributed by Stow to Dunbar, in which the chivalric, neofeudal grandeur of the city becomes the basis for a new vision of Tudor empire:

> London, thou art of townes *A per se*.
>   Soveraign of cities, seemliest in sight
> Of high renoun, riches and royaltie;
>   Of Lordes, barons, and many a goodly knyght;
>   Of most delectable lusty ladies bright...
>
> Gladdith anon, thou lusty Troynovant,
>   Citie that some tyme cleped was New Troy;
> In all the erth, imperiall as thou stant.[55]

While they supported the Tudor image, and reflected the late-feudal arrangements that enabled London to function as a "collective seigneur" through royal charter and privilege, the foundation-myth and its chivalric associations also had a wide appeal among the members of London's citizen class. The *Brut* chronicles, deriving from the foundation myth,

---

[53] *Albion's England*, 3.14, in *Works of the English Poets*, ed. Alexander Chalmers (21 vols. London, 1810), 4: 538.

[54] *The Minor Poems*, ed. H. N. McCracken (2 vols. 1934; rpt. London: EETS, 1961), 2: 777.

[55] *The Oxford Book of English Verse*, ed. Sir Arthur Quiller-Couch (New York: Oxford University Press, 1940), pp. 22–24.

were widely circulated in fifteenth-century London alongside the new civic chronicles, which typically began with the reign of Richard I, during which the mayoralty and commune began, and which dated each year from the inauguration of the Lord Mayor (October 29).[56] John Carpenter, a fifteenth-century clerk for the City of London, began the City custumal known as the *Liber Albus* (1419) by noting that London "possesses the liberties, rights, and customs of that ancient city Troy... All persons too that come here, of whatever condition they may be, whether freemen or serfs, obtain a refuge here, as well as protection and liberty."[57] Robert Fabyan, a late fifteenth-century City Sheriff, divided the two halves of his chronicle at the reign of Richard I by celebrating the longevity of a civic community "full kynde"

> To prynce and kynge
> That hath borne iuste rulynge
> Syn the fyrste wynnynge
> Of thys Ilande by Brute...
>
> Neuer yet caste downe
> As other many haue be
> As Rome and Carthage
> Hierusalem the sage
> Wyth many other of age
> In storye as ye maye se
> Chryst is the very stone
> That the cytye is sette vppon...
>
> This citie I meane is Troynouant
> Where honour & worshyp doth haunte
> Wyth vertue and ryches accordaunte.[58]

The assimilation of London's power and achievements to a neofeudal language of chivalry helped to establish a new "community of honor," a way of imagining the participation of the city and the merchant class in the process of nation-building. Caxton, the London publisher who initiated the new taste for chivalric materials in the Tudor age, held important positions for many years among the English merchants in Bruges, and it was, in fact, from mercantile contacts with Burgundian culture, Arthur Ferguson argues, that the sixteenth-century English taste for chivalry arose: "If the splendor of Burgundian chivalry rested on the profits of Burgundian commerce, it was the wool and cloth trade that kept Englishmen constantly in touch with Burgundy and rendered

---

[56] Antonia Gransden, *Historical Writing in England: Volume II: c. 1307 to the Early Sixteenth Century* (Ithaca: Cornell University Press, 1982), ch. 8.
[57] *The White Book of the City of London*, ed. H. T. Riley (London: Camden Society, 1862), p. 54.   [58] *Concordance of Histories* (1516), sigs. AA–AAv.

them all the more susceptible to the chivalric pretensions of the Burgundian court."[59] At the lavish London tournament of 1467, designed to celebrate the economic *rapprochement* between Burgundy and England, the Mayor and city magistrates occupied seats of honor.[60] And when Charles V paid his imperial visit to the City in 1522, he was confronted, at the Conduit in Cornhill, with an Arthurian pageant that made imperial counterclaims for London and its Prince.[61]

If, following "the total collapse of a settled court culture"[62] in the disastrous reigns of the mid-Tudor period, there was a hiatus in the tradition of "learned chivalry," the myths and motifs were sustained in popular form by London's citizen class, for whom the ideals of loyalty and service offered a means of cultural legitimation. A document of 1582, for example, announces that an Arthurian archery tournament, established under Henry VIII, "hath been greatly revived, and within these five years set forward at the great cost and charges of sundry chief citizens." Spenser's teacher, Richard Mulcaster, digresses from his *Positions* (1581) to remark upon "the friendly and franke fellowship of prince *Arthurs* knightes in and about the citie of *London* ... of late years ... reviv'd."[63] This or another Arthurian society, led by Hugh Offley, "a rich Citizein of London, free of the Leather-sellers Company," staged for the Queen "a costly show of Prince Arthur," and received in return her grateful promise that "she would love, maintain, and advance, her Citizens of the City of London."[64] A number of burlesques from *The Tournament of Tottenham* to *The Knight of the Burning Pestle* testify to the selective and highly improbable adaptations of chivalry to the urban sphere. Enabling Londoners to reflect with pride upon the origins of their city and its place in the history of culture, the decor of chivalry legitimized their standing in the realm, masked their novel economic pursuits as traditional loyalty, and provided a pageantic language of parity and reciprocity in which to negotiate their relationships to the crown and aristocracy.

---

[59] Ferguson, *The Indian Summer*, p. 19; see also Gordon Kipling, *The Triumph of Honour: Burgundian Origins of the Elizabethan Renaissance* (Leiden University Press, 1977), and "Henry VII and the Origins of Tudor Patronage," in *Patronage in the Renaissance*, ed. Guy Fitch Lytle and Stephen Orgel (Princeton University Press, 1981).

[60] Ferguson, *The Indian Summer*, p. 21.

[61] Millican, *Spenser and the Table Round*, p. 50.

[62] Roy Strong, *The English Icon* (New York: Pantheon, 1969), p. 1.

[63] W. M. or W. H., *A Remembrance of the Worthy Show and Shooting* (1582), cited by Millican, *Spenser and the Table Round*, p. 55; for Mulcaster, see p. 56.

[64] Richard Robinson, *A Learned and True Assertion* (1582), cited by Millican, *Spenser and the Table Round*, p. 59; for Hugh Offley and his show, see Millican, p. 61 and J. G. Nichols, *The Progresses and Public Processions of Queen Elizabeth I* (3 vols. 1829; rpt. New York: Burt Franklin, 1968), 2: 529.

Through its double determination, the myth of Troynovant and its chivalric decor provided Spenser with a basis on which to carry out the epic translation of ancient empire to modern Britain, a way of simultaneously celebrating the dynastic descent of "the antique Troian blood" (3.3.42) and affirming "the social contract ... the establishment of peoplehood, national boundaries, and national faith, and the manifestation of political destinies. "[65] The aim of Spenser's poem, as Maurice Evans aptly describes it, "is to make the line of history and that of myth one and the same, to make London identical with Cleopolis. "[66] But in the poem as it stands this projected convergence remains incomplete. To a degree unprecedented in earlier epic poets, Spenser separates the historical and fictional dimensions of his poem. History, and with it the emergence of a great capital city, exists primarily in retrospect or prospect, on the horizon of the poem, as it were; and this temporal suspension is figured in the spatial translocation of the narrative from Britain to Faeryland. Exiled from Britain, Arthur and Britomart are in effect exiled for a time from history, precisely at a point at which the history that leads to modern Britain is in jeopardy. While the Faery Queen Gloriana, a shadow of "the most excellent and glorious person of our soveraine the Queene," informs the existing poem by visionary anticipation and as a pervasive allegorical influence, the Briton Arthur never meets with her, and her historical embodiment remains in a distant future Britomart has yet to create. Faeryland, as Thomas Roche has said, "is like Augustine's City of God in that it exists morally as a state of being in men and metaphorically as a fictional world. It can be attained as a state of mind, but not as a human society because the time was and is not ripe. "[67]

What finally matters in the structure of Spenser's poem, however, is not the completion of the quest, the projected end or union, but what Angus Fletcher has called "the sense of threshold, the sense that great deeds contain within their forms the seeds of great truths. Viewed in this more provisional light, every episode possesses a typological direction. "[68] Spenser's historical vision is thus a function of a fictional technique in which the poet, "thrusteth into the middest, ... and there recoursing to the thinges forepaste, and diuining of things to come, maketh a pleasing Analysis of all." As a work that effects a *translatio*, a symbolic rite of historical transition, *The Faerie Queene* is itself a bridge

[65] James Nohrnberg, *The Analogy of "The Faerie Queene"* (Princeton University Press, 1976), p. 8.
[66] *Spenser's Anatomy of Heroism: A Commentary on "The Faerie Queene"* (Cambridge University Press, 1970), p. 20.
[67] *The Kindly Flame* (Princeton University Press, 1964), pp. 45–46.
[68] *The Prophetic Moment: An Essay on Spenser* (University of Chicago Press, 1971), p. 75.

or *limen* that mediates not only between the mythic past and historical present, but also, within that present, between feudal and statist alternatives. Written from within "the middest" of a crucial historical passage, the poem looks backward and forward to register the "density" of a "unique, critical moment of a nation's culture and history."[69]

The spiritual import of this moment emerges on Book 1's Mount of Contemplation, in Spenser's contrast between the New Jerusalem, "the Citie of the great King" (1.10.55), which extends its "loftie towres vnto the starry sphere" (1.10.56), and Cleopolis, wherein "that fairest *Faerie Queene* doth dwell" (1.10.58), "for earthly frame, / The fairest peece, that eye beholden can" (1.10.59). The well-known contrasts between these symbolic cities[70] – between the predestinarian city "God has built / For those to dwell in, that are chosen his" (1.10.57) and the noble earthly city haunted by those "that couet in th' immortall booke of fame / To be eternized" (1.10.59) – elaborate upon a problem both the Bible and Augustine pose in urban metaphor: the conflict between the New Jerusalem and Babylon, the City of God and the City of Man.

Brought to "A litle path ... / Which to goodly Citie led his view," the newly–regenerate Redcrosse is, with the poet himself, dazzled by a visionary fabric

> Whose wals and towres were builded high and strong
> Of perle and precious stone, that earthly tong
> Cannot describe, nor wit of man can tell.   (1.10.55)

The jewelled splendor of this sight dims the merely crystalline lustre of "great Cleopolis," the Faerie Queene's "city of glory" that until this moment both hero and poet had thought

> The fairest Citie was, that might be seene;
> And that bright towre all built of cristall clene,
> *Panthea*, seemd the brightest thing, that was:
> But now by proofe all otherwise I weene;
> For this great Citie does that far surpas,
> And this bright Angels towre quite dims that towre of glas.   (1.10.58)

Although its crystal tower of Panthea is associated by name with the Roman Pantheon and thus with the earthly city, where joy, Augustine

[69] Frank Kermode, "Spenser and the Allegorists," in *Shakespeare, Spenser, Donne* (London: Routledge and Kegan Paul, 1971), p. 22.

[70] See especially Isabel Rathborne, *The Meaning of Spenser's Faeryland* (1937; rpt. New York: Russell and Russell, 1965), pp. 106–107; Carol V. Kaske, "Spenser's Pluralistic Universe: The View from the Mount of Contemplation," in R. C. Frushell and B. J. Vondersmith, eds., *Contemporary Thought on Edmund Spenser* (Carbondale: Southern Illinois University Press, 1975), pp. 127–147; Paul J. Alpers, *The Poetry of "The Faerie Queene"* (Princeton University Press, 1967), pp. 118, 348; and Hankins, *Source and Meaning in Spenser's Allegory*, pp. 107–114.

noted, is "but as glass, bright and brittle, and evermore in danger of breaking," Cleopolis is "for earthly frame, / The fairest peece, that eye beholden can" (1.10.59). And while its temporal glories will finally "vanish into nought" (1.10.62), Redcrosse, momentarily blinded to earthly sights by this vision, must "turne againe / Backe to the world" at the Mount of Contemplation's foot. *Georgos*, St. George, is a "man of earth" (1.10.52), a British ploughman's foundling who is doubly exiled both from the heavenly city at time's end and the ideal fairy capital to which he lends his allegiance. His descent from the mountain marks his entry into the "painefull pilgrimage" (1.10.61) of history, and his restoration of Eden, lord of both East and West, gives a typological coherence to the historic struggle that remains incomplete in Britain at the moment of the poem's writing. The urban festival that celebrates the restoration of Eden to his throne equates the recovery of Edenic origins with the redemption of the Israelite capital, Jerusalem,[71] thereby completing the structural parallel between the Legend of Holiness and its Biblical subtext, which begins with expulsion from a garden world and ends in the "great citie" to which "the Kinges of the earth shal bring their glorie and honour" (Rev. 21:10, 24).

To this latter verse the Geneva Bible attaches the gloss that "Here we se ... that the Kings & Princes are partakers of the heauenly glorie, if they rule in ye feare of the Lord." Spenser's defense of this proposition draws heavily on the symbolism of Apocalypse, pitting the Constantinian, imperial claims of the English Crown and Church against those of the papal emperor who "high hath set his throne where *Tiberis* doth pass" (1.2.22). Through this apocalyptic urban typology, which suggestively contrasts Babylon and the New Jerusalem, London and Rome, Spenser shares with Augustine a visionary mode that transforms history into "an exquisite poem set off with antitheses."[72]

The overwhelming height and distance of the Heavenly City, that "durst so high extend / Her loftie towres vnto the starry sphere" (1.10.56) – "too high a ditty for my simple song" (1.10.55) – contrasts decisively with the false erectness of Lucifera's House of Pride, "mounted ... full hie," but built on sand, "Whose wals were high, but nothing strong, nor thick" (1.4.4–5). Through this contrast, Spenser defines the Christian purposes that will differentiate his own epic from "The antique ruines of the *Romaines* fall" (4.5.49) – those melancholy afterimages that linger out their dead-end cultural lives in Lucifera's

---

[71] "The prophets," James Nohrnberg observes, "compare the restored Israel to Eden (Isa. 51: 3; Ezek. 36: 55); and Spenser's Eden, like the one in Revelation, is metropolitan," p. 179.

[72] *The City of God*, tr. Marcus Dods (New York: Modern Library, 1950), 11.18.

basement (4.5.49, 51). Though distanced from it, however, Cleopolis does resemble the New Jerusalem, and in beholding this City of God Redcrosse looks as much across as up from the Mount of Contemplation, perceiving there a kind of reciprocity and connection, as "The blessed Angels to and fro descend / As commonly as friend does with his friend" (1.10.56). As a scene of *conversio*, Spenser's departs significantly from Augustine's, which also orients itself to Virgil.[73] Unlike the Pauline text ("put ye on the Lord Jesus Christ, and take no thought for the flesh" – Rom. 13: 14) that supersedes Augustine's early reading in Virgil, replacing the classical *libido dominandi* with a love for the City of God,[74] the Pauline text that forms the motto of Spenser's legend ("Put on the whole armour of God" – Eph. 6: 11) concerns the charity and compassion of the Christian community, wherein men are members of one another and by God's "workemanship created ... vnto good workes, which God hath ordeined, that we shulde walke in them" (Eph. 2: 10).[75] Reinforced at the House of Holiness by the teachings of Charissa and of Mercie and her seven corporal works, this reorientation to the Augustinian City of God enables Spenser to redefine, rather than repudiate, the epic and its urban vision. As the embodiment of this new vision, the conjunction of the New Jerusalem and Cleopolis balances the remoteness of divine purpose with a sense of its intimate and continuing presence in history; it establishes an order for *The Faerie Queene* to imitate and forms a threshold for the poem's representation of the epic rite of passage.

In Book 2, with the contrasting chronicles of Faeryland and Britain and the contrasting capitals of Cleopolis and Troynovant, Spenser begins to elaborate upon that passage, bringing his poem closer to "a palpable material, natural history ... closer to ideas of economy, wealth, maritime exploration, imperial expansion, political dominion."[76] Extending uninterrupted down through seven hundred generations to the present reign of Gloriana, Faeryland's history, like the Bible, begins in a garden and ends in a city. The building of Cleopolis, a key development in faery legend, is both a model for the historic evolution of all cities and an ideal that, in its own emergence, Troynovant must approximate."[77] In

---

[73] On the debt of Augustine's historical vision to Virgil's, see Brooks Otis, "Virgil and Clio," *Phoenix* 20 (1966), 59–75.

[74] See *Confessions* 1.13; cf. *City of God*, 1.1, 14.28.

[75] The particular import of the Ephesians text is discussed by Kathleen Williams, *Spenser's World of Glass: A Reading of "The Faerie Queene"* (Berkeley: University of California Press, 1966), p. 33.   [76] Fletcher, *The Prophetic Moment*, p. 85.

[77] The early history of Cleopolis, as Thomas Roche has said, is "the story of every civilization, of man establishing himself in society ... The details of the Elfin chronicle ... were meant to convey the general idea of the evolution of 'the city,'" *The Kindly Flame*, p. 37. I derive my idea that Troynovant must "approximate" this ideal – that Troynovant is London in its literal, historical existence, while Cleopolis is London in its

the course of its construction – from Elfinan "who layd / Cleopolis foundation first of all," to Elfiline who "enclosed it with a golden wall," to Elfant who "all of Christall did *Panthea* build," and to Elfinor, who "built by art vpon the glassy See / A bridge of bras" (2.10.72–73) – Cleopolis acquires the principal features of the cityscape of Troynovant mentioned in the poem – its walls (2.10.46), towered skyline (4.11.27–28), and bridge (3.9.45).[78] More importantly, the order in which these monuments are constructed parallels the historical migration of civilization from Troy to Rome, to Troynovant. Elfiline's wall, evoking the foundational act by which Tros, Romulus, and Lud gave their names to the capitals of these three civilizations, symbolizes a common cultural inheritance. Elfant's tower of Panthea alludes both to the Roman Pantheon and to the Roman addition to Trojan culture. The third and crucial monument, however, is the one left by Elfinor, who "built by art vpon the glassy See / A bridge of bras, whose sound heauens thunder seem'd to be" (2.10.72–74). Spanning the glassy sea that in Revelation separates St. John from God's throne and that in the Geneva Bible is glossed as "this brittle and inconstant worlde,"[79] this bridge, for which there is no Trojan or Roman equivalent, completes the building of Cleopolis and points forward to that "wonder of the world," the bridge by which London or Troynovant carries civilization forward.

But within the British history itself there is no bridge that crosses the glassy sea before God's throne. The British chronicle suddenly breaks off at an "vntimely breach" as it reaches the historical moment of its reader, King Arthur. It is the fate of Arthur, like the other British heroes of the chronicle, to inherit and inhabit the condition of historical discontinuity. "In the end was left no moniment / Of Brutus" (2.10.36), the founder of Troynovant, the chronicle declares. It is not the founder, but Lud, a later figure of passage in the "middest" of history, who carries out the renewals that change the name of Troynovant to London and who leaves

> endlesse moniments of his great good:
> The ruin'd wals he did reaedifye
> Of *Troynouant*, gainst force of enimy,
> And built that gate, which of his name is hight,
> By which he lyes entombed solemnly.   (2.10.46)

It is, significantly, these urban monuments, and not Lud's progeny – "two sonnes, too young to rule aright" – which sustain his "famous

politically and morally ideal existence – from J. W. Bennett's view that "Faeryland is an ideal realm of which England is often the material counterpart," "Spenser's Muse," *JEGP*, 31 (1932), p. 214.
[78] As demonstrated by Isabel Rathborne, *The Meaning of Spenser's Fairyland*, pp. 106–120.   [79] Cited in Hamilton's note, p. 271.

memory" and make for continuity between past and future. Lud's reconstruction stands, with the acts of the lawgiver Donwallo and a few others, for the recoveries and renewals that sustain historic purpose amid the overwhelming disasters of British history.

Unsure of his identity and destiny, and exiled from Britain to Fairyland, Arthur searches unsuccessfully for the ideal Faery Queene, Gloriana, whose historical counterpart in the poem's temporal scheme is a yet unborn descendant who lies on the other side of the "vntimely breach" between Arthur's own death and the resumption of the line by Britomart and Artegall. Like the young historical Christ poring over the prophets, reading of his place in prophecy, Arthur is moving toward an understanding that he is "sonne and heire vnto a king, / As time in her iust terme the truth to light should bring" (1.9.5). Only in the very broad perspective of a faith in things unseen – the perspective of reading history with God's eye [80] – can the seemingly random and destructive cycles of British history be seen to participate in a purposeful, linear continuity like that of Faerie civilization. Arthur and Britomart are, in a sense, the bridge across the "vntimely breach" they inhabit, which is why they are the poem's two visionary readers of British history and prophecy, respectively.

In the spatio-temporal disjuncture – the "vntimely breach" – that is the locus of their visionary reading, Spenser opens up the vast "meanwhile..." that is the workspace of his poem and his culture. This is, in Angus Fletcher's terms, a pro-fane or labyrinthine time that lies proleptically "before" the templar completion of all things. It is also, in Jacques LeGoff's terms, a natural time, "both eternally renewed and perpetually unpredictable," allowing for the secular innovations of mercantile and civic time.[81] It is, finally in Benedict Anderson's terms, the simultaneous time and space that is "the technical means for 'representing' the *kind* of imagined community that is the nation."[82]

The widening of historic vision in the reading of the Faerie and British chronicles is framed, significantly, by the narrower alternatives of the Cave of Mammon and the Bower of Bliss, which represent both the opposite dangers of excessive care and carelessness and the misreadings of historic purpose that these dangers generate. Like the mercantile London Robert Crowley called "An hell with out order" and which

[80] David Lee Miller, *The Poem's Two Bodies: The Poetics of the 1590 "Faerie Queene"* (Princeton University Press, 1988), pp. 203–206.

[81] "Merchants' Time and Church's Time in the Middle Ages," in *Time, Work, and Culture in the Middle Ages*, tr. Arthur Goldhammer (University of Chicago Press, 1980), p. 35.

[82] *Imagined Communities: Reflections on the Origin and Spread of Nationalism* (London: Verso, 1983), p. 30.

Bishop Aylmer accused of bowing to "the might of Mammon,"[83] Mammon's is a realm of "worldlings" (2.7.8.); its storehouse of "huge great yron chests and coffers strong" (2.7.30) evokes the city Stow called "the principall store house, and Staple of all commodities within this Realme,"[84] while its sooty atmosphere and Bosch-like "hundred fornaces all burning bright" (2.7.35) evoke "the new furnaces of the Elizabethan industries, about whose chimneys, with their dark Satanic smoke, there was already much feeling."[85] By contrast, the voyage to the Bower, with its Gulf of Greedinesse, Quicksand of Vnthriftyhed, and Whirlepoole of Decay, is an extended exploration of prodigal *dépense*, of "lustfull luxurie and thriftlesse wast," "lost credite and consumed thrift" (2.12.7–9).[86] The Bower's enclosed garden, "arbers," and "banket houses" (2.12.83) recall the suburban London "harbers... bowres" and "banquetting houses" in which moralists like Stubbes complained that the age's social butterflies were wont to "play the filthie persone" (pp. 87–88). From opposite extremes, then, the two realms figure the critical socioeconomic transition that was leading sixteenth-century moralists to pit merchants against gentlemen, covetousness against prodigality, bourgeois accumulation against aristocratic *dépense*.

Within and between themselves, the Cave and Bower offer false versions of beginnings and ends that attenuate historic process, reducing it to purposeless cyclicality. Claiming to "poure out vnto all, / ... all this worldes good" (2.7.8), Mammon portrays his busy furnaces as "the fountaine of the worldes good" (2.7.38) and his storehouses as "the worldes blis, loe here the end" (2.7.32). Like Mammon's, Acrasia's realm is both a false source and a false end. The "most daintie Paradise on ground" (2.12.58), "more sweete and holesome than Eden selfe" (2.12.52), it is also the "sad end... of life intemperate" (2.12.85). The Bower's lulling effects of amnesia and inertia are summed up in the enchanting Song of the Rose, where the cyclical flourishing and decay of bud, leaf, and flower, collapsed into "the passing of a day," epitomize the unredeemed historical rhythms of the *Briton moniments*. To read, with Arthur and Britomart, past these false starts and ends, is to discover a widened horizon in which *eros* and *imperium*, garden and city, may yet

---

[83] Robert Crowley, "Of Allayes," in *Select Works*, ed. J. M. Cowper (London: EETS, 1872), lines 193–204. See Paul Seaver, *The London Lectureships* (Stanford University Press, 1970), p. 129.

[84] *The Survey of London*, 1: 12. On several occasions, Stow describes the conversion of confiscated Church properties to storehouses; see 1: 125–126, 131, 263.

[85] Evans, *Spenser's Anatomy of Heroism*, p. 71.

[86] See esp. Martha Craig, "The Secret Wit of Spenser's Language," in A. C. Hamilton, ed., *Essential Articles for the Study of Edmund Spenser* (Hamden, Conn.: Archon Books, 1972), pp. 313–333.

paradoxically be one. Such reading from the "middest" creates a new order from the cycles of the old, creates a new history to be inhabited and settled, "Formerly grounded, and fast setteled / On firme foundation of true bountihed" (2.12.1).

When, from the other side of Britain's dynastic breach, Britomart takes up from Arthur the poem's visionary burden, it is, significantly, to contrast Troynovant not with its ideal counterpart, Cleopolis, but with its historical predecessor, Rome. In contrast to Paridell, who cannot complete the story of Troy's afterlife, Britomart recalls how the virtuous Aeneas "was not in the Cities wofull fyre / Consum'd" (3.9.40) but, burning with a purer flame, survived to found the second Troy from which the third descends:

> There, there (said *Britomart*) a fresh appeard
> The glory of the later world to spring,
> And Troy again out of her dust was reard...
> But a third kingdome yet is to arise...
> That in all glory and great enterprise,
> Both first and second *Troy* shall dare to equalize.

> It *Troynouant* is hight, that with the waues
> Of wealthy *Thamis* washed is along
> Vpon whose stubborne neck, whereat he raues
> With roring rage, and sore him selfe doth throng,
> That all men feare to tempt his billowes strong,
> She fastned hath her foot, which standes so hy,
> That it a wonder of the world is song
> In forreine landes, and all which passen by,
> Beholding it from far, do thinke it threates the skye.

> The *Troian Brute* did first that Citie found,
> And Hygate made the meare thereof by West,
> And Ouert gate by North: that is the bound
> Toward the land; two riuers bound the rest.
> So huge a scope at first him seemed best,
> To be the compasse of his kingdomes seat:
> So huge a mind could not in lesser rest.   (3.9.44–46)

While the triumphant posture of London Bridge figuratively effects the epic *translatio* to Britain, it does not, like Elfinor's "bridge of bras," span the "glassy sea" before God's throne, nor does it, like the visionary golden bridge of *The Ruines of Time*, span "the Sea from one to other side" (line 548). Instead, it barely holds the raging river in check, not so much abridging time, or leaping to its nether end, as surfing upon it. It stands in precarious relation to gigantic powers, a point emphasized in the odd fact that the bridge "stands so hy" that "all which passen by, / Beholding it from farre, do thinke it threates the skye." The appearance of overreaching may only be the overly apocalyptic effect of beholding the bridge from too great a distance; but Elfinor's bridge of brass, oddly, makes a sound that "heauens thunder seem'd to be," and the precarious height of London's bridge, together with the river's "roring rage," may be Spenser's way of invoking those sons of Babel who sought to build a bridge too far, "a city and a tower, whose top may reach unto heaven" (Gen. 11: 4).

This threat of overreaching becomes a central concern in the capital's next appearance, in the river marriage of Book 4, where it appears not in relation to its historical predecessors but in relation to its contemporary British neighbors. In this version, Troynovant appears as the crown of the Thames,

> like to a Coronet
> He wore, that seemed strange to common vew,
> In which were many towres and castles set,
> That it encompast round as with a golden fret.

> Like as the mother of the Gods, they say,
> In her great iron charet wonts to ride,
> When to *Ioues* pallace she doth take her way:
> Old *Cybele*, arayd with pompous pride,
> Wearing a Diadem embattild wide
> With hundred turrets, like a Turribant.
> With such an one was Thamis beautifide;
> That was to weet the famous Troynovant
> In which her kingdomes throne is chiefly resiant.   (4.11.27)

As the circular, mural crown of Cybele (see Figs. 2–4), Troynovant as *urbs* becomes in the river pageant the microcosm and center of a terrestrial *orb* or *mundus*. The wedding procession in which river and city take part unfolds the history of culture, from the "most famous founders ... Of puissant Nations" (4.11.15), to the exploratory incursions of Britain's empire into the New World (4.1.22). The procession of rivers, which "anthropomorphizes the land and civilizes it,"[87] placing culture in the world of time, and artifice in the world of nature, thus forms a fitting prelude to the exaltation of Troynovant.

In addition to mythopoeia and numerology, however, politics and economics provide another structure of significance in the catalogue. In addition to rivers, the passage names "many a city, and ... many a towne" (4.11.34) – the major population or trading centers of the realm, as well as every English river navigable for trade at the turn of the

---

[87] Harry Berger, Jr., "Two Spenserian Retrospects: The Antique Temple of Venus and the Primitive Marriage of Rivers," *TSLL*, 10 (1968), 18.

century.[88] All of these personified attendants practice an exemplary political and economic deference to the London-crowned Thames:

> They all on him this day attended well;
> And with meet seruice waited him about...
> ... both him honour'd as their principall.   (4.11.30)

This deference is a tribute to the transformation of sixteenth-century London into the capital of an expanding trading empire, a transformation that nevertheless disrupted the traditional economy of England's countryside, outports, and provincial towns. Throughout the sixteenth century, London's domination of the "common wealth" had become an increasingly central theme of complaint. The city's extraordinary growth at the expense of the provinces was the focus of particularly hostile criticism.[89] Spenser's answer to this criticism in the river-marriage, where London becomes quite literally a *caput orbis terrarum*, is to emphasize the innovative force of London in the creation of a unified nation–state and empire. In establishing this point, the river-marriage draws heavily upon the new nationalistic (and perhaps distinctively British) genre, the poetic river-pageant, invented by England's chief patriotic anatomists, John Leland and William Camden. Leland's *Cygnea Cantio* (1545) pays tribute to "the high walls of lofty Troynovant,"[90] while Camden's fragmentary *De Connubio Tamae et Isis* asserts, in view of London's "Palaces" and "stately towres," "That now with Romane Tyberis the Tamis may well compare."[91] In Michael Drayton's later nationalistic river-poem, the *Poly-Olbion* (1612), London's destined greatness as an *entrepôt* is justified by its ideal geographic situation on the Thames:

> *Tames* his either Banks, adorn'd with buildings faire,
> The City to salute doth bid the Muse prepare.
> Whose Turrets, Fanes, and Spyres, when wistly she beholds,

---

[88] See T. S. Willan, *River Navigation in England* (London: Oxford University Press, 1936), pp. vi and 146–147; cf. H. C. Dorby, ed., *A New Historical Geography of England* (Cambridge University Press, 1973), p. 291.

[89] Merchants, MPs, and local officials from the provinces frequently addressed to the Crown such petitions as the following: "As the city [London] is grown to be exceedingly populous, the consumption must be great; it is supplied principally from some few shires adjoining, which are generally much annoyed, for by the daily carrying away of their commodities, the prices of those which remain are very much raised. As they of London receive great benefits from their neighbours, so they should benefit them."

[90] "alta Trenovanti / Celsi...moenia" (echoing Virgil's prophetic *altae moenia Romae*, 1.7), in *Cygnea Cantio* (1545), in *The Itinerary of John Leland*, ed. Thomas Hearne (Oxford: 1769), p. 13.

[91] *Britannia* (1610), p. 419. For the relation of Leland's and Camden's poems to Spenser, see Jack B. Oruch, "Spenser, Camden, and the Poetic Marriages of Rivers," *SP*, 64 (1967), 606–624; C. G. Osgood, "Spenser's English Rivers," *Transactions of the Connecticut Academy of Arts and Sciences*, 23 (1920), 65–108.

> Her wonder at the site, thus strangely she unfolds:
> At thy great Builders wit, who's he but wonder may?
> Nay: of his wisdom, thus, ensuing times may say;
> O more then mortall man, that did this Towne begin!
> ... As in the fittest place, by man that could be thought,
> To which by Land, or Sea, provision might be brought.
> And such a Road of Ships scarce all the world commands,
> As is the goodly Tames, neer where Brute's City stands.
> Nor any Haven lies to which is more resort,
> Commodities to bring, as also to transport.[92]

Writing a generation after Spenser, and in the shadow of growing opposition to the absolutism of the Stuart state,[93] Drayton immediately responds to this picture of the burgeoning economic power of the capital by deploring the misappropriation by a class of newly powerful upstarts, of the "publique wealth" London should help to circulate:

> Our kingdome that enricht (through which we flourisht long)
> E're idle Gentry up in such aboundance sprong,
> Now pestring all this Ile: whose disproportion drawes
> The publique wealth so drie, and only is the cause
> Our gold goes out so fast, for foolish foraine things,
> Which upstart Gentry still into our Country brings...
> ... Merchants long train'd up in Gayn's deceitful schoole,
> And subtly having learn'd to sooth the humorous foole,
> Present their painted toyes unto this frantique gull,
> Disparaging our Tinne, our Leather, Corne, and Wooll;
> When Forrainers, with ours them warmly cloath and feed,
> Transporting trash to us, of which we nere had need.   (16.341–358)

In opposition both to the economic domination of London and to the centralized absolutist state it helps to support, Drayton adheres to an apparently backward-looking and nostalgic ideal of "authority... not centered but dispersed," a "land-centered vision," in which the land and its individual owners, rather than the dynasty, become the basis of dominion, the embodiment of "impersonal and historically transient authority."[94] Yet insofar as this decentered power is secured by the orderly juridico-political apparatus of a modern state which the growth of London had helped to create, Drayton's is paradoxically a neofeudal rather than a strictly regressive ideal. The paradox is reflected in his simultaneous glorification and critique of London's economic power,

[92] *Poly-Olbion*, 16.313–340, in *Works*, ed. J. William Hebel (5 vols. Oxford: Shakespeare Head, 1933), 4: 321.
[93] See David Norbrook, *Poetry and Politics in the English Renaissance* (London: Routledge and Kegan Paul, 1984), ch. 8.
[94] See Richard Helgerson, "The Land Speaks: Cartography, Chorography, and Subversion in Renaissance England," *Representations*, 16 (Fall, 1986), pp. 65, 74, 62.

and his solution is to sacrifice the concentration of power to its distributive effects.

By contrast, Spenser's earlier response to the overdetermined process and contradictory results of London's growth is to sacrifice the distribution to the concentration of power, to emphasize the "meet seruice" by which the provinces and outports do "honour" to London as to "their principall." In this approach to London's domination of the realm, Spenser follows the logic of George Peele's *Descensus Astraea* (1585), the first surviving published text of the London mayoral pageants that would in the next quarter-century elaborate a new ideology for the city:

> The honest Franklin and the Husbandman
> Layes downe his sackes of corne at Londons feet,
> And bringes such presents as the countrie yeeldes.
> The pleasant Thames...
> For Londons good convayes with gentle stream,
> And safe and easie passage what she can...
> For Londons aid the Country giues supplie
> Of needful things, and store of euery graine.[95]

Placing Britain's rivers in subjection to the Thames, and insisting they "owe vassallage / To him, as to their Lord, and tribute pay" (4.11.29), Spenser explicitly defends in neofeudal language London's innovative contribution to the progressive cultural force of a new nation–state. But in this earlier defense, there is an implicit sympathy with the concentrated force of absolutism which Drayton, connecting it with the later corruptions of court and City, explicitly rejects. For Spenser, a just and stable order is inseparable from the primitive and violent hierarchy that establishes it. Cybele, to whose primitive and exotic "Turribant" Spenser likens the mural crown of Troynovant, stands as much for the dynamism and power as for the stabilizing effects of the civilizing process. The "troublous noyes" and "perilous tumult" that greet the arrival of Spenser's other Cybele, Cambina, confirm these former associations (see Fig. 4); arriving in "a charet of strange furnishment," drawn by "two grim lyons" (4.3.38–39), she imposes concord on the tournament of Satyrane through a primitive and terrifying violence:

> as she passed through th'vnruly preace
> Of People, thronging thicke her to behold,
> Her angrie teame breaking their bonds of peace,

---

[95] *The Description of England* in Holinshed's *Chronicles of England* (1577), sig. 1v. George Peele, *The Device of the Pageant Borne Before Wolstane Dixie, Lord Mayor of the Citie of London*, October 29, 1585, in J. G. Nichols, *The Progresses and Public Processions of Queen Elizabeth I*, 2: 447–449.

> Great heapes of them, like sheepe in narrow fold,
> For hast did ouer-runne, in dust enrould,
> That thorough rude confusion of the rout,
> Some fearing shriekt, some being harmed hould. (4.3.41)

Like the arrival of Cambina, the marriage of rivers, with its interplay of fixity and flux, towns and rivers, London and neighbors, simultaneously celebrates a novel civic order and the political violence from which it arises.

To compare this vision of dynamic concord with the New Jerusalem of Book 1 – where "Angels to and fro descend / ... As commonly as friend does with his frend" (1.10.56) – is to weigh the burdens the poem has accumulated as it travels toward contemporary history. As a jewelled mural crown, Troynovant has become in Tasso's terms an epic "ornament" adorning the body of the nation. At the same time, the feminine bridge that completed the *translatio* of Book 3 has become a mere masquing property, yielding to the masculine Thames and his "vassals." Through this gender switch, Troynovant has helped to effect a transition to the state and empire.

Bringing the prophesied emergence of Troynovant up to the contemporary present in its relations with the kingdom, the river-marriage of Book 4 also marks the first point in the poem that the whole British landscape enters Faeryland. But with this coalescence of the poem's two landscapes, a sense of destiny fulfilled is balanced by a sharpening dissonance between real and ideal. The convergence of Cleopolis and Troynovant within the same historical space – the space of Britain and the reader, where Westminster and London do not precisely coincide – begins to underline the disparity between radical justice and radical power, between the emergence of a new politico-juridical *imperium* and the extensive "vassalage" this entails. Already in Book 3, where Troynovant seems to threaten the sky, a potential for conflict emerges when Paridell responds to Britomart's account of Brute's founding of Troynovant by observing that

> His worke great *Troynouant*, his worke is eke
>   Fair *Lincolne*, both renowmed far away,
>   That who from East to West will endlong seeke,
>   Cannot two fairer Cities find this day,
>   Except *Cleopolis*. (3.9.51)

To the extent that Cleopolis and Troynovant begin to jostle for the same space, Paridell's exception suggests a potential conflict, within the historic present, between Troynovant–London and Cleopolis–Westminster – whose crystal tower of Panthea has suggested to some readers the Henry VII Chapel at Westminster Abbey, with its royal tombs and perpendicular Gothic glass.[96] In prophetic terms an ideal simulacrum of Troynovant, Cleopolis would thus begin to represent, *within* the historical horizon, an alternative in tension with it. As in the map of Middlesex in Drayton's *Poly-Olbion*, where personified figures of London and Westminster, both wearing mural crowns, appear side-by-side (see Fig. 5), or in Dekker's *The Dead Tearme* (1608), where London and Westminster debate for pride of place,[97] the divergence between the two cities marks a site of overdetermination, a liminal zone where the emergence of a new civil order can also be seen perpetuating the very Babylonish past of violence, pride, and tyranny from which it would be free.

Dynasty and destiny

In Book 5, as Britain becomes an imperial state acting on the stage of international power struggles, the prophetic counterpoint between Cleopolis and Troynovant yields to an equation (and reduction) of the two to Mercilla's palace. As the nearest approach to the seat of power in either Faeryland or Britain, Mercilla's palace "is a realization of the long sequence of allusions to Cleopolis or Troynovant, that is, to a capital city – no such court or city appears in the poem hereafter."[98] This radical concentration of power in Mercilla's court appears to justify and support the culmination of a Tudor apocalypse in the international exploits that conclude the legend.

Yet Spenser's effort to project a Tudor apocalypse abroad exhibits a distressing tendency to revert from European politics to domestic economy, from Satanic threats of foreign tyranny to the internal dangers of rebellion. As Artegall is repeatedly and egregiously delayed by the domestic problems that stand in the way of his mission as international justicer, his difficulties figure those of a modern state asserting its destined greatness abroad while failing to achieve a stable order from within. A force of modernization, the concentration of power essential to the Tudor apocalypse is also potentially regressive in a violence inimical to domestic legal right. As Milton later understood, the projection of violence abroad confirms the "blessedness" of British power by concealing its violence at home.[99]

[96] See, e.g., Hamilton's note on 1.10.58, and Hankins, who maintains that in Troynovant and Cleopolis, "London and Westminster are separate entities," *Source and Meaning in Spenser's Allegory*, p. 201.   [97] See below, p. 360.

[98] Nohrnberg, *The Analogy of "The Faerie Queene"*, p. 404.

[99] Patriotism, Milton noted, had "heretofore, in persuance of fame and forren dominion, spent it self vain-gloriously abroad; but henceforth we may learn a better fortitude, to dare to execute highest Justice on them that shall by force of Armes endeavour the

Pollente and the egalitarian Giant, found at opposite ends of the "Bridges passage" to the Rich Strond in the second canto (5.2.4), perhaps best exemplify the challenges to domestic order in this modern state. If, "Hauing great Lordships got and goodly farmes / Through strong oppression of his powre extort" (5.2.5), Pollente represents, at the monopolistic extreme, the extension of feudal tyranny through the extortionate apparatus of a state not fully freed by absolutism from a customary past, then the mobs and the Giant, who will "Lordings curbe, that commons ouer-aw" (5.2.38), represent at the opposite, levelling extreme the dangerous solvency in a new order where feudal structures have eroded. In both cases, the demand is for a radical and absolute power, represented in the monarch, which can harmonize these conflicting tendencies with true and radical justice.

The theoretical basis for this justice is royal prerogative, or equity, which, as Frank Kermode points out, exalts the Roman, imperialist view of the sovereign will over law. By implicitly elevating the new Tudor prerogative courts – Chancery and Star Chamber – over common law, Spenser's allegory translates the *supplement* of Equity in common law into the primary or originary power of the sovereign who rules in God's stead.[100] Even while it imputes an insufficiency to established law, the charismatic supplement of Equity professes to serve the meliorative purpose of reform: it is "better to reforme, then to cut off the ill" (2.10.1). In Spenser's Legend of Justice, however, the principle is epitomized in Mercilla's decapitation of Duessa. The inseparability of justice and power, reform and violence,[101] is upheld from the beginning of the legend, when the "vertuous race" of antiquity (represented in the primitive Hercules and Bacchus) is said to have reformed by having "cropt the branches of the sient base, / And with strong hand their fruitfull rancknes did deface" (5.1.1), to the end, when Artegall undertakes to "reforme that ragged Common-weale" by having Talus "search out" all rebels and "inflict most grievous punishment" (5.12.26).[102] The beheaded Pollente, Radegund, and Mercilla, the dismembered Munera and Geryoneo, the shattered Giant, Malengin, and Soldan all taste the violence of equitable reform.

The Legend of Justice is Spenser's attempt to depict reform as the

oppressing and bereaving of Religion and their liberty at home," *The Tenure of Kings and Magistrates* (1650), in *The Complete Prose Works of John Milton*, ed. Don M. Wolfe (8 vols. New Haven: Yale University Press, 1953–82), 3: 238.

[100] *Shakespeare, Spenser, Donne*, pp. 50–57.

[101] Goldberg points out that "reformation and cutting off form a single act," "The Poet's Authority: Spenser, Jonson, and James VI and I," in Stephen Greenblatt, ed., *The Forms of Power and the Power of Forms*, special issue of *Genre*, 15 (1982), p. 85.

[102] Geryoneo also has his arms hacked off as if "pruned from the natiue tree" (5.11.11).

outcome of an evolution from primitive, prelegal conditions (the world before Astraea's departure) to a secure and legal political establishment (where Artegall and Arthur make war on foreign powers). Yet the legend's uncertain oscillations between reform and violence, justice and force, maintain a fundamental continuity between the two.[103] The mythical passage from foundational violence to the juridical power of the state, Gilles Deleuze and Felix Guattari argue, requires a transitional moment when the violence internalized by the state must project itself in its purely negative, exterior, and unassimilable form.[104] Such a moment occurs in the palace of Mercilla, when Duessa (the thinly disguised pretender, Mary Queen of Scots) is beheaded at the behest of a sovereign word. Yet this moment of projected opposition is also a moment of semic evaporation, where the antinomial logic of romance yields to what Fredric Jameson sees as its foundational contradiction, namely, that "my enemy can be thought of as being *evil* (that is, other than myself and marked by some absolute difference, when what is responsible for his being so characterized is quite simply the *identity* of his own conduct with mine."[105] No more than the savage Artegall, discredited at legend's end, does Mercilla herself negotiate unscathed the passage from violence to the peaceful state that internalizes and redeploys it. In the double and divided blood of the royal progeny in Mercilla–Duessa, dynastic succession shows its unreliability, its potential to undermine the very pattern of cultural *translatio* and political perfection it claims to perpetuate. The most modern bearer of civilization, the monarchy is paradoxically regressive in its violence, inseparable from the feudal past its law would dissolve, and lacking in the means to assure its perpetuation. During the very Armada crisis that Spenser allegorizes, a bellicose pamphleteer had whipped up patriotism by appealing to the neochivalric and apocalyptic motifs that are the basis of Spenser's legend:

What enterprizes did famous King Arthur attempt?... What cities and peoples did he conquer? ...there shall be no decay, no leading into captiuitie, nor complayning in your streetes. Yee shall be blessed in the cittie and in the field.

But, like Spenser as well, his patriotism faltered over the "lettes and impediments... to this excellent defence" – the "dissention and emu-

---

103   Stephan Batman, for example, argued that the serpent symbolized not only "the prudence of Laws, well to gouerne common Wealthes," but also the "oppression which proceedeth from the kinge, from nobility, from spirituality, from Officers in authority," *The Golden Booke of the Leaden Goddes*, p. 16; quoted in Jane Aptekar, *Icons of Justice: Iconography and Thematic Imagery in "The Faerie Queene"* (New York: Columbia University Press, 1969), pp. 90–91.
104   *A Thousand Plateaus: Capitalism and Schizophrenia*, tr. Brian Massumi (Minneapolis: University of Minnesota Press, 1987), p. 355.
105   *The Political Unconscious*, p. 118.

lation ... in the Common weale" that had "shewed vnto vs our owne wants, ... stirred vp our mindes to looke to our selues."[106]

If, in the climax of Mercilla's palace, the poem comes closest to identifying Faeryland and Britain, it does so through an identification of Mercilla with the poet's Queen, an identification that also reduces these two vast civilizations and histories to a sovereign's prerogative word. And with this reduction there is also the strongest sense of a divergence – as in Spenser's Renaissance epic predecessors – between the durability of culture and the unreliability of dynastic succession. Potentially a link between Cleopolis and Troynovant, Mercilla's palace ultimately reinforces the distinction between the two because Troynovant cannot be reduced to a political body which is exclusively the monarch's. The palace, as Spenser notes, is finally "forraine land" to Arthur and Artegall (5.9.37).[107] Their final conquests, like the palace itself, bear witness to a continuing foreignness within the bodies of the state and poem.

Thus, as it moves closest to the real, historic cities of Europe – to Antwerp, or Paris, or Westminster – *The Faerie Queene* paradoxically moves furthest from its earlier "visions of the city." These visions – the symbolic contrasts of the New Jerusalem with Cleopolis, of Cleopolis with Troynovant, and of Troynovant with first and second Troy or with its domestic neighbors – help to organize the fabric of the poem and to establish its stature as a cultural monument. The Legend of Justice abstracts these visions into the figure of Mercilla, absorbs the symbolic edifice – the walls, the towers, the bridges – into a cult of personality. The once "huge ... scope" that Brutus traced "to be the compasse of his kingdomes seat" contracts into the narrow space of Mercilla's palace. The city, the bearer of prophetic and historic meaning, has become the seat and object of power.[108]

It is perhaps in view of this narrowed identification that the final Book of *The Faerie Queene* marks in many respects a retreat from the poem's epic thesis, its confrontation with history, and its urban vision. It is *from* the court that Calidore undertakes his seemingly regressive route in the legend:

---

[106] Anthony Marten, *An Exhortation to Stirre vp ... Faithfull Subiects to Defend their Country* (1588), sigs. D4v, E2, F1v, C2v.

[107] See T. K. Dunsheath, *Spenser's Allegory of Justice in " The Faerie Queene"* (Princeton University Press, 1968), pp. 188–222.

[108] In one way or another this is emphasized by most of Spenser's interpreters. One of the clearest statements of the theory is in Michael O'Connell, *Mirror and Veil: The Historical Dimension of Spenser's "Faerie Queene"* (Chapel Hill: University of North Carolina Press, 1977), pp. 155ff.; see also Joanne Craig, "The Image of Mortality: Myth and History in *The Faerie Queene*," *ELH*, 29 (1972), 538–542.

> Him first from court he to the citties coursed,
> And from the citties to the townes him prest,
> And from the townes into the countrie forsed,
> And from the country back to priuate farmes he scorsed.
>
> From thence into the open fields he fled,
> Whereas the Heardes were keeping of their neat.

Calidore's is not, however, a route of flight, but of quest. Insofar as the pastoral "noursery / Of vertue" yields perfect "patterne" of civility, Calidore's return to pastoral sources is also an *extension* of *The Faerie Queene*'s epic thesis, a continued movement forward into the public sphere and the political and social virtues that shape it. Yet this forward movement finally extends the poem's crisis without fully resolving it.

For Spenser's use of pastoral in the support of epic claims there are imposing Virgilian precedents. Aeneas' visit to the site of Rome, and to the rude society of Evander and his Arcadians, for example, forms a pastoral interlude that links two Golden Ages, the rustic Roman past and its glorious imperial future.[109] A similar connection of pastoral nostalgia with imperial destiny in Virgil's fourth eclogue became a seminal model for Christian interpreters of history, who linked the human origins of Eden with the final triumph of the New Jerusalem, using the Edenic *locus amoenus* to prefigure its supplantation by the heavenly city.[110] In keeping with this sort of typology, Spenser's courtesy grows on a humble "lowly stalke," but "brancheth forth in braue nobilitie, / And spreds it selfe through all ciuilitie" (6 Proem 4). In its polar extremities of sheepfold and court, therefore, the Legend of Courtesy aspires to reconcile a number of antinomies: the deepest recesses of the mind and solitary integrity with the most subtle and refined reciprocities of deference and demeanor,[111] the unadulterated simplicity of nature with the consummate satisfactions of culture, the inspiring and creative powers of leisure with the necessary labor of sustaining civilization against the siege of Fortune. In its rescue and restoration of Pastorella, Calidore's turn from pastoral reflection to active heroism takes the form of an Orphic adventure, thereby forging a link between lyric grace and civilizing labor and connecting, in the manner forecast by *The Ruines of Rome*, the pastoral and epic extremes of the Virgilian poetic model.

In many respects, however, this is less the establishment of a continuum or line of development than the assertion of a tautological

---

[109] See Otis, *Virgil: A Study in Civilized Poetry*, p. 337.

[110] See, for example, Giuseppe Mazotta, *Dante, Poet of the Desert* (Princeton University Press, 1979), p. 145.

[111] Nohrnberg places special emphasis on the superficiality of "reciprocities," *The Analogy of "The Faerie Queene"*, p. 709.

identity – "a marriage between the lowest and the highest," as it is called in Sidney's *Arcadia* – in which the polar extremes of courtliness and natural virtue converge in a mirror relationship and exclude the refractory middle ground, the dense historical phases and layers of privilege and power that actually separate them. "The essential trick of the old pastoral," William Empson observes, is "to imply a beautiful relation between the rich and poor," and to justify the superiority of the former by identifying them with the humble virtues of the latter: "the qualities most associated with the court turn up in the pastoral world apparently the characteristics of the life of nature – only to be transferred to the court through a magical discovery."[112]

In effecting this transition, however, the Legend of Courtesy also performs disjunctive acts of exclusionary violence. In becoming, on Mt. Acidale, a poem of Gloriana's triumph, it must "displace" (6.10.20) the graceful vision of Colin Clout, just as, in the manner of Virgil's first eclogue, it must exclude the shepherd Meliboe in order to effect the celebratory project of a hardened Tityrus-Immerito. As Julia Lupton points out, Spenser's tale of Meliboe conforms in many ways to the Renaissance tradition of conflating the unhappy exile of Meliboeus with Tityrus' triumphant return from Rome, thereby making pastoral the scene of a new beginning in the face of civilization's failures.[113] Having abandoned the sheepcote for the "roiall court" in order to "sell my selfe for yearly hire," Meliboe becomes disillusioned with "this worlds gay showes" and returns to make a second pastoral start for himself, realizing that "each vnto himselfe his life may fortunize" (6.9.24, 27, 30). In Spenser's legend, however, this meliorative sequence is counterbalanced by a simultaneity that juxtaposes loss and gain in the manner of Virgil's paradoxical contrast of Meliboeus and Tityrus. Calidore's quest is discontinuous with Colin Clout's loss, just as Pastorella's fortunate return is discontinuous with the fate of Meliboe, who is "spoyld ... of all he had" before being "slaine ... with many others beside" (6.10.40; 6.11.18).[114]

The destruction of Meliboe's realm is perpetrated by the brigands, who, like the earlier Salvage nation, represent a primitive, pre-civilized brutishness in need of civilizing; but also like the Salvage nation, the brigands are, as Lupton indicates (p. 132), post-civilized exiles or borderers. Just as the former steal "Into their neighbours borders" (6.8.35), so the latter prey upon "their neighbours, which did nigh them

[112] William Empson, *Some Versions of Pastoral* (1935; rpt. New York: New Directions, 1974), pp. 10–11; Humphrey Tonkin, *Spenser's Courteous Pastoral: "The Faerie Queene" VI* (Oxford University Press, 1972), p. 290.
[113] "Home-Making in Ireland," p. 123.   [114] See ibid., p. 138.

border" (6.10.39): in each case, the potential to be conquered by the new force of civilization is created by exclusion from the borders of a civilization already established. The point is underlined by a further parallel: if Meliboe is "led away" with the intrusion of the excluded brigands, he is "slaine" with the arrival of "a sort of merchants" that "skim those coastes" (6.11.9). For all its emphasis on new beginnings, the legend thus retains the paradoxical sense of pastoral belatedness – of failure, exile, displacement, and complaint. If, in Spenser's earlier pastoral complaints and ruins poems, the sense of lateness and failure was a response to earlier civilizations, it is now aroused as well by the emergent civilization celebrated in *The Faerie Queene*, a poem which has begun to contain its own ruins.

The delicate and exclusive focus of Book 6 produces the sense, as Nohrnberg has said, "of a variety of separate individuals, set apart from one another throughout a common landscape in which each occupies his own 'discreet' space – like so many eremites in so many niches."[115] The *Faerie Queene*'s final vision of grace thus contrasts distinctly with its first, in the New Jerusalem, where God's people are "Saints all in that Citie sam" (1.10.57).[116] The openness of the New Jerusalem, where "the blessed Angels to and fro descend ... As commonly as friend does with his friend" (1.10.56), forms the threshold of a poem that is itself open to history and to the labor that makes the city "fairest of all earthly thing" *The Ruines of Rome*, 1.14). Trojan Brute once traced the outline of a city "To be the compasse of his kingdomes seat" (3.9.46). This was a circle that would survive the "vntimely breach" in the British chronicles and be "sought / Of marchants farre, for profits therein praysd" (3.10.5). But the fragile circle of Mt. Acidale fails to tolerate even Calidore's "lucklesse breach" (6.10.29).

Not just because it is a courtly poem, but because it represents the city in a transitional phase, when that city extends the past even as it helps to dissolve it, *The Faerie Queene* tends to identify the city with royal power and aristocratic interests and culture. In the sixteenth-century dialogue, *Cyvil and Vncyuile Life* (1579), a country gentleman observes that he has heard that "in Court and Cittie" the "manner of liues doo much resemble one thother"; he receives from a city-dweller the reply that "so they doo in deed, I meane the Gentlemen, and not the Marchants or

[115] *The Analogy of "The Faerie Queene"*, p. 660.
[116] According to Van der Noot's gloss, the four sides of the New Jerusalem signify that "none of what so euer kindred ... shall haue either preferment heere in this citie, or be lesse regarded, for whether he be from East or the West, from the North or the South rich or poore ... he shall be received of God," *A Theatre for Voluptuous Worldlings* (1569), pp. 81–82.

Mechanicall people, for their trade (as you can conceaue) is turned an other waies" (sig. ĸiv). As he approaches the roots of civilized order in his final legend, Spenser seems to resolve the transitional nature of the city by similarly resolving the epic connotations of the city into the court, the *renovatio* of Troynovant–London into the power of Cleopolis–Westminster. Frank Kermode observes that "the first condition of pastoral is that it is an urban product"; but Raymond Williams notes that it is the function of pastoral "to promote superficial comparisons and to prevent real ones."[117] The natural integrity of Spenser's shepherds and the graceful vision on Mt. Acidale thus justify the more advanced forms of civilization, but they effectively conceal the novel bases on which those forms increasingly were built – the movement of population and wealth from country to city, the development of capital, social mobility, the facilitation of the emergence of the state.

To turn from Spenser's heroes to his lesser creations, however, is to discover the true epic breadth of the poem's world, a world that includes or alludes to "Clarkes" (5.10.1) and a "Bayliffe-errant" (6.7.35); a surgeon (4.11.6), a "schoolmaistresse" (3.6.1), and beadsmen (1.10.36); a "maister Cooke" and a "Kitchin Clerke" (2.9.31); watchmen (1.11.13) and keepers (6.12.6) and messengers (1.12.24); monks (6.12.24) and priests (1.3.17); "Bargemen" (7.7.35), a "boteman" (2.12.17) and pilots (2.7.1) and sailors (1.3.31) and beaten mariners (1.3.31); fishermen (2.10.6) and merchants (2.10.5) and a butcher (6.12.35); many instances of the "cunning Craftesman" (2.9.41): blacksmiths (4.5.53) and goldsmiths (4.6.20) and painters (3 Proem 2), and a mason (3.8.37); porters and footmen (1.12.34) and tax collectors (5.2.6); widows and orphans (1.10.43) and beggars (1.4.3) and Courtesans (3.7.58) and thieves. "Sky-threating towres" (5.10.23) and courtly palaces dominate Spenser's urban vistas as his heroes dominate the social sphere, but like the social backdrop of his poem, Spenser's landscape also includes humbler settings: inns and churches; schools, a "schoolehous" (1.10.18), and hospitals; bridges and harbors, a storehouse and sheds; walls and pillars and steeples and gates and streets. And for this landscape there is a whole material substrate of brick and mortar and timber and glass and nails and conduit pipe; cheese and bread and milk and wine and tobacco; brass, iron, steel, lead, and copper-wire; coaches and wagons and wheels; clocks and compasses and cobbled shoes; linen and arras and silk. Here, as in its epic celebration of *translatio*, *The Faerie Queene* is not just a "booke...to fashion a gentleman or noble person," but, in Milton's terms, a poem "exemplary and doctrinal to a nation."

[117] Kermode, *English Pastoral Poetry* (1952; rpt. New York: Norton, 1972), p. 14; Williams, *The Country and the City* (New York: Oxford University Press, 1973), p. 54.

As in the genre of urban description, so in Spenser's *œuvre*, one final consequence of the transhistorical vision of the social body is the emergence, from within that visionary body, of a new sense of personal identity, secured in space and time by a sense of cultural achievement. One final configuration of the river and the city appears in Spenser's *œuvre*; it shapes the poet's meditative progress toward London in the *Prothalamion* (1596). The progress, significantly, is by water, and begins

> When I whom sullein care,
> Through discontent of my long fruitlesse stay
> In Princes Court, and expectation vayne
> Of idle hopes, which still doe fly away,
> Like empty shaddowes, did aflict my brayne,
> Walkt forth to ease my payne
> Along the shoare of siluer streaming *Themmes*...   (lines 5–11)

In the temporal flow of "streaming *Themmes*" the poet seeks release from the time-serving cares of his "fruitlesse stay" at court. The waters lead the way

> To mery London, my most kyndly Nurse,
> That to me gaue this Lifes first natiue sourse:
> Though from another place I take my name,
> An house of auncient fame.
> ...whereas those bricky towres,
> The which on *Themmes* brode aged backe doe ryde,
> Where now the studious Lawyers haue their bowers
> There whylome wont the Templer Knights to byde,
> Till they decayd through pride.   (lines 128–136)

Both the naming of "mery *London*" and its personification as "my most kyndly Nurse" contribute to the consoling and relatively unguarded moment when the poet unveils his name and accepts the city as his cultural heritage.[118]

This moment of identification, like the visions of Troynovant in *The Faerie Queene*, significantly reverses the configuration of river and city, yielding a vista in which the city's "bricky towres...on *Themmes* brode

[118] In so doing, Spenser takes his place beside such citizen–writers as Caxton, who pauses to remember London as "my moder / of whom I haue receyued my noureture & lyuynge," Prologue to *Caton*, in *the Prologues and Epilogues of William Caxton*, ed. W. J. B. Crotch (London: EETS, 1928), p. 77, or the pseudo-Chaucerian poet of *The Testament of Love*, who confesses his love for "the citee of London, that is to me so dere and swete, in whiche I was forth growen; (and more kyndely love have I to that place than to any other in erthe...)," *The Complete Works of Geoffrey Chaucer*, ed. Walter W. Skeat, (7 vols. 1897; rpt. London: Oxford University Press, 1935), 7: 27–28. Alice S. Miskimin notes that Usk's *Testament* was "printed in all the sixteenth-century *Works* [of Chaucer] as authentic" *The Renaissance Chaucer* (New Haven: Yale University Press, 1975), p. 92.

aged backe doe ryde." In this symbolic triumph over mutability, London is invested with the power of cultural endurance; as Harry Berger, Jr., has said, it "figures man's historical environment" and, as the objectification of the human spirit, "outlasts its makers." This is confirmed by the otherwise strange mention of the "studious Lawyers" who succeed the Knights Templars and thus replace "chivalric force" with "legal persuasion" (p. 519). The approach toward London thus effects an imaginative transition toward the emergence of a modern, secure, and stable political order.

This imagined cultural transition finds a poetic counterpart in the refrain of the poem, "Sweete *Themmes* runne softly, till I end my Song." The refrain, like the city itself, is a consoling if partial triumph over mutability; together, both consolations express a symbiotic relation between the order of the city and the civilizing effects of poetic song. The Orphic poet who civilized with his song, it was said, possessed as well the power to halt the flow of rivers.[119] In the *Prothalamion*, the city only manages to ride the river's back, and the poet only momentarily retards and tames its flow; but these twin achievements balance the tide of mutability and human failure with consoling hopes for cultural endurance.

These hopes bring to fruition both a Virgilian career and an Orphic preoccupation with the city that began when Spenser, like the Camden whom he praises, first tried "To see the light of simple veritie, / Buried in ruines" (*The Ruines of Time*, 171–172). As if to acknowledge its cultural function as a fiction of settlement, one of the unknown encomiasts of *The Faerie Queene* passed over the Vergilian claims of the Proem to praise its author as "this Bryttane *Orpheus*." In so doing, he wisely adopted Spenser's own configuration of city and river and thus, uncannily anticipating the refrain of the *Prothalamion*, portrayed the writing of *The Faerie Queene* as a triumphant act of Orphic reconstruction, a recreation of a city that would endure against the flow of time:

> Fayre *Thamis* streame, that from *Ludds* stately towne,
> Runst paying tribute to the Ocean seas,
> Let all thy Nymphes and Syrens of renowne
> Be silent, whyle this Bryttane *Orpheus* playes.

[119] Cesare Ripa interprets this latter power as a variation of the former, for when Orpheus "stops the flow of rivers," he demonstrates the power of poets to curb "dishonest and lustful men who, when they are not kept back by the force of language from their infamous lives, run without any restraint as far as the sea, which is the regret and bitterness which usually come suddenly upon the carnal pleasures," *Iconologia* (Padua, 1603), p. 140; Cf. Boccaccio, *Genealogia deorum gentilum libri*, 1: 245.

If a cause of the incompleteness of *The Faerie Queene* was the inability of the author to see beyond the contradictions of his moment to the end of things, the obverse achievement is his postponement of an end, the sense of expectancy and futurity that opens out from the coexistence and interanimation of the social possibilities his poem puts in play. A dialectically open work, *The Faerie Queene* expresses, in its shifting plot and multiple generic orientations, the contradictions of its moment, producing a complex vision of the social order that may be said to represent "to divers persons, at divers stations, diverse forms." Reflecting on the permanently unstable and self-constituting dynamics of an urbanizing, capitalizing society, it derives its complex vision of the social order not from *a priori* forms of permanence but from a recognition of the conflicting forces out of which that order arises. It situates a critical time and place in a profane, continuing, unapocalyptic rhythm of negotiation.

This is a pattern found elsewhere in London's fictions of settlement. It is found, for example, in literature of the criminal underworld, where Robert Greene's recognition that "all conditions and estates of men seek to live by their wits"[120] breaks down the confines of orthodox morality and exposes as merely positional the differences that organize a world in transition. It is found in the history of the Jacobean stage, where economic competition, personal ambition and rivalry, different repertories and different social audiences produce, in the "War of the Theaters," what might better be called a romance, an agonistic process of exchange and recombination that elaborates social consciousness by opening the vision and bias of individual plays and repertories to engagement with their alternatives. It is found in pamphlet lore – in Thomas Nashe's *Lenten Stuffe* (1599), for example, where the freedom of the marketplace becomes a model for all human exchange, creating a progressive utopia whose alpha is not its omega and whose continuing livelihood is based upon the principle that "one or two there pockets up not all the pieces."[121] It is found everywhere in Thomas Dekker's many portraits of London, where the traditional languages and types of allegory, homiletics, and feudal social theory alternate with portraiture of a quotidian world, bestowing on London a permanence opposed to the demonic fixities of sinfulness or class strife. Dekker's is typically a romance voyage, sailing past the "creekes, rocks, gulfes, and quicksandes" of the "black shore of mischief"[122] – we may think of Spenser's Rock of Vile Reproach, Gulf of Greediness, and Quicksand of Unthrifty-

---

[120] *The Defence of Cony-Catching*, in A. B. Grosart, ed., *Life and Complete Works* (15 vols. London: Huth Library, 1881–1883), 11: 51.   [121] *Works*, 3: 160, 168.
[122] *Non-Dramatic Works*, ed. A. B. Grosart, 3: 66.

hood (2.12.8, 9, 18) – in order to take the measure of those critical hot spots where London's life hardens into the fixity of contradiction or antagonism. But his goal, like that of other romance heroes, is to encounter and comprehend these scenes of concentrated meaning without himself becoming demonized or fixed by them, to apprehend the world morally without letting moralism harden into ideological rigidity or apocalyptic hysteria. In helping to widen out a space in which his culture could reflect upon itself, Spenser may be said to have joined, from a courtly perspective, in the work of creating a common fiction of settlement.

5   Scripts for the pageant: the ceremonies of London

A tale of two cities: the symbiosis of ceremonial forms

The theatricalization of London's traditional civic ceremonies was an essential development in the expansion of celebratory literature and myth that justified the city's increasingly dominant role in the social order. Throughout the eight-hundred-year history of the London mayoralty, some form of ceremony has accompanied the annual inauguration of the City's chief official. But in this *longue durée* of civic custom, the Tudor–Stuart period occupies a special place, for it was only in the 1540s that the processions which have continued from at least the fifteenth century to the present began to be accompanied by pageants and speeches scripted by leading writers for London's newly emergent public theaters. The new prestige of the innovative "inaugural show" was the result of several factors, including both the expansion of civil power that accompanied the decline of religious ceremony at the Reformation, and the general inflation of ceremony that was part of the "imaginative refeudalization" of culture throughout sixteenth-century Europe.[1] But another major factor was the process that links the inaugural shows to the larger body of the urban literature of the Renaissance – an effort to comprehend and justify the transformation of traditional English society by a new form of communal life, a type of urban settlement unprecedented in its scale and dynamism.

The context for this development was the late-feudal arrangement by which localities enjoyed their limited freedoms at the pleasure of the Crown, which endowed them with liberties and immunities in exchange for tribute, service, and conformity to prevailing socio-economic norms. London's inaugural ceremonies, for example, took place only after the mayor-elect had been approved and taken his oath of fealty to the Crown.

---

[1] Frances A. Yates, "Elizabethan Chivalry: The Romance of the Accession Day Tilts," *JWCI*, 20 (1957), 4–25. See also Roy Strong, *Art and Power: Renaissance Festivals 1450–1650* (Woodbridge, Suffolk: The Boydell Press, 1984), p. 19; Edward Muir, *Civic Ritual in Renaissance Venice* (Princeton University Press, 1981), p. 59.

This was no token arrangement; Henry III vetoed a dozen mayors in his long reign.

At this interface between different jurisdictions, social orders, and ways of life lies the significance of the new scripted civic pageants of the Renaissance. The most elaborate and costly inaugural shows were staged in the Jacobean and Caroline regimes, and their use was discontinued altogether in 1702.[2] In the 800-year history of the mayoralty, the 160-year interval in which the City elected to endow its greatest ceremony with speech, opting for what Thomas Heywood called a "great loud voyc'd inauguration,"[3] was marked by an important change in mental framework, which bestowed upon London – its far-flung economy, freedoms, new modes of life – a leading role in shaping the destiny of the individual and the nation. This is reflected in the historical and formal relationships between the "loud voyc'd inauguration" and its closest counterpart, the pageantic entry of a monarch into the city. Elaborate scripts and pageants began regularly to accompany the London coronation entries of monarchs in the late fourteenth century, a period of rivalry in City–Crown relations that roughly coincides with the early consolidation of London's status as a capital and dominant metropolis – with the settlement of the established form of the City's constitution, the incorporation of its major guilds, the consolidation of the City oligarchy, and a general escalation in civic ceremony.[4]

That these events were not coincidental is suggested by later relationships between the mayoral inauguration and the royal entry. Charles II's full-scale pageantic entry into London in 1661 was "the last of its kind in English history."[5] Charles II was also the first monarch to pay London the compliment of regularly attending its inaugural shows and feasts.[6] In 1702, the date when the inaugural show spoke for the last

---

[2] An attempt to revive the show was made in 1708, when Elkanah Settle prepared pageants and speeches, but the show was not held. See Robert Withington, *English Pageantry: An Historical Outline* (2 vols. 1926; rpt. New York: Benjamin Blom, 1963), 2: 86. My summary of the decline of the entries and inaugural shows is based on Withington, esp. 1: 253, where he connects the "disuse" of the royal entry to the "custom of a state visit to the Guildhall on the first Lord Mayor's Day in each reign."

[3] *Londini Status Pacatus* (1639), in *Dramatic Works*, ed. R. H. Shepherd (6 vols. 1874; rpt. New York: Russell and Russell, 1964), 5: 363.

[4] See Michael Berlin, "Civic Ceremony in Early Modern London," *Urban History Yearbook* (1986), pp. 16–18; Mervyn James, "Ritual, Drama, and the Social Body in the Late Medieval English Town," *Past and Present*, 98 (1983), 25.

[5] Howard Erskine-Hill, *The Augustan Idea in English Literature* (London: Edward Arnold, 1983), p. 216.

[6] In the reign of William and Mary Celia Fiennes reported in her diary that the Lord Mayor typically "invited ye King and Court to dinner, which sometimes they accept but mostly refuse, because it puts the Citty to a vast Charge," *Through England on a Side-Saddle in the Time of William and Mary* (London, 1888), p. 242, quoted in Withington, *English Pageantry*, 2: 67.

time, Queen Anne established what has ever since remained the unbroken custom that the beginning of an English monarch's reign should be marked by the monarch's attendance at the next inauguration of a Lord Mayor. The establishment of this custom, together with the nearly simultaneous decline of the royal entry makes the silence of the mayoral inauguration after 1702 speak whole volumes.

In a symbiotic manner, the royal entry and the inaugural show elaborated in ceremonial terms the complex relationships between two distinct but interconnected political domains. In mediating between these domains and their distinctive cultural values, both ceremonies suspended everyday norms, producing the anti-structural condition Victor Turner has called "liminality." Performed in London's public spaces on the most solemn of communal occasions, both ceremonies submerged the distinctive segments and echelons of society in a ritual "communitas," a quasi-sacred condition of solidarity expressing the deepest and most basic values of the collectivity.[7] But the meanings generated in this ceremonial communitas were at the same time institutionalized and consolidated at the centers of the different spheres between which they mediated. As Turner puts it, the ceremonial power of communitas

is put into the service of normativeness almost as soon as it appears... The experience of communitas becomes the memory of communitas, with the result that communitas itself in striving to replicate itself historically develops a social structure, in which initially free and innovative relationships between individuals become converted into norm-governed relationships between social personae. (pp. 45, 47)

The structuring and political encoding of communitas is already evident, for example, in the organized repertoire of roles and symbols that quickly developed within the royal entry ceremony itself; but it is even more apparent in the socio-political uses to which the ceremony was put. Though the ceremonial advent of a monarch was symbolically marked as an *initium seculi felicissimi*, in which London became a kind of New Jerusalem and its complex social order a unified host of equal and eternal souls, this ritual miracle served to reinforce specific socio-legal norms – the domination of the City by the Crown, of the polity by neofeudal principles, and of the social order by aristocratic blood.

At the same time, however, ceremonial communitas also bears with it potentially liberating effects; it represents, in Turner's words, "the latent system of political alternatives from which novelties will arise" (p.

[7] "Liminal to Liminoid in Play, Flow, and Ritual: An Essay in Comparative Symbology," in *From Ritual to Theater. The Human Seriousness of Play* (New York: Performing Arts Journal Publications, 1982), p. 54.

52). A powerful group may use communitas values to consolidate its dominance, as did the court when English monarchs entered London. But "the key communitas values shared by both groups but put into abeyance by the politically successful one may later become resurgent in the latter... Communitas tends to generate metaphors and symbols which later fractionate into sets and arrays of cultural values" (p. 50). The royal entry developed from and shared in many aspects of London's own local ceremonies and civic traditions. It is therefore not surprising that incipient within its distinctive form were possibilities that were developed in very different ways by its major counterpart, the inaugural procession of the City's Lord Mayor. The history of the two major forms suggests that London's leaders became increasingly aware of these possibilities and found a basis for self-definition in them, simultaneously distancing themselves from the structural norms enforced by the entry and consolidating themselves around bourgeois alternatives. These alternatives took form in the scripts developed for the inaugural shows, in which the static tableaux and arches of the royal entry gave way to a tumultuous succession of processing images, and in which the hieratic, typological, and magical representation of timeless mysteries yielded to more "discursive" types of "argument" – to non-mystical representations of historical, moral, and political causes and effects and to public reasoning about matters of state. This discursive or argumentative thrust emerged naturally enough from the tendency of ceremony to *laudando praecipere* – to teach by praising. But with its emphasis on sharing, exchange, and reciprocity, the discursive teaching of the inaugural show tended to become, through a kind of meta-liturgical awareness, a general model of the innovative kinds of human relationships the inaugural shows extolled. Annual variations in an ever-widening repertoire of myths, motifs, and ideas reinforced a sense that history, the community, and its values were all human productions, arising from an ongoing civilizing process.

The sixteenth-century emergence of the inaugural show, when the City elected to add speech and spectacle to a traditional liminal rite, was thus a symptom of a larger change, the passage of a traditional society into the complex, diversified, and individualized functions of early capitalism. Commissioned (or not commissioned, as the choice might be) by individual companies to celebrated writers in London's new entertainment industry, published in cheap pamphlet form, and fraught with messages for a variety of constituencies, the inaugural shows are traditional liminal forms which nonetheless bear the incipient marks of liminoid phenomena – an emphasis on the individual as potentially opposed to the collective, a sense of privilege in making free with the social heritage, an awareness that the values and expressions of particular individuals and groups compete with one another on – and thus together form – a "free" market that is the core of common life.[8] In the arguments and symbols that it developed in order to justify the rule of London's oligarchic elite to a variety of constituencies, the Lord Mayor's Show inaugurated a more profane, material time, a secular vision of the city that gave wider scope to individuals in shaping their surroundings in the pursuit of their particular ends.[9] Here, as elsewhere in the history of London's ceremonies, the potential for innovation was not anti-structural but proto-structural, an anticipation – and a making – of the specialized functions, motives, and mobilities of the early modern individual, who, no longer wholly circumscribed by the city's local community, nevertheless bore the inscription of the city within himself.

The structural, systemic nature of these innovations is all the more apparent in light of the ceremonial circumstances in which they emerged. The history of London street pageantry is practically identical with the history of collaboration and conflict between the twin jurisdictions of the Crown and the City. The earliest royal street ceremonies to make use of pageantry date from the troubled reigns of Edward II and Richard II,[10] and they marked a new level of London's counterweight to the sovereignty of English kings. Recounting the events that led to Richard II's deposition, Froissart recalled that in the reign of Edward II "Les citoiens de Londres ... par lesquels tout le royaume d'Angleterre se ordonne et gouverne" had instigated the return of Queen Isabella and her party; without the aid of London, he added, "ils ne fuissent jamais venus au dessus de leur emprise."[11] So it was also to be in the reign of Richard II: "Les citoiens de Londres, comme chiefs de royaume d'Angleterre, et puissans que ils sont," helped to bring about Richard's fall (16: 161).

In the 1580s, one of those decades of unusually tangled City–Crown relations that coincided with an escalation of London pageantry, the

---

[8] I have here slightly modified several of the attributes Turner associates with "liminoid" phenomena, "Liminal to Liminoid," pp. 52, 55.

[9] See Muriel Bradbrook, "The Politics of Pageantry: Social Implications in Jacobean London," in Anthony Coleman and Anthony Hammond, eds., *Poetry and Drama 1570–1700: Essays in Honour of Harold F. Brooks* (London: Methuen, 1981), pp. 73–74.

[10] Stow mentions a pageant in 1236 for Eleanor of Provence, *A Survey of London* (1598; 1603), ed. C. L. Kingsford (1908; rpt. Oxford: Clarendon Press, 1971), 1: 95. On this (probably apocryphal) procession and the processions and pageants of 1298–1327, most associated with Edward II, see Withington, *English Pageantry*, 1: 124–127.

[11] *Œuvres*, ed. K. de Lettenhove (25 vols. Brussels, 1867), 16: 158–159. On the role of London as kingmaker, see M. McKisack, " London and the Succession to the Crown in the Middle Ages," in R. W. Hunt, W. A. Pantin, and R. W. Southern, eds., *Studies in Medieval History Presented to Frederick Maurice Powicke* (Oxford: Clarendon Press, 1948), pp. 76–89.

anonymous author of the *Apologie of the Cittie of London* similarly remarked that "London is a mighty arme and instrument to bring any great desire to effect, if it may be woon to a man's deuotion."[12] Though he claimed that in the demise of Edward II and Richard II "London neuer led the dance, but euer followed the pipe of the Nobilitie," the author added that these were among the kings who had "been heauie Lordes to London" (2: 215, 217). By the Tudor–Stuart period, there remained an important token of London's earlier role in kingmaking: the Lord Mayor – who "with yn London" was "nexte unto the kynge in alle maner thynge" – "became the greatest officer in England at the demise of the Crown, all royal offices being vacant until reconfirmed."[13]

A background of jurisdictional and constitutional ambiguity thus accounts for the quasi-official function of the royal entry ceremony, according to which the City of London was privileged to offer the popular acclamation essential to the making of a king. With very few exceptions, a full-fledged pageantic royal entry to London was a one-time affair for any given monarch.[14] In significant contrast, however, to such ceremonies as royal entries in Paris, held after the coronation at Rheims,[15] or the papal *possesso* in Rome, held after the consecration ceremony,[16] the London entry took place on the day prior to the coronation ceremony at Westminster.[17]

Writ large in this sequence of events is the Germanic influence that distinguished many Western from Eastern coronation rites by giving a role to the populace and to elite ritual specialists in the making of a king.[18]

---

[12] I give Stow's shorthand designation as the title of this work, which was printed as an appendix to his 1603 *Survey of London*, 2: 206.

[13] *Gregory's Chronicle*, in *The Historical Collections of a Citizen of London in the Fifteenth Century*, ed. James Gairdner (London: Camden Society, 1876), p. 223; Bradbrook, "The Politics of Pageantry," p. 63.

[14] Gordon Kipling, "Richard II's 'Sumptuous Pageants' and the Idea of the Civic Triumph," in *Pageantry in the Shakespearian Theater*, ed. David M. Bergeron (Athens: University of Georgia Press, 1985), p. 85.

[15] Lawrence M. Bryant, *The King and the City in the Parisian Royal Entry Ceremony: Politics, Ritual, and Art in the Renaissance*, Travaux d'Humanisme et Renaissance, 216 (Geneva: Droz, 1986), p. 30.

[16] Charles L. Stinger, *The Renaissance in Rome* (Bloomington: Indiana University Press, 1985), p. 53; cf. Peter Partner, *Renaissance Rome, 1500–1559* (Berkeley: University of California Press, 1976), p. 193, André Chastel, *The Sack of Rome, 1527*, tr. Beth Archer (Princeton University Press, 1983), pp. 207–215.

[17] That this was an English formality recognized as such is evident from the case of Henry VI, whose coronation followed English rather than French precedent, taking place at Rheims *after* an entry into Paris; see Bryant, *The King and the City in the Parisian Royal Entry Ceremony*, p. 158.

[18] See Janet L. Nelson, "Symbols in Context: Inauguration Rituals in Byzantium and the West in the Early Middle Ages," *Studies in Church History*, 13 (1976), 97–119. Cf. Ernst Kantorowicz, *Laudes Regiae* (Berkeley: University of California Publications in History, 33 [1946]), 79–80.

In the entry ceremonies that preceded the coronation, London retained for the City and the English commons a prominent liturgical role in the rite of coronation. In the entry ceremony, the monarch passed westward through the city and along by the City hierarchy that lined Cheapside, before being greeted by the clergy within Paul's Churchyard and then escorted to Westminster for coronation on the following day. This procession was a structural parallel and symbolic anticipation of the coronation rite itself, in which the monarch was presented for popular acclaim in the nave of Westminster Abbey before being escorted to the high altar for anointing by the clergy.[19] The entire two-day sequence, moreover, was symbolically compressed into the climax of the London entry at the western end of Cheapside, where symbolic crownings were represented in pageant form before the eyes of London's chief officials.

As the chief city of the realm, London was a microcosm in which the joyous reception of the monarch by the City represented an ideal relationship for the nation. "In respect of the whole Realme," said the author of the *Apologie of the Cittie of London*, "London is but a Citizen and no Citie, a subiect and no free estate ... gouerned by the same law that the rest of the realme is ... London differeth not in substance, but in ceremonie, from the rest of the realme." But this meant, he added, that "it onely is found fit and able to entertaine strangers honourablie, and to receiue the Prince of this realm worthily" (2: 206–207, 214). London's primacy as representative of the commons was thus asserted at the Londinium Arch at Fenchurch Street for the entry of James I: depicted above the Genius of the City and the motto "THE KINGS CHAMBER" was the figure of British Monarchy, "fitly ... placed," Ben Jonson noted, "as in the proper seate of the empire: for so the glorie and light of our Kingdome, M. Camden, speaking of London, saith, shee is, *totius Britanniae Epitome, Britanniciq. Imperij Sedes, Regumque Angliae Camera.*"[20] In this symbolic primacy, however, lay the basis for both collaboration and conflict between the different jurisdictions, ways of life, and historical potential of the Crown and the City.

The same ambiguities characterize ceremonials for the other party to the relationship, the City. The Lord Mayor was annually chosen by the

---

[19] The record of the coronation ceremony for James I, for example, places the *collaudatio* before the unction and crowning; see *The Progresses, Processions, and Magnificent Festivities of King James the First*, ed. John Nichols (4 vols. 1828; rpt. New York: Burt Franklin, n.d.), 1: 231–232. The actual political force of the acclamation is better summed up in an account of Queen Mary's coronation, *The Chronicle of Queen Jane and Two Years of Mary*, ed. J. G. Nichols (London: Camden Society, 1850), p. 31.

[20] *B. Jon: His Part of King James his Royall and Magnificent Entertainement in Passing to his Coronation*, in *Works*, ed. C. H. Hereford and Percy and Evelyn Simpson (11 vols. Oxford: Clarendon Press, 1925–52), 7: 83–84.

Court of Aldermen (popularly nominated in their wards and holding office for life) from the two candidates nominated in the Guildhall by the Court of Common Hall, London's largest popular assembly. Yet the basis for this oligarchical, elective arrangement was – like the many charters pertaining to London's liberties and jurisdictions – the essentially feudal result of a royal grant, the 1209 charter of King John, by which Londoners were permitted to elect from among themselves a mayor who would take his oath before the king or his justiciars. In the Tudor–Stuart period, London's mayor took his oath and received the insignia of office at the Guildhall on the Feast of Saints Simon and Jude (October 28); but just as the coronation of a king took place only after a passage through the streets of London, so by custom the actual rule of the new Lord Mayor only took effect on the morrow after the Feast of Saints Simon and Jude, when he returned to the City after taking an oath of fealty before the monarch or the Barons of the Exchequer in Westminster.[21] As the Recorder, or chief legal officer of the City, put it on presenting Sir Cuthbert Buckle for oath before Queen Elizabeth in 1593, "we enjoy our jurisdictions and privileges derived from your imperial crowne, the onely well-spring of all authority, justice, and jurisdiction."[22]

On the whole, the ceremonies of the royal entry and the mayoral inauguration contributed to a strong and stable symbiosis, establishing a mental framework that accommodated the novel forces of urbanization to traditional visions of the social order. Each ceremony established a circle of custom and neofeudal consensus around the interface between two potentially divergent systems of government and society. This was in keeping with the mutual interests of the two jurisdictions. The Tudor regime was heavily dependent on the good will of the City. The City's wealth was a source of financing more dependable than Parliament. The City companies provided a ready mechanism for raising subsidies, and City merchants provided the Crown with loans and backed its foreign credit. The City's stable and efficient government not only secured the Crown's authority, but enabled it to carry out ambitious programs and policies. The City's manpower, for example, provided 10 percent of the

---

[21] Thus the *Liber Albus*, a custumal of 1419, notes that even after the new mayor has taken his oath at the Guildhall, "in case of urgent necessity it would be the duty of the past Mayor, for the rest of such day, to exercise the functions of his office in public and abroad; seeing that he was not fully discharged from his office until such time as the Mayor succeeding in his stead had been accepted of his Lordship the King, or the Barons of the Exchequer, or the Constable of the Tower," p. 22.

[22] "The Recorder of London's Speech to Queen Elizabeth, after the election of Sir Cuthbert Buckle to be Lord Mayor, 1593," in John Nichols, ed., *The Progresses and Public Processions of Queen Elizabeth* (London, 1823), 3: 228.

nation's military force between 1585 and 1602.[23] In recounting the "zealous love and dutie" of communities throughout the realm during 1588, Stow thought it invidious "to single out the admirable dexterity and the bounty of any one particular place"; nevertheless, in proceeding to explain how the City doubled the number of men and ships requested by the Crown, Stow noted that "euen as London, London-like gaue president, the whole kingdome kept true ranke and equipage" in its contributions to the war-effort.[24]

In exchange for its support of the Crown, London enjoyed not only its traditional liberties and privileges, but special concessions and contracts that enabled it to secure control over England's overseas trade. Such control became increasingly urgent as the international markets ceased to expand. The Crown's support was essential, moreover, in protecting the City's interests against anti-monopolistic lobbies in Parliament, where members of the entrepreneurial gentry and representatives from the beleaguered outports and provincial towns brought increasing pressure to bear against the exclusionary trading practices of Londoners.[25] The interdependency between City and Crown, enabling Londoners to prosper economically, helps to explain the new prestige bestowed by the developing inaugural shows upon the mayoralty, which was dominated by an elite of international traders.

Public ceremonies were thus an occasion on which City and Crown could celebrate their *rapprochement* while underlining the needs and obligations that defined their relationship. In royal entries, for example, the City companies and officials who, dressed in full livery, lined the processional route in orderly ranks, formed an essential buffer between the tumultuous crowds in the background and monarch and nobility in the procession; they served as a symbolic reminder of the City's essential mediation in the task of government. At the same time, when the City's chief officials offered their gifts and speeches in the climactic ceremonies at the end of Cheapside, the monarch responded by passing a sword or sceptre to the Lord Mayor, who then carried it before the monarch for the remainder of the procession. By this means, the special status of London and the mayoralty was affirmed.[26] Both in royal entries and in the

[23] Frank Freeman Foster, *The Politics of Stability: A Portrait of the Rulers in Elizabethan London* (London: Royal Historical Society, 1977), p. 137.

[24] *The Annales, or Generall Chronicles of England, Begun First by Maister Iohn Stow, and After Him Continued ... by Edmund Howes* (1615), p. 744.

[25] Robert Brenner, *Merchants and Revolution: Commercial Change, Political Conflict, and London's Overseas Traders, 1550–1653* (Princeton University Press, 1993), pp. 56–57, 200–208.

[26] I owe these two points to R. Malcolm Smuts, "Public Ceremony and Royal Charisma: The English Royal Entry in London, 1485–1642," in *The First Modern Society: Essays*

annual inaugural shows, the prestige of both Crown and City was ideally enhanced. The inaugural shows typically paid tribute to the monarch at whose pleasure the Lord Mayor served,[27] just as the royal entries glorifying monarchs assumed and enhanced the City's magnificence and prestige.[28]

Even so, such ceremonies always negotiated distance and difference. Just as monarchs used the granting of charters as a means of wielding power and exacting tribute – "to speak the plaine truth," said the *Apologie of the Cittie of London,* "the princes have taken hold of small matters, and coyned good summes of money out of them" (2: 214) – so the pageants of the Lord Mayor's Shows frequently extolled the precedents, charters, and liberties London had wrested from English kings. The neo-feudal ethos of the pageants only thinly concealed a rivalrous relationship, in which merchants liked to represent themselves as the peers of kings. Because both the entry and the inaugural show negotiated ceremonially between two jurisdictions, the relationships between the two ceremonial forms were bound to articulate – and perhaps to sharpen – the conflict between different forms of rule, different styles and modes of life, different perceptions of time, history, and the place of the city and individual within them. As in formal descriptions of the city, and as in Spenser's epic, the ceremonial negotiation between the City and the Crown, framed in the transitional language and logic of neofeudal harmony, was a cultural *limen* that produced new concepts and thereby effected historical change.

The ceremonial route and its syntax

The individual pageant scaffolds and allegorical tableaux of the eight major royal entries from 1501 to 1604 and the more than two dozen surviving Lord Mayor's Shows from 1585 to 1639 offer historical interpreters well over two hundred opportunities for fine-tuned topical analysis of the events, policies, agendas, and regnal styles that shaped individual regimes.[29] In addition to their political and artistic signifi-

in History in Honour of Lawrence Stone, ed. A. L. Beier, David Cannadine, and James M. Rosenheim (Cambridge University Press, 1989), pp. 72–73.

[27] See, e.g., Anthony Munday, *Cruso-Thriambos. The Triumphs of Gold* (1611), in David M. Bergeron, ed., *Pageants and Entertainments of Anthony Munday: A Critical Edition* (New York: Garland, 1985), p. 117.

[28] See, e.g., Lydgate's *Ordenaunces ffor the Kyng made in the Citie off London,* in Henry Noble MacCracken, ed., *The Minor Poems of John Lydgate. Volume 2: Secular Poems* (London: EETS, 1934), ll. 510–12, 524–30.

[29] For general treatments of Tudor pageantry see Strong, *Art and Power,* and Sydney Anglo, *Spectacle, Pageantry, and Early Tudor Policy* (Oxford: Clarendon Press, 1969). For the regnal style and policies of James I, see Jonathan Goldberg, *James I and the*

cance, however, the two major forms of London street ritual – the coronation entry and the mayoralty show – served the deeper ceremonial function of mediating between historically divergent tendencies and forces. Just as important as topical reference, then, is the shape and meaning of each form as the two evolved in a longer historical perspective. The deeper ritual syntax and symbolism of the forms, and the cultural work they carried out, are in fact a basis for the historically specific meanings elaborated at individual pageant stations and in individual entries.

Insofar as they were rites of passage for individuals assuming high office, London's civic ceremonies had a personalistic, topical side; but at least one scholar has emphasized "how *impersonal* these exhibitions are."[30] Whether they formed a *limen* for the status elevation of a monarch or a mayor, the streets of London also formed a *limen* between two jurisdictions, thereby performing, through the both/and logic of liminal ceremony, the cultural work of negotiating between the either/or claims of potentially divergent or even incompatible interests, powers, and institutional structures. In the formality with which they performed this work, and to some degree apart from the topical meanings they express, the urban ceremonies of London shared with other rituals the liturgical quality Roy Rappaport has called *invariance*, a *canonical* quality of timelessness that enables the participants in the ritual to transmit but not themselves to encode the permanent meanings the ritual embodies. Performance of the ritual thus substantiates a traditional form or order, even while that order informs and hallows the historical instance being celebrated.[31] Each performance of a London ceremony, then, not only celebrated a historical instance but substantiated a canonical ceremonial order.

The canonical status of the royal entry ceremony is reflected in Henry VIII's command to the mayor and citizens "to see the citie ordered and garnished with pageantes in place accustomed" for the reception of Anne Boleyn.[32] It was not simply hindsight that enabled Stow to write that in 1522 London prepared for the entry of Charles V "after the manner as is vsed for a coronation"; at the time, the precedent-minded aldermen commanded William Lily, who wrote the Latin verses for the entry, to

Politics of Literature (Baltimore: Johns Hopkins University Press, 1983), pp. 28–54; Graham Parry *The Golden Age Restor'd: The Culture of the Stuart Court, 1603–42* (New York: St Martin's Press, 1981), pp. 1–21.

30   Withington, *English Pageantry*, 1: 180.

31   "The Obvious Aspects of Ritual," in *Ecology, Meaning, and Religion* (Richmond, Calif.: North Atlantic Books, 1979), pp. 176, 179, 193, 194, 200–201.

32   Edward Hall, *The Union of the Two Noble and Illustre Famelies of Lancastre & Yorke* (1548), p. 798, quoted in Withington, *English Pageantry*, 2: 10.

bring them "to this court that they may be entered for a precedent hereafter."[33] Certainly by the reign of Elizabeth precedent had clearly established the processional route, its major stations, and even its ceremonial syntax.

Uncrowned monarchs entering the City on the eve of their coronation spent the night before the entry in the Tower of London, processing on the following day through Tower Street and up Mark Lane to Fenchurch Street, along Fenchurch Street to Gracechurch Street as far as Cornhill, and then along Cornhill and the main route through the Poultry and Cheapside to St. Paul's. The last phase of such processions led down Ludgate Hill and Fleet Street, and out through the City's boundary at Temple Bar to Westminster. Alternatively, entries for crowned foreign monarchs and English monarchs previously crowned abroad or returning from victory abroad began at the gate to London Bridge, passing up Gracechurch Street and then along the same processional route, usually ending, in this case, at St. Paul's itself. The main pageant stations of the latter route were already reduced to crisp summary by the time of Henry V's victorious return from Agincourt in 1415:

agenns his comynge was ordeyned moche ryalte in London: that is to weten, at London Brigge, at ye Conduyt in Cornhill, at the greet Conduyt in Chepe, and at ye Crosse in Chepe was mad a Royall Castell with Angells and Virgynes, syngynge there jnne. And so ye kyng and hise presoners of Frensshmen reden throgh London vn to Westminster.[34]

The stations for the former route were similarly outlined in a ceremonial order issued by the Court in order to compensate, on the occasion of Elizabeth of York's coronation, for the "litill knolege" of how monarchs "shuld be seruide."[35]

In the entry route, then, an invariant liminal center was surrounded by slightly different preliminal and postliminal routes and procedures (see Map).[36] Foreigners, or previously crowned or victorious monarchs, met their first pageant while passing through the defensive outwork at the

---

[33] Stow, *Annales*, p. 517; London Court of Aldermen, *Repertories* 4: 135; both passages quoted in Withington, *English Pageantry*, 1:175. This evidence controverts Arthur Kinney's claim that there was "little or no precedent" for Elizabeth I's coronation entry, *Elizabethan Backgrounds: Historical Documents of the Age of Elizabeth I* (Hamden, Conn.: Archon Books, 1975), p. 7.

[34] Harleian MS. 565, quoted in Edward Tyrrell, *Chronicles of London Bridge by an Antiquary* (London, 1827), pp. 221–222; cf. Grafton's summary of the route for Charles V's 1522 entry, *Chronicle or History of England* (London, 1809), p. 323.

[35] *A Ryalle Book off the Crownacion of the Kinge, Queene, and the Creacion of a Prince*, in Francis Grose and Thomas Astle, eds., *The Antiquarian Repertory* (4 vols. London, 1807), 1: 303.

[36] Victor Turner, *The Ritual Process: Structure and Anti-Structure* (Ithaca: Cornell University Press, 1969), p. 94.

southern end of London Bridge. At this preliminal station, male monarchs were typically confronted by fearsome giant effigies, a kind of communal face or mask, a "shield for the living commune that protected it from threatening foreign intrusions into the psychic and social interior."[37] An apotropaic defense against the dangers of foreignness or recent war was raised in the giant "full grym of syght" who met Henry V, in the "geaunt ... off looke and chere sterne as a lyoun" that met his son, in the Samson and Hercules who hung a chain across the way of Charles V and Henry VIII in 1522, or in the City palladia, Corineus and Gogmagog, who stood before Philip II "come custodi della citta."[38]

By contrast, the preliminal pageant that greeted pre-coronation entrants to the City was typically at Fenchurch Street, where children, often dressed as angels, offered songs of greeting in a very different ceremony of humiliation.[39] From the point where they subsequently converged in Gracechurch Street, the alternative routes coincided until they reached St. Paul's, where they once again diverged into postliminal alternatives. For crowned victors and entrants, and foreigners not being crowned (Henry V, Henry VI, Henry VII, Charles V), the culminating rite was the singing of the *Te Deum*, followed by a return to normalcy with sequestration at a palace or seat of power such as Westminster, Bridewell, or the Bishop of London's palace at Lambeth. For precoronation entrants, the procession always continued in its postliminal phase along the route to Westminster, with a final pageant at the Fleet Conduit and, in at least two cases, with a significantly postliminal appearance by the giant palladia who appeared at London Bridge in the preliminal phase of the alternative route.

[37] Muir, describing the defensive function of pageantry in general, *Civic Ritual in Renaissance Venice*, p. 233.

[38] Poem on the Battle of Agincourt, incorrectly ascribed to Lydgate, in *A Chronicle of London from 1089 to 1483*, ed. Edward Tyrrell (London, 1827), p. 231; Lydgate, *Ordenaunces ffor the Kyng*, in *The Minor Poems, Volume Two: Secular Poems*, lines 75, 79; Corpus Christi MS 298, cited by Anglo, *Spectacle, Pageantry, and Early Tudor Policy*, p. 191; *La Solenne et felice intrata delli Serenissimi Re Philippo, et Regina Maria d'Inghilterra, nella Regal Citta di Londra* (n.p. 1554?), cited in Anglo, p. 327. The author of the Agincourt poem explains the giants were "To teche the Frensshe men curtesy," but their association with the defense of the City's powers and liberties was stressed in an alternative account of the Henry V entry: "there stood on high a figure of gigantic magnitude, fearlessly looking into the King's face, as if he would do battle; but on his left hand, were the great keys of the City hanging to a staff, as though he had been Gate-keeper," Latin MS Cottonian Julius E.IV., art. 4., tr. in Tyrrell, *Chronicles of London Bridge*, p. 223.

[39] An interesting, and perhaps politically significant confusion between the standard preliminal alternatives occurs in one record of Queen Mary's greeting at Fenchurch Street; records agree that an enthroned child met her here, but Machyn adds that there were "iiij grett gyants," *The Diary of Henry Machyn*, ed. J. G. Nichols (London: Camden Society, 1848), p. 45.

Most striking, however, is the coincidence of the two routes in a common, central, liminal phase. In this phase they shared a common set of pageant stations, which began at the top of Gracechurch Street at the corner of Leadenhall, and followed, from the Conduit or Tunne in Cornhill to the Little Conduit at the gate into Paul's Churchyard, the main East–West route through the city. A basic syntax of pageant stations was clearly laid out around the same invariant landmarks, the cisterns – the Conduit in Cornhill, the Great Conduit at the head of Cheapside, the Little Conduit at Paul's Gate – and the standards – the Standard and the Cross in Cheapside (see Figs. 10, 11a–d) – that punctuated the route. At these stations, and chiefly at the cisterns – where normally the city's life welled up to be gathered by appprentices of a morning, and where water turned to wine during entries – nature, culture, and grace converged in pageant form. The polygonal architecture, niches, and parapets of these structures readily accommodated the pageants built on, around, or near them. All date from the mid-fourteenth to the mid-fifteenth century, the same period in which the ceremonial forms themselves evolved.[40]

Progress along this central, liminal portion of the route, moreover, was analogical or graduated; the ceremonial temperature shot up exponentially toward the culmination of the route, between the Great Conduit, Cross and Standard in Cheapside (see Fig. 12) and the Little Conduit at the gate into Paul's Churchyard (see Fig. 13), where the symbolically climactic pageants unfolded themselves before the eyes of the City's chief officials.[41]

The climactic ceremonial events at the end of Cheapside and the entry to the Churchyard were governed by a logic and set of ritual habits that made this the City's most sacred ceremonial space (see Map). It is recorded in the London custumal called the *Liber Albus* (1419) that on the major religious feasts of All Saints (November 1), Christmas, St. Stephen's Day (December 26), the Circumcision (January 1), Epiphany (January 6), the Purification of the Virgin (February 2), and St. John the Evangelist (May 6), the mayor, sheriffs, aldermen and their liveries processed to evening services at St. Paul's from the Hospital and Chapel of St. Thomas de Acon, founded by the family of the London worthy St. Thomas à Becket, and located opposite the Great Conduit in Cheapside.

[40] Glynne Wickham, *Early English Stages 1300–1600* (3 vols. New York: Columbia University Press, 1959–1981), 1: 58.

[41] For the ascending echelons of city officials and the invariant placement of the City's leaders at the head of Cheapside, see, e.g., Holinshed, *Chronicles of England, Scotland and Ireland* (1587), pp.507–508; Corpus Christi MS 298, quoted in Withington, *English Pageantry*, 1: 175–176; *Ioannis Lelandi ... Collectanea*, ed. Thomas Hearne (7 vols. London, 1744), 4: 310.

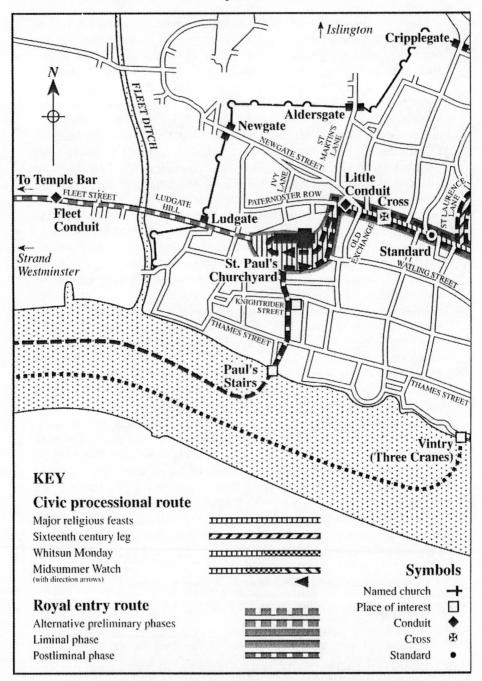

Map. Processional routes for major civic observances, royal entry
route, and route of the Lord Mayor's inaugural show

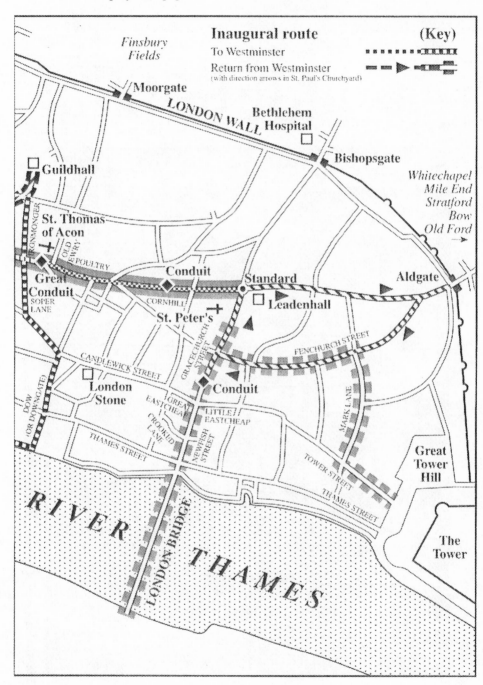

Finsbury Fields

Inaugural route (Key)

To Westminster

Return from Westminster
(with direction arrows in St. Paul's Churchyard)

Moorgate

LONDON WALL

Bethlehem Hospital

Bishopsgate

Guildhall

Whitechapel Mile End Stratford Bow Old Ford

IRONMONGER

St. Thomas of Acon

OLD JEWRY

POULTRY

Great Conduit

SOPER LANE

Conduit

CORNHILL

Standard

Aldgate

Leadenhall

St. Peter's

FENCHURCH STREET

CANDLEWICK STREET

GRACECHURCH STREET

London Stone

Conduit

DOW FOR DOWNGATE

EASTCHEAP

GREAT EASTCHEAP

LITTLE EASTCHEAP

MARK LANE

CROOKED LANE

NEWFISH STREET

THAMES STREET

TOWER STREET

Great Tower Hill

THAMES STREET

R I V E R

LONDON BRIDGE

T H A M E S

The Tower

228

Fig. 10. Cornelius
Dankerts, attr. to
Augustine Ryther
(c. 1633)

1 Gracechurch St.
Conduit
2 Fenchurch St.
Conduit
3 Leadenhall
4 St. Peter in
Cornhill
5 Tunne in Cornhill
6 Great Conduit
7 St. Thomas de
Acon
8 Guildhall
9 Standard in
Cheapside
10 Cheapside Cross
11 Little Conduit and
Paul's Gate
12 St. Paul's

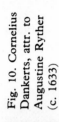

Fig. 10 Map-view of London, showing processional route and pageant stations. Cornelius Dankerts (c. 1633)

St. Thomas de Acon and St. Paul's, the two *termini* of the great thoroughfare of Cheapside, therefore defined the central portion of the City's most important ceremonial route. St. Thomas de Acon, whose high altar was still believed in Tudor times to mark the spot on which Thomas à Becket was born on the feast of Thomas the Apostle, was dedicated to a famous Londoner who had inspired the first major description of London (by his biographer William Fitzstephen in 1184) and whose cult made London the embarkation point for the second-most important pilgrimage in Christendom.[42] Stow listed Becket first among the "worthie Citizens" he celebrated in the *Survey* (1: 105), and Becket's effigy adorned the City's official seal until the suppression of his cult in 1539.[43] After its suppression, the cult of Becket – a London-born Thomas martyred by a royal Henry – became a focal point for Londoners opposed to the Reformation, and while the feast of Becket's namesake, the Apostle Thomas, ceased to be observed religiously, it became the occasion when the Lord Mayor and every alderman was to "sit in his ward in his violet gowne and cloake furred," presiding over the Wardmote Inquest, at which, "theoretically, every householder could take part in civic government."[44]

In St. Paul's, at the other end of the processional route, the most important shrine was the tomb of Bishop William, a heroic defender of the City's feudal liberties. Stow, who listed the occasions of the Lord Mayor's "going to Paules" in the *Survey*, explained the "Lord Mayors cause of repayre to Paules" in his *Annales*, where he observed that

through the great sute and labour of William the Norman, then Bishoppe of London, King William graunted the Charter and liberties to the same William Byshop, and Godfrey Portgreue and all the bourgies of the Cittie of London, in as large forme as they enioyed the same, in the time of Saynt Edward before the Conquest: in reward whereof, the Cittizens haue fixed upon his graue, being in the middest of the West Ile of Saint Paules, this Epitaph following.

> These Marble monuments to thee thy Cittizens assigne,
> Rewardes (O Father) farre vnfit to those deserts of thine,
> Thee vnto them a faithfull friend, thy London people found,
> And to this towne, of no small weight, a stay both sure and sound:
> Their libertie restorde to them, by meanes of thee haue beene,

---

[42] For the view that Becket was born on the site of the altar, Henry Wriothesley, *A Chronicle of England During the Reigns of the Tudors*, ed. William Douglas Hamilton (2 vols. London: Camden Society, 1876), 1: 87.

[43] Stow, *Survey*, 1: 315; on the suppression of the cult of Becket, see Susan Brigden, *London and the Reformation* (Oxford: Clarendon Press, 1989), pp. 291–292.

[44] *The Ordre of My Lorde Maior, the Aldermen & the Shiriffes, for Their Meetings Throughout the Yeere* (1621), p. 20; Foster, *The Politics of Stability*, p. 37.

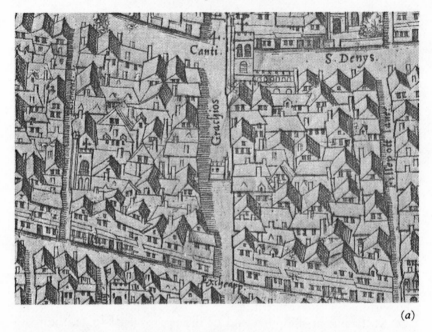

(a)

(b)

Fig. 11 Copperplate map (c. 1560) (details)
(a) Gracechurch Street Conduit
(b) Conduit in Fenchurch Street

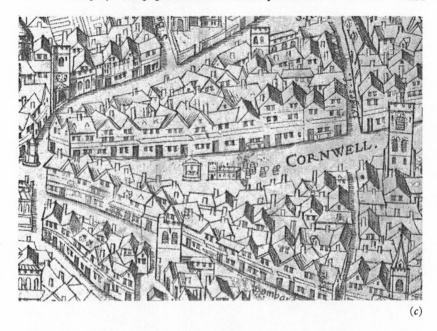

(*c*)

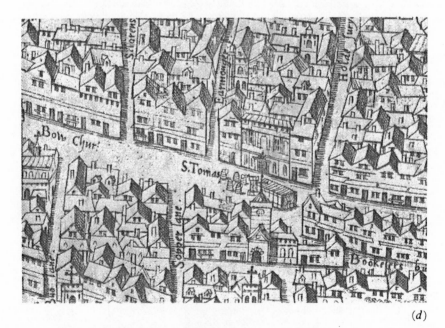

(*d*)

(*c*) Conduit and Tunne in Cornhill
(*d*) Great Conduit in Cheapside, with St. Thomas de Acon

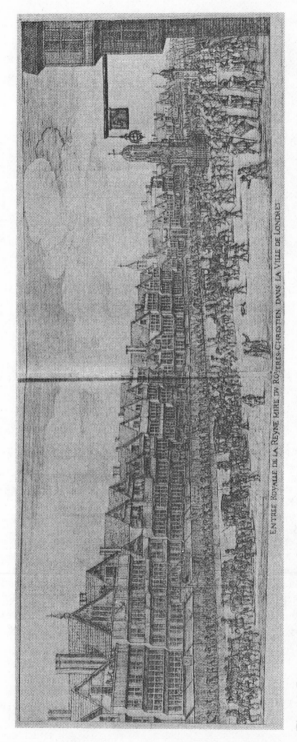

Fig. 12 Procession showing the Cross and Standard in Cheapside. J.-P. de la Serre, *Histoire de l'entrée de la Reyne Mère* (1637)

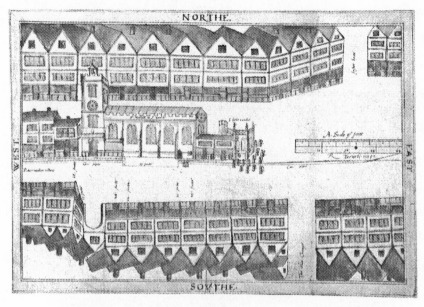

Fig. 13 The Little Conduit, with Paul's Gate. Ralph Tresswell (c. 1585)

Fig. 14 Personification of London receiving the Emperor Constantius Chlorus. Gold medallion (c. 306 AD)

Fig. 15 Coronation Procession of Edward VI. S. H. Grimm (1785) after 1547 original

Fig. 16 Procession to St. Paul's, 1614

Fig. 17 Londinium Arch. Stephen Harrison, *Arches of Triumph* (1604)

Their publike weale, by meanes of thee, large gifts haue felt and
seene.
Thy riches, stocke, and beauty braue, one houre hath them supprest,
Yet these thy vertues and good deedes, with valor euer rest.[45]

The civic importance of these two shrines explains not only the
processions on religious feast days, but the rituals that, until the
sixteenth-century development of the inaugural shows, marked the
inauguration of London's mayors. In its account of these rituals, the
Liber Albus was merely following the much older precept of the *Liber
Ordinationum*, which explained that after the inaugural feast, the mayor
"offered prayers at St. Paul's for Bishop William, ... led the aldermen in
ritual chant at the Becket grave and in a torchlight procession through
Cheap to the house of St. Thomas."[46] After the Reformation, when the
hospital of St. Thomas de Acon was suppressed and its chapel came
under the control of the Mercers, City officials continued to process on
most of the traditional major feasts, beginning at the Guildhall, but
following the same route along Cheapside, from the foot of Ironmonger
Lane at the corner of the Mercer's Chapel to St. Paul's.[47] And though
sixteenth-century ceremonial orders make no mention of prayers at
Bishop William's tomb, City officials continued to doff their gowns
before entering and to circle the cathedral before donning them again.
Thus, while one pole of the ceremonial axis, the Chapel of St. Thomas de
Acon, had been secularized and replaced by the Guildhall, its main spine
of the processional route, and probably much of its traditional meaning,
remained the same.[48]

The meaning of this central civic axis was reinforced by its incorporation into a longer one (see Map), reserved in the fifteenth
century for the first Monday in Whitsuntide, when the City officials
processed along the entire main spine of what was also the coronation
route, from St. Peter's in Cornhill, at the corner of Gracechurch Street
and opposite the Standard in Cornhill, to St. Paul's, where "the hymn
Veni Creator was chaunted by the Vicars to the music of the organ in
alternate verses; an angel meanwhile censing from above." [49] This civic

---

[45] *Survey*, 2: 190; *Annales*, fos. 108–109.
[46] Gwyn A. Williams, *Medieval London: From Commune to Capital* (London: Athlone, 1963), p. 30.
[47] Stow, in 1603, listed the same seven feast days: "1. Alhallowen day. 2. Christmasse day. 3. Saint Stephens day. 4. Saint Iohns day. 5. New years day. 6. Twelfe day. 7. Candlemasse day," 2: 190; by 1621, however, the ceremonial calendar published by the City listed only "all Saints day, Christmas day, Twelfth day, and Candlemas day," *The Order of my Lord Maior, the Aldermen, and the Shiriffes, for their Meetings ... Throughout the Yeere* (1621), sig. B2v.
[48] See Michael Berlin, "Civic Ceremony in Early Modern London," *Urban History Yearbook* (1986), p. 21.   [49] *Liber Albus*, p. 26.

238   *Literature and culture in early modern London*

occasion, "when the Mayor and Aldermen went to the Church of St. Peter in Cornhulle to proceed thence through the City to St. Paul's according to ancient custom,"[50] was a boundary-setting ceremony like the Roman Terminalia, focused not on the city's outer boundaries,[51] but on its two historically sacred spots, the twin hilltop churches (and former Roman temple-sites) of St. Peter's in Cornhill, "thought to be the Cathedral of Restitutus, the Christian Bishops See...in the Raigne of great Constantine,"[52] and St. Paul's, founded in the reign of Ethelbert, "wherein Melitus began to bee Bishop in the yeare 619" (Stow, 2: 127). Located at the eastern and western ends of the main city thoroughfare, these twin churches, of Roman and Saxon Christendom respectively, were the anchors of the central, definitive portion of the civic ceremonial route and part of the City's topographical self-image (see Figs. 5 and 15).

After the Reformation, the Pentecostal processions were reduced to the ceremony of the Lord Mayor's and aldermen's attendance of Monday and Tuesday sermons at St. Paul's.[53] Up to 1541, however, the Pentecostal route was retained as the central portion for the marching of the Midsummer Watch on June 24 and 29, when, with their pageants borne before them, the mayor and sheriffs led the City's constables and militias

> from the litle Conduit by Paules gate, through west Cheape, by ye Stocks, through Cornhill, by Leaden hall to Aldgate, then backe downe Fenchurch streete, by Gracechurch, aboute Grasse church Conduite, and vp Grasse Church streete into Cornhill, and through it into west Cheape again, and so broke vp. (Stow, 1:102)

This longest of the civic routes (see Map), in keeping with its military, boundary-setting function, went all the way to the City's eastern gate. This route, too, was hallowed by custom. Stow unearthed the probable origins of the route in the account he took from the *Liber Custumarum* of the rights of Robert Fitzwater, one of the twelfth-century *barones* of the City. In time of war, Fitzwater, the City bannerer, was to receive from the mayor and aldermen at the West door of the cathedral the City's banner of St. Paul. The leaders and commons of the City were then to assemble and "go vnder the Banner of Saint Paul, and the said Robert shall bear it himself vnto Aldgate," where a council "taken in the Priorie

---

50   *Calendar of Letter-Books of the City of London. Letter-Book H*, ed. R. R. Sharpe (London, 1907), p. 188.
[51] Although the Whitsun Monday procession was followed on the next two days by processions that led the common folk of Middlesex eastward, through Newgate to St. Paul's, and the common folk of Essex westward, through Cheapside to the same destination.
[52] *The Theatre of the Empire of Great Britaine* (London, 1676), fo. H2.
[53] "If my Lords pleasure be to goe," *The Order of My Lord Maior* (1621), sig. B5v.

of the trinitie near vnto Aldgate" was to complete the City's military plans (1: 63–64). Originating at St. Paul's, Londoners' traditional "place of assembly to their folkmotes," where their "common bell" was rung that "all the inhabitants of the citie might heare and come together" (1: 325), and terminating at the priory of Holy Trinity, whose Prior, "according to the customes of the Citie did sit in Court and rode with the Maior, and his brethren the Aldermen, as one of them ... vntill the yeare 1531" (1: 123), the route of the Midsummer Watch took in literally all of the coronation route, as, on its westward return leg, instead of merely retracing the eastbound leg and following the logically efficient return route through Lombard Street to Cheapside, it turned into Gracechurch Street – even to the extent of looping southward around the Gracechurch Street Conduit – so that it might incorporate *both* royal entry routes, taking the turn at St. Peter's in Cornhill that opened onto the main series of pageant stations leading to St. Paul's.[54]

Civic myth and custom had thus established a hallowed ceremonial route between London's two main hilltops. At one end lay the old St. Peter's and the main crossroads of London;[55] at the other end lay the ceremonial heart of the metropolis at St. Paul's. Stow remarked that with the building of the Norman cathedral and the enclosing of its churchyard, "the high and large street stretching from Aldegate in the East, vntill Ludgate in the West [i.e., the Cornhill–Poultry–Cheapside thoroughfare] was in this place ... crossed and stopped vp" (1: 35; cf. 1: 118), requiring passage through or around the enclosed churchyard in order to exit the city. The entry to the churchyard at Paul's Gate, opposite the Little Conduit, marked the *limen* to an enclosed sacred space – with its cloister decorated with the Dance of Death, its famous outdoor pulpit cross, and its schoolyard – which in turn enclosed the cathedral itself. Here was the holy of holies for a London conceived on the model of the Temple of Jerusalem (see Fig. 16). According to Samuel Purchas, "that which the Face is to the Bodie; the Eye to the Face, the Sight to the Eye, that is London to England; and as the Spirits to the Eye, so should this holy place be to London."[56]

---

[54] A manuscript account of the Midsummer Watch presented to the Lord Mayor and aldermen in 1585 by John Montgomery offers an account of the procession route that concurs entirely with Stow's, including the remarkable loop southward around the Gracechurch Conduit, Harley MS 540, ed. Frederick R. Furnivall, in *Harrison's Description of England in Shakespeare's Youth* (Part IV. The Supplement, no. 2 London: Chatto and Windus, 1908), p. 403.

[55] "From St Georges in Southwark to Shoreditch north and south; and from Westminster to St Katherines or Ratcliff, west and east, is a cross of streets, meeting at Leadenhall," Thomas Gainsford, *The Glory of England* (1618), p. 258.

[56] *The Kings Towre, And Triumphal Arch of London. A Sermon Preached at Pauls Crosse, August 5, 1622*, sig. F5v.

On ceremonial occasions, therefore, the customary processional route helped to link the city's open, outdoor public spaces, forming a single interior of contiguous ritual zones.[57] Processions might be longer or shorter, but all converged toward the same final phase. They all reached their climax as they followed the stretch of Cheapside from St. Thomas de Acon and the Great Conduit to the Little Conduit and Paul's Gate, the scene of civic processions on all major religious holidays and, not incidentally, the leg that became the climactic phase of the Lord Mayor's inaugural show. Here, leading up to the Cathedral which Speed had said "assumed that dignity" from "the Temple of Diana," which Stow's contemporaries believed "had beene a Temple of Iupiter" (Stow, 1: 333), and which Stow called "ye beawty of ye syte of London, ye beawty of ye hoole Reallme,"[58] was where the standing ranks of London's officials came to a head during royal entries. Here, in the "high and most principall streete of the cittie" (1: 117), where "diuers Iustings were made" in the reign of Edward III, was the "fayre building of stone," still used in Stow's day, from which monarchs and ambassadors were accustomed to "beholde the shewes of this Citty, passing through West Cheap" (1: 257, 268). Here, in the space that civic custom defined as theirs and the City's, the officials made their presentations and the climactic pageants unfolded. For the entry of Henry VI, the eastern side of a pageant, facing the King as he progressed down Cheapside, represented the earthly family trees of Saints Louis and Edward, while the western, reverse side depicted the greater glories of the Tree of Jesse. Lydgate explained

> This was the cause in especyall,
> For next to Paulis, I dar well specefye,
> Is the partye most chieff and princypall,
> Callyd of London the chirche cathederall,
> Which ought off reson to devyse to excuse,
> To alle thoo that wolde ageyn it ffroune or muse.
>
> (*Ordenaunces ffor the Kyng*, lines 419–425)

Michael Drayton made a more secular version of the same point in the account of James I's coronation entry he wrote under the patronage of the Goldsmiths, where he claimed that if London was the "souerein Citie" of Britain, Cheapside was London's "first and absolutest place,... the Starre and Iewell of the land."[59]

---

[57] André Chastel, "Le lieu de la fête," in Jean Jacquot, ed. *Les Fêtes de la Renaissance* (Paris: Centre National de la Recherche Scientifique, 1956), 1: 419–424.

[58] "Stowe's Memoranda," in *Three Fifteenth-Century Chronicles*, ed. James Gairdner (London: Camden Society, 1880), p. 116.

[59] In *The Progresses, Processions, and Magnificent Festivities of King James the First*, 1: 406–407.

The segmentation of London's ceremonial interior formed a running conceit in Dekker's account of James' entry. The Tower, Dekker noted, was a "with-drawing Chamber" from which the King "stept presently into his Citie of London, which for the time might worthily borrow the name of his Court-Royall." The architecture led analogically inward and upward. As he passed from Gracechurch Street and Cornhill into Cheapside, the King passed from "the great Hall to his own Court Royall" to "*The Presence Chamber*." The head of Cheapside was where the "other happy Spirits" – the City's rulers – "higher vp in these Elizian fields awaited for his presence." As he passed from the climactic pageant at the Little Conduit into Paul's Churchyard, James entered "into the closet or rather the priuy chamber to this our Court royall: through the windowes of which he might behold the Cathedrall Temple of Saint Paule."[60] In Dekker's architectural trope, as in other respects, the decor of James I's entry was largely secular; but in its underlying structure it followed the liturgical patterns long-established by civic ritual. Through traditions of ritual performance, the City of London had established the principles of a templar order; as they reached the end of Cheapside, London's street ceremonies approached the quasi-liturgical consummation of a "ceremony of truth," a ceremony that binds "the hero to a fortunate, if strenuous destiny," and that typically takes the form of a betrothal.[61]

The king's advent: miracle and discourse in the royal entry

As they reached the climax of their central phase at the end of Cheapside, the royal entries enacted a dual convergence – a spiritual union between temporal rule and divine providence, and a political bond between prince and people. The formal political undertakings that here transpired between the City and the prince formed an immediate prelude to symbolic crownings and enthronements in which were figured the mystical marriage of Christ to his bride in the New Jerusalem. The history of the royal entry amounts to an ongoing elaboration and modification of this typological symbolism, all of it emanating from, and oriented to, this climactic ceremonial space – a space which also became a cultural *limen*, a site of political negotiation.

---

[60] *The Magnificent Entertainment: Giuen to King Iames ... Vpon the Day of his Maiesties Tryumphant Passage ... Through his Honourable Citie (and Chamber) of London* (1604), in *The Dramatic Works of Thomas Dekker*, ed. Fredson Bowers (Cambridge University Press, 1955), 2: passim.   [61] Angus Fletcher, *The Prophetic Moment*, pp. 22, 20.

This history originated with the single pageant constructed for the coronation of Richard II in 1377:

a kind of castle had been constructed, having four towers, in the upper part of the shopping street called Cheapside (*in superiore parte Fori venalium quod 'Cheap' nuncupatur*): and from two of its sides wine flowed abundantly. In its towers, moreover, four very beautiful maidens had been placed ... one in each of the four towers. On the King's approach, ... they scattered golden leaves in his path and, on his coming nearer, they showered imitation gold florins on both him and his horse. When he had arrived in front of the castle, they took gold cups and, filling them with wine at the spouts of the said castle, offered them to him and his retinue. In the top of the castle, and raised above and between its four towers, a golden angel was stationed holding in its hands a golden crown. The angel had been devised with such cunning that, on the king's arrival, it bent down and offered him a crown.[62]

Beneath the surface of this ritual crowning lay a wealth of Biblical symbolism equating Richard with Christ the King, anointed into power by the Holy Spirit in the shape of a dove (Mark 1: 10; Luke 4: 18; John 1: 32–3; Acts 10: 38; Isaiah 61: 1) and received as king into Jerusalem as the way was strewn with palms before him (Matt. 21: 8; Mark 11: 8; Luke 19: 36).

This Biblical symbolism was elaborated in the 1392 pageant–entry by which the City of London attempted to lay to rest its quarrel with Richard over the municipality's rights of self-governance: "betwene seynte Poules & the crosse in chepe þere was made a stage ... And an Aungell come a downe from þe stage on hye bi a vyse and sette a croune vpon ye Kynges hede."[63] Richard Maidstone's account of the occasion declared that evil counsel "had estranged" the "city's spouse, its king and master" (*tuum regem, sponsum, dominumque tuumque*), but now no detractor's tongue "could overcome the bride-groom's longing to enter his bridal chamber." The whole city was adorned like the New Jerusalem, "as if art had painted a new heaven."[64] After a thanksgiving ceremony at St. Paul's, the King passed a final pageant at Temple Bar, where St. John gestured with his finger, *agnus et ecce dei*, equating Richard with the divine Spouse and Savior Christ.

The entire pageant embodied that blend of classical ceremony and Biblical symbolism Ernst Kantorowicz has called "the king's advent":

[62] Thomas of Walsingham, *Historia Anglicana*, ed. H. T. Riley (2 vols. London, 1863–64) 1: 331; tr. in Wickham, *Early English Stages*, 1: 54–55.

[63] Bodleian MS Ashm. 793, fos. 128b–129, quoted in Withington, *English Pageantry*, 1: 130.

[64] Maidstone, *De Concordia inter Regem Ric II et Civitatem London*, in *Political Poems and Songs*, ed. T. Wright (2 vols. London: Longmans, Green, 1859–61), 1: 282ff., tr. in Wickham, *Early English Stages*, 1: 64–71.

Whenever a king arrived at the gates of a city, the celestial New Jerusalem seemed to descend from heaven to earth. It is as though, through the magic balm of the Anointed, both king and city are transformed as they approach one another; every terrestrial city becomes another Jerusalem at the Advent of the anointed, and the ruler by his entry becomes more and more a likeness of Christ.[65]

It was in keeping with this advent pattern, and with Tertullian's view that the greatest pageants were those devoted to "the advent of the Lord ...or the city of the New Jerusalem,"[66] that London was "ornamented with jewels like New Jerusalem (*quasi nova Ierusalem monilibus ornata*)" for the reception of Edward II and his queen.[67]

During the fifteenth century, with the consolidation of London's civic order and fabric, further aspects of this seminal advent pattern were extensively elaborated for the magnificent London entries of Henry V and Henry VI. At London Bridge, Henry V was greeted as a type of Christ entering Jerusalem: "'benedictus' thei gan synge; / *Qui venit in nomine domini*, goddys knight" (Matt. 21:9). Along the main portion of the route, pageants depicting heavenly visions of English saints and other "Patriarkes" (Cornhill), the "XII apostelys" and "XII kynges" (entrance to Cheapside) established new dimensions of the advent analogy. The symbolism of these pageants probably derived from the Office of the Dying in the Roman Ritual, which pairs with the *profectio*, or prayer for the departure of the soul, an *adventus*, or prayer for the arrival of the anointed soul in heaven:

May your soul, which is departing from the body, be met by the brilliant host of Angels, may it be received by the court of Apostles, welcomed by the triumphant army of resplendent Martyrs, surrounded by the lilied array of rubiate Confessors, greeted by the jubilant choir of Virgins, and embraced by blessed peace in the bosom of the Patriarchs.[68]

Likened to an anointed soul entering heaven, the King was also hailed and censed as a savior at the climactic pageant just before St. Paul's in Cheapside: "'Nowell,' 'Nowell,' all the gon syng. / vnto Poules thanne rood oure kyng."[69]

The 1432 entry of Henry VI likened the King's salvific presence to David's entry into Jerusalem:

[65] "The 'King's Advent' and the Enigmatic Panels on the Doors of Santa Sabina," *Art Bulletin*, 26 (1944), 210.
[66] *De spectaculis*, quoted in *The Complete Prose Works of John Milton*, ed. Don M. Wolfe (8 vols. New Haven: Yale University Press, 1953–82), 1: 489–490 n.
[67] William Stubbs, ed., *Chronicles of Edward I and II* (RS 1: 1882), p. 152, quoted in Kipling, "Richard II's Sumptuous Pageants," p. 88; also Kantorowicz, "The 'King's Advent,'" p. 210.   [68] Quoted in Kantorowicz, "The 'King's Advent,'" p. 207.
[69] Harleian MS 565, in Tyrrell, *A Chronicle of London from 1089 to 1483*, p. 232.

And lyke for Dauyd affter his victorie,
  Reioyssed was alle Ierusalem,
So this Citee with laude, pris, and glorie,
  For ioye moustred lyke the sonne beem,
  To yeve ensample thurgh-out the reem.[70]

According to Lydgate's poem on the occasion, the entry reached its climax in Cheapside, when the young King passed from "a castell bilt off iasper grene"(line 394), an image of the heavenly Jerusalem (Rev. 21: 11), to an enthroned likeness "Indeuysible made off the Trinite" near "the partye most chieff and princypall, / Callyd off London the chirche cathederall" (lines 431, 422–423).

The approach to this epiphany began, however, as the monarch received blessings from Nature, Grace, and Fortune, who were flanked on one side by the Seven Gifts of the Holy Ghost and on the other by the Seven Gifts of Grace. These, along with other personified virtues later in the pageant, mark the first appearance of the moral allegories that, in the *speculum principis* tradition, became a regular feature of subsequent pageants. Although *laudando praecipere* was a traditional function of pageant tributes, in Henry's entry, the traditional function of moral and political counsel was subordinated to the typological thrust of the advent pattern. The virtues, in other words, were not treated morally, as desiderata, but magically and mystically, as attributes emanating from the *roi thaumaturge*, the anointed savior–king, or as gifts descending from God to him through the *vota* or good wishes of the people. It was the monarch's charismatic approach to such moral tableaux that endowed them with animation and speech, just as his presence caused the city's conduits to run miraculously with wine. The entering monarch was thus the bearer of *felicitas* or good fortune, the anointed one whose touch or presence *facit esse felicem* (cf. *Aeneid* 6.229, 7.750).[71] Because the Seven Gifts of the Holy Ghost were among the spiritual graces which, by analogy with the ritualistic chrism of confirmation, a king received upon being anointed,[72] Henry VI was typologically cast as a *christomimetes*, a "living image" of both the human, incarnate Savior and spiritual, ascended Christ entering the New Jerusalem.

To be sure, Henry VI was exhorted by a pageant of the arts – symbolic of human labor and learning – to remember his Lord, "Syth ye be iuges other ffolke to deme" (l. 271). And in keeping with civic logic, this advice

[70] *Ordenaunces ffor the Kyng made in the Citie off London*, lines 22–26.
[71] H. S. Versnels, *Triumphus: An Inquiry into the Origin, Development, and Meaning of the Roman Triumph* (Leiden: E. J. Brill, 1970), pp. 367–372.
[72] Marc Bloch, *The Royal Touch: Sacred Monarchy and Scrofula in England and France*, tr. J. E. Anderson (London: Routledge and Kegan Paul, 1973), p. 114.

led to a climactic exhortation at the Great Conduit, just before the King
entered Cheapside, where two judges and seven sergeants, advised that

> Honour off kyngys in euery mannys siht,
> Off comyn custum lovith equyte and riht.   (lines 298–299)

Yet even this pointed exhortation was softened by a typological
invocation of the Psalmist's blessing on Israel's King, *Deus iudicum tuum
regi da, et iusticiam tuam ffilio regis* (Ps. 72: 1).

The seven major entries of the Tudor period drew heavily on the
liturgical elements laid out in this very full entry of Henry VI. Like the
1432 entry, they incorporated the new "discursive" elements – the
genealogical tableaux and allegories of virtues and arts – that provided a
kind of "secular," non-mystical orientation toward historical, moral,
and political matters. But they also typically followed the 1432 entry in
subordinating these to the fundamental spiritual mysteries of the
"advent." Royal genealogies almost always occurred in the earliest
phases of the Tudor entries, before they reached the sacred–civic axis
along Cheapside. Moreover, despite their historical import, such dynastic pageants were usually dramatized in terms that emphasized the
divine, providential mystery of the royal line of descent.[73] Pageants of
personified virtues, in the Tudor period usually stationed at the Conduits
in Cornhill and Cheapside, after the dynastic pageants and at the
beginning of the climactic phase of the Cornhill–Cheapside axis, were
likewise adapted to the pattern of the advent of the blessed one. The
entire series of Beatitudes, for example, was staged for Elizabeth in order
to emphasize her fulfillment of the prophecy in Isaiah 11: 2.

The moral and dynastic desiderata of these early phases of the entry
were thus usually linked to the spiritual mysteries and analogies that were
the heart of the ceremony. The political import of these typological
mysteries was exemplified in the climactic pageant of Catherine of
Aragon's entry, where the depiction of God enthroned at the Standard in
Cheapside transformed the city into a sacred temple:

> In thys my chirch I am allway Recydent,
> As my chyeff tabernacle and most chosyn place,

---

[73] See, e.g., *The Noble Triumphant Coronation of Quene Anne* (Wynkyn de Worde, 1533),
in Edward Arber, ed., *An English Garner* (8 vols. London, 1877–96), 2: 47; and *English
Verses and Ditties at the Coronation Procession of Queen Anne Boleyn, An English Garner*,
2: 52–53. *The Procession of King Edward the VIth from the Tower to His Pallace at
Westminster*, in *Ioannis Lelandi ... Collectanea*, ed. Thomas Hearne (London, 1744), 4:
315–316.

>Among these goldyn candylstykkis which Represent
>My catholyke chyrch shynyng affore my fface.

The function of this divine presence was to legitimize the earthly rule of Henry VII:

>Owir Soverayn lord the kyng ryall
>May be Resemblid, to the King Celestiall
>As well as any prynce, erthly now lyving
>Syttyng among, the sevyn candylstykkys Royall.[74]

Few of the Tudor entries climaxed quite so spectacularly, but most ascended to symbolic crownings, heavenly visions, or mystical manifestations of holy kingship. In all of the entries, the monarch's advent was a salvific event, a *renovatio* or *initium seculi felicissimi*. Even when Charles I belatedly received entry, postponed at his coronation in 1625, upon returning from Scotland in 1641, a personified London could still greet the monarch and his spouse with the observation that "Some gods are come, to make a heav'n of me."[75]

The biblical dimensions of the advent were further underlined by the use of children to welcome Anne Boleyn, Edward VI, Mary, Elizabeth, and James at the first pageant station in Fenchurch Street. Under the rule of Hadrian, children had been used to represent the *natio* of Judaea, to signify "*Iudaea renascens*, the New Jerusalem or Aelia Capitolina founded after the Jewish rebellion."[76] Their use at the threshold to the London pageants, alluding to Christ's entry into Jerusalem "and the children crying in the Temple, and saying, Hosanna to the son of David" (Matt. 21: 15), similarly dramatized the renewal brought about by the entry of a messiah.

The messianic pattern had always culminated at the heart of the processional route, along Cheapside. Yet this segment, which occupied the center of London's own civic ceremonies, was also the locus for another sort of ideology in the entries. Between the two apocalyptic Cheapside pageant stations of 1392, Richard II had received a harangue from the City officials who lined this stretch of the route, an oration in which there was never "the least hint that London was wrong in the initial quarrel or that there was any justification for Richard's arbitrary conduct."[77] Henry VI, as well, had here been reminded of the "comyn

---

[74] *The Great Chronicle of London* (Guildhall Lib. MS. 3313), ed. I. D. Thornley (London: George W. Jones, 1937), pp. 308–309.

[75] *Ovatio Carolina, The Triumph of King Charles* (1641), in *Somers Tracts*, (13 vols. London, 1809–15), 4: 151.

[76] Kantorowicz, "The 'King's Advent,'" p. 213; see also Jocelyn M. Toynbee, *The Hadrianic School: A Chapter in the History of Greek Art* (Cambridge University Press, 1934), pp. 119–121.   [77] Wickham, *Early English Stages*, 1: 70.

custum" by which kings love "equyte and riht." Though accommodated to typological patterns and removed mysteries, the allegorical virtues, arts, and trees of the pageants always contained a tacit discursive element, a residue of topical reference, moral reasoning, and historical and political argument.

This potentially desacralizing awareness of the political causes and effects governing the ceremony became increasingly prominent in the Tudor period. The reception of Catherine of Aragon, for example, established what thereafter became a faithfully observed custom. Between the Temple of God at the Standard and Catherine's final symbolic enthronement beside Prince Arthur at the Little Conduit, Catherine was greeted by London's Lord Mayor and Recorder, and

hard such wordis of salutacion and welcomyng as þe Recorder then to hyr utterid in the name of the mayer & of the comynalte of the Cyte, and afftyr convenyent thankis by hir chanceler to the Mayer & comynalte of the Cyte govyn, she held on her progresse passyng by the aldyrmen syttyng on horsbak in scarlet tyll hir Grace cam vnto the lytyll cunduyt at the ffere ende of Chepe.[78]

Beginning with the entry of Anne Boleyn, perhaps the most discursively explicit up to that time, a further element was added to the City's speeches: "midway between" the two ends of Cheapside,

the Recorder of London received her before the Aldermen ... saluting her Grace, with a humble and loving proposition, presenting her Grace with a rich and Costly purse of gold, and in it a thousande marks ... to whom she gave great thanks.[79]

The City had presented a gift to Henry VI in Westminster on the day after his entry, but Anne Boleyn's entry established what thereafter became another unbroken custom – the insertion into the climactic phase of the entry of symbolic gift-giving by the City's own representatives. The offering of gifts was then followed in a ceremony in which a sword or sceptre was passed from the royal entrant to the mayor of London, who then preceded the entrant for the remainder of the procession.[80] At the heart of their enactment, the mysteries of the advent were henceforth balanced by a conspicuous display of the underlying discursive realities, the process of give-and-take by which groups with different interests "carry on exchange, make contracts, and are bound by obligations."[81]

The City of London, as attested by its careful records of precedents, loyal services, and charters, had always been conscious of the causes and

---

[78] *Great Chronicle of London* , p. 307.   [79] *The Noble Triumphant Coronation*, p. 48.

[80] Smuts, "Public Ceremony and Royal Charisma," p. 73.

[81] Marcel Mauss, *The Gift: Forms and Functions of Exchange in Archaic Societies*, tr. Ian Cunnison (New York: Norton, 1967), p. 3.

effects that linked the two jurisdictions. But that this view of the relationship should have become so symbolically conspicuous – and increasingly a matter *for* discourse – in the early Tudor period is no accident. It was just two years after Anne Boleyn's entry, in 1535, that the first triumphal pageant, belonging to the Mercers, was carried before Sir John Allen at his mayoral inauguration. And it was at just this time that such pageants began to speak. One of the last of the suppressed pageants of the Midsummer Watch – that of 1541 – was the first to have made use of speeches. By 1553, the mayoral shows had "goodly speeches," and by 1575 William Smith described as a typical feature of the inaugural procession, a pageant "whereuppon by certayne fygures and wrytinges, some matter touchinge justice, and the office of a maiestrate is represented."[82]

Of increasing importance throughout the Tudor period, London's discourse to the monarch actually transformed the advent trope into a trope of covenant in the remarkable entry of Elizabeth I. The covenantal aspect of the ceremony was underlined at the very beginning of Elizabeth's entry, at Fenchurch Street, where the Queen was exhorted in remarkably secular terms to

> behold what this thy town
> Hath thee presented at thy fyrst entrance here:
> Behold with how riche hope *she ledeth thee* to thy crown.
> Behold with what two gyftes she comforteth thy chere.[83]

Implicit within the miraculous, atemporal advent types and analogies of Elizabeth's entry was an alternative language of political and moral reasoning about the ongoing political life of City and Crown. The glorious advent symbolism was thus balanced by a symbolism of precedent, pact, and covenant, in which "the promises and blessinges of almightie god made to his people" (p. 24) became a model for Elizabeth's commitments to the people of London and England. At the first pageant in Gracechurch Street, for example, a family tree depicting Elizabeth's descent from Henry VII and Elizabeth of York was offered not primarily as a genealogical emblem of dynastic legitimacy but as a political token of a quasi-covenantal "uniting of the houses of Lancaster and Yorke" (p. 19). The essential point was not that Elizabeth was heir to Henry VII but that she was "heire to agreement." The point was sealed with such Latin

[82] *A Breefe Description of the Royall Citie of London, Capitall Citie of This Realme of England* (BM Harleian MS 6363), printed in Nathan Drake, *Shakespeare and His Times* (1838; rpt. New York: Burt Franklin, 1969), p. 424.

[83] *The Quene's Majestie's Passage through the Citie of London*, in Arthur F. Kinney, ed., *Historical Documents of the Age of Elizabeth I* (Hamden, Conn.: Archon Books, 1975), p. 16; italics mine.

tags as *omnium gentium consensus firmat fidem* (p. 21). In a quite literal sense, Elizabeth became the "heire to agreement" when at this point she "promised, that she would doe her whole endeavour for the continuall preservation of concorde" (p. 20).

At the Cornhill Conduit, where many other monarchs were graced with spiritual gifts, Elizabeth received what was unmistakably a political lesson. The protestant doctrine of godly rule combined with a critique of the Marian regime in "The Seate of worthie Governance," where an effigy of the Queen was enthroned above four virtues – "Pure Religion, Love of Subjects, Wisdom, and Justice" – treading on their opposites – "Superstition and Ignorance ... Rebellion and Insolencie." The pageant represented not simply a temporal agenda but also an apocalyptic fulfillment of millenarian hopes – the "utter extirpation of rebellion, and ... *everlasting* continuance of quietnes and peace" (p. 210). Nevertheless a different sense of time, history, and causality emerged in the almost simultaneous explanation that the Queen "should syt fast in the same ... seate of governement ... *so long as* she embraced vertue and helde vice under foote" (pp. 21, 23–24).

Subsequent events in the entry brought to a head the intersecting forces – and the alternative models of City–Crown relations – that became an underlying feature of the climactic portion of the route. The climactic Little Conduit pageant, in which Truth and his daughter Veritas, bearing a Bible with the motto *Verbum veritas* in her hands, emerged from a grotto between the two hills of *Ruinosa Respublica* and *Respublica bene instituta*, very deliberately restaged a controversial feature of the genealogical Fenchurch pageant for Philip II, in which the protestant author of the pageant, Richard Grafton, had given offense by representing Henry VIII as having in his "hande a booke, whereon was wrytten *Verbum Dei*."[84] By resurrecting this censored pageant of a few years earlier, the City of London reaffirmed its commitment to the Henrician Reformation. With her shrewdly theatrical response that "Tyme hath brought me hither" (p. 26), Elizabeth gracefully transformed the political lesson lurking in this version of a great Tudor icon – the frontispiece to the 1539 Great Bible – into an image of her own epiphany as the vessel of revealed truth, a providentially ordained daughter who was the temporal fulfillment and incarnation of the Revelation.

Yet another set of analogies lay beneath those of Elizabeth the Daughter of Henry and Truth the Daughter of Time. If the Scriptural

---

[84] *Chronicle of Queen Jane and Mary*, p. 78; on the controversy and Grafton's role in both the Great Bible and the Philip II entry, see Anglo, *Spectacle, Pageantry, and Early Tudor Policy*, pp. 329–330.

Verbum Veritas descended from Henry–Time to Elizabeth–Truth, it also descended from the City of London itself. As Elizabeth approached the Little Conduit pageant station, and "understoode that the Byble in Englishe shoulde be delivered unto her: *she thanked the Citie for that gift, and sayd that she would oftentimes reade over that booke*" (p. 26; italics mine). The covenantal basis of the exchange was then immediately underlined, for the Queen – restrained from sending an attendant to take the Bible – was prevented from receiving the book until

by appointment, the right worshipfull master Ranulph Cholmley, Recorder of the citie, presented to the Quene's majestie a purse of crimosin sattin richly wrought with gold, wherein the citie gave unto the Quene's majestie a thousand markes in Gold, and master Recorder did declare brieflye unto the Quene's majestie, whose wordes tended to this ende, that the Lord maior, hys brethren, and comminaltie of the citie, to declare their gladnes and good will towardes the Quene's majestie, did present her Grace with that gold, desyering her grace to continue their good and gracious Quene. (p. 26)

Significantly, Elizabeth responded to this gift, as she did throughout the entry, in discursive kind, highlighting the genuine political exchanges and contractual logic that counterbalanced the advent pattern:

I thanke my lord maior, his brethren, and you all. And whereas your request is that I should continue your good ladie and quene, be ye ensured, that I wil be as good unto you, as ever quene was to her people. No wille in me can lacke, neither doe I trust shall ther lacke any power. And persuade yourselves, that for the safetie and quietnes of you all, I will not spare, if nede be to spend my blood. (p. 27)

A strong thread of discursive political exchange thus ran side-by-side with the emerging typological patterns in this entry. Repeatedly the reporter of the entry emphasized the quasi-contractual undertakings, the promises and assurances which, depending on the perspective taken, either manifested the charismatic magnificence of the monarch whose pleasure it was to grant them or demonstrated the power of the city to extract them.[85] To an extent unprecedented in earlier examples, the whole entry was conceived by its reporter as comprising in its elements a connected discourse of moral and political reasoning: interspersed summaries related each pageant to the ones preceding, stressing that "the matter ... dependeth of them that went before" (p. 29).

[85] Elizabeth's promises are recorded on pp. 19, 24, 32, 37, 38. For a view that emphasizes the charismatic nature of the entry and, implicitly, of these promises, see Clifford Geertz, "Centers, Kings, and Charisma: Reflections on the Symbolics of Power," in Joseph Ben-David and Terry Nichols Clark, eds., *Culture and Its Creators: Essays in Honor of Edward Shils* (University of Chicago Press, 1977), 152–171.

This discursive emphasis appears in one further feature dating from the entry of Elizabeth's mother, Anne Boleyn. If Anne's entry established both the gift-giving ceremony and a new degree of discursiveness, it also added further pageantry to the postliminal phase of the monarch's passage out of the City, from St. Paul's to Temple Bar: every entry after Anne's (except, possibly for Mary's – for which the records are sketchy) stationed a pageant at the conduit in Fleet Street, and in later entries at Temple Bar as well. The Fleet Street pageants were, typically, devoted to specific policy agendas. Edward VI, for example, was in Fleet Street exhorted to follow the protestant policies of his father, to become "After old David, a young King Solomon."[86] The typological afterglow was even stronger in the Fleet Street pageant representing Elizabeth as Queen Deborah enthroned, but it was balanced by a literal representation of the secular political process. Deborah was "richlie apparelled in Parliament robes" and flanked by effigies of "the Nobilitie ... the Clergie, and ... the Comminaltye." This was, as one motto declared "Debora the judge and restorer of the house of Israel, Judic. iv," but it was also, as another model without Biblical authority declared, "Debora, with her estates, consulting for the good Governement of Israel."

The discursive exchange in the later Tudor entries was reinforced by the strange reappearance of the ancient City palladia at the very limit of the City's jurisdiction at Temple Bar. Both Philip II and then Elizabeth were confronted at the Bar by twin giants – identified in Elizabeth's entry as "Gotmagot" and "Corineus" – the city palladia who had stood in apotropaic defiance at the initial entry of many earlier monarchs. Because these figures manifested the City's might and defiant spirit, their new role at Temple Bar was especially significant. In both cases, the giants bore up a discursive summary of the entire "argument" of the entry, "a bryffe rehearsall of all the sayd pagauntis," "theffect of all the Pageantes which the Citie before had erected."[87] It is as if in moving their position the City had found – as the entry form developed – a new meaning in the strength of its giant representatives. As elsewhere in Europe, where the giant effigies of towns came to symbolize "the imposition of culture and authority," the power of Gotmagot and Corineus now rested not so much in being "grym of syght" as in drawing and inscribing powerful conclusions.[88] In the case of Elizabeth's entry, the giants were summing up the point explicitly declared at the climactic *Verbum Veritas* pageant

[86] *Lelandi ... Collectanea*, 4: 321.
[87] *Two London Chronicles*, in *Camden Miscellany*, 12: 38; Kinney, *Elizabethan Backgrounds*, p. 35.
[88] Walter Stephens, *Giants in Those Days: Folklore, Ancient History, and Nationalism* (Lincoln: University of Nebraska Press, 1989), p. 41.

– "wordes do flye, but wryting doth remaine." Issued in novel printed form, the pamphlet account of the entry amounted to a written record of the promises Elizabeth had made. Perhaps Sidney had it in mind when he wrote a few years later that "No kings be crowned, but they some covenants make."[89]

The different meanings that had come to inhabit the entry form are perhaps epitomized in the differences between the contributions for the entry of James I by Ben Jonson, court poet, satirist, private theater dramatist, and masque-designer, and Thomas Dekker, degraded pamphleteer, romancer, popular theater workhorse, and author of several mayoral pageants, including one of the two most splendid in the history of the form. For Dekker as for Jonson, the King's advent marked a *renovatio*, "a Regeneration, a new birth."[90] But for Dekker, the animation of the City at the King's approach was not so much an effect of royal influence as the manifestation of London's inherent vitality. At many points, Dekker's account looks more like the report of an anthropologist than a liturgical handbook. The causes and effects enacted by the ceremony, its economic basis and political efficacy, come repeatedly to the fore. According to a pair of present-day anthropologists, the danger in all ceremony is

the possibility that we will encounter ourselves making up our conception of the world, society, our very selves. We may slip in that fatal perspective of recognizing culture as our construct, arbitrary, conventional, made by mortals. Ceremonies are paradoxical in this way. Being the most obviously contrived forms of social contact, they epitomize the made-up quality of culture and almost invite notice as such. Yet their very form and purpose is to discourage untrammeled inquiry into such questions.[91]

For Dekker, as for other pageant-writers commissioned by the London companies to script the annual inaugural shows, it was precisely this meta-liturgical awareness of the invented-ness of the shows – an awareness of historical development, political ostentation, and material preconditions – that was a source of interest. In his account of the *production* of the pageants Dekker lays bare the materials and labor – the nuts and bolts and flimsy scaffolding, the political patronage and committee-work – that lay behind the ceremonial performance of

---

[89] *Astrophil and Stella* 69, l. 14, in *Sir Philip Sidney*, ed. Katherine Duncan-Jones (Oxford University Press, 1989), p. 181.   [90] *Dramatic Works*, 2: 254–255.
[91] Sally Moore and Barbara G. Myerhoff, "Introduction: Secular Ritual: Forms and Meanings," in *Secular Ritual* (Assen: Van Gorcum, 1977), p. 18; quoted in Richard C. McCoy, "'Thou Idol Ceremony': Elizabeth I, the Henriad, and the Rites of English Monarchy," in Susan Zimmerman and Ronald F. E. Weissman, eds., *Urban Life in the Renaissance* (Newark, Del.: University of Delaware Press, 1989), p. 254.

miracles. For Dekker, it was this autonomous power – the material and efficient causes of urban labor – that accounted for the postdiluvian recovery of the city from the plague on the occasion of the entry:

Hee that should haue compared the emptie and vntrodden walkes of London, which were to be seen in that late mortally-destroying Deluge, with the thronged streetes now, might haue belieued, that vpon this day, began a new Creation, and that the Citie was the onely Workhouse wherein sundry Nations were made. (2: 258–259)

The different agencies at work in the entry were sharply contrasted in the alternative preliminary pageants designed by Dekker and by Jonson, for the Bars without Bishopsgate and Fenchurch Street respectively. Dekker's device "should haue serued at his Maiesties first accesse to the Citie" (2: 254) on his arrival from the North, but it was "prevented" by the King's adherence to a route and program that honored Jonson's Fenchurch arch as the first in the entry series; "his Maiestie not making his Entrance (according to expectation)," Dekker's opening contribution was "layd by" (2: 257). This cancelled "first Offring of the Citties Loue" at Bishopsgate was itself, however, a device of "prevention," as St. Andrew and St. George, riding "in compleate Armour," were confronted by the female Genius of London, who "Intersepts their Passage" to greet the King (2:254). Repeating the classic advent gesture that brought a city's female Genius outside the walls to greet an arriving ruler (see Fig. 14), Dekker's Genius took an implicitly critical stance toward the aristocratic, chivalric, and martial spirit of union as it was represented in the two knights. She asked,

> why you beare (alone) th'ostent of Warre,
> When all hands else reare Oliue-boughs and Palme...
> When Troyes proud buildings shew like Fairie-bowers...
> And when soft-handed Peace, so sweetly thriues,
> That Bees in Souldiers Helmets build their Hiues? (2: 255)

In a speech modelled on John of Gaunt's great hymn to England in Shakespeare's *Richard II*, she identified herself as the representative of a different decorum and agency,

> This little world of men; this pretious Stone,
> That sets out Europe...
> This Iewell of the Land; Englands right Eye:
> Altar of Loue; and Spheare of Maiestie:
> Greene Neptunes Minion, 'bout whose Virgin-waste,
> Isis is like a Cristall girdle cast.
> Of this we are the Genius; here haue I,

Slept (by the fauour of a Deity)
Fourtie-foure Summers and as many Springs,
Not frighted with the threats of forraine Kings.
But held vp in that gowned State I haue,
By twice Twelue-Fathers politique and graue:
Who with a sheated Sword, and silken Law,
Do keepe (within weake Walles) Millions in awe.   (2: 256)

Having established the political causes – the "sheated Sword" and "silken Law" – that uphold the powers of the weak, the Genius then urged the monarch to enter the city, "In name of all these Senators, (on whom / Vertue builds more, then those of Antique Rome)" (2: 257).

Jonson's Fenchurch arch, by contrast, subjected the city to the monarch's own messianic agency. The source of Jonson's sniffy differences with Dekker on the gender of London's Genius[92] was neither pedantry nor personal friction but the inherent ambiguity in the relationships negotiated by the entry ceremony. By placing a male Genius of London beneath a female representative of *Monarchia Britannica* on the Fenchurch Street arch (see Fig. 17), Jonson stressed that with his coronation James I married himself not to London but to the independent, royal institution of the monarchy, to whose *Theosophia* or divine wisdom the City and its virtues were subject. The point was reinforced on the frieze by a quotation from Martial's epigram (8.36.12) on Domitian's palace:

PAR DOMVS HAEC COELO,
SED MINOR EST DOMINO.

Taken out of Martial, and implying, that though this citie (for the state, and magnificence) might (by Hyperbole) be said to touch the starres, and reach vp to heauen, yet was it farre inferior to the master thereof, who was his Maiestie; and in that respect vnworthy to receiue him. (7: 83)

The establishment of priorities, however, was not so much the point of the Fenchurch arch as a requirement of the decorum it shared with the entry as a whole, which used solar myths and Virgilian prophetic patterns to present the King's advent as a once-and-for-all salvific event, the inauguration on earth of a great *pax Iacobi*. The face of the Italians' arch at Gracechurch Street, for example, combined an image of Henry VII bestowing the sceptre on James I with Anchises' culminating charge to Aeneas (*Aeneid* 6.851–852, quoted at the end of James' own *Basilikon Doron*) on the inauguration of a reign of peace. The program was

---

[92] Cf. Dekker, *The Magnificent Entertainment*, in *Dramatic Works*, 2: 254–255 and Jonson, *B. Jon: His Part of King James his Royall and Magnificent Entertainment*, in *Works*, 7: 85.

reinforced by Virgilian mottoes hailing the King as the light of Troy (*Aeneid* 2.281) and the god who has wrought peace (*Eclogues* 1.6). The reverse of the Gracechurch pageant lauded James as the *fortunate puer* (*Eclogues* 5.49), a latter-day Apollo whose rule includes an *Imperium in Musas*. Governed by the arts of peace, the Four Kingdoms of Britain would voice in unity the fixed will of destiny (*Eclogues* 4.47), while every land would bear all fruits (*Eclogues* 4.39). Dekker's paradisal *Nova faelix Arabia* arch at Soper Lane end (i.e. Great Conduit) reinforced the magical notion of the anointed monarch as the bearer of *felicitas*. As a successor to Elizabeth, James was here hailed as a Christlike "sacred Phoenix" who brings "To England a new Arabia, a new Spring." The Christian, typological dimension of this recovered paradise was underlined in a song proclaiming that "Troynovant is now no more a Citie / ... Troynovant is now a Bridall Chamber" (2: 279–280). A proclamation of *iam regnat Apollo* – from Virgil's messianic fourth eclogue (4.10) – announced the approach of the climactic Little Conduit pageant, where James was epiphanically lauded as the deified Daphnis–Caesar – *deus, deus ille* (*Eclogues* 5.58–64).

Yet a different logic ran in tandem with this ascending series of miraculous events. By 1604, apparently, the City's discursive claims on this central portion of the route were sufficiently strong to raise hackles at such miracles as might make "Troynovant... now no more a Citie," for Dekker's program noted that "some, (to whose setled iudgement and authoritie the censure of these Deuices was referred,) brought (though not bitterly) the life of those lines into question" (2: 281). Dekker's elaborate defense of the trope was hardly necessary, however, in view of the traditional ceremonial corrective inset between the two paradisal pageants in Cheapside. As had become the custom, in the presence of "all the Aldermen, the Chamberlaine, Town-clarke, and Counsell of the Citie," the monarch was presented with the City's gift (in this case a gold cup) and a speech by the City Recorder:

Come therefore O worthiest of Kings as a glorious Bridegrome through your Royall chamber: But to come nearer, *Adest quem querimus*. Twentie and more are the Soueraignes wee haue serued since our conquest, but Conqueror of hearts it is you and your posterities, that we haue vowed to loue and wish to serue whilst London *is* a Citie. (2: 282)

Even as London was being symbolically transformed into a *nova faelix Arabia* or *hortus euporiae* through the eschatalogical miracle of the king's advent, the different ideology of mundane exchanges, causes, and effects that *did* make "Troynovant... a Citie" were also coming into discursive prominence. With its Virgilian text and classical figures like Pomona and

Ceres, the climactic *hortus euporiae* that followed at the Little Conduit continued the classical Golden Age motif of the entry as a whole; but its use of Euporia, Chrusos, Argurion, and the Seven Liberal Arts linked it also with the trade pageants that were playing an increasingly important role in the contemporary Lord Mayor's Shows. The different decorum of the latter prevailed when the causes of this paradisal vision of plenty were traced to sources other than the grace of the royal person, to whom the pageant was offered

in name of the Praetor, Consuls and Senators of the City, who carefully pruine this garden, (weeding-out al hurtful and idle branches that hinder the growth of the good,) and who are indeede, *Ergatoi pistoi*, faithfull Laborers in this peice of ground. (2: 288)

Ergatoi pistoi: the phrase may have been intended to echo the classical distinction between the acclaim bestowed upon the *soter*, the superhuman god or hero who performed messianic miracles, and the lesser *eugertes*, the civic benefactor whose name was set in stone for continued helpfulness.[93] Used to characterize the maintainers of this symbolic paradise, the phrase placed an ergonomic emphasis squarely on the deeds, the shared labors, that sustained the city. This thread of argument followed James into Paul's Churchyard, where an oration by "one of maister Mulcaster's Schollers"[94] from the Mercers' school entreated the monarch in the name of

his Royal Sonne Henry (Prince of vnspeakable hopes,) he would a little suffer his eie to descend and behold our Schoole, and therein to prouide that those who are but greene in yeeres, and *of equall age* with that his Princelie issue, may *likewise* receiue a vertuous education. (2: 293; italics mine)

The likenesses drawn here – matters of exchange and reciprocity rather than typological analogies – were reiterated in the concluding plea that the King "suffer his royall name to be rolled amongest the Citizens of London, by vouchsafing to be free of that worthie, and chiefest Society of Mercers" (2: 294).

Dekker's song for the postliminal phase at Temple Bar portrayed the entry as a procession through the streets of heaven, but even this miraculous event contained a different dimension: as the song acknowledged, the occasion of James' entry was not in fact his coronation, which

[93] Arthur Darby Nock, "*Soter and Eugertes*," in Sherman E. Johnson, ed., *The Joy of Study: Papers on New Testament and Related Subjects Presented to Honor Frederick Clifton Grant* (New York: Macmillan, 1951), pp. 127–148.

[94] If Mulcaster had indeed been connected with the authorship of Elizabeth's entry, his conspicuous mention here, forty-five years later, would further have underlined the means by which the city sustained its own good life.

had taken place a year earlier, but the King's opening of his first
Parliament:

> ... Ioue and all the states,
> Of Heau'n, through Heau'ns seauen siluer gates
>   All in glory riding ...
> Which starry Path being measur'd ouer,
>   The Deities conuent
>   In Ioues high Court of Parliament.   (2: 299)

In view of the dynamics the entry form had come to embody, it was
perhaps not inappropriate that, in contrast to his predecessor, King
James but dourly "endured the days brunt with patience, being assured
he should never have such another."[95] As the protagonist of the entry
ceremony, the monarch was the symbolic focus of an emblematic series
of moral, genealogical, and theological messages. This series, however,
increasingly took the form of a discursive whole (a change in which the
recent practice of publishing entry narratives perhaps played a symptomatic role), a process of undertakings in which the monarch was in
some respects as much interlocutor and recipient as agent and symbolic
focus. This was a function of a deeper ceremonial ambiguity. As a
ceremony in which differences between alternative jurisdictions, ways of
life, and visions of society were negotiated, the entry was the sort of
liminal event where potentially conflicting structures, expectations, and
discursive modes were held together in suspension. In this suspension,
especially in the central phase of the entry, the potentially divisive
structures that organized different modes of politico-legal–economic life
were transformed by a spirit of *communitas* into a basis for dialogical
reflection on social unity, on the ideals and desiderata of the nation.[96]
Social relationships were clarified even while myth and ritual were
elaborated.[97]

To be sure, the dangerous and potentially anarchic aspects of this
communitas were amply hedged "with prescriptions, prohibitions, and
conditions."[98] The hieratic, hierarchical nature of the tableaux and the
theophanic, eschatalogical conceptions of the basic advent metaphor
supported a *normative communitas* that diminished the role of dialogue,

---

[95] Arthur Wilson, *The History of Great Britain* (1653), pp. 12–13, quoted in David M.
Bergeron, *English Civic Pageantry 1558–1642* (Columbia, S.C.: University of South
Carolina Press, 1971), p. 75.

[96] See esp. Victor Turner, "Liminality and the Performative Genres," in John J.
MacAloon, ed., *Rite, Drama, Festival, Spectacle* (Philadelphia: Institute for the Study
of Human Issues, 1984), pp. 19–27; and Turner, *The Ritual Process*, pp. 95–96.

[97] I am adapting Turner's view that in ceremony "we find social relationships simplified,
while myth and ritual are elaborated," *The Ritual Process*, p. 167.

[98] Ibid., p. 109.

reasoning, and exchange. Because only the monarch and his entourage moved past each of the stationary pageants, the potential for dramatic development and discursive connection was strictly limited. No spectator along the route could likely witness more than a single pageant, almost any one of which could be taken as a Biblical, moral, historical, or theophanic version of the same underlying miraculous event – the descent of God's blessings through the ritual advent and coronation. The very spirit of unity wrought by such blessings – as London became an Edenic New Jerusalem or City of the Saints – tended to obliterate the different interests and identities that might generate critical consciousness. The entry was shaped (and ultimately functioned) to serve the interests of structure by inspiring awe and obedience.

Nevertheless, the *normative* communitas enforced by the entry also involved an element of *ideological communitas*, the symbolic representation of social and political ideals in which there lay the potential for exchanging "explicitly formulated views on how men may best live together in comradely harmony."[99] Though it served to reinforce the *status quo*, the ceremony also contained within itself the potential for further change. As Turner observes, one group may use the consensus built around the myths and rituals of communitas to rationalize and consolidate its domination of another; but "the key communitas values shared by both groups but put into abeyance by the politically successful one may later become resurgent in the latter... Communitas tends to generate metaphors and symbols which later fractionate into sets and arrays of cultural values."[100] In the discursive events that transpired along Cheapside, in the threads of reasoning developed along the way, and in the form of the entry itself lay the basis for the alternative ceremonial forms and functions by which the city defined and inscribed itself in the hearts of its citizens.

From ritual to myth in the civic year

In contrast to the royal entry, a once-and-for-all event that marked an *initium seculi felicissimi*, the inaugural ceremony that evolved into the Elizabethan and Jacobean Lord Mayor's Shows was an annual occasion. As Thomas Heywood put it in the show for 1637, "the Dominion of the greatest Magistrates, which are Kings and Princes, ought to be perpetuall; but of the lesse which be Praetors, Censors, and the like, only Ambulatory and Annual."[101] From this basic contrast follow many of the

---

[99] Ibid., p. 134.   [100] "Liminal to Liminoid in Play, Flow, and Ritual," p. 50.
[101] *Londini Speculum* (1637), in *Dramatic Works*, 4: 304.

major formal differences that distinguish the Lord Mayor's Shows: the staging of the Lord Mayor's Show on the model of a triumph, rather than a procession past static arches and tableaux, so that each pageant was incorporated into a procession that, by its conclusion, formed a continuous and complete sequence visible in its entirety to all and any spectators who lined the culminating portion of the route; a correspondingly greater emphasis on narrative and discursive continuity, making visible a sequence of moral, historical, and political causes and effects; a stronger meta-liturgical dimension, i.e., a tendency of these causal discourses to articulate the functions of the ceremony and the history from which it emerged; a sharpened awareness of the reciprocities – the sharings and exchanges – mediated by the ceremony, such that the discursiveness of the ceremony could itself be offered as a general model of human relationship; an ever-widening repertoire of myths and motifs, which, through so many annual variations, produced a sense of history and meaning as human products; a wider latitude between the centripetal and centrifugal functions of the ceremony, resulting in a greater variety of messages directed to a greater variety of groups and interests whose identity was recognized as distinctive without being divisive.

The meaning of all these formal properties, however, lay in the political arrangements – the sharing and exchange of offices – that made the ceremony an annual event. The anonymous Elizabethan Apologist for the City of London wrote that in the metropolis there had never "been any strong faction, nor any man more popular than the rest, forasmuch as the gouernment is by a Paterne, as it were, and alwayes the same, how oftensoeuer they change their Magistrate" (Stow, 2: 206). Writing at the same time as the anonymous Apologist, another unidentified defender of the city asserted that the greatness of London was that

so populous a citie, conteyning by true estimation more then 500 thousandes of all sortes of inhabitants [was] managed not by cruel viceroyes, as in Naples & Millaine, neither by a proud Podesta, as be most cities in Italie, or insolent Lieutenants or presidentes, as are sundry Cities in France, ... but by a man of trade or a meare merchant, who notwithstanding, during the time of his magistracie, carieth himselfe with that honourable magnificence in his port, and ensignes of state, that the Consuls, Tribunes, and praetors of Rome ... neuer bare the like representation of dignitie.[102]

The power of the ceremony, then, lay in its celebration of the continuity maintained through annual changes in the City's chief magistrate: "though the maine Authoritie of Government (in hym) may be sayd to

---

[102] *A Breefe Discourse, Declaring and Approuing the Necessarie and Inuiolable Maintenance of the Laudable Custemes of London* (1584), sigs. a7–a7v.

dye: yet it surviveth in other Pellicanes of the same brood, and so it reacheth to them in the same manner.''[103] Constitutional mechanisms and ritual observances maintained at an early point for Londoners one of the most difficult and fragile institutions of civilized communities, a respect for electoral procedures that ensured that duly chosen candidates would be allowed to serve, and willing to relinquish, their offices at the appointed times. The ceremonial oath-takings that governed every level of the City freedom, guild life, and civic hierarchy[104] culminated in the elaborate transitional protocols of the mayoralty, when the outgoing and incoming mayors exchanged elaborate deferences to mark the transfer of authority.

It is important here to distinguish between the different kinds of ritual represented in the royal entry and in the inaugural show that developed in connection with the mayor's installation. Both were of course liminal rites in the sense that each involved negotiation between the potentially conflicting jurisdictions of Court and City: just as the monarch passed through the City on the way to coronation in Westminster, so the Lord Mayor received his pageant upon return from his swearing in before the monarch's representatives at Westminster. The royal entry, however, was a *life crisis* rite, an obvious passage from one status to another for the monarch, certainly, but also a major crisis for English society as a whole, an irreversible, non-cyclical passage from a known state of affairs into a new and unknown era. Election was of course also a *rite de passage* for the Lord Mayor; but in a more fundamental sense the inaugural ceremonies were a *calendrical rite*, a periodic collective ceremony, linked to an annual cycle of events, which renewed the ongoing life of the community by re-enunciating its most basic principles.[105]

What reconciled change with continuity in this annual rite was the rotation or exchange of positions, on a basis of parity, within the City hierarchy. According to the City Recorder who presented the mayor-elect Sir John Spencer at the Exchequer in 1594, the annual election of the mayor had several meanings:

To the Magistrate; it putteth him in minde that he is to rule Men, and his Fellow Citizens; to rule them not after his will, but according to the laws; to rule, not alwaie, but for a time, and for no longer tyme then only one yeare; then to lay

---

[103] Anthony Munday, *Chrysanaleia: The Golden Fishing: or, Honour of Fishmongers*, in *Pageants and Entertainments of Anthony Munday*, p. 107.

[104] See Brigden, *London and the Reformation*, p. 27; James Knowles, "The Spectacle of the Realm: Civic Consciousness, Rhetoric and Ritual in Early Modern London," in J. R. Mulryne and Margaret Shewring, eds., *Theatre and Government Under the Early Stuarts* (Cambridge University Press, 1993), pp. 163–164.

[105] For this distinction, see Victor Turner, "Liminality and the Performative Genres," p. 21, and *The Ritual Process*, p. 168.

downe his office ... and to become a Member, and noe Head, as ready to obey as he was willing to command.

To the well-disposed Cittizens; to stirr them up to ascend the same degrees that hath advanced others to that honourable dignity, when they see the self-same way for them as it was for others to attayne the same, which is from vertue to vertue, from service to service, from one office to another.[106]

A later verse encomiast observed more simply that

> ... every year they change Lord Maior
> To show their mutual love,
> And that in power they equal are,
> And none the other above.[107]

By its very nature as a gift-giving ceremony, the inaugural rite acknowledged this reciprocal office-sharing arrangement. Gift giving played a large role both within individual guilds and companies and in the City government as a whole. The mayor, sheriffs, and other officials maintained by privilege the carefully restricted right to bestow liveries and other gifts.[108]

The Lord Mayor's Shows were themselves a major instance of such gift-exchange. Unlike royal entries, they were not a production of the City government, but of the individual guild from whose membership the mayor had been elected in a given year. Commissioned and paid for by the "bachelors" of the company, scores of whom were raised to this livery from the lower yeomanry whenever a company's candidate was elected mayor,[109] the show was the company's gift to one of its illustrious members. It was also, along with the mayor-elect himself, the company's contribution to the City as a whole. Spices, comfits, and sweetmeats (in the case of the Fishmongers, fish) were strewn to the crowds along the route in token of the larger gift bestowed by "that company / Whose love and bounty this day doth declare."[110] Such largesse was a desirable symbol of a company's status. As with the earlier sponsorship of Corpus Christi pageants in medieval English towns, changing guild sponsorship of the inaugural show expressed "diachronic changes within the social body ... It projected a symbolism of temporal mutation." The changing fortunes and prestige of companies were reflected in changing spon-

---

[106] *The Recorder of London's Speech, on Presenting the Lord Mayor, Sir John Spencer, to the Lord Chief Baron and his Brethren of the Exchequer, 1594*, in John Nichols, ed., *The Progresses and Public Processions of Queen Elizabeth*, 3: 256.

[107] *London's Praise, Or, The Glory of the City* (1685), in Hyder Rollins, ed., *The Pepys Ballads* (Cambridge, Mass.: Harvard University Press, 1929), 3: 222.

[108] For these privileges, see *Liber Albus*, p. 26, and Stow, *Survey*, 2: 187–195.

[109] Steven Rappaport, *Worlds within Worlds: Structures of Life in Sixteenth-Century London* (Cambridge University Press, 1989), p. 229.

[110] Anthony Munday, *The Triumphs of Re-United Britannia*, in *Pageants and Entertainments*, p. 6.

sorship of the inaugural shows; "equality, change, and mobility" were thus symbolically integrated with a continuing stress on "status, hierarchy, and the role of authority."[111]

The civic principles of parity and reciprocity on which the gift of the pageant was based were recognized in another central feature of the ceremony, the feast at the Guildhall, hosted by the new mayor and sheriffs as a gift to their companies and the City.[112] As year by year the office passed from man to man and the sponsorship of the show from company to company, the exchanges of the ceremony – the gift of "bachelorhood," the show itself, the pamphlets commemorating it (published at the guild's expense and distributed to its members), the feast hosted by the mayor and sheriffs – nostalgically returned the advanced politico-economic rule of the city to a symbolic basis in the mutuality of quasi-feudal bonds and undertakings. As Middleton's personification of Love reminded Sir William Cockayne in 1619,

> There's no free gift but looks for thanks at least;
> A love so bountifull, so free, so good,
> From the whole city, from thy brotherhood –
> ... Expect some fair requital from the man
> They've all so largely honor'd.[113]

There is no concealing either the realities masked by this nostalgia or the fundamentally centripetal function of such exchanges – their tendency to consolidate the rule of the City's elite on the basis of a neofeudal ethos. The rise of the mayoral inauguration and its show to pre-eminence in London's civic year reflected the increasing domination of the City by a few elite companies, the cultic elevation of the Lord Mayor, and a widening gap between the leading City merchants and the expanding body of middling shopkeepers, artisans, journeymen and apprentices who constituted the great majority in the citizen class. The official sponsorship of the inaugural shows by London's leading companies was meant to uphold their increasingly exclusive privileges at the very time when these were coming under heavier attack from the outports and in Parliament. The mayors whose rule was celebrated in the shows were no mere London guildsmen but royal concessionaires and investors in the leading international trading consortia. The election to "bachelor" status of those guildsmen who could afford to subsidize the shows marked an important distinction between the men of substance who

---

[111] Mervyn James, "Ritual, Drama, and the Social Body in the Medieval English Town," pp. 34, 38.

[112] For a description of the feast, see William Smith, *A Breefe Description of the Royall Citie of London*, in Drake, *Shakespeare and His Times*, p. 424.

[113] *The Triumphs of Love and Antiquity (1616)*, in *Works*, ed. A. H. Bullen (8 vols. New York: AMS Press, 1964), 7: 330.

might eventually attain the livery of their companies and the lesser artisans and shopkeepers who never would.

Nevertheless, reciprocity and exchange within the City's elite – its discourses and dialogues, its office-sharings, substitutions, causal chains of obligation, – were offered in the inaugural shows as a general model of the means by which urban life perpetually renewed itself. Not only did the shows attempt to reinforce authority at the apex of the social pyramid by inculcating ideals of obedience and cooperation at its widening bottom; in celebrating commensality and the glory of the City's *cursus honorarum*, they provided the lower echelons of Londoners with a genuinely innovative and compelling model of civic and economic achievement.

As an annual rite of transition and renewal, the inaugural ceremony drew meaning from its place in the cycle of customary ritual practices by which the civic elite defined the city's ideals. Custumals like the *Liber Albus* and *Liber Ordinationum* devoted considerable attention to outlining the ceremonial year.[114] In the 1590s, City officials paid for a new transcription of the former, but by this time the City was also periodically issuing printed calendars and prescriptions for the major civic rituals.[115] In 1574–75 Thomas Norton, the City Remembrancer, prepared a manuscript version of such a document for the new Lord Mayor, noting that "things ... have their prescribed times, and so be set under the titles of every severall monethe," and advising that "it is good ... to read over the monethes that shall next followe, to see yf anie thinge in the moneth followinge do require preparation or warnynge in the monethe present."[116]

The mayoral inauguration played a crucial role in the annual cycle of ceremonies. In London, the civic year was divided into two semesters.[117] During one half of the year, City officials participated in a series of processions between St. Thomas de Acon and St. Paul's (later, between the Guildhall and St. Paul's), beginning with the Feast of All Saints (November 1) and continuing with the fixed holidays of the Christmas season (Christmas, New Year's Day, Epiphany, Candlemas) and the moveable feasts that followed Easter (Ascension Day, Pentecost, and

---

[114] For rites recorded in the *Liber Ordinationum* (fol. 174), see Williams, *Medieval London: From Commune to Capital*, p. 30.

[115] The first such calendar was published by John Day in 1568.

[116] *Instructions to the Lord Mayor of London, 1574–75*, in *Illustrations of Old English Literature*, ed. J. Payne Collier, (3 vols. London, 1866), 3: 14–15.

[117] I am indebted to the account of such a pattern at Coventry by Charles Pythian-Adams, "Ceremony and the Citizen: The Communal Year at Coventry 1450–1550," in Paul Slack and Peter Clark, eds., *Crisis and Order in English Towns 1500–1700: Essays in Urban History* (London: Routledge and Kegan Paul, 1972), pp. 57–85.

Corpus Christi, which could be dated as late as June 24). These were the major liturgical feasts, keyed to the events of Christ's life, and tracing a complete Christological cycle from Christmas to Corpus Christi – a feast whose symbolic relevance to the body politic made it the occasion of the great medieval town play cycles. The second semester began with the Midsummer Watch, held on the Feasts of John the Baptist (June 24) and Saints Peter and Paul (June 29). This outdoor festival, the explicit function of which was the mustering of the City's government, police, and defenses, marked the beginning of a civic semester that culminated with the inauguration of the mayor on October 29.

Prior to the Reformation, the Midsummer Marching Watch, rather than the inauguration, was the primary rite of civic renewal. Part *terminalia* or boundary-setting rite, the Watch was also a kind of lustration or purgative ceremony whose major purpose may "have been literally to carry fire through the streets."[118] Stow reports that the Watch was a time for reconciliation and renewing communal attachments: bonfires were so called because of the "good amitie amongest neighbours that, before being at controuersie, were there by the labour of others, reconciled, and made of bitter enemies, louing friendes, as also for the vertue that a great fire hath to purge the infection of the ayre" (1: 101).

It was on this occasion, marking the end of the religious and the beginning of the civic semester, rather than on the inauguration in October,[119] that pageant wagons, sponsored by the companies of the Lord Mayor and sheriffs, formed part of the procession: "the Mayor had besides his Giant, three Pageants, each of the Sheriffes had besides their Giantes but two Pageants, ech their Morris Dance" (Stow, 1: 103). A few of these pageants were honorific conceits based on the names of officials, but the majority were devoted to Biblical subjects (Jesse, Solomon, Christ's Disputation) or to saints and cults (John the Evangelist, Our Lady and St. Elizabeth, the Assumption, Corpus Christi, St. Margaret, St. Blythe, St. Thomas Becket, St. Ursula).[120]

The suppression of the Midsummer Watch by royal edict in 1539 coincided with a major change in the October inauguration and its place in the civic year. Undoubtedly a factor in the suppression was the

---

[118] Ibid., p. 72.

[119] There were, apparently, some pageants in fifteenth-century inaugurations, but they were suppressed by an order of October 23, 1481 forbidding any "disguysyng nor pageoun ... as it hath been used nowe of late afore this time," *City of London Calendar of Letter-Books, Letter Book L*, ed. R. R. Sharpe, p. 187; see E. K. Chambers, *The Elizabethan Stage* (1923; rpt. Oxford: Clarendon Press, 1951), p. 135.

[120] See Withington, *English Pageantry*, 1: 38–41, and *A Calendar of Dramatic Records in the Books of the Livery Companies of London 1485–1640*, ed. Jean Robertson and D. J. Gordon (Oxford: Malone Society, 1954), pp. xx–xxii.

hostility of the Reformation agenda to traditional forms of piety and festivity.[121] However, this suppression did not, as it did in combination with economic decline at Coventry and other towns, mark an absolute waning of civic ceremonial.[122] On the contrary, the economic decline of the provincial towns, like the Reformation itself, was in many ways a manifestation of London's relative advance in political and economic strength. Accordingly, the suppression of the Midsummer Watch in London resulted in an amplification of civic ceremony in other forms. After the Reformation and the suppression of the Watch, Midsummer Day continued to mark the beginning of a series of secular, political events that culminated in the October inauguration – the election of the sheriffs on June 24; their swearing-in on Michaelmas eve; the mayoral election on Michaelmas; the presentation of the sheriffs to the Lord Chancellor on the day following. All of these events were neatly dovetailed as a run-up to the climactic events of October 28–29, which completed the staffing of the City government just in time for the beginning of the religious year on November 1. Coinciding with the ancient Celtic New Year of Samhain, the mayoral inauguration was part of a transition from the civic to the religious semester, a transition that straddled All Souls' and All Saints' Days, feasts which together represent the two extremes of Christian cosmology, where *communitas* and *hierarchy* confront each other.[123] It was well-suited, then, to reconciling change with continuity, community with rule.

Other important changes accompanied this ceremonial shift. Pageants first appeared in inaugural processions in 1535, and they became a regular feature of the October ceremonies from about 1540, almost immediately upon the suppression of the Midsummer Watch.[124] By 1575 William Smith could characterize the inaugural procession in general as having a "pageant of tryumphe rychly decked, whereuppon by certayne fygures and wrytinges, some matter touchynge justice, and the office of a maiestrate is represented."[125] The most important change was the new

---

[121] On the suppression of the Watch, see Stow, *Survey*, 1: 103, and Wriothesley, *A Chronicle of England During the Reigns of the Tudors*, 1: 100.

[122] For the impact of economic decline on ceremony in provincial towns, see Charles Pythian-Adams, "Urban Decay in Late Medieval England," in Philip Abrams and E. A. Wrigley, eds., *Towns in Societies: Essays in Economic History and Historical Sociology* (Cambridge University Press, 1978), pp. 159–186.

[123] See Turner, *The Ritual Process*, pp. 181–182. Before it became the date of the inaugural presentation, October 29 was the date of the mayoral election.

[124] See *A Calendar of Dramatic Records in the Calendar Books of the Livery Companies of London*, ed. Robertson and Gordon, p. 37. Machyn's reports from the 1550s all refer to the use of pageants; see *The Diary of Henry Machyn*, pp. 48, 73, 96, 118, 155.

[125] *A Breefe Description of the Royall Citie of London*, in Drake, *Shakespeare and His Times*, p. 424.

prominence of a discursive element – the "fygures and wrytinges" upon the pageants, certainly, but even more crucially the "goodly speeches" that began to accompany the pageants. While the pageants of the Midsummer Watch may occasionally have made use of painted "scriptures" and singing,[126] the evidence suggests that throughout most of their history these (mainly religious) pageants were without speeches. That the accompaniment of the new inaugural pageants with speeches was not simply an accident of shifting the pageants from June to October, but part of a more deliberate and pervasive escalation in civic ceremony at this time, is reflected in the fact that one of the last Midsummer Watch pageants, that of 1541, made use of speeches for the first time.[127] The survival of the first inaugural pageant texts, by an anonymous writer in 1561 and by Richard Mulcaster in 1568, as well as the commissioning of texts from Mr. "Grimbald" (i.e., Grimald?) in 1556 and James Peele in 1566,[128] substantiate a picture of new attempts to disseminate, more widely and in verbal form, the ideology of the City's elite, which had hitherto been confined to a customary ritual framework. If Mervyn James is right in thinking that the absence of a major Corpus Christi play cycle in London reflects the unusual stability of the City government and the lack of a "serious challenge to the dominance of a self-co-opting elite,"[129] then the escalation of civic ceremony in the mid-Tudor period would suggest not only that "the consolidation of the oligarchic form of government"[130] was in constant need of reinforcement, but that this consolidation also led the increasingly powerful leaders of London to address themselves in new ways to the kingdom at large.

Coinciding as it did with the economic and ceremonial decline of the provincial towns and outports in the 1540s, this ceremonial escalation expressed a new degree of civic assertiveness, as London rose to greater prominence in the national economy and consciousness. The use of the first inaugural pageant in 1535, and the use of speeches in 1541, like the new discursive element that made its first appearance with the coronation entry of Anne Boleyn in 1533, show the City oligarchy flexing its muscle and framing an ideological response to the varieties of Tudor complaint that at just this time were identifying London as the central force in the catastrophic transformation of the traditional English landscape and social order. The first royal entries and civic ceremonies, as recorded in

---

[126] As, for example, in 1519; see *A Calendar of Dramatic Records in the Calendar Books of the Livery Companies of London*, ed. Robertson and Gordon, p. 4.

[127] The Drapers paid Thomas Streeton for coaching child actors "after that the matter were set out by him and another," Ibid., p. 33.

[128] Ibid., pp. 40, 42–44, 46, 48–50.

[129] "Ritual, Drama, and the Social Body," p. 41.

[130] Berlin, "Civic Ceremony in Early Modern London," pp. 17–18.

the *Liber Albus*, had emerged in tandem at the beginning of the fifteenth century, when, "in the aftermath of the social and political upheavals of the later fourteenth century, the government of the liveries and the city became entrenched into a strict hierarchy which ensured the domination of a class of elite merchants by means of artificial ceremonial restrictions on participation in government." In the same way, the further escalation of mayoral ceremonies in 1530–40 emerged in tandem with a further consolidation of power by London's leaders through restrictions on the livery and the definitive establishment of the Twelve Great Livery Companies.[131] While securing oligarchic domination of the City, however, these developments also consolidated London's leading role in the modern national economy. The habit of styling London's chief official the "*Lord* Mayor" – thereby insisting on his theoretical parity with the rank of Earl – became common in internal communications around 1535–40; but it began to be used externally, and in a systematic way, in 1545, the publication date of Henry Brinklow's *Lamentacyon of a Christen Agaynst the Cytye of London*.[132]

While it reflected both the increasing domination of the national economy by London and the increasing domination of London by the mercantile elite, the cultic elevation of the mayoralty was a response to increasing frictions between the City and the Crown, as the leaders of the former sought to chart an independent, if not always consistent, course amid the changing tides of the state-sponsored Reformation. The ability of the Crown and Privy Council to enforce religious changes required the cooperation of London, whose leaders and populace were themselves deeply divided on religious questions. In order to enforce its policies the Crown often threatened, and sometimes resorted to, interference in the City's government. Henry VIII had threatened the City's liberties both in the aftermath of the Buckingham affair and at the time of his marriage with Anne Boleyn. In 1551 Edward VI threatened "to call in" the liberties of London, while at the accession of Mary the Lord Mayor was warned by the Privy Council that he would be forced to "yield up his sword" if he could not maintain peace in the city. In the later 1530s, Thomas Cromwell was successfully manipulating the City leadership, causing William Hollis, a Catholic conservative who, as senior alderman, was next-in-line for the mayoralty, to be "put by" in favor of candidates, proven loyalists like John Allen (1525, 1535) and Ralph Gresham (1537), who supported the reforms of Crown and Council. Cromwell's maneuvers provoked an official protest that the commons should "have their free election as they have used afore this time,"[133] and it may be that the

---

[131] Ibid., p. 18.   [132] See Withington, *English Pageantry*, 2: 13.
[133] Brigden, *London and the Reformation*, pp. 163–164, 211, 240, 250, 321, 518, 529.

escalation in mayoral inaugural celebrations – with the first use of pageants in 1535 and their regular use beginning in 1540 – was the City's response to incursions into its jurisdiction.

With the 1580s, there are indications of a further conscious escalation in the inaugural ceremony, an escalation that coincided with an apparent heightening of tensions between the City and both Crown and Parliament. The expenses for the Ironmongers' pageant of 1566 had included "5s. to the printer for printing of posies, speeches, and songs that were spoken and sung by the children in the pageant."[134] This is the only record of printing, however, until the mid-1580s, after which were printed the first extant pageants – George Peele's for 1585 and 1591, and Thomas Nelson's for 1590 – as well as one other, Peele's for 1588, now lost. There are fuller records of pageants for 1581, 1584, 1586, and 1587 as well, but the telling change is the consistent use of the print medium, from this point on, for disseminating the civic ideology of the pageant.

Challenges on a variety of fronts to London's expanding privileges and powers probably influenced the City's elaboration of the inaugural shows during the 1580s. A particularly troublesome issue was London's domination of foreign trade. The stagnation in the international cloth markets at mid-century led London's elite Merchant Adventurers to lobby for more exclusive privileges, including restrictively high entry fines in the 1550s and a favorable charter in 1564. However, the ascendancy of London's leading Merchant Adventurers, whose domination of the mayoralty in the 1560s may be reflected in nascent mayoral shows of that decade, was almost immediately challenged in Parliament in 1563 and 1566; by 1581 serious lobbying and a trade boycott were required to turn back a bill in Parliament against the monopoly of London Merchant Adventurers.[135] It was in the early 1580s also that the Privy Council began to take up in a formal way the complaints being lodged by the provincial towns and outports against London's growing monopoly on trade, and in 1587–89 a "Discourse of Corporations" was declaring that the trade of London "hath eaten vp all the rest of the Townes and havens of England."[136] Yet even as the supremacy of the London Merchant Adventurers began to wane, the mayoralty was

---

[134] *A Calendar of Dramatic Records in the Calendar Books of the Livery Companies of London*, ed. Robertson and Gordon, p. 46.

[135] T. E. Hartley, *Proceedings of the Parliaments of Elizabeth I* (Wilmington: M. Glazier, 1981–), 1: 488; G. D. Ramsay, *The City of London in International Politics at the Accession of Elizabeth I* (Manchester University Press, 1975), p. 49; Robert Ashton, *The City and the Court, 1603–1643* (Cambridge University Press, 1979), p. 88; G. R. Elton, *The Parliament of England* (Cambridge University Press, 1986), pp. 256–257.

[136] R. H. Tawney and Eileen Power, eds., *Tudor Economic Documents* (3 vols. London: Longmans, Green 1924), 3: 274.

dominated in the 1580s by men like Edward Osborne (1583), Thomas Pullison (1584), George Barne (1586), Martin Calthorpe (1588) and Richard Martin (1589), who were powerful lobbyists in Crown and Council for the emerging Mediterranean and Eastern import trades – the Spanish (1577), Turkey (1580–81), Venice (1583) and Levant (1592) Companies – that would dominate the City hierarchy up to the first Civil War.[137] Throughout the course of these developments, London's elite were always seeking to defend and expand the prestige of the metropolis – often against attacks like those of Robert Wilson's interlude *The Three Ladies of London* (c. 1584), in which Lady Lucre's triumph over her sisters Love and Conscience was accompanied by sharp remarks about London's developing trade with "Moors, Turks and Pagans" and about the sleights with which the City "fetched away" adverse legislation in Parliament.[138]

At the same time, the City of London government found itself embroiled with the Crown in numerous negotiations and controversies. The Queen's first proclamation against further building in the City was issued in 1580, and in 1586, the City's failure to solve the problems of growth – which was a "great misliking" to the Queen – resulted in an inquiry by the Privy Council.[139] The appearance of the seditious *Leicester's Commonwealth* on the streets of London in 1585 provoked a tart note from the Council to the Lord Mayor, expressing the Queen's indignation against the infamous libels spread against the Earl.[140] In the same decade there were frictions between the City and the Crown and Privy Council over the garbelling of spices, the toll on victuals, and the jurisdiction of the Tower.[141] Stow had noted the ambiguous and potentially divisive relations between City and Crown when he called the Tower "a Citadell, to defend or commaund the Citie" (1: 159). The troublesome litigation of the 1580s was an episode in a history of intermittent conflict over the Tower that extended from the quarrels of Henry III with the City in 1247 to the explosive struggle over the Tower Lieutenancy in December 1641.

All of these developments were the context for a new civic assertiveness in the 1580s. Some of the most impassioned defenses ever written on behalf of the City – the anonymous *Apologie of the Cittie of London* and

[137] Robert Brenner, *Merchants and Revolution: Commercial Change, Political Conflict, and London's Overseas Traders, 1550–1653* (Princeton University Press, 1993), pp. 17–18.
[138] *The Three Ladies of London*, in *Dodsley's Old English Plays*, ed. W. C. Hazlitt (12 vols. London, 1874), 6: 306, 277.
[139] *Acts of the Privy Council* (March 2, 1586), n.s. 14: 356.
[140] *Calendar of State Papers Domestic, Elizabeth I, 1581–1590* (London, 1865), p. 248.
[141] See Ian W. Archer, *The Pursuit of Stability: Social Relations in Elizabethan London* (Cambridge University Press, 1991), pp. 36–37.

the *Breefe Discourse ... of the Laudable Custemes of London* (1584) – date from this period and concern themselves with the defense of London's special privileges and liberties. The Apologist explicitly undertook "to aunswere the accusation of those men, which charge London with the losse and decay of many (or most) Citties, Corporate Townes and markets within this realme" (Stow, 2: 211). The surviving fragment of *Londons Complaint*, conjecturally dated 1585, pleads for recognition or reinstatement of the "immunities ... large and ample liberties" granted to the City by "Illustrious kings." Stow mentions other documents written on behalf of the City at about this time, a book on purprestures and overbuilding "exhibited ... to the Mayor and communaltie" by one W. Patten, "a learned Gentleman, and graue cittizen" (1: 83), and in 1585 a "commendation" of the suppressed "marching watch in the Cittie vpon the euens accustomed" by a "graue citizen ... John Mountgomery" (1: 103). The attempt to revive the Midsummer Watch, together with the escalation of the inaugural ceremonies, points to a heightened sensitivity to ceremony in the decade. As in 1392, an attempt to improve uneasy relations may have been behind the unusual step of according the monarch a second splendid reception in 1584.[142] Even so apparently simple a matter as the cancellation of an inaugural ceremony by the City in 1580 produced a two-year give-and-take between Westminster and London, in which the City dourly asserted that "it had not been used to obtain permission to Her Majesty or the Council to omit the feast."[143]

The heightened importance of civic ceremony coincided with measures on the part of the City to consolidate its legal and ritual heritage. The office of the Remembrancer, charged with the maintenance of customary practices and ceremonies, was created in 1571. The City had begun to issue its printed ceremonial calendars in 1568, and in 1596 the Court of Aldermen required "notes to be set down in writing and hanged in the Guildhall what things appertain either by charter, usage, Acts of Common Council or by custome to be yearly done."[144] In the later sixteenth century the Corporation was involved as well in extensive efforts to consolidate its archives, ordering the recopying of the *Liber Albus* and other custumals, the sequestering of records, and the search for lost registers and papers.[145]

[142] *A Famous Dittie of the Ioyful Receauing of the Queens Most Excellent Maiestie by the Worthy Citizens of London* (1584), in *Black-Letter Ballads and Broadsides, 1559–1597* (London: Joseph Lilly, 1870), p. 182.
[143] *Index to the Remembrancia*, ed. W. H. Overall, pp. 206–207.
[144] Piers Cain, "Robert Smith and the Reform of the Archives of the City of London, 1580–1623," *London Journal*, 13: 1 (1987–88), 11.   [145] Ibid., passim.

The emergence of the first extant inaugural show pamphlets in connection with these circumstances clearly reflects a heightened civic consciousness and ceremonial assertiveness on the part of London's leaders. Not surprisingly, then, there were several important innovations in the early surviving pageants by Peele and Nelson that emphasized both the discursive potential of the Lord Mayor's Show and its formal and ideological divergence from the royal entry ceremony. First, Peele's *Descensus Astraeae* (1591) contains a *speech on the water delivered in the morning at my Lord Maiors going to Westminster*.[146] This is the first instance of the pageants that developed as a result of a transformation of the processional route which had occurred in the fifteenth century, when the earlier horseback journey through Newgate to Westminster and back gave way to the voyage of the Lord Mayor and the companies to and from the royal seat by barge. As the later shows developed, the Lord Mayor's return landing at the city became the occasion not only for the first pageant but for a whole repertoire of symbolism underwriting the discursive nature of the form. As the roughest and most boisterous of the pageants, the arrival by water was a fittingly tumultuous and unsettled transitional event, marking the successful negotiation of the troubled waters between the two jurisdictions. But more, at this *limen* between sea and land lay the occasion for all manner of reflection on boundaries and transitions, opportunities for symbolizing the relation between outside and inside, chaos and order, territory and shelter, the larger realm of world trade and politics and the city's inner stability, the strifeful microcosmos of London's vast society and the inner circle of the civic elite, the active life of politics and inner moral life of the citizen. The rite of arrival, moreover, provided the occasion for constructing narratives of arrival, myths and stories enacting the historical passage from nature to urban culture, from the violence of a pagan creation to the serenity of Christian community, from a barbarous past to a civilized present.

The title of Peele's *Device of the Pageant Borne Before Wolstane Dixie* indicates that while as yet there were few pageants, they were borne before the mayor as in triumph, providing the basis for the later construction of longer discursive strings, as four or five pageants were inserted to form a continuous sequence by the end of the day's events. A standard syntax, moreover, was dictated by the route and its meaning (see Map). The installation of a kitchen in the Guildhall in the early sixteenth century meant that it had replaced the Lord Mayor's house as the site of the feast. The route to the Guildhall was from Baynard's Castle (Paul's Wharf) north to Paul's Chain, and from there through the

---

[146] *Life and Minor Works*, ed. Charles T. Prouty (3 vols. New Haven: Yale University Press, 1952), 1: 218.

Churchyard (where one or two pageants joined later shows) to Cheapside and St. Lawrence Lane (the site for what were usually the last two pageants in the later shows). Most crucially, the post-feast return route from the Guildhall to St. Paul's led down St. Lawrence Lane and then along Cheapside to the Little Conduit, retracing, as the older civic processions from St. Thomas de Acon to St. Paul's had earlier done, the climactic portion of the royal entry route to St. Paul's.

In the full-fledged Jacobean shows the pageants were performed and inserted into the procession on the way to the Guildhall feast, in a sequence that ran from Paul's Wharf and Paul's Chain, through the one or two pageant stations of the Churchyard, to the last stations at the Little Conduit and St. Lawrence Lane end or the Cheapside Cross. However, in the most splendid of the shows, performed in 1611–16, the Little Conduit and Cheapside pageants appear to have joined the procession in reverse sequence, when the Guildhall feast had been completed and the Mayor's retinue was returning westward along Cheapside for evening prayers at St. Paul's.[147] Even in the more usual pattern, when the Cheapside pageants joined the procession on its eastbound leg toward the Guildhall feast, it was only on the westbound return, which duplicated the climactic phase of the entry route, that "the whole fabric of the Triumph"[148] was finally and fully assembled. In "Cheapside; at which place the whole Triumph meets," the inaugural procession of the mayor became most strikingly a formal alternative to the royal advent, as the City's chief official went "accompanied with the Triumph before him, towards St. Paul's, to perform the noble and reverend ceremonies which divine authority religiously ordained."[149]

Finally, this very public culmination in the City's main ceremonial space gave way to a very different destination and sense of destiny, as following the evening service the mayor returned "by torchlight to his own house, the whole Triumph placed in comely and decent order before him."[150] In contrast to the royal entry's postliminal passage to Westminster, this final passage of "the whole body of the Solemnity"[151] to the private hearth of an individual citizen within the City's walls defined a very different sort of destiny, a different sense of history and its possible outcomes.

[147] See, e.g., Munday's *Chrysanaleia* (1616), and Dekker's *Troia-Nova Triumphans* (1612).
[148] Middleton, *The Triumphs of Health and Prosperity* (1626), in *Works*, 7: 409.
[149] Middleton, *The Triumphs of Honor and Industry* (1617), in *Works*, 7: 305; *The Triumphs of Love and Antiquity* (1619), in *Works*, 7: 329.
[150] Middleton, *The Triumphs of Love and Antiquity*, in *Works*, 7: 409.
[151] John Squire, *Tes Irenes Trophaea, or The Tryumphs of Peace* (1620), in *Progresses, Processions, and Magnificent Festivities of King James the First*, 4: 626.

Rudiments of the mythmaking that would support this sense of destiny, finally, were also adumbrated with the publication of the first inaugural pageants of the 1580s. Peele's pageants extolled a general neofeudal ethic, subordinating City to Crown in the loyal service by which London "dooth... yeeld / Her selfe her welthe with hart and willingnes / Unto the person of her gracious Queene."[152] In Nelson's 1590 pageant for the Fishmongers, the neofeudal decor provided for a very different understanding of the sources of the City's greatness, by focusing on the figure of William Walworth, the legendary Fishmonger whose virtuous deeds were alleged to have produced the privileges that distinguish the City:

> I slew Iacke Straw, who sought my kings disgrace,
>   and for my act reapt honors of great price,
> First knight was I of London you may reade,
>   and since each Maior gaines knighthood by my deede.
>
> Yea for that deed to London I did gaine,
>   this dagger here in armes giuen as you see,
> I won my companie this creast which doth remaine,
>   this to my selfe and my posteritie ...

It is to be vnderstood that sir William Walworth pointeth to the honors wherewith the king did endue him, which were placed neere about him in the Pageant.[153]

Using history and civic mythology to produce a meta-liturgical account of the efficacious emblems gracing the ceremony, Nelson's pageant was an early contribution to the wave of civic mythmaking that followed the ceremonial escalation of the 1590s and that became a staple in later scripts for the pageant. *The Life and Death of Jack Straw* (1593), which may originally have been connected with the same Fishmonger mayoralty of 1590,[154] was an early instance of what became a corpus of works, associated mainly but not exclusively with the popular theater, devoted to the magnanimity, virtue, and chivalric elan of worthy Londoners. In plays like *The Book of Sir Thomas More*, Dekker's *The Shoemaker's Holiday*, and Heywood's *Edward IV*, *If You Know Not Me You Know Nobody*, and *The Four Prentices of London*, there emerged a whole gallery of urban luminaries whose virtues equalled or outshone those of nobility

---

[152] *The Device of the Pageant Borne Before Wolstane Dixie* (1585), in *Life and Minor Works*, 1: 210.
[153] *The Device of the Pageant, set forth by the Worshipful Companie of Fishmongers, for the right honorable Iohn Allot: established Lord Maior of London* (1593), sigs. A3v–A4.
[154] See Robert Withington, "The Lord Mayor's Show for 1590," *PMLA*, 30 (1915), 110–115, and David M. Bergeron, "Jack Straw in Drama and Pageant," *The Guildhall Miscellany*, 2: 1 (1968), 459–463.

and kings. Walworth was among the illustrious merchant–heroes celebrated in Richard Johnson's compilation of the *Nine Worthies of London* (1592), and in the gallery of famous Londoners assembled in Heywood's *If You Know Not Me, You Know Nobody*. He reappeared along with others in Richard Niccols' *Londons Artillery* (1616), which devoted an entire canto in its praise of London to "those sons of fame / Whose deeds do now nobilitate her name" (pp. 54–55). Richard Whittington took his important place in citizen mythology with the registration of a play and ballad in 1605,[155] while Deloney's *Jack of Newbury* (1597), "showing the great worship and credit which men in this trade have formerly come to," became the basis for a whole mode of citizen romance and for a wealth of advice books pointing apprentices the way to greatness.[156] Popular dramatists like Munday and Middleton, who incorporated such mythology into mayoral pageants commissioned by the City's leading companies, became the occupants of a new patronage office, the City Chronologer, whose task was not only to invent "honourable entertainments for this City," but "to collect and set down all memorable acts of this City and occurrences thereof."[157]

The neofeudal ethic of loyalty, chivalric service, and communal solidarity developed in these civic mythmakers sought to normalize the socially disruptive effects of the new urban order, accommodating an acquisitive citizen mentality to the values of traditional English society, even while it masked the mobility and aspirations of entrepreneurs as manifestations of a nobility comparable with high birth. The true social functions of citizen myth and morality were soon enough unmasked by city comedy, as a play like *The Knight of the Burning Pestle* (1609) demonstrates (see pp. 467–469 below). But with its mixture of moral and historical causation – its emphasis on the virtuous deeds and historical events leading to a felicitous present – civic mythology was both a logical by-product of the escalation of ritual and a fitting means for elaborating that ritual in the form of a discourse that might annually be told and re-told.

---

[155] See C. M. Barron, "Richard Whittington: The Man Behind the Myth," in E. A. J. Hollaender and W. Kellaway, eds., *Studies in London History Presented to Philip Edmund Jones* (London: Hodder and Stoughton, 1969), pp. 197–248.
[156] See Louis B. Wright, *Middle-Class Culture in Elizabethan England* (Chapel Hill: University of North Carolina Press, 1935), ch. 2; Laura Caroline Stevenson, *Paradox and Praise: Merchants and Craftsmen in Elizabethan Popular Literature* (Cambridge University Press, 1984), pp. 108–129; L. C. Knights, *Drama and Society in the Age of Jonson* (1937; rpt. New York: Norton, 1968), ch. 8.
[157] R. C. Bald, "Middleton's Civic Employments," *MP*, 31 (1933), p. 67.

The impression of the figure: the meaning of the inaugural script

At the same time that it elaborated civic ideology, the "Annual argument" of the Lord Mayor's Shows also instantiated a liturgial order, re-establishing the underlying forms and meanings which the ceremony embodied. Even while it celebrated what Munday called "the *Creation* of her worthy Consuls and Magistrates,"[158] the liturgical order of the London shows also acted as what Roy Rappaport calls a "paradigm of creation that represents (re-presents) the primordial union of form and substance."[159] To a far greater extent than the royal entry, the Lord Mayor's Show emphasized this creational function, recognizing in "those yearly ceremonial rites which ancient and grave order hath determined"[160] the actual forms and customary practices by which the "Annual argument" was constructed. All of the surviving Jacobean and Caroline shows printed not only the spoken verses but also an elaborate prose commentary describing the devices and incidentally reviewing the history and function of the ceremony, its various customs and liturgical features. In both prose and verse, the pamphlets provided a running meta-liturgical commentary on the features of an event that was "usuall every yeare."[161] Implicit in this self-awareness was a powerful sense that the inaugural ceremonies were "a debt payd to Time and Custome," an annual observance of highly traditional orders: "as Time warranteth, so Custome confirmeth."[162]

But just as important as reverence for civic tradition was something like its opposite, a historical and anthropological awareness that the performance of the inaugural show functioned as a creational act that established and reaffirmed a new historical order. Thomas Dekker, for example, explained that "in former ages" the Lord Mayor

was not Encompast with such Glories, No such Firmaments of Starres were to be seen in Cheap-side: Thames dranke no such Costly Healthes to London, as he does now. But as Troynovant spred in Fame, so our English Kinges, shined vpon her with Fauours. In those home-spun Times, They had no Collars of SS, no Mace, Sword, nor Cap of Maintenance. These came by degrees, as *Addimenta Honoris*, additions or Ensignes of more Honour, Conferd by seuerall Princes on this Citty.[163]

[158] *Cruso-Thriambos* (1611), in *Pageants and Entertainments*, p. 51; italics mine.
[159] "The Obvious Aspects of Ritual," pp. 193–194.
[160] Middleton, *The Triumphs of Truth* (1613), in *Works*, 7: 258.
[161] Munday, *The Triumphs of Reunited Britannia* (1605), in *Pageants and Entertainments*, p. 15.
[162] Dekker, *Troia-Nova Triumphans* (1612), in *Dramatic Works*, 3: 230; Heywood, *Londini Emporia* (1633), sig. A2.
[163] *Londons Tempe* (1629), in *Dramatic Works*, 4: 102.

The performance of the show was thus an occasion for rehearsing the history of its emergence. This meta-liturgical dimension of the "Annual argument" meant that the printed show was no mere script for the particular mayor's pageant but "a booke of all those Ceremonies, which this great Festiuall day hath prouided to Atttend vppon him, and doe him honour."[164] Such a book provided not only the evidence on which a modern anthropologist or historian might reconstruct the ceremony; it also adumbrated the very mode of thought – the profane, desacralizing logic – with which the anthropologist or historian might analyze it.

A crucial aspect of this meta-liturgical awareness is the insistence that the Lord Mayor's Shows were formally modelled on the Roman triumph. When the City Recorder, Sir Henry Montague, presented the new mayor to the King in 1607, he observed that the Roman custom that good governors "should with triumphall ornaments enter the Citie" was both "a recompence of their payns, and to others an encouragement."[165] As the "ancient Romaines, ... the first Creators of Consuls and Senators for publike rule and honorable government, used yearlie triumphall showes and devices, to grace their severall Inauguration," so London, Munday argued, "devis'd and continued the like love and carefull respect, at the Creation of her worthy Consuls and Magistrates."[166] The belief that "the triumphs of the Romans exceed all their other shows"[167] was certainly fundamental to the parallel. But just as crucial were the Republican origins of the triumph, the use of the ceremony to mark annual elections of Rome's new officials. Authors of the London shows commonly insisted upon the mayor's "free Election, (without Emulation or competitorship)," and in 1631 Heywood took the conflict between the kings and populace of Rome as a model for the relationship with the Crown from which London's liberties emerged. "In processe of time the Tarquines being expeld ... the prime soveraignty remain[ed] in the consuls," who created the "*praetor vrbanus*, or Maior"; as "Camillus the sonne of Marcus" was the first *praetor* styled *ius honorarium*, Heywood explained, so "the first *Praetor* or L. Maior appointed to the Government of this Honourable Citty of London, was Henry Fitz Allwin, advanced to that Dignity by King Iohn, Anno. 1210."[168] By insisting on the "yearlie" nature of the Roman triumph, and by taking

---

164 Dekker, *Britannia's Honour* (1628), in *Dramatic Works*, 4: 83.
165 Nichols, ed., *The Progresses ... of King James the First*, 2: 155–157.
166 *Cruso-Thriambos* (1611), in *Pageants and Entertainment*, p. 51. Cf. Webster, *Monuments of Honor* (1624), in *The Complete Works of John Webster*, ed. F. L. Lucas (London, 1927), 3: 317.
167 Holinshed (1808), 4: 466, quoted in Kipling, "Triumphal Drama: Form in English Civic Pageantry," *RenD*, 8 (1977), p. 41.
168 *Londons Ius Honorarium* (1631), in *Dramatic Works*, 4: 268, 270.

the *processus consularis* rather than the miltary triumph as the primary model, the authors of the London shows were at least implicitly reversing the Roman history of civic ceremony, returning the miraculous advent to its origins in annual rites of republican renewal.[169]

They were also reinforcing a point implicit in the formal differences between the royal entry and the inaugural triumph. In contrast to the former, the latter was not a once-and-for-all salvific miracle, but an annual renewal in an ongoing history of political actions and changes. Part of the meta-liturgical dimension of the shows was a consciousness that the pageants were not, as in the coronation entry, fixed tableaux and arches stationed along the route, but elements inserted seriatim into the moving procession itself. According to the logic of the triumphal trope, as each new element took its place in the procession, it was understood as following from but also superseding the one before it. In London's inaugural shows, as the Lord Mayor processed "From court to court before you be confirm'd / In this high place,"[170] his progress thus formed a narrative or symbolic sequence of events or stages. In contrast to the monarch's passage through a series of tableaux, however, the mayor's progress stressed this sequentiality, as each mobile pageant joined the procession, displacing the ones before it in pride of place, just before the Lord Mayor. Moreover, as the procession reached its climax along Cheapside to St. Paul's, and again on the way to the mayor's house in the evening, the magistrate was preceded "by the whole body of the Solemnity,"[171] a narrative or symbolic chain recapitulating the phases of the mayor's progress, but now (in contrast to the arches of the royal entry) visible to all of the populace lining the route and seen as coming to its *telos* in the figure of the new Lord Mayor himself. A trope of historical sequence and succession thus lurked beneath the protocol that

> In great Processions many lead the way
> To him, who is the triumph of the day.[172]

Contrasting with the hieratic mysteries revealed at the stages in the royal entry, this continuous discursive chain was appropriate to a form

[169] On the republican origins of the triumph in the *processus consularis*, see Versnels, *Triumphus*, pp. 284, 302; Georges Dumezil, *Archaic Roman Religion*, tr. Philip Krapp (2 vols. University of Chicago Press, 1970), 1: 287–290; A. H. J. Greenidge, *Roman Public Life* (London: Macmillan, 1901), pp. 156–158; W. Warde Fowler, "Jupiter and the *Triumphator*," *Classical Review*, 30 (1916), 153–157.

[170] Middleton, *The Triumphs of Honor and Virtue* (1622), in *Works*, 7: 364.

[171] John Squire, *Tes Irenes Trophaea* (1620), in *Progresses…of King James the First*, 4: 626.

[172] Robert Herrick, "To Doctor Alabaster," lines 3–4, in *The Complete Poetry of Robert Herrick*, ed. J. Max Patrick (1963; rpt. New York: Norton, 1968), p. 338.

whose function was so explicitly an annual renewal of the civic order. The inaugural shows exemplify what Mircea Eliade has called the tendency of traditional renewal rites to "re-enter the time of origin" and to repeat the paradigmatic act of the creation, the "passage from chaos to cosmos."[173] Devoted to the historical and moral causes of London's greatness, the pageants were able to accomplish their function – "to shut up the year past... and open to the yeare future" – by discursively "remembring things past, and predicting what was futurely to come."[174] The most common temporal tropes in the mayoral pageants, moreover, were not eschatological, like those of the royal entries, but cyclical, profane, and continuing – the four seasons and, especially because the mayoralty rotated among London's Twelve Great Companies, the months and the signs of the Zodiac.

Such tropes served, moreover, to reinforce the civic ideology by naturalizing another cause of London's greatness – the actions and accomplishments of the citizen body. "Time, and your Merit," Heywood told one mayor, "have call'd you to this Office and Honour."[175] To a far greater extent than royal entries, the inaugural shows stressed the merits and effects of labor and virtuous action.[176] In their praise of virtuous acts and labor, the shows often rebuked aristocratic privilege, asserting that it was "more faire and famous... to be made, then to be borne Noble, for that Honor is to be most Honored, which is purchast by merit, not crept into by descent."[177] In the humble origins of London's Lord Mayors lay a "fire that may shame the best perfection," for as one of Middleton's personified virtues put it, "Industry is the life-blood of praise: / To rise without me, is to steal glory."[178] Both the legendary heroes and the civic forebears who adorned the pageants were alike "worthies... that have got honour by their labours and deserts."[179] A conscious departure from the enthroned effigies of the royal entries may have been a purpose in Middleton's 1617 pageant, in which Reward

[173]   *The Sacred and the Profane: The Nature of Religion*, tr. Willard R. Trask (New York: Harcourt Brace Jovanovich, 1959), pp. 77, 88.
[174]   Heywood, *Londini Status Pacatus* (1639), in *Dramatic Works*, 5: 364.
[175]   *Londini Sinus Salutis* (1635), in *Dramatic Works*, 4: 285.
[176]   Gail Kern Paster stresses "the emphasis in these pageants on service and responsibility, on the labors of the magistrate's office," and notes "the extent to which the pageants ministered to the city's self-esteem by challenging aristocratic assumptions that birth, courtly grace, and royal favor matter most of all... The city affirms its order as essentially self-perpetuating and a greatness that is the product of its own life in time," *The Idea of the City in the Age of Shakespeare* (Athens: University of Georgia Press, 1985), p. 149.
[177]   Heywood, *Londons Ius Honorarium*, in *Dramatic Works*, 4: 267.
[178]   *The Triumphs of Honor and Industry* (1617), in *Works*, 7: 295, 298.
[179]   Middleton, *The Sun in Aries* (1621), in *Works*, 7: 340.

offered the new Lord Mayor the empty throne in the Castle of Fame and Honour but Justice forbade him to seat himself because

> Great works of grace must be required and done
> Before the honour of this seat be won.
> ... There must be merit, or our work's not right.[180]

As in the royal entry, the temporal process traced in the mayoral shows was understood as leading up to a felicitous present, just as the processional sequence of the pageants led literally to the new Lord Mayor, invested in the City's hard-won regalia: "behold this Scarlet worne / And Sword of Iustice this in publike borne; / The Cap of Maintenance, Collar of Esses."[181] Just as the shows gestured toward their own liturgical components and functions, so they provided a running commentary on the physical surroundings in which they occurred, the "Grammer Schooles... Free-Schooles, Hospitals, Almes-Houses, Lectures, and Exercises"[182] endowed by mayors and companies both past and present. Frequent gestures also incorporated, as evidence of what history had wrought, the ceremony's spectators and participants – not only the mayor but "these grave Senators," the aldermen; "this honour'd Company" that supplied the mayor and the pageant; the liveries of the Twelve Great Companies and of the "full three score" guilds of the City; the seventy poor men who received gowns and marched with the sponsoring company; the City militias; the crowds of witnesses who "on tip-toe stand."[183] Taken together, these echelons offered citizens both a living, contemporary image of the entire social body and an exemplary canvass of all the ranks and stages in the civic *cursus honorarum*, which, theoretically open to all citizens, extended from "th' apprentice seuen yeares seruitude" to

[180] *The Triumphs of Honor and Industry* (1617), in *Works*, 7: 303–4.
[181] Heywood, *Londini Artium & Scientiarum Scaturgio* (1632), sigs. B2v–B3. Even in the climactic phases of the royal entry along Cheapside, London remained very much a real, untransformed, historical and political landscape, as the City's officials made their discursive claims on royalty. Perhaps to a greater extent than the countryside in Elizabeth's rural entertainments, the London entry remained *both* "literal and symbolic," as Helen Cooper claims in "Location and Meaning in Masque, Morality, and Royal Entertainment," in David Lindley, ed., *The Court Masque* (Manchester University Press, 1984), p. 141. Cooper thus endorses Jean Wilson's view that in their pageantry "the Elizabethans are not dealing with play worlds. What they are doing is transforming the real one," *Entertainments for Elizabeth I* (Totowa, N.J.: Rowman and Littlefield, 1980), p. 43. Even less, however, is the real world symbolically transformed in the inaugural shows.
[182] Heywood, *Londini Artium & Scientiarum Scaturgio* (1632), sig. B.
[183] Middleton, *The Triumphs of Integrity* (1623), in *Works*, 7: 388; Taylor, *The Triumphs of Fame and Honor*, sig. A8; Munday, *Himateia-Poleos* (1614), in *Pageants and Entertainments*, p. 73; Heywood, *Londini Sinus Salutis* (1635), in *Dramatic Works*, 4: 291, *Londini Speculum*, in *Dramatic Works*, 4: 313; Munday, *Cruso-Thriambos* (1611), in *Pageants and Entertainments*, p. 57.

> the graue gowne, and the Liuery-Hood,
> Till, (in the end) by merit, paines and care,
> They win the grace to sit in Honours chaire.[184]

The lifetime's achievement that led to the present mayoralty, more-over, was a model for the larger history being celebrated, the lifetime of the city, "the way / That led thee to the glory of this day."[185] The very fabric of the city, its major buildings and monuments, entered the pageant scripts as visible evidence of what London had produced by the worthy efforts of its citizens. In Munday's *Cruso-Thriambos* (1611), a former mayor, Nicholas Farringdon, awakened from his pageant tomb to recognize "these gates he built, this ward of him took name," while in Middleton's *Triumphs of Truth* (1613), Time gestured to the nearby Paul's Cross pulpit, where weekly "Truth's celestial harmony thou shalt hear."[186] The pageants paid frequent tribute to the civic officials who gave the city its present landscape,[187] and a host of London landmarks took their place in the continuing history of a city

> Who in her age, grew pregnant, brought abed
> Of a New Towne, and late deliuered...
>   her Cathedrals, temples new repairing,
> An act of true devotion, no man sparing.[188]

Contemporary London was thus for Middleton "virtues fair edifice," a monument in which the City's worthies had "Erected fair examples, large and high, / Patterns for us to build our honors by."[189] The underlying theme of this edifying story was the power of virtuous effort to improve and extend by constant renewal: "ruins built agen / 'Come better'd both in monuments and men."[190] But the *telos* of this pattern of renewals was always to "descend... to the modern use" of ancient and honorable things.[191]

This historical trajectory was complicated, however, by the variations that naturally developed as different authors annually retraced it under the sponsorship of different companies. To retrace the route to the present was "againe to view / Old customes kept, and (in them) things anew."[192] Despite its origins as a traditional liminal rite, the inaugural show was in certain respects a liminoid form, an entertainment authored by the luminaries of the public theaters, the new leisure industry of the

---

[184] Taylor, *The Triumphs of Fame and Honor*, sigs. A8–Bv.
[185] Middleton, *The Triumphs of Truth* (1613), in *Works*, 7: 237.
[186] See, for example, Munday, *Pageants and Entertainments*, p. 56; Middleton, *Works*, 7: 250.   [187] Middleton, *Works*, 7: 342, 303.
[188] Heywood, *Londini Speculum* (1637), in *Dramatic Works*, 4: 316.
[189] *Works*, 7: 345, 390.   [190] Ibid., 7: 346.   [191] Ibid., 7: 385; cf. 404.
[192] Heywood, *Londini Emporia* (1633), sig. B.

expanding metropolis.[193] Economic competition and artistic rivalry among these authors, as between the sponsoring companies themselves, made it necessary not "to runne againe in the same course of antique honor: but rather to jumpe with time, which evermore affecteth novelty, in a new forme."[194] Annual variations in the performance had the potential for undermining the ideological project of the shows; their constantly varied symbolism made "allegory self-consciously problematic, self-reflexive, and therefore no longer allegorical."[195] For the pageant-writers, necessity was always the mother of invention and of sometimes forced and improbably exotic symbolism – never more so than when Heywood represented London's government with an Elephant, asking

> What Hieroglificke can men invent,
> Embleame or Symbole, for a Government
> In this high nature, apter or more fit
> Devis'd before, or to be thought of yet?[196]

But if annual innovations produced a sense that meanings were constructed and provisional, the main effect was not to destabilize the civic ideology but to refine and adapt it, producing a peculiar sense that history was a continuing process of exchange and transformation to which all might contribute. As the mayoralty and the show itself rotated from company to company, each show contributed to a common fund of lore its own version of the route to the present, highlighting the particular contribution of the sponsoring company, its past luminaries and its present activities, to the common life: "Fame hath them All en-rold / On a Large File (with Others,) And their Story / The world shall reade, to Adde unto thy Glory."[197] Each new mayor was to "spend the Houres to inrich future story / Both for your own grace and the Cities glory."[198]

This discursive pattern was a model for history itself, which the writers typically presented as a process of simultaneous refinement and dispersion, a centripetal movement of consolidation, producing more and more advanced kinds of order, which nevertheless took form as a centrifugal diversification, an increase in the possibilities for exchange and combination. Munday's 1614 pageant for the Drapers, for example,

---

[193] On the paradoxes that arise from the City's patronage of playwrights, see Theodore B. Leinwand, "London Triumphing: The Jacobean Lord Mayor's Show," *Clio*, 11 (1982), 137–153.

[194] Munday, *Metropolis Coronata* (1615), in *Pageants and Entertainments*, p. 87.

[195] Michael D. Bristol, *Carnival and Theater: Plebeian Culture and the Structure of Authority in Renaissance England* (New York: Methuen, 1985), pp. 62–64.

[196] *Londini Artium & Scientiarum Scaturgio* (1632), sig. B4v.

[197] Dekker, *Troia-Nova Triumphans* (1612), in *Dramatic Works*, 3: 241–242.

[198] Heywood, *Londini Status Pacatus* (1639), in *Dramatic Works*, 5: 365.

showed how the trade "hath branched it selfe into divers other Companies, and of one entire trade or Mysterie, is become many."[199] Through the theme of industrial diversification, the process of urbanization was represented as the historical conversion of nature into the ever more refined and proliferating forms of culture. Munday's "Orferie" or gold mine, a trade-pageant for the Goldsmiths in 1611, took note first of the "Pioners, Miners, and Delvers" who "doe first use their endeavour and labour, to come by the Ore" hidden deep beneath the Mount of "*Cthoon*, or *Terra*, the breeding and teeming Mother of all Golde." But the pageant followed the refinement of the ore "into Ingots or variable form," which "descend to divers other dexterous Artezans; as the Mint-Maister, his Coyners, and divers others, who make them to serve in publike passage for generall benefit." In its "publike passage for generall benefit," the gold was further "brought into...variant substances," passing in turn to "the Jeweller, Lapidarie, Pearle-Driller, Golde-Smith, and such like."[200]

Enacted with variations each year, the discursive trajectory of the pageants remained – unlike the atemporal miracles of the entries – essentially open-ended and incomplete; it did not lead to the end of time but traced a profane and continuing route through it. The pageants shared with traditional renewal rites an agonistic structure, in which the "passage from chaos to cosmos" was enacted as a primordial battle between creative and destructive forces. Personified vices, practically non-existent in royal entries, played a major role in the inaugural shows, as did constant symbols and reminders of the "dayes of disturbance and rough combustion" from which the city had emerged.[201] Giants, pagan deities, and exotic infidels usually presented themselves in the early stages of the triumph, to be superseded by later representations of London's Christian virtues and civic harmony. But evil, disharmony, and social ills remained an embarrassing challenge to the city even as its virtues were being extolled. Middleton's pageants, sponsored by such Puritan-dominated companies as the Grocers and the Skinners, were especially frank in their allusions to contemporary vices threatening the City's rulers, ills like "epicurism," "plenty coop'd up and bounty faint and cold," counselors "that only mind their ends, but not their end," "oppression, cozenage, bribes, false hires," "usuring," and "Envy, detraction of all noble right."[202] The mayor's year in office, "the Chronickle of a dangerous year," was often represented as a perilous

[199] *Himateia-Poleos* (1614), in *Pageants and Entertainments*, p. 73.
[200] *Cruso-Thriambos* (1611), in *Pageants and Entertainments*, pp. 52–53, 59.
[201] Munday, *Cruso-Thriambos* (1611), in *Pageants and Entertainments*, p. 53.
[202] *Works*, 7: 257, 306, 319, 361, 406.

voyage amid "rocks, gulfs, quicksands," for which ancient voyagers like Jason and Ulysses were offered as exemplars.[203] Nowhere during the day's proceedings were London's mayors exempt from reminders of human limits, which as Gordon Kipling has suggested were conveyed most forcefully in the final speech of the shows, when the mayor was ushered into his house with sobering exhortations on the challenges of the year ahead.[204]

The agonistic basis of renewal rites also manifested itself in saturnalia, in elements of license and indulgence that embody the threat of a potential reversion back to primordial chaos.[205] The inaugural show was a much rougher affair than the royal entry, never more so than in the opening water pageant, which Dekker characterized as so much "Powder and Smoake."[206] Squibs and volleys of ordnance combined with jostling for priority among the company barges to produce a scene so chaotic that Middleton usually declined to lay his hand to the water pageant, leaving it instead for Munday, whom he despised.

Things were hardly better on land. The route of the procession was not railed, as in the royal entry; instead, a cadre of whifflers, green-men, devils, and beadles was pressed into service to clear the way ahead with staves and fireworks, while throwing sweetmeats to the crowd.[207] The vices and evils depicted at the pageant stations, moreover, were not left behind but incorporated into the processions. Roman custom dictated that only the *triumphator*, or entering victor, could bring the *spolia opima*, the enemy captives and arms, within the city of Rome. "Loaded ... with enemy power, dangerous," the *spolia opima* had a "hostile and dangerous magic, of which only the victor had nothing to fear."[208] The incorporation of symbolic evils into a triumphal sequence borne through the city before the mayor revealed the city's faith in its own virtues and destiny. Yet the incompleteness of this destiny was figured frequently in setbacks, delays, and saturnalian eruptions of chaos that occurred along the way. Incorporating vice and tumult, the shows thus traced a moral and historical trajectory that "may be said beginning still," a profane progress that tended toward but remained short of the sort of apocalyptic fulfillments celebrated in the royal entries. The shows inaugurated a profane, material time, a continuing medium in which human labor was the basis for historical changes and transformations.

---

[203] Dekker, *Troia-Nova Triumphans* (1612), in *Dramatic Works*, 3: 240; Middleton, *The Triumphs of Health and Prosperity* (1626), in *Works*, 7: 406.
[204] "Triumphal Drama," pp. 52–54.
[205] Eliade, *The Sacred and the Profane*, pp. 78–80.
[206] *Troia-Nova Triumphans* (1612), in *Dramatic Works* 3: 247.
[207] See Busino, *CSPV* (1617–19), 15: 59.   [208] Versnels, *Triumphus*, pp. 309, 311.

The effects of labor made themselves felt spatially as well as temporally, as the passage from chaos to cosmos was frequently registered in spatial contrasts between inside and outside, center and periphery, shelter and territory. The shows were in one respect centripetal, celebrating the power and values of the City's innermost mercantile elite and justifying their domination of the municipality. Nevertheless, in their treatment of moral and political challenges, they also addressed the domains that lay beyond this inner sphere – most obviously and immediately, of course, through the poor men who marched with the sponsoring company and received its charity, the unwashed hordes of non-citizens who sustained the city's economy. More broadly, they addressed the many different kinds of spectators observing the procession, including the "Strangers ... of all forraigne Nations" and the "streames of Nobility and Gentry, run with the Tide hither."[209] They addressed, too, the territory beyond the City's jurisdiction, the rival power to the west, and, most crucially, the outports, countryside and provincial towns of the realm and the remote and far-flung global outposts where the increasing power of the urban center was, paradoxically, most apparent. The shows were a journey to the center, to the Guildhall and the Lord Mayor's door, but the power and security of the center were a function of its domination of an extended territory – a domination carried out economically and politi-cally by trade, religiously by conversion, and discursively by the inscription of the city's values and influence in the hearts and minds of individuals circulating "freely" in the world.

Occupying the boundary where London met the extra-urban world beyond, the waterside pageants that began the journey to the interior initiated a series of transitions, from past to present, chaos to cosmos, nature to culture. In the first place, the mayor's water journey to and from Westminster completed a negotiation between two rival juris-dictions. The mayhem of this opening phase – with its fusillades and volleys, "divers Sea-fights and skirmishes"[210] – gave release to the tensions and anxieties that surrounded this dangerous passage between different jurisdictions. The pageants took a sometimes ambivalent approach toward the Crown, as in John Taylor's wonderfully ambiguous assertion that the inauguration "plainly showes / The Kings illustrious greatnesse whence it flowes."[211] Heywood focused the issue as a contrast between two cities: "in the one, the right honourable the lord maior

[209] Heywood, *Londini Artium & Scientiarum Scaturgio* (1632), sig. B; Dekker, *Troia-Nova Triumphans* (1612), in *Dramatic Works*, 3: 231.
[210] Munday, *Cruso-Thriambos* (1611), in *Pageants and Entertainments*, p. 51.
[211] *The Triumphs of Fame and Honor* (1634), sig. A3, in Sheila Williams, "A Lord Mayor's Show by John Taylor the Water-Poet," *Bulletin of the John Rylands Library*, 41 (1959).

receaveth his honour, so in the other he takes his oath; yet London may be presumed to be the elder, and more excellent in birth, meanes, and issue; in the first for her antiquity, in the second for her ability, in the third, for her numerous progeny."[212] In the heroic voyages of the water shows – Jason, Ulysses, Hercules – the mayor was symbolically lauded as "our Jason, Londons glorie, / Now going to fetch that fleece of Fame, / That ever must renowne your name."[213]

The heroic task of urban settlement was dramatized in the arrival of pagan deities and giant forms in this phase of the ceremony. Munday's 1605 pageant for the Merchant Taylors set a crucial precedent for later shows in this regard, depicting in its water pageant the settlement of Britain, as Neptune and Amphitrite, "who first seated their son Albion in this land," arrived to witness "what happy successe hath thereon ensued." In recognition that "times have altred former harshe incivilities, bringing the state to more perfect shape of majesty," this pageant of arrival gave way to the giant descendants of Albion, Goemagot and Corineus, the City palladia, from whose creational agon emerged the founding of Troynovant by Trojan Brute, who "built... my New Troy, in memories / Of whence I came, by Thamesis faire side."[214] The movement from sea to land, nature to culture, was appropriately figured in the many amphibian mascots, pagan gods, giants, and heroes that adorned the water shows. Such figures rarely appeared at the later pageant stations, where they were generally superseded by English heroes and civic worthies, by trade pageants, and by the homelier personifications of Christian and political allegories.[215] The meaning of these pagan deities lay in their primitive, pre-Christian, protean–creational aura.

The waterside era of creation usually took the form, however, of a contract or tribute through which London's power over the Thames and the realms to which it led became the basis for the city's magnificent destiny. A Virgilian sense of this destiny colored John Squire's 1620 water pageant, in which Oceanus promised that

> My care that shall be for ever to attend
> Your wealthy bottoms to your coasts apace;
> And this my promise I will never end

---

[212] *Londini Porta Pietatis* (1638), in *Dramatic Works*, 5: 263.
[213] Munday, *Metropolis Coronata* (1615), in *Pageants and Entertainments*, p. 89.
[214] *The Triumphs of Reunited Britannia* (1605), in *Pageants and Entertainments*, pp. 3–9.
[215] The most notable exceptions are the appearance of Apollo at St. Lawrence Lane in Middleton's 1621 show and of Titan and Apollo at the Little Conduit and St. Lawrence Lane in the 1629 show by Dekker; it could be argued, however, that the late appearance of such solar deities conforms to the general pattern of ascent from the primitive and primordial to more highly civilized forms.

> Nor breake, untill your wealth and states surmount
> Tagus' unvalued sands in the account.[216]

Webster celebrated London's mastery of a vast maritime territory by depicting "a faire Terrestrial Globe" at Paul's Wharf, in which were seated "seauen of our most famous Nauigators ... who haue made England so famous in remotest partes of the world."[217] Jason's return with the Golden Fleece, a hoary favorite of the Drapers, dating back to the early sixteenth century, appropriately combined the prospect of gain with the hero's taming of the fiery bulls to make sea-going trade the preeminent civilizing act. But few pageant ships arrived at Paul's Wharf without their due lading of riches, neither the Goldsmiths' fleet of 1611, the 1616 Fishmongers' Busse, the "well-built Ship" of the "esteemed Company of Haberdashers" in 1620, nor the 1634 Clothworkers' Barge.

Like these pageants of arrival, the "Island of Lemnos" created by Munday for the Ironmongers in 1618 enacted through its giant forms the transition from primordial matter to civilized form. From the primitive mining of ore to the forging of implements of war, husbandry, navigation, and commerce, the pageant traced the pattern of civilization in the processing of

> Steele and Iron: which as they refine
> From the earths Oare, So to all Lands they send,
> And all Artes else do bounteously befriend.[218]

The civilized, refining act of trade was embodied, finally, in the savages and infidels who sometimes replaced the pagan gods and heroes of the water show. In a Paul's Wharf pageant for the Grocers, "A company of Indians" was "set at work in an Island of growing spices," while "a rich personage presenting India, the seat of merchandise" was flanked by Traffic and Industry to demonstrate that the "several nations where commerce abounds / Taste the harmonious peace so sweetly sounds."[219] The recently established forts of the East India Company were represented in 1613 by "five islands, artfully garnished with all manner of Indian fruit trees, drugs, spiceries, and the like, the Middle island with a fair castle especially beautified."[220] Jason returned to the Drapers in 1623 with "Sixe Tributarie Indian Kings" in order to support the theme that virtue is "like light struck out of darkness."[221]

Following the incorporation of the water pageant into the procession,

---

216 *Progresses ... of King James the First*, 4: 621.
217 *Monuments of Honor* (1624), in *Dramatic Works*, 3: 317.
218 *Sidero-Thriambos* (1618), *Pageants and Entertainments*, pp. 126–128.
219 Middleton, *The Triumphs of Honor and Industry* (1617), in *Works*, 7: 297–299.
220 Middleton, *The Triumphs of Truth* (1613), in *Works*, 7: 239.
221 Middleton, *The Triumphs of Integrity* (1621), in *Works*, 7: 385, 387.

the arrival at the pageant stations in Paul's Churchyard marked a symbolic conversion of the barbarous past and exterior territory into a civilized present and center. A royal Moorish entourage bowed "their bodies to the temple of St. Paul" in 1613, signifying their conversion by

> English merchants, factors, travellers,
> Whose Truth did with our spirits hold commerce,
> As their affairs with us.[222]

In 1622, "a black personage representing India... the Queene of Merchandise" was presented personified Knowledge by "commerce, adventure, and traffic, three habited like merchants" in token of the conversion

> which first came by you,
> By you, and your examples, blest commerce,
> That by exchange settles such happiness.[223]

In Paul's Churchyard, too, it was typically native sons like William Walworth and Nicholas Farringdon, early contributors to the city's greatness, who commonly replaced the pagan gods, heroes, and savages at this point, to mark the shaping of a local polity won from English kings. The political consolidations represented in the Churchyard sometimes drew upon the tradition of personifying cities as matriarchs, figures whose maternal affection (bestowed equally upon all her off-spring) gave to the fundamentally patriarchal hierarchy of the urban elite an aura of parity and solidarity. Adorned with the mural crown of "Steeples, Towers, and Turrets," and bearing a twelve-branched tree signifying "the twelve Superior Companies," the Genius of the City in *Britannia's Honor* (1628) dramatized the motto "*Viuite Concordes*, Liue in Loue: or, Agree in one." Placed at the gates of a model of London in 1634, the "ancient Matron" personifying the city declared that all

> True Citizens are the true Cities sonnes...
> Worke on, my lads, and you in time may be
> Good members of this Honour'd Company.

As figured in the feminine persona, the city's power to incorporate and unify extended further in Heywood's *Ius Honorarium* (1631), where the city matron sat "in the first and most eminent place" of a triumphal chariot, surrounded by "the chiefe Cities of the Kingdome," in recognition that London "incorporates many into one, / And makes unanimous peace, content and joy."[224] Webster's Churchyard Temple of

---

[222] Middleton, *The Triumphs of Truth* (1613), in *Works*, 7: 248–249.
[223] Middleton, *The Triumphs of Honor and Virtue* (1622), in *Works*, 7: 358–359.
[224] *Dramatic Works*, 4: 274–275; this pageant was not in Paul's Churchyard but in the "upper part of Cheapside," presumably near the Little Conduit.

Honor extended the maternal image even further in "a person representing Troynouant or the City, inthroned, in rich Habiliaments; beneath her, as admiring her peace and felicity, sit fiue eminent Cities, as Antwerpe, Paris, Rome, Venice, and Constantinople."[225]

In many ways, the gender and transhistorical nature of the personified metropolis unified the city at the expense of history, smoothing temporal and social discontinuities into an ideal supra-temporal identity. In keeping with the other Churchyard forms of conversion and consolidation, this marked a kind of closure, before the pageants opened out a second time along Cheapside, where the proliferating forms of modern economic life – the works and products of the city – were dramatized in tributes to the sponsoring companies. Many of these pageants were historical, depicting contributions to London's fabric and government by former officeholders of the company. Middleton especially favored pageants of this kind, in which the corollary to the consolidation of London's good government was a wealth of patronage, endowment, building, and bequests, "Good works and noble, for the City's grace."[226] Others, however, extolled the glories of trade and its benefits for all. The favored tactic was to represent the trades as branching out into an ever-diversifying variety of subsidiary occupations. Like his splendid 1611 Orfery, Munday's 1614 pageant of Old Drapery linked the industrial process of refining raw matter to the socio-economic process of expansion, gracing the Little Conduit with the mundane miracles by which the "mysterie" of Drapery became "the benefit of divers trades or occupations, Carding, Spinning, Weaving, Fulling, Rowing, Shearing, Dressing, Dying, Tentering, and what else appertained to woollen cloath."[227] Taylor made the same point for the Clothworkers in 1634, and Heywood for the Ironmongers in 1629. In such pageants, London answered its critics, demonstrating through images of economic diversification that urban growth was not the cause of decline in agrarian prosperity, but a source of wealth and energy

> Which through our Kingdomes large Dominions flowes,
> By founded Schooles, by Commerce, by Proiect layd.
> For thrifty Bargaine and all competent gayne,
> As well arising from the Hand as Brayne,
> London the Mother and the Fountain stil'd.[228]

But more importantly, as year by year the inauguration rotated among the companies, the Cheapside pageants also elaborated a sense of fraternal

---

[225] *Monuments of Honor* (1624), in *Dramatic Works*, 3: 319.
[226] *The Triumphs of Love and Antiquity* (1619), in *Works*, 7: 323.
[227] *Himateia-Poleos* (1614), in *Pageants and Entertainments*, p. 81.
[228] Heywood, *Londini Artium & Scientiarum Scaturgio* (1632), sig. c v.

reciprocity and mutual dependency, which justified the city's division of
the socio-economic order into an ever-widening range of possibilities. At
the Little Conduit in 1613, London and Religion were flanked on
London's Triumphant Mount by Liberality and Perfect Love, the latter
of which held "a sphere, where in a circle of gold is contained all the
Twelve Companies arms, and therefore called the Sphere of True
Brotherhood, or *Annulis Amoris*, the Ring of Love."[229] In the Jacobean
shows, all twelve Great Companies were linked in rings and zodiacs
symbolizing exchange and mutual dependency. The fraternal themes of
the show served the centripetal function of justifying the rule of an
exclusive elite; but at the same time, the model of equality and reciprocity
included a different, centrifugal logic. In 1635, as tensions between
greater and lesser companies were deepening, Heywood went at least so
far as to extend the franchise in the civic zodiac to all sixty of the City's
companies; the mayor had

> full three score, about your state to shine:
> For every Company's a Starre this day, –
> All enioy one like Freedome, all are Free.[230]

This twofold movement, inward and outward, reached its culmination
in the final major pageant of the triumph sequence. This was usually a
templar structure, a mount or bower, castle or sanctuary marking the
arrival at peace and harmony at the end of the triumphal procession and
at the heart of the city. Though it sometimes represented, in all its glory,
the triumph of the English nation, all of England's powers and estates
united in the monarch,[231] this arrival usually took the form of a more
temporary respite and refuge. The peace realized was not the eschatological state that made the city a New Jerusalem but a local shelter from
the violent and incomplete history continuing outside the center. In
1620, John Squire's Peace "bare the modell of London" in her lap to
show that she was "placed here by a divine decree, / Within this
Commonwealth, and chiefly here / Within this Citty."[232] Surrounded
by the world's "Vproares, ... Famines, and ... hellish brood of Warres,"
the Sun's Bower of Dekker's *Britannia's Honor* (1628) found "no Peace
but here. O blessed Land!"[233] The peace, felicity, and plenty that closed
the triumph were thus the uniquely virtuous works of Londoners, whose

---

[229] Middleton, *The Triumphs of Truth* (1613), in *Works*, 7: 252–253.
[230] *Londini Sinus Salutis* (1635), in *Dramatic Works*, 4: 291.
[231] See, e.g., the Castle of Fame or Honour in Middleton's *Triumphs of Honor and Industry* (1617), or Webster's 1624 Monument of Gratitude.
[232] *Tes Irenes Trophaea*, in *Progresses ... of King James the First*, 4: 625.
[233] *Dramatic Works*, 4: 95; cf. Heywood, *Londini Status Pacatus* (1639), in *Dramatic Works*, 5: 373.

"gratitude and pious cares / Striue to entaile them to Vs, and our Heires."[234] Middleton concluded the pageant sequence of the 1617 Grocers' show by reminding the mayor that "Great works of grace must be required and done / Before the honour of this seat be won."[235]

In view of the continuing history that surrounded it, the ideal templar city was not so much realized on the streets of London as inscribed within the souls of its inhabitants, directing their course in a process not yet finished. Sitting in a "Crystal Sanctuary," Middleton's Integrity remarked in 1623 that "The temple of an upright magistrate / Is my fair sanctuary, throne and state."[236] The center of Webster's 1624 pageant depicting the philanthropic Londoner Thomas White's

> Christian heart;
> Faith kept the center, Charity walkt the round,
> Untill a true circumference was found;
> And may the Impression of this figure strike
> Each worthy Senator to do the like.[237]

The "impression of the figure" in the heart was a variation on the protestant theology of the migratory temple, the typological thinking that equated the Temple's outer court with the Old Testament, the inner court with the New Testament, and the wandering Ark with the sojourning souls of militant believers.[238] The London preacher Daniel Featley explained that the "triumphes and pompous shewes we see... but *en passant*, carried in procession, not staying anywhere" figured "the militant church in this world... carried with the wings of an Eagle from Country to Country."[239] The theology of the invisible migratory temple, as embodied in the mayoral shows, did not invalidate communal life, but extended its influence beyond the walls of the visible community. The Globe of Honour that concluded Middleton's *Triumphs of Honor and Virtue* (1622), for example, opened to reveal the culmination of the show in "the inward man, the intentions of a virtuous and worthy breast"; but the outside of this sphere – in a sense the obverse of its inner core – represented

the outparts of the Globe, showing the world's type in countries, seas, and shipping, whereon is depicted or drawn ships that have been fortunate in this kingdom... as also that prosperous plantation in the Colony of Virginia and the

---

234 Heywood, *Londini Status Pacatus* (1639), in *Dramatic Works*, 5: 373.
235 *Works*, 7: 303.
236 Middleton, *The Triumphs of Integrity* (1623), in *Works*, 7: 391–392.
237 *Monuments of Honor* (1624), in *Dramatic Works*, 3: 325.
238 See Barbara K. Lewalski, *Protestant Poetics and the Seventeenth-Century English Lyric* (Princeton University Press, 1979), p. 142.
239 *The Embleme of the Church Militant ... preached in Mercers Chapel*, in *Clavis Mystica* (1636), sig. Dd.

Bermudas, with all good wishes to the Governors, Traders, and Adventurers into these Christianly reformed islands.

By the 1630s, the city had in some respects ceased to serve as a boundary between worlds within and without: the pageants acknowledged the declining influence of the local commune and its guilds by lauding the City's leaders for their membership in the new far-flung syndicates and consortia.[240] Bypassing and rendering obsolete the traditional government and companies of the City, corporations like the East India, Levant, and Muscovy Companies had superseded the North-European-oriented Merchant Adventurers in importance and had dominated the City of London government since the end of the sixteenth century. The chief financiers of the Stuart Crown and the chief beneficiaries of its patronage and protection, the leaders in these Eastern and Mediterranean trades were coming under increasing pressure in the 1630s from the lesser merchants and shopkeepers who were beginning to prosper in the new Puritan-dominated colonial trade with America. Gaining influence with Londoners opposed to the religious policies and unparliamentary rule of Charles I, the new American tradesmen were attempting to interlope in the markets of the conservative elite and were challenging the traditional ties between the City leadership and the Crown.

In attempting to defend both the political authority and trading franchises of the traditional elite, however, the shows of the 1630s laid a new stress on international commerce that paradoxically dissolved and disseminated earlier ideals of urban settlement. While they sought to justify the rule of an exclusive elite of merchant capitalists, the shows adopted an expansionist social vision and a rhetoric which, appealing to and drawing on the influence of the new colonial traders, reflected an historical process that was wrenching mercantile practices free of the local arrangements by which they had been restricted. In 1633 for example, Heywood made it clear that Ralph Freeman's achievement lay not in his membership in the lowly Clothworkers but in his investments in syndicates "whose Factors in both Indies lye / The East and West." His pageant culminated, however, not with these vast global dealings but in the innermost core of man's civilized virtues, represented in a Bower of Blisse that was "an Embleame of the future Happinesse, which not

---

[240] In 1637, for example, Richard Fenn was praised for his membership in the Merchant Adventurers, "as also of the Levant, or Turkey, and of the East India Co.," *Londini Speculum*, in Heywood, *Dramatic Works*, 4: 307–308. Henry Garway, Draper, was lauded for "the multiplicity of your Commerce ... in the Low Countries, France, Spaine, Italy, Venice, East India; and moreover in Greene-land, Muscovy, and Turkey, of which three notable societies you are at this last present Governor," Heywood, *Londini Status Pacatus* (1639), in *Dramatic Works*, 5: 358, 307.

onely all iust and vpright Magistrates, but euery good man ... especially aimeth at." Not just the pageant, but in a sense the history of the inaugural show, was summed up in Heywood's punning declaration that "euery good man" follows Freeman in seeking to arrive at "yon celestiall Tower, / Which aptly may be titled Freemans Bower."[241] As the pageants made their final journey to the mayor's private domicile, they dissolved the city only to reinscribe it in the soul, creating a new journey and destination, in which the

> honour'd brest,
> Shall (maugre shelues and rocks) your passage clear,
> And bring you to the Port, to which you steare.[242]

In their elaboration of a profane and continuing history, a history leading both outward toward the commercial and spiritual conquest of the globe and inward toward the economic and spiritual freedom of the individual citizen, the London mayoral shows derived, from their negotiation with the ceremonial symbolism of the monarchy, new rationales for the city and its bourgeois pursuits. As in Spenser's epic, where the neofeudal symbiosis of London and the Crown was delineated in terms of a cultural *translatio* or civilizing process, the ceremonies of London negotiated, through their sense of a secular history of moral causes and effects, both a balance between political domains and ideals and a transition between historical eras. While contributing to a conciliatory sense of settlement and thus to the sedentary process of urbanization, the cultural *limen* of ceremony effected social change and pointed toward new developments. As in descriptions of London, where the negotiation of neofeudal compromise through the transhistorical appeal of communal persona and gender yielded finally to a sense of historicized personhood and alienation from the monster city, the ceremonies of London led finally toward innovations – global expansion and economic individualism – in which the traditional civic commune would be eroded by a metropolitanism whose influence transcended its physical boundaries. In their post-Restoration guise, London's mayoralty shows entered a period of notable decline, some of it immediately reinforced by the burning of St. Paul's Cathedral in 1666, which altered both the procession route and the ceremonies. But the rebuilding of the Cathedral did bring with it a return of the older patterns, which were forever altered by more deeply rooted changes – the movement of the waterside show to Westminster, the replacement of the triumphal narrative with fixed pageant stations, the replacement of the concluding

[241] *Londini Emporia* (1633), sig. c.
[242] Heywood, *Londini Sinus Salutis* (1638), in *Dramatic Works*, 4: 298.

evening's prayers at St. Paul's with indoor entertainments at the Guildhall, often attended by the king and aristocrats, where merry drolleries mocked Puritans and other unsophisticates. Excluded from this feast, the majority of liverymen repaired "to their respective halls to dinner,"[243] while bachelors feasted themselves separately, in turn.

These new arrangements reflected not only the city's growth, but more importantly, the structural changes that accompanied it – a turn from civic community toward bourgeois privacy, a social stratification and widening gap between labor and capital, a new, cosmopolitan role of national influence for the latter. It is not surprising that with the accomplishment of these changes, perhaps epitomized in royal attendance at the Guildhall feast, the mayoral shows, which had only begun to speak in 1540, had by 1702 ceased speaking altogether. These long-term developments were supported by the forces of metropolitanism discussed in Part 4, but the way to them was prepared in the new ethical techniques that developed alongside the Elizabethan–Jacobean neofeudal fictions of settlement. These are the subject of the Part that follows.

---

[243] Thomas Jordan, *The Triumphs of London* (1678), p. 178; the pattern was already established, however, in 1660; see John Tatham, *The Royal Oake* (1660), p. 106.

Part III

Techniques of settlement

6 "To be a man in print": pamphlet morals and urban culture

Word and sword: techniques of settlement

In the descriptive, epic, and ceremonial modes that formed the encomiastic literature of Renaissance London, the novel forces of urbanization were harnessed, in "fictions of settlement," to new visions of a national community. In its growing wealth, power, and splendor, London became the symbol of a providential destiny that reconciled nature with culture, justice with power, and the feudal past with a commercializing present and future. By means of these fictions, the life of feudal society was extended in the new form of the absolutist state, centered in the capital. Embracing the interests and ideals of a widening variety of status groups and institutions, the capacious and broadly consensual nature of these neofeudal "fictions of settlement" helped to effect orderly change by stabilizing and containing its potentially solvent effects.

Yet in the very process of effecting change, encomiastic fictions of settlement also encountered and uncovered discontinuities and contradictions, incompatibilities between the traditional order and the new. These manifested themselves in the emerging challenges to traditional descriptive techniques, in the difficulty of effecting the epic passage from past to present, and in the productive tensions between royal and civic ideologies in urban pageantry. In each case, the very instabilities in fictions of settlement registered the momentum of the sedentarizing process, the tendency of technical and ethical innovations to outstrip the capacity to contain them.

A widely recognized feature of the urbanizing process is the behavioral transformation that accompanies demographic and structural changes.[1]

---

[1] This three-part terminology is the basis for Jan de Vries' recent study of *European Urbanization, 1500–1800* (Cambridge, Mass.: Harvard University Press, 1984), pp. 10–13. The general case for the behavioral bias in the history of urban sociology is summarized by Don Martindale's Introduction to Max Weber, *The City* (New York: The Free Press, 1958).

As the American urban sociologist Robert Park observed, urbanization is "accompanied by corresponding changes in the habits, sentiments, and character of the urban population."[2] During some phases of urbanization, such changes become exponentially related to urban growth; as Jan de Vries observes, "the cultural impact of cities... grew more than proportionally with their size."[3] The disproportion is perhaps better put in terms of qualitative change: "the mobility of a population is unquestionably a very large factor in its intellectual development."[4] Such intellectual development includes the moral techniques – the modes of identity-formation, systems of belief, habits of deportment and civility, means of aggression and defense – that motivate and discipline massive cohabitation, making urban life endurable, viable, desirable.

It is such qualitative changes that, destabilizing the encomiastic fictions of Renaissance London, helped to generate the contemporary body of grotesquerie and satire, the vast and sudden outpouring of seriocomic pamphleteering, popular mockery, verse satire and epigram, and public comic theater that emerged from the metropolis at the end of the sixteenth century. The theoretical difference in kind that separates praise and blame is in practice largely a matter of emphasis and degree within a structural symbiosis. Such a symbiosis links the praise and blame of Renaissance London, both of which, in varying degree, were written from within the same neofeudal framework and both of which, in varying degree, registered the novel and disruptive effects of the ubanizing process. Fictions, in their ideological functions, are of course social and ethical techniques, just as moral techniques involve fiction-making. As compared with the more sharply polarized political and polemical climate of either the early Reformation or the Civil War, moreover, the late sixteenth and early seventeenth century represented a period of considerable fluidity and flexibility, corresponding, in fact, to a structurally overdetermined and socially transitional situation. Both praise and blame participated in and contributed to this same transitional process. Nevertheless, differences in emphasis amounted to what may be said to be differences in kind. If, as Louis Wirth maintained, the attitudes, ideals, and values that constitute "urbanism" are dependent for their "development and extension" on the technical resources of "urbanization,"[5] then the realm of urban grotesquerie, comedy, and

---

[2] "The City: Suggestions for the Investigation of Human Behavior in the Urban Environment" (1916), in Richard Sennett, ed., *Classic Essays on the Culture of Cities* (Englewood Cliffs: Prentice-Hall, 1969), p. 110.
[3] *European Urbanization*, p. 154.   [4] Park, "The City," p. 106.
[5] "Urbanism as a Way of Life" (1938), in Sennett, ed., *Classic Essays on the Culture of Cities*, p. 148.

satire – with its connection to such technical innovations as the literary marketplace, the urbanization of folklore, popular dissemination, and the cult of individualism – represents a more truly novel emphasis and thus potentially a difference in ethical, social, and political kind. The difference is perhaps summed up in George Herbert's dictum that "Courtesie growes in the court; news in the citie."[6] Written largely without patronage and sometimes against the obstacles of official censure, this literature was – in what is often seen as its new "realism" – at once a critique of courtly literary fashion and of traditional modes of social and discursive authority. Its innovations represented a response to the inadequacies of traditional institutions and concepts to an urbanizing world.

In the face of rapid and disruptive urban growth, and by the terms of human experience and moral need, the traditional institutions of the City and the official Church were proving organizationally adequate but morally and discursively wanting. Commanding sufficient force and loyalty – at least up to the Civil War – to hold the population to obedience, neither could supply a positive, innovative moral content adapted to the unsettled, mobile conditions of life in the capital. Innovative as they were in other respects, the merchant class and its rulers formed a gerontocracy conservative in its neofeudal outlook and not, in any case, closely affiliated with the large portion of London's population that did not possess the freedom of the City. Only when the values of this group were transformed by their dissemination in pamphlets, plays, and pageants by popular writers did they begin to have wide-spread appeal and innovative potential.

Doctrines like vocation and stewardship, and above all the late sixteenth-century development of protestant casuistry,[7] represent a similar moral innovation among churchmen, but the system of belief that had appealed so strongly to the youthful and dispossessed at the Reformation[8] had become less compelling in its prescriptions for urban life. The London clergy, for example, complained in 1581 that their preaching against usury merely caused angry parishioners to withhold their tithes.[9] In Robert Wilson's interlude *The Three Ladies of London* (c.

---

[6] "The Church-Porch," line 292, in *Works*, ed. F. E. Hutchinson (1941; rpt. Oxford: Clarendon Press, 1970), p. 18.

[7] See Camille Wells Slights, *The Casuistical Tradition in Shakespeare, Donne, Herbert, and Milton* (Princeton University Press, 1981).

[8] See Susan Brigden, "Youth and the English Reformation," in Paul Slack, ed., *Rebellion, Popular Protest and the Social Order in Early Modern England* (Cambridge University Press, 1984), pp. 77–107, and K. V. Thomas, "Age and Authority in Early Modern England," *Proc. Brit Acad.*, 62 (1976), 1–46.

[9] Richard L. Greaves, *Society and Religion in Elizabethan England* (Minneapolis: University of Minnesota Press, 1981), p. 609.

1584), the victory of the wicked Lady Lucre over her sisters Love and Conscience proved the point that in London "there never was more preaching and less following, the people live so amiss."[10] Thomas Wilson's *Discourse upon Usury* (1582) recounted how London merchants jocularly invited preachers to their tables in gratitude for their having dissuaded their competitors from the practice of usury.[11] In another anecdote, a grasping merchant complacently accepts as merely part of the system his university-educated son's preaching against usury:

I cannot justly blame my Sonne for that he hath done, for it is as well his profession, to speake against usury, as it is my occupation to follow it, otherwise he might want matter to speake on, and both my selfe and my Son might lacke money to live on: proceed therefore my Sonne, quoth this goldfinder, and see you spare not to invent damning arguments against such as live by loane, and I hope that in time this will become my trade alone.[12]

Nowhere, however, was the limit of the preachers' moral authority more apparent than in the language of crisis and in the literal sense of "monstrosity" in which they typically portrayed the anomalies, disruptions, and innovations of London's burgeoning life as portents of impending doom, shakings in the very foundations of civilized life. To judge from the sermons of the more extreme preachers, London's fate hung daily in the balance, poised precariously between promises of fulfillment in the New Jerusalem and the threat of cataclysm and everlasting destruction.

The large body of popular, secular, urban literature – of ballads, plays, pamphlets, and satires – that emerged between 1580 and 1620 may be seen as an alternative response to this moral and discursive impasse, an alternative whose effect was to articulate an urbane mentality of settlement. "Men are men," Thomas Nashe declared, "and with those thynges must be moued, that men wont to be mooued"; this, he added, required a rhetoric and ethic that would probe London's life "more searchingly then common Soule-Surgions accustome."[13] Linked to the practices and dynamism of the marketplace by the publishing trade and the new public theater industry, and belonging to no established institutions, the pioneering professional writers of the early modern age in England were "liminary–luminaries" whose uncertain, marginal status was inseparable from their development of highly mobile forms

[10] *The Three Ladies of London*, in *Dodsley's Old English Plays*, ed. W. C. Hazlitt (12 vols. London, 1874), 6: 287.   [11] Ed. R. H. Tawney (London, 1925), pp. 325–326.
[12] George Phillips, *The Life and Death of the Rich Man Lazarus* (1600), quoted in Helen C. White, *Social Criticism in Popular Religious Literature of the Sixteenth Century* (New York: Macmillan, 1944), pp. 222–223.
[13] *Christes Teares ouer Ierusalem* (1593), in R. B. McKerrow, ed., *The Works of Thomas Nashe* (5 vols. 1904; rpt. Oxford: Basil Blackwell, 1966), 2: 80.

and styles.[14] Their work is profane in Angus Fletcher's sense of being pro-fanum, before the calamity of apocalypse;[15] it seeks, in Nashe's words, "to build vertue a Church on that foundation that the Deuil built his Chappell" (*Works*, 1: 305), and it postpones calamity by making London a profane and "intricate laborinth"[16] to be negotiated by being read.

The ways in which this project involved a mutual shaping of mores and discursive modes by way of deviance from authoritative norms is best demonstrated in the development of the seriocomic prose pamphlet, not so much a form or genre as a new medium and technology based on "rhapsodic stitching," on the "decomposition and recomposition" of established discursive models and motifs.[17] Mobilizing both the language and structures of pulpit oratory and the genrism of humanist poetry, pamphleteering was, as Nashe put it, "duncified 'twixt diuinity and poetrie" (*Works*, 5: 231). Yet its performative, provisional clowning cleared a space in which destabilized conventions, both moral and verbal, yielded new interpretations of a changing urban scene. With a highly self-conscious sense of the materiality of discursive practice, pamphleteering erected itself on the rubbish heap of preaching and complaint, "fitting well-worn materials into neat patterns. It was a substitute for technology, and gave the same feeling of control. Experience is reduced to adage, thought to a familiar manipulation."[18] Because, in its fiction of "anatomizing," it drew upon such standard structural topoi as the deadly sins, the estates, and the professions, pamphleteering mimicked many of the conservative, neofeudal features of traditional sermon and complaint, especially their animus toward novelty and their sense that

[14] I borrow the term "liminary–luminary" from Jean-Christophe Agnew, *Worlds Apart: The Market and the Theater in Anglo-American Thought, 1550–1750* (Cambridge University Press, 1986), p. 115. The standard accounts of professional writing are Sandra Clark, *The Elizabethan Pamphleteers: Popular Moralistic Pamphlets, 1580–1640* (Rutherford: Fairleigh Dickinson University Press, 1983); Edwin H. Miller, *The Professional Writer in Elizabethan England* (Cambridge, Mass.: Harvard University Press, 1959); Phoebe Sheavyn, *The Literary Profession in the Elizabethan Age*, 2nd edn. J. W. Saunders (New York: Barnes and Noble, 1967); Margaret Spufford, *Small Books and Pleasant Histories: Popular Fiction and Its Readership in Seventeenth-Century England* (Cambridge University Press, 1981).

[15] *The Prophetic Moment: An Essay on Spenser* (University of Chicago Press, 1971).

[16] Barnabe Rich, *Favltes, Favltes, and Nothing Else but Favltes* (1606), ed. Melvin H. Wolf (Gainesville: Scholars' Facsimiles and Reprints, 1965), sig. E.

[17] Walter Ong, "Oral Residue in Tudor Prose," in *Rhetoric, Romance, and Technology in the Interaction of Expression and Culture* (Ithaca: Cornell University Press, 1971), pp. 34–35. W. Parkes thus refers to seriocomic prose writers as "Pamphlet stitchers" whose work was "Now drawne to a large multiplication," *The Curtaine Drawer of the World* (1612), sigs. B2v–B3.

[18] John Carey, "Sixteenth- and Seventeenth-Century Prose," in Christopher Ricks, ed., *English Poetry and Prose, 1540–1674* (London: Barrie and Jenkins, 1970), p. 364.

contemporary ills could be cured by the recovery of that better past that had somehow been mislaid.

But from this mimicry new possibilities, a sense of historical change and moment, also emerged. Often highly educated but lacking patronage and place, the professional pamphleteers occupied an ambiguous position of estatelessness that corresponded in many ways to the ambiguous place of London itself during the transition to capitalism. Regarded, in Sidney's slight, as "base men with servile wits ... who think it enough to be rewarded of the printer," and exploiting the very conditions *The Shepheardes Calender*'s E. K. blamed for making "our English tonge a gallimaufery and hodgepodge,"[19] the pamphleteers typically devoted themselves to the sensations and phenomena of liminality, to the ephemera of gossip and controversy, to the London demimonde and criminal underworld, to the exchanges and combinations of the marketplace, to the monstrous portents of social crisis and disaster, and to the promotion of their own work. In the decoding of the feudal order and the deterritorializing of the economy by these phenomena, the seriocomic rhapsodes also found the means for deconstructing the authority of prevailing modes of discourse, confronting them with their origin in and their reproduction of material life and its practices. Geared to the constant adjustments of the marketplace, seriocomic prose was unusually sensitive to the flux of social life as well. Like the marketplace, which institutionalized crisis as a permanent condition, social life was retooled in pamphleteering to the tempo of crisis. It is, as Robert Park observed, "the existence of a critical situation which connects what were otherwise mere information into news."[20] Hence Dekker's observation that "Books are strange a commoditie; the estimation of them riseth and falleth faster than the exchange of money in the low countries."[21] Writing, in John Danby's terms, "down" Fortune's Hill to a popular, heteroglot audience that was itself being created by the impact of London and by the writing profession, the pamphleteers empowered themselves through pariahhood and heterodoxy, parleying the status of placeless, degraded urbanites into uninventoried forms of gentleness, creating distinctively experiential modes of authority and authorship,[22] making it possible in

[19] Sidney, *Apology for Poesie*, quoted in David Margolies, *Novel and Society in Elizabethan England* (London: Croom Helm, 1985), p. 13; see also J. W. Saunders, "The Stigma of Print: A Note on the Social Bases of Tudor Poetry," *Essays in Criticism*, 1 (1951), 139–64; Charles C. Mish, "Black Letter as a Social Discriminant in the Seventeenth Century," *PMLA*, 68 (1953), 627–630.   [20] "The City," in Sennett, p. 107.

[21] *Jests to Make You Merry*, quoted in F. O. Waage, "Dekker: Plays and Pamphlets," *RORD*, 26 (1983), 25.

[22] See Robert Weimann, "*Fabula* and *Historie*: The Crisis of the 'Universall Consideration' in *The Unfortunate Traveller*," *Representations*, 8 (1984), pp. 23–24; cf. M.

the fullest sense of Dekker's wonderful phrase, "To be a man in Print."[23] This was a manhood not so much autonomous as positional, deeply implicated, through its self-recognizing mobility and ephemerality, in the languages, relations, processes, and potential of the urban marketplace. Geared to the tempo by which, "in a day & a night" Greene was reputed to "haue yarkt vp a Pamphlet,"[24] this mode of subjectivity also defined for the city itself a new temporality, a rhythm of profane and continuing historicity that made it possible to *represent* unsettlement as itself a settled and "natural" condition. In "indeauouring by their pennes to set vpp lightes, and to giue the world new eyes to see into deformitie,"[25] these moralists may also be said more profoundly to have given the world new eyes with which to see.

This was, in many ways, a transgressive enterprise, and its full meaning only emerges when set against the modes of discursive authority out of which it emerged. An important achievement of the Tudor state was its successful domination of London through its influence on the City government and its control of the Church and pulpits. London's Court of Aldermen, together with the City's leading companies and their elaborate apparatus provided for the extraction of Crown revenues, the enforcement of law and policy, and when needed, the raising of force. Reinforced by a system of court patronage and sponsorship which provided for the award of honours, offices, and commercial privileges, London's civic institutions were circumscribed by a jurisdictional boundary which at once licensed and limited the city's autonomy. To be sure, this was a flexible boundary, open to compromise and easily crossed by informal contacts, legal expertise, and the movement of capital. But mutually profitable collusions were disguised by a theory of political subordination, so that quite revolutionary economic changes took place under the aegis of a limited political arrangement.

Along with the City government, Church and pulpit were essential to the structure of authority in London. The Crown's control over the Church was extended to the pulpit not only through the promulgation of the *Homilies* and the refusal to license nonconformist preachers, but also

---

Foucault, "What is an Author?" in Josue V. Harari, ed., *Textual Strategies* (Ithaca: Cornell University Press, 1979), pp. 141–160.

[23] *The Wonderfull Yeare. 1603.*, in *Non-Dramatic Works*, ed. A. B. Grosart (5 vols. London, 1884), 1: 78.

[24] Nashe, *Works*, 1: 287, quoted in Murray Roston, "Grub Street," in *Sixteenth-Century English Literature* (New York: Schocken Books, 1982), p. 103. On the sense of temporality in sixteenth-century "news" and pamphleteering, see also Lennard J. Davis, *Factual Fictions: The Origins of the English Novel* (New York: Columbia University Press, 1983), chs. 3–4.

[25] Barnabe Rich, *The Honesty of This Age* (1614), ed. Thomas Wright (London: Percy Society, 1843), 11: 3–4.

through the active recruitment of propagandists to occupy London's leading pulpits, such as those at St. Mary Spital and Paul's Cross, where sermons were regularly attended by the mayor and aldermen in all their regalia on religious holidays. It must be stressed again that London's leading families exercised a degree of autonomous influence on city preaching through their control of benefices and their sponsorship of parish lecturers.[26] Nevertheless, the authorized form of preaching was dictated by the bishops of the Church, or at critical times in concert with the Privy Council.[27] The pulpit at Paul's Cross was occupied by the bishops when Parliament was in session and was otherwise under the patronage of the Bishop of London; Bishop Aylmer called it "my chaire."[28] An early eighteenth-century description of the Paul's Cross preachers applies equally well to the sixteenth century: "The Persons that are to preach these Sermons, are from time to time appointed by the Bishop of London, and are chosen out of such as either have been or are of either of our Universities, by turns."[29]

The structure of authority represented in the coalition between London's magistracy and preaching clergy thus had profound consequences not simply for the stability of the Tudor state, but for the way life was lived and mentally experienced in the metropolis. It is not simply that Londoners were subject to a downward flow of information, but that much of this discourse originated outside the city, in institutions whose values and structures were in some ways alien to the city's own institutional life, and especially to newer developments. London's magistrates were, for example, charged with enforcing a body of parliamentary statutes and royal proclamations regulating work, wages and prices, dress, and consumption, building, disorder, and deviance. But these did not represent a positive moral content so much as a series of ad hoc reactionary measures against the accelerating pace of social change. Only indirectly – through their adherence to conservative, still largely feudal values – could they be said to express a social vision, and this vision became less credible with time, and with such developments as the lifting of the statute against interest in 1571. The City's medieval

---

[26] At the official end, city fathers disputed the Bishop of London's right to appoint the preachers of the Spital sermons and resisted re-endowing the Paul's Cross lectures in 1581, Millar MacLure, *The Paul's Cross Lectures, 1534–1642* (Toronto University Press, 1958), pp. 11–12. On the civic sponsorship of parish lecturers, see Paul S. Seaver, *The Puritan Lectureships* (Stanford University Press, 1970).

[27] See Alan Fagar Herr, *The Elizabethan Sermon: A Survey and a Bibliography* (1940; rpt. New York: Octagon Books, 1969), ch. 4.

[28] MacLure, *The Paul's Cross Lectures*, p. 113.

[29] Richard Newcourt, *Repertorium Ecclesiasticum Parochiale Londinense* (2 vols. London, 1708–10), 1: 4–5, quoted in MacLure, *The Paul's Cross Lectures*, p. 11.

custumals and civic traditions of course embodied the wisdom of the
past, but London could claim no members of its ruling elite – no Salutati,
Bruni, or Pirckheimer – who combined office and eloquence in such a
way as to transform the city's ideals into inspired literary monuments.[30]
Until, under the influence of the new professional writers, it found
increasingly articulate expression in mayoral pageants and popularization
in citizen drama, the citizen ethic remained the insular morality of a
powerful but somewhat inarticulate urban elite; directed to the citizen
class rather than the urban populace as a whole, it could not embrace the
larger dimensions of urban experience.

"Where there is no vision the people perish,"[31] Sampson Price told
the Paul's Cross audience in 1616, when for more than half a century
London's preachers had been claiming for themselves an authoritative
role in shaping the city's life. Though always a troubled relationship, the
alliance of clergy and magistracy, word and sword, came to represent a
powerful model of moral and discursive authority. Among the more
potent of its political manifestations were not simply the city's pulpits,
used for reading proclamations, and delivering important news as well as
preaching, but the parish vestries, essential to the city's governance, and
the periodic Wardmote Inquest, which regulated economics, social
harmony, physical maintenance, and all the minuter species of moral
turpitude.

It was against the background of authority vested in the alliance of
cleric and magistrate, religion and regulation, that the professional
writers developed the novel morality of the secular pamphlet form. Some
measure of the difficulty this involved is reflected in Ben Jonson's
observation that writing was only economically successful when practiced as an accoutrement to careers in "the Law, and the Gospel."[32] In
the decade following Elizabeth's succession, the suppression of unlicensed preaching[33] went hand in hand with an extensive campaign to

---

[30] A point made by Frank Freeman Foster, *The Politics of Stability: A Portrait of the
Rulers in Elizabethan London* (London: Royal Historical Society, 1977), p. 5. On civic
ideology as ritual, however, see above, pp. 258–264.

[31] *Ephesus Warning Before Her Woe* (1616), p. 62.

[32] "Poetry in this latter Age hath prov'd but a meane Mistresse, to such as have wholly
addicted themselves to her, or given their names up to her family. They who have but
saluted on the by, and now and then tendered their visits, shee hath done much for, and
advanced in the way of their professions (both the Law, and the Gospel) beyond all they
could have hoped, or done for themselves, without her favour," *Discoveries*, in *Works*,
ed. C. H. Hereford and Percy and Eveln Simpson (11 vols. Oxford: Oxford University
Press, 1925–52), 8: 583, quoted in Phoebe Sheavyn, *The Literary Profession in the
Elizabethan Age*, p. 5.

[33] In restricting the subjects of sermons, Elizabeth proclaimed that assemblies to hear
preaching, "specially in the city of London" gave rise "amongst the common sort [to]
not only unfruitful dispute in matters of religion, but also contention and occasion to

outline and defend the terms of the Elizabethan settlement from the nation's pulpits, including the essential one at Paul's Cross. Not until the mid-seventies did preachers begin frequently to address themselves to the moral life of the metropolis, and when they did so it was primarily to inscribe their authority in that life. London was typically compared to Biblical cities blessed with prophets, and the city's failure to heed its preaching clergy was represented as a form of apostacy. As Henry Smith told his parishioners at St. Clement Danes,

> The city of Jerusalem had never so many prophets crying at once in her streets as this city wherein we dwell, though the ox which treadeth out the corn hath often been attempted to be muzzeled, even of those which tread not at all ... Here is the college of the prophets, here is the voice of the crier, here dwells the seer, though he be hated, and scorned, and contemned for his pains.[34]

Where the word is "plentifully preached, and the people wilfully negligent," Thomas White warned in 1577, "there is deepe damnation and vtter destruction shortly to be looked for."[35] By an inexorable, self-fulfilling logic, London's sufferings were interpreted as punitive signs which further validated the preachers' authority. Anthony Anderson, in a plague sermon at the Cross in 1581, explained that God had set "his correcting hande to London, ... as thereby reproving our wante of fruite. And nowe he stirreth vppe the courage of his Prophets (the godly Preachers whiche truly feare him) with one consent to sound, as it were, the soleyme blaste of a laste visitation."[36]

In asserting that it was "a great and publique taske for the Lords Voices to Cry unto a Citie," London's preachers claimed to be driven by the inspirational force of a Scripture directly addressed from God to London:

> when the Lords Voices, out of this and such like publike places, cry vnto your Citie, blame not the Voices, for the Voices, they of themselves are slow enough to cry vnto a Citie ... blame me not, though I (who am the meanest of Gods Voices) show vnto you how the Lords quarrel with this Citie in my Text [Micah 6:9], agrees in some sort to this famous Cittie.[37]

---

breach common quiet," *Documentary Annals of the Reformed Church of England*, ed. Edward Cardwell (2 vols. Oxford University Press, 1844), 1: 209, quoted in Seaver, *The Puritan Lectureships*, p. 204.

[34] "The Art of Hearing," *Works* (2 vols. Edinburgh: James Nichol, 1866), 1: 319; cf. James Bisse, *Two Sermons* (1581), sig. D3; William Fisher, *A Godly Sermon Preached at Paules Crosse* (1592), sigs. A5–A7; Sampson Price, *Ephesus Warning Before Her Woe* (1616), pp. 3–10, 53; Francis White, *Londons Warning, by Jerusalem* (1619), pp. 6–8.

[35] *A Sermon Preached at Paules Crosse, November 1577* (1578) sig. A6; cf. John Field, *A Godly Exhortation by Occasion of the Late Iudgement of God at Paris Garden* (1583), p. 2.

[36] *A Sermon Preached at Paules Crosse* (1581), sig. D.

[37] *Londons Warning, by Jerusalem* (1619) pp. 40–41; last sentence slightly emended for sense.

The presence of divine authority in preaching justified an institutional arrangement in which the "watchfull Senators of this great Citty" should "give all encouragement to this holy exercise ... So long as the currant of the Gospell shall engirt your Cittie, well are ye, and happy shall yee be."[38] The city's government was obliged not only to support preaching but to follow the guidance of preachers in carrying out its functions. Magistrates, William Holbrooke preached, "Shold not beare the sword for naught, or be like a player vpon the stage, to play his part and away."[39] Rather, it was the duty of London's magistrates, said Thomas White, "to play both the Phisition and Surgeon ... and thrust diligently your sword of iustice in, to launce out all coruption and baggage which is gathered in the bowels" of the city.[40]

The ideological relation of the word to the sword accounts for the peculiar rhetoric of preaching on civic themes, which typically addressed itself simultaneously to the cure of souls and to the counsel of secular authority. In their addresses to London's populace, the preachers thus performed what MacLure has called "a sort of weekly 'check-up'" (p. 121), meant to purge the audience of error. Because it was understood that the Paul's Cross sermons were delivered "principally for the governours of this Honourable Cittie,"[41] this check-up took the institutional form of prescriptions on the social order. John Stockwood, for example, called on London's magistrates to "kepe in your several warde a carefull and diligente watche to meete with such abuses as highly offende God, and are directly againste his maiesties lawes, amongst the rest these ..."[42]

The divinely authorized alliance between preaching and power thus required an elaboration of scripture in terms of conventional models and theories of social order. As they applied their texts to the city's ills, preachers typically fell back on such traditional homiletic structures as the decalogue or the seven deadly sins, which were summoned up and discarded as the need arose, usually in combination with such equally venerable structures of complaint as the estates and their degrees or the professions.[43] However, the prominence of certain motifs – such as the

---

[38] David Price, *Maries Memoriall, A Sermon Preached at St Maries Spittle* (1616), p. 30.
[39] *Loves Complaint, for Want of Entertainment. A Sermon Preached at Paules Crosse* (1609), p. 16.   [40] *A Sermon Preached at Paules Crosse ... 1577* (1578), sig. F7.
[41] Roger Ley, curate of St. Leonard's Shoreditch (c. 1619), cited in MacLure, p. 121.
[42] *A Sermon Preached at Paules Crosse on Bartholomew Day* (1578), pp. 85–86.
[43] William Cupper's plague sermons of 1592 thus ran first through London's violation of the ten commandments and then traced the corruption in various estates and degrees, *Certaine Sermons Concerning Gods Late Visitation* (1592). Comparing London to Sodom, Adam Hill's plague sermon of the same period demonstrated that Sodom's sins were manifest in terms of the decalogue, the seven deadly sins, and the estates and professions, *The Crie of England* (1595).

pairing of prodigality and avarice and the invocation of the destruction of Biblical cities – betokens a sense of contemporary social crisis.

The pairing of prodigality with covetousness, first of all, implicitly defined a contemporary social boundary even while it excoriated traditional moral extremes. These two forms of moral deviance destabilized the mythical boundary, in a status system based on land, by means of which the influence of the city could still be contained. In Elizabethan sermons prodigality was almost invariably the sin of gentry abandoning their estates, while covetousness was just as invariably the sin of overweaning and usurious merchants. Because the modern credit relationships linking countryside to city were intolerable to late-feudal notions of standing and stability, prodigal gentlemen and covetous merchants were polarized as opposite forms of moral deviance. The erosion of traditional society by the urban convergence of aristocratic *dépense* and bourgeois accumulation manifested the dangers of the city as a catalyst of socio-economic change. The three duties of London's magistrates, William Cupper proclaimed, were to reform disorders offensive to God, to "take away the wonderfull prodigallitie of this time," and to bridle covetous "usurers, also brokers, badgers, & hucksters & such like locustes that eat vp the poore."[44] According to William Fisher, magistrates were to restrain the "excess of dyet and excess of apparel" in "Epicures, Bellygods," and "proud Poppies," and at the same time to oppose "every harde hearte, every Churlish Nigarde, every pinchyng Myser, every greedy Vsurer."[45] The corrosive social effects of these moral extremes was the basis for Thomas White's attack on the deviance of Gentlemen and Merchants from their proper roles:

the Commonwealth hath no cause to bless ... them, who first have taught our Gentles, to degenerate from their noble Auncestors, to leave their houses in the Countrye for the most part of the yeare, and to keepe Ordinaries heere in the Cittie, without neede: a tricke of more then Ordinarie Gentlemen. But Vsurie, is the Marchants fault, Gentlemen cannot be charged therwith ... To cleare this Citie, if euerie man were bonde to excercise the trade wherof he is free, Poore Companies woulde not then decaie so fast, as Vsurers should be driven to sue for a Corporation for themselves, for while they are no Corporation, they are Free of all Companies, and this casting of your money into the Banke, will cast a banke about this Cittie in the end, and then you may goe purchace Aceldama.[46]

Like that of many London preachers, White's underlying concern was to uphold a weakening distinction between the older virtues of feudal loyalty and rural hospitality of the unfallen countryside, on the one hand,

[44] *Certaine Sermons* (1592), pp. 342–343.
[45] *A Sermon Preached at Paules Crosse* (1580), c8–d2.
[46] *A Sermon Preached at Paules Crosse* (1589), pp. 38–39.

and the mean cycles of debt and credit in the capital on the other. Linked by an elaborate system of patronage to the Universities and to the court, the Paul's Cross preachers, and indeed most of London's licensed clergy, were themselves members of a gentry that depended for its support increasingly on the sort of commercial wealth generated by London. When they offered their preaching of the word as counsel to the sword, they were also calling on London's magistrates to maintain the fictional boundaries that would secure their traditional standing while concealing its changing socio-economic basis.

A sense of socio-economic crisis is reflected, too, in the many sermons that tied London's fate to that of Biblical cities.[47] On the one hand, as center of reformed preaching, London was potentially a Jerusalem to which "God hath sent his prophets and teachers...that from it all the towns and villages about might receive instruction & light, like a becon which standeth upon a hill, and is seen ouer all the country."[48] Having both "her owne Ordinary with store" and "her solemne Assemblies furnished with the choise of Vniuersitie and Countrie, to speake vnto her," London was "the very Arke of the presence of God, aboue all other places of this land."[49] On the other hand, London was like those "Greater Cities" that "for theyr contempte,...haue more plentifull tast of hys plages before other places."[50] Typologically, London's trials and sufferings linked it in apostasy to a host of fallen cities in sermons on *The Most Lamemtable* [sic] *Destruction of Ierusalem* (1584), *Gods Mercie and Jerusalems Miseries* (1609), *Abrahams Sute for Sodome* (1612), *Ephesus Warning Before Her Woe* (1616), *Londons Warning by Laodiceas Luke-warmenesse* (1619), *Londons Warning, by Jerusalem* (1619). The *Homilies* encouraged believers to interpret strange events and disasters as the result of "God's anger at the vices of the community,"[51] and London's preachers were quick to seize on freak occurrences and recurrent plague outbreaks as signals of God's wrath.[52] Strictly speaking, such monstrosities and prodigies were portents, or warnings of punishments that might be avoided, rather than judgements.[53] But the tendency of many preachers "to sound, as it were the soleyme blaste of a laste visitation"[54]

---

[47] See Patrick Collinson, "The Protestant Town," in *The Birthpangs of Protestant England* (London: Macmillan, 1988), pp. 28–32.   [48] Henry Smith, *Works*, 1: 319.

[49] Thomas Jackson, *The Conuerts Happines* (1609), p. 30.

[50] Stockwood, *A Sermon Preached at Paules Crosse on Bartholemew Day* (1578), p. 23.

[51] Keith Thomas, *Religion and the Decline of Magic* (New York: Charles Scribner's Sons, 1971), p. 83.

[52] Favorite events with preachers were the burning of Paul's steeple in 1561, the supernova of 1574, the earthquake of 1579, and the collapse of Bear Garden bleachers in 1583.

[53] Thomas, *Religion and the Decline of Magic*, pp. 89–90.

[54] Anthony Anderson, *A Sermon Preached at Paules Crosse* (1581), sig. D.

to London betokened a sense of crisis and a divided consciousness as to the city's moral significance.

The tonal register of city preaching was typically high and narrow, seldom including the sort of derisory or sceptical tones that would question or deconstruct the social frame within which preaching was conducted. Denunciations of deviants from the social model of complaint – usurers, extortioners, rapacious landlords, prodigal gentry, and the varieties of vagabonds – were thus entirely common, while pointed attacks on the structure of society were not.[55] While it was "not vndecent for a prophane writer to be iestyng and merie spoken," it was "mete for a man of god rather to wepe then to iest."[56] The sharp distinction preachers maintained between these decora meant that laughter was typically seen as an unacceptable and dangerously rivalrous form of social commentary. The clerical campaign against the Elizabethan theatres was in this regard part of a larger campaign against all unlicensed and derisive social comment, including the new seriocomic medium of the topical prose pamphlet, in which popular clowning and bedevilment amounted to a critique of the sobriety of orthodox forms of counsel.[57]

By 1592, as the Marprelate pamphlets and the social pamphlets of Lodge, Greene, and Nashe were emerging to great popularity, the pamphlet had thus joined the theater as an outlaw form of discourse. Worse than ignorant preachers, Henry Cupper complained, were the

manie priuate persons tickeled with vaine-glorie, blinded with self-loue, bewitched with gaine, or such lyke carnall affections ... bold in the pride of their wittes vppon the reading of a fewe bookes, or the hearing of a fewe Sermons, to thrust foorth a Pamphlette vnto the worlde, neuer reuerencing the graue censure of learned men, ... and venturing vppon those things whereunto, neither their skill, nor calling, will giue anie warrant to their consciences.[58]

Like the theater, the pamphlet was at bottom a discourse unauthorized by Scripture. But in both cases, the complaint that people "bestow more time ... in the writings of men, then in the sweete and pretious word of God himselfe," (Cupper, sig. A5) was based upon a not-so-subtle institutional competition for discursive authority between preachers and

---

[55] Henry Smith did wax sceptical at Paul's Cross when he openly "mused what text to take in hand, to please all, and to keep myself out of danger" (*Works* 2: 323); though not intended to appease, Smith's denunciation of sins, from usury and rentracking to starching collars, playing cards, and sleeping in church got him into no personal difficulty.

[56] Thomas Drant, *Horace his Arte of Poetrie, Pistles, and Satyrs Englished* (1567), sig. A3.

[57] I am indebted in what follows to the larger view taken by Russell Fraser, *The War Against Poetry* (Princeton University Press, 1970).

[58] *Certaine Sermons Concerning Gods Late Visitation in the Citie of London* (1592), sig. A4v.

popular moralists. Henry Crosse, for example, objected that if any godly writers

> set forth any notable book of divinitie, humanitie, or such like, they are in no request, but to stop mustert pots, & what is the reason but this, euery stationers shop, stal, & almost euery post, giues knowledge of a new toy, which many times intercepts the vertuous discipline of a willing buyer.[59]

John Stockwood and other Paul's Cross preachers were fully aware of their proximity to the stationers' stalls in the Churchyard and Paternoster Row, which sold "filthy bookes, wherwith this Churchyard swarmeth in this clear light of the Gospel."[60] William Vaughan objected that England's youth were made rebellious by the pamphleteers' arsenal of "taunts and temptations fraught with satyricall scoffes, with scurrility, with Scogins sports, with amorous allurements, deuised by the deuill." In the age of commercial print, it had become the devil's plan to train youth "to detract, to lash out fearefull othes at euery other word, to reade baudy ballads, books of his own Apostles, ... our English cast-awayes."[61] The ancients censored unlicensed criticism, said Gosson, because "they would not have the life and behaviour of the citizens, subiect eyther to a Poets' inkehorne, or a Players tongue, but to the Seate of justice."[62] Munday explained that sin "ought not be revealed openlie," but left to the authority of the Church, which is "appointed to reform manners, and execute discipline" (p. 119).

The dual and exclusive authority of word and sword was neatly summed up in Henry Crosse's modern version of the social estates, where all legitimate callings reduce "into these two, either in minde or in body, the Magistrate, Minister, and such as holde publique and sacred places ... others are manuell or mechanicall" (sig. R3). The intended effect of exclusive alliance of word and sword was to marginalize secular moralists – "our English cast-awayes" – as men without calling.[63] Lodge, whose reply to Gosson's *The School of Abuse* was "forbid ye publishing" by "ye godly & reuerent," was subsequently portrayed by Gosson as "little better than a vagrant, looser then liberty, lighter than vanitie it selfe."[64] Literary professionals who lived "by plaies and such like," Perkins maintained, were men of "no calling at all."[65] Thus

---

[59] *Vertues Common-wealth*, sig. P.

[60] *A Sermon Preached at Paules Crosse on Bartholomew Day* (1578), p. 147.

[61] Vaughan, *The Golden-Groue* (1600), sigs. P2v, I3v.

[62] *Plays Confuted in Five Actions* (1582), in Arthur F. Kinney, ed., *Markets of Bawdrie: The Dramatic Criticism of Stephen Gosson* (Salzburg Studies in English Literature 4, 1979), p. 165.   [63] Ibid., p. 196.   [64] Ibid., p. 141.

[65] Perkins, *Works* (1603), sigs. 4K3–4K3v. Cited in Jonas Barish, *The Antitheatrical Prejudice* (Berkeley: University of California Press, 1981), p. 113.

marginalized, professional writing was situated at the frontiers of aberrant mobility: it was either likened to the practices of "vsurers and extorcioners, which ... exhaust ... the purses" of their clients,[66] or castigated as "a continuall monument of London's prodigalitie and folly."[67] Vaughan attacked "the apish spleen of certain English Pamphleters" as the prodigal offerings "of their greene wittes, or as we vulgar say, their wilde seed Oates."[68] At the same time, the professional literary entertainer was an avaricious marketeer who preferred "wordes before matter, shewe before substance";[69] he was "like to a Marchants finger, that standes sometime for a thousande, sometime for a cypher,"[70] and his goal was to "sucke up the bottome of ... young Prodigals superfluities."[71] Like the playwrights, "our Pamphleters" were "detracting and deluding Alchymists" who presided over a discursive no man's land, tempting readers to "leave their honest callings" and "live idlely." This was a monstrous discursive "Laborinth" of "prodigious vanitie."[72]

The suppression of this realm required a return to a more stable discursive norm, "a zeale in authoritie, to banish them; a diligence in Preachers to pursue them."[73] It was Northbrooke's hope that "God will so move the hearts of magistrates, and loose the tongue of the preachers in such godly sort ... that both with the sw!orde and the worde such vnfruitfull and barren trees shall be cut doune" (p. 103). This alliance was, however, only a theoretical bulwark against the emergence of a new form of discourse, an urban and urbane mode of moral expression. As such, it represented merely one side of what was becoming a triangular situation, in which preachers would be forced to compete with clowns for the ears and minds of the urban audience.

Prodigality and the language of romance

In their approach to London, the secular moralists of the sixteenth century took many of their cues from the evolving language of complaint and from the paradigmatic relation between social criticism and authority developed by preachers. The imitation of the homiletic pattern was

---

[66] Crosse, *Vertues Common-wealth*, sig. Q. Fraser argues that both usury and the theater were seen as opposed to an ethic of thrift, industry, productivity, and hard assets, *The War Against Poetry*, p. 113.

[67] *A Sermon preached at Paules Crosse ... 1577* (1578), sigs. A2, c8.

[68] *The Golden-Groue*, sig. P.   [69] Cupper, *Certaine Sermons*, sig. A5.

[70] Gosson, *Plays Confuted*, p. 147.

[71] *This World's Folly* (1615), sig. B3, cited in Fraser, *The War Against Poetry*, p. 133; cf. Rankins, *A Mirrour of Monsters* (1587), sigs. E2v–E3v; John Northbrooke, *A Treatise of Dicing, Daunsing, Plays, and Interludes* (c. 1577), ed. J. P. Collier (London: Shakespeare Society, 1843), p. 84; White, *A Sermon* (1578), sig. c7v.

[72] Rankins, *Mirrour*, sig. c2 ff.   [73] Gosson, *Plays Confuted*, p. 158.

perhaps most slavish in the growing body of popular ballads which admonished Londoners

> Ye bryng the curse of God, dayly on your heade,
> Which shall fall vpon you, as heuy as any lead ...
> Repent ye Cyttizens of London.[74]

Urging that "London leaue thy wicked trade,"[75] these ballads typically drew their moral authority from "The fall of many cities greate / ... As sacred scriptures doth repete."[76] Countless ballads interpreted both the fall of Biblical cities and contemporary prodigies as portents of impending punishment for London's sins.[77] As Thomas Beard explained, "great and populous cities are ... blameable for glutting and ouer-charging themselues with sins ... for in steed of being a patterne and direction vnto others of wisedome and good gouernment, as they ought, they are for the most parte examples of folly and vanity."[78]

The follies and vanities indicted were many, but like the preachers, many popular moralists – for whom there were few vernacular prose models other than preaching – gravitated toward the pair of prodigality and covetousness. "Of all the vices that is, and are vsed," Henry Carr observed, none doo more resemble one an other, then these two."[79] Imputed, respectively, to the gentle and burgher classes, these paired forms of moral deviance defined the faultline in a social fabric threatened by change. A variety of works in verse and prose paired Avarice and

[74] William Samuel, *A Warnynge for the Cittie of London* (1550).

[75] William Birch, *A Warnyng to Englande, Let London Begin : To Repent Their Iniquitie, or Flie from Their Sin* (1565).

[76] John Carr, "Citezein of London," *A Larum Belle for London* (1573).

[77] Surviving examples by the prolific John Barker include *Of the Horyble and Woful Destruccion of Ierusalem* (c. 1569) in J. P. Collier, ed., *Illustrations of Old English Literature* (3 vols. 1866), 1: 13–17 and *The Great Earthquake* (c. 1580), in *Old Manuscript Ballads and Songs*, pp. 39–42. Hyder Rollins, *Analytical Index to Ballad Entries in the Registers of the Company of Stationers of London* (Chapel Hill: University of North Carolina Press, 1924) includes the following (volume and page numbers refer to Edward Arber, *A Transcript of the Registers of the Company of Stationers of London* [5 vols. London, 1875–77]): (51) *Alarme to England [or to London]*, 1578, 2: 338; (1528) *Looke London Looke to be Warned, &c.*, 1578, 2: 333; (327) *Comme from the Plaie, Comme from the Playe : the House Will Fall so People Saye : the Earth Quakes Lett Vs Hast Awaye*, 1580, 2: 368; (340) *The Common Crie of London*, 1580, 3: 382; (663) *An Ernest Admonycon to Repentance vnto England especially to London*, 1580, 2: 369; *The Iudgement of God*, 1580, 3: 370; (1838) *A Godly Newe Ballat, Mouing Vs to Repent by Example of ye Earthquake Happened in London*, 1580, 3: 367; (2224) *Quake, Quake, yt is Tyme to Quake, when Towres and Tounes All Doo Shake per Elderton*, 1580, 2: 369; (564) *A Newe Ballad of the Destruccion of Ierusalem*, 1586, 2: 454; (2877) *A warninge or Lamentation to London of the Dolefull Destruccion of Fayre Ierusalem*, 1603, 3: 236. See also E. D. Mackerness, "'Christs Teares' and the Literature of Warning," *ES*, 33 (1952), 251–254.

[78] *The Theatre of Gods Iudgements : Or, a Collection of Histories* (1597), p. 462.

[79] *The Ruinous Fal of Prodigalitie*, sig. c4.

Prodigality to paint the portrait of an age of acquisition, which was "neuer more couetouse, nor...neuer more addicted vnto riotousnesse."[80] The crucial and debatable "question, betweene the covetous and the prodigall,"[81] became the basis not only for popular morals but for a stage debate that ran from the *Contention Betweene Liberalitie and Prodigalitie* (pub. 1602) to *The Merchant of Venice* (c. 1597) and beyond.

Because preaching was virtually the only vernacular prose model for secular moralists, they tended to follow preachers in justifying their enterprise as a discursive service to the authority of the sword. A supplementary source for this strategy was the legend, first popularized in Sir Thomas Elyot's *Image of Governance* (1541), of the Roman Emperor Alexander Severus, who "vsed many tymes to disguise him selfe in diuers strange facions," and "wolde one day haunte one parte of the citie, an other day an other parte."[82] In the fiction of magistrates who tour their realm incognito or appoint secret censors and informers to report on corruption, the writers of late Elizabethan London found an enabling device that provided both a theoretical justification and a practical rhetorical model for probing the contemporary scene. In Thomas Lupton's utopian realm of *Mauqsun*, magistrates "would walk in the streetes early and late." In *Look on Me London* (1613), a late example of the cony-catching genre so profoundly influenced by this testimonial rhetoric, Richard Johnson portrayed himself as "an honest Englishman, ripping vp the Bowels of Mischiefe, lurking in the sub-urbs & Precincts." He praised his dedicatee, Sheriff Thomas Middleton, for conducting "visitations in the sub-urbs and out-places of the precincts of London, to enquire after evil livers, and by justice to root out iniquity."[83]

---

[80] Ibid., sig. C. Compare the pairing of Avarus and Prodigus in T. A., *The Massacre of Money* (1602), and *Of the Belly and the Back* in W. Auerell, *A Maruailous Combate of Contrarieties* (1588).

[81] "John Dando" and "Harrie Hunt" (pseud.), *Maroccus Extaticus: Or, Bankes Bay Horse in a Trance* (1595), ed. E. F. Rimbault (London: Percy Society, 1863), p. 15.

[82] *The Image of Governance* (1541), in *Four Political Treatises*, ed. Lillian Gottesman (Gainesville: Scholars' Facsimile and Reprints, 1967), p. 310. A history of this motif, to which I am much indebted, is found in Mary Lascelles, "Sir Thomas Elyot and the Legend of Alexander Severus," *RES*, n.s. 2 (1951), 305–318 and *Shakespeare's "Measure for Measure"* (London: Athlone, 1955), esp. pp. 23, 96–103. See also G. K. Hunter, "English Folly and Italian Vice: The Moral Landscape of John Marston," in *Jacobean Theatre*, ed. John Russell Brown and Bernard Harris (1960; rpt. New York: Capricorn Books, 1967), p. 101; Josephine Miles, *The Problem of "Measure for Measure"* (New York: Barnes and Noble, 1967), and Leonard Tennenhouse, *Power on Display: The Politics of Shakespeare's Genres* (New York: Methuen, 1986), ch. 4.

[83] Lupton, *The Second Part and Knitting vp of the Boke Entitled Too Good to be True* (1581), sig. T4. Johnson, *Look on Me London* (1613), ed. J. P. Collier, *Illustrations of Early English Popular Theatre* (London, 1864), t.p. and p. iii. No less influential than legends were the actual procedures of inquest and visitation; see, for example, the letter from William Fleetwood, Recorder of London, to Burghley, on his undercover discovery of

In keeping with the logic of such older complaints as *The Complaynt of Roderyck Mors* (1542), *The Supplication of the Poore Commons* (1546), Crowley's *Informacion and Petition* (1549), or *Pyers Plowmans Exhortation* (1550?), the informer's rhetoric implied that a true picture of society, suppressed by bureaucratic intermediaries, could only be gained through the (fictional) authority of the moralist's "first hand" experience.[84] The fictional perspective of the informer–reporter was later exploited and ironized in the presenter and disguised-justice plays of Middleton and Shakespeare and in the commentaries of such stage satirists as Thersites, Malevole, and Bosola. But, as in the urban reportage of Greene, Nashe, and Dekker, these ironic uses of the reporter's perspective developed from an earlier alliance between the moralizing observer and political authority. This alliance made it possible for the pamphleteer to become "a great corrector of the vices and abuses of his time ... tho' not in sacred orders."[85]

Among the first of the popular prose comedians to open the relation of word and sword to the marginalized standpoint of the professional writer were George Whetstone and Thomas Lodge. Still laboring under the need to justify their exploration of urban life, they adopted the enabling fiction of writing in the service of magisterial power, but their claims as moralists and reporters were based not on the transcendent authority of Scriptural prophecy but on the more problematic authority of their personal experience as victimized participants in the scandal of contemporary London life. Writing in the only semi-fictional personae of prodigal gentlemen burned in the attractive candleflame of London, Whetstone and Lodge adopted a position even more socially partisan than the preachers who insisted on an asymmetrical or "hierarchical" contrast between genteel prodigality and mercantile avarice. Yet their very partisanship – the necessity of self-defense – also depended on a new degree of self-implication, on self-justifying narratives in which the city becomes the unavoidable scene of inevitably "educational" (and literarily productive) encounters with vice. This implication in the urban

a training school for young cutpurses, Lansdowne MS. 44, art. 38, ed. H. Ellis, *Letters Illustrative of English History* (3 vols. London, 1824), 2: 296–298.

[84] A prose gloss by the authors of *A Myrrorre for Magistrates* (1559) pleads with "Magistrates, that they maye ratifie our olde freedome" on the grounds that through the poets' license to complain rulers "should have knowen what the people myslyked and grudged at, (which no one of theyr flatterers eyther would or durst have tolde them)," ed. Lily B. Campbell (1938; rpt. New York: Barnes and Noble, 1960), p. 359. The passage is discussed in Annabel Patterson, *Censorship and Interpretation: The Conditions of Reading and Writing in Early Modern England* (Madison: University of Wisconsin, 1984), p. 13.

[85] Anthony à Wood, describing Philip Stubbes, *Athenae Oxoniensis*, ed. P. Bliss (4 vols. Oxford: Ecclesiatical Society, 1848), 1: 645.

scene, together with a contaminated rhetoric which alternates between counselling imperilled peers and castigating urban adversaries, remained in many ways a source of contradiction for Whetstone and Lodge. Yet it opened up for such later writers as Greene, Nashe, and Dekker the possibility of deploying the traditional terms of moral and social analysis with a skeptical, ironic regard for their ultimately linguistic and fictionally malleable nature.

Whetstone's *Mirour for Magestrates of Cyties* (1584) and Lodge's *An Alarum against Vsurers* (1584) are alike not only in assailing London's depletion of gentlemen's purses, but also in attempting to establish for their authors a literary standing that will make good on previous personal failings. Whetstone, the son of a wealthy London haberdasher with ample country holdings, complains that "no man was euer assaulted with a more daungerous statageme of cosonage than my selfe, with which my life & liuing was hardly beset." He dedicates his work to London's Lord Mayor, "to showe my selfe worthy of my deceased father, who liued longe in good Credite amonge you."[86] Lodge, the second son of a colorful Lord Mayor who scandalously went "banquerout in his maioralitie to the grete slandar of the citie," offers the public service of his work as evidence against the personal slander of Stephen Gosson, who had labelled Lodge "a vagarant person, visited by the heuy hand of God, lighter then libertie, & looser then vanitie."[87]

Profligacy thus authenticates the very compensatory service for which it creates the need; but furthermore, the prodigal's perspective is offered as an implicitly critical alternative or supplement to the ineffectual guidance of the clergy. Whetstone, for example, notes that "the godly Diuines, in publique Sermons, and others, in printed Bookes, haue (of late) very sharply inuayed against Stage playes ... But, there are in the Bowels of this famous Cities, farre more dangerous Playes" (sig. G4v). Whetstone acknowledges that "by the testimonie of Holy writ ... magistrates haue on Earth, the names and places of Goddes," but he quickly adds that their perspective is limited: because their "sightes are not inuisible," it is "necessarie, that you haue visible Lightes, in obscure Corners." Lodge asserts that the municipal authority of word and sword are powerless against London's deviants: "neither honourable may controll them, nor diuine admonition reclaim them." The reason "such desolation is not perceiued" is not a lack of law and preaching but an

---

[86] *A Mirour for Magestrates of Cyties ... and Herevnto, is Added, A Touchstone for the Time: Containyng: Many Perillous Mischiefes, Bred in the Bowels of the Citie of London* (1584), sigs. K4, B.

[87] *An Alarum against Vsurers* (1584), in *The Complete Works*, ed. Edmund Gosse (4 vols. Glasgow: Huntlerian Club, 1883), 1: 14, 6.

inexperience of the "pretie collusions these cunning merchants can finde
to infringe" upon both law and pulpit (p. 36). Just as "Orpheus can
describe Hell, better then Aristotle," Whetstone explains, so direct
experience makes "the sight of one eye" superior to "the attention of ten
eares." To the authorities' question, where "haue I knowledge, of these
concealed Abuses?" the Orphic Whetstone tartly answers, "forsoothe,
In Hel" (sig. A3v).

In describing the machinations through which "the Marow & strength
of this happy Realme, ... the Abilitie of the Gentlemen, is much weakened
and, almost wasted" (Whetstone, sig. A4), both Lodge and Whetstone
follow the standard complaint procedure by coordinating status with the
sins of avarice and prodigality to produce the stereotypical contrast
between merchants' "cruelty, and Gentlemens folly" (Lodge, p. 50). In
keeping with the Emperor Severus' two-pronged campaign "to instruct
the youth" and "to abate the number" of Rome's dangerous predators,
Whetstone's double purpose is to preserve the health of gentlemen and to
expose evils in London (sig. B2). Lodge's purpose, similarly, is both to
amend the offense and to warn potential victims "to shunne the scorpion
ere she deuoureth" (p. 3). These dual tasks require a double rhetoric:
Whetstone offers his work to both the London authorities and the
gentlemen of the Inns of Court, while Lodge alternately addresses the
authorities, potential gentle victims, and vicious usurers. As prodigals,
both engage in the rhetoric Richard Helgerson has called "a three-way
conversation... One young man admonishes another while an old man
listens"[88]

This divided rhetoric is not, however, symmetrical. In Alexander
Severus' twin addresses, for example, Rome's citizens are threatened
with prosecution, while prodigal gentlemen are financially reinstated and
forgiven, because "Prodigalitye, is so sharpe a vengeance, as there
needeth no Lawe to chastise the Prodigall man" (Whetstone, sig. E). The
position that ungentle merchants should "exceede not the boundes of
your popular state" (sig. D2) or prey upon "that which is the portion of
more profitable subiects," thus reflects the claim which both writers
make to gentle status. But the more crucial asymmetry stems from their
necessarily apologetic stance toward prodigality itself. While the pur-
ported task of these works is to show gentlemen "the true image of a
rebellious sonne, and the rewarde of contempte of parents" (Lodge, p.
28), the authors' semi-fictional status as prodigals enables them to offer
not only moral advice but also practical, self-justifying guidance on
surviving the urban perils to which gentlemen must inevitably be

[88] *The Elizabethan Prodigals* (Berkeley: University of California Press 1976), p. 68.

exposed. Whetstone's *Mirour* does not show young gentlemen their faces
so much as it "showeth you a large hole to see Daye"; it will "guide you
as safe, as the Clue of the Threede did Theseus, in the Laberinth" (sig.
Bv). The labyrinthine city thus becomes a romance realm where young
gentlemen inevitably encounter threats to their integrity. The necessity
of such encounters arises from the fact that for modern gentlemen
London's Inns of Court have become "the first intertayners of your
Lybertie," the ritual passageways to success in an increasingly urbanized
world: "the wanton Alectues, which you (continually) behold, are not
vnlike the Sirens Inchauntments (were Poets faynings true:) you
continually walke by the Adamant Rockes, which drawe Siluer and Gold,
as fast as Iron and Steele" (sig. A3). While it might be preferable if "the
Innes of the Court, were farre from Dicyng-houses," the historical
necessity that "*you can not be thus separated*" calls instead for an ability
to read the landscape.

London thus becomes a shadowy and dangerous landscape, a moral
realm characterized by "sudden alterations of temperature, mysterious
heightenings, local intensities, sudden drops in quality, and alarming
effluvia, in short, the whole semic range of transformation scenes
whereby, in romance, higher and lower worlds struggle to overcome each
other."[89] Authors who claim to read this world must be prepared to
acknowledge that its enticements "in very deed are many" (Whetstone,
sig. I4). The deception of merchants, confidence-men, gamesters, and
prostitutes lurks everywhere, "in Cheapside, and other principall
streetes" (sigs. Kv–K2). These dangers are invisible to the authorities
because "official culture is founded on the principle of an immoveable
and undying hierarchy in which the higher and the lower never merge."[90]
In order to negotiate this tricky urban world where high and low *do*
merge, the writer is forced to become a social renegade. His ability to read
this landscape comes neither from the patrimonial donor-culture that
subjects him to urban temptations nor from the tempter culture which
would devour him. It comes rather from his marginal status as a
victim–participant: his in-law counsel derives from personal experience,
from his outlaw absorption in the urban scene. This absorption gives him
his biography and enables him to speak.

Lodge's *Alarum* actually pits two maimed patrimonies against each
other in order to generate this independent urbanist perspective. Having
fallen into debt through a series of temptations, a prodigal son is

---

[89] Fredric Jameson, "Magical Narratives," in *The Political Unconscious: Narrative as a
Socially Symbolic Act* (Ithaca: Cornell University Press, 1981), p. 112.
[90] M. Bakhtin, *Rabelais and His World*, tr. H.Iswolsky (1968; rpt. Bloomington: Indiana
University Press, 1984), p. 166.

summoned home from London and lectured by his father, who urges him to "weigh the iudgement of God, and let that terrifie thee." Yet the father also confesses that it was because "my honour shuld haue beginning in thee alone, and be continued by thy offspring" that his son was "by mee brought to the Innes of Court, a place of abode for our English Gentrie" (pp. 20–21). The father then "returneth him to the Innes of Court again," in the hypocritical manner of Nashe's "carefull Fathers" who "send their Chyldren to thys Citty, ... like those that in Affrick present theyr children (when they are first borne) before Serpents: which if the children (they so present) with their first sight scare away the Serpents, then are they legitimate, otherwise they are Bastards."[91] The prodigal's moral integrity and independence are thus maintained not simply at the expense of urban moneylenders but at some cost to the whole idea of a gentle patrimony:

Among ye rebblement of such as we finde to haue falne in their youth, how many experienced men find we at yeares of discretion? who hauing only ye name of gentrie left them to promote them to honor, & finding no releefe any way, are inforced either in forren countries to end their liues miserably & desperately, some more vngratious, are a pray for ye gallous, choosing rather to die with infamie, then to liue to beg in miserie. (p. 19)

Lodge further undermines the authority of the gentleman's patrimony through a second speech of paternal advice, this time from a usurious merchant, whose adopted son the prodigal becomes when he is forced by poverty to join the usurer's schemes against other gentlemen:

The world at these dayes is such (my friend) as there is smal respect had of those which haue nought, and great honour attributed vnto them, that will most neerly looke vnto themselues: which I perceiuing, haue giuen my selfe (as naturally men are inclined to seeke after glory) to the hoording vp of riches, to the end my posteritie might be raised vp, and my fathers name (which as yet is of no accompt) might by my meanes become worshipfull. (p. 30)

The gentleman–father who declares "my honour should haue beginning" in his prodigal son and the usurious father who would enrich a son "of no accompt" begin to coalesce, thereby undermining the basis of the status-system. The prodigal son, freed by this loosening of status barriers, learns to negotiate the resulting ambiguities, which give the urban labyrinth its semic strangeness. London's underworld denizens are advised by their trainers and patrons to "fashion your selfe to feede humours" and "be verie circumspect." Young English gentlemen are advised by Lodge to "trust not to apparent goodes, beleeue not credulously ye faire spoken" (pp. 32, 47). Two moral codes begin to ape

---

[91] *Christes Teares ouer Ierusalem*, in *Works*, 2: 96.

each other in a society where "the dissolution of one familie, is the setting vp of another" (p. 40).

The more crucial distinction in Lodge's *Alarum* is not the social one between merchants and gentlemen but the generational one between the prodigal urban moralist and the older, paternalistic order. The moral potential of the new generation derives precisely from its immersion in, complicity with, a scene of urban exploitation. A new type of moralist and a new type of urban landscape come into being in a mutually productive relationship. This relationship is summarized in Lodge's closing address to his own creations, the London deviants whose crimes have brought the author into being, by giving him "matter to write on":

How happy were I that hauing lesse cause, might haue lesse matter to write on? And haplesse are you, if not won with these warnings, you giue more occasion to be written. (p. 52)

Lodge thus flourishes the power of his credible testimony against his urban adversaries, asserting that "he that made you knoweth you, and he whom you offend can (and will) punish you" (p. 49). Yet Lodge would never have achieved this discursive power to "know" and "punish" without his complicit status as offender, which provides his "matter to write on." A new kind of author and a new kind of subject come into being symbiotically. As a new means of exploring the urban labyrinth, the combination of in-law and outlaw perspectives establishes Lodge's brilliant mercenary enterprise. The urban sociologist Robert Park observes that "neither the criminal, the detective, nor the genius has the same opportunity to develop his innate disposition in a small town that he invariably finds in a great city."[92] The genius of the pamphleteers was to have combined the outlaw and inlaw perspectives of the criminal and the detective, thereby creating a new image of the great city of London and a new sense of its moral challenges.

Ghosts: projects and projections of Nashe and Greene

None of London's pamphleteers contributed more than Robert Greene and Thomas Nashe to transforming the socio-economic marginality of popular writing into the basis for a new form of urban literature. Their literary projects were so intertwined with their reputations as prodigals and "prandial libertines"[93] that they came to exemplify both the dangers of bohemian dissipation and the scandal of literary professionalism. Through their flagrant notoriety, they also served as posthumous models – enabling figures, or "ghosts" – who underwrote a whole new body of

[92] "The City," in Sennett, *Classic Essays on the Culture of Cities*, p. 126.
[93] Bakhtin, *Rabelais and His World*, p. 297.

urban literature that derived its secular, urban morality and urbane style from an intimacy with largely unexplored portions of the city's landscape.

At once a linguistic, literary, and moral innovation, the comic prose of Greene and Nashe depended foremost on its contamination of the traditional humanistic canons of Ciceronian prose with the base element of popular idiom, marketplace, and theater. The boundary between these humanistic and popular extremes was seldom fixed or stable in a society where popular religion, the relative novelty of print, a potent oral culture, and limited schooling combined to prevent domination by learned humanism or neo-classical genrism. Conversely, the literate use of popular culture was never a liberation from humanist and courtly orthodoxy, whose lineaments are still visible in the ethical priorities and biases of the pamphleteers. Yet Nashe and Greene created an inter-oriented prose in which no centrifugalities of idiom, aristocratic or bourgeois, learned or popular, could dominate.[94] With their imitators and successors, they established both a profession, and, with it, a heteroglot idiom – a language and a medium that subjected the mundane and the everyday to higher forms of order, even while, under the pressures of the everyday, those structures were made to yield new forms of life.

That such previously marginal comic prose should have been felt not simply as a challenge to familiar structures but as productive of new possibilities made it more, not less, disturbing. It was staging a discursive "descent" to have implied, as in effect these writers did, that the language, style, and morals of the nation and the self were to be fashioned not simply in the traditional discursive arenas – the pulpit, the school-room, the aristocratic household, and the court – but in the streets of London, in its theater and its popular press. In moving these previously subordinate realms from the margins to the center of consciousness, the professional pamphleteers acquired, and in fact exploited, a kind of dual status as discursive liminaries who bedevilled orthodoxy by interpreting the world through its urban underbelly. They were cultural luminaries who derived their authority from their sensational outlaw experience and marginal social status. In the works of their contemporaries, Nashe and Greene lived out a lingering perdition as wandering ghosts and demonic acolytes not simply because their lives were scandalous and their writings influential, but because the very dynamics of their literary project created and demanded this status for them.

[94] Jonathan Crewe, for example, notes that Nashe's prose is at once "unassailably learned rather than vulgar" and yet "never less than popular art," *Unredeemed Rhetoric: Thomas Nashe and the Scandal of Authorship* (Baltimore: Johns Hopkins University Press, 1982), pp. 17–18.

Greene and Nashe acquired their reputations in quite different ways. In Greene's case, an apparently genuine dissipation became the basis for a protracted literary repentance. Greene's own late works, moving gradually from retraction of his wanton romances to cautionary tales of prodigality to (apparently) frank autobiography, were subsequently extended, in posthumous works by his contemporaries, into a pamphlet saga that included *Greenes Mourning Garment* (1590), *Greenes Neuer too Late* (1590), *Greenes Farewell to Folly* (1591), *The Repentance of Robert Greene* (1592), *Greenes Groats-worth of Witte, Bought with a Million of Repentance* (1592), *Greenes Vision: Written at the Instant of his Death* (1592), *Greenes Newes Both from Heauen and Hell* (1593), *Greenes Funeralls* (1594), *Greene in Conceipt, New Raised from his Graue* (1598), and *Greenes Ghost Haunting Conie-Catchers* (1602). The retrospective coherence of this repentance-saga, which so resembles the "stretching Adios" of the prostitutes attacked in these very pamphlets,[95] invites but does not answer speculation as to Greene's own motives. But in his related project, the half-dozen enormously successful cony-catching pamphlets of 1591–92, Greene more openly exploits his wayward career as both the motive and the authoritative basis for his exposé of the underworld: "now ripe daies cals on to repentant deedes... odde mad-caps I haue been mate too, not as a companion, but as a spie to haue an insight into their knaueries."[96] The justification for Greene's dissipation is the authority he acquires in the sequels, as the rogues and criminals who read his pamphlets admit they "cannot discouer more then hee hath laid open."[97]

By contrast, though Nashe drew heavily on popular culture for his style and program, and though he flaunted the "wantoning humour" that was true "Pierce a gods name,"[98] he was never fully at ease in the prodigal's role. His anxiety with his marginal status – which shows up in his coolness toward Greene, in his often supercilious contempt for lesser hack writers, and in his bitterness at his lack of preferment – accounts in large part for the mixture of horror and delight with which he regards the powers of his own voice. Despite their differences, however, the authorial strategies of Greene and Nashe formed a composite on whose dynamics their detractors and advocates were agreed. Both the friends and the enemies of Greene and Nashe placed a premium on their literary–social marginality and their exploitation of it.

[95] *A Disputation Betweene a Hee Conny-catcher and a Shee Conny-catcher* (1592), *Life and Complete Works*, ed. A. B. Grosart (15 vols. London: Huth Library, 1881–83), 10: 199.
[96] *A Notable Discouery of Coosnage* (1591), *Works*, 10: 5–6.
[97] *A Disputation...*, *Works*, 10: 206.
[98] *Nashes Lenten Stuffe* (1599), *Works*, 3: 151–152.

This marginality is, for example, an essential point for Gabriel Harvey, in whose slanders both the deceased Greene and the living Nashe are said to exercise a kind of ghoulish or demonic influence:

Greene (although pitifully blasted, & how woefully faded?) still flourisheth in the memory of some greene wits, wedded to the wantonnesse of their own fancy, and inamored vppon euery new-fangled toy: and Pierce Pennilesse (although the Diuels Oratour by profession, and his Dammes by his practise) in such a flush of notable good fellowes, cannot possibly want many to read him.[99]

For Harvey, the baneful liminality of the "blasted" Greene and the demonic Nashe is at once an offense to morals, society, and letters. The scandal of Greene is the association between "his dissolute and licentious living" and his "impudent pamphletting, phantastical interluding, and desperate libelling" (pp. 19, 20). Even while Greene's writing over-reaches itself, "contemning of Superiours, reviling of other, and defying all good order," it descends to the base element of professional and popular writing, to the "goodfellowship, and bad conditions... of the riming, and scribbling crew" (pp. 14–15). Greene lives by his "running Head, and the scribbling Hand, that neuer linnes putting-forth new, newer, & newest bookes of the maker" (p. 37). Similarly, Nashe's dissolute life "daily feedeth his stile; and his stile notoriously bewraieth his life."[100]

Harvey links Greene and Nashe to the ballad hackwork of Elderton and Deloney; but with striking consistency, he associates their literary-social marginality primarily with that of the recently deceased comic entertainer, Dick Tarlton. Harvey sneers at Greene's "piperly Extemporaizing, and Tarletonizing" and regrets he cannot sue this "king of the paper stage" who has "played his last part, & gone to Tarleton" (*Foure Letters*, pp. 18, 20). He taunts Nashe for "the very Timpanye of his Tarletonizing wit" and charges that "his gayest flourishes are but... Tarleton's trickes, or Greene's crankes,... his jestes but the dregges of common scurrilitie, or the shreds of the Theatre, or the of-scouring of new pamflets."[101] Nashe's *Pierce Pennilesse* (1592), he adds, derives from Tarlton's sub-literary example, touched up by Nashe's own subterranean experience; it is

not Dunsically botched vp, but right-formally conueied, according to the stile, and tenour of Tarleton's president, his famous play of the Seauen Deadly Sinnes ... and is now pleasurablie interlaced with diuers new-founde phrases of the

---

[99] *Foure Letters & Certaine Sonnets* (1592), ed. G. B. Harrison (London: The Bodley Head, 1922), pp. 7–8.
[100] *Pierces Supererogation: Or, A New Prayse of the Old Asse* (1593), p. 45.
[101] *Foure Letters*, p. 42; *Pierce's Supererogation*, p. 66.

Tauerne: and patheticallie intermixt with sundry dolefull pageantes of his own ruinous, & beggerlie experience. (*Foure Letters*, p. 45)

The "Tarletonizing" Harvey associates with Greene and Nashe was not simply a clever sobriquet, but, as its participial form suggests, a discursive and moral practice, a way of life. Like Greene and Nashe, Tarlton led a ghostly afterlife in many contemporary works,[102] not simply because he was famous or influential but because the rhetoric of liminality he developed underwrote his continued presence in the work of others. In *Tarltons Newes out of Purgatorie* (c. 1590), Tarleton's ghost appears to Robin Goodfellow "near the backside of Hogsdon" and explains that anyone who takes him for a devil

is a Calvinist; what, doo you make heauen and hell *contraria immediata* – so contrarie that there is no meane betwixte them, but that either a mans soule must in poste haste goe presently to God, or els with a whirlwind and a vengeance goe to the devil! Yes, yes, my good brother, there is a *quoddam tertium*, a third place that all our great grandmothers haue talkt of, that Dant hath so learnedlye writ of, and that is purgatorie.[103]

Enabling Tarlton to unfold his subsequent jests and novella, the posthumous, ghostly status that prolongs his literary life is not simply an ambiguous moral condition but a figure for his self-authorizing, heteroglot mode of expression – his way of standing between divided and distinguished worlds.[104]

The first English actor to achieve lasting fame and influence, "Tarlton" was both a fictionalized clownish rogue and a performing artist. As Robert Weimann explains, his achievement was to have used his represented self for serious "non-fictional" purposes. As he became a national institution he enjoyed "a certain detachment from the plebeian and rural forms of culture from which he had sprung. This allowed him to adapt traditional forms to the needs of a popular Renaissance theatre."

---

[102] For example, Tarlton interrupts the devil's business with a ditty in *Greenes Newes Both from Heauen and Hell* (1593), ed. R. B. McKerrow (London: Sidgwick and Jackson, 1911), p. 58, and he plays a major role in Chettle's *Kind-Hart's Dreame* (1594), discussed below. His ghost appears as prologue to Percy's *Cuck-Queanes and Cuckolds Errants*, and a ballad entered in the Stationers' Register for August 20, 1590 is called " a pleasant Dyttye Dialogue wise between Tarltons Ghost and Robyn Good Fellowe"; see C. R. Baskervill, *The Elizabethan Jig* (University of Chicago Press, 1929), pp. 96–104.

[103] *Tarleton's Jests, and News out of Purgatory*, ed. J. O. Halliwell (London: Shakespeare Society, 1844), p. 56.

[104] My account of Tarlton is based on Baskervill, *Elizabethan Jig*, Robert Weimann, *Shakespeare and the Popular Tradition in the Theater* (Baltimore: Johns Hopkins University Press, 1978), pp. 186–189 and W. J. Laurence, "The Underrated Genius of Dick Tarleton," *Speeding up Shakespeare* (London: Argonaut Press, 1937).

Through his dramatic self-depiction, Weimann adds, he developed his extradramatic function as a festive mocker, crossing "the boundary between a represented world and the here-and-now world he shares with the audience."[105] He thus parlayed his plebeian lineaments into an artistic autonomy;[106] as Simplicity, the ballad-seller in *The Three Lords and Three Ladies of London* (1590) puts it, "the fineness was within, for without he was plain."[107] The cultural authority of his popular fictional image is figured in such formulaic titles as *Tarltons Toyes* (ent. 1576), *Tarltons Tragicall Treatises* (1578), *Tarlton's Jig* (n.d.), *Tarltons Newes out of Purgatorie* (c. 1590), *Tarltons Jests* (1611), "Tarletons Farewell," "Tarletons Recantacion," and "Tarletons Repentance."[108] Tarlton's cultural authority is inscribed in these titles by virtue of his fictional status as clown; in a sense, it matters little whether he actually wrote (or performed) *Tarltons Jests*, because his fictional identity as comic, roguish protagonist has become a popular reality that authorizes the jests as his. It cannot be accidental that the popular name of Greene also authorizes the variously authentic, doubtful, and pseudonymous works in the series of *Greenes Farewell to Folly*, *Greenes Groats-worth of Witte*, *Greenes Newes Both from Heaven and Hell*, *Greene in Conceipt, New Raised from his Graue*, and *Greenes Ghost*. Nor can it be accidental that Nashe entitled his praise of the red herring *Nashes Lenten Stuffe* and posthumously lent his name to such later works as *Tom Nash His Ghost* (1640–44).[109] In each case, the popular persona serves as a *limen* not only between fiction and life, but also between the degraded status of popular entertainment and the lustre of literary fame and cultural authority. These figures became posthumous luminaries precisely because they were liminaries who

---

[105] Weimann, *Shakespeare and the Popular Tradition*, pp. 186–189.
[106] Michael D. Bristol, *Carnival and Theater, Plebeian Culture and the Structure of Authority in Renaissance England* (New York: Methuen, 1985), p. 140. Among other things, Tarlton and Greene may have shared the same underworld woman. Tarlton reputedly died in dissipation at the Shoreditch house of "Emma Ball, a woman of bad repute" (DNB), while according to Harvey, Greene employed a ruffian called "cuttinge Ball ... to leavy a crew of his trustiest companions, to guarde him in danger of Arrestes" and kept "the foresaid Ball's sister, a sorry ragged queane, of whome hee had his base sonne, *Infortunatus Greene*" (*Foure Letters*, p. 20). See Janet E. Biller, "A Link Between Greene and Tarleton," *AN&Q*, (1968), 151.
[107] W. C. Hazlitt, ed. *Dodsley's Old English Plays*, 6: 398.
[108] The last three titles do not survive, but see Arber, *Transcript of the Registers of the Company of Stationers*, 2: 500, 526, 531; see also D. Allen Carroll, "Who Wrote *Greenes Groats-worth of Witte* (1592)?," *Renaissance Papers* 1992, ed. George Walton Williams and Barbara J. Baines (Raleigh: Southeastern Renaissance Conference, 1993), pp. 69–78.
[109] *Tom Nash His Ghost* was first used as a subtitle for John Taylor's *Differing Worships* (1640), a work in which Nashe does not in fact appear. His ghost delivers monologues, however, in the anonymous *Tom Nash His Ghost* (1642), and in Taylor's *Crop-eare Curried, or, Tom Nash His Ghost* (1644); see *Works*, ed. McKerrow, 5: 45–47.

successfully negotiated the preexisting boundaries between life and art, entertainment and literature, outlaw urban setting and in-law society.

The moral ambiguity of such liminary exploitation of the marginalized realms of popular culture and mundane urban life is reflected in the common associations between "Tarletoning" and the equally liminary status and tactics of the popular stage Vice.[110] Like Tarlton, who probably often played the role,[111] the Vice was a hybrid figure who derived his extradramatic moral authority from his dramatic, representational status as a demonic, roguish villain: the very corruptions he enacted lent authority to his boasting catalogues, sermons, and moral asides. The mixed commitments of the Vice, as rogue and moral commentator, placed him at the *limen* between outlaw and in-law worlds. An ambiguous creature who ingratiated himself with his victims by alternately posing as their servant and preceptor, he exposed their follies in asides to audiences and sometimes betrayed them to the authorities in the play.[112] By the mid-sixteenth century, the Vice, previously a denizen of hell, had become a denizen of the London underworld as well.[113]

---

[110] Bernard Spivack, *Shakespeare and the Allegory of Evil* (New York: Columbia University Press, 1958), p. 135; I draw much of my summary of the Vice from Spivack, chs. 5–9, and from Weimann, *Shakespeare and the Popular Tradition*, pp. 151–159; Charlotte Spivack, *The Comedy of Evil in Shakespeare's Stage* (Rutherford: Fairleigh Dickinson University Press, 1973); Robert C. Jones, "Dangerous Sport: The Audience's Engagement with the Vice in Moral Interludes," *Ren.P.*, n.s. 6 (1973), 45–64; Alan C. Dessen, *Shakespeare and the Late Moral Plays* (Lincoln: University of Nebraska Press, 1986), chs. 1–2; David Bevington, *From "Mankind" to Marlowe* (Cambridge, Mass.: Harvard University Press, 1962).

[111] The anti-Martinist pamphlet *A Whip for an Ape* (1589), for example, observes "Now Tarleton's dead the Consort lackes a uise," in John Lyly, *The Complete Works* ed. R. Warwick Bond (3 vols. Oxford: Clarendon Press, 1902), 3: 419; cited by Weimann, *Shakespeare and the Popular Tradition*, p. 158.

[112] For example, in Ulpian Fulwell's *Like Will to Like* (1568), Nichol Newfangle not only exposes the knavish sinners to Severity, but provides the judge with the halters to hang them. *Dodsley's Old English Plays*, ed. Hazlitt, 3: 354.

[113] He leads *Mundus et Infans'* Manhood through Eastcheap, Hazlitt, *Dodley's Old English Plays*, 1: lines 916–38); he escapes London's jails in several works: W. Wager, *Enough is as Good as A Feast*, ed. Mark R. Benbow (Lincoln: University of Nebraska Press, 1967), lines 360–362; *Hick Scorner* (c. 1515–16), ed. Ian Lancashire (Baltimore: Johns Hopkins University Press, 1980), lines 660ff.; *Youth* (1513?), in *English Morality Plays and Moral Literature*, ed. Edgar T. Schell and J. D. Schuchter (New York: Holt Rinehart, Winston, 1969), lines 229–255; he roams London's streets (in *Hick Scorner*, lines 663–684; *Lusty Juventus*, p. 78); he debauches Impacient Poverty's Prosperity in London's stews (*Impacient Poverty* (1560) in *Lost Tudor Plays*, ed. J. S. Former [London: Early English Drama Association, 1907], p. 332ff.); he leads *Lusty Juventus* "about the town" with a pudding. On the use of the urban underworld in moralities, see esp. Normand Berlin, *The Base String: The Underworld in Elizabethan Drama* (Rutherford, N. J.: Fairleigh Dickinson University Press, 1968), ch. 2; see also Lois Potter, "The Plays and the Playwrights" in the *Revels History of the English Drama*, ed. N. Sanders, R. Southern, T. Craik, and L. Potter (8 vols. London: Methuen, 1980), 2: 153–154 and Schell and Schucter, Introduction, p. xx. The larger connections between

It was not simply the unsavory cachet of the Vice that made him a model for comic prose comedians, but his ontological mobility and his range of expressive devices – his performative diatribes, his improvisatory uses of such homiletic structures as the deadly sins and the estates, his alternately flattering and adversarial stance toward his audience, his appropriation of the extra- and sub-literary popular urban forms for the purposes of cultural commentary, his exploitation of authorial aliases combining virtue and vice, his polyvocal and heteroglot rhetoric. The techniques by which the Vice converted "homiletics into a theatrical art by inverting it into irony, satire, innuendo, by charging it with scornful laughter" applied equally to Greene's and Nashe's urban comic prose. The Vice's tendency to dominate the stage, "prefacing and coordinating each part of his activity with his explanatory and triumphant monologues"[114] was identical in many respects to what L. C. Knights describes as the exhibitionism of "Elizabethan Prose":

> The argument is conducted by invective and ridicule ... Often, ... an interlocutor is imagined as present, and there are pages which can only be understood if we realize that certain sentences – there is no typographical distinction – come from the opposition side. The pamphleteering method is, in short, the method of spoken dialectic. Popular writing is largely, like verbal fencing, an exhibition of skill, and the writer, like an improvisator on the stage, takes care to call attention to a particular display of agility.[115]

It may not have been simply the discursive prominence and power of the pulpit and the theatre, but their coalescence in the marginal figure of the Vice that accounted for the fact that the principal authorial roles for the popular prose writers were those of the preacher and the clown.[116]

---

devils and city comedy tricksters are explored in Wendy Griswold, "The Devil's Techniques: Cultural Legitimation and Social Change," *American Sociological Review*, 48 (1983), 668–680.

[114] B. Spivack, *Shakespeare and the Allegory of Evil*, p. 189, which I also paraphrase in the first clause of this sentence.

[115] *Drama and Society in the Age of Jonson* (1937; rpt. New York: Norton, 1968), p. 311.

[116] "The role of author ... did not exist, so the writer tried on the various masks of preacher and clown for the first two centuries" of printing, Marshall McLuhan, *The Gutenberg Galaxy: The Making of Typographic Man* (University of Toronto Press, 1962), p. 136; cf. pp. 201–202. In his *Elizabethan Grotesque* (London: Routledge and Kegan Paul, 1980), Neil Rhodes develops McLuhan's and Walter Ong's insights on the oral models of clowning and preaching along somewhat different lines to produce a theory of the grotesque as a seriocomic "mixture of buffoonery and moral stridency," p. 53. I am indebted, however, not only to his superb discussion of the residue of these discursive models in Nashe and Shakespeare, but also to his theoretical framework, which, like Robert Weimann's account of the *productive* interorientation of humanism and popular culture, attempts to derive a productive *combinatoire* from what he sees as the more one-sided theories of satire and (especially Bakhtinian) saturnalia. His book thus takes a somewhat more useful though no more profound approach than Jonathan Crewe's

Like Tarlton, who parlayed his origins in a popular stratum into an expressive autonomy, Nashe and Greene exploited the popular idiom of homiletic clowning, not so much to dissociate themselves from the intellectual and social orthodoxies of humanist and courtly literature, as to redefine and invigorate these orthodoxies for the purpose of a widened and more viable social ethic. Philip Stubbes objected that no one could be "a wiseman, that plaieth the part of a foole and vice" (1: 146), but Nashe responded to Harvey's charge that he had borrowed the technique of *Pierce Pennilesse* from Tarlton by asserting that it was no blemish for a writer "to begin where the Stage doth ende, to build vertue a Church on that foundation that the Deuill built his Chappell" (1: 305). Like the stage actors whom the puritan Philip Stubbes labelled "doble dealing ambodexters" (1: 141), the pamphleteers improvised a verbal and social mobility that not only bridged "the emerging social distinctions but actually seemed to thrive on their contradictions"; their manner fostered what Weimann has called "a relative blurring of class alignments and a certain kind of double-edged social criticism" (p. 159).

This social criticism, written from the marginalized standpoint of popular urban culture, amounted to a new but troubling form of ethical wisdom. Bridging the traditional strata of social rank and expression, it gave its practitioners a unique and ambiguous stature – a new autonomy as men in print, but with it, a criminal and infernal aura of transgression. The urban pamphleteers thus haunted the London landscape in the double guise of demigods and demon Vices. In *Greene's Newes Both from Heaven and Hell* (1593), for example, Greene's ghost explains how, "for the writing of my bookes," he "was first banished from Heaven for my ouer much parciallitie" to vice and "nowe exiled from hell, for my too much playnenesse" against it.[117] At once too plain and yet not plain enough, not pure enough for heaven or black enough for hell, Greene becomes "the maddest Gobline…a walking spyrite, restlesse and remedilesse to wander through the world" (60–61). Dekker later associated this fate with the whole tribe of popular writers, whom he described as "Goblins … so like Ghosts in white sheets of paper, that the statute of Rogues may unwittingly be sued upon them because their wits haue no abiding place, and yet wander without a passe-port."[118]

Unredeemed Rhetoric: Thomas Nashe and the Scandal of Authorship, in which the clash between rhetorical orthodoxy and unorthodoxy represents not so much a productive liminality as a deconstructive *aporia* that leaves Nashe between the devil and the deep blue sea. One is prompted to ask, with Tarlton, whether these *contraria immediata* should be so Calvinistically opposed as to preclude a *quoddam tertium*.

[117] B. R. (Barnabe Rich?) *Greenes Newes Both from Heaven and Hell* (1593), ed. R. B. McKerrow (London: Sidgwick and Jackson, 1911), p. 60.

[118] *The Wonderfull Yeare. 1603.*, in *Non-Dramatic Works*, 1: 79–80.

From this liminal, estateless, and mobilized perspective, pamphleteer-ing performed its particular kind of bedevillment, calling up from the marginalized limbo of popular culture and the urban underworld the repressed voices of society's critics. In *Greene in Conceipt* (1598), the ghostly Robert Greene, "a well-proportioned man suted in deaths liuery, *who seemed to write as fast as I could read,*" serves as news correspondent between London and the Elysian fields that harbor "Diogenes, Menippus, & all the ancient Cynicks, with as many of our modern humorists as haue iumpt with them."[119] In Henry Chettle's *Kind-Harts Dreame* (1592), the tooth-drawer Kind-Hart, a popular London figure who eventually enjoyed his own afterlife, is visited by the ghosts of Greene, Tarlton, and several other famous London rogues and entertainers, all of whom attack the in-law enemies of pamphleteers, the sanctioned hucksters who have "fauour from authority" (p. 50). Nashe's direct address to the devil in *Pierce Pennilesse* opens a channel of communication between London and the underworld. In the opening Epistle, where he contemplates writing "to the Ghost of Robert Greene, telling him, what a coyle there is with pamphleting on him after his death," Nashe announces that he might later follow up his address to the devil by writing "the returne of the *Knight of the Post* from hel, with the *Deuils* answer to the *Supplication*" (1: 153–154). This announcement authorizes a large posthumous correspondence, in which Nashe's imitators exploit the satiric possibilities of the links Nashe had forged between London and hell. In *The Returne of the Knight of the Post from Hell* (1606), a straightfaced author whom Dekker regarded as a puritan objects to the infernal prospects that Nashe's pamphleteering opened up for his imitators:

The most famous wittes [will] fall to display the vulgar humours of deiected natures ... others lesse powerfull seeking to flye with their feathers shall rippe vppe all the graues of Scurrilitie & common market places of filthines, & therewithall so ouer presse and loode all eares & attentions, that as if there was nothing but follie, worthie the chronickling, all vertuous actions shall be eyther forgot or vnspoke of. (sigs. F3v–F4v)

At once an offense to language, to morals, and to the social establishment, the opening of discourse to the repressed realms of scurrility and marketplace filth made the authorship of pamphlets a kind of crime.[120] Pamphleteers became what Humphrey King called "publicans and sinners, (or sinners in publique) in that infortunate Art of Printing."

[119] Ed. A. B. Grosart, *Occasional Issues* (London, 1878), 8: 97, 99.
[120] According to Michel Foucault "Texts, books, and discourses really begin to have authors ... to the extent that authors become subject to punishment, that is, to the extent that discourse could be transgressive," "What is an Author?", p. 148.

According to King, himself the clownish "king of the Tobacconists" to whose "capering humour" Nashe dedicated his unpatronized *Lenten Stuffe*, the new urban writers "torment the Print daily" by a contaminating satiric manner that claps "a paire of French spurres on the heeles of Vice to rowell ope the wombe of that resty [sic] Iade Iniquity, [to] let all the loath-some guts & garbidge of his panch issue out to putrifie and infect the fresh aire of Pauls Church-yard."[121]

Dekker, for one, delighted in the possibilities opened by this contamination. Published almost simultaneously with *The Returne of the Knight of the Post*, his own *Newes From Hell* (1606) pays tribute to the merry heterodox vein of "ingenious, ingenuous, fluent, facetious, T. Nash" and boasts that "with the coniuring of my pen, al Hell shall breake loose."[122] The purpose of the infernal perspective in this pamphlet, which links the landscape of hell with that of London, is "to give the world new eyes to see into deformitie."[123] In a later version of the same work, where the deceased Nashe himself bears the devil's message all the way to heaven, the ghosts of "Marlow, Greene, and Peele" laugh to see "Nash (that was but newly come to this colledge,) still haunted with the shape and satyricall spirit that followed him heere vpon earth."[124]

In what is perhaps the darkest portrait of Nashe's project of bedevillment, T. M.'s *The Black Book* (1604) depicts an infernal messenger returning the devil's answer to Nashe's suburban London deathbed:

In this infortunate tiring-house lay poor Pierce upon a pillow stuffed with horse-meat; the sheets smudged so dirtily, as if they had been stolen out of Saint Pulcher's Churchyard when the sexton had left a grave open, and so laid the dead bodies wool-ward: the coverlet was made of pieces a' black cloth clapt together, such as was snatched off the rails in King's street at the queen's funeral... poor Pierce began to stretch and grate his nose against the hard pillow; when after a rouse or two, he muttered these reeling words between drunk and sober, that is, between sleeping and waking: – I should laugh, i'faith, if for all this I should prove a usurer before I die, and have never a peny now to set up withal. I would build a nunnery in Pict-hatch here, and turn the walk in Paul's into a bowling alley: I would have the Thames leaded over, that they might play at cony-holes with the arches under London Bridge. Well (and with that he waked), the devil is a mad knave still.[125]

[121] *An Halfe-Penny-Worth of Wit, in a Penny Worth of Paper, Or, The Hermites Tale* (3rd edn. 1613), sigs. A4, A2v.   [122] *Non-Dramatic Works*, 2: 101–102.
[123] Barnabe Rich, *The Honestie of this Age* (1614), ed. Thomas Wright (London: Percy Society, 1843), p. 115.
[124] *A Knights Coniuring*, ed. E. P. Rimbault (London: Percy Society, 1841) 5: 76–77.
[125] *The Works of Thomas Middleton*, ed. A. H. Bullen, (8 vols. rpt. New York: AMS Press, 1964), 8: 24–26.

The seriocomic mutterings of the dying Nashe lend vitality to this enfleshed ghost, who was in 1604 a living dead man. His "reeling words between drunk and sober" mock the devil as a knave even while they knavishly refigure London as a Utopian rogues' paradise. But the profound degradation of the scene registers the considerable cost of becoming the devil's correspondent and of playing, rhetorically, his advocate.

In demonstrating to the literary world what "immortallitie" has "to doe with mucke," Nashe adapted his literary manner to the perspective of the "despised and neglected" (1: 157) – to the prodigal Pierce Pennilesse, to the "infortunate" Jack Wilton, a former "appendix or page" to nobility; to the fugitive and author of the *Lenten Stuffe*; and ultimately to the persecuted Christ, "a mean-titled man" who "kept company with Publicans and sinners, the very out cast of the people ... but made all he spake or did preparatives to his Embassie" (2: 18). Like Christ, sent "to scrape on a dunghill for Pearle, where nothing will thrive but Toad-stooles," Nashe attempts to convert the dross of mundane London life to literary gold. Any man, Nashe notes, can "write in prayse of Vertue and the seuen Liberall Sciences, ... and fetch water out of the Thames; but [to] ... wring iuice out of a flint, thats Pierce a Gods name, and the right tricke of a workman" (*Lenten Stuffe*, 3: 151–152). For Nashe, such "quintessing" was not only a commercial enterprise but a heroic calling to the role of prophet in the age of print: "Moyses Strooke the Rock and water gusht out of it" (2: 23).

Yet this prophetic role was compromised by its necessarily transgressive exposure of the nature of traditional signifying practices, by its insistence "on the pre-emptive power of contingency" and on "the ascendancy of mercenary over ideal order" (Crewe, p. 26). Nashe's literary self-empowerment consequently took the form of isolation, pariahhood, and discursive exile. In robbing language of its innocence Nashe performed the guilty act that enabled but also tainted his project from the start; the self-proclaimed Messiah was implicitly a self-condemned rhetorical deviant.

Nashe's antagonism toward established authority and established modes of expression was intended to clear a new discursive space for the estateless wits of the London demimonde, literary prodigals who were in traditional terms "vnfitte for any calling in the Common wealth" (1: 37). In Nashe's view, the traditional authorities had failed to meet the moral challenge of a changing society. "Men are men," Nashe argued, "and with those thinges must bee moued, that men wont to be mooued." The moral significance of London's dynamic life needed to be probed "more searchingly than common Soule-Surgions acustome" (1: 80), but the degraded urban generation most fit to undertake this exploration was rejected by a power structure, patronage system, and economy that allowed "no wit nor courage." The hypocritical failure of the traditional authorities to address the actual experience of urban life accounted for the fact that "a great number had rather heare a iarring blacke-sant, than one of theyr balde Sermons" (*Christes Teares*, 2: 123).

The "extemporall veine" that Nashe commended over "our greatest Art-masters deliberate thoughts" in the Preface to *Menaphon* (1598) was thus defined in oppositional and transgressive relation to traditional morality and expression. The challenges of survival in the lively urban setting fostered, according to Nashe, a much needed rhetorical mobility: "a secular wit that hath liued all dayes of his life by *What doe you lacke?*" was "more iudiciall in matters of conceit then our most quadrant crepundios, that spit *ergo* in the mouth of euery one they meete" (3: 314–315). In keeping with this logic, Nashe staked his authority as writer, moralist, and urbanist on his own outlaw status – his prodigality, rebelliousness, and degraded professional career:

> I yeeld that I haue dealt vpon spare commodities of wine and capons, I haue sung George Gascoigne's Counter-tenor; what then? Wilt thou peremptorily define that it is a place where no honest man or Gentleman of credit ever came? Hear what I say; a Gentleman is neuer throughly entred into credit till he hath beene there; & that Poet or Nouice, be hee what he will, ought to suspect his wit, and remaine halfe in a doubt that it is not authenticall, till it hath beene seene and allow'd in vnthrifts consistory.
> *Grande doloris ingenium.* Let fooles dwell in no stronger houses than their Fathers built them, but I protest I should neuer haue writ passion(?) well, or beene a peece of a Poet, if I had not arriu'd in those quarters. (*Strange Newes*, 1: 310)

What such experience bestowed upon the writer was not only a measure of human sympathy but an anti-idealistic understanding of the ways in which language – a system for exchange and combination – is integrated with the material and social fabric of urban life. The dense materiality of Nashe's own language, his use of technical argot, popular idiom, base comparisons and original coinages – perhaps summed up in his own verb, to "palpabrize," (2: 115)[126] – reflects an unusually developed sensitivity to the material life and social practices in which language, ideas, and social structure originate.[127] At the heart of Nashe's

---

[126] Rhodes, *Elizabethan Grotesque*, pp. 25–26. I am much indebted to Rhodes' careful discussion of Nashe's style.

[127] Nashe perhaps epitomizes what L. C. Knights has called the way in which "Elizabethan prose reflects a way of living ... its language retained many more of the primitive functions of speech than are to be found after the seventeenth century. Not only was the

understanding of language and society are the pressures of commercial writing, "the exigences of the commercial press" (Crewe, pp. 25–26), which lay bare the ways in which language is a mobile and negotiable currency. Nashe's own improvisatory mode of verbal production – which extends, expands, modifies, and supplements the objective verbal order of "substantiues" – actually destabilizes that order by confronting it with the material life and practices in which it originates and for which it purports to provide the authoritative account. For Nashe, language does not embody truth but enacts the processes – of negotiating, exchanging, domineering, defying, cozening, cursing, and coercing – by which society is always being constituted.

Thriving on positionality, discord, and division, Nashe's penetration of the "too-to compound Cabalistic substance" (2: 80) of traditional morals and expression was thus profoundly oppositional and transgressive, at once a reforming and corrosive service to public life. In his most popular work, *Pierce Pennilesse*, which confesses that the transgressive writer "neuer comes to his answere before the offence be committed," Nashe creates for himself an authorial identity by offending society (1: 240–241). The greatest of Tom Nashe's Literary Offenses in this pamphlet was, in Harvey's words, to have played the "Diuels Oratour" (*Foure Letters*, p. 8), to have taken the devil as a patron and addressed to him a flattering praise in acknowledgment of his power.[128] By the logic of the paradoxical encomium, Nashe's *Supplication* is thus a praise and celebration of the seemingly indefensible – of the devil's domination of a world in change and of the wonderful opportunities this creates for the writer. From the world's fallenness Pierce Pennilesse extrapolates an urbane ethic appropriate to it – even if this means that "sooth and verity" as traditionally understood, must be sent to "walk melancholy in Marke Lane."

Based on the seven deadly sins, the *Supplication* reflects Nashe's typical preference for such native and often "literal" models of discourse as the sermon (*Christes Teares*), complaint (*Pierce Penilesse*), interlude (*Summer's Last Will and Testament*), and chronicle (*Lenten Stuffe, The Unfortunate Traveller*).[129] As a harangue on "the lamentable condition of our Times," the *Supplication* feigns to depart from the basic premise of

relation of word and thing, word and action, far more intimate ... a large number of Elizabethan words and phrases are the direct equivalent of action," Appendix A, "Elizabethan Prose," in *Drama and Society in the Age of Jonson* (1937; rpt. New York: Norton, 1968), pp. 305–306.   [128] Crewe, *Unredeemed Rhetoric*, p. 46.

[129] Ibid., passim.; Stephen S. Hilliard, *The Singularity of Thomas Nashe* (Lincoln: University of Nebraska Press, 1986), ch. 3, and Ann Rosalind Jones, "Inside the Outsider: Nashe's *The Unfortunate Traveller* and Bakhtin's Polyphonic Novel," *ELH*, 50 (1983), 61–81.

traditional complaint – that an ancient order of vertue and hospitality, when "the Yeomandry had beene better to passe" has been overturned and voided by an acquisitive anti-order that promotes "Carterly vpstarts" (1:159–160). But the *Supplication* finally maintains, in contrast to tradition, that "it argueth a very rusty witte, so to doate on worme-eaten Elde" (1:185). In fact, the urban, bourgeois, and acquisitive arch-villains in Piers' gallery are sinners not so much in the traditional, positive sense as in their relational opposition to the youthful, disillusioned generation of Piers, which their oppression has created. Envy, for example, is "a iolly lusty old Gentleman" who troubles "the streame, that Poets and good fellowes may [not] drinke" (1:183, 185). Wrath is a powerful "Iudge or a Iustice," an agelast deaf to Tarlton's jesting, a "great personage of the Court" who revenges comic insult, or a "dul-headed" divine who "holds them fantasticall fooles that haue wit" (1:187, 190, 192). "Master Diues" Gluttony is a London Magnifico whose greed forces "poor Scholers and Souldiers to wander in backe lanes and the out-shiftes of the Citie, with neuer a rag to their backes" (1:199, 200, 204).

The domination of the world by these ancient and hideous tyrants, moreover, is effected by the pompous authority of official language. Greedinesse is "attyrd in a Capouch of written parchment buttond doune before with Labels of wax," and his breeches are "bumbasted like Beerbarrels, with statute Marchants and forfeitures." Wrathful judges make "Newgate a Noune Substantiue" (1:187), while "sterne spirited Saturists" empower themselves with "domesticall Sermons" (1:192). Even London's wealthy Gluttons had rather "put vp a Supplication to the Parliament house, that they might haue a yard of pudding for a penie, than desire (with the Baker) there might be three ounces of bread sold for a halfe a penie" (1:202).

Viewing the social order as institutionalized rivalry and strife, Piers thus reinterprets the bipolar ethics of traditional complaint in positional terms. He does not advocate the traditional virtues, but engages a potentially ceaseless and ungrounded Oedipal rivalry[130] for possession of "Ladie London," this "great grandmother of Corporations, Madame Troynovant" (1:216, 181). Piers' demonic defense of the indefensible does not condemn the unstable grotesqueries of the mercenary age but welcomes them, provided that they do not empower "Sparage Gentlemen and chuff-headed Burghomasters" (1:174) but instead serve Piers' effort to "strip these golden asses out of their gay trappings" (1:242).

---

[130] Margaret Ferguson, "Nashe's *The Unfortunate Traveller*: The 'Newes of the Maker' Game," *ELR*, 11 (1981), 175.

Sin is thus merely a misappropriated ethical potential that Piers turns into personal virtue (1: 278). Drunkenness, for example, becomes the underworld virtue opposed to the in-law vice of gluttony, enabling a prodigal like Piers "to write admirable verses, and to have a deepe casting head, though he were neuer so verie a Dunce before" (1: 208).[131] Similarly, by contrast to the slothful stationer who monopolizes the printing trade, the "liuelie, wanton, yoong Gallant," he concludes, "is like to prooue the wiser man, and better member of the Common-wealth": he "haunts Plaies, & sharpens his wits with frequenting the company of Poets ... and lookes into all Estates by conuersing with them in publike places" (1: 210). The estatelessness of Piers and his like occasions a useful resentment and restlessness; it unsettles complacent "securitie, peace, quiet, tranquillitie: when we have no adversarie to prie into our actions, no malicious eye, whose pursuing our priuate behauior might make vs more uigilant ouer our imperfections then otherwise we would be" (1: 211).

The malicious "eye" of Piers thrives on adversity – in fact requires the preemptive domination of the world by the devil in order to derive his perspective and being. That domination takes the form of discursive contingency and freedom, the absoluteness of the always relative authority of anyone's word. Sinfulness and strife are no longer, as in traditional complaint, aberrancies or disfunctions of the normal social order; rather, they constitute that order and are intrinsic to its functioning. In concerning himself with this positional order and its functioning, Piers effects a transition from religious moralizing to satiric analysis, from allegory to "realism."[132]

By definition and from all time, then, the social order – epitomized in the city – is the devil's domain: "we maie with small labour cast our nets where we list: yet are we not so at our disposition, but that we are still commanded by Lucifer" (*Pierce Pennilesse*, 1: 229. cf. 1: 217). Hence Nashe's conjectural question in *The Terrors of the Night*: "if in one man a whole legion of diuells haue bin billeted, how manie hundred thousand legions retaine to a Terme at London?" (1: 349). In *Christes Teares*, London becomes a supercharged romance realm, a "seeded garden of sinne, the Sea that sucks in all the scummy channels of the Realme" (2: 158). The reading of this demonically changeful landscape requires the different temporal sense of the urban pamphlet, which is geared to thrive on the division and diversification of the familiar (Clark, p. 218 and

---

[131] Cf. *Preface to Menaphon, Works*, 3: 321–322.
[132] See, e.g., G. R. Hibbard, *Thomas Nashe* (Cambridge, Mass.: Harvard University Press, 1962), p. 71; Hillyard, *The Singularity of Thomas Nashe*, p. 87; Clark, *Elizabethan Pamphleteers*, pp. 66, 202, Rhodes, *Elizabethan Grotesque*, ch. 4.

passim). "Newe Herrings, new, wee must Crye, euery time wee make our selues publique, or else we shall be christened with a hundred newe tytles of Idiotisme" (pp. 191–192). As the devil's domain, the mercenary urban order helps to situate the pamphleteer in a new discursive economy. "Our wits now a daies", said Thomas Lodge, "are waxt verie fruitfull, and our Pamphleteers more than prodigall;... and euery corner is tooke vp with some or other pennilesse companion that will imitate any estate for a twopenny almes."[133] In this new enterprise, to "runne through the estates of our Citie" is to "play the worldling a while to please thee... What estate shall we deal with first?" Pamphleteering teaches "sinne in discoursing and discovering it."[134]

In *Christes Teares ouer Jerusalem*, Nashe connects the timely novelty of pamphleteering with the positionality of the social structure when he dedicates himself "to the prosternating and enforrowing the *frontiers* of sinnes" (2: 80) – to a portraiture of vice in its latest and most modern forms, at the interface or boundaries of contact, exchange, and domination that define an agonistic and competitive society:

the rich Cittizen swells against the pryde of the prodigall Courtier; the prodigall Courtier swels against the welth of the Cittizen. One Company swells against another, and seekes to intercept the gaine of each other: nay, not a Company but is deuided in it selfe. The auncients, they oppose themselues against the younger, & supresse them and keepe them doune all that they may. The yong men, they call them dotards, & swel and rage, and with many othes sweare on the other side, they will not be kepte vnder by such cullions, but goe good and neare to out-shoulder them. (2: 83–84)

Euery man heere in London is discontent with the state wherein hee lives. Euery one seeketh to vndermine another. No two of one trade, but as they are of one trade, enuy one another. Not two conioyned in one office, but ouerthwart & emulate one another. (2: 131–132)

In London, the ritch disdayne the poore. The Courtier the Cittizen. The Cittizen the Countriman. One Occupation disdayneth another. The Merchant the Retayler. The Retayler the Craftsman. The better sort of Craftsman the baser. The Shoomaker the Cobler, the Cobler the Carman. (2: 135)

In a devastating passage that had to be cancelled in the second edition, Nashe demonstrates that the crucial taxonomic terminology that distinguishes gentlemen and merchants (and thus defines the boundaries of the city within the social order) is in fact a purely positional terminology, an adversarial language of domination and abuse:

---

[133] *Scillaes Metamorphosis* (1589), in *Works*, 1: 4.
[134] Lodge, *Catharos. Diogenes in His Singularitie* (1591), *Works*, 2: 14, 95.

Is it not a common prouerbe amongst vs, when any man hath cosend or gone beyond vs, to say, Hee hath playde the Merchant with vs? But Merchants, they turne it another way, and say, Hee hath playd the Gentleman on them. The Snake eateth the Toode, and the Toode the Snaile. The Merchant eates vp the Gentleman, the Gentleman eats vp the Yeoman, and all three do nothing but exclaime one vpon another. (2: 159)

This is the mobile, relativized condition on which the heteroglot idiom of the marginalized urban writer thrives; for it unsettles the false settlement of the established order, voids its "too-to compounde Cabalisticall substance" and exposes it for the arbitrary construct that it is. Evil is essentially rootless, as Nashe's circular logic repeatedly insists. Only the mobilized, secular morality of the urban pamphleteer can penetrate the "damnable paradox" that connects material and discursive practices, the "vnder-hand cloaking of bad actions with Common-wealth pretences".[135] The core of this paradox is the mutual support of wealth and doctrine, or what Nashe calls Abundance and Atheism. Atheism is "the roote that nourisheth all the branches of security" (2: 122) and yet "Tis nothing but plenty and abundance that makes men Atheists"(2: 120). Sheltered by patronage and the isolation of university life, the educated ministers sent up to London for occasional preaching "are not halfe so wel acquainted as them that liue continually about the Court and Citty, how many followers this damnable paradox hath" (2: 122). Preachers and traditional moralists merely "fitte vs with a cheape religion ... being covetous your selues, you preach nothing but covetous doctrine" (2: 107). By contrast, Nashe's own racy idiom, with its "humaine Metaphors and similitudes" (2: 128), its "puft vp stile" and "prophane eloquence"(2: 183), turns the bottom of the social order – the urban underbelly – to God's purposes:

Hee which out of the barrainest and basest parts of his Lords dominion shall accumulate and leuy to his Treasury a greater tribute then he hath out of his richest Prouinces, shall hee not (of all other) doe him the most remunerablest seruice? (2: 128)

The precondition for this liberating manner is the freedom of exchange provided by the professional literary marketplace, a freedom that Nashe celebrates in *Nashes Lenten Stuffe* (1599). Dedicated "neither to rich, noble, right worshipfull, or worshipfull, of spirituall or temporall," but to the "capering humour" (3: 149) of Nashe's prandial companion, the hack-writer Humphrey King, Nashe's mock-praise of the bourgeois town of Yarmouth constructs a Utopian civilization of free exchange

---

[135] *Pierce Pennilesse*, in *Works*, 1: 220.

around the professional writer's ironized word. Like all paradoxical encomia, Nashe's is a seriocomic effort to transvalue values – to "wring iuice out of a flint," find "remedies of tosted turues against famine" (3: 152, 178), and otherwise extract a plenitude from the world's dearth. Having written himself into exile from London, Nashe re-discovers in provincial Yarmouth the simple but invaluable commodity that is both the red herring and the seriocomic word.

"So fast and weather-beaten that it hath nowe no anchor-holde left to cleaue vnto," Nashe's personal condition is identical with the original state of Yarmouth itself, "which, hauing but as it were a welte of land, or as M. Camden cals it, *lingulam terrae*, a little tong of the earth, betwixte it and the wide Maine," nevertheless "sticks not to mannage armes and hold his owne vndefeasably against the vniuersall vnbounded empery of surges" (3: 157). In the "Chronographycal Latine table, which they haue hanging vp in their Guildhall," Nashe discovers his "Sea-Rutter," a time/table by which to reconstruct Yarmouth's seriocomic Genesis – the "apostacie of the sands from the yalping world," and the migrations of "whole tribes of males and females" who "bargd it thither, to build and inhabite" (3: 163). The history reconstructed from this table is a pattern of "ebbs and flowes," of constant spatio-temporal movement, so that Yarmouth's Alpha is not its Omega (3: 160). The constant changes and displacements of history force Nashe to stick by Yarmouth, abandoning the "Profligated labor" of a larger survey of all coastal towns, which would demand too much "reuoluing meditation and raueling out... (as raueling out signifies Penelopes *telam retextere*, the vnweauing of a webbe before wouen and contexted)" (3: 168).

The text woven by Nashe himself praises an "Elizian... habitation" for the "common good it communicates to the whole state" (3: 169). That good is the system of exchange Yarmouth generates, even from the time of the town's first enclosure against an elemental chaos, when "thronging theaters of people... hiued thither about the selling of fish and Herring... and there built their sutlers booths and tabernacles, to canopie their heades from the rhewme of the heauens, or the clouds dissoluing Cataracts" (3: 162). Yarmouth's constitution reflects this original freedom of exchange:

All common wealths assume their prenominations for their common diuided weale, as where one man hath not too much riches, and another man too much pouertie... To this *Commune bonum* (or every horse his loafe) Yarmouth in propinquity is as the buckle to the thong, and the next finger to the thumbe; not that it is sibbe or cater-cousins to any mungrel *Democratia*, in which one is all, & all is one, but that in her, as they are not al one, so one or two there pockets not vp all the peeces. (3: 168)

The foundation of this glorious civilization – "if there be any plentifull world, it is in Yarmouth" (3: 171) – is the humble, Lenten food, the red-herring or stockfish:

Doe but conuert... the slenderest twinckling reflexe of your eie-sight to this flinty ringe that engirtes it, these toured walles, port-callized gates, and gorgeous architectures that condecorate and adorne it, and then preponder of the red herrings priority and prevalence, who is the onely vnexhaustible mine that hath raised and begot all this. (3: 174)

From "the red herings priority" comes all the glory of Yarmouth, a Utopian community that rivals London itself; it "empals our sage senatours or Ephori in princely scarlet as pompous ostentyue as the Vinti quater of Lady Troynovant" (3: 175). The red herring is both the generator of circulation and the medium of communication; on the foreign exchange it brings in "a great deale of goode trash," it augments her Majesty's tributes and customs, and it increases England's famous navigation in unpathed waters (3: 180). And yet the essential value of the herring is its lack of value, its use as a food of Lenten denial, which in turn gives meaning to Carnival and plenitude: it is but the "shooing horne for a pinte of wine ouer-plus" (3: 184). Its very worthlessness, then, makes it the quintessential object and medium of desire. "Our dapper Piemont Haldrick Herring... draweth more barkes to Yarmouth bay, then [Helen's] beautie did to Troy" (3: 185). It is so desired that in "droues the gouty bagd Londoners hurry down and die the watchet aire of an yron russet hue with the dust that they raise in hot spurd rowelling it on to perform compliments vnto him" (3: 186). Worthless until "gilded" by smoking, the red herring becomes a "true flying fish... because he is so portable" (3: 192). There is an "inlinked consanguinitie twixt him and Lady Lucar" (3: 44). He is "euery mans money" (3: 179).

As a figure for all media of exchange – currency, language, marketplace – the herring negotiates between lack and plenitude, desire and fulfill-ment; he makes and unmakes gods. Contrary to what mythographers maintain, the tyrant Dionysus did not strip the golden coat from an idol of Jupiter but ate the golden herring that had been set up in Jupiter's stead. A god who can be uncrowned and eaten, the herring is yet an ever-renewable divinity, for "so revengefull a iust Iupiter is the red Hering" that shortly afterwards Dionysus was chased from his throne "to become a frowning pedant or schoolemaster" (3: 194).[136] The herring is elected king of the world of fish because if he ever aspires to tyranny he can be

---

[136] For this point, as for my reading of *Lenten Stuffe* in general, I am indebted to Bristol, *Carnival and Theater*, ch. 6.

easily deposed. And yet he has, in all his humility, the power to raise an unholy, demystifying stink in the Papal chambers.

Whatever the proverbial status of the red herring in his time, Nashe was perfectly aware that "to draw on hounds to a sent, to a redde hering skinne there is nothing comparable" (3 : 221).[137] And so he represents the ironies of his own professional writing in the

ieast of a Scholler in Cambridge, that standing angling on the toune bridge there, as the country people on the market day passed, secretly bayted his hook wyth a red Herring with a bell about the necke, and so conveying it into the water that no man perceived it, all on the sodayn, when he had a competent throng gathered about hym, vp he twicht it agayne, and layd it openly before them; whereat the gaping rurall fooles, driuen into no lesse admiration than the common people about London some few yeares since were at the bubbling of Mooreditch, sware by their christendomes that, as many dayes and yeeres as they had liued, they neuer sawe such a myracle of a red hering taken in the fresh-water before … Let them looke to themselues as they will, for I am theirs to gull them better than euer I haue done; and this I am sure, I haue distributed gudgeon dole amongst them, as Gods plenty as any stripling of my slender portion of witte, farre or neere. (3 : 212–213)

At the same time, however, the deceptive gudgeon dole of which Nashe boasts is a golden gift. Its uncrowning nonsense, like the worthless herring, is a portable, valuable commodity that can generate a market of free exchange and give true measure: "for doo but rubbe a kanne or quarte pot round about the mouth wyth it … the beere shal neuer foame or froath in the cupp, whereby to deceyve men of their measure" (3 : 221). A great prandialist and debunking enemy of the foam or froth by which men are defrauded of good measure, Nashe chooses to fish the fresh, inland waters that are *his* red herrings' domain. The professional writer and the urban waters in which he fishes, Nashe implies, are as little regarded by the contemporary world as were fishermen and the sea by ancient poets. Plautus labelled fishermen mere "hungerstarued gubbins or offales of men," and Ovid regarded the sea as "a slippery companion … a place like Hel, good for nothing but to perish periurers" (3 : 225). But as Nashe notes, the fishermen hitherto neglected by poets "are the predecessors of the Apostles … for your seeing wonders in the deepe, you must be the sonnes heires of the Prophet Ionas." After *Nashes Lenten Stuffe*, they will also be this degraded poet's boon companions and the feisty defenders of *his* "hungerstarued Muse," ready to lash and hew about them "when you heere mee mangled and torne in mennes mouthes about this playing with a shettlecocke, or tossing empty bladders in the air" (3 : 225).

[137] Hibbard, *Thomas Nashe*, p. 237.

Cony-catching: anatomy of anatomies

I cannot but wonder master R. G. what Poeticall fury made you so fantasticke, to write against Cony-catchers? Was your braine so barraine that you had no other subiect? or your wittes so dried with dreaming of loue Pamphlettes, that you had no other humour left, but satirically with Diogenes, to snarl at all mens manners: You neuer founde in Tully nor Aristotle, what a setter or a verser was.[138]

Whether Cuthbert Cunny-Catcher is the creation of Robert Greene or of some unknown contemporary,[139] his question is central to Greene's cony-catching enterprise. In fact, the very existence of such a fiction-alized rogue reader as Cuthbert is a partial indication of the motives behind Greene's project, an extended apologia and example of the powers of fiction-making. As Greene himself hints more than once, the fictional artistry of these pamphlets at once conceals and flaunts its actual intentions.

The most explicit motive is the same one that underlies Greene's many published repentances: the cony-catching pamphlets turn Greene's personal degradation into a public service. The models for this project are not the straight-faced classical preceptors, Aristotle and Tully, but those classical ironists whose discursive wisdom was wedded to the demonstrative pattern of their lives. To be sure, the names Greene actually cites for precedent – Socrates, Diogenes, Ovid, Horace, Mar-tial[140] – are not so much peripheral as central to the ironized classicism favored by Elizabethans. But in Greene's understanding they are not simply penitents, but subversives who challenge classical orthodoxies by putting them to the test of experience. This is why they serve as guiding lights to Greene's innovative efforts to resituate writing in relation to the streets of London, to transform the social taxonym of "gentleness" into a moral attribute available to himself and the range of his readers, and to

---

[138] "Cuthbert Cunny-catcher," *The Defence of Cony Catching, Or a Confutation of Those Two Iniurious Pamphlets Published by R. G.* (1592), *Works*, 11: 50.

[139] Greene's authorship of the *Defence* is disputed by C. E. Saunders, *PMLA*, 48 (1933), 392ff. and by I. A. Shapiro, "An Unexpected Earlier Edition of *The Defence of Conny-Catching*," *The Library*, 3rd series 18 (1963), 88–112. Greene's authorship is defended by E. H. Miller, "Further Notes on the Authorship of 'The Defence of Cony-Catching' (1592)," *N&Q*, 97 (1952), 446–451; Daniel Parker, "Robert Greene and 'The Defence of Conny Catching,'" *N&Q*, n.s. 21 (1974), 87–89; and David Margolies, *Novel and Society in Elizabethan England* (London: Croom Helm, 1985), p. 134.

[140] Diogenes "from a counterfait Copier of money, became a currant corrector of manners," and "Socrates age was vertuous though his prime was licentious," *A Notable Discouery, Works*, 10: 5. Greene's is "the reformation of a second Ovid," and Greene will "with Horace sit downe & dine with his satyres"; Horace "writ wanton Poems, yet the grauest embraced his Odes, and his Satyres. Marcial had many lasciuious verses, yet none rejected his honest sentences," *Greenes Mourning Garment* (1590/1616), *Works*, 9: 121, 124, 221.

reappropriate the pieties of humanism for a viable urbanism. In half-comic parody of Scaeuola, who demonstratively mutilated his own hand to save Rome from Porsenna, Greene confesses that if his self-humiliating *Mourning Garment* "could *make a man ciuill*, what care I, though I ... deliuered preceptes out of tubbe?"[141] As Greene's imitator Dekker later put it, the indecorous underworld is "drawne to the life, of purpose that life might be drawne from it."[142]

The repentance pamphlets which accompany the cony-catching pamphlets trace an arc of moral development through which prodigality humanizes the soul as it becomes increasingly identified with the base pursuits of popular pamphlet and theatrical writing.[143] Greene's early *Mourning Garment* (1590) is a conventional prodigal son tale, except for the attention it lavishes on the hero's degradation in the city's "consuming labyrinth" (*Works*, 9: 178); but Greene's *Neuer Too Late* (1590) and its sequel valorize the degradation of the prodigal hero, whose experience takes him from bourgeois responsibility and domestic bliss to dissipation in the "Laborynth" of Troynovant. As Greene's prodigal hero falls "in amongst a companie of Players," and sees "a meanes to mittigate ye extremitie of his want," he thinks "it no dishonour to make gaine by wit, or to get profite by his pen" (8: 33, 104, 129). The thinly disguised "Roberto" of the *Groats-worth of Witte* (1592), "famozed for an Arch-paimaking-poet," and fallen "to a low ebbe," converts his filial errors into paternal wisdom as he bequeathes his ten commandments to the world. Roberto's moral bequest to the world has conspicuously economic underpinnings. He devises his project only as he looks upon his last groat: "O now it is too late, too late to buy witte with thee: and therefore will I see if I can sell to carelesse youth what I negligently forgot to buy" (12: 137). This is not to say, however, that his decalogue – "remember those that want," "Oppresse no man," "Beware of building thy house to thy neighbours hurt" – is fraudulent. Rather, the economic motive purges the repentence and conversion of naivety, emphasizing the liberating consciousness of the world's fraudulence to which Roberto comes in the not coincidental company of rogues and playwrights:

[141] *Works*, 9: 220; Scaeuola is cited in *The Second Part of Conny-catching*, *Works*, 10: 67.
[142] *The Belman of London* (1609), in *Non-Dramatic Works*, 3: 67.
[143] The arc is not as smooth as it might be: *Greene's Mourning Garment* was registered November 20, 1590, while *Greene's Neuer Too Late*, dated 1590 by its title page, was apparently not registered; the authorship of Greene's *Groats-worth of Witte* (1592), moreover, is disputed. For arguments against Greene's authorship, see Saunders, "Robert Greene and His 'Editors,'" and the work of Warren B. Austin, as reported by Louis Marder, "Greene's Attack on Shakespeare: A Posthumous Hoax?" *Shakespeare Newsletter*, 16: 4 (1966), 29–30, and Austin, "The Posthumous Greene Pamphlets," *Shakespeare Newsletter*, 16: 5–6 (1966), 45.

His companie were lightly the lewdest persons in the land, apt for *pilferie,*
periurie, forgerie or any great villanie ... By these he learned legerdemaines of
nips, foysters, connicatchers, crossbyters, lifts, high Lawyers, and all the rabble
of that vncleane generation of vipers: *and pithily could he paint out their whole*
courses of craft. (12: 134–135; italics mine)

The scandal of the scribbling profession – its immersion in the fraudulence of theater, marketplace, and "common haunted places" (10: 207)
– is thus the basis for the special authority with which Greene addresses
the world.

Greene's prodigal descent to the world of rogues and players enables
him to expose the dynamics of credit and credibility in the urban
marketplace. Greene explains that it was only "after I had ... driuen my
selfe out of credit with sundry of my frends" that "I became the Author
of Playes, and a penner of Loue Pamphlets, so that I soon grew famous in
that qualitie, that who for trade growne so ordinary about London as
Roben Greene?" (12: 173). The undoing of the socially creditable Robert
is thus the making of the morally credible Robin Greene, an outlaw
author, Tarltonesque bedevilling goblin, and discursive Robin Hood.

It is frequently remarked that Greene's cony-catching pamphlets
rapidly evolve from reportage to more palpable fiction.[144] As Greene
gradually abandons the elaborate taxonomical and lexical apparatus of
underworld sociology he turns to "merry jests" and eventually to the
voices of the rogues themselves, who criticize and threaten Greene,
defend themselves, and, in the cases of Ned Browne and Nan the
prostitute, narrate their own adventures. This supplanting of the official
sobriety of taxonomy with the gay deceptions of fiction corresponds to
Greene's movement from an in-law to an outlaw point of view, to a
deepening recognition that the structures, beliefs, and practices which
govern social interaction are themselves constituted by mutual investment, confidence, and credit.[145]

Greene's urbanism, based on the dynamics of fiction-making, thus
tends (in the name of orthodoxy) toward a transformation of orthodox

---

[144] Normand Berlin, for example, notes that Greene "progressively moves away from the
presentation of direct information for the sake of cleansing England to a presentation
of picaresque narrative for its own sake," *The Base String,* pp. 25–26; see also J. C.
Jordan, *Robert Greene* (New York: Columbia University Press, 1915), pp. 109–117,
and Clark, *Elizabethan Pamphleteers,* pp. 50–55. A refreshing exception to the general
pattern is Virginia L. Macdonald, who argues that from the beginning Greene writes
fiction with the serious purpose of exploring "the hypocrisy of reputable society,"
"Robert Greene's Innovative Contributions to Prose Fiction in *A Notable Discovery,*"
Shakespeare Jahrbuch (Weimar), 117 (1981), 127–137.

[145] Agnew, *Worlds Apart,* thus regards the rise of cony-catching literature as part of the
"crisis of representation" accompanying the proliferation of market practices; see esp.
pp. 60, 67–68.

moralizing into what Bakhtin has called the strain of "novelness," the force of discursive heterogeneity that opens a closed environment to new possibilities of exchange and combination:

Opposed to the *lie of pathos* accumulated in the language of all recognized and structured professions, social groups and classes, there is not straightforward truth (pathos of the same kind) but rather a gay and intelligent deception, a *lie* justified because it is directed precisely at *liars*. Opposed to the language of priests and monks, kings and seigneurs, knights and wealthy urban types, scholars and jurists – to the language of all who hold power and who are well set up in life – there is the language of the merry rogue, wherever necessary parodically reprocessing any pathos, but always in such a way as to rob it of its power to harm.[146]

It is obvious that even while they mirror the other social anatomies of the period, the taxonomies of rogues, from Awdeley and Harman to Greene and Dekker, are also analogous in their techniques to those of popular drama and that through these analogies they underline the theatrical nature of social reality. Dekker, for example, notes that cony-catchers have a "kind of Play of theirs, they call the Barnards Law. To act which Knauish Comedy of Wily-Beguily, 5. Persons are required, and those are, 1. The Taker, 2. The Cozen, 3. The Verser, 4. The Barnard, 5. The Rutter ... The Stage on which [the Rutter] playes the Prologue, is either in Fleetstreete, the Strond, or in Poules, and most commonly in the afternoone."[147] When Greene writes of "a Foist *performed* in Paules" (10: 114) he evokes a commonplace of Elizabethan thought – the *theatrum mundi* – to analogize the deceptions practiced in all walks of life by "those who, though they kept on the right side of the law, most of the time indulged in activities whose spirit and nature were very much akin to those of the acknowledged underworld."[148] Rogues are by necessity actors who hold up a most unflattering mirror to in-law society. "Like as law, when the terme is truely considered, signifieth ye ordinance of good men," Greene observes, so bad men have "a multititude of hateful rules, as it were in learning" (10: 33).

If it is obvious that the taxonomy of the underworld anatomizes the rest of society, it is perhaps less obvious that it also anatomizes the cony-catching genre itself. The anatomy of the most basic and pervasive of all underworld tricks, Barnard's Law, not only provides a synoptic plotline for the narratives which illustrate it; it also glosses the fictional dynamics

---

[146] "Discourse in the Novel," in *The Dialogic Imagination*, ed. Michael Holquist (Austin: University of Texas Press, 1981), pp. 401–402.

[147] *The Belman of London*, in *Non-Dramatic Works*, 3: 125–126.

[148] Gamini Salgado, *The Elizabethan Underworld* (1977; rpt. Gloucester: Alan Sutton, 1984), p. 47.

of the crime reporter's entire project. The pamphleteer shares with other rogues the practice of gaining the confidence of his dupes by warning them in advance of the "villanies and knaueries in his owne profession" (10: 179). One such warning is the compensation for profligacy Greene's pamphlets repeatedly profess. But another is Greene's freeze-frame anatomy of Barnard's Law.

Barnard's Law is the first ruse Greene analyzes in his earliest work; the version of it described in the earliest of all English crime pamphlets, Gilbert Walker's *Manifest Detection* (1552), is what Greene calls "cony-catching," and it remains the archetypal underworld deception for all later writers.[149] As Greene explains, it is an art "many yeeres agoe ... put in vse ... wherein as in the Arte of Cunny-catching, foure persons were required to perfourm their coosning commodity. The taker-vp, the Verser, the Barnard and the Rutter" (10: 9–10). These four roles resemble strikingly the roles required for Greene's own fictional strategy in the pamphlets. "The Taker vp," who first hooks the victim, is a worldly sophisticate who "seemeth a skilful man in al things, who hath by long trauell learned without Booke a thousand pollicies to insinuate himself into a man's acquaintance" (10: 10). Such personal experience is precisely the ground on which Greene defends his own credibility just four pages earlier when he remarks, "To be briefe, Gentlemen, I haue seen the world and rounded it, though not with trauell, yet with experience" (10: 6). The Verser, however, next gains the victim's confidence by feigning to be "a man of more worshippe then the Taker vp, and hee hath the countenance of a landed man" (10: 10). This is the man who feigns hearty country manners and neighborly concern – in short, the reformed, public-spirited, honest Greene who claims "I am English borne and I haue English thoughts" (10: 6), the noble Scaeuola who thinks "no pains nor danger too great that groweth to the benefit of my countrie" (10: 69). The pivotal figure in the trick is its namesake, the Barnard or fake victim, a seeming loser who actually holds all the cards. This is the victimized Greene, maligned by critics for his base style and matter (10: 71), threatened by the crooks he exposes (10: 90–91),

---

[149] *A Manifest Detection of the Most Vile and Detestable Vse of Dice-Play*, in A. V. Judges, ed., *The Elizabethan Underworld* (London: George Routledge & Sons, 1930), p. 47. Strictly speaking, in Greene's version, Barnard's Law ("a drunken cosenage by cards") differs from Cony-Catching Law ("cosenage by cards," 10: 37) in that it adds to cony-catching (which Walker called Barnard's Law) a fourth conspirator, the Rutter, or ruffian, who creates the diversionary scuffle that enables his companions to escape. As I argue below, this final diversion is a significant addition on Greene's part; but otherwise Frank Aydelotte is correct in saying that between the two laws "there is really little difference," *Elizabethan Rogues and Vagabonds* (Oxford: Clarendon Press, 1913), p. 89.

physically attacked "in the Saint Iohns head within Ludgate" (10: 236) – the Greene who nonetheless uses his suffering and degradation to underwrite his authority and gain his readers' confidence. As Dekker later explained, "the Bernard is the chiefe Player, for hee counterfets many parts in one, and is now a drunken man, anon in another humour, and shifts himselfe into so many shapes, onely to blind the Cosen, and to feede him with more delight, the more easily to beguile him" (3: 126). This is an atavistic version of the Vice, the luminary–liminary empowered by his underworld connections, the part Greene shares with cony-catchers, the putative victims in the game of pamphleteering.

The final part belongs to the Rutter (or rubber), the low-life ruffian who stages a distracting scuffle as the final diversionary tactic that will seal the game's success. This figure, Greene's own creation, is a simulacrum of Greene the diverting jester and raconteur, indeed, of the diversion and diversionary tactics of fiction itself. It has been noted that like other kinds of seriocomic prose, underworld pamphlets – perhaps because of their heterogeneous nature – tend to have problems with closure.[150] It is taken as a sign of these difficulties that Greene, Nashe, and Dekker all typically conclude their pamphlets with a jest. Greene's earliest crime pamphlet concludes with such a diversion ("Now Gentlemen by your leaue, and heare a merry iest," 10: 38), and the tendency of their sequels to merge more and more fully with jest-book tradition is taken by many as a sign that the whole genre is not serious but diverting. However, the failure to appreciate the seriousness of Greene's diverting jests is a failure to see in his anatomy of fiction the extent to which fictional "diversion" is a serious de-railing of more priviledged forms of discourse, a low-life "roughing up" of monological structures that yields a more heterogeneous urbanism. Even Thomas More, whose *Utopia* was driven by a humanist's desire to rationalize the city, turned in his later works to the tradition of merry jests to epitomize the common life. Greene's tendency to give his cony-catching project over more and more conspicuously to fictional diversions may be seen as a groping toward the ultimately diverted and diverting form of the heteroglossal novel.

It remains in this little allegory to identify the fifth man of Barnard's Law, to whom Dekker gives the name of "the Cozen." The obvious candidates are "the young Gentlemen, Marchants, Apprentices, Farmers, and plain Countreymen" – the audience invariably inscribed on the title-pages of these works. The fiction, in other words, is that the

[150] Clark, *Elizabethan Pamphleteers*; Rhodes, *Elizabethan Grostesque*; on Dekker, Marie-Thérèse Jones-Davies, *Un peintre de la vie londonienne : Thomas Dekker* (2 vols. Paris: Didier, 1958), 2: 124.

audience of cony-catching pamphlets are themselves conies who live in fear of the unclassified tramp and who stake their honesty on their adherence to the roles dictated by a social order that is already discredited, not only by its parody in the taxonomy of rogues, but also by its dissolution into the single, total readership declared on the title-page. The existence of this heteroglot readership implicitly acknowledges the power of the city to attract and reconstitute classes, estates, and professions. And it acknowledges the writer's power to assist this process with the help of print and literacy. In contrast to such sober dupes, the professional writer and the cony-catcher share an understanding of their own, more intense, estatelessness. Both are – in a frequently repeated formula – men "about London," who "liue Gentleman-like of them-selues, hauing neythere money nor Lande, nor any lawfull meanes to maintain them."[151] One of Greene's major strategies was to have transformed the reporter's status, to have replaced the sober magistrate, Thomas Harman, arch-persecutor and taxonomist of rogues, with the degraded professional writer. This enabled the reporter to share many traits with his specimens, among them a fluency in the argot of street, tavern, and alley. But the most striking resemblance is the ability to parlay estatelessness into authority, in short, a social competence or versatility that is not simply a parody but a realistic reconstitution of the encyclopedic ideals of humanism. It is true of both rogue and urban writer that "there is no Arte but he will haue a superficiall insight into, and put downe euerie man with talke"; this souped-up version of the logophiliac ethos is perhaps epitomized in the raffish *uomo universale* Ned Browne, whose many talents include the manufacture of high-explosive letter-bombs.[152]

This simultaneous exploding and exploiting of literalism is what makes the cony-catching pamphlet – even more than its subject-matter – the perfect scam. Both cony-catcher and writer profess to read the urban populace, to "interpret their conceipts, and...decipher their qualities," to behold people "a farre off...and to know their qual-lities."[153] In view, however, of the unreliability of conventional cate-gories, the reading is always done in the conditional mood, and it must always be prepared to improvise in response to contingency. Cony-catchers devise "their methods...according to the man they aim at." Given the writer's similar method, the potential for comic escalation of

---

[151] *The Blacke Bookes Messenger* (1592), in *Works*, 11: 29; cf. *A Notable Discouery*, *Works*, 10: 40, and S. R., *Greenes Ghost Haunting Conie-Catchers* (1602), sig. B3.

[152] *The Blacke Bookes Messenger*, *Works*, 11: 28–29; cf. *Greenes Ghost*, sig. B3.

[153] *A Notable Discouery*, 10: 6; Dekker, *Lanthorne and Candlelight*, in *Non-Dramatic Works*, 3: 180.

the game's complexity is immense. As Greene's most avid readers, his cony-catcher adversaries become locked with him in an ever-spiralling pattern of reading and retaliation. "Impouerished by the late editions of their secret villanies," they devise "new methods how to fetch in their Connies and to play their prankes" (10: 88–89); they even secure, Greene complains, "a scholler ... to make an inuectiue against me ... in disparagement of *my credit*."[154] The counter-measures required of Greene make cony-catching – both invisible (Greene does not concern himself with the more visible half of the tradition, vagabondage) and protean – the perfect subject for professional writing:

> If I shoulde spend many sheets in deciphering their shifts, it were friuelous, in that they be many, and full of variety: for euery day they inuent new tricks, and such queint deuices as are secret, yet passing dangerous, that if a man had Argus eyes, he could scant prie into the bottom of their practices. (10: 35)

The stable, vertical orientation of the social taxonomy is thus turned on its side to yield a proliferation of quasi-theatrical roles unfolding in an open-ended temporality. Like the marketplace, geared to daily shifts in prices, the tempo of "news" is that of perpetual crisis. The reading of the urban underbelly is thus "news" that must be constantly updated to encompass matters earlier "past ouer, vtterlie vntoucht" or matters never "till this yeare discouerd."[155] The fixed, objective terms of social description give way to the hucksterish argot of destabilizing comparatives and superlatives; the constantly updated supplements attempt to fill an essential vacancy with "a third, and more necessarie part (10: 144), with things "neuer heard of in any of the former bookes" (11: 3), with "more strange villanies than euer were till this yeare discouerd."[156]

In one sense, this deepening of the world's opacity contradicts the promise to penetrate it with an interpretive key, "to acquaint you with the signification of the termes, in a Table" (10: 34), or to make the world negotiable by drawing "forth a perfect Map."[157] Yet the "perfect Map" Dekker's in-law Belman draws is based upon what turns out to be an outlaw devil's account of his "Iland voyage" through London's streets. The overlap between the voices of the Belman and the devil in *Lanthorne and Candlelight* is in fact part of the larger difficulty of overcoding a map onto a realm that asks to be experienced as a fictionally unfolding labyrinth.[158]

[154] 10: 101; italics mine. The "scoller" is quite possibly Greene himself, but see note 139 above.   [155] Greene, 10: 67; Dekker, 3: 173.
[156] Dekker, 3: 175. The destablizing effect of marketplace comparatives is discussed in Bakhtin, *Rabelais and His World*, p. 170.
[157] Dekker, *Lanthorne and Candlelight*, in *Non-Dramatic Works*, 3: 302.
[158] Greene remarks that Troynovant "is to young Gentlemen, like the Laborinth, whereout Theseus could not get without a Threed, here be such Minotaures as first deuour the threed." *Greenes Neuer Too Late*, 8: 104.

The project of mapping the labyrinth is thus a thin excuse for sailing "the black shore of mischiefe" and exploring the suburban "caues, where monsters are bred vp to deuoure the Cities them-selues."[159]

It is, then, worth bearing in mind again that Greene associates the diversionary "roughing up" of his terminal jests with the Rutter's scuffle that turns the trick in Barnard's Law. A favored device for beginning this scuffle is to drop a key. Greene himself lets fall the key to his own project when he explains that cony-catchers always warn their victims before they ensnare them. Greene illustrates the point with the story of a cony-catcher, masking as a gentleman in St. Paul's, who relates to his chosen victim "a very solemne tale of villanies and knaueries in his profession": "a very especiall friend of mine," he explains, was robbed even though he had hidden his gold watch closely on his person. The present victim naively reveals how much better his own gold chain is hidden on his person, whereupon the cony-catcher bids farewell, returns disguised, and "let[s] fall a keie," which precipitates the struggle in which the victim is robbed. This story merits attention, the cony-catching Greene confides to his unwary readers, for the gentleman robbed "is my very good friend" (10: 175–180). The key to Greene's project, then, is the diversionary roughing-up accomplished on the occasion of its putative provision of a sober, taxonomic key to the underworld. Yet this roughing-up is also a way of getting at valuables without a key, and it has analogies with the art of picking locks, the Black Art which Greene illustrates in an autobiographical narrative. In order "to haue an insight" into the art, Greene invited a picklock to "my Chambers":

I shewed him my Deske, and asked him if he could pick that little lock that was so well warded ... and ere I had turned fiue times, his hand was refling in my Deske very orderly. I wondred at it, and thought verily that the Deuill and his Dam was in his fingers. (10: 129)

Yet as Dekker later explained, this simple trick "is not that Black Art, by which men coniure up Spirits, and raise Diuels in Circles ... but ... to fetch away money where it lies" (*The Belman of London*, 3: 137). Greene's own artistry is not so much akin the the devil's as to the boasting Ned Browne's: "The most expert and skilfull Alchumist, neuer tooke more pains in experience of his mettals, the Phisition in his simples, the Mechanicall man in the mysteries of his occupation, than I haue done in plotting precepts, rules, axiomes, and principles" (*The Blacke Bookes Messenger*, 11: 20). In "plotting Plaies," Nashe was to recall, Greene "was his craftes master" (3: 132), but it is Greene's creation, the master-plotter and illusionist Ned Browne, who claims to be "the first that

---

[159] Dekker, *The Belman of London*, 3: 65; *Lanthorne and Candlelight*, 3: 267.

inuented the letting fall of the key" (*The Blacke Bookes Messenger*, 11: 23).

The roughing-up of Greene's diverting jests – of his whole project – is the aggression his fictions inflict on orthodoxy. It consists in part of an increasingly explicit preference for the relatively more knowing and less harmful deceptions of cony-catchers over the more vicious and unconscious hypocrisies of their victims. The poetic justice that gives cony-catchers their comeuppance in the early *Notable Discouery* has already become, in *The Second Part*, a comic aggression against such conventional butts as millers, haberdashers, mercers, goldsmiths, lawyers, scriveners, and vain women. By the third part, given over wholly to merry tales, the victims are those who stand on and exploit their status – an "honest Citizen" who falsely accuses and imprisons his maid (who subsequently dies in her cell) in order to assuage his ill feelings, a "gentle" lawyer to country clients who attempts to coax a whore to his chamber, a gentleman given to "rash pride and simple credulitie," a broker "cunningly ouerreached by as craftie a knaue as himselfe" (10: 155–160, 175, 185). Still later, the victims of Ned Browne and Nan – cross-biters both – are by definition moral hypocrites. Much of the subversive power of these tales lies in their encouragement of the reader to "imagine himself as the robber,"[160] the figure who, as Dekker says, "stands vpon both Wit and Manhood" (*Belman*, 3: 150). And the endings of the tales occasion release by reducing social difference to ethical sameness. But perhaps the greatest subversion lies in the raising of tensions by the wary, confrontational readings and counter-readings of motive and status that occupy the body of the jest. If the typical conclusion of the jests is a triumph for coherence and cohesion – for the solidarity of perpetrator and victim in crime, the body of the jests is commonly a scene of social conflict, entanglement, or disorientation.[161] They turn on awkward,

---

[160] "Stories of successful cheats [are] 'mery' because the reader imagines himself as the robber," William Empson, *Some Versions of Pastoral* (1938; rpt. New York: New Directions, 1974), p. 57. See also Brian Gibbons' view that the cony-catching pamphleteer "invites his readers to enjoy, vicariously, the pleasures of knavery, and then to enjoy the pleasure of self-righteous condemnation of it," "A Minor Genre: The Coney-Catching Pamhlet," Appendix 2 in *Jacobean City Comedy* (2nd edn. London: Methuen, 1980), p. 163.

[161] "The lasting, unchanging part of the joke, that which grips both teller and listener, is deep within the body of the joke – a basic situation of cuckoldry, seduction, impotence, castration, disease, and death, which are closely related, as common metaphorical equivalents, to oppression and poverty," Ronald Paulson, *Popular and Polite Art in the Age of Hogarth and Fielding* (Notre Dame University Press, 1979), p. 76. "The important and universal elements of the joke have all been delivered before the punch line is reached," Gershon Legman, *Rationale of the Dirty Joke* (New York: Grove Press, 1968), 1: 139, also cited by Paulson. See also Keith Thomas, *TLS*, January 21, 1977, 77–81.

sometimes painful confrontations between the powerful and the impotent, the wealthy and the poor, the established and the marginal. Greene's tales accomplish their most "diverting" work in these tense moments, in the wary reading and counter-reading of motive and status by paranoid individuals.

On occasion, the cony-catchers are allowed to air their own views of society. Greene's early *Notable Discouery*, borrowing from Walker's *Manifest Detection*, permits one cony-catcher to remark that

fewe men can liue vprightly, vnlesse he haue some pretty way, more then the world is witness to, to helpe him withall: Think you some lawyers could be such purchasers, if all their places were short, and their proceedings iustice and conscience? that offices would be so dearely bought, and the buiers so soone enriched, if they counted not pilage an honest purchase? or do you think that men of handie trades make all commodities without falsehood, when so many of them are become daily purchasers? who so hath not some sinister way to helpe himselfe, but foloweth his nose alwaies straight forward, may well hold vp his head for a yeare or two, but ye third he must needs sink, and gather the wind into begers hauen.[162]

The true dialogizing force of the genre, however, lies not in the license it extends to outlaws to criticize their in-law betters – "fox-furred gentlemen," lawyers, and grasping craftsmen[163] – but in the analogy drawn between the in-law and outlaw worlds. This analogy substitutes for the myth of status the "natural" premise that acquisitiveness governs all forms of contemporary life:

all conditions and estates of men seeke to liue by their wittes, and he is counted wisest, that hath the deepest insight into the getting of gaines: euerything now that is found profitable, is counted honest and lawfull: and men are valued by theyr wealth not by their vertues. (*Defence*, 11: 51)

The cony-catching pamphlet is thus a kind of totalizing anthropology. It explores the systematic ways in which aggression and acquisitiveness can generate an entire social structure: "their conditions: their lawes amongst themselues: their degrees and orders: their meetings, and their maners of liuing, (both men and women)" (Dekker, *Belman*, 3: 68). The structural analogies between in-law and outlaw society are not meant simply to assimilate the latter to the former, but to penetrate the "exclusionary conventions developing within the class and market structures of English capitalism," and to expose "the multiple and shifting intentionalities concealed behind the outward face of all

---

[162] *A Notable Discouery*, 10: 34; cf. *A Manifest Detection*, in Judges, *Elizabethan Underworld*, p. 38. Greene's version is perhaps milder than Walker's: it omits "noblemen" and "merchants."

[163] See, e.g., S. R., *Martin Markall the Beadle of Bridewell* (1610), in Judges, *Elizabethan Underworld*, pp. 391–392.

exchange."[164] The in-law world is implicitly challenged once it is revealed that the order of the underworld consists of "nothing else but certaine Acts and Rules, drawne into heads (in an assembly of damned Wretches) for the vtter vndoing of Men, and confusion of a Weale Publike" (*Belman*, 3:117). As the genre develops, the organization of the underworld expands to include legal proceedings against authors, moral decalogues ("Thou shalt see me want nothing, to which thou canst help me"), and dynastic chronicles "of the Regiments of Rogues ... and How They Haue Succeeded One the Other Successiuely."[165]

With these later developments the genre extends its exploration to the instabilities of the documenting, classifying, authorizing word in "this Printing age of ours" (*Lanthorne and Candlelight*, 3:177). Dekker, the pamphleteer most sensitive to the phenomenon of counterfeiting, specializes in the potentially fraudulent ledger-demesne[166] of socio-economic accountability, certification, and credit. Dekker's are literate rogues who "carry a Certificate or passport about them," exploiting various forms of "counterfeit License" or "pattents – which are counterfeit." Their talents are epitomized in the Jackman, "so cunning sometimes that he can speake Latine: which learning of his, lifts him vp to aduauncement, for ... his office is to make counterfet licenses" (*Belman*, 3:96, 102, 110, 104). In the later *Lanthorne and Candlelight*, the criminal advancement of learning extends more troublingly into author-ship and literacy themselves: Faulconers, "with an Alphabet of letters which they carry about them, being able to print any man's names (for a Dedication)" exchange recycled pieties – "especially a Sermon, or other matter of Diuinity" – into common currency (3:245–246). Meanwhile, "counterfet Maisters of that *Noble Science of Writing*" falsely promise "in foure and twenty houres" to teach any base soul "to write as fair and as fast as a country Vicar" (3:294). Thus are the most orthodox and creditworthy uses of the word revealed as matters of production and reproduction. In *Martin Markall*, the fool's voyage to a utopian paradise – a motif originating in the mad taxonomies of Brant and Barclay – passes through a realm conceived entirely as a product of the age of print:

A very fair city, called Vanita, beautiful to the eye, but of no permanence, for it is built after such a slight manner, that they are fain to re-edify their houses, walls and temples euery yeare anew. This city is gouerned by a woman called Madonna

---

[164] Agnew, *Worlds Apart*, pp. 68–69; it is Agnew, however, who also claims that the underworld pamphlets are a "fictional act of settlement," an "effort to assimilate an otherwise erratic pattern of itinerancy and trespass into a more familiar notion of deliberate, if dubious, guild activity," p. 65.

[165] *Martin Markall*, in Judges, *Elizabethan Underworld*, p. 388; pseudo-Dekker, *O per se O* (1612), in Judges, pp. 377–378; *Martin Markall*, in Judges, pp. 411ff.

[166] This brilliant pun is Agnew's, *Worlds Apart*, p. 70.

Instabilita ... Their city walls seem to be made of changeable taffeta; their houses of painted papers of sundry colours. They are busied all day about nothing but inventing of new fashions, of tires, garments, behaviours, speeches, words, and oaths. (Judges, p. 400)

The ultimate parody of the classifying word is perhaps embodied in the canting taxonomies of the underworld (Gentry Mort, a Gentleman; Rome-mort, a Queene). The language of cant takes careful note of social striations (to "cutt bene" = to speake gently) and it supports its own tradition of social complaint:

> The Ruffin cly the nab of the Harmanbeck,
> If we mawnd Pannam, lap or Ruff-peck,
> Or poplars of yarum: he cuts, bing to the Ruffmans,
> Or els he sweares by the light-mans,
> To put our stumps in the Harmans.
> The ruffian cly the ghost of the Harmanbeck,
> If we heaue a booth we cly the Ierke.[167]

For Dekker even more powerfully than for Greene, the curse of crime becomes a kind of discursive blessing when it bedevils in-law sobriety. The countryside rogues' lair of *The Belman of London* is at once a simulacrum of hell and a merry, festive image of the carnivalized marketplace. "A farre off," Dekker sees only "certaine cloudes of smoake, whose vapours ascended vp so blacke and thicke into the element, as if the Sighes of Hell had burst the bowels of the earth." Yet closer up he witnesses a festive banquet, with "as much stirring, as commonly is to be seene in a Booth, vpon the first day of the opening of a Fayre" (3: 77–79). The marginalized denizens of the realm are paradoxical figures – "they are all freemen, yet scorne to liue in Citties: great trauellers are they, and yet neuer from home." They enable the world itself to be reimagined under the aegis of praise–abuse.[168] In the Uprightman's festive oration, the world's in-law and outlaw poles are not simply reversed[169] but productively realigned to yield a new and striking form of morality:

---

[167] "The Diuell take the Constables head, / If we beg Bacon, Butter-milke or bread, / Or Pottage, to the hedge he bids vs hie, / Or Sweares (by this light) ith stockes we shall lie. / The Deuill haunt the Constables ghoast; / If we rob but a Booth, we are whipt at a poast," 3: 199–204.

[168] For the paradoxical oration in praise of thieves, see also *A Sermon in Praise of Thieves and Thievery* (Lansdowne MS 98 and MS Cott Vesp. a xxv), in Edward Viles and F. J. Furnivall, eds., *The Fraternitye of Vacabondes* (London: EETS, 1869), pp. 92–95.

[169] Stephen Greenblatt observes that such reversals, whereby the "forces of order" are "revealed as themselves dependent on dissembling and betrayal and the vagabonds ... as primitive rebels against the hypocrisy of a cruel society," are "at the very heart of the rogue literature," *Shakespearian Negotiations: The Circulation of Social Energy in Renaissance England*, (Berkeley: University of California Press, 1988), p. 51.

What though there be Statutes to Burne vs i'th eares for Rogues? to Syndge vs i'th hand for pilferers? to whippe vs at posts for being Beggers; and to shackle our heales i'th Stockes for being idle vagabondes? What of this? Are there not other Statutes more sharpe then these to punish the rest of the Subiects, that scorne to be our companions? What though a prating Constable, or a red nosd beadle say to one of vs, Sirra Goodman Rogue, if I serued you well, I should see you whipped through the towne? Alas! Alas! Silly Animals! if all men should haue that which they deserue, we should do nothing but play the Executioners and tormentors one of another. (3: 89)

Under its paranoid fictional pretexts, the anatomy of cony-catching is essentially a genre of fearlessness, particularly in its glorification of the urbanity of the man who goes lousy, lame, unregarded, and unrewarded: "The whole kingdome is but his Walke, a whole Cittie is but his parish." (3: 10) Perhaps only in certain kinds of pastoral – of which the cony-catching pamphlet is a variation – does one find a similar potential to make "the classes feel part of a larger unity or simply at home with each other."[170] And yet the underworld pamphlet seems more effectively than pastoral to frame its morality as a form of being-in-the-world, to reconstrue timeless moral antimonies in the profane and ambiguous terms of a bedevilled temporal world. As Dekker later wrote, after seven years in debtors' prison,

There is a Hell named in our Creede, and a Heaven, and the Hell comes before: If we looke not into the first, we shall neuer liue in the last. Our tossing vp and doune (here) is the Sea, but the land of Angels is our Shoare.

This "necessary" sequencing in the urbane morality of the cony-catching genre does not so much modify pastoral as replace it, just as Greene and his followers concealed the rural origins of vagabondage and of its first anatomists by insisting that the underworld's deceptions take root in London, from which they are "generally dispersed through all England" (*Notable Discouery*, 10: 29). The hellish feast–fair on which Dekker stumbles in fact aborts *The Belman of London*'s opening bad-faith pastoral feint at finding the "blessed life! patterne of that which our first Parents lead" (3: 70). The contamination of the world by the city's baneful influence, of nature by the shifting forms of urban culture, thus actually effects a reconciliation with the world: "All places being therefore haunted with euill Spirits, I forsooke the fieldes and the

---

[170] Empson, *Some Versions of Pastoral*, p. 199. This positive, productive task must have been one basis for the enormous, widespread appeal of the cony-catching genre, unless one is to suppose that all of the "young Gentlemen, Marchants, Apprentices, Farmers, and plain Countrymen" who made up its audience were unable to learn – as cony-catching victims usually do – from the experience of being had. This is a genre in which the victim is supposed to feel guilty of the crime perpetrated on him.

Mountines, and took my journey back againe to the Citie, whose customes (both good and bad) I desired to be acquainted with" (3: 113).

This reconciliation with the shifting structures of urban life, which put the traditional social order in abeyance, is what enables the threadbare poet Robert Greene "a waste good and an vnthrift," to take upon himself a newly defined mantle of gentleness, to substitute himself as the authoritative judge of English society.

The continuing city: Dekker's heterocosm

Gabriel Harvey charged that Nashe's urbane idiom was a base, unliterary manner, "but lenten stuff, like the old pickle hering."[171] In several respects, the comic prose pamphlet was in fact a Lenten form. A meagre living for disenfranchised writers whose only other source of income was the theater, the pamphlet tended to flourish when the theaters were closed and all of London was threatened with Lenten-like returns of the plague. The city's moral and physical health thus stood in inverse proportion to the vitality of the pamphlet form. Under normal conditions, London's carnivalian prosperity was a professional writer's Lent; under these conditions, Dekker observed, writing could not "yet be made Free! no, no, there is no good doings in these dayes but amongst Lawyers, amongst Vintners, in Bawdy houses, and at Pimlico. There is all the Musick (that is of any reckning) there all the meetings, there all the mirth, and there all the mony."[172] Conversely, the pamphlet-writer's prosperity was based on sensational disasters, sudden economic changes, disruptions in the social order, and other anomalies, which provided timely subject-matter; even disruptive social changes were helping to constitute a socially broader readership. Unprecedented in pace and scale, these instabilities made painfully apparent the lack of an abiding, obligatory rationale to justify the city's prolific life. The unsettling influence of such urban-generated phenomena as poverty, crime, vice, disease, dearth, rampant acquisitiveness and social mobility – against which preachers, for example, invoked such traditional theories as providence, the three estates, or the deadly sins – was for pamphleteers an opportunity to reflect in new ways on the permanently unstable, self-constituting dynamics of an urbanizing, capitalizing society.

[171] *Pierces Supererogation*, p. 66.
[172] *Worke for Armourers* (1609), in *Non-Dramatic Works*, 4: 97; cf. *Newes from Gravesend: Sent to Nobody*: "How much happier had it bin for them, to have changed their copies, & from Sciences bin bound to good Occupations, considering that one London Occupier (dealing vprightly with all men) puts vp more in a weeke, than seuen Bachilers of Art (that euery day goe barely a wooing to them) do in a yeare," in F. P. Wilson, ed., *The Plague Pamphlets of Thomas Dekker* (Oxford: Clarendon Press, 1925), p. 68.

As a group, the pamphleteers tended to derive their rationales for the city not so much from *a priori* forms of permanence as from the dynamism of the city itself. In the very conditions of social instability and intensified economic exchange they saw the production of viable and valid meanings and thus a potential for a kind of human permanence. Geared to a specific time, place, and economy, the urbanism of the pamphleteers rendered an account of the city perhaps no more adequate than the symbolic viewpoints (religious, feudal, classical) it sought to modify. But it was in many respects a novel rationale, more inclusive in its social appeal – which is to say, more open to the production of new, empirical meanings – than the self-enclosed symbolic frameworks of religion, feudalism, or even burgher ethics. Pamphlet urbanism was an alternative morality, developed at a crucial, transitional phase in the history of captalism and of London's growth. It offered a broad, consensual basis on which a diversifying society and readership might remain at ease while reflecting critically upon itself and its apparent instability.

Dekker's first pamphlet, *The Wonderfull Yeare. 1603.*, was devoted to that year's devastating plague, and nearly all of Dekker's subsequent London pamphlets examine the city under the Lenten aspect of social disaster – they are all concerned with war, famine, pestilence, social conflict, and hard times.[173] From the condition of turmoil, real or impending, Dekker seeks abiding rationales for urban existence. Like other pamphleteers, Dekker often makes parasitic use of the traditional symbolisms of complaint – of homiletic structures like the seven deadly sins, of taxonomies of the estates, professions, degrees, and underworld. Yet Dekker integrates these with the very different strategy of reading the city representationally, reading it, that is, for the embodiment of natural, permanent rhythms in change, for the timelessness of the ephemeral itself, for the anticipations of carnivalian plenitude even in the actuality of Lenten deprivation.[174] A writer less sophisticated and less socially conflicted than Nashe, Dekker tends like Nashe to envision a London permeated by the production and exchange of meanings; but he regards this process not so much in the grim manner of *Pierce Pennilesse* or *Christes Teares* as in the gay spirit of Nashe's late *Lenten Stuffe*. It is easily forgotten that the paradoxical praise is even more the *métier* of Dekker than of Nashe, perhaps because Dekker's paradoxes are less sharp, more genial, and typically mundane – there is perhaps some

---

[173]   John Carey observes that with the development of literary interest in the plague, "a complex arose for which Nashe had developed the perfect medium," "Sixteenth and Seventeenth-Century Prose," p. 381.

[174]   See Jones-Davies, *Un peintre de la vie londonienne*, 2: 19.

justice (and certainly a critique of bourgeois thinking) in Muriel Bradbrook's charge that Dekker was "something of a moral sloven."[175] Yet Dekker's discovery of a paradoxically abiding beauty in the city's turbulent and troubled life, his recognition of a stable center amid change, was not at all an obvious one, nor is the pictorial manner in which it is realized – its "truth to nature" – literarily or philosophically naive. Indeed, the moral force of Dekker's urbanism is apparent both in his mastery of heterogeneous modes of composition and in his awareness of the ambiguous, provisional quality of the "natural" meanings the city may be seen to represent.

Despite their grim, macabre detail and their homiletic digressions, Dekker's plague pamphlets could never be mistaken for anything but seriocomic prose rhapsodies. Dekker's *Wonderfull Yeare*, like its successor, is "not sorely," but only "somewhat infected" by the plague; its dedication promises that "If you read, you may happily laugh" (1 : 76). Some of Dekker's laughter arises from the degrading horror and trenchant cosmic ironies of the medieval grotesque, and he sometimes luxuriates in a decadent and sentimental pathos.[176] Yet in the main Dekker's is the rejuvenating, health-giving laughter of medical theory,[177] a "mirth...both Phisicall and wholsome against the Plague" (1 : 76). This laughter "diverts" the traditional, symbolic meanings of death "on the merry winges of a lustier winde... to arrive at some prosperous shore" (1 : 110).

The carnivalized treatment of Lenten matters is epitomized in the "merrie Corpulent Host" of *The Meeting of Gallants at an Ordinarie* (1604). This tavern-keeping raconteur, like many of Dekker's Londoners, rides out the plague in London and commodifies it in the merry tales which are at once his, and Dekker's, stock-in-trade; he is

an honest Host about London, that hath barreld vp newes for Gallants, like Pickled Oysters, marry your Ordinarie will cost you two shillings, but the tales that lie in Brine will be worth sixpence of the money: for you know 'tis great charges to keepe Tales long, and therefore he must be somehwat considered for the laying out of his Language. (Wilson, p. 118)

Like the Nashe of the red herring, Dekker's "fatte Host" traffics clownishly in degraded Lenten matter, laying out a language that is both

---

[175] *The Growth and Structure of Elizabethan Comedy* (1955; rpt. Baltimore, Penguin, 1963), p. 134.
[176] Like "Souldiers, who at the end of any notable battaile, with a kind of sad delight... [make] the remembrance euen of tragicall and mischieuous euents very delectable," 1 : 118.
[177] See, e.g., Laurent Joubert, *Treatise on Laughter*, tr. Gregory David DeRocher (University of Alabama Press, 1980), pp. 16, 126–128; cf. Glending Olson, *Literature as Recreation in the Middle Ages* (Ithaca: Cornell University Press, 1982), ch. 5.

a terrible groping in the dark and a foretaste of carnival abundance: the host's pickled tales are kept like "Anchovies to rellish your drinke wel" (p. 121).

Like his contemporaries, Dekker exploited the material basis of his profession and its analogies with commerce. Some of the Liberal Arts' "chymicall & Alchymicall raw disciples," he notes, "haue learnt...to distill gold and siluer out of very Tauerne-bushes, old greasy knaues of Diamonds, the dust of bowling Allyes, yea, & like Æsops Gallus Gallinacaeus, to scrape precious stones euen out of dung-hils" (*Newes from Graues-end*, Wilson, p. 68). Dekker proclaims himself one of those writers

that being free of Wits Merchant-venturers, do euery new moone (for gaine onely) make 5. or 6. voyages to the Presse, and euery Term-time (vpon Booksellers stalles) lay whole litters of blind inuention...he is not much to be condemned that hauing no more Acres to liue vppon than those that lie in his head, is euery hour hammering out one peice or other out of this rusty Iron age. (3: 178)

A counterfeiter and parodist without parallel, Dekker shares with Greene a fine sense of the gullish proclivities of his audience, consumers to whom writers "are as much beholden" as such morally dubious entrepreneurs as "Vintners, Players, and Puncks." The commercial analogies are pushed to their limits in Dekker's many tales of plague-time commerce. In *The Wonderfull Yeare*, a sober country village is confronted by the embarrassing fact of a dead Londoner in its midst. Like another group of villagers in *The Meeting of Gallants*, who devise "certaine long instruments" to dispose of a similar embarrassment (Wilson, p. 127), these countrymen pay a wretched tinker, commissioned as the grave-digger, with ten shillings "tyed to the end of a long pole and deliuered (in sight of all the Parish, who stood aloofe stopping their noses" (1: 144). But as Dekker warns, "long devices take soonest infection," and such elaborate machinery as might be devised for dealing with the plague is contrasted with the merry commercial impulse of the tinker, who leaves the scene "crying aloud," not unlike Dekker himself, "Haue ye got any more Londoners to bury, hey downe a downe dery, haue ye any more Londoners to bury?" (1: 145).

Even in the depth of its misfortune, London exhibits a mock-festive prosperity, with "Bells ringing all about London, as if the Coronation day had beene halfe a yeare long" (*The Meeting of Gallants*, Wilson, p. 116). 1603, Dekker notes, became "a rare worlde for the Church, who had wont to complaine for want of liuing" (*The Wonderfull Yeare*, 1: 114). In *The Meeting of Gallants*, "Coffiners and Sextons" dominate the economy, becoming "the Lawyers of the last Vacation" (Wilson, p. 132).

The savagery with which the plague is economically exploited reflects not only on the parasites who profit by the disease, but also on the everyday commerce whose logic they merely adopt. With his typically potent material sense, Dekker notes how death is woven, literally, into the fabric that is the basis of London's life; the most "dangerous and perilous Trades," he explains, are those "that had any woollen about them, for the infection being for the most part a Londoner, loued to be wrapt warme, and therefore was said to skip into woollen cloathes" (*The Meeting of Gallants*, Wilson, p. 117). Life and death, Lenten plague and carnivalian commerce, are not so much incompatibles as convertible opposites, so that a proclamation announcing a reopening of the Westminster law term merely signals a shift in demand for the perpetual marketplace: "Now Cookes begin to make more Coffins than Carpenters, and burie more whole meate then Sextons" (*Meeting of Gallants*, Wilson, p. 116). If, in such a thoroughly ambiguous treatment, roast meat forever loses some of its savor, death also loses some of its sting. Even when experiencing the worst of urban life, Londoners body forth a kind of carnivalian life, as they go "miching and muffled vp & downe, with Rue and Wormewood stuft into their eares and nosthrils, looking like so many Bores heads stuck with branches of Rosemary, to be serued in for Brawne at Christmas" (*The Wonderful Yeare*, 1: 112).

Though he shares with his preaching contemporaries a fascination with cities "rooted vp and swept from the face of the earth,"[178] Dekker seems to part with them in promising his London audience a city that continues – and has its justification – here. *London Looke Backe* (1630) ends with the Pauline observation that "the World is our common Inne, in which we haue no abyding: It stands in the Road-way for all passengers"; but the same work opens with a very different analogy:

This World is a Royall Exchange, wher all sorts of men are Merchants ... Princes, Dukes, Earles, Lordes, Clergymen, Iudges, Souldiers haue their Trading in particular Marchandizes, and walke euery day for that purpose vpon this Old Royal Exchange ... They talke in seuerall languages, And (like the murmuring fall of Waters) i[s] the Hum of their seuerall businesses: insomuch that the place seemes Babell, (a confusion of tongues.) The best, (yet most incertaine) Commodity, which all these Merchants striue for, is Life. (p. 199)

The Exchange is a form of settlement that partakes in some degree of the unsettled rhythms of pilgrimage. Dekker stresses this in the portrait of Sturbridge Fair with which old mother London concludes her oration in *The Dead Tearme* (1608). Like busy Yarmouth, Nashe's little *lingua terrae* rising from the yalping seas, Sturbridge is a

---

[178] *A Rod for Run-awayes* (1625), in Wilson, *Plague Pamphlets*, pp. 140–141; cf. *The Seuen Deadly Sinnes of London* (1606), in *Non-Dramatic Works*, 2: 9.

quarter of the Land, to which from all other partes men in multitudes repayre, to suck the sweetnesse of honest gaynes, and so to increase their wealth. It is a place, where (in a large field) a Citty as it were is in a fewe dayes builded vppe, and so quickly raysed, as if it had been done by Enchantment, and in a few daies it is afterwardes pulled down, no memory remayning of it, nor Monument to shewe that there it stoode: though whilst the earth beareth it vppe, there be Fayre streetes, so filled with people, that they seeme to bee paued euen with the feete of men: whilest on either side, shops are so furnished and set forth with all rich and necessary commodities, that many coming thyther, haue taken that place for my selfe, and haue not stucke to call it by the name of little London, so like do they sweare it hath beene vnto me. (4: 79)

If the marketplace is the means by which Dekker links urban life to nature's ebbs and flows, it is also a means of softening the social boundaries that some regarded as the faultlines of a coming cataclysm. In *The Dead Tearme*, the matronly persona of London, 1,110 years older than Westminster, calls on her greater wisdom to absorb the challenges of the latter, preventing their "Enter-view" (4: 8) from hardening into a symbolic hierarchy of class-based contrasts, populace vs. privilege, plain thrift vs. power. The newly bureaucratized fastness of an ancient lordly class, Westminster complains of the seasonal disruptions, especially the Long Vacation, which punctuate the thriving periods of the law terms and of royal residence; she languishes "in the height and lustiest pride of summer," when London "allurest the people from all the corners of the Land, to throng in heapes, at thy Fayres and thy Theators" (4: 22). The upstart capital would abolish the seasons of vacancy and "haue all these foure Riuers of the law, run into one stream, without any stoppings or turnings" (4: 28). London, the sempiternal marketplace which has "had Negotiation with all the Nations that be in the world," pleads rather for the mundane rhythms of reciprocity and exchange that form the world's economic, moral, and natural law:

If the moyst-handed Isis the Thames (who, takes the names from Thame & Isis), shold send all her melted Siluer to the insearchable and vnknowne Treasury of Neptune, (into which all Riuers pay their custome) and should neuer haue an profitable Returne of it, how soone would she grow poore? Or if the Sea-god ... should do nothing but pour his gifts into the lappe of that his Christall bosom daughter, how soone would her swimming too hie in riches, make her forget her selfe? ... we should lie drowned in her greatnes, as other partes of the land would be ouerwhelmed in thyne, if thou haddest what thou desirest and coueteth. (4: 61)

It is this rhythm of the marketplace that finally links London and Westminster in a new reciprocity: "wee are growne so like and euerie day doe more and more so resemble each other that many who neuer knew vs before, woulde sweare that we were all One" (4: 70). Natural resemblence (and hence exchangeability) thus overrides symbolic difference and softens social antagonism. In the ruthless social structures and social boundaries that Nashe regarded as the "frontiers of sinne" Dekker sees a jovial as well as sinister feast:

men shall be bought and sold like Oxen and Calues in Smithfield, and young Gentlemen shall be eaten vp (for daintye meat) as if they were pickled Goose, or baked Woodcockes ... Courtiers shall this dismall yere feed vpon Cittizens, & cittizens on the contrary-side lay about them like tall trencher-men to deuoure the Courtiers. (*The Rauens Almanacke* (1609), 4: 207)

Throughout Dekker's pamphlet *œuvre*, the presence of such saturnalian motifs in the savage turmoil of London helps to transform the threat of an ever-impending cataclysm into a shifting, but continuing, pattern of losses and recoveries, failures and triumphs. Dekker's pamphlets always flirt with catastrophe, not only with plague but with the whole series of edifying (and newsworthy) disasters comprised in the Litany's catalogue of famine, war, and pestilence. All three of these, personified, blaze "their seuerall Euills" in *The Meeting of Gallants* (1604), and they contribute to the title-page of *The Rauens Almanacke. Fortelling of a Plague, Famine, and Ciuill Warre* (1609). London becomes a city under figurative siege in *A Rod for Run-awayes* (1625), in *The Seuen Deadly Sinnes of London* (1606) and *Worke for Armourers* (1609, t.p.). *A Knights Coniuring* (1607) opens with a tempest that threatens to become "a second deluge" and sends Londoners scrambling for their almanacs.[179] Yet all these works mingle disaster with festive resiliency, often following the movement of the plague pamphlets from grim description to merry jest.[180] The impending class Armageddon of *Worke for Armourers*, for example, is averted by an uneasy but semi-festive truce, an anti-apocalyptic recognition that rich and poor

were two Nations so mighty and so mingled together, and so dispersed into all the parts of the world, that it was impossible to seuer them ... The Armies hereupon broke vp, the Siege raised, the City gates set wide open. Shop-keepers fell to their old *what doe you lacke*: the rich men feast one another (as they were wont) and the poore were kept poore still in pollicy, because they should do no more hurt. (4: 165–166)

[179] Ed. E. F. Rimbault, (London: Percy Society, 1841), pp. 8–9.
[180] The seven-day siege of *The Seuen Deadly Sinnes of London* is also, for example, a seven-day triumph, "appointed to receive these seuen Potentates" (2: 17). The opening psychomachia of *A Strange Horse-Race* modulates into a "misticall Masque of Catchpols" and a "Bankrouts Banquet" (3: 363, 369), while Dekker awakens in amazed delight from the infernal dream-visits of *Newes from Hell* and *A Knights Coniuring*. In *The Dead Tearme*, Westminster's complaint yields to London's encomiastic self-portrait.

In *The Wonderfull Yeare*, the potentially cataclysmic death of Queen Elizabeth is subsumed, like the disasters in Dekker's other works, into a pattern of continuity that links the rhythms of nature with the orderly, year-to-year regulation of London's civic life:

Shee came in with the fall of the leafe, and went away in the Spring ... she was borne vpon a Lady Eue, and died vpon a Ladye Eue: her Natiuitie & death being memorable in this wonder: the first and last yeares of her Raigne by this, that a Lee was Lorde Maior when she came to the Crowne, and a Lee Lorde Maior when she departed from it. (1: 92–93)

Dekker's typical movement from disaster toward equilibrium corresponds with several related movements, from satire to saturnalia, from sober categories and taxonomies to grotesque realism, from literal report and counsel to conscious counterfeiting, picture- and fiction-making. These movements are in a manner one. Dekker's cony-catching pamphlets and mock-almanacs, together with *The Guls Horne-booke* and parts of the plague pamphlets, all masquerade as practical advice manuals and non-fictional documentaries.[181] Their ostensible practical purport provides the pamphleteer with both a motive and an expository framework. Motive and framework tend to unfold parodically, however, edging the apparent clarity of Dekker's satire toward saturnalia, his schemes and categories toward dilated description, his practical intentions toward rhapsodic celebration. As *The Guls Horne-booke*, for example, follows the daily round of its hero from the privacy of his chambers to London's fashionable public haunts, Dekker moves through several modes of discourse, from a crude opening satire on the deadly sins, to a more subtly satiric view of manners in the form of a mock-courtesy book, to the public saturnalia that hold his deepest interest – the "Poets Royall Exchange ... so free in entertainment ... that your Stinkard hath the selfe-same libertie to be there in his Tobacco-Fumes, which your Courtier hath" (2: 247).

Throughout Dekker's pamphlets, the swarming public scene, interweaving the destinies of groups and individuals, constitutes a new and durable truth (to nature) quite different from the allegorical truth of traditional complaint. In *The Seuen Deadly Sinnes of London*, for example, the languages of allegory and neofeudal hierarchy alternate with portraiture of the quotidian world to bestow on London a sense of permanence opposed to the demonic fixities of sinfulness or class strife. The abstract, allegorical sins are represented as alien powers besieging

---

[181] Jones-Davies observes that "toutes ces brochures se presentent comme les guides," *Un peintre de la vie londonienne*, 2: 120.

"this little world of people" (2: 70), strange visitors who are essentially "forreners that liue without the freedome of your Citty" (2: 27). Against such specious demons London asserts its own forms of endurance. Sloth, must contend against the overwhelming hubbub of a lively metropolis:

> How then dares this nastie, and loathsome sin of Sloth venture into a Cittie amongst so many people? who doth he hope wil giue him entertainment?... for in euery street, carts and Coaches makes such a thundering as if the world ranne vpon wheeles: at euerie corner, men, women, and children meete in such shoales, that postes are set vp of purpose to strengthen the houses, least with iustling one another they should shoulder them downe. Besides, hammers are beating in one place, Tubs hooping in another, Pots clinking in a third, water- tankards running tilt at a fourth: here are Porters sweating vnder burdens, there Merchants-men bearing bags of money, Chapmen (as if they were at leape-frog) skippe out of one shop into another: Tradesmen (as if they were dauncing Galliards) are lusty at legges, and neuer stand still: all are as busie as countrie Atturnyes at an Assizes: How then can Idleness thinke to inhabite here? (2: 51)

Such scenes are ordered not by theological or social schemes but by the temporal rhythms of the urban routine that has come to seem like nature itself. The alternation of daylight and nocturnal scenes in *The Seuen Deadly Sinnes of London*, itself an *opus septem dierum* (2: 3), is a favorite Dekkerian device, repeated in the "gloomy Midnight" and sunrise scenes of *The Wonderfull Yeare* (1: 104–109) and in the approach toward London's twilight curfew in the major cony-catching pamphlets (3: 113, 295). The daily round organizes both *The Guls Horne-booke* and the devil's visit to a debtors' prison in *Villanies Discouered* (1616, H4v). The complaints of Westminster are resolved not simply by London's reconciliation of change with continuity but also by her reference to the four winds, the seasons, and the tidal rhythms of the Thames (4: 20, 22, 28, 61–64).

Dekker's use of mock-prognostication, however, is his most striking evocation of the natural rhythms to be found in urban life. A staple of Elizabethan comic prose, and perhaps pioneered by Nashe,[182] the mock-almanac was used by secular pamphleteers to burlesque the unduly sober and portentous methods of astrology by applying them to matters of obvious and mundane routine. Yet the principal reference of the genre was not to the pseudo-science it parodied but to the mundane routines that it predicted with a mixture of cynicism and resignation.[183] Adam

---

[182] F. P. Wilson, "Some English Mock Prognostications," *The Library*, 4th ser. 19 (1938), 6–43. McKerrow's edition includes Adam Foulweather's *Wonderfull, Strange and Miraculous, Astrological Prognostication* (1591), but McKerrow claims to "have been unable to discover any reason whatsoever for" considering it an authentic work of Nashe (*Works*, 5: 138); cf. Wilson, "Some English Mock Prognostications," p. 23.

[183] See Clark, *Elizabethan Pamphleteers*, p. 271.

Foulweather, for example, set the pattern with his advice that the summer

beginneth when the wether waxeth so hot that beggers scorne barnes and lie in the field for heate, and the wormes of Saint Pancredge Church build their bowers vnder the shadow of Colman hedge ... bottle Ale shall be in great authoritie ... Tapsters this quarter shall be in greater credite then Coblers ... Butchers are like to make great hauocke amongst flies ... Young Gentlemen shall creepe further into the Mercers Booke in a Moneth then they can get out in a yere; and ... sundry fellowes in their silkes shall be appointed to keepe Duke Humfrye company in Poules. (*Works*, 3: 392)

In their mundane readings of the heavens, typically "calculated for the Meridian of London," the mock-prognosticators portrayed the city as an animated, hylozoic realm where cosmic forces make their constant presence felt. The author of *The Owles Almanacke* (1618) noted that many of the signs of the zodiac "are to be seene hanging in the middle of Cheapside; for there's the Ram, the Bull, the Crab, Capricorne, &c."[184] Anthony Nixon's *Strange Foot-Post* (1613) opened with a vision of "the Metropolitan Cittie of the World, seeming indeed like Heauen it selfe" (BV). The entire cosmic zodiac was resituated in the mundane London landscape – Aries as "the Ramme in fleetstreet," Aquarius as "the sign of the Water-bearer", and "the seauen Planets" as the "seauen Gates of this Cittie." [185]

As Bakhtin has it, such mundane cosmologies uncrown the stars, "give time and the future a different coloring, ... transform the accent to the material bodily life"; like comic riddles, they transform the dread of eschatalogical expectation into a "gay monster."[186] Thus Dekker's *Rauens Almanacke* completes its dreadful prophecies of *Plague, Famine, and Ciuill Warre* (t.p.) by predicting a cataclysm which is nothing more earth-shaking than the annual mayor's pageant – by which Londoners celebrate the enduring cycles of their civic order:

vpon the verie next day after Simon and Iude, the warlike drum and Fife shall be heard in the verie midst of Cheapside, at the noise whereof people (like mad-men) shall throng together, and run vp and downe, striuing by all meanes to get into Mercers and Gold-Smithes houses, and to such height shall this land water swell, that the 12. Conduits themselues are like to be set one against another, and not only the Lord Maior, Sheriffes, and Officers, but also many of the Nobilitie of the land shall haue much adoe, with their troopes of horse, to breake through

---

[184] *The Owles Almanacke ... Calculated as Well for the Mirth of London, as Any Other Part of Great Britaine* (1618), ed. Don Cameron Allen (Baltimore: Johns Hopkins University Press, 1943), p. 28.

[185] Sigs. B2–B2v; cf. *Platoes Cap* (1604), sigs. B2–B3; *The Owles Almanacke*, pp. 39–40, 63–64.   [186] *Rabelais and His World*, pp. 234, 237.

the disordered heapes of Tradesmen and others, that will on that fearful day be assembled together. In vaine shall it be for any man to *Cry peace*, nothing will be heard but noise, and the faster that fire-workes are throwne amongst these Perditious children, the lowder will grow their rage, and more hard to be appeased. (4: 211–212).

Animated by a saturnalian energy that often verges on frenzy, such scenes are nevertheless an important emblematic means by which Dekker expresses "sa vision juste des qualites robustes et durables de la race anglaise."[187] Yet despite their association with natural and cosmic forces, these emblems are relatively inarticulate. The confidence they express comes not so much from an elaborate, rigorously argued rationale as from a largely unexamined allegiance to extra-official and hitherto sub-literary traditions – to the local civic heritage and artisan ethic Dekker also celebrates in his plays and pageants, to a naive faith in the fundamental justice of the marketplace, to a temporal sense formed by popular culture and consciousness, resistant alike to the false permanence claimed by official regimes and to the imagined apocalyptic consequence of their demise.

There is a fatalism in Dekker's praise-abuse, a diminished sense of responsibility, that makes him seem at times the first urban voyeur. Dekker's "longing desire to get the true pictures" (3: 115) of his world often puts him in the position of the furtive or fugitive observer. In *The Belman of London*, Dekker takes the view of an underworld banquet from "an vpper loft where (vnseene) I might (through a wooden lattice that had the prospect of the dyning roome) both see and heare all that was to be done or spoken" (3: 80). The tailor who accompanies the *Hornebooke*'s Gull to St. Paul's to view fashions shares Dekker's hidden standpoint, when, "stepping behind a piller to fill his table-bookes with these notes, [he] will presently send you into the world an accomplisht man: by which meanes you shall weare your clothes in print with the first edition" (2: 235). When Dekker looks into the "perspective glasses" of chronicles to see "kingdomes and people afarre off," he seems to be looking into the *speculum vitae* of rhetorical tradition; yet his vantage point does not depend so much on his social or moral standing as on a purely accidental, felicitous location in time and space: "this makes me call to memory the strange and wonderfull passing of a Coach that scudded through London the ninth of August, for I put the day in my Table-booke, because it was worth the registering."[188]

---

[187] Jones-Davies, *Un peintre de la vie londonienne*, 2: 19.
[188] *The Meeting of Gallants*, Wilson, *Plague Pamphlets*, p. 117; cf. *A Rod for Run-awayes*, Wilson, p. 146. See also Jones-Davies, *Un peintre de la vie londonienne*, 2: 8.

Dekker's pictorial manner seems at times a logical extension of the marginality of the urban pamphleteer, a reduction of the ambiguous and embattled status of a Greene or a Nashe to the comfortable but impotent anonymity of the urban bystander.[189] Unlike Greene or Nashe (or Lodge or Whetstone, for that matter) – whose education and ambition made their professional, urban pamphleteering a transgressive prodigal practice – Dekker could in fact claim no better role for himself than that which London, with its fluid roles and structures, mixed audiences, and professional genres offered. Dekker's pamphlet morality cannot be charged with "basic indifference to its origins in admonitory literature." But his works do lack the "sense of crisis in the authorial persona" to be found in earlier pamphleteers. His exploration of the London landscape is largely free of the professional's social shame or the satirist's guilty complicity. He does not share with Greene or Nashe a sense of responsibility for the mental structures he at once deploys and undermines in his survey of the London scene.

This is not to say that Dekker's portraits of the city are without moral structure or purport. On the contrary, though Dekker often expresses his intention to "get the true pictures" or "to paint and delineate to the life" (1: 103), his strongest pictorial analogies are to the moral grotesque. A group of cony-catching banqueters are like "so many Anticks" in "a dutch peece of Drollery" (3: 87); a banquet of London prodigals forms a similar grotesque: "you must take out your writing tables, and note by the way, that euery roome of the house was a Cage full of... wilde fowle, ... birds all of a beake, not a Woodcocks difference among twenty dozen of them" (3: 87).

The consequence if not the actual cause of becoming such a moral spectacle is to have become morally fixed and visibly conspicuous in a realm where invisibility, mobility, and anonymity are of the essence. Dekker's is always a romance voyage, sailing past "the creekes, rocks, gulfes, and quick-sandes" of the "black shore of mischief" (3: 66) or "alongst the shore of the Ile of Guls" (2: 204), in order to visit those critical hot-spots where the city's dynamic life and inhabitants harden into demonic fixity. By a series of more than merely clever puns, the middle aisle of St. Paul's becomes a "mediterranean Ile" which is both "the onely gallery, wherein the pictures of all your true fashionate and complementall Guls are" (2: 230) and also a mid-earth plenum that is the

---

[189] It corresponds also to the diminishing presence of the narrator, and a concomitant emphasis on representation over presentation, both of which David Margolies attributes to the professional writers' gradual resolution of the problems of voice and address created by the development of printing, *Novel and Society in Elizabethan England*, pp. 27–44.

commercial romancer's paradise, a "Mediterannean Sea, in which as well the Merchant hoysts vp sayles to purchase wealth honestly, as the Rouer to light vpon prize uniustly" (2: 51). Dekker's goal, however, like that of certain romance heroes, is to encounter and comprehend these scenes of concentrated meaning without himself becoming demonized or fixed by them, to apprehend the world morally without letting the moralism of his pamphlets harden into the ideological structures and homiletic functions from which the form emerged.

The pamphlet form, with its heavy moral residue but flexible idiom and now open form was perfectly suited to this balancing act. *A Strange Horse-Race*, perhaps Dekker's strangest pamphlet, is a building in which

euery Roome (though all be but meane) hath some Picture to delight you ... The maine plot of my building is a Moral labyrinth; a weake thred guides you in and out: I will shew you how to enter, and how to pass through, and open all the Roomes, and all the priuate walkes, *that when you are come to them*, you may know where you are: and these they be – Yet I will not; I know it is more pleasure to finde out the conceitfull-deceits of a Paire of Tarriers, then to haue them discouered. The pleasure be yours, the Tarriers are mine. (3: 312–313; italics mine)

As a reading of this, or any, pamphlet by Dekker reveals, the terrier's design is less important than the pleasurable, instructive recognition of the places passed; the total design of the labyrinth is less essential than the moral experience of recognizing, at any given moment, the room one occupies within it.

The virtue of Dekker's pamphlet morality is perhaps best understood in contrast to the more "binding" uses of language he repeatedly attacks. Dekker's fascination with counterfeit and parody, especially his comic exploration of the uses of print and writing by cony-catchers, bespeaks a profound skepticism toward the final documenting, verifying, classifying, authorizing word by which domination of the social order is established. Dekker notes in one of his pamphlets that "wee are most like to God that made vs, when we shew loue one to another, and doe most looke like the Diuell that would destroy vs, when wee are one anothers tormentors" (2: 72). The first half of the formula is crucial but unremarkable; the second is a caution equally to all of those – officials, taxonomers, even satirists – who fix themselves demonically by inscribing the signs of their domination on others. Dekker's writerly credential for returning the devil's answer to Pierce Pennilesse is simply that he is the one kind of writer who is not a scrivener, lawyer, schoolmaster, or other tormentor. It is around the "binding" words of these latter functionaries that truly dangerous demons tend to gather. In London's taverns, for example, one "thinkes verily that the men are coniuring" with their talk of "Statutes, Bonds, Recognizances, Fines, Recoveries, Audits, Rents, Subsidies, Sureties, Inclosures, Liueries, Indictments, Outlaries, Feoffments, Iudgements, Commissions, Bankerouts, Amercements "(2: 245). The longest mock-document in Dekker's *œuvre* is the devil's own "last and onely Will" (3: 335). The Bankrupts' Banquet which concludes the *Strange Horse-Race* is a paper feast at which the main dishes are, in more than one sense, binding: "Bondes, a binding meate... Bils, binders too... Iudgements lie heauy in the stomacke." These binding documents must therefore be accompanied by condiments "good against those Binding and Restringent dishes" – "Purging-comfits" and "Annis-seed-comfits, beeing exceeding good to procure Long-winds" (3: 371–373). The unpaid supplier of these loosening sweets is a "poore rotten-tooth'd Comfit-maker," the pamphleteer himself, who closes the work with a joyful celebration of the impossibility of closure and the inexhaustible riches of his urban subject: if all the water in the Thames were ink, and all the

fethers vpon Swans backes were pens, and all the smoky sailes of westerne barges, were white paper, & all the Scriueners, all the Clarkes, all the School-maisters, & all the Scholers in the kingdome were set a writing, and all the yeares of the world yet to come, were to be imploied in that businesses: that inke would be spent, those pens grub'd close to the stumps, that paper scribled all ouer, those writers wearied, and that time worne out, before the shiftes, ledger-demaines, conueiances, reaches, fetches, ambushes, traines, and close vnder-minings of a Bankrout could to the life be set downe...

> My Muse thou art so merry,
> When wilt thou say th'art weary?
> Neuer (I know it) neuer,
> This flight thou couldst keep euer:
> Thy shapes which so do vary
> Beyond thy bownds thee carry.   (3: 377–378)

The seriocomic vitality of Dekker's prose is at once a product of this writer's capacious and resilient professionalism, of the possibilities which had come to inhere in the medium, and of a vision of the city in which familiar moral and social patterns, tested for the natural truth they represent, are always being realized and undermined simultaneously. Mediating between the languages of sin and civility, Dekker's pamphlets seem at once to fulfill and to render obsolete the responsibilities of complaint morality, to condemn and yet to naturalize London's destabilizing effect on society, morals, and expression. The polyglot tendencies of the professional pamphlet form, which flourished alongside those of the popular theater, owed their existence to a peculiarly fluid phase not only in language and literature but also in the socio-economic development of London. Between the mid-sixteenth and early seventeenth centuries, the necessary functions of the economy – production, trade, law, and administration – were each organized according to the different principles of London's different artisanal, mercantile, legal, and courtly communities. Yet by the early seventeenth century, the relatively cohesive relationships between these functions and communities were being broken down by several factors – by the inflation of honors and a burgeoning court bureacracy, by the growing influence of court syndicates on capitalism and foreign trade, by the correspondingly diminished power of London's guilds and artisans, and by a deepening alienation of London's merchant class from the economic practices, foreign policy, and moral and religious tone of the Stuart court.

The later history of the seriocomic prose pamphlet is thus a history of a waning consensus in neofeudal urban culture, and with it, the emergence of a more thoroughly modern, but exclusionary, metropolitan mentality. While cony-catching pamphlets continued to be reissued and updated, *Pierce Pennilesse His Supplication* was the only Elizabethan comic pamphlet to receive a seventeenth-century edition, and the newer works published by Dekker's lesser contemporaries demonstrate an inability to orchestrate the different responsibilities, languages and audiences which had been essential to the life of comic prose. Unable to reconcile traditional morality with contemporary urbanity, in-law analysis with out-law foolery, the reading of the map with the experience of the labyrinth, most later pamphlets settle for one or the other of these extremes. At one extreme, such pseudo-homiletic works as *The Glasse of Mans Folly* (1615) and *This Worlds Folly* (1615) follow the vein of Stubbes' *Anatomie of Abuses*, combining their petrified morality and ostentatious biblicism with invectives against more urbane " Sarcasticall scorners, that reioyce in Sodisme" and with predictions of the "imminent dissolution, or conclusive dissolution of this foolish doting worlde, since vniuersally it is but an vndigested Chaos of outrageous enormities."[190] At the other extreme, popular entertainers like John Taylor or Barnabe Rich rework a tired comic soil, contenting themselves with being "almost lost … in this intricate labyrinth of abuses" and ruefully admitting that "if I hit the trueth, it is but chance medley."[191]

Most revealing, finally, are works like *The Man in the Moone* (1609) or Anthony Nixon's *Strange Foot-Post* (1613), in which these different tendencies sit side by side as wholly separate discursive strands. These strands represent not simply a skeletal anatomy of the disintegrating

---

[190] *The Glasse of Mans Folly* (1615), sig. H4v; cf. *This Worlds Folly* (1615), sig. B4v.
[191] Rich, *Favltes, Favltes, and Nothing Else but Favltes* (1606), sigs. E, P2.

heteroglot body but a small chronicle of the absorption of its original responsibilities into the new, urbane manner of character-writing and "alcove realism."[192]

The Man in the Moone, for example, is essentially a collection of separately etched characters, but each character is approached through several discursive perspectives. These are represented by Mockso, a "pert Iuuinall," who describes the physical appearance of each in the comic manner of a traditional grotesque; by Opinion, a secular, urbane moralist who can "anatomize any ones condition at the first sight"; and by Fido, a traditional homilist who speaks in authoritative Roman print rather than the black-letter of the first two. What is remarkable is that each strand of discourse should be so faithful to the tone and diction of the different strata intertwined in the prose of the great pamphleteers – in the voice of Mockso, to the intensely physical detail and ritual paratactic structures of the popular stage clown; in the voice of Fido, to the second person counsel, feudal disposition, and appeals to god and nature of the preacher; in the voice of Opinion, to the calculated parallelisms, antitheses, and classical allusions of the urbane connoisseur of manners, whose epigrammatic conclusion identifies him as a prac-titioner of the newly fashionable, classically inspired genre of character writing. It is, in a sense, the disparity between the first and second speakers, between the clown and the preacher, between the physical and the spiritual, that creates an opening for the responsible, urbane, but finally rancid and condescending voice of Opinion.

In the work of Greene, Nashe, and Dekker, pamphlet urbanity had been a means of containing and orchestrating a wider range of discursive possibilities, a range which actually embraced both the clownish and the homiletic. But here the urbanity of Opinion emerges as a distinct alternative to the heteroglot idiom of the marginal man. Opinion's is the accomplished poise of the character-writer, who was in fact to claim from the hack pamphleteers the title and authority of urban moralist. It is similarly the new voice of "Opinion," in Anthony Nixon's *Strange Foot-Post* (1613), that pronounces the final dismissive glosses on the characters and deviants represented both by the narrator and in their own voices. The fate of pamphleteering is perhaps summed up in "Opinion's" treatment of a Malcontent, who "ioggeth along," in the narrator's description, "spurning the pauement as if he were angry with it." The Malcontent's own voice, strangely, is not that of the Marstonesque satyr–satirist, but that of a pamphleteer who inhabits outlandishly traditional modes:

---

[192] Bakhtin, *Rabelais and His World*.

Couetousness is become a Tradesman, and Pride his wife. Drunkenness the onely sociable companion, & Lechery the sole good fellow: Gluttony is a great man, & Envy a younger brother ... Oh Sodome, thou wast fired for thy sinnes ... *O Tempore*, [sic] *Oh mores!*

The traditionalist is deprived of his urbanity by the more urbane "Opinion," who dismisses him with the high and haughty manner of the character-writer, right down to the last, defining word:

The Welfare of others is his bane, & their ruine his Balsamum...He is a Misanthropos, which hateth men, a Narcissus which loueth not women, a Diogenes which carpeth at will, a malitious Mal-content. (sigs. Fv–F2v)

Though this urbane dismissal of the carping, hypocritical moralist may be said to have emerged from the saucy manner of the Elizabethan pamphleteers, it is divorced from the polyvocal and resonantly traditional context of their work and, in a manner, quite opposed to it. Urbanity has here entered a narrower range, and fallen prey to a kind of *genrism*. It has become more exclusively the province of a particular class of urbanite and a privileged mode of expression. Disdainfully, it proclaims a freedom from the moral necessity of writing satire. The following chapter will demonstrate that a movement toward this new urbanity was anticipated in the contemporaries of the pamphleteers, the Elizabethan verse satirists. The movement was thwarted, however, by the forces of consensus and the traditional limits and inhibitions that prevailed in this transitional period of London's history. But this movement would be completed only later, with the waning of the Elizabethan symbiosis of cultures and the emergence of a new metropolitan mentality and a new form of utopianism dedicated to the cultivation of the pleasures of the town.

7   Essential difference: the projects of satire

The art of discrimination

Along with the development of seriocomic prose, the sudden development of verse satire at the end of the sixteenth century represents an
alternative form of ethical innovation in response to the disorienting
effects of urbanization on traditional values. In *The Arte of English
Poesie*, published in 1589, but written perhaps twenty years earlier,
George Puttenham could find few exemplars of the genre practiced by
"Lucilius, Iuvenall, and Persius among the Latines": the sole author of
English satire – a genre "more like to sermons or preachings then
otherwise" – was "he that wrote the booke called Piers plowman." By
contrast, Francis Meres, writing in 1598, could connect with the Roman
satirists a number of new contemporary figures: "Lodge, Hall of Imanuel
Colledge in Cambridge; the Authour of *Pigmalions Image and Certaine
Satyrs* [i.e., Marston]; the Author of *Skialetheia* [i.e., Guilpin]."[1] With
the appearance of this new generation of writers, satire, which had been
but a "childe of Playne dealing and Simplicitye" in Gascoigne's *The
Steel Glas* (1576), had become by the turn of the century a laureate
master-genre charged with policing the entire literary system:

> The Satyre onely, and sharpe Epigrammatist,
> (Concisde Epigramme, and sharpe Satyrist)
> Keepe diet from this surfet of excesse.[2]

Despite the varied backgrounds and careers of the verse satirists, and
despite their obvious debt to such popular forms as seriocomic prose and

[1] Puttenham, *The Arte of English Poesie*, ed. Gladys Doidge Willcock and Alice Walker
(Cambridge University Press, 1936), p. 26; Meres, *Palladis Tamia*, ed. D. C. Allen
(New York: Scholars' Facsimiles and Reprints, 1938), p. 283v.

[2] Gascoigne, *Works*, ed. J. W. Cunliffe (2 vols. 1907; rpt. New York: Greenwood Press,
1969), 2: 144; Guilpin, *Satyre Preludium*, in *Skialetheia or A Shadowe of Truth, in
Certaine Epigrams and Satyres* (1598), ed. D. Allen Carroll (Chapel Hill: University of
North Carolina Press, 1974), p. 61. Gascoigne's distinction between poetry and satire is
discussed in Bernard Harris, "Men Like Satyrs," in J. R. Brown and Bernard Harris,
eds., *Elizabethan Poetry* (New York: St. Martin's Press, 1961), p. 179.

stage comedy, the self-canonizing center of formal verse satire was perhaps unique in its assertive genrism, in its insistence (without reference to continental models or popular traditions) on its classical pedigree and its attempt to dictate the laws of its reception.[3] To an unprecedented degree, the new verse satire asserted its difference from other literary kinds. In doing so it defined itself as *the* medium for discrimination, for the moral and social judgement that could establish differences no longer given or apparent in contemporary social life.

To the degree that formal verse satire insisted on its classical antecedents it insisted as well on its novel ethical tasks and peculiar modes of vision. This is why the verse satirists, despite their debts and borrowings, typically took a dismissive posture toward the professional prose moralism exemplified by Nashe and other pamphleteers.[4] The tendency to disclaim debts to native models, together with a pointed evocation of classical models and an affected indifference toward readers, was a way to elevate the verse satirists' amateur status and higher social standing above the scandalous professional careers of downwardly mobile hacks like Greene and Nashe.[5] These strategies also served the pursuit of laureate ambitions and authority, the initiation of a poetic career modelled on that of Horace and directed against such irresponsible amateur genres as the sonnet and such outmoded and blunt moral instruments as traditional complaint and seriocomic prose.[6]

By its self-definition, at any rate, formal verse satire was distinguished not by its resemblance to other forms but by its difference from them.[7]

---

[3] On the well-defined sense of genre, see Wesley Milgate's Introduction to his edition of Donne's *Satires, Epigrams and Verse Letters* (Oxford: The Clarendon Press, 1967), p. xvii.

[4] In this respect J. B. Leishman is mistaken in his claim that formal verse satire is no different from other contemporary satiric forms, "that the particular form chosen – prose satire, verse satire, 'humours' comedy, prose Character – is, in a sense, almost accidental," Introduction to *The Three Parnassus Plays* (London: Ivor Nicholson & Watson, 1949), p. 45. On the debt of the verse satirists to the satiric prose of Nashe, see John Peter, *Complaint and Satire in Early English Literature* (Oxford University Press, 1956), p. 132; and C. S. Lewis, *English Literature in the Sixteenth Century* (Oxford University Press, 1954), p. 474.

[5] Hall's many attacks on Nashe are discussed in Arnold Davenport's Introduction to the *Collected Poems* (Liverpool University Press, 1949), pp. xliv–xlvii; see also Davenport's "The Quarrel of the Satirists," *MLR*, 37 (1942), 123–130. For the amateur status of the satirists, see John Wilcox, "Informal Publication of Late-Sixteenth-Century Verse Satire," *HLQ*, 13 (1949–50), 191–200; see also Alvin Kernan, *The Cankered Muse: Satire of the English Renaissance* (1959; rpt. Hamden, Conn.: Archon Books, 1976), p. 39.

[6] Ronald J. Corthell, "Beginning as a Satirist: Joseph Hall's *Virgidemarium Six Bookes*," *SEL*, 23 (1983), 47–60; see also Anthony Caputi, *John Marston, Satirist* (Ithaca: Cornell University Press, 1961), p. 33.

[7] Despite his view that the verse satirists are too varied in their work to constitute a movement, Bernard Harris acknowledges that the differences between prose and verse

Hall paid tribute to "angry Skeltons breath-less rimes" but insisted on calling himself the first "English Satirist."[8] Even Lodge, a pioneer of seriocomic prose who was accused of having "his oare in euery paper boate," declared that his verse satires were written "in that forme, wherein no man might chalenge me with seruile imitation."[9] Formal difference implied other differences: the literary historical differences within the form (such as those between Horace and Juvenal) by which satirists could establish their slant toward antiquity and toward each other; the different modes of perception and signification which distinguished satire from native complaint; the social, intellectual, and moral differences which supposedly distinguished the verse satirists from their urban contemporaries.

It was of course paradoxical to assume that the formality of classical verse satire conferred distinction – the formal heterogeneity of the classical *satura* or *farrago* is notorious. The verse form brings to bear a full gamut of structures and devices, in an effort "to contain the multitude of conflicting attitudes that any great city requires its citizens to perceive."[10] What governs the haphazard deployment of these resources is the discursive relationship between satiric spokesman and audience at a particular place and time. This relationship involves a wealth of rhetorical structures and cultural assumptions, but more immediately striking is the opposite impression of unmediated spontaneity which these support. All that is "formal" in verse satire originates in the impression of a personal, uncompromising voice:

> Whatever the color of my life, write I must.   (Horace, *Satires*, 2.1.60)

> I have a wayward wit and must have my laugh out.
> (Persius, *Satires*, 1.11–12)

> Must I not have my fling?   (Juvenal, *Satires*, 1.51–2)

satire are not "merely formal, for the work of young men such as Donne, Sir John Davies, Guilpin, and Marston, or of Joseph Hall of Emmanuel College, is markedly different in temper from that of the University Wits. That these men began a new satirical movement is attested by Francis Meres in 1598," "Dissent and Satire," *Shakespeare Survey*, 17 (1964), p. 130.

[8] *Virgidemarium*, in *Collected Poems*, 6.1.76; 1 prol. 4; see also Arnold Stein, "The Second English Satirist," *MLR*, 38 (1943), 273–278.

[9] *The Complete Works*, ed. Edmund Gosse (4 vols. Glasgow: Huntlerian Club, 1883), 3: 6; for the charge against Lodge, see *The Pilgrimage to Parnassus, with the Two Parts of 'The Return from Parnassus'* , ed. W. D. Macray (Oxford, 1886), p. 80, cited in Hallet Smith, *Elizabethan Poetry*, (Cambridge, Mass.: Harvard University Press, 1952), p. 80.

[10] Angus Fletcher, "The Distractions of Wit in the English Renaissance," in *Colors of the Mind: Conjectures on Thinking in Literature* (Cambridge Mass.: Harvard University Press, 1991), p. 61; for a good account of the range of structural devices, see esp. Mary Claire Randolph, "The Structural Design of Formal Verse Satire," *PQ*, 21 (1942), 373.

Shall I, nones slaue, of high borne, or rais'd men,
Fear frownes? (Donne, *Satires*, 4. 162–163)

I am my selfe, so is my poesie.
(Marston, *The Scourge of Villanie*, "To Detraction," line 24)[11]

My lines are still themselves, and so am I. (Guilpin, *Skialetheia*, 6.10)

While the satirist is in part motivated by the simple imperative – *quid faciam?* (Horace, *Satires*, 2.1.44–46) – of correcting the world's folly and corruption, he draws special force from the subjective angle of his moral vision. Thus Hall chides "the world, that did *my thoughts* offend" ("Defiance to Envy," lines 113–114), while Marston vows to "plague and torture whom I list" (*SV*, 2.1.10). "Shall I lend eare to other," Guilpin asks, "and myne owne priuate Muses musicke smother?" (1.3–4).

Taking precedence over abstract moral schemes, this subjective judgement confronts the world in apparently immediate, improvisatory fashion. The satirist's judgements emerge dramatically, often with an "unplanned extempore effect… A point seemingly at issue is debated and then settled – right before the reader's eyes. A 'truth,' that is, is recorded in the act of being established."[12] Many factors led the Elizabethans to cultivate the effects of immediacy – the Socratic, dialectical nature of Horace's later satires,[13] the Stoic association of forthright expression with truthfulness and moral self-possession,[14] an impatience with the *a priori* structures of traditional complaint,[15] and a correspondingly empirical emphasis on fresh perceptions. But the primary factor was the assertion of moral difference, the claim to an unprecedented moral liberty and autonomy.[16] The couplet form was for Marston a "friendly ayde of *my* designes," enabling him to "freely range" (34, 36). Hall's satiric muse sought to surpass "former Satyrs in her libertie" (3 Prol. 1, 11–12).

[11] Marston's poems are cited from *Poems*, ed. Arnold Davenport (Liverpool University Press, 1961). References to Marston's *Certain Satyres* and *The Scourge of Villanie* will hereafter be abbreviated as *CS* and *SV*, respectively.
[12] Doris C. Powers, *English Formal Satire: Elizabethan to Augustan* (The Hague: Mouton, 1971), pp. 17, 19.
[13] See, e.g., Powers, *English Formal Satire*, p. 26; David L. Sigsbee, "The Disciplined Satire of Horace," in *Roman Satirists and Their Satire*, ed. Edwin S. Ramage, David L. Sigsbee, and Sigmund C. Fredericks (Park Ridge, N.J.: Noyes Press, 1974), p. 77; and W. S. Anderson, "The Roman Socrates: Horace and His Satires," in *Essays on Roman Satire* (Princeton University Press, 1982), pp. 13–49.
[14] Sam H. Henderson, "Neo-Stoic Influence on Elizabethan Formal Verse Satire," in *Studies in English Renaissance Literature*, ed. Waldo F. McNeir (Baton Rouge: Louisiana State University Press, 1962), pp. 56–86.
[15] Peter, *Complaint and Satire*, p. 113.
[16] On the *volonté d'indépendance* of the satirists, see Louis Lecocq, *Le satire en Angleterre de 1558 à 1683* (Paris: Didier, 1969), p. 32.

By grouping satires of variable length in books of varied size and number, the Elizabethans followed the ancients in writing satires rather than satire.[17] The clever use of titles, epigraphs, and allusions – often subjecting some *locus communis* to ironic scrutiny – emphasized the reassessment of moral and social order according to improvised premises and idiosyncratic perspectives. The "strangely haphazard" imitation of classical satire by the Elizabethans merely extended the ancient experimentation of mixed styles and effects in the interest of authorizing the satirists' personal perspectives.[18] The debt to classical satire was profound,[19] but Marston could still extol his own "free-bred poesie" (6.99–100).

In formal verse satire, then, the "hard" rhetoric of trope, analogy, and abstract framework is apparently subordinated to the softer, performative rhetoric – the "haecceity"[20] – of the inflected voice. What Donne most wanted from classical satire, Arnold Stein observes, "was the tradition for licensed freedom of movement," the personal authority "to produce telling recognitions of the rightness or wrongness of what he presented."[21] Whether characterized negatively as a "great vogue of facile criticism," or more positively as the quest for a decorum adapted to the needs of moral independence,[22] Elizabethan formal satire aspired to that

---

[17] Randolph, "Structural Design," discusses the issue of grouping satires; my distinction between satires and satire is based on Ronald Paulson, *The Fictions of Satire* (Baltimore: Johns Hopkins University Press, 1967), p. 4.

[18] "Strangely haphazard," Peter, *Complaint and Satire*, p. 117; on mixed styles, Raman Selden, *English Verse Satire, 1590–1675* (London: Allen & Unwin, 1978), pp. 45–47, 55.

[19] The most thorough census of borrowings remains R. M. Alden, *The Rise of Formal Satire in England Under Classical Influence* (1899; rpt., Hamden, Conn.: Archon Books, 1962). Harold F. Brooks argues that "the imitations are never more than contributory to the poem as a whole," "The 'Imitation' in English Poetry, Especially Formal Satire, Before the Age of Pope" (1949), in *Die Englische Satire*, ed. Wolfgang Weiss (Darmstadt: Wissenschaftliche Buchgesellschaft, 1982), p. 245. For classical influence in Donne's satires, see Niall Rudd, "Donne and Horace," *TLS*, 22 March 1963; Howard Erskine-Hill, "Courtiers Out of Horace: Donne's *Satyre IV* and Pope's *Fourth Satire of Dr. John Donne, Dean of St Paul's, Versifyed*," in *John Donne: Essays in Celebration*, ed. A. J. Smith (London: Methuen, 1972), pp. 273–307; Heather Dubrow, "'No Man is an Island': Donne's Satires and Satiric Traditions," *SEL*, 19 (1979), 71–83; Y. Skikany Eddy and Daniel P. Jaeckler, "Donne's 'Satyre I': The Influence of Persius' 'Satire III,'" *SEL*, 21 (1981), 111–122. See also Arnold Stein, "Joseph Hall's Imitation of Juvenal," *MLR*, 43 (1948), 315–332. For a characterization of Marston's "scanty first-hand acquaintance with classical satire," see Arnold Stein, "The Second English Satirist," *MLR*, 38 (1943), 273–278.

[20] See Thomas M. Greene, *The Vulnerable Text: Essays on Renaissance Literature* (New York: Columbia University Press, 1986), p. xiv.

[21] "Voices of the Satirist: John Donne," *Yearbook of English Studies*, 14 (1984), p. 74.

[22] Negatively, Harris, "Dissent and Satire," pp. 131–132; positively, Roma Gill, "A Purchase of Glory: The Persona of Late Elizabethan Satire," *SP*, 72 (1975), 408–414.

state of self possession Marston punningly called the "true iudging eye," or the "vnpartiall eye":

> What is honest, you may freely thinke,
> Speake what you thinke, and write what you doe speake,
> Not bound to servile soothings.[23]

Ben Jonson similarly claimed the satirist "alone canst judge, so alone dost make."[24] Donne's satire rose spontaneously from "my precious soule" (4.156), and Marston's from "my soule an essence metaphysicall" ("To Detraction," lines 11–12.). According to Guilpin, the satirist's ability to judge came from Reason,

> the soules bright *Genius*,
> Sent downe from *Ioues* throne to conduct vs
> In this lifes intricate daedalian maze.   (Guilpin 6.13–15)

Yet it is in just this apparent inwardness that the moral persuasiveness of ancient satire reveals itself as overdetermined, as funded by a harder rhetoric of cultural tropes and assumptions (the ideal mean, the virtues of dialectic, the Republican virtues and heritage, patrician privilege, and the ethical resources of friendship). These vary with each satirist, but even so basic a device as conversational or epistolary address reveals how much the ancient satirist draws on societal and cultural support. Horace can name his discriminating friends (*Satires*, 1.10.81–91), address his *boni* (2.2.1), or celebrate the inner circle where "est locus uni / cuiusque suus" (1.9.51–52). Persius can praise the concord that links his judgement with others' (5.45–6). Even Juvenal can converse with his Umbricius or Persicus, or find diminished consolation in the Roman *virtus* that ends the tenth satire. There is a *laus* that balances the satirist's *vituperatio*, a metacommunication which implicitly celebrates shared values, or what Donne called "a confident community of those things which we know."[25]

The conventions of familiar address in Elizabethan satire indicate a desire to situate moral judgement in a similarly shared social ground.

---

[23] Marston, *The Fawn*, 1.2, in *The Plays of John Marston*, ed. H. Harvey Wood (Edinburgh: Oliver and Boyd, 1938), 2: 158.

[24] Ben Jonson, Epigram "To John Donne," in *The Complete Poems*, ed. George Parfitt (1975; rpt. New Haven: Yale University Press, 1982), p. 67; cf. Lodge's claim to "have written, as I have read: so read, as I can iudge" (*Works*, 3: 7). See also Horace, *Satires*, 2.6.75–78, Persius, *Satires*, 5.104.

[25] *Letters*, p. 121, quoted in Arthur F. Marotti, *John Donne, Coterie Poet* (Madison: University of Wisconsin Press, 1986), p. 22; Marotti makes brilliant use of the concept of "metacommunication," borrowed from Gregory Bateson, *Steps to an Ecology of Mind* (New York: Ballantine Books, 1972), p. 178.

The persistent use of *indicatio* also implies a society of discriminating minds; it not only summons up illustrations with spatio-temporal immediacy but also draws a moral distinction between "that-over-there" and "you-and-me-here."[26] In contrast to the persona in complaint, typically "a clerk or plebeian moralist" who can only lament at the corruption above his lowly station,[27] the verse satirist shares with his implied audience a social as well as moral high ground from which to condescend. Thus the "comical satire" of the turn-of-the-century private theaters, which adapted the spirit of court revelry to the persona of the verse satirist, invited the privileged audience to join a spokesman–satirist in ridiculing the "others," – "usurers, merchants, *nouveaux riches*, fawning parasites, upstart courtiers, and puritans."[28] Crites, Jonson's satirist in *Cynthia's Revels*, is reassured by Mercury that his "ironical confederacy" will be licensed by the virtue of the elite:

> The better race in court
> That have the true nobility call'd virtue,
> Will apprehend it as a grateful right
> Done to their separate merit.   (5.1)

The epilogues and prologues of many comical satires bear witness, however, to the fragile nature of this elite sociability in the theater.[29] Similarly, the Elizabethan verse satirists' elaborate prefaces, postscripts, proems and programmatic statements reflect more than the convention of the satirist's apologia;[30] in their failed attempts to inscribe an ideal readership, in their wavering between the merits of obscurity or plainness, mirth or scourging, they demonstrate a genuine inability to define a stable style or to substantiate the satirist's judgement by appeal to a sustaining social terrain. Marston would exclude the "swarme of Idiots" from an idealized audience of "diviner wits, celestiall soules, / Whose free-borne mindes no kennel thought controules" (p. 98). But in

---

[26] Walter J. Ong, "The Writer's Audience is Always a Fiction," in *Interfaces of the Word: Studies in the Evolution of Consciousness and Culture* (Ithaca: Cornell University Press, 1977), pp. 62–66; Annabel Patterson notes that Hermogenes regards as a feature of the condescending or vehement style "the figure of *Indicatio*," whereby "one may attack one's victims with pronouns (*hic, iste, ille*), which are denigrating by their rejection of personality as well as by their brevity," *Hermogenes and the Renaissance: Seven Ideas of Style* (Princeton University Press, 1970), p. 107.

[27] Peter, *Complaint and Satire*, p. 112; Selden, *English Verse Satire*, p. 48.

[28] Michael Shapiro, *Children of the Revels: The Boy Companies of Shakespeare's Time and Their Plays* (New York: Columbia University Press, 1977), p. 50; see also O. J. Campbell, *Comicall Satire and Shakespeare's "Troilus and Cressida"* (San Marino: Huntington Library, 1938), passim.

[29] See Shapiro, *Children of the Revels*, pp. 70–79.

[30] Lucius Shero, "The Satirist's Apologia," *Classical Studies in Language and Literature*, ser. 2: 15 (1922).

his and other Elizabethan satires, the rhetoric of shared ethos is undermined by a rhetoric of isolation – by the tendency of apostrophes to moral abstractions to replace social address, by the degeneration of second-person confreres into third-person targets, by the decline of intimate wit into declamation. If these latter two tendencies suggest a resort to Juvenalian precedent, this is not so much a matter of choice as of necessary compensation for a failed Horatian sociability. A pattern not found in classical satire but crucial to the Elizabethans is the urgent but futile attempt to win over a young companion, a mirror of the speaker, at the very moment he is being lost to the world's folly.[31] The urgency of the task underlines the absence of a secure ethos. If for the Elizabethans the satiric heritage comprised a range of possible strategies, the extremes of which are Horace at his most secure and poised and Juvenal at his most isolate and enraged, then the latter was a compensation for the failure to create within contemporary society a durably Horatian ideal. The early Horatian experiments of Donne and Lodge, together with the widespread epistolary fashion and the Horatianism of Jonson, which followed the more Juvenalian works of Hall, Marston, and Guilpin, suggests that the formal difference of verse satire resided in its attempt to establish moral and social difference. As Ben Jonson put it, "Rare poems ask rare friends" and those who "like them ... must needfully, though few, / Be of the best."[32]

The power of discrimination was meant to enable the satirists to prosecute the world extemporaneously, without reliance on traditional moral frameworks. Marston, for example, rejects all muses but "my Genius" (*SV* proem lib. 3). Eschewing allegorical schemes and moral systems, the satirists sought to identify and discriminate among the world's ills in more immanent terms, by means of improvised comparisons. They negotiated for a self-possessed moral standing *within* the world. The strength of this position was the ability to weigh greater and lesser, tolerable and intolerable evils.

The problem, however, was that unsupported by persuasive social or cultural tropes, the soul's comparisons yielded not so much a moral scale as a slippery, bottomless slope. Comparison became an exercise in diminishing perspectives, while reasonable concessions became gestures of retreat rather than of balanced certitude:

[31] Examples would be Donne's "fondling motley humorist" (Satire 1), the version of Hall first addressed by Marston (*Certain Satyres*, 4), or Guilpin's Fabian (Satire 3).

[32] "To Lucy, Countess of Bedford, with Mr. Donne's *Satires*," in *The Complete Poems*, p. 66. Richard C. Newton relates Jonson to the satirist's attempt "to gather about himself a literate and moral community which shares with him the strength and moral insight necessary to remain upright even in the midst of the worst corruption," "'Goe, Quit 'hem all': Ben Jonson and Formal Verse Satire," *SEL*, 16 (1976), p. 106.

> Sir; though (I thanke God for it) I do hate
> Perfectly all this towne, yet there's one state
> In all ill things so excellently best
> That hate, towards them, breeds pitty towards the rest.   (Donne 2.1–4)

The Elizabethan satirists, in other words, were socially vulnerable, lacking not only the models of community Horace finds in the elite circle of Maecenas and in his own balanced soul, but even (with the possible exception of Hall) the potent nostalgia with which Juvenal evokes the unextinguished memory of communal ideals in order to give the lie to the present. The residual influence of medieval complaint did occasionally engender fitful evocations of traditional ideals of place, degree, obligation, service, and plain English virtue. But such conservation rarely became, as W. S. Anderson has shown it does for Juvenal, a compositional source of stability equivalent to Horatian poise.[33]

In Elizabethan satire, the act of moral discrimination was animated by opposing tensions, for which Horatian poise and sociability and Juvenalian rage and lament were rough exemplars. Even as the satirists sought to ground their moral improvisations in the possibility of a shared ethos, they were thrust back upon a sense of moral isolation. Unable to establish the essential difference that would separate a moral center "here" from what is "there," the satirists' perspective was forced from the inside to the outside of the elite circle of honor and distinction, condemned to the haecceity of an alien world that was only "there." On occasion the satirists responded to this experience, as did Juvenal, with a conservative resort to the traditional ideals of complaint, or to myths – like pastoral virtue or the Golden Age – which offered an alternative to the corrupted spatio-temporal "there" of the contemporary world. Yet, with the partial exception of Hall, the satirists typically surpassed Juvenal in their despairing perception that in the present such myths were without foundation. Indeed, the perceived absence of such foundations was the fundamental premise of verse satire, the reason for its rejection of received moral frameworks and its assertion of the essential difference of subjective discrimination. The fragility of this difference is reflected in the fact that the major works in this highly self-conscious, individualistic

---

[33] Anderson, "Studies in Book I of Juvenal," in *Essays on Roman Satire*, pp. 252–253. On Juvenal's movement toward balance, see W. S. Anderson, "Anger in Seneca and Juvenal," in *Essays on Roman Satire*, pp. 293–361. Many commentators note, however, that these "ideal" moments are undercut by irony and exaggeration. See Sigmund C. Fredericks, "Juvenal: A Return to Invective," in Ramage, Sigsbee, and Fredericks, *Roman Satirists*, pp. 158–159 and H. A. Mason, "Is Juvenal a Classic?" in J. P. Sullivan, ed., *Critical Essays on Roman Literature: Satire* (London: Routledge & Kegan Paul, 1963), pp. 93–176.

genre were published anonymously or not at all. This would-be laureate master-genre actually sustained no careers, existed only to be given up. Hence its peculiarly naked, vulnerable inflection: " Seeke true religion. O where?" (Donne, 3.43).

To claim simply that "the Elizabethan satirist was a strange, twisted character, and the poets seemed to have delighted in multiplying his peculiarities"[34] is crudely to summarize stylistic effects which emerged from a complex series of intentions. The tensions between poise and extravagance, self-defense and self-consuming aggression may be universal to satire,[35] but they took a particular shape in Elizabethan satire, a shape dictated both by the satirists' peculiar situation in the social structure of Elizabethan London and by their corresponding analysis of socio-linguistic order.

Hallett Smith has said that the sources of Elizabethan satire "are not literary or philosophical; they are social and economic."[36] Yet the developments he summarizes – agrarian change, inflation, poverty, the dissolution of the monasteries, new commercial practices, monopolies – show relatively little direct impact on verse satire, either on its targets or on its apparently associational, non-analytic, improvised construction.[37] Constructed from a series of often stereotypical portraits, verse satire, Peter complains, is "like nothing so much as a string of epigrams" (p. 165). The Elizabethan satirists differ from their Roman predecessors, J. B. Leishman concludes, in their inability to generalize, in the "absence of clear outline and plan, a tendency to pile detail upon detail and to present us with just one damned thing after another" (pp. 111, 121). "No author of Elizabethan satire had a clear idea of what was basically wrong with his society" is the verdict of Kernan (p. 86).

Yet the improvised, associational structure of verse satire – its preference for metonymy over metaphor – is in fact an analytical instrument strikingly appropriate to the represented superficiality of the social types most often condemned. And this fit between social type and mode of figuration serves a sometimes deep and pointed reflection on society. While denying the satirists any scientific percipience, Kernan allows that "the traditional fools and villains" which the Elizabethan satirist "displays in his satires *do* have an innate similarity ... The common butts of the new satire are the members of the rising middle class ... and if the

---

[34] Kernan, *The Cankered Muse*, p. 89.
[35] See pp. 29–35, and Michael Seidel, *Satiric Inheritance, Rabelais to Sterne* (Princeton University Press, 1979), pp. 11–23.   [36] *Elizabethan Poetry*, p. 194.
[37] Wesley Milgate, for example, characterizes the typical subjects of Donne's satires as "in the worst sense, imitative ... the stock-in-trade of Roman satire, and indeed of sermons, homilies, and moral writings throughout the ages," *Satires, Epigrams, and Verse Letters*, p. xviii.

creation of this rogues' gallery was a somewhat sporadic and not entirely
conscious process, it was not haphazard" (pp. 86–87). Not so much the
representatives of a consolidated "middle class" as the mobile and
anomalous groups who were, in the midst of an urbanizing society, "en
transfert de classe,"[38] the common targets of verse satire are the many
varieties of "gilded vagabonds";[39] they range upward from farmers,
merchants, and their sons and downward from courtiers, lawyers and
their offspring. All of them swarm like flies around London.

Donne's satires are a thorough census of such estateless or pretentious
urbanites: the motley humorist and the swaggering captains, perfumed
courtiers, well-favored dancers, tobacconists, and fashion-mongers he
idolizes (1); a broking lawyer (2); merchant venturers who fear the
spiritual quest (3); slime-bred courtiers (4), foolish suitors and corrupt
officials (5). Hall and Guilpin concern themselves with similar strata,
while Marston, three-quarters of whose targets come from the gentry,[40]
compiles a swollen catalogue of broking gents, Italianate gallants,
monopoly-hunters, usurers, swaggerers, lawyers, painted ladies, plagiarizing pedants and prodigals.

On the surface, at least, the threat embodied in these figures is not their
systematic violation of social norms but their manipulation of appearances to satisfy personal ambition. To be sure, their estatelessness
reflects a general discomfort with social mobility. For Hall, at least,
personal ambitions are seen as well to have a devastating impact on the
unprotected victims of the new economy. But in general the emphasis
falls not on social injustice but on fraudulence, hypocrisy, dissimulation,
and pretence. These are the sorts of falsehood against which the satirists,
exercising the privilege of immediate, personal judgement, assert the
essential difference that marks the access to truth in the soul of the
satirist. With "truth on my side," Hall aims to clear "the worlds eye
bleared with these shameless lies" (prol. lib. 1, lines 5, 17), and Marston
claims the glory of "tearing the vaile from damn'd Impietie" (*SV*,
proem. lib. 1, line 18). The title of Guilpin's *Skialetheia. Or, A Shadowe
of Truth, in Certaine Epigrams and Satyres* proclaims allegiance to the
ideal of establishing verity.[41] The idea of exposing falsehood is of course
well adapted both to the medical theories which associated satire with

---

[38] Lecocq, *Le satire en Angleterre*, p. 81.

[39] H. V. Routh, "London and the Development of Popular Literature," in *The Cambridge
History of English Literature*, ed. A. W. Ward and A. R. Waller (15 vols. Cambridge
University Press, 1907–33), 4: 363.

[40] Philip J. Finkelpearl, *John Marston of the Middle Temple: An Elizabethan Dramatist in
his Social Setting* (Cambridge, Mass.: Harvard University Press, 1969), p. 90.

[41] On the ideal of "verity" as a stylistic decorum of satire, see Patterson, *Hermogenes and
the Renaissance*, pp. 118–121.

surgery, cauterizing, and catharsis,[42] and to the idea that satire punishes as it tells the truth, stripping folly naked and making the ears of its victims glow with shame.[43] But it is also the essence of the satirist's power to discriminate, to define through the exclusion of falsehood the authentic values and community with which he identifies.

The types of falsehood exposed are many and rarely distinguished systematically by the satirists themselves. The deepest engagement, however, is with those forms of simulation which empty social surfaces of the power to signify true worth, thereby depriving the satirist of any visible community with which to identify. The least problematic form of falsehood is dissimulation, a pretence not to be or to have what one in fact is or has. As Bacon put it, dissimulation is a feigning "in the negative, when a man lets fall signs and arguments that he is not what he is."[44] Dissimulations are perpetrated by hypocrites – *quedam sunt, et non videntur*, in the formula Marston takes from Epictetus.[45] Their false identity is easily broken down to yield the traditional core of vice or folly which is being dissimulated. The satirists often claim to be exposing "vizar-fac't, pole-head dissimulation" (Guilpin, 1.57), inciting their muse to open up "the hidden entrailes of ranke villanie" (*SV* proem lib.1, line 17) or to "unmask" the "vgly face of vice" (Hall, prol. lib. 1, line 20). Yet the instances where the stripping of disguise yields the name of a traditional vice or evil are relatively few – there is probably no single figure in all of Donne's satires who reduces to such a stable core of motive.

A significantly more common form of falsehood is counterfeiting, the substitution of the guise for the reality, the pretense of having or being what one lacks or is not. Bacon called it a feigning "in the affirmative, when a man industriously and expressly feigns and pretends to be that he is not."[46] Apes and pretenders – *quedam videntur, et non sunt* in Marston's scheme (*CS* 1) – abound in the satires. Their presence is a symptom of the transition from a symbolically obligatory social order to a semiotics of fashion. The satiric preoccupation with upstarts and counterfeiters recognizes in social mobility the troubling possibility of misrepresen-

---

[42] See Mary Claire Randolph, "The Medical Concept in English Renaissance Satiric Theory: Its Possible Relationships and Implications," *SP*, 38 (1941), 125–157.

[43] See Jonson, *Every Man Out of his Humour*, in *Works*, 3: 428; Hall, *Virgidemiae*, 4.1.36. The idea of satire as a scourge or lash is a commonplace enshrined in many titles. Guilpin notes that satire is more effective than preaching because it does not simply admonish but also punishes, thus encouraging reform, *The Satyrs Whipper his Pennance in a White Sheete* (1601), in A. Davenport, ed., *The Whipper Pamphlets* (Liverpool University Press, 1951), p. 43.

[44] "Of Simulation and Dissimulation," in *The Essays*, ed. John Pitcher (Harmondsworth: Penguin, 1985), p. 77.   [45] See notes to *CS* 1–3.

[46] "Of Simulation and Dissimulation," p. 77.

tation. As the distribution of wealth and the spread of mobility invalidate such closed systems as the estates, professions, and degrees by opening access to the visible means by which status is signified, the immediate, obligatory, sacramental signs of social order become the arbitrary media of circulation in a competitive system of fashion.[47] This transformation is written into the stategies of Elizabethan seriocomic prose, where traditional models of social order are stripped of their timeless significance and revealed (and deployed) as the temporal instruments by which a changing society represents itself.

But if it denies the transparent, iconic relation between sign and status, style and substance, the idea of true or false representation nevertheless assumes the possibility of intelligible mediation between social image and reality. If gold does not signify social worth, then perhaps it does at least signify wealth. The feigned or counterfeit appearance, therefore, can still be understood as merely a false representation of the real, "natural" relationships between the signs used by a society and the priorities they signify. In verse satire, the presence of a core of moral truth or natural fact underlying appearance motivates the writer to discriminate between the counterfeit and the genuine representation. The satirists thus resort to the honored techniques of juxtaposition, parody, and the classic norm[48] in order to expose the "slie dissemblance stamp" which gives "a sunne-shine title to a lampe" (Guilpin, 1. 121–122). Marston, for example, exposes the social counterfeits in the first of his *Certaine Satyres* by invoking the various ideals (compliment, courtship, true heroic spirit – lines 19, 28, 119) they ape. And in his satire on "Humours," where he lashes a series of pretty fools who imitate "that which is but Gentries ornament" (*SV* 11.189), he explicitly juxtaposes real and counterfeit gentility. Donne juxtaposes literary originality to the counterfeiter who spews out others' works "As his owne things" (2.25–28), and his third satire turns on the juxtaposition between true spiritual courage and its worldly counterfeits. Throughout Hall's satires, new-made men are exposed as inept imitators of true courtesy (3.3), charity (3.4), and hospitality (5.2), thus laying themselves open to parody. The techniques of juxtaposition and parody imply the pervasive presence of classic norms, the existence of deep-seated grounds of judgement toward which the satirist's discriminations point as vehicle to tenor.

[47] Jean Baudrillard, *Simulations*, tr. Paul Foss, Paul Patton, and Philip Beitchman (New York: Semiotext(e), 1983), pp. 84–85.

[48] I take these terms, and their contrast with simulation (which, following Baudrillard, I substitute for the term "counterfeiting"), quotation, and connoisseurship from Hugh Kenner, *The Counterfeiters: An Historical Comedy* (1968; rpt. New York: Anchor Books, 1973), pp. xi–xii.

Yet this metaphoric evocation of moral substance through appeal to classic norms is threatened by a more potent falsification, the sort of simulation that abolishes all sense of difference between true and false, real and imaginary. If the semiotics of representation allows for counterfeiting, it nonetheless "leaves the reality principle intact: the difference is always clear, it is only masked" (Baudrillard, p. 5). Simulation, by contrast, is a mode of signification governed not by underlying truth but by relationships among signs themselves. Simulated realities are produced from the nuclear, genetic potential of signs. The social practices, manners, and codes which in a semiotics of representation are oriented, as means to ends, to the order of values they signify, become oriented instead, as products to process, to the potential they contain for recombination and mutation (Baudrillard, pp. 110–111). As the satirists are forced against their will from community to isolation, from the premise that truth and virtue have a social realization in the world toward the ultimately political act of doubting that moral substance inheres in the mechanisms of social order, it is as if they move from a semiotics of representation to a semiotics of simulation. These different semiotic frameworks help to polarize the dialectical battle with society which the poems dramatize, a battle between society's promise to accommodate virtue and the dark suspicion that society is entirely – only – what it appears to be: a concatenation of self-generating and self-perpetuating roles, structures and functions without moral foundation.

The latter possibility finds expression in Marston's survey of those who are what they appear to be – *quedam et sunt, et videntur* (*CS* 3), but it is evident, too, in the techniques which supersede the representational devices of juxtaposition, parody, and classic norms – the techniques of simulation, phosphorescent quotation, and connoisseurship. What disables the ploy of juxtaposing the social counterfeiter to the genuine is the more radical scenario where all of civilized life becomes a simulated or substitute reality, where

> Nothing but cossenage doth the world possesse,
> And stuffes the large armes of his emptines. (Guilpin, 1.83)

In this case, the world's social organization is a self-reproducing semiotic matter which simulates, and thereby supplants, real moral being with "naught but clothes, and images of men, / But sprightles truncks" (Marston, *SV*, *In lectores*, lines 59–60). The power of *seeming to be* – of displaying all the signs of that which one would desire to be thought to be – thrusts Marston's Cynick Satirist, searching London for a true human being, toward the dismal conclusion that

> These are no men, but Apparitions,
> Ignes fatui, Glowormes, Fictions,
> Meteors, Ratts of Nylus, Fantasies,
> Colosses, Pictures, Shades, Resemblences.   (*SV* 7.13–16)

For Marston, as the social process displaces truth and being, the world is seen to have "lost thy soule, for naught but shades I see, / Resemblences of men inhabite thee" (*SV* 7.141–142). In this darker scenario, ritual surfaces and routines possess the power to construct a simulated reality, to "make Christen-soules" (Hall, 2.5.4–5). Where the signifier is taken as the signified, the whole order of creation is anthropomorphically reversed:

> Almighty men ... can their Maker make,
> And force his sacred body to forsake
> The cherubines, to be gnawne actually,
> Deuiding individuum, really.   (*SV* 2.84–87)

Where reality is not so much counterfeited as simulated, and juxtaposition is therefore impossible, Marston can only confess that his inamorato Lucian is "no Janus, but substantial," and that his foppish Duceus is "no accident, / But reall, reall" (*SV* 3.73, 85–86). The soul and its power to discriminate are thwarted by a proliferation of sixteenth-century automata, "Idols, Puppets, Exchange babies" (Guilpin, 2.11). According to Marston's Cynick Satirist,

>   puppets, painted Images,
> Haberdashers shops, torchlight maskeries,
> Perfuming pans, Dutch ancients, Glowe-wormes bright
> ... soile our soules, and dampe our reasons light.   (*SV* 7.180–183)

In a world where "All are players," there is no longer any pretence; acting and counterfeiting yield to automatism, a mechanic operation of the spirit wherein

> As in some Organ, Puppits dance above
> And bellows pant below, which do them move.   (4.185)

Waxwork figures, Donne argues in one of his most penetrating tropes, "flout our Presence" – our ruler and our being – by sharing our own hyperreal ontology; we are, he claims, "at London...Just such gay painted things, which no sappe, nor / Tast have in them" (4.171–173). When Donne's lawyer Coscus reconstitutes the English landscape "In parchments then, large as his fields," the essential ontological difference which separates map from terrain, signifier from signified, dissolves into one seamlessly perfect surface. Coscus can make whatever landscape he likes.

Without the possibility of juxtaposition, parody thus becomes indistinguishable from original. The satirist must resort to what Kenner
calls "phosphorescent quotation," the mere reproduction or recording
of what cannot be exposed as falsified or distorted. Hall is the master of
this technique, but Donne uses it in his fourth satire to attack a slime-
bred courtier whose speech cannot be placed or exposed as false but only
quoted. Unlike the speech of Coscus, which can still be heard as a
distortion of classic amatory and legal norms (and thus rhetorically
parodied by the satirist), the courtier's speech is not a deviation but itself
an all-consuming norm. As the courtier speaks the satirist finds his own
moral being eroded:

> for hearing him, I found
> That as burnt venom'd Lechers doe grow sound
> By giving others their soares, I might growe
> Guilty, and he free. (4.133–136)

The differences between juxtaposition and simulation, parody and
quotation, entail a movement toward a purely presentational concern
with surfaces. Caught up in this movement, the satirists risk losing sight
of classic norms in their connoisseurship of simulations. The hyperreality
of the surface, of affections, poses, types, and tinsel trappings, is a trap for
satirists. It pushes them toward what Eliot called "poetry of the surface,"
or what Wyndham Lewis labelled an "orgy of externals."[49]

Unlike its epigrammatic companion-form, which attempts to re-order
the world's surface in telling schemes and abstract symmetries, verse
satire makes its discriminations primarily on the basis of tropes.[50] Yet
these tend more toward the obsessional associations and contiguities of
simile and metonymy than toward the liberating transports of metaphor.
The part or attribute suffices to characterize a state of being which runs
no deeper than its outward signs. Marston's London usurer, for example,
is a completely metonymic being, "*naught* but budge, old gards, browne
foxe-fur face. / *He hath no soule*, the which the Stagerite / Term'd
rationall" (*SV* 7.65–67).

Thus, instead of joining or contrasting orders of significance, metonymy merely leads the satirists across the surface of the one and only
discourse given by society itself.[51] Simile becomes primarily a measure of

---

[49] T. S. Eliot, "Ben Jonson," in *Selected Essays* (New York: Harcourt Brace & World,
1960), p. 132; Wyndham Lewis, "The Greatest Satire is Nonmoral," in Ronald
Paulson, ed., *Satire: Essays in Modern Criticism* (Englewood Cliffs, N. J.: Prentice-
Hall, 1971), p. 78. [50] Powers, *English Formal Satire*, p. 53.
[51] For a contrast between metaphoric "joining a plurality of worlds" and metonymic
"movement within a single world of discourse," see René Wellek and Austin Warren,
Theory of Literature (New York: Harcourt Brace, 1942), p. 200.

satiric connoisseurship, and the attempt to negotiate essential moral difference by comparison digresses into a catalogue of contiguous surfaces. The swaggering manner of Marston's Martius, for example, implies no classic norm so powerfully as it declares its association with other surfaces; his hacked dagger-blade proclaims

> It slew as many as figures of yeares
> *Aqua fortis* eate in't, or as many more,
> As methodist *Musus*, kild with Hellebore
> In autumne last, yet he beares the male lye
> With as smooth calme, as *Mecho* rivalrie.   (*SV* 1.1–8)

As C. S. Lewis said of Donne, "instead of a norm against which the immediate object of satire stands out, we have vistas opening on corruption in every direction."[52]

The techniques of incidental satire – comparison, parenthesis, digression, catalogue – were inherited from Roman satire, but their prominence in Elizabethan satire has important implications. First of all, the restriction of reference to social surface by means of simile, association, and comparison reinforces the substitution of the satirists' subjective "eye" for the moral metaphorics of complaint. It reinforces, too, the bias which interprets the world through its appearances. The result is a "scientific" concern with fashion, a descriptive analysis of social functions, mechanisms, and relationships. Kenneth Burke points out that insofar as the figure of metonymy shares with science a concern "with operations rather than with substances," it becomes necessarily the "reduction of some higher or more complex realm of being to the terms of a lower or less complex realm of being."[53] Like scientific method, Elizabethan verse satire reproduces itself in the world it analyzes: metonymically focused on the mediation of status by style and surface, it reduces classical *humanitas* to the cultural rules and materials by which the effects of moral existence are produced.[54]

For this radical ethical position there is a correspondingly radical view of the social order: metonymy encourages daringly improvised comparisons across the boundaries of status. The strutting and talking of

---

[52] *English Literature in the Sixteenth Century*, p. 470. For another such metonymic "vista," see Hall, 4.2.37–48.

[53] Appendix D, "Four Master Tropes," in *A Grammar of Motives* (New York: George Braziller, 1955), pp. 505–506.

[54] Kenner observes that "Swift's age was groping its way to a principle familiar to ours, that you can be said to understand a process thoroughly if you know how to instruct a machine to carry it out. ('To understand is to construct,' said Da Vinci.) This makes a related proposition seem plausible: to the extent that you can simulate an organism, to that extent you understand what it is," *The Counterfeiters*, pp. 12–13.

Donne's lawyer Coscus, for example, leads by association upward and across the comparable counterfeitings which together found a whole society:

> Now like an owlelike watchman, hee must walke
> His hand still at a bill, now he must talke
> Idly, like prisoners, which whole months will sweare
> That onely suretiship hath brought them there,
> And to' every suitor lye in every thing,
> Like a Kings favorite, yea like a King;
> ... Bastardy abounds not in a Kings titles, nor
> Symonie and Sodomy in Churchmens lives,
> As these things do in him; by these he thrives. (2.65–76)

For Marston, as for Donne, there is often no end to comparison. Marston achieves his satiric penetration not by moving from surface to depth but by moving across associated surfaces and types until nothing remains. Within a few lines, Flavia's blush leads to the highest places:

> *Flauia* would blush to flout
> When *Oppia* calls *Lucina* to help her out.
> If she did thinke, *Lynceus* did know her ill,
> How Nature, Art, how Art doth Nature spill.
> God pardon me, I often did auer
> Quod gratis, grate, the Astronomer
> An honest man, but I'le do so no more,
> His face deceau'd me; but now since his whore
> And sister are all one, his honestie
> Shall be as bare as his Anatomie,
> To which hee bound his wife, o packstaffe rimes!
> Why not, when court of starrs shal see these crimes? (*SV*, 1.32–43)

The devastating social disillusionment with the "court of stars" probably includes a reference to the gossip Aubrey later recorded about the greatest Elizabethan stargazer, Sir Philip Sidney: "there was so great love between him and his sister that I have heard old gentlemen ... say that they lay together."[55] In a sense, Marston would have had to invent such rumors had they not already existed. Working by analogy and contiguity, the magic of Marston's figures is at once imitative and contagious: metaphorically it evokes the essential moral difference which is the satirist's judgement, but by the power of association it effectively rules out any *rapprochement* between this judgement and the social order.[56] If the first of these tendencies represents the satirist's attempt to

---

[55] Davenport quotes the rumor "reluctantly" in his edition, p. 273.
[56] On imitative and contagious magic, see Sir James Frazer, *The Golden Bough: A Study in Magic and Religion* (abr. edn. New York: Macmillan, 1940), p. 12.

conserve a moral refuge, the second reveals how "little is truly conserved in the satiric rendering of human behavior."[57]

"Poetic vaine circumference": the isolation of the satirist

The tensions within verse satire reflect a social structure which placed the satirists at the very outside boundaries of privileged circles and communities of honor – the nobility, the court, the City commune, the legal profession. Like the professional prose moralists who influenced them, the major verse satirists were (with the exception of Hall) marginalized urbanites, yet with an essential difference. In contrast to Greene, the son of a Norwich saddler, Nashe, the son of a rural clergyman, or Dekker, the descendant of Dutch weavers, the satirist stood higher in the mobile ranks of Elizabethan society, in an echelon wealthier, more urbanized, and somewhat closer to the state apparatus.[58] Donne was the son of a wealthy London ironmonger (who had left him £3,000 at his birth) and was descended on his mother's side from the Lord Chancellor, Sir Thomas More. Marston was the son of a prominent Reader, Bencher, and Treasurer of the Middle Temple. Guilpin was the son of a bureaucrat in the Court of Exchequer. Lodge, the only writer of popular prose in this group, was significantly the son of a Lord Mayor of London and, unlike the university-educated Nashe and Greene, a sometime resident of Lincoln's Inn. The residence of all the satirists but Hall at the Inns of Court – and hence their proximity to the powerful and to the means of preferment within the capital – accounts for the assertion of literary and social difference in verse satire, for its pointed disdain of popular and professional writing.[59] Unlike the pamphleteers, the satirists ended their lives in respectable careers, Marston and (probably) Guilpin as clergymen, Donne as Dean of St. Paul's, and Hall as a bishop.

London's Inns of Court offered their members a community which was in many ways autonomous but at the same time contiguous with London's competing centers of wealth and power. Unlike the universities, which still retained strong affiliations with the Church and the old

---

[57] Seidel, who also notes that "the author's preference for the surfaces of things goes deeper than he imagines," *Satiric Inheritance*, pp. 21–22.

[58] See Phoebe Sheavyn, *The Literary Profession in the Elizabethan Age*, 2nd edn. J. W. Saunders (New York: Barnes and Noble, 1967), p. 128; Edwin H. Miller, *The Professional Writer in Elizabethan England* (Cambridge, Mass.: Harvard University Press, 1959), pp. 7–10.

[59] The relation of verse satire to the milieu of the Inns is treated by Finkelpearl, *John Marston of the Middle Temple*, chs. 2 and 7; Marotti, *John Donne: Coterie Poet*, pp. 27–118; and Anthony Caputi, *John Marston, Satirist*, pp. 6–22.

clerical estate, the Inns were geared toward the novel, diversifying professions created by London's burgeoning administrative, financial, and mercantile functions. To a greater degree than university-educated civilians, the Inns' common lawyers made careers in a variety of ways, as "accountants, financiers, entrepreneurs, and land agents."[60] The location of the Inns, at the threshold between Westminster and London, court and City, symbolized both their autonomy and their multiple affiliations with the constituent elements of the capital's life. In the fifteenth century, Fortescue had stressed the autonomy by noting that "the place of study is not in the heart of the city itself, where the great confluence and multitude of the inhabitants might distract them in their studies; but in a private place, separate and distinct by itself, in the suburbs."[61] By the seventeenth century, however, when the area around the Inns had become more closely interwoven with the urban fabric, William Dugdale emphasized instead the steady traffic of clients that made scholarly cloister and urban crossroads nearly indistinguishable: "the Students," he said, "may as quietly study in the open streets, as in their Studies."[62] After remaining steady since the fifteenth century, the population of the Inns increased by 30 percent in the last quarter of the sixteenth century.[63] Some of the growth reflects the increasing use of the Inns as finishing schools, fashionable residences, and entrances to careers for aspiring gentlemen, whose amateur status distinguished them from the practicing benchers and professional students. The *Gesta Grayorum*, the Gray's Inn Revels for 1594–95, advises young members to "frequent the Theatre, and such like places of Experience; and resort to the better sort of Ord'naries for Conference, whereby they may... become accomplished with Civil Conversations, and able to govern a Table with Discourse."[64] Such matters as wit, reveling, fencing, dancing, and the mastery of fashion were not recreational but vocational; as Dugdale put it, the members practised "such... exercises as might make them more seviceable to the King's court."[65]

The City's merchant oligarchy, to which the leading benchers were tied by office, investment and marriage, was another influence on experience at the Inns. The competing pressures of these different power structures accounts in part for the peculiar ethos of the Inns, an ethos

[60] Wilfred R. Prest, *The Inns of Court under Elizabeth I and the Early Stuarts, 1590–1640* (Totowa, N. J.: Rowman and Littlefield, 1972), p. 22.

[61] *De Laudibus Legum Angliae*, cited in Finkelpearl, *John Marston of the Inner Temple*, p. 4.   [62] *Origines Juridiciales* (1671), quoted in ibid., p. 10.

[63] Ibid., p. 10; by Prest's estimate, there was a more than 100 percent increase between 1550 and 1600, *The Inns of Court*, pp. 5–7.

[64] *Gesta Grayorum*, ed. Desmond Bland (Liverpool University Press, 1968), p. 41.

[65] Quoted by Finkelpearl, *John Marston of the Inner Temple*, p. 9.

consisting not so much of a positive content as of a range of improvised responses to different social possibilities. The Gray's Inn Revels nicely illustrate the fundamental ambivalence that tended to arise from these juxtaposed possibilities. In this festive work, the elaborate ceremonies and proceedings of the mock Prince Purpoole and his many functionaries are at once a satiric parody and a serious rehearsal for the courtly and administrative roles the revellers hoped one day to take up. The mixture of mockery and seriousness in these simulations at once exposes office, status, and power as fictions and endorses them as realities.

It does no service to the Inn's revellers or to satirists to reduce their ambivalence to the envy and bitterness of "those whose ambitions were frustrated and who yearned to involve themselves more deeply in the social environments they pretended to scorn."[66] This merely glosses the surface of an inner struggle to locate by discrimination a social framework that could accommodate the essential moral difference demanded by the individual soul. Life at the Inns epitomized the power of urban life to transform a structure of obligations into a range of opportunities and choices. According to Richard Brathwait, social awareness and moral self-possession enabled the gentleman to view "the City, with a princely command of his affections. No obiect can draw him from himselfe; or so intraunce his thoughts, as to admire ought seruilely."[67] The difficulty was that a powerful sense of moral consequence still attended an act of choice for which few traditional moral guidelines were available. If there is a condescension in the Inns of Court ethos which suggests a "confident sense of belonging to an elite in a world of gulls" (Finkelpearl, p. 73), it is also true that the multiplying definitions of gallants, gulls, humorists and fantastics in the late Elizabethan period reflects a genuine malaise, a fundamental uncertainty as to where *gaucherie* ends and exquisiteness begins.[68] The typical scenario in Elizabethan satire dramatizes random encounters forced on the individual in public spaces which are un-mediated or overmediated by rules and expectations – in antechambers and at thresholds, in presence rooms, and above all "in London streets" (*CS* 3.10) or "along in London way" (Hall, 3.5.5). The resort to caricature and broad typification compensates for raw exposure to streets that "swarme / With troupes of men" (*SV* 7.3–4), to a "Chaos of rude sounds... / Compos'd of seuerall mouthes and seuerall cries" (Guilpin, 5.43–45).

The Inns were in fact notorious for posing temptations and challenges while offering little firm guidance; as Francis Lenton put it, a student

[66] Marotti, *John Donne : Coterie Poet*, p. 39; cf. O. J. Campbell, *Comicall Satire*, pp. 59–61.
[67] Richard Brathwait, *The English Gentleman* (1630), pp. 451–452.
[68] Lecocq, *Le satire en Angleterre*, p. 88.

arriving at the London Inns from the university had "crept from the cradle of learning to the court of liberty...from his tutor to the touchstone of his wits ... he is his own man now."[69] By the later sixteenth century, the legal societies had abandoned their oversight of the "personal lives and extramural behavior of the members," and, unlike the universities, they offered no tutorial system.[70] The study of the common law was largely empirical and not easily simplified or abstracted. Mootings and mock-debates likewise stressed empirical and improvisatory skills. The same bias is reflected in John Hoskins' manuscript *Directions for Speech and Style* (c. 1599), a textbook formulation of the Inns' cult of concision and wit. For epistolary invention, Hoskins notes, "*There can be no rules* of more Certainty or precepts of better direccion given yow, then Coniecture can lay downe of all the seueral occasions of all pticular mens lives and vocacions."[71]

In verse satire, as more broadly in the discourse of the Inns, the improvisations of the discriminating subject replaced more traditional rules, but with little compensating sense of moral infallibility. Francis Bacon, who languished for years at Gray's Inn while awaiting patronage, and whose twelve 1597 *Essaies* canvassed the major topics of wordly morality, complained that contemporary divines were failing to prepare a new generation for the complexities of moral choice: "The word (the bread of life) they toss up and down, they break it not. They draw not their directions down *ad casus conscientiae*; that a man may be warranted in his particular actions whether they be lawful or not."[72] Nashe, too, had complained of preachers who offered their congregations "Bread made of stones" because they were "not halfe so wel acquainted as them that lyue continually about the Court and Citty" with the threat of unbelief (2: 122–125). William Perkins' *Discourse of Conscience* (1596) was the first of several casuistical works which began to answer the needs of everyday morality; perhaps not surprisingly, the typical English version of casuistry came to occupy a position midway between the traditional alternatives of tutiorism and probabilism in its balance of moral imperative against the openness of choice.[73]

The dynamics of choice and discrimination in verse satire thus hinged

---

[69] *The Young Gallants Whirligigg* (1629), p. 3; quoted in Prest, *The Inns of Court*, p. 141.

[70] Prest, *The Inns of Court*, p. 138.

[71] *The Life, Letters, and Writings of John Hoskyns, 1566–1638*, ed. Louise Brown Osborn (1937; rpt. Hamden, Conn.: Archon Books, 1973), p. 118.

[72] "An Advertisement Touching the Controversies of the Church of England," in *The Letters and Life of Francis Bacon*, ed. James Spedding (7 vols. London: Longmans, 1861–72), 1: 92, quoted in Camille Wells Slights, *The Casuistical Tradition in Shakespeare, Donne, Herbert, and Milton* (Princeton University Press, 1981), p. 5.

[73] See Slights, *The Casuistical Tradition*, pp. 7–14.

upon the diversification of social alternatives by the rising importance of London. The conceptual distinction of country, court, and city has been shown to be a novel deformation of the feudal model of the three estates, worked upon that model by attempts to explain the impact of London on English society (chapter 2). But in contrast to the model of the three estates, the newer model is shaped by boundaries which are understood as permeable and therefore not wholly obligatory. Country, court, and city continue to imply status boundaries as well as characteristic duties and obligations, economic and administrative spheres. Generated, however, by the conceptual emergence of the city, with its anomalous exchanges and recombinations, the model of country, court, and city implies mobility and choice. This is reflected in the spatial orientation which is the basis of the new model, and wholly lacking in the old. The city, in other words, precipitates a spatial orientation because the mobilities it creates open for some the possibility of choice at any critical moment in time.

It was probably in the seventies, the first decade of the Inns' literary importance, that the model of country, court, and city entered the poetry of moral choice. Its emergence can be traced by way of a pair of poems from the Greek Anthology which had been translated into Latin in Erasmus' *Adagia*. Posidippus' epigrammatic survey of "the ways of life," and the answer to it by Metrodorus, were first Englished by Nicholas Grimald, who follows the sixteenth-century habit of rendering Metrodorus' *ein agore* (in the marketplace) as "law courts" but otherwise faithfully reproduces the series of environments common to both poems:

> What race of life runne you? what trade will you
>   assaye?
> In courts, is glory gott, and witt encreased daye by
>   daye,
> At home, wee take our ease, and break our selues rest:
> The feelds our nature doo refresh with pleasures of the
>   best.[74]

By contrast to Grimald, the version of Metrodorus' answer in Puttenham's *Atre of English Poesie*, published in 1589, but composed sometime between 1569 and 1585, adopts the new schema gaining currency as a model for England's ways of life:

[74] *Tottel's Miscellany*, ed. Hyder Rollins (2 vols. Cambridge, Mass.: Harvard University Press, 1928), 1: 105. Grotius' Latin translation in Firmin-Didot's edition of the Greek Anthology renders *agora* as "law courts," while Ronsard is the first to equate it with the royal court; see Herbert Grierson, "Bacon's Poem 'The World': Its Date and Relation to Certain Other Poems," *Essays and Addresses* (London: Chatto and Windus, 1940), p. 223 n.1.

What life list ye to lead? in good Citie and towne
Is wonne both wit and wealth, Court gets vs great
   renowne:
Countrey keepes vs in heale, and quietnessse of mynd.[75]

This three-part version of life's choices by Puttenham, who was a member of the Middle Temple, enjoyed a wide currency among the later Inns of Court wits. In Bacon's poem on "The World," for example, it helps to elaborate Posidippus' challenge:

Yet since with sorrow here we live opprest,
   what life is best?
Courts are but only superficial Schools,
   to dandle Fools:
The rural parts are turned into a Den
   of savage men:
And where's a City from all vice so free,
But may be term'd the worst of all the three?[76]

A manuscript reply, modelled on Metrodorus, concludes its reversal of Bacon's estimates by exclaiming that "the trim Cities Plenty-horne imparts / Treasures to all, but above all, her Arts,"[77] while an epigram to Henry Wotton by Thomas Bastard contrasts the dullness of "the Country or the towne" to the excitements of the court, "happy London, Englands fayrest eye."[78]

Donne's longest epistle to Henry Wotton adapts the three-part model to a careful definition of the poise with which urbane souls negotiate the world's perilous waters:

Life is voyage, and in our lifes wayes
Countries, Courts, Towns are Rockes, or Remoraes;
They breake or stop all ships, yet our state's such,
That though than pitch they staine worse, wee must touch...
     But Oh, what refuge canst thou winne
Parch'd in the Court, or in the country frozen?
Shall cities, built of both extremes, be chosen?...
Cities are worst of all three; of all three
(O knottie riddle) each is worst equally.[79]

In many of Donne's epistles, the distance and difference between one place and another frames the issue of choice by which writer and distant

---

[75] *The Arte of English Poesie*, ed. Willcock and Walker, pp. 205–206.
[76] "A Poetical Essay," in Francis Bacon, *The Essays*, Appendix. 5, pp. 286–287.
[77] Printed in Grierson, "Bacon's Poem 'The World,'" pp. 226–227.
[78] *Chrestoleros. Seuen Bookes of Epigrammes*, (1888; rpt. New York: Burt Franklin, 1967), p. 35.   [79] *Satires, Epigrams, and Verse Letters*, ed. Milgate, p. 71, lines 7–20.

addressee are united in moral concern and social privilege.[80] Donne's
epistle to Guilpin, for example, contrasts Guilpin's repose in Suffolk to
Donne's distaste for the summertime in London, when "pleasures
dearth our City doth possess."[81] But it ends by freeing both men to
exploit both environments, to range like bees, gathering the sweets of the
"garden" of the countryside and retailing them in the hive and
warehouse of London. More successfully, perhaps, than the satires, the
epistles celebrate what is at once a social and moral privilege, the
privilege of being "our selues in our selues." In one sense, this renders
environment moot: "To rome / Giddily, and bee euery where, but at
home, / Such freedome doth a banishment become."[82] But in another
sense it empowers the writer and his like-minded associates to negotiate
independently with a variety of choices:

> in the worlds sea, do not like a corke sleepe
> Upon the waters face; nor in the deepe
> Sinke like a lead without a line: but as
> Fishes glide, leauing no print where they passe,
> Nor making sound, so, closely thy course goe.[83]

In a reply to one of Donne's epistles, Sir Henry Wotton celebrates the
commonplace that "It is the mind that makes the mans estate / For euer
happy or unfortunate."[84] In the mature epistolary manner of Donne,
Jonson, and their associates he transforms this commonplace into a
persuasively urbane negotiation with the world.

The emergence of such poems is part of a broader process of
urbanization, a process which includes the moral challenges of a mobile
society as they were felt at the Inns of Court and embodied in the writing
of verse satire. The work of each satirist yields a different mode of
negotiating with the world, from Donne's cool participatory stance, to
Hall's affected naivety, to Marston's mixture of insolence and rage. Yet
in each case, the act of satiric discrimination moves between, on the one
hand, the representational possibility of weighing truth against falsehood, real virtue against social counterfeit, and, on the other hand, the
darker simulational possibility that no such differences exist.

Donne's satires pit an anti-social moral integrity against the fear of
social isolation, an attempted moral accommodation to society against a
sweeping indictment of it. As they attempt to "mediate the claims of

---

[80] See, e.g., the epistle "To Mr. R. W." (ibid., p. 64); the second and third epistles
"To Mr. T. W." (pp. 60–61); and the epistle "To Mr. I. L." (p. 68).
[81] Ibid., p. 64, line 7.
[82] "To Mr. Rowland Woodward," ibid., p. 69, lines 19, 28–30.
[83] "To Sir Henry Wotton," ibid., p. 72, lines 53–58.
[84] Quoted in Grierson, "Bacon's Poem 'The World,'" p. 234.

individual conscience and external power,"[85] Donne's five satires
converge on the conflict between an iconoclastic singularity of soul and
"the search for a safe and unafflicted vision of the truth,"[86] a vision of the
truth compatible with the pursuit of office and the attempt to reform the
world. As he moves in his satires through a series of moral problems and
social environments, Donne attempts to reconcile his perceptions to his
imagined status in the social structure, to his dramatized roles as
scholar–wit, jurist, theologian, courtier, and office-holder.[87] Yet in the
course of the five satires his penetration more and more deeply toward the
inner circles of his society pushes him, as satirist, further and further
toward that soulful isolation which alone can authenticate his being and
vision. To the extent that the simulation of virtue usurps the reality, the
satirist's only truthful act must be a confession of his inability to
represent a social order where the differences between true and false,
feigned and counterfeit no longer matter. Thus, if the prevailing note of
the scholar–wit of the first satire is Horatian, that of the privileged royal
officeholder of the fifth – a man "most richly / For seruice paid,
authoriz'd" – is paradoxically a self-isolating Juvenalian rage:

> O Age of rusty Iron! Some better wit
> Call it some worse name, if aught equall it;
> Th'iron Age *that* was, when justice was sold; now
> Injustice is sold dearer farre.   (5.35–38; italics mine)

Throughout Donne's satires, the attempt to reform the world through
the negotiation of compromises and discriminations is thwarted by the
world's erosion – through a kind of "stream-effect" – of all moral
potential.[88] In the first satire, the scholar–satirist seeks to reclaim the soul
of his worldly friend by establishing a clear and firm distinction between
the motley humorist's foolish connoisseurship and the moral judgement
that can separate a "fine silken painted foole" from "a grave man" (lines
97, 79). Yet apart from the speaker, no other such man is found in this
survey of freaks, fiddlers, and dancers, performing apes and elephants,
Indians, comedians, and whores under glass. The contagion of surfaces
has eliminated "men of sort, of parts, and qualities" (line 105). As the

---

[85] Ronald J. Corthell, "Style and Self in Donne's Satires," *TSLL*, 24 (1982), p. 157;
cf. Dwight Cathcart, *Doubting Conscience: Donne and the Poetry of Moral Argument*
(Ann Arbor: University of Michigan Press, 1975), p. 4.

[86] Richard C. Newton, "Donne the Satirist," *TSLL*, 16 (1974), p. 440.

[87] These are the roles identified by M. Thomas Hester, *Kinde Pitty and Brave Scorn: John
Donne's "Satyres"* (Durham: Duke University Press, 1982), pp. 4–5.

[88] On the motif of betrayal in the poem, and the corresponding shift from second person
address to third-person narrative, see Barbara L. Packer and Max Patrick, "Two
Hollow Men: The Pretentious Wooer and the Wayward Bridegroom of Donne's *Satyre
I*," *Seventeenth-Century News*, 33: 1–2 (1975), p. 11.

distracted survey of details suggests, discrimination mocks itself by
becoming a connoisseurship of surface; the once obligatory symbolism of
rank, talent, and worth has vanished. The triumph of surface over depth,
contiguity over analogy, easily wins the humorist away from the scholar:
his soul evaporates like his own breath on the surface of a pane of glass,
a surface which is at once the window through which he sees his
"plumpe, muddy whore" and the mirror on which his image is
reflected:[89]

> At last his love he in a windowe spies,
> And like light dew exhal'd, he flings from mee
> Violently ravish'd to his lechery.   (lines 106–108)

In Donne's second satire, the poet is himself increasingly estranged
and isolated by the encroaching, simulative tactics of the lawyer Coscus.
Coscus expands himself through

> words, words, which will teare
> The tender labyrinth of a soft maides eare,
> More, more, then ten Sclavonians scolding, more
> Then when winds in our ruin'd Abbeyes rore...
> Shortly (as the sea) hee' will compasse all our land...
> Peecemeale he gets lands, and spends much time
> Wringing each Acre, as men pulling prime.
> In parchments, then, large as his fields, hee drawes
> Assurances, bigge, as gloss'd civill lawes,
> So huge, that men (in our times forwardnesse)
> Are fathers of the Church for writing less.   (lines 57–60, 77, 85–90)

By analogy with revisions in the canonical texts by protestant theologians,
Coscus' rewriting of the social landscape effectively prevents traditionally
"vouch't Texts" from being heard. There is no resisting the power of
those who can at will cancel the "shrewd words, which might against
them clear the doubt." Unlike Horace, who has no trouble maintaining
his faith in satire against the warnings of the lawyer Trebatius, the
urbane satirist who began Donne's satire with a superior contempt for
the town becomes by the end a dispossessed plaintiff lamenting the loss
of traditional moral ground:

> Where are those spred woods which cloth'd heretofore
> Those bought lands? not built, nor burnt within dore.
> Where's th'old landlords troops, and almes? In great hals
> Carthusian fasts, and fulsome Bachanalls
> Equally' I hate; meanes blesse; in rich mens homes

---

[89] For my reading of this glassy surface and its relation to the hairy "coarse attire" of the
scholar–satirist, I am indebted to Thomas Docherty, *John Donne, Undone* (London:
Methuen, 1986), pp. 111–112.

> I bid kill some beasts, but no Hecatombs,
> None starve, none surfet so; But (Oh) we' allow
> Good workes as good, but out of fashion now,
>   Like old rich wardrops; but my wordes none drawes
> Within the vast reach of th' huge statute lawes.   (lines 103–112)

The satirist's embittered contrast between "my words" and the "vast reach of th' huge statute lawes" perhaps endows him with an isolate integrity, a truthfulness which not even the laws' persecution can touch. But the ambiguous syntax also suggests that his word lacks the power to prosecute, that its impotence in the face of the law's power makes it not worth persecuting.[90]

In its attempt to locate religious truth, Donne's third satire continues to seek accommodation between the soul and worldly powers,[91] only to conclude, against the possibility of compromise, that

> As Streames are, Power is; those blest flowers that dwell
> At the rough streames calme head, thrive and prove well,
> But, having left their roots, and themselves given
> To the streames tyrannous rage, alas, are driven
> Through mills, and rockes, and woods, and at last, almost
> Consum'd in going, in the sea are lost:
>   So perish Soules, which more chuse mens unjust
>   Power from God clay'md, then God himselfe to trust.
>   (lines 103–110)

The world is governed by a perilous stream-effect, whereby souls are uprooted, brought to the turmoil of the surface, swept along and "consum'd in going."

The perils of this stream-effect are most potent in Donne's two final and darkest satires. In the fourth, Donne's disturbing return to Horace 1.9 and to his own first satire, the slime-bred courtier who assaults the speaker lays down a challenge which goes to the heart of the satirist's being. The satirist goes to court confident of his own capacity for moral discrimination, but as the astonished satirist falls under the spell of the courtier's gossip, this guilty knowledge invades him, making his very consciousness a form of political transgression:

[90] Hester, who measures Donne's satires by the standard of Biblical prophecy, finds Donne's stance at the end of the poem "an exemplary alternative for the abuses criticized," *Kinde Pitty and Brave Scorn*, p. 52. But Clayton D. Lein, who places Donne against classical models, finds the satire suffused with an "exceptional moral nihilism," "Theme and Structure in Donne's *Satyre II*," *CL*, 32 (1980), 150. Frank Kerins concurs with Lein in declaring that in the poem "the imaginative constructs of wit reveal themselves as no more than moral and intellectual failures," "The 'Businesse' of the Satirist: John Donne and the Reformation of the Satirist," *TSLL*, 26 (1984), 45.

[91] For a reading which stresses this accommodation, see Thomas V. Moore, "Donne's Use of Uncertainty as a Vital Force in *Satyre III*," *MP*, 67 (1969), 41–49.

> I more amas'd then Circes prisoners, when
> They felt themselves turne beasts, felt my selfe then
> Becomming Traytor, and mee thought I saw
> One of our Giant Statutes ope his jaw
> To sucke me in; for hearing him, I found,
> That as burnt venom'd Leachers doe grow sound
> By giving others their soares, I might growe
> Guilty, and he free.   (lines 129–136)

After a failed attempt at recuperation, the speaker is left trembling in fear at the magnitude of his discoveries and the isolation and impotence these discoveries bring upon him:

> I shooke like a spyed Spie. Preachers which are
> Seas of Wit and Arts, you can, then dare,
> Drowne the sinnes of this place, for, for mee
> Which am but a scarce brooke, it enough shall bee
> To wash the staines away; Though I yet
> With *Macchabees* modestie, the knowne merit
>   Of my worke lessen: yet some wise man shall,
>   I hope, esteeme my writs Canonicall.   (lines 237–244)

For a Catholic poet whose sense of dispossession and fear of persecution color his whole approach to the court, the heroic Maccabeus sustains a fundamental conviction of integrity. But as in *Satyre II*, where "Good workes" are disallowed as out of date, so here the satirist's "worke" lacks the official canonization which would give it authentic moral standing within the existing, protestant power-structure.

Not even the attainment of office under the Lord Keeper Egerton in 1597 was sufficient to accommodate Donne's satiric vision to the realities of power. On the contrary, Donne's fifth satire, on the corruption of officeholders, is his most corrosive penetration to the heartless center of the social order. Jests and tears both prove inadequate to this exploration, which opens not with conversational banter but with a solitary apostrophe to the Muse. The motifs of the satire – the "wrech'd"-ness of "Suiters misery," and the "wicked"-ness of "Officers rage" – are not so much Horatian extremes as poles in a cycle of social competition: "Each thing, each thing implyes or represents" (line 12). Quite uncharacteristically, Donne attempts to ground these poles in an extended moral metaphor:

> man is a world; in which, Officers
> Are the vast ravishing seas; and Suiters,
> Springs...
> They are the mills which grinde you, yet you are
> The winde which drives them; and a wastefull warre
> Is fought against you, and you fight it.   (5.13–15, 23–25)

In desperation, the poet asks whether the chain of causes may be broken off short of its end:

> Greatest and fairest Empresse, know you this?
> Alas, no more then Thames calme head doth know
> Whose meades her armes drowne, or whose corn o'rflow. (lines 28–30)

The damning answer to this question, more typical of old-fashioned complaint than of verse satire, contrasts the blissful serenity at the source of power with the distant havoc power wreaks. Unlike the third satire, the fifth imposes no theoretical distinction between orders of being in order to stop the stream-effect, to separate the source from the violence of the flow. The remainder of the satire compounds this problem by working its way along a stream which is everywhere connected and yet nowhere navigable to the source that can render justice.

> Powre of the Courts below
> Flow from the first maine head, and these can throw
> Thee, if they sucke thee in, to misery,
> To fetters, halters; But if th' injury
> Steele thee to dare complaine, Alas, thou go'st
> Against the stream, when upwards: when thou' art most
> Heavy' and most faint; and in these labours they,
> 'Gainst whom thou should'st complaine, will in the way
> Become great seas, o'r which, when thou shalt bee
> Forc'd to make golden bridges, then shalt see
> That all thy gold was drown'd in them before;
> All things follow their like, only who have may' have more.
>
> (lines 45–56).

Donne's indictment here leads to no witty escape; it puts him in first-person plural relationship to all excluded victims, who may only obey a distant and inscrutable power:

> she is established
> Recorder to Destiny, on earth, and shee
> Speakes Fates words, and but tells us who must bee
> Rich, who poore, who in chaines, who in jayles. (lines 70–73)

Donne confessed in a letter to Wotton that "to my satyrs there belongs some feare ... Therefore I am desirous to hyde them with out any recording of them or their maker."[92] The rhetoric of Donne's satires engenders fear because its critique of the social order finally runs deeper than intended. It eliminates the possibility of compromise with the world by showing that there are no safe waters in which worldlings may glide,

---

[92] *Selected Prose*, ed. Evelyn Simpson, Helen Gardner, and Timothy Healy (Oxford: Clarendon Press, 1967), p. 111.

"leaving no print where they passe." The would-be Horatian sophisticate can only take up an uncouth and humble morality as he watches his more ambitious hopes vanish before him. Disillusioned and isolated, the satirist is left to

> moralize
> Esops fables, and make tales, prophesies.
> Thou' art the swimming dog whom shadows cosened,
> And div'st, neare drowning, for what vanished.   (lines 88–91)

Like this final one, all of Donne's satires tend to end on a note of surprised disillusionment, as if, in the process of unfolding, they exhaust all hope in the project of selection and refinement they set out to perform. By a process of elimination that cannot be halted, the discriminatory quest for a moral refuge within the social order finally consumes the very goal it seeks. Moral substance fades from the world of the poems "like light dew exhal'd" (1.107); as the questing poet inevitably feels him "selfe then / Becomming Traytor," he shares the fate of all souls "consum'd in going"; he is left groping for "what vanished."

The erosion of safe moral ground is equally the outcome at the opposite end of the satiric spectrum, in the more deliberately archaic satires of Hall. Unlike the marginalized environment of the Inns of Court, the refuge of Emmanuel College offers Hall's satirist a positive, traditional ethical content. Though it has a modest Horatian potential, Hall's scholarly status has deeper affinities with the old-fashioned integrity of the clerical estate and thus with the conservative conventions of complaint:

> To what ende did our lauish auncestours,
> Erect of olde these stately piles of ours?
> For thred-bare clerks, & for the ragged Muse
> Whom better fit some cotes of sad recluse?
> Blush niggard Age, and be asham'd to see
> These monuments of wiser ancestrie.   (2.2.1–6)

Hall retains a deep allegiance to the traditional subjects of complaint – enclosure, rack-renting, usury, simony, the decline of hospitality – and this bias is reflected in his preference for "renowmed *Aquine*" (i.e., Juvenal) over Persius and Horace (5.1.1–10). He cultivates packstaff plainness (3 Prol. 4), "gall-weet words and speeches rude" (2 Prol. 5), and the scourging manner "that shoots sharpe quils out in each angry line" (5.3.2). Hall would thus seem to have defined a native English equivalent for Juvenal's compulsive stance. Like Juvenal at the Porta Capena, Hall stands upon ground once hallowed by his culture and continues to insist on being heard:

Pardon ye glowing eares; Needs will it out,
Tho brazen wals compas'd my tongue about,
As thicke as wealthy Scrobioes quick-set rowes
In the wide Common that he did enclose.   (5.1.1–4)

Yet despite the measure of stability implied by Hall's gravitation toward the examples of Juvenal and native complaint, his satires share with those of his Inns of Court contemporaries a fundamental rootlessness. Their techniques are not so much the conservative instruments of juxtaposition, parody, and classic norm as the more unsettled and unsettling devices of counterfeit, quotation, and satiric connoisseurship. Readers who criticize Hall's satires as complacent and simple-mindedly conservative[93] miss their elegiac note, their sense of powerlessness to resurrect the past, and their truly wide-eyed astonishment as they gaze on an almost wholly alien world. Hall's satires typically define a situation of discursive exile and deracination, as the satirist is forced to abandon his former pastoral domain ("Defiance to Envy," lines 79–114), to bear up against the lofty scorn for "the home-spun threed of rimes" (1.6.1), and to sing without the aid of the Muses, who have deserted "Grantaes naked side" for the more fashionable, lucrative, salacious waters of "the tyded Thames and salt Medway."

The miscellaneous literary satires of Hall's first book thus cohere in their condemnation of what Nashe had celebrated as the urbanization of the language.[94] Modern writing produces a cultural amnesia, and Hall's elaborate prefatory matter, prologues, and postscript attempt to protect his satires from the new mercenary culture which would make them unreadable. Wherever he turns, Hall finds the moral past reduced to fading inscriptions, "figures half obliterate / In rain-beat Marble" (4.3.9–10). Heaven-descended laws were engraved by Themis "deepe in during Marble-stone / ... But now their Characters depraued bin" (2.3.4–7). Even "th'heauens vniuersall Alphabet" has been recoded as the "mock-art" of astrology (2.7.1).

If Hall follows Juvenal and the traditions of complaint in jogging the faulty memory of a forgetful age, his juxtapositions are short-circuited by the present's power to simulate a past more suitable to its own purposes.[95] Mechanical reproduction produces an alarmingly diminished but otherwise indistinguishable substitute for a grander past. The effacement of the genuine by its simulation is epitomized for Hall in the legend that an

---

[93] See, for example, the harsh verdict of Lecocq, *Le satire en Angleterre*, pp. 402–403, 427.
[94] The capital's literary life creates the "Shame that the Muses should be bought and sold" (1.3.57); Parnassus is "turned to the Stews" and "Cytheron hill's become a Brothel bed" (1.2.17, 19). Mercenary motives touch the theaters (2.3; 2.4), ersatz humanists (1.6.17) and hacksters like Nashe (1.9.7–8).   [95] See, e.g., 4.2 and 4.3.

ancient writer reproduced the entire *Iliad* on a parchment inside a nutshell (2.2.35–54). Like Swift's Lilliput, the world of Hall's satires is not so much a deviation from the human norm as a tellingly diminutive reproduction of it: in his paltry offspring, for example, the counterfeit gallant Gallio will but "giue the world yet one dwarfe more" (4.4.104). As if to emphasize the diminished world the Elizabethan age has created from the past, Hall's striking use of classical epigraphs leaves heroic and idyllic tags hanging like outsized clothing upon modern dwarfs.[96]

If this last technique suggests a poetic of juxtaposition and classic norms, the use of quotation in Hall's satires suggests the opposite techniques of counterfeiting and connoisseurship. Hall is a stranger in a strange land, a naive pilgrim–reader who records with astonishment the puzzlingly modern signs he encounters. His wandering takes him "along in London way" (3.5.5) and to the usual high places in the satirists' itinerary. But if, unlike Donne's unhappy satirists, he is never contaminated by his journey, this is because he is always denied entrance to the inner sanctum. Hall is left waiting on many thresholds, invited once and ever after excluded from a courteous citizen's table (3.3), passing by the freshly painted doorposts of the proud burgess Palemon, waiting outside the chambers of the furtive Lollio (4.2.72), standing with the "penylesse penitent" who "beats his faint fist" at a usurer's door (4.5.60–61), sharing the humiliation of Trebius, locked out of Virro's hall at festive seasons (5.2.105–112), watching Villius' hide-bound son ride in his carriage "through the Cheape" (5.4.14). Denied entrance to these privileged spaces, the satirist reads and quotes the signs and wonders inscribed on their surfaces. He contemplates the tomb of great Osmond, designed "Egyptian wise, / *Rex Regnum* written on the *Pyramis*" (3.3.6–7); he reads the "*siquis* patch'd on Pauls Church dore" (2.5.1); he describes the grim sculptural visage of Gotmagot, the London *palladium*, as "some frowning post, / The crab-tree Porter of the Guild-Hall gates" (6.1.8–9). The arch-image of the satires is perhaps Hall's arrival with his reader at the overdecorated, locked entrance of a proud estate:

> Beat the broad gates, a goodly hollow sound
> With doubled Ecchoes doth againe rebound...
> Thou shalt discerne vpon the Frontespice,

---

[96] *Arcades ambo* (Virgil, *Eclogues*, 7.4) becomes the motto for the miserly Lollio and his son (4.2). In keeping with Strabo's diminished replica of Homer, *Fuimus Troes* (*Aeneid*, 2.235), *Heic quaerite Troiam* (*Aeneid*, 5.637), *Possunt quia posse videntur* (*Aeneid*, 5.231) and *Vix es nostra* (Ovid, *Metamorphoses*, 13.140) underwrite such modern forms of greatness as Pride in ancestor (4.3), inhospitable ostentation (5.2), and deficit budgets (5.4). Gallio's is the mock-chivalric motto *Plus beau que fort* while Plato's *koina philon* (*Laws* 866a) becomes the punning motto of enclosers (5.3).

OGDEIS EISITO grauen vp on hie,
A fragment of old Platoes Poesie:
The meaning is, Sir foole ye may be gone,
Go backe by leaue, for here way lieth none.   (5.2.53–66)

The reading of such surfaces depends less on juxtaposition than on quotation. An advertisement on the door of St. Paul's suffices to embody the literate being of its writer, "a Churchman, that can seruice sey, / Read fast, and faire, his monthly Homiley / And wed, and bury, and make Christen-soules" (2.5.3–5). The unframed, free-standing verbatim of another advertisement constitutes a complete satire in itself (2.6). Hall prefers quoting to arguing. Man's nature being worsened by his possession of reason (4.3.80–83), the satirist stands to gain more by the former than the latter. Hall's relatively few conversational satires are outnumbered by those containing such monologues as a squire's attack on learning (2.2) or Torcullio's defense of usury (4.5). The phosphorescent quotation of these monologues relies on the capacity of perfectly straightforward claims to mock themselves.

Not because he was an Augustan *manqué* but because he realized possibilities inherent in the Elizabethan form, Hall violates the literary–historical commonplace that the violent, embittered, half-hircine satyr–satirist of the Elizabethan age was a vernacular crudity mercifully dissolved by the ironic, detached techniques of Augustan parody, portraiture and irony.[97] Resort to these latter techniques was already a potential inherent in the Elizabethans' self-isolating critique of a society ordered on the model of simulation. Hall's use of these techniques accounts for the free-standing, parodic character of his satires – for the resemblance of his earlier satires to short, descriptive epigrams and for the tendency of his later, longer satires to concentrate, like epigrams, on single figures. Hall inclines toward the epigram not for its formal resources of schematic wit and barbed conclusion – these he does not manage well – but for its economy of characterizing detail.[98] Despite their brevity, Hall's satires are, as Jonson said of Harington's and Owen's epigrams, not so much epigrams as narratives.[99] As Hall traces the progress of a play from its inception in a drunken hack's brain to the curses of the departing audience (1.3), or as he describes a dinner (3.3) or a doorway (3.4) or a runaway wig (3.5), the descent of liquor through the body (3.6) or the immoral rise of an ambitious family (4.2; 5.4), he abandons the subjective tasks of discrimination and comparison for a

[97] See, e.g., Paulson, *The Fictions of Satire*, p. 92; cf. Kenner, *The Counterfeiters*, p. xiii.
[98] Lecocq, *Le satire en Angleterre*, pp. 410–411.
[99] *Conversations with Drummond of Hawthornden*, in *Works*, 1: 133, 138.

purely presentational technique: with straight face, he lets events follow out their own arc toward self-parody. Perhaps partly in response to Marston's attacks on the first installment of the *Virgidemiae*, Hall moved in the final three books closer toward the declamatory manner of Juvenal and the conservatism of native complaint.[100] But this cannot be said to have occurred apart from a sophisticated exploration of the vulnerabilities of verse satire in his age, an exploration that finally defined Hall's status as that of an isolated and defeated outsider.

Marston condescendingly marvels that the "squint-ey'd sight" of Hall's harsh and sweeping Juvenalian manner "Could strike the world's deformities so right," but he cautions against Hall's undiscriminating extremism, for "Loue, nor yet Hate, had ere true iudging eye" (*CS* 2.37–40). Marston affects to favor the "vnpartiall eye" (p. 105). The sobriquet of "snaphaunce [i.e. hair-trigger] Satyrist," a nimble improviser, is for Marston the "tytle which my iudgement doth adore" (*CS* 2.2–4). He imagines an equally adaptable adversary who argues *pro nunc* and "pay'th me with snaphaunce quick distinction" (*SV* 4.130–132). These aspirations, together with his search for a comprehending audience,[101] his revival of Stoic tenets, and his animus toward social counterfeiters, all reflect an attempt to articulate through satire "a system of practical morals suited to the needs of contemporary man."[102]

By attacking the "vile detraction" of Hall's satires, Marston positions himself against the scourging manner, assuming a degree of social refinement and literary discrimination that Hall by implication lacks. Comparing Hall's self-proclaimed thunder to the braying of an ass, Marston portrays Hall as a benighted lout whose undiscriminating slander cannot touch the pure and privileged center of the Elizabethan culture:

> Who cannot raile? what dog but dare to barke
> Gainst Phoebes brightnes in the silent dark?   (*CS* 4.9–10)

By Marston's logic, Hall's sweeping attack on his Elizabethan contemporaries fails to respect the special license that according to Sidney's *Apologie for Poetry* gives the privileged golden poetry of the Elizabethan court its true distinction:

---

[100] Hall would have to have seen, or heard of, Marston's satires in manuscript; *Virgidemiae* 4–6 were registered on March 30, 1598, while Marston's *Certain Satyres* were not registered until May 27 and *The Scourge of Villanie* until September 8.

[101] Scott Colley, "Marston, Calvinism, and Satire," *Medieval and Renaissance Drama in England*, 1 (1984), 89.

[102] Michael Higgins, "The Convention of the Stoic Hero as Handled by Marston," *MLR*, 39 (1944), 339.

> For tell me Crittick, is not Fiction
> The soule of Poesies inuention?
> Is't not the forme? the spirit? and the essence?
> The life? and the essential difference? (*CS* 4.87–90)

In seeking to uphold the "essential difference" that separates "the soule of Poesies inuention" from degraded simulacra, Marston places a utopian faith in the "true iudiciall style," whose "vnvalued worth / Shall mount faire place, when Apes are turned forth" (11.50–53). This is a discriminating ideal realized intermittently throughout the satires, from the first of the *Certayne Satyres – quedam videntur, et non sunt* – to the last in *The Scourge of Villanie*, on the humorous "vainenes of fayre Albions youth" (11.187). The "essential difference" between the truthful intuitions of the poet's soul and spurious illusions that drive social pretenders is likewise an informing principle of Marston's attack on counterfeits in *Totum in toto* and *Fronti nulla fides*.

Yet as the uncertain course of the latter satire suggests, the capacity of society to host or embody virtue can become instead its capacity to simulate and thereby extinguish it. The initial disparity between face and moral substance – and hence the original truth of the despairing Juvenalian motto – eventually becomes the more disturbing equation of the two, the absorption of substance into surface. The prefatory verses to *The Metamorphosis of Pigmalions Image* had already identified Opinion, in mock-praise, as "The soule of Pleasure, Honors only substance / ... Whom fleshly Epicures call Vertues essence." In keeping with this equation, Marston's most explicitly Juvenalian satire, *Difficile est satyram non scribere* (*SV* 2), laments the extreme possibility that the discrimination of moral nuance is no longer possible (44–47). The hideous possibility that "appetite ... *Hatcheth the soule*" (4.110–102; italics mine) manifests itself in many of the later satires, in figures whose entire being is defined by their surface:

> He's nought but clothes, & senting sweet perfume,
> His very soule, assure thee, Linceus,
> Is not so big as an Atomus:
> Nay, he is sprightlesse, sence or soule hath none. (7.41–44)

> He's naught but budge, old gerds, browne foxe-fur face.
> He hath no soule. (7.65–66)

> Why, he is naught but huge blaspheming othes,
> Swart snout, big lookes, mishapen Swizers clothes, ...
> Infeebling ryot, all vices confluence
> Hath eaten out that sacred influence
> Which made him man. (7.116–22)

Alas, her soule struts round about her neck,
Her seate of sence is her rebato set,
Her intellectuall is a fained nicenes
Nothing but clothes, & simpering precisenes   (7.176–79)

His very soule, his intellectuall
Is nothing but a mincing capreall.   (11.23–24)

... this Eccho that doth speake, spet, write...
                              ... whose very soule
Is but a heape of Iibes.   (11.90–93)

His guts are in his braines, huge Iobbernoule,
Right Gurnets-head, the rest without all soule.   (6.41–42)

Like Hall's, one critic observes, Marston's satires "formally resemble the plague-bill lists, recounting the separate deaths of the human spirit that accompany the emergence of new competitive ways of London life."[103] The later satires of *The Scourge of Villanie* concern themselves increasingly with a soulless wilderness of monkeys, an "apish Age" (5.116) of "apish schollers, pedants, gulls" (10.17). Degraded writers labor with "Apish skips" (4.60), lovers would be their "Mistres smug Munkey" (8.129), while every fool "in veluet cloake" is "yet still an Ape" (6.72). The result is not so much a defense of the real virtues being aped as a dissolution of that reality by the process of aping. "Fie," the satirist asks, "whether doe these Monkeys carry mee?" (9.100).

Unlike Donne's satirist, who negotiates near the sources of power, and unlike Hall's, who pointedly situates himself outside of such centers, Marston's satirist approaches the high places with great reluctance and circumspection. But his brief forays, usually disguised in mythological fable, suggest that soullessness has usurped the very seat of power: "Shape-changing Proteans, damned Briareans," he complains, "dare vnto Ioues Pallace creepe" (*CS* 5.2–4). It is not surprising, then, that Marston's most trenchantly political satire, *Parua magna, magna nulla* (*CS* 5) modulates into his most extensive imitation of the execrable Hall; it amounts, in fact, to a reworking of the latter's ironic reversal of Juvenal's sweeping tenth satire. Marston's imitation ends with the sense of futility which makes "my Satyre stagger in a doubt, / Whether to cease, or els to write it out" (167–168).

The pervasive doctrine of Marston's satires, that the spiritual powers of the soul are gradually extinguished in their confrontation with the world, has a figurative dimension which is clearly political. The soul,

[103] Angus Fletcher, *Colors of the Mind: Conjectures on Thinking in Literature* (Cambridge, Mass.: Harvard University Press, 1991), p. 61.

"not subiect to mortalitie" (11.206), becomes a monarch "scorn'd and reiected, thrust from out his seate" (11.216), an exiled ruler forced to abandon the body to "sensuall / Base hangers on" (8.198–199), a Lord challenged by a "parliament of sense" in which "the sensual haue preheminence" (11.133–134; cf. 8.177–178), and, in the figure always favored by the tradition of complaint, a virtuous tenant evicted from "his Land-lordes muddy slime" (8.192). The descent from the soul to the slime, reversing Pico's neoplatonic ascent,[104] becomes the destined path of those who foolishly attempt to negotiate a compromise between the soul's integrity and the corrosive effects of human society:

> Beasts sence, plants growth, like being as a stone,
> But out, alas, our Cognisance is gone. (7.201–202)

Marston elsewhere hymns the praises of that state wherein there are "No suburbes all is Mind."[105] But in the satires, the search for the "essential difference" that is mind ends in a realm that is entirely suburbs, "a Poetick vaine circumference" (*SV* 10.82). The expulsion from center to periphery exemplifies the fate of verse satire itself, a genre that in seeking to stabilize a changing world could only underline its radical instability, its social impotence, and its literary marginality.

Proverbs, epigrams, and urbanity

The fate of the Elizabethan satiric enterprise is further demonstrated in the formal problems of the epigram, a form that was practiced widely throughout the English Renaissance but that enjoyed, along with formal verse satire, a particular vogue beginning in the 1590s. Epigrams were written in many forms on a variety of subjects, but, as in verse satire, the number dealing with the life of London began to form a large and distinctive subclass by the end of the sixteenth century, in keeping with T. K. Whipple's generalization that the epigram "thrives best in the atmosphere of metropolitan literary circles ... It flourishes in urban air and in coteries."[106]

Like verse satire, the epigram represented to its late Elizabethan practitioners new laureate potential recovered from classical poetry. Donne's early poetry included both epigrams and satire, and Guilpin's *Skialetheia, or ... Certaine Epigrams and Satyres* (1598) inaugurated the

---

[104] Marston's anti-Platonism is the subject of A. D. Cousins, "The Protean Nature of Man in Marston's Verse Satire," *JEGP*, 79 (1980), 517–529.

[105] *Perfectioni Hymnus*, in *Poems*, ed. Davenport, p. 179.

[106] T. K. Whipple, *Martial and the English Epigram* (Berkeley: University of California Publications in Modern Philology, 10: 1925), p. 284.

tradition of publishing both forms together.[107] Most epigrams written in this early satiric vein were a raw variety compared with the poised and polished work Jonson would soon reckon "the ripest of my studies."[108] "Epigrams," said Richard Hayman, "are like Satyrs, rouhg [sic] without."[109] Insofar as they were "Satyres reduc'd to an Epitome,"[110] epigrams also shared many of the tensions of verse satire: just as verse satire aspired to become a laureate master genre but instead became the scourging vein of popular moralists like George Wither and degraded professionals like Richard Brathwait and John Taylor, so the barbed, satiric epigram passed from the hands of distinguished amateurs – "the clamorous frie of Innes of court"[111] – to professionals associated with the Inns, like Henry Parrot and William Gamage, and to uneducated popular writers like Taylor and Samuel Rowlands.

This tension between laureate ambition and popular influence animates the history of the form. In many respects the formal resources of epigram – its compression, concision, and point – were well adapted to the *volonté d'indépendance* of the verse satirists, their ethical project of examining society with "Snaphaunce quick distinction," a verisimilar *haecceity* liberated from the outmoded framework of moral anatomy. The epigram's highly schematic resources of antithesis and balance lent an illusion of definition, stability, and authority appropriate to the new laureate ambition of the satirists. Schematism was also, however, a prime resource in the traditional forms of social anatomy and complaint – Weever called his volume *Epigrammes in the Oldest Cut and Newest Fashion* and later complained that contemporary epigrammatists merely "skipt vp and downe from one estate to another, like a Squirrel in a tree."[112] Thus, if the tendency of verse satire to slide into superficial metonymic series represented both a swing from Horace to Juvenal and a return to the native manner of complaint, this was congruent with a similar slippage of epigrammatic schematism in the direction of popular oral sources. Much more obviously than formal verse satire, the epigram simultaneously inhabited both center and margin of late Elizabethan

---

[107] See, e.g., Richard Middleton, *Epigrams and Satyres* (1608); John Taylor, *The Sculler: or Gallimawfry of Sonnets, Satyres, and Epigrams* (1612); Richard Brathwait, *A Strappado for the Diuell: Epigrams and Satyres* (1615); Henry Parrot, *The Mastive, or Young-Whelpe of the Old-Dogge: Epigrams and Satyrs* (1615); Henry Fitzgeffrey, *Satyres and Satyricall Epigrams* (1617); Henry Hutton, *Follies Anatomie: or Satyres and Satiricall Epigrams* (1619).

[108] Dedication "To ... the Most Noble William, Earl of Pembroke," *Epigrammes* (1616), in *The Complete Poems*, p. 33.   [109] *Quodlibets* (1628), p. 61.

[110] Sir Aston Cockayne, "To Sir Andrew Knyveton, My Wives Brother," in *Small Poems of Divers Sorts* (1658), p. 158.

[111] *The Poems of Sir John Davies*, ed. Robert Krueger (Oxford: Clarendon Press, 1975), p. 130.   [112] *The Whipping of the Satyre*, 1601, in *The Whipper Pamphlets*, p. 6.

literary culture. It overlapped with primarily oral forms such as ballads, jests, and proverbs, all of which were part of the popular culture of Renaissance London. Indeed, the two main tendencies of the London epigram – its tendency to borrow names, places, types, and allusions from a common fund of popular wisdom and its tendency to order this complex lore in precise and telling formulations – arise from the conflicting traits of proverbs and epigrams respectively. While both genres belong in certain respects to the same oral substrate, and both include a topographical variety devoted to peoples and places, proverbs and epigrams are divided by a formal and creative tension. The protean character of the proverb, a function of its theoretically oral and often metaphorical nature, proves resistant to incorporation by the schematizing power of the epigram, a theoretically lapidary form in which writers frequently attempted to order an imaginative vision of London by encoding commonplace materials into revealing nutshell formulas. To study this creative tension, a tension between tropes and schemes, really, is to trace the reciprocal influences between oral and printed media, between popular and imposingly classical forms.

But in the epigram on London, those different strands of influence contribute to conflict – a conflict between order and the mystery that order would contain, between a literary perspective and the vision of the world it would frame. For epigrammatists who wrote on London, that uncontainable mystery was not the ineffable sublime but its antithesis, a terrifying and unknowable world of material and social profusion. Despite the ambitions of its early practitioners, the epigram failed to detach itself, as a genre of distinction, from its oral and popular substrate. This failure was a result of the overdetermination of this literary code by the social and material forces participating in its genesis. Not until the creation of a broader social mode in the work of Jonson and his successors did the epigram secure its place as a genre of distinction in a complex of laureate "literature" in control of, and thus fully adapted to, the urban environment. Just as Jonson's development of an anti-satiric stance replaced the metonymic simulation-effects of the lashing satire with a new ethical security, so his treatment of the epigram marshalled its schematic resources to produce a new trope of inter-legitimation, the illusion of a positive moral substance and urbane sophistication (see pp. 497–508 below).

In both the rhetorical handbooks and the many Renaissance collections of proverbs, epigrams and proverbs share a loose family resemblance. They belong to an elastic category of aphorisms, maxims, apophthegms, and sententiae which serve both the decorative ideal of copiousness and the logical rule that ancient or common testimony bears repeating.[113] Proverbs and epigrams were basic tools in the pursuit of eloquence; both were collected and both were used in schoolroom exercises. But beneath these loose associations lie certain formal similarities. James Howell, one of the great seventeenth-century collectors of proverbs, observed that "the chief ingredients that go to make a true proverb" are "Sense, shortnesse, and salt."[114] It would be an act of charity to say that these qualities abound in the epigrams of the Elizabethan–Jacobean satirists; but if, as Hoyt Hudson once suggested, we take the will for the deed, then the aim of most epigrammatists might be summed up in Timothe Kendall's description of the epigram as "pithie and pleasant... pretty, short, witty, quicke, and quipping."[115] All of these associations, however, were the basis for a more deeply dialectical relationship, which hinged on some essential differences between the two forms.

First, unlike the epigram, whose many graphological qualities attest to its evolution from lapidary epitaphs and inscriptions, proverbs were linked more closely, in theory at least, to oral tradition. They were, it was said, the *vox populi*, the voice of the people. Even Erasmus, who drew on written sources and thus collected learned rather than popular adages, insisted that his materials originally belonged to "the accepted idiom and daily coin of language."[116] If not *a priori* then at least *a fortiori*, Renaissance proverbs were thought to belong more to speaking than to writing.

Second, unlike the epigram, which is a literary form, the proverb is technically not a genre but a figure of speech. Throughout his writings on the subject, Erasmus insists on the figurative darkness or obscurity of proverbs. Proverbs conceal a hidden truth; they signify something other than what they say.[117] Like the cryptological forms with which they were frequently connected – emblems, devices, and posies – proverbs wrap in figurative darkness a hidden truth that must be unfolded or explicated by exactly the sort of learned commentary Erasmus writes on proverbs in

---

[113] Erasmus indicates his awareness of the family resemblance between proverbs and epigrams when he singles out "noteworthy epigrams" for inclusion in the 1508 *Adagia*; see Dedication to *Adagiorum Chiliades* (1508), trans. R. A. B. Mynors and D. F. S. Thompson, in *The Collected Works of Erasmus* (University of Toronto Press, 1974–), 2: 141. Cf. the Dedication to *Collectanea* (1500), trans. R. A. B. Mynors and D. F. S. Thompson, in *The Collected Works*, 1: 157.

[114] *Paroemiographia* (1659), in *Lexicon Tetraglotton* (1660), unpaginated preface.

[115] *Flowers of Epigrammes* (1577; rpt. New York, 1967), p. 9; see Hoyt Hudson, *The Epigram in the English Renaissance* (Princeton University Press, 1947), p. 2.

[116] Dedication to *Collectanea*, 263–264; cf. Howell's defense of the proverb as "the Philosophy of the Common People," unpaginated preface to *Paroemiologia*.

[117] "Quid sit paroemia," *Adagia*, *Opera Omnia*, ed J. LeClerc (10 vols. Leiden, 1703–6), 2: col. 11.

the *Adagia*. Thus, by the figures of thought that lie at their center, proverbs are again distinguished from the type of epigram that dominated in the work of the Inns of Court satirists, a type which relied primarily not on tropes but on clever schemes of repetition, balance, and antithesis, and on witty concluding turns like *epiphonema* and *acclamatio*.

These first two attributes of the proverb, its oral and metaphorial nature, are related to a third, which has to do with the sense of place proverbs often convey. The first two attributes constitute a paradox: proverbs are the voice of the people, on everyone's lips, and yet they are enigmatic; they are well known but obscure. The key to this paradox is that proverbs can sometimes be ethnospecific. They do not always belong to *the* people, but to peoples, to languages and cultures situated in specific place and time. By insisting on just this link between proverbs and the cultures to which they belonged, Erasmus could justify his proverb collection as an archaeological adventure. Unfolding the figure of a proverb was for Erasmus a matter of restoring dead metaphors to life; and this in turn was a matter of reconstructing cultural contexts, of tracing allusions that were in theory oral commonplaces before they were written mysteries.[118] Proverbs could thus disclose the *ethos* of a culture; they were, as Henry Peacham said, "the Summaries of maners, or, the Images of humane life." Erasmus claimed that, like certain wines, proverbs are not easily exported from their place of manufacture. Sir Francis Bacon declared more flatly that "the genius, wit, and spirit of a nation are discovered in its proverbs."[119]

Laden, then, with the sort of cultural residue that always makes language a barrier, proverbs often make explicit what is elsewhere implicit in a language: the values, beliefs, and aspirations of a community. Renaissance Londoners seem partly to have known themselves through a rich proverbial lore, of which there are still a few living reminders, such as "Billingsgate" or "Bedlam." To begin with the most homely economic truths, a sixteenth-century Londoner would understand that London Bridge was built upon woolpacks, and that London's power and privilege could be summed up in the phrase "Lincoln shall hang for London's sake." He would know that if he kept his shop it would keep

[118] Erasmus quotes Donatus' claim that the proverb "est accomodatum rebut temporibusque," *Opera Omnia*, 2: col. 11. The intellectual consequences of such timeliness for Erasmus' view of antiquity are explored by Margaret Mann Phillips, *Erasmus on His Times: A Shortened Version of the "Adages" of Erasmus* (Cambridge University Press, 1967), pp. ix–xi. See also Daniel Kinney, "Erasmus' *Adagia*: Midwife to the Rebirth of Learning," *Journal of Medieval and Renaissance Studies*, 2 (1981), 169–192.

[119] Peacham, *The Garden of Eloquence* (1593), p. 30; the passage does not appear in the 1577 edition. Erasmus and Bacon are cited in Archer Taylor, *The Proverb* (1962; rpt. Bern: Peter Lang, 1985), pp. 166–167.

him, that wax, linen cloth, and fustian made a fair shop but no gain, that patience in adversity would bring him to Three Cranes in the Vintry, but that playing the merchant would get him nowhere. If rich enough, he might whet his knife on the threshold of the Fleet. From his experience of civic life he would know that in his stateliest walk he was paced like an alderman; he might hope to dine as well as the Lord Mayor; if content with his lot, he would not change places with him, but in nasty generalizations he would always make an exception of him. He might know someone as old as St. Paul's, as lame as St. Giles' Cripplegate, as melancholy as Moreditch, or as tenacious as a St. Anthony's pig. He knew Cheapside was the best garden, but he would never seek a woman in Westminster, a servant in St. Paul's, or a horse in Smithfield. He was chary of St. Martin's ware (rings made principally of copper) and Smithfield bargains. A house in Turnagain Lane would be the place to mend his ways, as would the dry parish of St. Peter's the Poor, where he could find "no tavern, alehouse, or sign at the door." He knew that if too much went down Gutter Lane it might well come up again, but that going up Holborn backwards was a one-way trip to the Tyburn gallows. If he walked penniless in Mark Lane, he might mutter in Bear-Garden, or worse, Billingsgate; but these would be as useless as pissing in the Thames. Among the maladies to be avoided were the Lombard fever (debt to bankers) and (after 1630) the Covent Garden ague. Finally, if he were incapable of fathering a child, he would, in imitation of all those worthies who passed from their apprenticeship into the worshipful City companies, be enrolled as "free, of Fumblers' Hall."[120]

Through expressions like these, Londoners formed an image of themselves in which style was an aspect of local wisdom. Their proverbs amounted not only to a repository of wisdom, but also to a repertoire of ready phrases, concise formulations, antithetical and serial schemes that were themselves the marks of an urban eloquence. Urban proverbs typically aspire to the condition of epigrams because epigrams satisfy the impulse to label and anatomize, but also because epigrammatic devices reflect and foster the nimble, antagonistic, aggressive wit that traditionally marked a speaker as urbane.

Unlike the proverb, the epigram was recognized as an explicitly urban form. The English epigrammatists were typically gentlemen of a wide swallow, and their poems treated a variety of topics, but a major strand

[120] I have gathered most of these proverbs from the collections of Clarke and Howell, and from Thomas Fuller, *The History of the Worthies of England*, ed. P. Austin Nuttall (3 vols. London: T. Tegg, 1840), 1: 340–350. Literary uses and variants are recorded in M. P. Tilley, *A Dictionary of the Proverbs in England in the Sixteenth and Seventeenth Centuries* (Ann Arbor: University of Michigan Press, 1950), and in V. S. Lean, *Collectanea* (4 vols. Bristol, 1904), 1: 134–145.

of their work was colored by the spirit invoked by Sir John Davies when he sends his "merry Muse unto that merry towne, / ... Where all good wits and spirits love to be."[121] By the end of the sixteenth century, the Latin epigrams of Martial had become the nearest classical equivalent to what English poets regarded as their own sense of urbanity.[122] But it would be as mistaken to equate English with Roman urbanity as to trace the London of the English epigram to Rome. The merchants, aldermen, apprentices, decayed gentlemen, and precise parsons of the London epigram belong just as surely to the mobile urban culture of the Renaissance as do the native forms of raillery and jest which, along with Martial, helped to shape the genre. The Roman orator Quintilian associated urbanity with the verbal mastery of a tricky situation (6.3.102–112), but in the Renaissance this mastery had as much to do with burgherly and genteel aspiration as with Roman oratory. Ensuring survival in the competitive urban society and economy, witty improvisation was the equalizer that stamped its owner as a member of the community. From well before Boccaccio up through the seventeenth century, the timely mastery of circumstance in "quick answers," "conceited jests," "flashes and whimsies" (each the title of a jestbook) stands synecdochically for the range of aggressive personal powers that make citizens adversaries, but which can also reconcile them in equalizing laughter. The point may be illustrated with two examples, the first from Salimbene's thirteenth-century Florentine chronicle, the second from a seventeenth-century English jestbook:

One day in winter, when Detesalve (a Franciscan friar) was walking about the city of Florence, it happened that he fell flat on the frozen ground. Seeing this, the Florentines, who are great jokers, began to laugh. One of them asked the friar who was lying there if he would not like to have something put under him. To

---

[121] "Ad Musam," *Epigrammes and Elegies* (?1590), in *The Poems of Sir John Davies*, p. 129. Thomas Bastard asks more simply whether the epigrammatist's wit can flourish outside of "London, England Fayrest eye," *Chrestoleros. Seuen Bookes of Epigrammes* (1598), ed. A. B. Grosart (London, 1880), p. 19.

[122] See, for example, Bastard, *Chrestoleros*, p. 7; Henry Parrot, *The Mous-Trap* (1606), sig. c4v; and Everard Guilpin, *Skialetheia* (1598), p. 44. The Latin term *urbanitas* could signify a broad possession of culture and refinement, as Cicero's use of the plural form *urbanitates* (*Familiares*, 16.21.7) suggests; urbanity retains this sense when equated with "good behauiour" in the anonymous "Apologie of the Cittie of London" (c. 1580), in Stow, *Survey*, 2: 198. See also the anonymous "Precepts of Vrbanity," in *The Dr. Farmer Chetham Ms.*, ed. A. B. Grosart (2 vols. Manchester, 1873), 2: 142–150. But Roman writers also associated *urbanitas* more narrowly with a manner of speaking, and Quintilian, drawing on the lost treatise *De Urbanitate* by the epigrammatist Domitius Marsus, equates *urbanus* with *iocus* (6.3.10), to show that it stands for a wittiness appropriate to time and place; Ben Jonson has in mind this sort of definition when he identifies the "true artificer" by asking "in Jest, what urbanity hee uses," *Timber.Or, Discoveries*, in *Works*, 8: 588. See Edwin S. Ramage, *Urbanitas: Ancient Sophistication and Refinement* (Norman: University of Oklahoma Press, 1973).

which the friar answers, yes, the wife of him who asked. When they heard this, the Florentines did not take it amiss but praised the friar, saying: Good for him, he is one of us![123]

One passing through Cheapside, a poore Woman desired his charity, he disregarding the woman kept on walking, and by and by let a fart: the woman hearing it said much good may it do your worship, he hearing her say so, turnes his backe and gives her a tester; she thank't him and told his worship that it was a bad wind that did blow nobody good.[124]

Through urbanity of this homely, native sort Londoners learned to identify the epigram as a social act as well as a literary genre, a form of street wisdom as well as a Roman importation. From John Stow's translation of Fitzstephen's twelfth-century *Descriptio Londinae* they could learn that for centuries London schoolboys had been "nipping & quipping their fellowes ... with Epigrams and rhymes" (*Survey*, 1: 72). Stow himself paused over several venerable epigrams in which clever language compensated for the disequilibrium of city life. Thus the overweening goldsmith Jasper Fisher found his ostentatious house immortalized with those of other parvenus in "Kirkbyes Castell, and Fishers Folly, / Spinola's Pleasure, and Megses glorie" (1: 154). Four Aldermen forever linked in epigram were "Ramsey the rich, Bond the stout, / Beecher the gentleman and Cooper the lout."[125]

The lapidary neatness of such formulaic barbs parodied the memorial inscriptions from which the ancient epigram allegedly evolved and which Londoners found throughout their environment, on walls, gates, tombs, and monuments. Through these inscriptions, wealthy citizens and officials sought to make the urban space an articulate order. At the Steelyard, which had housed the merchants of the Hanseatic League, Londoners could read that "Gold is the father of flattery, born of sadness; he who lacks it mourns, he who has it fears" (*Aurum blanditiae pater est, natusque doloris / Qui caret hoc, moerit, qui tenet, hic metuit*). And over the portal of the Leadenhall, its builder, the irrepressible Simon Eyre, summarized his remarkable career in the candid admission, *Dextra Domini exaltavit me.*[126]

But the impulse to immortalize by inscription could just as well become the satiric impulse to fix a neat, indelible image in a last, unanswerable word. Thus the worthy Sir Thomas Gresham, who built

---

[123] Translated in Erich Auerbach, *Mimesis*, trans. Willard R. Trask (Princeton University Press, 1953), p. 215.

[124] Robert Chamberlain, *Conceits, Clinches, Flashes, and Whimsies* (1639), sig. D1.

[125] Richard Johnson, *The Pleasant Conceits of Old Hobson the Mery Londoner* (1607) in *Shakespeare Jest-Books*, ed. W. Carew Hazlitt (3 vols. London, 1864), 3: 9.

[126] Nathan Chytraeus, *Variorum in Europa itinerum deliciae* (Herborn, 1592), p. 766; Stow, *Survey*, 1: 154.

the Royal Exchange but left his sedate tomb uninscribed, failed to escape the facetious epitaph of John Hoskins:

> Here lyes Gressam under the ground
> as wise as fifty thousand pound
> he never refused the drinck of his freind
> drincke was his life and drunck was his ende.[127]

The wealthy Italian merchant Horatio Pallavicino was similarly subjected to ridicule:

> Here lies Horatio Palavecene,
> Who robb'd the Pope to lend to the Queene;
> He was a thief. A Thief! thou liest;
> For whie? He robb'd but Antichrist.
> Hym death wyth besome swept from Babram,
> Into the bosom of ould Abraham;
> But then came Hercules with his club,
> And struck him down to Belzebub.[128]

The parody of inscriptions was carried to its logical conclusion when the epigram was actually posted as a sign or memo. Stow records that in St. Paul's, under the "most sumptuous monument" of Sir Christopher Hatton, which overshadowed those of the more popular Sir Philip Sidney and Sir Francis Walsingham, "A merry poet writ thus. 'Philip and Francis haue no Tombe, / For great Christopher takes all the roome'" (1: 338). The jestbook hero Tarlton scrawled his salty epigrams on the wainscoting, bearing out Puttenham's view that the epigram "is but an inscription or writting made as it were vpon a table, or in a windowe, or vpon the wall or mantell of a chimney in some place of common resort ... as now in our tauernes and common tabling houses ... many merry heades meete, and scrible with ynke with chalke, or with a cole such matters as they would every man should know, & descant vpon."[129] "Horace's" "bitter epigrams" are said in Dekker's *Satiromastix* (1602) to have been "disperst amonst the gallants in seuerall coppies" (3.1.240–241), and Jonson–Horace receives his comeuppance when he is forced to swear he will not "fling Epigrams" when "you Sup in Tauernes" (5.2.328–330).[130] In the series of incidents that led to his expulsion from the Middle Temple for brawling, young John

---

[127] *The Life, Letters, and Writings of John Hoskyns*, p. 171.
[128] W. H. Overall, ed., *Analytical Index to ... The Remembrancia ... of the City of London* (London, 1878), p. 55n.
[129] *Tarlton's Jests* (1611), in *Shakespeare Jest-Books*, 2: 216; Puttenham, *The Arte of English Poesie*, p. 54.
[130] *The Dramatic Works of Thomas Dekker*, ed. Fredson Bowers (4 vols. Cambridge University Press, 1953), 1: 344, 383.

Davies found himself libelled in epigrams "set up against him in all the famous Places of the City, as Queen-Hithe, Newgate, the Stocks, Pillory, Pissing Conduit; and (but that the Provost Marshall was his inward friend) it should not have missed Bridewell."[131]

These physical manifestations extend two impulses implicit in the poetics of the London epigram: first, an impulse to define the indefinite or fix the elusive in formulas; and second, an impulse to *be* definitive by inscribing that formula literally or metaphorically "on" the matter defined. The potential contribution of these impulses to the London epigram emerges most clearly in a related form, the epigram upon a proverb. Taking its name from a collection by the early sixteenth-century London jester, John Heywood, the epigram upon a proverb is an easily recognizable two-part form, in which a proverb of potentially indefinite extension is limited by a more pointed comment:

> *Children must learn to creep ere they go*:
> In the spittle old knaves learn to do so.[132]

By definition, such an epigram contains at least one trope – the proverb "on" which it is written. But this is most clearly so when the proverb is a metaphor, embodies some hidden truth, and thus bears out the traditional association of proverbs with such "darker" figures as allegory and conundrum. In this case, epigrammatic commentary is written "upon" or "out of" the metaphoric content of the proverb. Heywood's commentaries frequently elucidate a proverb by constructing a context or specific situation to which it applies, and not uncommonly that context is London:

> *Fast bind, fast find*: Nay, thou were 'prentice bound,
> And yet rannest thou away where thou couldst not be found.   (p. 224)

Whereas Erasmus sought to disclose the hidden wisdom of proverbs by unfolding their obscure figures back to the contexts from which they arose, Heywood's epigrams anchor a free-floating commonplace by providing a culturally specific interpretation. Heywood thus appropriates for his community, London, a property of humankind.

In his *Descants upon Most English Proverbes* (1611), a work he links to Heywood's example, John Davies of Hereford repeatedly invokes the London setting to reveal the special significance of proverbs:

> "The Faire lasts all the yeare": so Londons doth;
> And yet most fowly lyes each house and booth...

---

[131] Benjamin Rudyerd, *The Prince d'Amour* (1660), pp. 78–79.
[132] *Three Hundred Epigrammes, upon Three Hundred Prouerbes*, in *The Proverbs, Epigrams, and Miscellanies of John Heywood*, ed. J. S. Farmer (London: EETS, 1906), p. 176.

"When thrifts in the towne, then some are in the field":
But London doth few such cittizens yeeld.[133]

Such epigrams are built around the two-part structure that Scaliger traced to lapidary inscriptions and epitaphs, and which he claimed corresponded to the relationship between a monument and the identifying words inscribed upon it.[134] Like the inscription on a monument, the epigram upon a proverb fixes the meaning of an otherwise obscure or mysterious figure. In its power to interpret the protean *vox populi*, the epigram upon a proverb is thus a model for the larger class of epigrams in which Londoners sought to define their own protean and mobile environment. In the London epigram, names, places, signs, phrases – in short, commonplaces *of* but also *in* the community – are first of all allusions. But as such, they function as figures; like proverbs, they provide the basis for epigrammatic commentary, in which the schematic resources of repetition and contrast organize names and places in revealing counterpoint. When Heywood was not writing topical epigrams on proverbs, he was often writing them on London, and especially on its names, signs, and places. In "Seeking for a Dwelling-Place" he composed a veritable *London A–Z*:

> Still thou seekest for a quiet dwelling-place:
> What place for quietness hast thou now in chase?
> London bridge? That's ill for thee, for the water.
> Queenhithe? That's more ill for another matter.
> Smart's key? That's most ill for fear of smarting smart.
> Carter lane? Nay, nay! that soundeth all on the cart.
> Powles chain? Nay, in no wise dwell not near the chain.
> Wood street? Why wilt thou be wood yet once again?
> Bread Street? That's too dry, by drought thou shalt be dead.
> Philpot Lane? That breedeth moist humours in thy head.
> Silver Street? Coppersmiths in Silver Street; fie!
> Newgate Street? 'Ware that, man! Newgate is hard by.
> Foster lane? Thou wilt as soon be tied fast, as fast.
> Crooked lane? Nay, crook no more, be straight at last.
> Creed lane? They fall out there, brother against brother.
> Ave Mary Lane? That's as ill as t'other.
> Paternoster Row? Paternoster Row?
> Agreed: That's the quietest place I know.   (pp. 283–284)

Appealing sometimes to a factual knowledge of the city and sometimes to the power of the pun, Heywood aligns names with associations in a

---

[133] *The Scourge of Folly ... Satyricall Epigramms ... Together with a ... Descant vpon Most English Prouerbes* (1611), in *The Complete Works*, ed. A. B. Grosart (3 vols. Edinburgh, 1878), 2: 41–42.   [134] *Poetices libri septem* (1561), p. 170A.

paradigm whose underlying principle is disclosed in the final couplet: London is a sick and noisome city much in need of prayer.

Like their acknowledged master Heywood, later epigrammatists commonly composed epigrams incorporating the proverbial significance of the signs, names, and places of London;[135] but the epigrams most revealing of their enterprise embody binary schemes or extended paradigms which articulate a moral structure for the city. In a simple binary example, Richard Niccols contrasts the Old Exchange, at one end of the city, with the New Exchange, at the other, in terms of an underlying opposition of credit and debt:

> Few gallants lately will, nor is it strange,
> Bargaine for needements in the new Exchange;
> For on the Strand, the new stands bleake and cold,
> And they are hot in credit with the old.   (sig. B8)

Henry Parrot similarly articulates the underlying connection of St. Paul's, the haunt of gentlemen at the west end of the City, to the Old Exchange, the haunt of merchants in the east:

> This observation seemes (quoth Fisco) strange,
> Why marchants walk in Pauls & knights the exchange;
> Belike the one seeks those their debts should pay,
> Whiles th'other goes to craue a longer day.   (*Epigrams*, sig. A4v)

Such binary distinctions could be subject to the interpolation of further elements, as when John Heath identifies the Middle Temple (the law and not the Church) as the true center off London life:

> Saint Peters and S. Pauls are in disgrace:
> The Middle Temple, that's the onley place,
> Whither both Citie and Countrey come,
> As to the Temple in Jerusalem.[136]

When extended into series, such oppositions could form a system capable of ordering whole categories of London experience by means of names:

> Bedlam, fate bless thee, thou wantst nought but wit,
> And hauing gotten that, we'r free from it;
> Bridewell, I cannot any way dispraise thee,
> For thou dost feed the poor, and jerk the lazie.
> Newgate, of thee I cannot much complain;

---

[135] Other examples of epigrams on signs and places by Heywood are those on the sign "Of the Three Cups," p. 248, on Turn-again Lane, p. 255, on Freshwharf, p. 278, and on Bridewell and Broken Wharf, p. 243.

[136] *The House of Correction, or Certayne Satyricall Epigrams* (1619), sig. c4v; cf. the similar interpolation by Sir John Harington, *Letters and Epigrams*, ed. Norman E. McClure (Philadelphia: University of Pennsylvania Press, 1930), p. 267.

> For once a moneth, thou freest men out of pain;
> But from the Counters, goodnesse it self defend us?
> To Bedlam, Bridewell, or to Newgate send us,
> For there in time, wit, work, or law sets free;
> But here, wit, work, nor law gets liberty.[137]

By thus transforming series into system, the epigram demonstrates its superiority, as a written form, to the voice. Antithesis, balance, and concluding turns contribute to stability and closure, and in this respect they distinguish the epigram from an oral form like the ballad, in which reliance on simple repetition often threatens to break free of limitation. Whether it takes the form of a narrative or the form of a list, the Renaissance ballad is based on a seriatim taxis; written to an already oft-repeated tune and dealing with familiar matters, it is printed on a single broadsheet which, turned over, reveals that there is almost always more, a second part. Like epigrams, these broadsheets were frequently posted, but inside, not outside, in taverns, inns, and ordinaries, where they were pasted wall to wall, ceiling to floor.[138] Though ballads often focus on the urban landscape, like epigrams, they do not so much resolve as magnify an already protean confusion:

> Roome for Company,
>   heere comes good fellowes,
> Roome for Company,
>   in Bartholomew Faire.
> Coblers and Broome-men ...
> Botchers and Taylors,
> Shipwrights and Saylors ...
> Tinkers and Brasiers,
> Glassemen and Glasiers ...
> Fidlers and Pipers,
> Drummes, Flagges, & Fiffers ...[139]

Unlike the ballad, which typically compiles from the urban landscape, the epigram selects and articulates its elements. At one time or another, nearly every epigrammatist who writes on London pauses to atack the "hated fathers of vilde balladrie," as if this endlessly proliferating form were the very nemesis of the epigrammatic enterprise, "so runnes their

---

[137] Sir John Mennes and James Smith, *Musarum Deliciae : or, the Muses Recreation* (1656), in *Facetiae*, ed. Edward Dubois and Thomas Park (2 vols. London, 1874), 2: 196. Cf. John Owen, *Epigrams*, trans. John Vicars (1618), sig. G7.

[138] See Tessa Watt, *Cheap Print and Popular Piety, 1550–1640* (Cambridge University Press, 1991), pp. 12, 148–149, 194.

[139] *Roome for Company* (1614), in *Pepys Ballads*, ed. Hyder Rollins (8 vols. Cambridge, Mass.: Harvard University Press, 1929), 1 : 52. Many ballads compile from the London landscape; a few examples are *Turner's Dish of Lenten Stuff* (1612), *Londons Ordinarie* (1605–28), *A Mad Crew* (1620), *A Merry New Catch of All Trades* (1624).

verse in such disordered straine."[140] By the turn of the century, as the
epigram had begun to pass from residents at the Inns of Court into the
hands of professional writers, the epigrammatists were beginning to link
their own genre, or at least their fellow practitioners, with the loathed art
of balladry. When Harington's Faustus objected that "long Epigrams are
dull,"[141] or when Ben Jonson complained that Harington's and Owen's
epigrams were merely narratives,[142] they were expressing what was
perhaps the epigrammatist's darkest nightmare: that in his effort to
define and thereby master a protean city, the neat limitation and closure
promised by the epigram would give way to endless confusion. The
longest poem in Jonson's collection of *Epigrams* (1616) is, significantly,
also the one devoted most exclusively to London, the scatological
nightmare "On the famous Voyage."[143]

The hope against such nightmares was that the epigram would put
everything neatly in its place. Thomas Bastard underlines the difficulty
of this task when he complains

> the subiect of my muse
> Is an huge taske and labour infinite:
> Like to a wildernesse or masse confuse.

Against this fluid, inarticulate confusion Bastard balances the epigrammatist's power "To drawe thee forth (Reader) a mappe of men" (p. 16).
In the schemes through which it lays out a microcosmic order, then, the
epigram treats the *urbs*, as a version of the macrocosmic *orb* or mundus.
This logic may have helped to justify the tendency to schematize, but its
deeper motivation lay in the bewildering confusion of London itself.

In the very crudest terms, the sudden deluge of epigrams in the period
1590–1630 coincided with a particularly rapid acceleration in the rate of
London's growth, when the population more than doubled. But the
statistics only superficially suggest the havoc wreaked upon the social
fabric by this burgeoning city. London's new opportunities had been a
major factor in upsetting the traditional order of the three estates,
knights, clergy, and commons, by adding two more, the burgess and the
gentleman, shadowy figures whose mobility fascinated social com-

---

[140] John Cooke, *Epigrams* (1604), sig. B1; cf. John Elsum, *Epigrams* (n.d.), sig. B1, Guilpin,
Skialetheia, p. 41, and Bastard, *Chrestoleros*, p. 78.
[141] *Letters and Epigrams*, p. 146.
[142] *Conversations with William Drummond of Hawthornden*, in *Works*, 1: 133, 138.
[143] For an argument that Jonson did not think of this poem as an epigram, see John
Hollander, *Vision and Resonance: Two Senses of Poetic Form* (New York: Oxford
University Press, 1975), p. 269; but cf. Alistair Fowler, *Kinds of Literature: An
Introduction to the Theory of Genres* (Cambridge, Mass.: Harvard University Press,
1982), pp. 156–157.

mentators. Within the twenty-six wards of the City proper, political and commercial institutions provided a measure of stability by restricting citizenship to those who inherited it by birth or who earned it through apprenticeship in one of the City guilds; but citizenship, and thus the right to trade within the City, could also be purchased by redemption, and enrollment in one guild rarely prevented the ambitious member from dabbling in the trade of others. The great consortia established in the course of the century, such as the Muscovy, Levant, and East India Companies, further eroded the traditional commercial structures.

Even more disturbing than the mobile subcommunities that flourished within traditional insitutions were the social groups for which there was little or no visible structure. Even before the Reformation, London was alleged to harbor invisible communities of itinerant preachers and mendicants who, their opponents claimed, had "craftely crept" into the social fabric and increased "not onely into a great nombre, but also ynto a kingdome."[144] After the Elizabethan Settlement, Puritan and Anabaptist conventicles formed similarly concealed communities, which the authorities repeatedly sought to identify lest they undermine the structures of power.[145] The authorities likewise attempted to impose signs on the invisible community of the infected in times of plague; and repeatedly they singled out the thousands of aliens – both traders and religious refugees, who swelled the city's population – as a threat to London's restrictive institutions.[146] By far the largest and most troubling community was the fraternity of vagabonds, the enormous class of casual laborers and masterless men, demobbed soldiers, orphans, paupers, prostitutes, and thieves who sought refuge from the authorities in the liberties and suburbs. The most eloquent attempts to label these people are the epitaphic entries of the thorough parish registers, begun at the order of Thomas Cromwell. The parish of St Botolph without Aldgate, for example, numbers among its burials the following:

Christian A vagrant that died at Mrs. Crews doore (11 July 1588).
A striplinge who dyed near the barens of broome (29 September 1590).

---

[144] Simon Fish, *A Supplication for the Beggars* (1529), ed. Edward Arber (London, 1878), p. 3. One of Fish's opponents, Thomas More, speaks in the same way about the sort of early protestant preacher who can be found "lurking about and teachynge hys gospell in corners," *The Apology* (1533), ed. J. B. Trapp, in *The Complete Workes of St. Thomas More* (15 vols. New Haven: Yale University Press, 1979), 12: 164.

[145] See, for example, H. C. Porter, *Puritanism in Tudor England* (London, 1970), pp. 75–94. For epigrams on the dangers of invisible congregations, see Francis Thynne, *Emblemes and Epigrames* (1600), ed. F. J. Furnivall (London, 1876), p. 81, and Harington, *Letters and Epigrams*, p. 267.

[146] F. P. Wilson, *The Plague in Shakespeare's London* (Oxford University Press, 1927), pp. 63–65; R. H. Tawney and Eileen Power, eds., *Tudor Economic Documents* (3 vols. London, 1924), 1: 308–310.

A creple that died in the streete before John Awstens doore (15 November 1596).
A mayde a vagrant unknowne (23 July 1597).
Margaritt a deafe woman who died in the streete (27 September 1597).
A poore man who died in a stable whose name we could not learne (3 January 1610).
Thomas priestman ... chylde ... spurned on the belly by a Boy about ye age of x yeares whose name was caled Jacke being masterles and whose surname was not knowne (May 25, 1589).[147]

Along with the dissenting and the diseased, these anonymous creatures were the object of frequent searches and identifying schemes. Like these schemes to articulate a social order without margins, the London epigram was a response to social change; by sorting names and places it laid a lucid order over an obscure substrate of possibilities. This principle held true even when the epigrammatist turned from topography to the city's social fabric. The simplest and by far the largest class of these epigrams sought to fix distinctions in terms of commonplace social types, such as merchants, tradesmen, parvenus, and prodigals, whose proverbial traits the epigram put in definitive form.[148] On a more complex level, epigrammatic schemes are sometimes used to lay out the relations between these types. Just as oppositions could help to define urban topography, so they could reinforce social distinctions or puncture specious unions in the making:

> The well-borne Museus wedded hath of late
> A butcher's daughter fat, for pounds & plate:
> Which match is like a pudding, sith in that
> He puts the bloud, her father all the fat.[149]

The greatest challenge to such typifying schemes comes from the mobile characters who inhabit the ever-widening interstices of the social fabric. Marginal and mysterious, they resist proverbial labels, and so cannot be explicated or "unfolded"; their relentless activity conforms to no one familiar model. Thus Harington's Lynus has "more trades then any man aliue; / As first, a Broker, then a Petty-fogger, / A Traueller, A Gamester, and a Cogger / A Coyner, a Promoter, and a Bawde." Similarly, his wealthy city widow is wooed in succession by "Two Alldermen, three Lawiers, five Phisitions, / Seavn Captains, with nine

---

[147] Thomas Forbes, *Chronicle from Aldgate: Life and Death in Shakespeare's London* (New Haven: Yale University Press, 1971), pp. 78–80.

[148] This type is especially prominent in Peacham's *Thalia's Banquet* (1620) and in Henry Hutton's *Follies Anatomie* (1619).

[149] John Davies of Hereford, from the lost *Wits Bedlam*, in *The Complete Works*, 2: 3. See also Joseph Martyn, *New Epigrames* (1621), sig. B2v; Parrot, *Epigrams* (1608), sig. D2; and Rowlands, *Humors Ordinarie* (?1604), in *Uncollected Poems*, ed. Frederick O. Waage, Jr. (Gainesville: Scholars' Facsimiles and Reprints, 1970), p. 25.

Poets, ten Musitions" (pp. 235, 292). Henry Parrot's Parnell "accompts
it deepest pollicie, / To shift her lodging every month at least."[150]

In cases like these, for which no simple social label will do, the
resources of topography again come into play. If by no other means, then
by association with the landscape, the individual whose identity is
obscure or disguised may be socially codified. Henry Parrot's Rufus, for
example, is a merchant "wondrous rich" but ultimately betrayed by his
untailored clothes, "such as Houns-dich and Long-lane supplies."[151]
Davies' young Ciprius is "more tierse and neat / Then the new garden of
th' olde Temple is," while his "smell feast Afer Travailes to the Burse
/ Twice every day the flying newes to heare."[152] Roger Sharpe's
Magnaninny and Richard Niccols' mysterious Basiliscus betray themselves by frequenting rowdy Turnbull Street, and the pretensions of
Brunus are punctured when Sir John Davies discovers his belongings
"At Trollups by Saint Clements church in pawne."[153] Richard West is
momentarily puzzled by the seemingly familiar face of a merchant's new
wife, but he decides, sardonically, that he must have seen her look-alike,
"her picture, at a bawdy house."[154] Parrot's Mistress Jane is even less
successful at shedding the former haunts that identify her:

> Naye fie how strange you make it mistris Iane,
> Will you not know your *quondam* tried friends?
> Remember since you lodg'd in Carter-lane
> Shall former kindnesse merit no amends?[155]

Where such topographical tactics are pursued, the binary schemes so
useful in sorting out the landscape can arrest the movement of a mobile
figure by at least fixing the poles between which he moves:

> Naeuia is one while of the Innes of Court,
> Toyling in *Brook*, *Fitzherbert*, and in *Dyer*.
> Another while th'Exchange he doth resort,
> Moyling as fast, a seller, and a buyer:
>   Will not he thriue (think yee) who can deuise,
>   Thus to vnite the law and merchandise?[156]

The most complex versions are again formed around extended paradigms, in which the number of commonplaces or activities to which a
person can be traced build up a set of typifying associations. The
convention of the "daily round," drawn from Martial, provides the most

---

[150] *Cures for the Itch* (1616), sig. B4v.   [151] *The Mous-Trap* (1606), sig. C3.
[152] *The Poems of Sir John Davies*, pp. 138, 147.
[153] Roger Sharpe, *More Fooles Yet* (1610), sig. C1; Niccols, *The Furies*, sig. B6; Davies,
Poems, p. 142.   [154] *Wits A. B. C., or a Centurie of Epigrams* (1608), sig. B4.
[155] *Epigrams* (1608), sig. G1v.   [156] Guilpin, *Skialetheia*, p. 50.

common device for such characterizations. Davies' Faustus and Fuscus follow the daily course of veteran dissolutes from tavern to playhouse to brothel (pp. 132, 146–147), while the circuit of Peacham's Lucius, which includes the top of St. Paul's, the Tower, and the Counter, identifies him as "the lately knighted Farmers sonne," newly arrived in London.[157] But while such lists can form a unified portrait, they can also defy the neat portraiture that is the epigrammatist's goal:

> As Caius walks the streets, if he but heare
> A blackman grunt his note, he cries *oh rare*!
> He cries *oh rare* to heare the Irishmen
> Cry pippe, fine pippe, with a shrill accent, when
> He comes at Mercers chappell; and, *oh rare*,
> At Ludgate at the prisoners plaine-song there:
> *Oh rare* sings he to heare a Cobler sing,
> Or a wassaile on twelfe night, or the ring
> At cold S. Pancras church; or any thing:...
> From Paris-garden he renewes his song,
> To see my L. Maiors Henchmen; or to see,
> (At an old Aldermans blest obsequie)
> The Hospitall boyes in their blew aequipage,
> Or at a carted bawde, or whore in cage:
> He'le cry, *oh rare*, at a Gongfarmers cart,
> *Oh rare* to heare a ballad or a fart:
> Briefly so long he hath vsde to cry, *oh rare*,
> That now that phrase is growne thin & thred-bare,
> But sure his wit will be more rare and thin,
> If he continue as he doth begin.

In one respect, Guilpin's Caius is neatly reduced and fixed by his own manic repetitiveness. And this is underlined by Guilpin's careful imitation of an epigram from Martial.[158] But on the other hand, through Caius' undiscriminating use of the phrase "oh rare," the city ceases to be an articulate space. The many varieties of experience collapse into the one potentially endless experience of perambulation. This experience is punctuated by sounds – the blackman's note, the pippin-seller's cry, the cobbler's song – and Caius' phrase rings its changes in the manner of a ballad refrain. Indeed, these fluid, oral traits threaten to dissolve the epigram's lapidary neatness into balladeering chaos: "Coblers and Broome-men, / Iaylors and Loome-men." The connection between this mobility-within-the-epigram and the metonymic simulation-effect of verse satire, where the soul is eroded by the environment, is perhaps summed up in Davies' epigram on Quintus, whose wit is

---

[157] *The More the Merrier*, sig A4. For the precedent, see Martial, *Epigrams*, 4, 8, 10, 70.
[158] *Skialetheia*, pp. 56–57, cf. Martial, *Epigrams*, 12.57.

> fled into his feete,
> And there it wanders up and downe the streete,
> Dabled in the durt, and soaked in the raine.[159]

No less than that of Quintus, the wit of Davies' epigram becomes mired in its own wayward, wandering feet.

As it comes to incorporate extended lists, the epigram thus approaches its limits; its own resources are worn as thin as Caius' threadbare phrase or Quintus' shoes. For such figures, whose very essence is movement, neither the landscape nor the epigram can provide firm boundaries. London's places, and implicitly the epigram's repetitive schemes, threaten to elude neat closure and to become instead an endless series. In an epigram by Thomas Freeman, the whole city becomes a monument in helter-skelter motion; the city's living landscape pitches the usual schematic contrasts forward into a narrative sequence:

> Why how now, *Babell*, whither wilt thou build? –
> The old Holborne, Charing Crosse, the Strand,
> Are going to St. Giles'-in-the-Field,
> Saint Katerne she takes Wapping by the hand,
> And Hogsdon will to Hy-gate ere't be long.
> London has got a great way from the streame.
> I thinke she means to go to Islington,
> To eat a dish of strawberrries and creame.
> The City's sure in Progresse, I surmise,
> Or going to revell it in some disorder,
> Without the walls, without the liberties,
> Where she neede feare nor Mayor nor Recorder.
> Well, say she do, 'twere pretty, yet 'tis pity,
> A middlesex bailiff should arrest the Citty.[160]

Freeman's attempt to close the poem grasps at the hope that some authoritative limit will set bounds upon the city. But his witty turn lays down the law as feebly as the Middlesex Sheriff; neither allays the menace of a coming breakdown, when the city will "revell it in some disorder."

At such points as this, the epigrammatists' attempt to encode the city shows the strain of the material and social factors that contribute to the making of epigrams but cannot be contained by them. As its neat devices begin to soften and expand, the epigram admits to a difference between the order it desires and the alien, mysterious life that order would contain. In one respect, this difference threatens to deprive the epigram of its power to signify. But in another respect, this same difference reveals an underlying motivation which the surface qualities of neatness,

---

[159] *The Poems of Sir John Davies*, p. 134.
[160] Thomas Freeman, *Rubbe and a Great Cast* (1614), sig. B3.

lucidity, and finish might otherwise conceal. Freeman or Guilpin or Davies are paradoxically successful when they fail, when they confess to forces known only by their unsettling effects. In their moment of vulnerability London epigrams show us a city which is neither wholly undepictable nor too neatly circumscribed, but an animated shadow cast by new and unfamiliar forms of life.

Among contemporaries, one sign of the epigram's failure was its rapid dissemination from amateur to professional writers, from educated gentlemen and lawyers to unsavory hacks like Taylor the Water Poet and the unfortunately named Henry Parrot. For the literary degeneration of lapidary neatness into broadsheet banality there was an edifying, comforting social parallel. If the rage began with figures like the Queen's godson, Sir John Harington, it was drawing toward its doom with figures like the literary prodigal Richard Brathwait, the creator of Drunken Barnaby's endless *Itinerary*. Yet Harington's Ariosto was as unsavory and prolix as Drunken Barnaby, and the earlier epigrammatists are linked to their followers in ways only partially concealed by the social distinctions that seemed to differentiate them. Nearly all of the first generation of epigrammatists – Davies, Guilpin, Bastard, Thynne, and Weever – were associated with the Inns of Court, which had recently become a reinvigorated source for the country's elite, but which were also becoming a source of popular and professional writers. Drawn to London by the promise of a living, the members of the Inns were themselves a mobile and in some respects a marginal class, searching for niches in a system that could be maddeningly unstable. The Inns produced their Egertons and Lees, their Chancellors and Lord Mayors, as well as their suburban bureaucrats, the Thynnes and Guilpins. But in William Goddard they produced a demobbed soldier and begging epigrammatist. For young John Davies, the son of a Wiltshire tanner, expulsion from the Middle Temple was a more immediate concern than the Attorney-Generalship of Ireland, which lay a dozen years down the road; and for Thomas Bastard, the end of the road was death "in a mean condition"[161] in a Dorchester madhouse.

If urbane aggressiveness was part of London life, it was essential at the Inns. The rising fashion for "quips and sentences and ... paper bullets" accords nicely with what is known of the mootings and adversarial practices at the Inns;[162] but these proceedings speak for the even more

[161] Anthony à Wood, *Athenae Oxonienses*, ed. Philip Bliss (4 vols. Oxford: Ecclesiatical Society, 1848), 2: 228.

[162] Shakespeare, *Much Ado About Nothing* (2.3.240). See R. J. Schoeck, "Rhetoric and Law in Sixteenth-Century England," *SP*, 54 (1957), 498–508, and Finkelpearl, *John Marston of the Middle Temple*, pp. 8–10.

deeply adversarial environment toward which they were a preparation. Despite their frequently acknowledged debt to Martial, London epigrammatists depart from Martial in one crucial respect: Martial almost always delivers his barbs to second-person victims in a deceptively genial first-person voice, but the London epigrammatist does so rarely. Rather, opting for the antiseptic third person, he effectively removes himself from his victim. If the occasional epigrammatist, like Davies, finds a personal voice and pose, the common failure of others to do so should be attributed not simply to ineptitude but also to the nature of the form, which tended implicitly to alienate the writer from the work and its reified subjects.

There is thus an ironic relationship between the commonplace and the definitive, between the community and the writer, between communal wisdom and the sometimes bitter knowledge of the poet. While distance and detachment seemed a necessary precondition for the ordered encapsulation of a tumultous common ground, they were no guarantee against the writer's defeat by the common. Despite the lapidary origins and aspirations of the epigram, despite its traditional goal of rendering things permanently memorable, the epigram sometimes led its practitioners into an obsession with their own ephemerality.[163] It was the destiny of the genre to wind up in the hands of hacks, but the genre had always, in fact, been treated as a species of throwaway culture. The earliest manuscript title of Davies' epigrams was "English Epigrammes Much Like Buckminsters Almanacke, Seruinge for all England, but Especially for the Meridian of the Honourable Cittye of London Calculated by John Dauis... An. 1594 in Nouember."[164] John Weever similarly remarked that "Epigrammes are much like vnto Almanacks seruing especially for the yeare for which they are made... being one yeare pend, and in an other printed: are past due before they come from the Presse."[165] Beyond the calculated *sprezzatura* of such remarks lies a deeper ambivalence about the form itself, an awareness that it perishes before the task it attempts. Bastard, who titled his collection *Chrestoleros*, or useful (*chrestos*) nonsense (*leros*), asked simply

> how shall mens, or manners forme appeare,
> Which while I write, do change from what they were? (p. 7)

The inability *topos* differs from the sonneteer's or visionary's; the epigram is confounded not simply by time, or fortune, or the might of the

---

[163] A paradox noted by Whipple, *Martial and the English Epigram*, pp. 360–362.
[164] Krueger, *The Poems of Sir John Davies*, p. 377.
[165] *Epigrammes in the Oldest Cut and Newest Fashion* (1599), ed. R. B. McKerrow (London, 1911), p. 13.

divine, but by a concrete mystery antithetical to the sublime. Seeking to elucidate this mystery, the epigram finds itself instead swallowed by it:

> An Epigram that's new, quick, tart, sharp, witty,
> Is like a wench that's new, faire, smooth, neate, pretty:
> Whilst they are new and fresh, they are respected:
> Once common (though still good) they are neglected.

As marginal, then, as a cast-off wench, John Owen's epigram,[166] like many by his contemporaries, admits, prudently perhaps, to its own likely failure. It is of course ironic that in confronting so rich, dense, and central a subject as London the writer should be forced to confirm his own ephemeral irrelevance. When Henry Parrot announced at the end of several hundred epigrams, "thus haue I waded through a worthless taske,"[167] he necessarily claimed for himself and his subject the reverse of what Spenser had claimed in extolling his "labour huge exceeding farre my might," his "Worke of labour long and endlesse prayse" (*The Faerie Queene*, 2.10.2; 1.11.7). Marginalized, in its relation to a still-powerful courtly bias, the epigram remained in troubling proximity to the base and degraded manner of professional writing and popular culture that it sought to master. Only with the continuing urbanization of the gentry and the gentrification of London in the seventeenth century would the epigram, in the work of Jonson and his successors, see its laureate ambitions fulfilled.

---

[166] Trans. Hayman, *Quodlibets*, p. 29.   [167] *Epigrams* (1608), sig. H4v.

8   The uses of enchantment: Jacobean city comedy and romance

Haunted houses: the interplay of comic forms in the theater repertory

The writer who described Queen Elizabeth's 1559 coronation entry declared that "a man ... could not better term the City of London that time than a stage," thereby indicating the theatrical potential of the urban environment on great ceremonial occasions, especially when manipulated by a monarch as theatrically shrewd as Elizabeth I. More than half a century later, however, John Donne could lay to rest as relatively ordinary a personage as Sir William Cockayne, a prominent citizen and Lord Mayor, with the observation that "this City is a great Theater, and he acted great and various parts in it."[1] It is perhaps as a result of this de-sacralizing spread of theatrical consciousness that the dramatist Edward Sharpham could see so much comic potential in the convergence of theatrical art with urban life:

> The Cittie is a Commodie, both in partes and in apparell, and your Gallants are the Actors: for hee that yesterday played the Gentleman, nowe playes the Begger; shee that played the Wayting-woman, nowe playes the Queane; and shee that played the Ladie, nowe playes the Painter. Then for their apparell, they haue change too: ... and hee that could scarce get Veluet for his Cape, has nowe linde his Cloake throughout with it.[2]

Providing numerous possibilities for social interchange, a variety of histrionic roles to be played, and a protean potential for mobility, conflict, and extravagant display, the city had become, during a period of rapid growth and change, an inherently dramatic – and in Sharpham's view comic – setting.

Although preachers attacked them and the City authorities attempted

---

[1] A Sermon Preached at the Funerals of Sir William Cockayne Knight, Alderman of London, December 12, 1626, in *The Sermons of John Donne*, ed. Evelyn M. Simpson and George R. Potter (10 vols. Berkeley: University of California Press, 1954), 7: 274.

[2] *The Fleire* (1607), 2.1.124–134, in Christopher Gordon Petter, *A Critical Old Spelling Edition of the Works of Edward Sharpham* (New York: Garland, 1986), p. 265.

at times to suppress them, the new theaters of London – the first of which opened in the northern suburbs in 1576 – became a vital institution in the city's life. They left a lasting impression in the minds of foreign visitors, justifying Thomas Heywood's claim that "playing is an ornament to the citty ... for what variety of entertainment can there be in any citty of christendome more than in London?"[3] Among the many striking developments in the new world of the London theater was the sudden outpouring at the end of the sixteenth century of comedies set within the precincts of the contemporary capital. Largely an innovation of popular, professional writers like Dekker, Middleton, and Jonson, whose work was also associated with the new developments in seriocomic pamphleteering and verse satire, the rise of so-called "Jacobean city comedy" was central to the development of a new urban literature and outlook. By 1642 there were in the theater repertory more than a hundred comedies set in London.[4]

Nevertheless, the social meaning of this remarkable literary development has proven notoriously difficult to determine. The sociohistorically significant artistic innovations do not reside in city comedy's anti-acquisitive attitudes, which are quite traditional, but in the new form in which these attitudes are expressed.[5] And yet the formal innovations of city comedy – the evocation of familiar urban settings in conjunction with a racy, colloquial idiom, the satiric delineation of social types and the rigorous plotting of intrigue – also represent a rediscovery of traditional comic decorum. Ben Jonson's famous promise to "show an image of the times" by depicting familiar persons and using "language such as men do use,"[6] innovates by invoking the ancient pseudo-Aristotelian dictum that the inconsequence of everyday life is the appropriate medium of comedy, which should "sport with human follies, not with crimes."[7] The intrigue plots of city comedy continue the ancient New Comedy tradition of pitting young, resourceful wits – who are often driven by erotic motives – against the obstacles of an obtuse and rigid authority. Characters rise from their coffins perhaps more often in

---

[3] *An Apology for Actors* (1612), in O. B. Hardison, Jr., ed., *English Literary Criticism: The Renascence* (Englewood Cliffs: Prentice-Hall, 1963), p. 226.

[4] Anne Barton, "London Comedy and the Ethos of the City," *The London Journal*, 4: 2 (1978), 160.

[5] G. K. Hunter, "The Idea of Comedy and Some Seventeenth Century Comedies," in *Poetry and Drama in the English Renaissance: Essays in Honor of Jiro Ozu*, ed. Nakanori and Tamaizumi (Tokyo: Kinokuniya, 1908), pp. 78–80; for an interpretation of city comedy in terms of its anti-acquisitive attitudes, see L. C. Knights, *Drama and Society in the Age of Jonson* (1937; rpt. New York: Norton, 1968).

[6] Prologue to the revised version of *Every Man in His Humour*, ed. J. W. Lever (Lincoln: University of Nebraska Press, 1971), p. 5.

[7] Hunter, "The Idea of Comedy," p. 77.

city comedy than in any other genre,[8] and in formalistic terms, if not in spirit, the genre bears a very close resemblance to traditional comic kinds.

One way, however, in which the form of city comedy elaborates upon contemporary social life is through its relationships to other forms – relationships, which, internalized as a particular comic dynamic, are the most historically revealing feature of the form. In keeping with Paul Hernadi's description of genre as a gestalt which invites us to emphasize certain features while suppressing others it potentially contains, city comedy may be regarded not as a topical island in the Jacobean theater but as a territory defined and animated by its boundaries with others. Brian Gibbons identifies as a salient feature of city comedy its rigorous "exclusion of material appropriate to romance, fairy-tale, sentimental legend or patriotic chronicle."[9] City comedy, especially those versions of it associated with private theater companies, is in fact actively concerned to discredit magic and romance as viable frameworks for the representation of the city. The incongruity of romantic illusion with urban reality is thus a major source of humor in the form.[10]

It is also a source of generic definition. In plays like Jonson's *The Alchemist* – where a character awaits the appearance of the Fairy Queene while gagged and locked in a privy – the antiromantic inscription of romance motifs serves the purpose of defining and cleverly enforcing generic boundaries. This active enforcement – which often takes the form of disenchantment or theatrical exorcism –makes it less appropriate to speak of exclusion than of what Anne Barton calls a "curious interweaving of realism with fantasy that was characteristic of the genre."[11] The forces of attraction and repulsion that govern this interweaving emerge from two outstanding developments in the first decade of the Jacobean theater – the nearly simultaneous rise in popularity of city comedy and romance, the latter represented by the revival and frequent reprinting of *Mucedorus*, by the writing of such plays as Rowley's *The Birth of Merlin*, Heywood and Chettle's *The Trial of Chivalry*, and Shakespeare's romances, and, more distantly, by the tragicomic experiments of Beaumont and Fletcher and by the magical

---

[8] The traditional significance of this common motif is pointed out by Anne Barton, "London Comedy and the Ethos of the City," pp. 160–161.

[9] *Jacobean City Comedy* (2nd edn., London: Methuen, 1980), p. 11; cf. p. 1.

[10] A typical example might be taken from *Eastward Ho* (1604), in which Petronel Flash, a "true knight–adventurer" sets off on a "prosperous voyage" to the romantic eldorado of Virginia, but winds up on the Isle of Dogs, a rubbish tip in a lower Thames marsh. Harry Levin treats this clash of idioms as an exemplary instance in "Two Magian Comedies: 'The Tempest' and 'The Alchemist,'" *ShS*, 22 (1971), p. 220.

[11] "London Comedy and the Ethos of the City," p. 161.

charm of the new court masque.[12] The performance of Beaumont's *Knight of the Burning Pestle* in 1607 perhaps epitomizes the emerging symbiosis of city comedy and romance in Jacobean London's rival theaters and repertories.

The continued popularity of an old warhorse like *Mucedorus* might seem to argue less for the novelty of romance than for its persistence as the dominant comic mode of the native English theater.[13] But the 1610 epilogue to the revived Elizabethan play, when compared with its original Induction, illustrates how a new consciousness of generic symbiosis, fostered by the rise of Jacobean city comedy, changed the meaning of romance by repositioning its comic potential. The Induction to *Mucedorus* in the 1598 edition had followed the traditional practice of opposing comic to tragic potential, contrasting Envy's threat to impose "a tragic end" with Comedy's promise to bring "things with treble joy to pass."[14] In the Epilogue added for the court performance of 1610, however, Envy threatens to undermine Comedy's happy resolution not through tragedy but through a different comic strategy – the strategy of making "thy fall my comic merriment" by securing "a leane and hungry neger poet... to write a comedy, / Wherin shall be composed dark sentences, / Pleasing to factious brains."[15] The decisive difference here – factiousness – is not so much a formal as a social one, a challenge to the common ethical assent that in the more traditional Comedy's view would "gain the love of all estates."

The effect of Envy's maneuver is to replace the traditional contrast between comedy and tragedy, grounded in enduring differences in the patterns of fortune and the hierarchical decora of nature, with a more purely positional system of competing comic possibilities. The Induction to Day's *Isle of Gulls* shows that by 1606 the Jacobean theater had discriminated the differing comic potential of "rayling and inuectiues," "bawdy and scurrill jests" and "quick mirth."[16] In *Every Man Out of His Humour*, Jonson similarly contrasts the satiric engagement of topical matters "near and familiarly allied to the time" with the more traditional romantic comedy of "some... cross-wooing." At the other end of the comic scale, Thomas Heywood, the author of many popular romances,

[12] Michael Shapiro, *Children of the Revels: The Boy Companies of Shakespeare's Time and Their Plays* (New York: Columbia University Press, 1977), pp. 189–204.

[13] See Alfred Harbage, *Shakespeare and the Rival Traditions* (New York: Macmillan, 1952), pp. 62–65; cf. Leo Salingar, *Shakespeare and the Traditions of Comedy* (Cambridge University Press, 1974), ch. 2.

[14] Ed. Charles Read Baskervill, Virgil B. Heltzel, and Arthur F. Nethercot, *Elizabethan and Stuart Plays* (New York: Henry Holt, 1934), Induction, lines 10, 40.

[15] For the identification of the "neger poet" with the satiric Jonson, see Harbage, *Shakespeare and the Rival Traditions*, p. 109.

[16] Ed. Raymond S. Burns (New York: Garland, 1980), lines 84–85, 142.

complained in 1608 that "nothing but Satirica Dictaeria and Comic Scommata are now in request."[17] This is all evidence of a major generic repositioning, a dialogue between comic forms and writers which elaborated the impact of urban life on the literary system. Jonson was perhaps the most vocal participant in this dialogue, with his attacks on "mouldy tale[s], ... stale / As the shrieves crusts," on "Tales Tempests, and such like drolleries."[18] But the epilogue to *Mucedorus* or the generic playfulness of Beaumont's *Knight of the Burning Pestle* demonstrate that the active remapping of the comic terrain was a bilateral venture.

The unresolved alterity of realism and romance is perhaps a timeless means by which literatures reflect upon themselves. To some extent it can be found in English dramatic theory before the rise of city comedy.[19] But the heightened visibility of romantic and farcical alternatives in early Jacobean theatrical modes reflects a sharpened awareness of the positional nature of generic frames of reference, a new consciousness of the social basis on which the frames of reality are constructed. The dynamic relations between city comedy and romance, whereby each attempts to exclude or appropriate aspects of its demonic other, were thus part of a collective cultural process, the structure of which can be read along the lines of "romance." As Fredric Jameson explains it, romance projects as imaginative antinomies – good and evil, self and other – that which at the historical level is a contradiction, namely, that "my enemy can be thought of as being evil (that is, other than myself and marked by some absolute difference) when what is responsible for his being so characterized is quite simply the *identity* of his own conduct with mine." Romance poses and resolves such contradictions by the logic of what Jameson calls "semic evaporations," the magical transformations and miraculous discoveries that dispel difference as a baleful illusion.[20] The historically contradictory experience of being both/and is imaginatively projected in romance as a logic of either/or, which is magically or

---

[17] Preface to the Reader, *2 Iron Age* (written c. 1608; pub. c. 1632), in *The Dramatic Works of Thomas Heywood* (6 vols. 1874; rpt. New York: Russell and Russell, 1964), 3: 351; quoted in Harbage, *Shakespeare and the Rival Traditions*, p. 110. See also Muriel Bradbrook, "Shakespeare and the Multiple Theaters of Jacobean London," in G. R. Hibbard, ed., *The Elizabethan Theater VI* (Hamden, Conn.: Archon Books, 1978), p. 94.

[18] "Ode to Himself," in George Parfitt, ed., *The Complete Poems* (1975; rpt. New York: Yale University Press, 1982), p. 282; Induction to *Bartholomew Fair*, ed. E. M. Waith (New Haven: Yale University Press, 1963), lines 115–116.

[19] See Harbage, *Shakespeare and the Rival Traditions*, pp. 69–70; Madeline Doran, *Endeavors of Art: A Study of Form in Elizabethan Drama* (1954; rpt. Madison: University of Wisconsin Press, 1964), pp. 172–178; George Rowe, *Thomas Middleton and the New Comedy Tradition* (Lincoln: University of Nebraska Press, 1979), p. 12.

[20] *The Political Unconscious: Narrative as a Socially Symbolic Act* (Ithaca: Cornell University Press, 1981), pp. 115, 118–119.

436	*Literature and culture in early modern London*

providentially resolved into one/and the same. This mode of imagining, Jameson adds, thrives during socio-economic transitions; it is fostered by the "psychic dispersal, fragmentation... and temporal discontinu- ities" that occur when "an organic social order [is] in the process of penetration and subversion, reorganization and rationalization" (p. 148).

In the way that it institutionalized the interplay of forms and genres – through cross-fertilization, competition, and self-reference – the Lon- don theater world produced something like a cultural romance, a narrative of social reconciliation resembling that Empsonian version of pastoral in which "the classes feel part of a larger unity or simply at home with each other."[21] Playing one set of comic (and hence social) possibilities against another, the Jacobean comic theater helped to resolve the demonic logic of either/or into the utopian possibility of one /and the same. Yet this exhilarating release from the confines of generic and social categories was also a terrifying exposure of the mobility of moral and social life, of the mere positionality of the differences which organize a world in transition. The very generic terms which made the city negotiable were understood, with increasing self-consciousness, as themselves the product – and in a sense as the precondition – of the city's mobile life; the discovery of the city's power to incorporate and unify was at one with the discovery of its (and the theater's) prolific heterogeneity, its production of laws, classes, and discursive differences.

The anxieties associated with this perception help to animate the interplay between community and competition in city comedy – the conflict between its amoral celebration of the common but always divisive pursuit of advantage and its moral abhorrence of the violations of community which such positional antagonisms involve. On the one hand, through the ruthlessly positional logic of intrigue, the authors of city comedy achieved, along with the contemporary pamphleteers and satirists, a novel insight into the social construction of reality, into the genesis and exploitation of the illusory differences and antinomies that organize and drive the social process. On the other hand, the playwrights were always at least residually motivated by the socially and morally unifying logic of romance – by a tendency to withhold moral assent from the anti-communal, positional logic on which intrigue thrives and by which intrigue proves demonically resistant to the establishment of a non-positional, socially unifying morality. Just as their residually romantic enforcement of moral justice and social harmony thrived on the suppression of ruthless intrigue, so their demystifying uses of ruthless intrigue thrived at the expense of the moral and social satisfactions of

[21] *Some Versions of Pastoral* (1935; rpt. New York: New Directions, 1974), p. 199.

romance resolutions. The rise of city comedy thus heightened awareness of the social process through a heightened sense of the theater's diversifying comic potential. The conflicted relations between intrigue comedy and romance, internalized by city comedy itself, provided the characteristic tensions of the new genre. These tensions produced what might be called a "romance" of the theater, in which two comic modes, reflecting on the city by reflecting on each other, both acknowledged and held at bay the positional relationship by which each framed its vision of the world. The relationship was productive not only of artistic conflict but also of new social and discursive possibilities which, by exchange and recombination, resolved conflict and contradiction, opening the potentially monolithic attitudes and bias of individual plays and modes to critical engagement with their alternatives.

If the interplay of comic modes developed *through* the Jacobean reflection on the city at a crucial period of transition, this reflection developed *in* the contemporary rivalry between London's public and private theaters. The tension between and within city comedy and romance played a central role in establishing and expressing the different positions these institutions represented; it helped to elaborate differences between polite and popular repertories, elite and heterogeneous audiences, conformist and critical sensibilities, between an audience "to whom the traditional romantic images of the city were familiar but not convincing, and a broader public audience who would not have accepted a purely satiric treatment of those images."[22] The so-called Jacobean "War of the Theaters" embodied many features of the socio-economic change which centered in London – fierce economic competition, individualistic rivalry and ambition, new modes of corporate organization and identity, conflicting class values and anxieties.[23] As a war, however, it also embodied the features of the battles and antagonisms of romance – projection, homeopathic and imitative magic, camouflage and mimicry, the symmetrical relationship between hero and demon, self and other, which can be read allegorically in the unfolding of contradiction through the dialogue of alternatives.[24]

At the height of their activity (and rivalry), London's theaters were, in effect, haunted houses, heterocosmic spaces where rival traditions, values, and generic expectations acted as spectral antagonists, undermining the claims of any play or repertory to represent or interpret society with authoritative force. Jonson's constant battle against the

[22] Susan Wells, "Jacobean City Comedy and the Ideology of the City," *ELH*, 48:1 (1981), p. 48.   [23] Harbage, *Shakespeare and the Rival Traditions*, p. 90.
[24] Angus Fletcher, *Allegory: The Theory of a Symbolic Mode* (Ithaca: Cornell University Press, 1964), chs. 1, 3, 4.

popular-theater taste for the "concupiscence of dances and antics" that "run away from nature," draws on his confidence that "a little touch of their adversary gives all that boisterous force the foil."[25] Yet at the same time, Jonson was conscious that his own novel manner was haunted by the ghostly emanations of popular romance and the public theater tradition. His *Cynthia's Revels*, for example, was haunted by the influential mode of Lyly's Chapel plays, "the *umbrae* or ghosts of some three or four plays departed a dozen years since and recently revived."[26]

Yet the agonistic magic by which different comic modes suppressed their rivals and established their power to represent included the potential for scenes of recognition, moments of semic evaporation when the alternatives were seen as interdependent positions in a common social ritual of interpretation.[27] At the interface of comic modes – and at the height of theatrical interplay between them – there were many moments and a few extensive interludes, such as *A Chaste Maid in Cheapside*, *The Knight of the Burning Pestle*, and *Bartholomew Fair*, where the comic representation of the city saw through itself to the underlying romance in which it participated, to the patterns of exchange and combination that are the means by which drama conjures with the conflicts and contradictions involved in social change. There was a relative absence of such insight both before the rise of city comedy and the War of the Theaters, when the predatory logic of the city was seen as alien to popular, romantic morality and social unity, and after their decline, when, with the weakening of the public theaters and the adaptation of their romantic modes to private theater tastes, the exploitative ways of the world were underwritten and excused, given a romantic aura and endorsement, as the means by which a master class upholds its moral birthright. At the moment of transition, however, city comedy permitted trenchant insights into social and discursive practice by permitting insight into the alterity of comic modes.

Earlier comedies in the mode of romance tended to suppress this insight. In Heywood's *Four Prentices of London*, for example, a positional

---

[25] *The Alchemist*, ed. Alvin B. Kernan (New Haven: Yale University Press, 1974), "To the Reader," pp. 20–21.

[26] Quoted in Harbage, *Shakespeare and the Rival Traditions*, p. 71.

[27] Theodore B. Leinwand, *The City Staged: Jacobean Comedy, 1603–13* (Madison: University of Wisconsin Press, 1986), writes interestingly about the way in which character stereotypes in city comedy are simultaneously exploited and undermined; he does not, however, relate this dislectical relationship between illusion and disillusionment to the interplay of comic genres, to the rivalry of companies or theaters, or to the marketplace conditions which formed the key link between social interdependence in London and imaginative interdependence on stage. On the theater *as* marketplace, see Douglas Bruster, *Drama and the Market in the Age of Shakespeare* (Cambridge University Press, 1992), esp. pp. 23–24.

rivalry between four London apprentices for the hand of their unrecognized sister comes close to the farcical scenario of exploitation that became the staple of Jacobean city comedy. Moreover, the absurd decorum of the play, in which the apprentices serve as squires in the crusades, contains the potential for the burlesque juxtaposition of high and low genres, styles, and social expectations by which Beaumont was to mobilize the interplay of comic modes in his *The Knight of the Burning Pestle*. What prevents the exposure of this indecorum in Heywood's play is the fact that the four apprentices actually *are* young noblemen, sons of the exiled Earl of Bulloigne; indeed, they finally recognize their blood ties as noble kinsmen by recognizing on their shields the fraternal emblems of the London guilds in which they have served apprenticeship. This utopian, unifying moment, which evaporates fraternal rivalry, simultaneously erases the social difference between burgher and nobleman. As in Heywood's *Edward IV* plays, where London's potentially rebellious apprentices are assimilated by a patriotic appeal to burgher ethics, and where King Edward's potentially farcical cuckolding of a London citizen is condemned as uncharacteristic of true English nobility, the suppression of social differences and inter-class rivalry depends upon the suppression of potentially farcical structures of exploitation by an inclusive, neochivalric ethic of loyalty, service, and moral nobility.

By contrast, it became a primary function of city comedy to exploit exactly this rivalrous potential. Concerned with the mimesis of a range of social ranks and functions and with the competitive struggle for wealth, position, and power between gentry and citizens, masters and servants, creditors and debtors, "city comedy individuates various forms of economic identity and brings each forward to be displayed in sexual or economic relations where inevitably one is either predator or prey."[28] Such farcical struggles may be treated in different ways, however: as false, ungrounded oppositions which may be romantically resolved by a socially unifying moral norm, or as themselves a universal norm perpetuated by false, romantic delusions and pseudo-utopian pursuits. In the latter alternative, which prevails in most city comedy intrigue plots, the basis of human relationship is the recognition that no "essential difference" separates in-law and outlaw pursuits, both of which are fundamentally exploitational. As one city-comedy scoundrel explains it,

> Our life methinks is but the same with others;
> To couzen, and be couzen'd, makes the Age.

[28] Leonard Tennenhouse, *Power on Display: The Politics of Shakespeare's Genres* (London: Methuen, 1986), p. 161. For the predatory cycle as a basic structure for city comedy's social mimesis, see also Gail Kern Paster, *The Idea of the City in the Age of Shakespeare* (Athens: University of Georgia Press, 1985), ch. 6.

> The Prey and Feeder are that Civill thing
> That Sager heads call Body Politick.
> Here is the only difference: others cheat
> By statute, but we do't upon no grounds.
> The fraud's the same in both.[29]

There is probably no city comedy in which these romantic and farcical, utopian and satiric possibilities are not in some sort of tension. But the dark, demystifying turn of Jacobean city comedy depended in many respects on the exploitation of the farcical potential that had been suppressed by the romantic bias of much earlier popular theater comedy.

Reflecting the continuing influence of the logic of romance on popular theater citizen comedy before the rise of the private theaters, Shakespeare's *The Merry Wives of Windsor* exemplifies the predominance of romance over farcical predation. The force that motivates the play's farcical mechanism is a struggle for advantage, conducted along class lines, in the stereotypical rivalry between aristocrats and citizens, between the roguish knight Falstaff and the jealous citizen Ford.[30] The play moves, however, toward a solution like those of Heywood, establishing an inclusive, communal ethos of moral gentility which resolves the false opposition between the two major antagonists. The marriage of the bourgeois Ann Page to the gentle-born Fenton moves the play beyond the exploitational potential in this gentleman's original intention to exploit her "father's wealth" (2.4.13); it creates, in its union between bourgeois and gentle youth, a model of moral gentility that transcends the class conflict between Falstaff and Ford.

Blinded by class bias, both Falstaff and Ford view life as a struggle to maintain or enhance their social position. Their antagonism takes the form of a false version of romance, in which each contender believes that he enjoys a charismatic, non-positional advantage over the demonized class position of the other. Falstaff, for example, believes himself endowed with the personal charm and social status to sweep up gullish citizens – who "shall be my East and West Indies" – and to "sail ... my pinnace to these golden shores" (1.3.69, 80). A stolid member of the local community who falls prey to no less fantastic a delusion, Ford sees in Falstaff's threat to his reputation an eruption of demonic witchcraft which must be laid to rest (3.2.39–43; 3.5.147–49). Falstaff and Ford

---

[29] William Cartwright, *The Ordinary* (1635/1651), ed. G. Blakemore Evans, *The Poems and Plays of William Cartwright* (Madison: University of Wisconsin Press, 1951), p. 286.

[30] I owe much of my comparison of *The Merry Wives of Windsor* and *The Shoemaker's Holiday* to G. K. Hunter, "Bourgeois Comedy: Shakespeare and Dekker," in E. A. J. Honigmann, ed., *Shakespeare and His Contemporaries* (Manchester University Press, 1986), p. 5.

thus share a common enchantment by the false oppositions of class bias. In his disguise as Master Brook, "a gentleman that have spent much" (2.2.16–61), Ford mirrors Falstaff's own fantasy of a gentleman's ability to "predominate over the peasant" (2.2.282), while in his disguise as the Witch of Brentford, Falstaff manifests Ford's fears of being demonically dispossessed of household authority "by charms, by spells ... beyond our element" (4.2.176–178). The fairy scene organized by the merry wives and performed by the community is thus a ritual exorcism that purges the mutually demonizing rivalry of Ford and Falstaff, uniting bourgeois housekeeping with the renewal of the gentle ideals of the chivalric Order of the Garter.[31] It expels from a united community the divisive threat which inheres in the mutual aggressions and suspicions of farce. In one sense, the exorcism of Falstaff is a farcical triumph, a pointedly unmagical solution of social problems by ordinary social means. But the forest setting and magical aura of the *dénouement* effect the socially magical triumph of an inclusive national ethos over the demonic spectre of competition; even while it acknowledges the social reality that "Money buys lands," the play affirms that "In love, the heavens themselves do guide the state" (5.5.232–233).

By uniting an even broader range of social types, from the maimed apprentice Ralph to the the King of England, Dekker's *The Shoemaker's Holiday* (1599) lays to rest in similarly romantic fashion a potential for class strife which the play identifies with the farcical cycle of predation. This potential is embodied in the conflict between the Earl of Lincoln and Sir Roger Oately, Lord Mayor of London, each of whom sees in the love of Lincoln's nephew Rowland Lacy for Oately's daughter Rose – a love opposed by both – a threat to his own standing by the aggressions of a class enemy.[32] Yet Lacy's disguise as a humble shoemaker is not a cynical maneuver but a romantic demonstration of the "many shapes" that "gods and kings" have devised "to compass their desired loves,"[33] Eyre's support for the match of Rose and Lacy, and above all the spectacular rise of Eyre himself, help to remove any hint of class exploitation from the affair. Lincoln and Oately, the would-be master-plotters of a comic urban agon are themselves made "two gulls"(16.150) by the combined forces of the shoemakers' chicanery and the King's proclamation that "love respects no blood, / Cares not for difference of birth or state" (21.105–106).

[31] See Hunter, "Bourgeois Comedy," p. 11.
[32] The class warfare is established most strongly in the opening scene, which receives an excellent reading by Joel H. Kaplan, "Virtue's Holiday: Thomas Dekker and Simon Eyre," *RenD*, n.s. 2 (1969), 103–122.
[33] *The Shoemaker's Holiday*, ed. R. L. Smallwood and Stanley Wells (Manchester University Press, 1979), scene 3, lines 1–2.

Furthermore, Lacy's participation in Eyre's fortune-making *coup* bestows a mantle of gentility on the Shoemaker's shrewd investment, and Eyre's use of deceit – a principal trait of his prototype in Deloney's *The Gentle Craft*[34] – is minimized by his festive sharing of the secret and the profits with his apprentices.[35] Reinforced by Eyre's voluble mock-romance idiom – "Prince am I none, yet am I princely born (7.50)" – the pancake feast which caps Eyre's career unites, in classless moral opposition to the demonic French, a nation which, as fraternal as a guild, includes royalty with "gentlemen of the Gentle Craft, true Trojans, courageous cordwainers"(26.146–147). As a tribute to the growing powers of urban status-groups, *The Shoemaker's Holiday* is a major contribution to the development of a neofeudal burgher ethos; but like many other strands in this development – the evolving City of London mayoral pageants, the emergence of a mythical past and gallery of London luminaries, the organization of London militias, the improbable urban revival of chivalry – it follows the neofeudal practice of disguising novel developments in archaic forms. Accommodated to the play's mimesis of familiar social life, the underlying idiom of romance more than adequately suppresses the social conflicts Eyre's rise implies; these are projected onto the demonically farcical Lincoln and Oately, and onto Eyre's ambitious wife, whom the shoemaker easily puts down with an "Avaunt, avaunt, avoid, Mephistophilus!" (22.54). And finally, by whitewashing the motives of Ralph's rival Hammon,[36] thereby saving Jane from "Hammon and the devil" (14.68), the play succeeds in fully expelling the demon of social conflict from its final moral feast.

In using an inclusive ethos to disarm the false differences that mobilize farce, *The Merry Wives of Windsor* and *The Shoemaker's Holiday* typify the mimesis of social interaction in such other early city comedies as *Every Man in His Humour* (1598/1616) and *Westward Ho* (1604). Jonson's comedy, following *The Merry Wives*, depicts a domestic rivalry between a jealous citizen and his gentleman adversaries. Both the elderly Kitely and Knowell, Sr., London merchant and suburban gentleman respectively, are demonically driven, by the stereotypical suspicions of their class, to regard London's mobile social life as a threat to their status and reputation. The same "extreme conceits" which lead Kitely to fear poisoning by his enemies (4.6.28) make Knowell wonder whether his son is "allied / Unto ... hellish practice" (4.4.20–21). The delusion of class

---

[34] Alexander Legatt, *Citizen Comedy in the Age of Shakespeare* (University of Toronto Press, 1973), p. 18.   [35] Kaplan, "Virtue's Holiday," p. 113.

[36] At 3.88 Hammon shows a letter which reports Ralph among the battle dead, while at 18.46 he explains apologetically that he was misled. As usual in plays of this kind, a genuine violation only seems to occur and then, as if by magic, is shown not to have occurred.

antagonism they share is finally exorcised with perfect farcical symmetry at Cob's house, when both men are simultaneously caught in the position of the imaginary "outlaw" offenders they have been pursuing. Justice Clement, presiding over the final rites which link Bridget and Edward Knowell in that form of true gentility which is "a grace peculiar to but a few" (3.1.18), also "conjure[s] the rest to put off all discontent" (5.1.262). This magical act is lightly touched, but, as in *The Merry Wives of Windsor*, it identifies the conclusion of the play's farcical events as an exorcism of farcical motivation; it cancels out the false, socially antagonistic version of romance with an ameliorative counter-version whose antinomies are both moral and socially inclusive.

Ritual exorcism of the false demons of class rivalry is central to *Westward Ho*, a play which is deeply (and specifically) indebted to *The Merry Wives of Windsor* for its recuperation of moral harmony from the threat of farcical division and motivation. In this collaboration, one of the earliest of private theater city comedies, Dekker and Webster produced what was perhaps the most immediate inspiration for the host of bitter city intrigue plays which appeared over the next decade.[37] The play's exorcism centers in the "magical" conversion of the merchant Justiniano's sexual and class rival, the Earl – a conversion which draws directly on the disenchantment of Falstaff. In its figurative delineation of comic alternatives, it provides a point of reference for later seduction intrigues in such near-contemporary city comedies as *Volpone* and *A Mad World My Masters*. The Earl is an old *roué* who has presumed on the basis of his social status that "Lords may do any thing"[38] by enlisting the aid of a "sorceress" (2.2.102), the bawd Birdlime, to seduce Justiniano's wife. His attempt "to Coniure" (4.2.7) with the faithful Mistress Justiniano reaches its climax when he entertains her, calling for incense, music, and a banquet and engaging in a rapturous Ovidian soliloquy on "the strong Magick of our appetite" (4.2.29). The comely figure whose mask the Earl removes, however, is not the wife but her bearded husband in disguise, in whose astonishing features the Earl sees the spectre of his own degradation – a "witch, hag... proud damnation... [a] fury... [a] Deuil... Succubus... Harpy"(4.2.56–76). Revealing the apparently dead body of his wife, Justiniano strikes the Earl dumb with shame as he brings his feigning wife back to life.

The amphibious decorum of the scene, so typical of the interface of

---

[37] See Michael Shapiro, *Children of the Revels: The Boy Companies of Shakespeare's Time and Their Plays* (New York: Columbia University Press, 1977), p. 218–219; cf. Hunter, "The Idea of Comedy," pp. 82–83.

[38] 4.2.12; I cite from *The Dramatic Works of Thomas Dekker*, ed. Fredson Bowers (4 vols. Cambridge University Press, 1955), vol. 3.

modes in city comedy, brings the mundane and the magical into sharp collision; it plays out the farcical *ronde* to its logical conclusion even while it demonizes this logic as alien to the unifying ethos the play romantically asserts in its opening claim that "Court, City, and Countrey, are merely as maskes one to an other" (1.1.227–228). The alterity of modes is, even in this borderline play, ultimately a hierarchy: the reconciliation between merchant and earl begins the final movement of the play outside London to the inn at Brentford, where all of the imagined exploitations are shown never to have occurred. The norm recovered is essentially that of bourgeois marriage. The social model of exploitation, figured in the relationship between nobleman and whore, is shown to be the demonic spectre of the utopian social model of reciprocity figured in marriage.

Much of the history of city comedy is a history of dissent against romance dynamics of the kind represented in Dekker's plays, an exposure of the positional logic – the bourgeois bias – which supports their apparently non-positional, utopian recovery of social and ethical harmony from the threat of purely adversarial struggle. *Eastward Ho* (1604), a collaboration by Chapman, Jonson, and Marston, is perhaps the earliest play to offer a systematic challenge, in the form of a parody that generates comic alternatives, to the semic transformations wrought by the neofeudal ethos of citizen comedy in its Dekkerian form. The parody turns on a morality-play contrast between the two apprentices of the sober London goldsmith Touchstone – gentle-born but upstart rebellious Quicksilver, whose prodigal habits manifest his scorn for his flatcap master, and the virtuous Golding, "a youth of another piece" (1.1.79) whose sober marriage to Touchstone's virtuous daughter embodies the utopian possibility of transforming social conflict into a moral harmony beyond status difference. If the insolent Quicksilver relishes socio-economic warfare ("How would merchants thrive, if gentlemen would not be unthrifts?" – 1.1.38–39), Golding espouses, like Dekker's Simon Eyre, a non-positional ethic of gentility:

> From trades, from arts, from valour honour springs;
> These three are founts of gentry, yea of kings.   (1.1.174–175)

As in earlier plays in the romantic citizen mode, where the exploitational motivation of figures like the Earl of Lincoln and Sir Roger Oately, or Falstaff, or the Earl of *Westward Ho* is represented as a negative, demonic image of genuine romance, the ambition of *Eastward Ho*'s upstart schemers to gain positional advantage takes form in false romantic fantasies of unlimited power and gratification. The fantasies are perhaps epitomized in Petronel Flash, whose involvement as a "knight adventurer" in a fantastic scheme to reap the utopian harvest of Virginia rests ultimately in his confidence as a master-manipulator, an exploiter who can "work in the wounds of others and feel nothing himself" (3.2.17–18).

Based, as it is, in an ethic of purely positional advantage, the demonic version of romance in these fantasies is subjected to an exorcism which is at once farcically ironic and romantically providential – the voyage founders on a rubbish tip on the Isle of Dogs. Yet the shipwreck merely returns the scoundrels to the city's orbit, and Quicksilver nimbly evades moral recuperation with the plucky claim that "I have some tricks, in this brain of mine, shall not let us perish" (4.1.224–226).

At the same time, the play exposes in the conventionally generous ethos of Touchstone and Golding the same pursuit of advantage they expose in others. Though Touchstone appears, like Simon Eyre, to rise above narrow ambition by chastizing his wife for it, he fails dismally at Eyre's ebullient idiom. He hails as a providential miracle (4.2.59–63) Golding's spectacular rise to eminence, a grotesque parody of the romantic success which enables Simon Eyre to transcend the class antagonisms of *The Shoemaker's Holiday*. And though Touchstone also hails as miracle the schemers' defeat, he uses the "place of a justicer" for positional advantage and self-empowerment: "I will charge 'em, and recharge 'em, rather than authority should want a foil to set it off" (4.2.197–198). His increasing hardness toward his enemies undermines the apparent moral pattern of the play. By way of parody it exposes the partisan interests of self and class which underlie the apparently romantic triumph of virtue over exploitation.

It may not be the case, as Harry Levin has said, that Dekker's Simon Eyre is "Shylock masquerading as Falstaff";[39] but *Eastward Ho's* Touchstone shows a Simon Eyre becoming a Shylock, a Ford never released from his rivalry with Falstaff. As he becomes more and more obsessed with revenge, Touchstone becomes more and more a figure in whose mouth the heroic idiom of romance savors of exploitative monomania and repression: "I will sail by you and not hear you, like the wise Ulysses... Away, you sirens... I have stopped mine ears with shoemakers' wax, and drunk Lethe and Mandragora to forget you" (5.4.1–17).

In the bland triumph of Golding's true gentility over Touchstone's self-serving morality, *Eastward Ho* completes its parody of earlier city comedies in the romance mode by mimicking in a purely formal way the ameliorative emergence of an inclusive ethos that – like the shoewax in Touchstone's ears – suppresses predatory exploitation. But as the

---

[39] Cited in Jonas Barish, *Ben Jonson and the Language of Prose Comedy* (1969; rpt. New York: W. W. Norton, 1970), p. 282.

ludicrous spectacle of Quicksilver's psalm-singing repentance suggests, it withholds moral assent from the content of this pattern, which has been shown to serve merely partisan interests in an unresolved social agon.

In pointed contrast to the comic technique of Dekker and Heywood, the sort of later city comedy written by Jonson and Middleton follows *Eastward Ho* by including potentially romantic representations of London's social life in order to expose their ritual foundations, the positionally partisan logic by which they exorcise as mere illusion the all-pervasive competition which the later plays represent as the true norm and reality. The plays of Middleton, which more than any other helped to define the new mode of city comedy based on intrigue and exploitation, reinforce their insistence on the endlessly positional pursuit of advantage in the city's mercenary environment with deliberately countervailing exorcisms of the false magic and morality of romance. As the revue-like structure of Middleton's early presenter-play *The Phoenix* (1603) suggests, Middleton's vision of the social order was indebted to the scourging manner of the verse satirists and Jonson's comical satires. From them Middleton derived the vision of an endlessly predatory cycle that concludes the early city comedy *Your Five Gallants* (1605):

Does my boy pick and I steal to enrich myself, to keep her, to maintain him? why, this is the right sequence of the world. A lord maintains her, she maintains a knight, he maintains a whore, she maintains a captain. So in like manner the pocket keeps my boy, he keeps me, I keep her, she keeps him; it runs like quicksilver from one to another.[40]

In his mature city comedies, from *Michaelmas Term* (1606) to *A Chaste Maid in Cheapside* (1613), Middleton integrates this predatory vision with a formula for producing witty endings that, while formally resembling those of more romantic comic modes, are marked by a disinvestment of sentiment and moral affirmation. This disinvestment is reinforced by the ritual exorcism of the romantic materials and structures deliberately embedded in their ruthlessly plotted intrigues.

In *Michaelmas Term*, the intrigue of "city powd'ring" that pits Master Easy, a "fair free-breasted gentleman" of Essex,[41] against the London linen-draper Quomodo is driven by a class rivalry – a "deadly enmity" (1.1.106) – between citizens and gentlemen. Easy's revenge of his gulling by Quomodo, achieved by his mastery of Quomodo's predatory tricks, adheres to the new comic pattern that awards youthful resourcefulness

---

[40] *The Works of Thomas Middleton*, ed. A. H. Bullen (8 vols. rpt. New York: AMS Press, 1964), 3: 3.2.100–107.
[41] 1.1.53–65; I cite from the edition of Richard Levin (Lincoln: University of Nebraska Press, 1966).

the victory over aged compulsion. In its drive toward closure, farce typically observes the rough justice of balance and symmetry, and Middleton entertains the possibility that a deeper moral justice inheres in the amoral pattern by which "wit destroys wit" (5.1.45). But this suggestion is balanced by a moral disinvestment from the play's conventionally new comic ending. The position occupied by Easy at play's end is not that of the morally upright but of the least subject to illusions. Maintained, as it is, in Quomodo's terms of exploitation, Easy's is the ambivalent victory of an urbane wit.

The play's ambivalence is reflected in its subplot, which, like those in the plays that would follow, introduces and deflates a romantic moral potential at odds with the play's exploitational logic. The subplot, in which two parents separately search for their lost children in an alien and "man-devouring city" (2.2.20), deliberately recalls the romance plot of Shakespeare's urban *Comedy of Errors*, and it anticipates *Pericles'* depiction of a father's arrival in the city which threatens his daughter with prostitution. It anticipates as well the romantic reconciliation of Orlando Frescobaldo with his daughter, the reformed prostitute Bellafront, in Dekker's *2 Honest Whore* (1608). As elsewhere in Middleton, however, the romance potential of the subplot is cruelly exploded, as the corruption of both parents and children by the city prevents recognition and moral recovery. The outcome of the subplot reunion is a ritual shaming rather than recovery and perpetuation of family identity.

The dismal outcome of the subplot's romance enhances Easy's comic triumph by contrasting the fantasy of romance with the rigor of urbane wit. But in Easy's triumph, "no meaningful code is given us to separate the pretender from the gentleman,"[42] and the explosion of the subplot merely underlines Easy's own lack of moral grounding. On the one hand, the return of Easy's land appears to underwrite his formal comic triumph with the social confidence that the "natural" possession of English wealth has been returned from an aged, grasping parvenu to its rightful, genteel heir: "the old king of city cozenage dies for a time and is immediately replaced by a new man."[43] But on the other hand, this comic fertility rite is consummated in ways that make Easy the mirror-image of the *senex* he replaces. Easy remains unmarried at play's end, joining the pattern of failed patrimony established by the subplot.

A Mad World, My Masters features an even more bizarre eruption of

---

[42] Richard Levin, *The Multiple Plot in English Renaissance Drama* (University of Chicago Press, 1971) p. 175; see also the Introduction to his edition of *Michaelmas Term*, p. xvii.

[43] Anthony Covatta, *Thomas Middleton's City Comedies* (Lewisburg: Bucknell University Press, 1973), p. 91.

romance than the questing parents of *Michaelmas Term* – the conversion from lechery of a young gallant, Penitent Brothel, by a succubus who takes the form of Brothel's mistress. In one sense, as Richard Levin notes, the Penitent Brothel plot "belongs to the same genre as the main action" insofar as it is "a straightforward comedy of intrigue pitting a wit against a gull."[44] But in another sense, the two plots diverge generically in their outcomes, as the incongruously literal appearance of the devil and the sincere repentances and reconciliations of the Brothel plot are set in counterpoint to the theatrical contrivances and predatory exploits that conclude the main plot – Follywit's deception of his wealthy uncle, Sir Bounteous Progress.

Like the *Merry Wives'* Falstaff and the Earl of *Westward Ho*, Middleton's Brothel raises, in the form of a clever gentleman's pursuit of a citizen's wife, the antiromantic spectre of the exploitation of class position. This spectre is seemingly exorcised in the typical romantic fashion, as the appearance of the terrifying succubus stirs the already remorseful Brothel to repentance. But this does not reverse the fact of citizen Harebrain's cuckolding by Brothel, and Harebrain's conciliatory embrace of his exploiters as holy souls merely extends the originally monstrous delusions under which he mistook his wife's adulterous act for a lesson in divinity. His peace with Brothel is as incongruous as the literal emanation of the spirit-world within the realm of city intrigue. The reconciliation between perpetrator and victim is treated finally as another in the play's many species of "comic madness."[45] The succubus episode thus inscribes within the play the antagonistic relations between the comedy of urban intrigue and the comedy of moral recuperation and inclusion. If the magical appearance of the succubus highlights man's moral instincts, it does so in order that Follywit's deceptions of his uncle in the main plot may underscore the power of manipulation to exploit such instincts. At the same time, the parody of moral change in Brothel's conversion underlines the absence of such change in the formally comic reversals that conclude the Follywit plot.[46] The succubus episode is thus at once a parody of the comic ethos which Middleton repudiates and a haunting spectre of the moral and social harmony that he cannot hope to achieve.

The Dampit subplot of *A Trick to Catch the Old One* (1605–6) is another of the demonic eruptions of a generic alternative that help to

---

[44] *The Multiple Plot*, p. 170.

[45] William W. Slights, "The Trickster–Hero and Middleton's *A Mad World, My Masters*," *Comparative Drama*, 3 (1969), p. 95.

[46] For the view that Brothel's conversion is not a parody but a serious comment on Follywit's amorality, see Charles A. Hallett, "Penitent Brothel, the Succubus, and Parson's *Resolution*," *SP*, 69 (1972), 72–76.

define the different comic vision of Middleton's main city comedy plots.[47] Though less successfully integrated than the subplots of the earlier plays, the Dampit "plot" – which traces what Richard Levin has called a "Hogarthian 'Usurer's Progress'"[48] and ends with his hellish deathbed ravings – contains in its archaic morality-play atmosphere the demonically "other" moral implications that might otherwise spill over into the main, urban intrigue plot. By comparison with Dampit's hellish demise, the usury and avarice of the main plot's antagonists, Lucre and Hoard, are freed to become the instruments of a more "purely" comic rivalry.[49] If, as a morally charged foil, the Dampit plot gathers into itself, in order to exorcise, the moral instincts that would disable the formally comic intrigues of the main plot, its parallels with the main plot's positional antagonisms reintroduces the possibility of moral judgement upon the connivances of Lucre, Hoard, and the clever Witgood. In this way the subplot does not simply use the strategy of generic opposition to define the unique slant of city comedy; it actually inscribes that strategy into the play's mode of vision. The subplot actually highlights the rivalrous, antagonistic, and positional means by which city comedy mimes the form of romance, ending happily or "fortuitously," while emptying such happiness of all illusions, sentiments, and moral biases.

The technique is carried to its logical conclusion in the greatest of Middleton's mature city comedies, *A Chaste Maid in Cheapside* (1613), where it yields the fullest insight into the role of theater itself as an institution of social exchange and combination, a place where, through the shifting positional relations of generic frames, ideologies and social biases are tested, negated, affirmed, and negotiated. The multilayered pursuit of flesh, money, and position in this play is so vicious and labyrinthine as to prevent identification with any comic hero and to make any comic triumph merely formal and provisional. In each of its plots the play embodies formally a potential for social renewal and moral transformation. In Touchwood Junior's successful suit of Moll Yellowhammer, the play raises prospects of a utopian social harmony

---

[47] Among the critics who note the role of the Dampit subplot in undermining the moral implications of the main plot are Legatt, *Citizen Comedy in the Age of Shakespeare*, pp. 57–58; Rowe, *Thomas Middleton and the New Comedy Tradition*, pp. 84–88; and R. B. Parker, "Middleton's Experiments with Comedy and Judgement," in *Jacobean Theatre*, ed. John Russell Brown and Bernard Harris (1960; rpt. New York: Capricorn, 1967), pp. 187–188.   [48] *The Multiple Plot*, p. 130.

[49] Legatt observes that "whatever moral outrage Middleton may have felt at the world he depicts is here drained off into a subplot which is never integrated with the main action of the play, but which at last succeeds in preserving the light tone of the main action," *Citizen Comedy in the Age of Shakespeare*, p. 58. With qualifications, Parker shares the view that the subplot is "used as a safety-valve for disgust," "Middleton's Experiments with Comedy and Judgement," p. 188.

that transcends the price put on Moll by her goldsmith father and by Touchwood's rival suitor, the *roué* Sir Walter Whorehound. Sir Walter's own morality-play conversion mimes the recovery of moral understanding from degradation "in the heart of the city of London."[50] The successful impregnation of Lady Kix, following the pattern by which romance secures a familial line of succession, enables the willing cuckold Sir Oliver Kix to proclaim formulaically "I am a man forever!" (5.3.1). Yet each of these formally romantic possibilities is undercut by the play's antiromantic bias: the young lovers' double resurrection from their coffins mocks the magic of romance by adapting it to the exploitational conventions of city comedy; Whorehound's apparent conversion is mocked by the Allwits' parallel plans to recuperate their worldly fortunes; the Kixes' progeny is mocked by its origins in the prodigiously fertile loins of Touchwood Senior.

Instead of aligning themselves into a stable hierarchy, the play's comic possibilities remain – like the play's dialectical imagery of fertility and sterility, feast and famine, Carnival and Lent – an unresolved alterity. Sir Walter, wounded, and smelling the fires of hell, takes his exit by proclaiming "Gamesters, farewell, I have nothing left to play" (5.1.148–149). But his moral dissent from the play-world is answered by Allwit's witty claim that "There's no gamester like a politic sinner, / For whoe'er games, the box is sure a winner" (5.1.167–168). In its allusion to the dicer's cup, Allwit's remark subordinates the moral standing of the players to the roll of the dice, to the shifting positions dictated by the random play of the game. If the remark undercuts with moral grimness the lovers' happy resurrection from their wooden coffins, it also links their coffins with the *pudendum*, underscoring the play's grotesque celebration of the lively, goading effects of fleshly pursuits. In the play's twin patterns of degradation and renewal, the twin comic potentials of romance and intrigue are recognized as symbiotic elements in a single, agonistic process. The unrestrained competitive pursuits of the marketplace drive a comic cycle of reciprocal torment and exploitation. Yet they also cohere in a circle of rough justice and theatrical community, a *locus* of exchange and combination whereby the city elaborates its own prolific life.[51] In *A Chaste Maid in Cheapside*, the theater becomes a

[50] *A Chaste Maid in Cheapside*, ed. R. B. Parker (London: Methuen, 1969), 1.1.94. Parker calls Whorehound's repentance "the strangest expression yet of the serious note of Penitent Brothel in *A Mad World My Masters*, the old father in *Michaelmas Term*, and the spectators of Dampit's death," "Middleton's Experiments with Comedy and Judgement," p. 191.

[51] For the view that in city comedy "two contradictory aspects of the marketplace – commerce and celebration – confront each other dramatically," and that "Middleton, more than other writers of city comedy ... understood the tensions between these two

model for the city itself: its generic give-and-take assures that the box – the "boxholder's" collecting till – is sure a winner.

Middleton's city plays bear a formal resemblance to romantic comic forms in their apparent resolution of social conflict and their ritual enactment of enlightenment and renewal. But as Walter Cohen points out, the formally utopian resolution of social conflict in many city comedies is balanced by a satiric awareness of the moral contradictions that remain unresolved – including the contradictions of a mercenary theater industry. The absence of a positive moral content in the formal comic solution reflects a "disjunction between the social assumptions and resolution of the plot, on the one hand, and the implicit moral judgement by the author, on the other."[52]

Based on the farcical logic of exploitation – on the always reversible mechanism of position lost and gained – the plays produce what is at once an exhilarating release from the illusion and fantasies that drive the city's predatory frenzy and an equally dizzying recognition that this frenzy is a universal condition. In the comic triumph of the best predator, they approach the sweeping retribution and enlightenment achieved in Jonson's comical satires and in the later presenter-plays derived from them; but, because of their merely formal investment in the triumph of the master-trickster, they are without the liability of comical satire's moral investment in the dubious authority of the satiric presenters (Asper, Criticus, Horace) and the powers (Elizabeth, Cynthia, Augustus) to which they attach themselves.[53]

The trickster's triumph through his mastery of exploitational technique reveals but does not transform the adversarial, competitive nature of urban life. The moral outcome is thus grim, "regardless of whether a given aristocrat emerges victorious... Cut off from its roots, the aristocracy, traditional ruler of the land, confronts the alien existence of the city."[54] There is, in the wit's defeat of the city's most aggressive predators, a comic revenge which might potentially support a socially utopian impulse to exclude the divisive influence of competition from society. But this impulse cannot be endorsed morally since the comic means that enable it – successful competition on the world's terms – betray it as a social gesture and illusion without moral foundation. The result, as George Rowe says of Middleton's intrigue plays is that "their

---

forms of common life," see Wells, "Jacobean City Comedy and the Ideology of the City," pp. 37, 58.

[52] *Drama of a Nation: Public Theater in Renaissance England and Spain* (Ithaca: Cornell University Press, 1985), p. 282.

[53] My reading of *Measure for Measure*, pp. 455–457 below, concerns itself in part with the liabilities of presenter-plays.   [54] Cohen, *Drama of a Nation*, p. 284.

content (and the responses called for by that content) contradicts their structure … Instead of participating in the concluding festivities, we tend to remain distanced and even somewhat puzzled by what we have just witnessed onstage."[55] This is why the positional relationship between ameliorative and farcical possibilities within city comedy and between city comedy and romance is not strictly symmetrical. Each set of possibilities tends to represent its vision of the world by demonizing as merely positional and illusory the vision represented by the other; but where farcical exploitation prevails over romance, even though it resembles formally the celebration of the reverse outcome, it is tinged with a greater ambivalence and regret at its own lack of moral content. Yet to insist on such a content would be to assert a false, class-biased antinomy. Like the verse satirists, the city comedians discovered in urban life a degree of arbitrariness, interchange, and mobility that undermined the possibility of identifying moral integrity with any portion of the existing social body. Yet unlike the satirists and the scourging presenters of the comical satires that descended from them, the city comedians learned better, through the theatrical marketplace, than to insist upon investing themselves in an "essential difference."

This was especially true as long as more romantic versions of comedy continued to hold the stage, alongside and in dialogue with the new city comedy. But the situation changed. Jonson's *Epicœne*, significantly set in the newly fashionable precincts of London's West End and deliberately narrowed in its social scale, achieves in its slick plotting and cool morality something like a reconciliation with the wholly provisional and clear-headed morality of the new urbane "wit." But only later in the history of city comedy, with the movement of the adult companies into the private theaters – and with the subsequent decline in theatrical dialogue – did the countervailing romance bias of the unifying bourgeois ethos fade from view. And only with the fading of this ethos, which is to say with the appropriation of a capitalist mentality by an urbanizing gentry, were the aristocratic tricksters of city comedy consistently absolved of their taint and invested with all the moral sympathy that heroes of romance attract. This development, coinciding with a more thorough gentrification of the metropolis and a new urbanization of the gentry, marked a decline in the dialectical "romance" of the the London theaters and the rise to prominence of a truly city-dominated metropolitan mentality. The new

---

[55] *Thomas Middleton and the New Comedy Tradition*, pp. 7–8. On the ambivalent relationship between morality and comic form in Middleton, see also Gibbons, *Jacobean City Comedy*, p. 89; R. B. Parker, "Middleton's Experiments with Comedy and Judgement," pp. 179–199; and Wells, "Jacobean City Comedy and the Ideology of the City," pp. 52, 58.

mentality increasingly accepted the illusions of predatory triumph as morally valid reality, forgetting and suppressing what the dialogue of Jacobean comic modes had revealed.

Understanding: the penetration of comic perspective

If the interanimation of comic perspectives could produce different highlights and shadows, different interpretations of the city in the form of theatrical representations, it could also, as the example of *A Chaste Maid in Cheapside* suggests, provide for insights into the interpretive nature of representation itself. As it redefined the relationships of comic genres and added to them, the representation of the city sometimes became for dramatists, and perhaps for their audiences, a means of exploring and understanding genre and its social functions. At certain crucial moments where the interface of comic possibilities is felt as such, the nature of the city is understood to lie in the process of the city's self-interpretation. Like the moment when a romance hero removes the helmet of his adversary to discover the face of his ally, such moments are at once dreaded and desired, postponed in order that the dissonance of contradiction may produce the meaningful clarity of oppositions, embraced for the potentially benign but also threatening insights the resolution of conflict may promise to provide.[56] In this respect, the interplay of comic possibilities offers a model both for discursive exchange and for the reciprocities of urban life itself.

In the case of Shakespeare, a generic collision or interface can sometimes be recognized by a habitual phrase – "I understand you not." Like the more common phrase, "be ruled by me," "I understand you not" (and its variants) is a conveniently compact and metrical way of annotating a positional relationship. What the phrase identifies in Shakespeare is not simply the pervasive misprision and partial comprehension that are the essence of drama, but the extreme point at which two moral positions inhabit what are almost literally two distinct languages. And this literal, linguistic difference is often allied with generic difference. In *Love's Labour's Lost*, just after the Princess has been devastated by news of her father's death, she responds thus to Navarre's indecorously witty renewal of his suit: "I understand you not, my griefs are double" (5.2.752). In *The Winter's Tale*, it is just as the play's two generic potentials come into sharpest conflict with Leontes' public arraignment of his wife that Hermione declares, "Sir, / You speak a language that I understand not" (3.2.79–80). (The line is nearly

---

[56] For both the example and the terms of my analysis I am indebted here to Jameson, *The Political Unconscious*, pp. 118–119.

identical with Mistress Mayberry's virtuous response to her husband's belief that she has succumbed to Featherstone's sexual farce: "Sir this Language, to me is strange, I vnderstand it not."")[57] The final, erotic language game of *Henry V*, though it lacks the precise phrasal annotation, might be taken as an extensive and literal demonstration that the conquest of a linguistic barrier tropes the crossing of a generic boundary. Henry's successful wooing of Katherine is the last and most striking of the many evaporations of semic difference by which this chronicle of war becomes romance.

An early instance that marks a collision of city comedy with romance comes in *The Comedy of Errors*. In the fourth act, as the play approaches its deepest confusions with his twin's escape from jail, the Syracusan stranger soliloquizes on the mysterious benefits showered on him, and closes by reverting to his favorite hypothesis that Ephesus is enchanted: "Sure these are but imaginary wiles, / And lapland sorcerers inhabit here"(4.3.10–11). His servant Dromio enters and engages him in verbal byplay on "the old Adam new apparelled," quibbling that he does not refer to "that Adam that kept the Paradise, but that Adam that keeps the prison... he that came behind you, sir, like an evil angel, and bid you forsake your liberty." Antipholus replies, "I understand thee not" (4.3.13–22).

The stranger's double-take points up the play's running gag – the generic disorientations that occur when a romance is interwoven with an urban, Plautine farce. But to some extent, the stranger's confusion must be the audience's. By the logic of Plautine farce Dromio is not speaking here of the mythical Adam that kept the paradise but of the literal Adam that keeps Ephesus' prison. Yet the stranger's perspective estranges this Adam of everyday life, who comes behind men like an evil angel and bids them forsake their liberty. On the one hand, the stranger experiences the familiar city of Ephesus as an enchanted realm where he is dispossessed of his identity and becomes some other. But the tight logic of Ephesus exposes the positionality of his romance vision. He is dispossessed because Ephesus is a world of consensual structures – economic and social – into which he fits so precisely as to be recognized as a familar inhabitant of that world. Ephesus is not demonic for him because it is magical but because it isn't; it has a meaning for the self, but is meaningful because it is so rigorously determined for the hero in social terms.

On the other hand, the stranger's Ephesian twin is in the end balked of his supposed mastery of just this socially determined world. With the

[57] *Northward Ho*, 1.3.79.

climactic emergence of his twin from the Abbey and the romance reunion of his parents, he comes to recognize, along with Ephesus, the genuine estrangement of such urban manipulations from the authentic selfhood represented by romance. If the play's framing of its Plautine farce with such romantic possibilities seems to establish a hierarchy between the two modes, the final, farcical jostling of the twin Dromios over just such precedence keeps in focus the generic alterity through which the play forces us to ask, "which is the natural man and which the spirit: who deciphers them?" (5.1.334–335).

The Comedy of Errors is an early example of a type of play that became more common in the early Jacobean era, following the rise of city comedy, the War of the Theaters, and the revival of romance – a type of play whose *raison d'être* actually hinges on the alterity of comic genres. In such plays, the opposition between different kinds of comic potential is not simply a dynamic that gives definition to form; it is also a medium for self-reflection, a means for giving visibility to the ways in which generic kinds and social relations are structured. It is also, significantly, the principal means by which the two greatest comedians of the age – Shakespeare and Jonson – spoke to each other.

In its urban texture and sour tone, *Measure for Measure* is perhaps Shakespeare's nearest approach to city comedy, yet in its concern with the redeeming powers of love, forgiveness, and paternal authority many critics have seen anticipations of the later romances. When, at the end of her second interview with Angelo, Isabella declares "I have no tongue but one," and beseeches the deputy to "speak the former language" (2.4.139–140), a linguistic and generic barrier has broken down and Isabella has come to understand her persecutor all too well. The former language of legalism Isabella had so successfully undermined in Angelo is now the one to which she retreats. At the very moment that she condemns the "perilous mouths / That bear in them one and the self-same tongue" for "Bidding the law make curtsy to their will," Isabella bends the world to her own tongue and will: "Then, Isabel, live chaste, and, brother, die; / More than our brother is our chastity" (2.4.173–185).

Jonathan Dollimore has suggested that the urban underbelly of Vienna exists not so much to express the carnivalian necessities of the flesh as to expose the discursive origin of authority in the demonizing differences it asserts.[58] It is not *for* nature but *against* the positional romance conducted by authority against its enemies that Pompey speaks when he observes

---

[58] "Transgression and Surveillance in *Measure for Measure*," in Jonathan Dollimore and Alan Sinfield, eds., *Political Shakespeare: New Essays in Cultural Materialism* (Ithaca: Cornell University Press, 1985), pp. 72–87.

that the merrier of two usuries is "put down while the worser is allow'd by order of law; a furr'd gown to keep him warm"(3.2.5–8). No one, of course, is immune from exploiting difference. Pompey's own willingness to change himself from an "unlawful bawd" to a "lawful hangman" is followed immediately by Abhorson's complaint that Pompey will "discredit our mystery," and the complaint is undercut when the Provost disallows the difference: "you weigh equally; a feather will turn the scale"(4.2.15–30).[59]

Lucio's opening conversation with Vienna's other gallants explores a series of self-interested differences – between the King of Hungary and Vienna, between the decalogue and its piratical revision, and between the witty insults of the gallants, between whom there goes but a pair of sheers. The scene, and in a sense, the play, is summed up when one gentleman protests, "Thou art always figuring diseases in me; but thou art full of error, I am sound" (1.2.53–54). The play repeatedly demonstrates Pompey's explanation to his mistress, "Though you change your place, you need not change your trade" (1.2.107–108). As Dollimore points out, the arbitrarily enforced fornication laws of Vienna do not so much address crime as they assert the power which shores up authority against its own vulnerability. The feared rod of law must be flourished, the Duke explains, lest liberty pluck justice by the nose and the baby beat the nurse (1.3.29–30).

It is against just such arbitrariness that Isabella speaks to such effect in her first interview with Angelo. Provoked out of her initial sympathy with law by her perception that Angelo might but will not pardon her brother, might but will not speak a word and call it back again, she comes on against the law, like a thing to be enskied, a romance heroine wielding heaven's high and unitary truth against the "little brief authority" (2.2.118) in which proud men dress themselves. Isabella seals her case by pushing Angelo toward the semic evaporation whereby he finds in his own bosom the demonic other, the fornicator whom he persecutes in the process of asserting his authority.

Angelo's second scene with Isabella should therefore be understood not only as a rape but also as an act of revenge, as an attempt to do to Isabella and to the language of conscience what Isabella and the language of conscience have done to him. Having had the earthly logic in which he robes himself exposed as partisan by the higher rhetoric of heaven, Angelo now turns that rhetoric on Isabella to expose the limits of her own position. Brought by Angelo's sophistry to admit the partiality of her own rhetoric, Isabella confesses that "to have what we would have, we

---

[59] On the changeability of social place in the play, see Jonathan Goldberg, *James I and the Politics of Literature* (Baltimore: Johns Hopkins University Press, 1983), pp. 238–239.

speak not what we mean. / I something do excuse the thing I hate, / For his advantage that I dearly love." "We are all frail," Angelo gloats (2.4.111–123). After this, Isabella can only feign misunderstanding of Angelo's intent, beseeching him to "speak the former language."

This is a linguistic and generic seduction, a crossing of the boundary between romance and city comedy, between one discursive truth and that which it would deny as its other: Isabella admits to the presence in her speech of that very positionality she demonizes in the law. It is this generic seduction that the Duke seeks to reverse by cloaking his romantic solution with a providential aura. But as Marilyn Williamson points out, the difference asserted by the Duke's romantic solution conceals what can be regarded as a more subtle repetition of Angelo's act: just as Angelo uses the powers of the law to force a rape on Isabella and projects his own guilt on Claudio, so the Duke uses his powers to force himself on Isabella while blaming this same crime on his demonic other, Angelo.[60] The solution to *Measure for Measure* takes place at the gates of Vienna; it respects the dynamics of this city and of the other cities being staged in the genre whose rise was exactly contemporary with *Measure for Measure*.

A seduction scene not unlike *Measure for Measure*'s in its delineation of generic boundaries – and written almost exactly contemporaneously by Shakespeare's most self-conscious theatrical rival – is *Volpone*'s attempted rape of Celia. The scene is remarkable for being at once so central to this play's exploration of the delusional excess of desire and so teasingly gratuitous to its plot. Celia provokes in Volpone an eruption of Protean, self-regarding desire which in its violence dwarfs the lesser depravities it is meant to epitomize. And yet despite Celia's seemingly catalytic role, this chaste, sacrificial romance heroine, together with her rescuer Bonario, proves to be a strangely inert element in the play's chemistry. Her anticlimactic response to Volpone's appeal is underlined by the play's first, false ending. While her inviolable virtue threatens to lead to Volpone's exposure before the *scrutineo*, it proves instead utterly powerless against the combined forces of knavery, corruption, and gullibility. In the end, it is to these forces, of which Mosca proves the better master, that Volpone falls. Why is this misplaced romance heroine, so similar to Spenser's Amoret or the lady of Milton's *Comus*, so central and yet so peripheral to Jonson's comic design?[61]

From *Every Man in His Humour*, through the comical satires, to *Bartholomew Fair*, the central device of Jonson's comic enterprise is the

---

[60] *The Patriarchy of Shakespeare's Comedies* (Detroit: Wayne State University Press, 1986), pp. 101, 107–109.

[61] Ann Barton is perhaps typical in remarking that "Celia and Bonario seem remarkably displaced," "London Comedy and the Ethos of the City," p. 106.

exposure of humors and vanities, the fluid, restless element of delusion by which false consciousness structures the world as romance.[62] This exposure is at one with Jonson's formal enterprise, which is to purge the contemporary theater of its own romantic consciousness. The famous prologue to the revised *Every Man in His Humour* contrasts Jonson's controlled decorum and contemporary scene with the improbable scene changes, temporal shifts, and other transformations which Jonson associates with the dramatic excess of his contemporaries.[63] The very materiality of this theater, with its false beards, rusty swords, squibs and rolling cannonballs is used to undercut its false illusions and to reinforce the mimetic validity of Jonson's own image of the times.[64] In his comical satires Jonson had given over the task of exposure to satiric spokesmen whose dubious authority was kept safe from delusional excess only through their association with such political authorities as Cynthia or Caesar. But in the great city comedies that followed, Jonson grounded satiric exposure in the logical, but purely structural authority of the predatory cycle itself.[65]

The Alchemist is Jonson's purest achievement in this vein, a play in which every manipulator's exploitation of positional advantage is in turn subjected to manipulation by another.[66] Lovewit's triumphant position at play's end marks not so much a change in the play's ethos as the most complete realization of it.[67] Each character proves gullible in believing himself invulnerable to the mere positionality he perceives as constituting the gullibility of others. Each character, in other words, inhabits a self-empowering romance, in which the fantasy of self-fulfillment and invulnerability which he shares with others is seen in others as only a demonically corrupt and self-deluding posture. Dapper and Drugger, who, as gentleman law-clerk and citizen tobacconist, are rivals by the

[62] Harry Levin, for example, remarks that "Jonson's comedy is concerned with the theory and practice of delusion," "Two Magian Comedies," p. 219.

[63] See Jonas Barish, "Jonson and the Loathèd Stage," in William Blisset, Julian Patrick, and R. W. Van Fossen, eds., *A Celebration of Ben Jonson* (University of Toronto Press, 1973), pp. 27–54.

[64] Peter Womack, *Ben Jonson* (Oxford: Basil Blackwell, 1986), pp. 38–39.

[65] See Douglas Duncan, *Ben Jonson and the Lucianic Tradition* (Cambridge University Press, 1979), p. 147; cf. Anne Blake, "'Sportful Malice': Duping in the Comedies of Jonson and Shakespeare," in Ian Donaldson, ed., *Jonson and Shakespeare* (London: Macmillan, 1983), p. 123.

[66] See Harry Levin, "Notes Toward a Definition of City Comedy," in Barbara Kiefer Lewalski, ed., *Renaissance Genres: Essays on Theory, History, and Interpretation* (Cambridge, Mass.: Harvard University Press, 1986), p. 142.

[67] Hunter, "Comedy, Farce, Romance," in A. R. Braunmuller and J. C. Bulman, eds., *Comedy from Shakespeare to Sheridan: Change and Continuity in the English and European Dramatic Tradition. Essays in Honor of Eugene M. Waith* (Newark: University of Delaware Press, 1986), p. 38.

conventions of city comedy, are shown to differ only in harboring the delusions appropriate to their class, Dapper in the vain belief that his birthright descends from the Fairy Queen, Drugger in the hope of being "called to the scarlet" (1.3.37) as the result of a magnetic advertising campaign. The more central and most gullish characters – Mammon, Ananias, and Surly – are the ones with the most sweeping dreams of an empowerment built on the mere positionality and vulnerability of others. Even the clever members of the "venter tripartite" (1.1.135), who knavishly control the gullish fantasies of their customers, base their Cockaigne-like republic on fantasies which ultimately prove vulnerable.[68] In his triumphant and conventionally in-law capture of Dame Pliant, Lovewit comes to occupy a position which differs in no essentials from that of the banished outlaw Dol.[69] The pattern demonstrates that the frenzied power struggles of Jonson's plays are a mimetic picture, but also a metaphoric vehicle whose tenor is the lie or false difference that separates self and other, knave and gull.[70] The frantic crescendo of the plays typically culminates with a sudden exposure which, like the end of an antimasque, dispels the profusion of roles and fantasies and yields to a common, unitary image of man's foolish "nature," a nature presumably the obverse of the better sense the plays implicitly commend.[71]

Yet as nearly every student of Jonson remarks, this literary and moral economy of reduction is subverted by a theatrical economy that thrives on a romantic investment in the superiority of the central villains to their lesser victims.[72] The intelligence and virtuosity of such characters not only propels the mechanism of the plays but resists the moral impulse to turn the mechanism against them; this hunger for an unavailable moral – as well as theatrical – transcendence induces Jonson's city comedy to declare its affinities with romance. It is to reveal and to deny just this affinity with romance that Celia exists.

Unlike his later descendant, Epicure Mammon, Volpone is not merely the most monstrously deluded dreamer of his play but also the central

[68] On the relation between fantasy and the ultimate vulnerability of the "venter," see Robert N. Watson, *Ben Jonson's Parodic Strategy* (Cambridge: Harvard University Press, 1987), pp. 135–137; Nancy S. Leonard, "Shakespeare and Jonson Again: The Comic Forms," *RenD*, n.s. 10 (1979), 66.

[69] Richard Horwich, "Wives, Courtesans, and the Economics of Love in Jacobean City Comedy," in Clifford Davidson, C. J. Gianakaris, and John H. Stroupe, eds., *Drama in the Renaissance* (New York: AMS Press, 1986), p. 269.

[70] Womack, *Ben Jonson*, p. 27.

[71] Thus Douglas Duncan, for example, notes that *Volpone* implicitly commends the Stoic self-possession which Volpone merely parodies, *Ben Jonson and the Lucianic Tradition*, p. 156.

[72] E.g., Leonard, "Shakespeare and Jonson Again: The Comic Forms,"; Barish, "Jonson and the Loathèd Stage," p. 43; Womack, *Ben Jonson*, p. 143.

consciousness controlling its moral structure. His classicism is not simply the degraded, lip-smacking mythologizing of Mammon's Novo Orbe speeches, but a palimpsest in which the desire to "cocker up my genius and live free" (1.1.71) still contains traces of the humanist ambition of being "noble, valiant, honest, wise" (1.1.27) and the platonic recognition of the power of "beauty's miracle" to raise man "in several shapes" (3.7.146–148). There remains something of the aspirations of the presenter–satirists of the comical satires in Volpone, and in his self-regarding theatrical excess something of their bad faith.

The play thrives on the life of Volpone's performance, on the assertion of the difference which enables him to cast and direct – in a sense to create – the follies of his victims. Volpone's success depends upon his antiromantic exposure of their hollowness; yet this exposure is for him a source of life and being, a sublime and fantastic exhilaration.

Dramatic resistance to Volpone's performative afflatus is most clearly associated with the horrendous Lady Wouldbe, who calls home to him the fact that his disguise as a sick man makes him as gullible and vulnerable as his Venetian victims. Volpone's second and climactic attempt to seduce Celia is immediately followed by Lady Wouldbe's deflating visit to the sickbed, when Volpone discovers his own desire not to be gullishly reduced by Lady Wouldbe to the role of a dying man but to live forever in triumphant projections of himself.

With the Ovidian raptures that accompany his attempted rape of Celia, Volpone acts out a hunger for transcendence within an ethos that can never offer more than poses and positions. But an equally powerful demonstration of this hunger and a more potent revelation of its consequence for Jonson's art emerges from Volpone's first attempt on Celia in the disguise of the mountebank, Scoto of Mantua.[73] The first expression of Volpone's desire for more than the farcical role-playing and exploitation which the play in theory provides, Scoto's self-promotion is also an exposure of the antithetical romance structure by which Jonson makes the truth of city comedy. Scoto begins, not unlike Jonson himself, with an attack on his competitors, "ground *ciarlatani*" who "come in lamely with their mouldy tales out of Boccaccio" (2.2.49–51). Echoing the neo-classical promise of *Volpone*'s Prologue to "mix profit with your pleasure"(line 8), Scoto boasts that his stage is set apart from the popular "clamors of the *canaglia*," and "shall be the scene of pleasure and delight; for I have nothing to sell, little or nothing to sell" (2.2.71–72). Scoto's remedy, like Jonson's humors technique, is one that "hath only power to disperse all malignant humours"; Scoto promises, in fact, "out

---

[73] Stephen Greenblatt has noted that "Volpone's Scoto seems to be a striking parody of Jonson himself," "The False Ending in *Volpone*," *JEGP*, 75 (1976), 103.

of the honourable hat that covers your head, to extract the four elements"
(2.2.95, 164). But most revealing is Scoto's exposure of the positional
logic by which Jonson typically contrasts the truth of his comedy to its
romance demon other: "But may some other gallant fellow say, 'O, there
be divers that make profession to have as good, and as experimental
receipts as yours.' Indeed, very many have essay'd, like apes, in imitation
of that which is *really and essentially in me*, to make this oil ... but when
these practitioners come to the last decoction, blow, blow, puff, puff, and
all flies *in fumo* ... For, whilst others have been at the balloo, I have been
at my book" (2.2.145–155, 165–166).

It is the restless desire Celia arouses in Volpone, the theatrically
excessive difference which sets him apart from the predatory pattern he
sets up and controls, that threatens to undermine the generic opposition
on which Jonson's whole antiromantic enterprise is based. His ability to
expose others in his performances is not a neutral act, but, in the
Aristophanic manner, an aggressive, protean, and erotic will-to-life, an
extravagant power of invention.[74] The positive, restless content of this
impulse accounts for the fact that Volpone's classical fantasia is aroused
by the sort of romance heroine that the urban ethos and classicism of
Venice should not logically provide. This dangerous desire must be
exposed as mere delusion: and so Volpone's brilliant but pathetic appeal
to Celia unfolds itself as a powerless tissue of fantastic but always empty
lies, roles, and poses. Immune to these, Celia can imagine as the only
alternative to the madman before her the virtuous gentleman that a man
of Volpone's age ought to be. This reminder of his age, limits, and
vulnerability prompts Volpone's physical attack. In order to limit
Volpone, to make him the gullish inhabitant of merely another delusion
– and thus to save the antiromantic bias of his play – Jonson is forced to
admit to the presence of romance at the very center of his work. The
momentary instability this creates is quickly controlled, as Celia's pallid
resistance gives way to the even more inert and stilted rescue by
Bonario.[75] The play returns to its equilibrium as both these misplaced
romance figures are easily disempowered by the farcical logic of
deception. In the end, Volpone's fall comes not through desires which
exceed the play's pattern of exploitation but by desires which epitomize
it. Seeking to press home the gullishness of others, he is made a gull
himself. He is not undone by Celia – there is, as Scoto might say, nothing

[74] Leo Salingar, "Comic Form in Ben Jonson," in *Dramatic Form in Shakespeare and His Contemporaries*, pp. 156–158, 167; cf. Barton, *Ben Jonson, Dramatist*, p. 114.

[75] For views which stress, alternatively, the theatrical and mortal implications of Bonario's intervention, see Clifford Leech, "The Incredibility of Jonsonian Comedy," in Blisset, Patrick, and Van Fossen, eds., *A Celebration of Ben Jonson*, p. 14, and Charles A. Hallett, "Jonson's Celia: A Reconsideration," *SP*, 68 (1971), 50–69.

"really and essentially in" her – but by Mosca, the fly, the utterly mercurial embodiment of the play's mimetic mechanism of deceit. A figure of pure negativity, Mosca erases the play's generic dependencies and heightens its power to represent by what Peter Womack calls the completeness of his absence.[76]

If the challenge of such ruthless logic to romance sours the tone of a play like *Measure for Measure*, it is answered by Shakespeare's response to city comedy in *Pericles*. Sold into prostitution as a result of lies told at Tarsus, Marina enters the fallen city of Mytilene, like Isabella before Angelo, or Celia before Volpone, to receive her instructions from a bawd. The bawd promises that by turning her chastity from its yet undiscovered royal course, Marina will divert herself with the city's diversity: You shall, she tells Marina, "taste gentlemen of all fashions ... you shall have the difference of all complexions. What, do you stop your ears?" (4.2.78–81). Marina's gesture, like that of Morose in Jonson's *Epicœne*, or of Middleton's Touchstone stuffing his ears with shoewax, is but her first resistance to the endlessly dividing and divisive language of the city. Morose's resistance proves futile, of course, but Marina's stiffens in response to the bawd's further antiromantic advice on the exploitation of illusion: "You have fortunes coming on you. Mark me: you must seem to do that fearfully which you commit willingly, despise profit where you have most gain. To weep that you do live as ye do makes pity in your lovers; seldom but that pity begets you a good opinion, and that opinion a mere profit" (4.2.116–121). Marina's response to this dissonance is simple and straightfoward: "I understand you not." The phrase marks a moment of transition, in which the possibility of romance is recuperated from its demon other, city comedy.

Trained up in music's letters, able to sing like one immortal and to dumb deep clerks with her admired lays, Marina is gifted with an education and a speech which, like her undiverted chastity and royal birth, carry on the succession of virtue through a demonically duplicitous world. In winning a verbal battle against the salacious innuendo of the corrupt governor Lysimachus, and thereby reversing Isabella's earlier confrontation with Angelo, Marina's innocent, riddling speech restores to language itself a fullness emptied by her father's Adamic penetration of Antiochus' incestuous riddle. Like Jonson the city comedian, Pericles reads this riddle as an empty mystification, a self-empowering lie which turns language back upon itself in order to conceal the hideous circularity of incest, the cannibalistic dead-end of the *uroburos*, the viper that feeds "On mother's flesh that did me breed."

[76] *Ben Jonson*, p. 72.

The threat of predatory circularity repeats itself in proud and starving Tarsus, where "Those mothers who, to nuzzle up their babes, / Thought nought too curious are ready now / To eat those little darlings whom they love" (1.2.42–44). Later in the play, by starving "the ears she feeds" and "[making] them hungry / The more she gives them speech" (5.1.112–113), Marina repeats her father's merciful feeding of Tarsus by restoring to language a fullness beyond difference. She becomes an alternative to Dionyza's lying cenotaph, a living "palace / For the crown'd Truth to dwell in" (5.1.121–122).

As the play moves through Pericles' lifetime and across the Mediterranean, it also moves down through history, narrating its way through the phases and styles of civilizations, from the primitive, riddling, oriental fall at Antioch, through a Tarsus associated with Troy, to the Greek Pentapolis, whose complaining fishermen and chivalric tournaments associate it with the Middle Ages. But it is finally in teeming Mytilene – which, with its whores and bawds, market and harbor, and crusty, colloquial idiom, evokes the contemporary urban scene both on and off the stage – that Shakespeare performs his most triumphant act of linguistic recuperation. Marina's conversion of the city is an act of outrageous indecorum, akin to musty Gower's indecorous use of "one language in each several clime" (4.4.5–6). This triumph over linguistic difference Gower identifies with a triumph over generic difference when his Prologue urges those "born in these latter times, / When wit's more ripe" to "accept my rhymes" (lines 11–12). Against this contemporary witty ripeness unto rottenness, Gower poses the dream of recovering from history's dispersion of discourse a genre beyond difference, a primal story that "hath been sung at festivals, / On ember-eves and holy-ales; / And lords and ladies in their lives / Have read it for restoratives" (lines 5–8). That city comedy should represent the difference against which the truth of romance asserts itself is a recognition not only of a widely respected generic boundary, but also of the power of urban life to make this difference meaningful.

Performed at court on All Saints' Day, 1614, one day after its Bankside premier at the Hope and three years to the day after the court performance of *The Tempest*, *Bartholomew Fair* appears, like Shakespeare's romance, to draw on that day's Evening Prayer readings from *Wisdom of Solomon*, 5 and *Apocalypse*, 19 to evoke the transforming prospects of truth revealed.[77] As the Induction's repudiation of "Tales, Tempests, and such like drolleries" suggests, however, this transformation is wrought not by the sublimation of differences and conflict into superhuman

[77] Robert N. Watson, *Ben Jonson's Parodic Strategy*, p. 167.

possibilities but by their adulteration into common folly and degradation. Ceres is not found welcoming her daughter's return to earth, as in Hermione's embrace of Perdita, but "selling her daughter's picture in gingerwork!" (2.5.10). The "stuff they are made on" is not such stuff as dreams are made on but "stale bread, rotten eggs, musty ginger, and dead honey, you know" (2.2.5–9).[78] While a change of heart may remove the spider from the bottom of the cup in Shakespearian romance, there is no such antidote for the material adulteration of the bottled ale at Jonson's fair: "Hath not a snail, a spider, yea, a newt been found there?" (2.6.12). The degradation materializes not around a sheepcote or desert isle but around Ursula's booth, a Circean "mansion" or "bower" (2.5.39) at which the oracular sign of the pig's head ("Here be the best pigs" – 3.2.63) summarizes the metamorphic magic of the fair's exchanges: "Here you may ha' your punk and your pig in state, sir, both piping hot" (3.2.63). The monstrous force conquered in the demonic bears and bear-spirits of *Mucedorus*, *The Winter's Tale*, and the old *Like Will to Like*[79] comes to preside over the play, as "Ursa major ... sit[s] in thy chair and give[s] directions" (2.5.175–176). She presides over a conversion scene that reverses that of *Pericles* and a whole tradition, as Win Littlewit and Dame Overdo are transformed into quail and plover, "fowl i' the Fair" (4.5.15), no longer able to tell "one man from another, but i' the dark" (4.5.52).

The outcome of these transformations, epitomized in Justice Overdo's recognition that he is "but Adam, flesh and blood" (5.6.95), mirrors Prospero's acceptance of his humanity,[80] but in reverse, not as a recovery of the species' universal potential but as a discovery of its common limits.[81] The intended morally redemptive act by which Overdo erroneously believes that "Adam hath offered satisfaction" (5.2.117) is actually a suicidal blunder giving purely arbitrary legal warrant to Quarlous, the knave who strips Trouble-All to an Adam left with nothing but Ursula's scalding pan to cover his nakedness.[82] At one level, the fair performs the festive, utopian task of uncrowning the false differences

---

[78] These and other of the play's allusions to Shakespeare's romances are noted by Thomas Cartelli, "*Bartholomew Fair* as Urban Arcadia: Jonson Responds to Shakespeare," *RenD*, n.s. 14 (1983), 151–172.

[79] Joel H. Kaplan, "Dramatic and Moral Energy in Ben Jonson's *Bartholomew Fair*," *RenD*, n.s. 3 (1970), 144n.

[80] Hunter, "Farce, Comedy, Romance," pp. 44–50; cf. Cartelli, p. 168.

[81] "What is revealed is not our common bond of humanity but the commonness, the baseness, and enormity of our humanity," Robert Ornstein, "Shakespearian and Jonsonian Comedy," *ShS*, 22 (1971), 46.

[82] Dame Overdo thus recapitulates the fallen Eve's desire to be joined in sin by Adam when, retching and shedding tears of shame, she asks "Will not my Adam come at me?" (5.6.71).

that separate its outlaw denizens from its in-law visitors. The communal solidarity which unites Ursula and her touts in competition against their persecutors and victims gradually becomes a model for the larger, degraded community that emerges when the fair has stripped away the the legal, familial, and status ties which bind the visitors against it.[83] The erosion of social difference coincides, as in Jonson's other city comedies, with the antiromantic, disillusioning removal of the fantastic, false antinomies that separate self and other.

While the final semic evaporations of *Bartholomew Fair* exhibit in a purely formalistic sense the festive inclusiveness of more romantic modes, their ritual function serves Jonson's anti-popular, humanistic purpose of representing truthfully the spectacle of folly.[84] Based, as it is, on an antagonistic exposure of romantic falsehood, this representation of truth is also shown to be positional in nature. The "dramatic construction of a convincing sense of reality," in other words, is balanced by a sense of "the provisional status of that reality."[85] When the puppet Dionysus lifts its skirt in defense of players, the "reality" revealed is not a positive truth but an absence, a blank nothing. The puppet does not insist upon the "difference" of theater's truth from Busy's puritanic madness, but upon the identity between Busy's antagonistic standpoint and his own:

Nay, I'll prove, against e'er a rabbin of 'em all, that my standing is as lawful as his; that I speak by inspiration as well as he; that I have as little to do with learning as he; and do scorn her helps as much as he. (5.5.97–100)

As the punning terms of the debate suggest, anyone's claim to a "lawful calling" derives its lawfulness and legitimacy from the incriminating name by which it "calls" its antagonist (5.5.45–60). In just this way, Jonson's representation of Bartholomew Fair is called into being by its parasitic opposition to romantic comic modes.

Jonson depicts the degrading showmanship and materiality of the popular romantic theater in Littlewit and Leatherhead's "ancient modern history of *Hero and Leander*, otherwise called *The Touchstone of True Love*, with as brave a trial of the true friendship between Damon and Pythias, two faithful friends o' the Bankside" (5.3.4–9). The action

---

[83] Thus Peter Womack observes that the business ethos which holds the atomized society of the fair's "masterless men" in loose and tolerant association "invades and disintegrates the structuring consciousness of the legal and domestic" society; "the context, so to speak, swamps the text," pp. 148–149; see also R. Levin, *The Multiple Plot*, pp. 203, 207–208.

[84] On this relationship between the festive dynamics of the play and the "broad humanist moral tradition that turns the Fair into a theater or a book," see Jonathan Haynes, "Festivity and the Dramatic Economy of Jonson's *Bartholomew Fair*," *ELH*, 51:4 (1984), p. 664.   [85] Cohen, *Drama of a Nation*, p. 297.

of the Punch and Judy drollery advances itself as a series of rivalries – between opponents no more different from each other than, say, Touchstone and Quicksilver, or the Four Prentices of London – each of which reconciles its parties only with the arrival of another antagonist on the scene. Leatherhead's commentary sums up the daemonizing logic which underlies both the puppet-show romance and *Bartholomew Fair* itself:

> *Though hourly they quarrel thus and roar with other,*
> *They fight you no more than brother does with brother.*
> *But friendly together, at the next man they meet,*
> *They let fly their anger, as here you might see't.*   (5.4.256–259)

The moral positions occupied both within the puppet-show romance and in the fair at large are no more absolute and independent of each other than the "sack and fresh herring" and the "Dunmow Bacon" with which the puppet-lovers compete for Hero's favor; like the Lenten and Carnivalian perspectives of Middleton's *Chaste Maid*, they are constituent elements of a self-perpetuating process, a continuing game of vapors.

Jonson's travesty of popular romance, both in the puppet show and in the play as a whole, assumes an alterity of vision, an alterity which the Induction locates within the socio-economic practice of London's theaters. The Author, who proposes to see through the deluded "jig-a-jog" of the popular shows[86] without himself being seen, has actually been placed in the theater by the Stage-Keeper, who calls attention to the Author's man, Brome, lurking behind the arras, and reveals that the Author himself has "kicked me three or four times about the tiring-house" (Induction, lines 7, 25). Jonson's representational manner can no more transcend its situation in the theater than Overdo – a frustrated classicist and would-be presenter–satirist in the mode of Duke Vincentio or Prospero – can avoid farcical entanglement in the fair. At every level, the classical position staked out in *Bartholomew Fair* requires an interminable engagement with the popular delusions it opposes. The play thus remains a popular entertainment "as full of noise as sport" (line 73), a Punch and Judy knockabout whose representational claims are finally linked to the "grounded judgements" of popular

---

[86] Francis Teague points out that the play actually offers many of the motifs presumably rejected in the old Stage-Keeper's list of favorites: "Cokes loses his clothes in 4.2, much as Tarlton claimed to have lost his at the cloth fair. Although Adam cannot beat Tarlton, Jonson does give marginal stage directions for his characters to fight six times in the play. And as in the Stage-Keeper's description, the three watchmen engage in a Dogberry-like dialogue with Trouble-all as they lock Justice Overdo in the stocks," *The Curious History of 'Bartholomew Fair'* (Lewisburg: Bucknell University Press, 1985), p. 34.

theater and, through them, to "the grounded judgements and under-standings" of the "understanding gentlemen o' the ground" (lines 50, 68, 42). The classical "understanding" which Jonson elsewhere rep-resents as an upholding, rising under, re-erecting or restoring of ideals[87] is here shown to emerge from, and in continuing connection to, the very popular traditions it corrects. Jonson's relation to his creation is not so much that of Prospero to the "demi-puppets" (5.1.36) of his "living drollery" (3.3.21), as that of Leatherhead to the "players minors" (5.3.71) who beat him over the head.[88] If there is genuine festive feeling in the play's ultimate inclusiveness, it is not a warm endorsement of the common condition represented but a sheepish acknowledgement of the means by which it is represented.

In 1613, six years after the commonly accepted date of its first performance but contemporaneously with Middleton's *Chaste Maid in Cheapside* and slightly earlier than the premiere of *Bartholomew Fair*, William Burre published *The Knight of the Burning Pestle* with an epistolary explanation that "the wide world ... for want of judgement, or not *understanding* the privy mark of irony about it (which showed it was the offspring of no vulgar brain) utterly rejected it" upon its first performance.[89] The interpretive challenges of the play's remarkably complex staging originate in Beaumont's satire on the bourgeois ethos and romantic tastes of London's citizens, a satire that juxtaposes an inset city intrigue play, *The London Merchant*, with interruptions by this play's on-stage citizen–auditors and by the rival play, *The Knight of the Burning Pestle*, that is staged by the London apprentice Rafe at the citizen's behest. When George the Grocer disrupts the Prologue of *The London Merchant* in order to protest against the "girds at citizens" performed in "this house," he and his wife Nell state their preference for the romance and chronicle modes associated with the popular work of Heywood and Dekker: "*The Legend of Whittington*; or *The Life and Death of Sir Thomas Gresham, with the Building of the Royal Exchange*; or *The Story of Queen Eleanor with the Rearing of London Bridge upon Woolsacks ... Jane Shore ... The Bold Beauchamps*" (Induction, lines 19–22, 51, 53). Having played in "*Mucedorus* before the Wardens of our company" (84), their apprentice Rafe performs, in *The Grocers' Honour, or The Knight of the Burning Pestle*, an unintentional parody of citizen tastes and values. When he leaves his shop to become a grocer-errant, the

---

[87] Richard S. Peterson, *Imitation and Praise in the Poems of Ben Jonson* (New Haven: Yale University Press, 1981), pp. 50, 52, 69, 74, 108–109.

[88] The contrast with *The Tempest* is noted by Levin, "Two Magian Comedies," p. 217.

[89] *The Knight of the Burning Pestle*, ed. Sheldon P. Zitner (Manchester University Press, 1984), Dedicatory Epistle to Robert Keysar, p. 51; italics mine.

orphan Rafe enacts a citizen's aspiration to have "a famous history...
written of his heroic prowess" (1.255–256). In his refusal of the King of
Cracovia's daughter in favor of the humble Susan, "a cobbler's maid in
Milk Street" (4.99), the unifying patriotic jingoism of "a hearty
Englishman" triumphs over class barriers. And as he leads the City's
militias in a Mile-End muster, Rafe epitomizes the connections between
civic pride and the romantic fictions of warfare and citizen chivalry.

The limitations of this ethos are underlined by the simultaneous
performance of the *London Merchant* plot – by the identification of the
Grocer and his wife with the stinting, hypocritical merchant–senex
Venturewell and with the inept suitor Humphrey, and by the collisions
between Rafe's improbable romance and the witty schemes of Jasper
Merrythought to win the hand of his master Venturewell's daughter
Luce. The incompatibility between the fantasy of Rafe's adventures and
the "realism" of Jasper's clever plot comes to a climax in Waltham
Wood, where Rafe's attempt at heroics ends with his farcical beating as
an "arrant noddy" by Jasper. The threat that Jasper's plot and presence
pose to Rafe's romance is felt by the citizens as an eruption of the
demonic, an "enchantment" through which the reality-principle reveals
Rafe's quest as the socially partisan fantasy it is (2.330–331).

In its use of generic differences to expose the social basis of citizen
romance, as in many small details, *The Knight of the Burning Pestle* traces
generic differences to their origins in the conflicting interpretations of the
city in the romance of the theaters. This "understanding" of comic
alterity, rather than the mere parody of romance, perhaps accounts for
the play's failure on the stage. Unlike *Eastward Ho*, where a pervasive
structure of exploitation simply undermines the moral structure of
romance, *The London Merchant* plot actually derives its exploitative,
farcical temper from its contrast with the romantic expectations and
counterplot of the citizens. As Jackson Cope has argued, *The London
Merchant* "would be ordinary domestic romance and bathos"[90] without
the even more fantastically romantic Merrythought and Jasper plots. *The
London Merchant* only becomes an antiromatic city comedy, in other
words, to the extent that the presence of the citizens' perspective makes
it so. In this sense, Beaumont's play is not simply a satire on bourgeois
tastes and values but an essay on comedy, an exploration of generic
boundaries, their limits, and their tendency to conceal their genesis in a
common social project.

This common rite of comic interpretation accounts for the festive,
ritual resemblances between the two plays within the play. Embodying

[90] *The Theater and the Dream*, p. 197.

the ritual rhythm of defeat and renewal, Rafe's adventures finally merge, in form if not in fact, with Jasper's. Struck down in his shop by Death, come "To cheapen *aqua vitae*" (5.321), Rafe rises to cool himself in Moorfields, where, after being struck down again, he rises to do his final "obeisance to the gentlemen" of the Blackfriars audience. Jasper rises thrice from the dead, to rescue his bride, to haunt Venturewell into repentance, and to reconcile his parents.[91] Rafe's final ritual performances, as May Lord and resurrected Everyman, do not so much overshadow the concluding scenes of *The London Merchant* as absorb them into a counterpointed but common festive rhythm. If Rafe's triumph as May Lord coincides with the depths of Venturewell's meanness, his death coincides with Venturewell's repentance and the modulation of *The London Merchant* into the romance mode. Jackson Cope argues that the clashing generic possibilities in Beaumont's play "are unified in a larger pattern which makes the ephemeral, topical satire on taste and naiveté a mere instrument to express the *eternal validity* of ritual action."[92] The resemblence of this unifying pattern to the dynamics of such other city comedies as *A Chaste Maid in Cheapside* and *Bartholomew Fair*, however, suggests that its validity is being understood as less "eternal" than discursive, as a product, that is, of the common, complex enterprise of London's comic stage.

The romance of the second generation

By the time *A Chaste Maid in Cheapside* and *Bartholomew Fair* were performed, and *The Knight of the Burning Pestle* published, in 1613–14, the War of the Theaters was over, and even the romance of comic alternatives which had helped produce these masterpieces was fading from sight. The decline of this theatrical romance has to do in part with the changed relationship between public and private theaters, which resulted from the gradual dissolution of the children's companies and the migration of popular theater companies to the private theaters. The Children of Paul's were dissolved in 1607, and the King's Revels, which possibly absorbed them, also disappeared after performing city comedies by Barry, Day, and Sharpham at the private Whitefriars in 1607–8. Also in 1608, the Children of Blackfriars, formerly the Children of the Revels, turned the private Blackfriars over to Burbage's adult troupe, the King's Men. Moved temporarily to the now-vacant Whitefriars, they were merged in 1613 with the Lady Elizabeth's Men, an adult troupe whose performances at both the public Swan and new Hope and the private

---

[91] Ibid., p. 202.   [92] Ibid., p. 203; italics mine.

Whitefriars mirrored the practice of the King's Men of performing at both the public Globe and private Blackfriars.[93] The adaptation of London's popular, adult companies to private theater modes and styles perhaps contributed to the strange, hybrid nature of *A Chaste Maid* and *Bartholomew Fair*, both performed by the newly amalgamated Lady Elizabeth's Men, the former at the Swan, the latter at the Hope. But in the longer run, as the former public theater troupes gradually abandoned their old audience and adapted popular modes to the more aristocratic tastes of the private theater audience, the consequence was a loss of insight into the comic theater's discursivity, a convergence of perspectives which invested city comedy intrigue plots with a new romantic significance.[94] No longer used to explode the false moral oppositions of popular romance and city comedy in the burgher mode, the formal triumph of the clever new-comedy gallants in later city comedy lost its satiric equivocality and became the morally approved way of resolving social competition. Without the influence of a countervailing logic, exploitation and the establishment of class difference became themselves endowed with a magical, romantic efficacy, a charismatic power to link moral superiority with class standing.

If it was the tendency of early, romantically disposed citizen comedies to present socio-economic exploitation and rivalry as a demonic threat overcome by neofeudal ideals of earnest acquisition, loyalty and service, it became the tendency of late city comedies to present such exploitations as the providential means by which urbane gentility claims its moral birthright. In both cases, the discursive function of romance structures was to relieve the dissonance between social tradition and economic innovation – to justify bourgeois values in the name of feudal ideals, in the first case; to justify the participation of the late-feudal nobility and gentry in the new capitalist economy, in the second. The noble, chivalrous merchants and citizens who romantically transcended the threat of social conflict at the opening of the comic dialogue between the theaters thus became with the decline of this dialogue the gifted, gracious

[93] Shapiro, *Children of the Revels*, pp. 28–29; Harbage, *Shakespeare and the Rival Traditions*, p. 36; Alexander Leggatt,"The Companies and Actors," in *The 'Revels' History of Drama in English. Volume III, 1576–1613*, ed. J. Leeds Barroll, Alexander Legatt, Richard Hosley, Alvin Kernan (London: Methuen, 1975), pp. 95–118.

[94] For the view that the public theater actors "abandoned their audience" in appealing to private theater tastes, see Cohen, *Drama of a Nation*, p. 275. Lee Bliss sees in the adaptation of popular romance to the private theater audience a "literary self-consciousness distinguishing this return to older, non-dramatic sources of inspiration. Naive, popular, and so-called escapist subject-matter is handled with great technical sophistication," "Tragicomic Romance for the King's Men, 1609–11: Shakespeare, Beaumont and Fletcher," in Braunmuller and Bulman, eds., *Comedy from Shakespeare to Sheridan*, p. 149.

aristocrats who magically turned financial intrigue to the support of their traditional birthrights. The contradictions between ideals and economic means were no less disguised in this second version of romance than in the first. But the change in the disguise, whereby a neofeudal resistance to social competition gave way to an urbane endorsement of it, reflects the contribution of city comedy to a major ideological transformation. In both their underlying dynamics and their occasional use of popular theater motifs, the late plays demonstrate the adaptation of romantic bias to new social purposes.

After *Bartholomew Fair*, for example, Jonson's city comedies make increasingly serious use of the romance bias and popular theater motifs his earlier plays had exploded. By sending the hapless devil Pug to tempt a London already worse corrupted than hell itself, *The Devil is an Ass* (1616) appears at first to continue the technique of Jonson's earlier plays, invoking outmoded popular devices in order to display, through comic incongruity, the impotence of conventional morality in a world governed by the predatory cycle. In his very absoluteness Pug is rendered both morally and representationally impotent by the city's mastery of illusions:

> They have their vices there, most like to virtues;
> You cannot know 'em apart by any difference.   (1.1.121–122)

The town-wit Wittipol's seduction scene at Mrs. Fitzdotterel's window, recalling Volpone's similar scene at Celia's window, suggests that Wittipol's manipulative control over the events of the play will, like Volpone's, finally be exploded as a merely positional advantage. Yet as the play develops, Wittipol is endowed with moral purpose and the grace of his class. His willingness to join Meercraft's plot against Fitzdotterel is only "for the mirth" (3.1.348), and the play's sentimental investment in Wittipol's gallantry culminates in the arch-romantic virtue with which, disguised as the Spanish Lady, he morally educates his friend Manley and protects Mrs. Fitzdotterel's marriage by rebuffing Fitzdotterel's advances: "Alas!," the Spanish Lady–Wittipol proclaims, "I understand not / Those things, sir" (4.3.62–63). Though witty and self-conscious, this invocation of a mock-Shakespearian romance virtue supports the moral bias of the play.

Fitzdotterel's plot of feigning possession by the devil is appropriately antithetical to this moral bias, assuming as it does the power of Fitzdotterel's plausible performance to manipulate morality: "'Tis no hard thing t' outdo the devil in: / A boy o' thirteen year old made him an ass / But t'other day" (5.3.125–127). But the moral reality and absoluteness of evil asserts itself against this pretence when Pug is carried off to hell by Satan in clouds of sulfur and brimstone. Unprecedented in Jonson's comic *œuvre*, this eruption of moral absolutes drives Fitzdotterel from his disguise, prompting him to expose, one by one, the degraded props – bellows, false belly, mouse – by which his theater and Jonson's had subjected vice and virtue to the power of illusion.

In the allegorical personages and morality-play structure of *The Staple of News* (1626), and in that play's satire on the topicality and journalistic realism of Jonson's earlier manner,[95] Jonson regrounds a typically predatory city comedy conflict – the rivalry between Pennyboy Senior and his nephew, Pennyboy Junior – in the traditional moral opposition between covetousness and prodigality. The resurrection of Pennyboy Canter, whose liberality defines an "urbanity" and "humanity" opposed to "aldermanity" (3 Intermean, lines 1–11), achieves both a moral revelation of the sort parodied in Overdo in *Bartholomew Fair* and a romance triumph of the questing parent such as Middleton had parodied in *Michaelmas Term*. Pennyboy Junior's affection for the motley Canter is ultimately revealed, at the latter's unveiling, as a hidden love for his true father.[96]

Pennyboy Junior's outwitting of the lawyer Picklock is not just the witty exploit of a town wit, but a belated "act of piety and good affection" that reconciles father and son (5.3.23–24) even while it transforms the father's fourth-act homily into a practical demonstration of the virtue of urbane wit. This moral triumph is magically reinforced by the fate of the usurious Pennyboy Senior, a morally demonic figure whose unsavory financial means and motives are excluded from the play's genteel ethos by his astounding moral conversion, as he is brought to repentance by a brother "restor'd to life" and "sent from the dead" to convert him (5.6.12, 32).

Pennyboy Junior's restoration of both his father and his patrimony repeats a fundamental pattern of Shakespearian romance, whereby children preposterously re-beget their own parents, offering, in the virtue of the second generation, the opportunity to correct the errors and recoup the losses of the first. Jonson's greatest embodiment of this formula, *The New Inn* (1629), uses the recreation of two lost daughters to reunite a noble family even while it resurrects the form of popular romance in a second-generation version that accommodates the merry but "low" decorum of the Host of the Light Heart Inn – where the sort

---

[95] For the view that *The Staple of News* is Jonson's effort to transcend the topicality of which his comedies (and 1616 *Works*) had made him the contemporary master, see Douglas M. Lanier, "The Prison-House of the Canon: Allegorical Form and Posterity in Ben Jonson's *The Staple of News*," in J. Leeds Barroll, ed., *Medieval and Renaissance Drama in England*, (1985), 2: 253–267.

[96] Barton, *Ben Jonson, Dramatist*, p. 249.

of broils and humors found in *Bartholomew Fair* are now kept "below the Stairs" (Arg. line 54) – to both aristocratic values and the noble purposes of platonic humanism. But the formula of moral renewal also appears in Middleton's later London comedies, where the amoral predatory pattern is replaced by the weighty moralism of melodrama, tragicomedy, and romance. In *Anything for a Quiet Life* (c. 1621), Sir Francis Cressingham's apparently corrupt remarriage and disinheritance of his children "as by cursed enchantment"[97] is reversed when, in his eldest son's heartfelt, melodramatic confrontation with his stepmother, it is revealed that the new Lady Cressingham's intrigues were simply a means of curing her husband's impecunious pursuit of gambling and alchemy. The coincidental restoration of marital order and property rights is parallelled by the Canter-like return of another gentleman–patriarch from the dead in order to correct his prodigal son.

Middleton's *No Wit, No Help, Like a Woman's* (1612/1657) comes closest to reinstating the patterns of familial romance he had parodied in *Michaelmas Term*. Philip Twilight prodigally squanders the ransom meant to redeem his captive mother upon his secret marriage to a tavern servant. But this is eventually set right by his mother's return and by the discovery that his wife is the changeling daughter of gentle Master Sunset, while Sunset's supposed "daughter," Jane, is in fact Twilight's lost sister, Grace. Twilight is saved from adultery and incest, as Lysimachus is saved from fornication by Marina, by the unmistakable nobility of the disguised Grace, who "Sings, dances, plays, / Touches an instrument with a motherly grace" (4.1.145–146). The romance discoveries are aided by the miraculous conversion of the wicked Lady Goldenfleece, who is brought "to see the spider... Even when my lip touch'd the contracting cup" (2.1.392–393). Class conflict dissolves in celebration of a gentle blood recovered and shared out in marriage, and not even the farceur's wit of Twilight's wily servant Savourwit can alter the providentially ordained course of the play's romance action.

The witty, cavalier exploits of the gentleman–heroes of Fletcher's London comedies are likewise underwritten by a logic that transcends social contradiction by reconciling comic irresponsibility with the gentleman's right to wealth and status. In *Wit Without Money* (1613), Vallentine's meritoriously carefree prodigality raises the threatening prospect that the hospitable estates of the "race of the Gentry" will pass to "some of the City" and be "turned into Cabbidge Gardens."[98] But when the wealthy widow Hartwell convinces Vallentine that wealth does

---

[97] *The Works*, vol. 5, 4.1.23–24.
[98] *The Dramatic Works in the Beaumont and Fletcher Canon*, gen. ed. Fredson Bowers, (8 vols. Cambridge University Press, 1985), vol. 6, 1.173–176.

not entail corruption, that "if my cloathes / Be sometimes gay and glorious" it does not follow that "My minde must be my Mercers too" (3.2.83–85), Vallentine is magically enabled to enjoy an Empsonian version of vagabond's pastoral, freed of the desire for wealth, while at the same time redeeming his mortgage, through his marriage to the widow, and saving his estate for worthy "Lance/let" and "Saint George" (5.2.10–25). Under the guise of celebrating "wit without money" Fletcher reconciles the apparent contradiction between the gentry's noble freedom and ideals and its necessary pursuit of wealth. The widow plot of *The Scornful Lady* (1614) functions similarly, as Loveless Junior's marriage to a wealthy widow further enriches him without altering his carefree ways. This triumph for the gentry is reinforced by the sudden, Pennyboy-like conversion of the usurer Moorecraft, who is won over to the prevailing genteel ethos of finding "constant meanes to riches without curses" (5.3.55–56).

Though Massinger's plays are much closer than Fletcher's to the classic intrigues of Jonsonian and Middletonian city comedy, they support a similarly genteel ethos through their conspicuous use of the formulas of popular romance – noble sentiment, melodramatic sensation, distressed feminine virtue, demonic opposition, providentially empowered comic manipulators, enchantment, magical effects, and children who redeem their threatened patrimony. In *A New Way to Pay Old Debts* (1629), the rewriting from Middleton's *A Trick to Catch the Old One* of a nephew's marriage prospects to recover his patrimony from a rapacious uncle is especially revealing of Massinger's sentimental bias and romanticizing technique. The "widow" of Wellborn's plot against his uncle is not the courtesan whom Middleton's Witgood had previously seduced but the genuine widow Lady Alworth, whose deceased husband the noble Wellborn has previously aided. The lightly touched problem of Witgood's change from whoring to romantic interest in Joyce Hoard is solved by Massinger's creation of a separate character, Wellborn's friend Alworth, who can carry on, without taint, a heightened romantic pursuit of Overreach's virtuous daughter Margaret. While collaborating in Wellborn's manipulative deceit of the London usurer Overreach, Lady Alworth nevertheless becomes his "Lady of the Lake, or Queene of Fairies";[99] her gracious Nottinghamshire household, with its trusty retainers and fabulous chef, defines the center of a rural paradise in which Overreach, "come from the Cittie" (2.1.81), remains an alien, demonic force. The illegitimate city origins that exclude Overreach from such noble society are confirmed by his fiendish attempt to sacrifice his

---

[99] *The Plays and Poems of Philip Massinger*, ed. Philip Edwards and Colin Gibson, (5 vols. Oxford: Clarendon Press, 1976), vol. 2, 2.1.134.

daughter's chastity for the merely positional advantage of connecting himself to Lord Lovell:

> OVERREACH: Virgin me no Virgins.
> I must haue you lose that name, or you lose me…
> MARGARET: I haue heard this is the strumpetts fashion Sir,
> Which I must neuer learne.
> OVERREACH: Learne any thing,
> And from any creature that may make thee great;
> From the Diuell himselfe.
> MARGARET: This is but Diuelish doctrine…
> OVERREACH: Stand not on forme,
> Words are no substances. (3.2.112–129)

As in Middleton and Rowley's *A Fair Quarrel* (1617), where the virtuous Jane Russell defies the "hellish plot" of her "cruel-smiling father"[100] and resists attempted rape by proclaiming "I understand you not" (3.2.87), Margaret's enforcement of linguistic barriers gives moral and generic substance to the social differences on which the play turns. The drawing of swords between Wellborn and Overreach marks an unmistakably melodramatic collision of morally as well as socially polarized forces. The means by which Wellborn is released from Overreach's bonds is not a clever ruse like Witgood's precontract in *A Trick to Catch the Old One*, but the magic of Marral's use of disappearing ink. Coming as a result of the converted Marral's confession that "I Haue a conscience, not sear'd vp like" Overreach's (5.1.210), this strikingly literal example of the phenomenon Jameson calls "semic evaporation" absolves Wellborn of the chicanery that taints Witgood's victory and reinforces his recovery of financial and social standing with a positive moral content. Marral's miraculous, Pennyboy Senior-like conversion is balanced, finally, by Overreach's descent into the sort of hellish madness – "furies" come to "scourge" his "ulcerous soule… before the iudgement seate!" (5.1.367–369) – that Middleton had bracketed into the marginal figure of Dampit.

Unlike Overreach's demonic madness, the post-prandial indigestion of the London magnate Sir Thomas Bitefigg provokes, in Cartwright's *The Ordinary* (1635/1651), a "death-bed" repentance and conversion that enables the impoverished nobleman Littleworth to recoup his fortune through marriage to Bitefigg's daughter. Like Alworth's marriage to Margaret Overreach, this marriage marks an inter-legitimation of the merchant class and gentry through a common moral nobility that makes "riches usefull, free discretion." In Massinger's *The City Madam* the socio-economic necessity which binds the London merchant family of

---

[100] *The Works*, vol. 4, 1.1.382–383.

Sir John Frugal to the noble family of Lord Lacey becomes the basis of a similar moral solidarity. In Sir John Frugal's Prospero-like plot to exorcise both the corrupting influence of wealth on his brother Luke Frugal and the bad grace of social climbing in his vain wife and daughters, the point established is "Not that riches / Is or should be contemn'd," but that "the distinction / And noble difference" which separates true gentry from mere parvenus is gentility "in your abundance, good in plentie"(1.3.48–58). Sir John's reclamation of his patriarchal right is carried out literally by the secular causation of a city comedy intrigue, but in both decor and underlying design it works in the manner of romance. It endows a social solution with moral authority, establishing, in the exposure of Luke Frugal and the correction of Frugal women, the proper reciprocity and inter-legitimizing balance "'twixt the City, and the Court" (5.3.155).

In later comedies of the Caroline period, the romantic recuperation of the moral virtue of the gentry through the medium of city intrigue amounts to a process of social conversion, an urbanization of genteel attitudes that corresponds to the physical gentrification of London itself. In Brome's *The Weeding of Covent Garden* (1632), the *Pericles*-like rescue of a young gentlewoman from the hands of London bawds and the moral recovery of a gentleman's two sons from prodigality and puritanism, respectively, combines with a number of interclass marriages to integrate citizens and gentry in a common respectability. The process is paralleled by the moral and physical "purging" of the new Covent Garden piazza, a "new plantation" whose first underworld explorers are displaced by the "better sort" of merchants and gentry who colonize and cleanse the district. Similarly, in Brome's *The Sparagus Garden* (1635/1640), the new "plantation" of this London pleasure-garden, "an Island of two Acres," forms the polite backdrop for reconciliation and intermarriage between dignified merchants and gentry. Shirley's gentrified *Hyde Park* (1632/1637) is the scene for the Whorehound-like conversion to true nobility of the lecher and gambler Lord Bonvile, for the purgative exposure and correction of rakish gentleman–butterflies, and for a gentleman's apology for attempting to cuckold a London merchant who is "not / born so unequall" to "suffer / His poor affront." In Nabbes' *Tottenham Court* (1633/1635), set in the fashionable resorts of Marylebone Park, where "'twas customary for Gentlemen to have early revels and rendevous," the romance-like recovery of genteel fortunes and manners, together with proofs of citizen virtue, expels the twin urban threats of class rivalry and genteel dissipation. Nabbes' *Covent Garden* (1632/1638) similarly offers "no abuse of the Place"; instead, the natural virtue and winning ways of the impoverished gentleman Artlove enables him to link his hereditary status to the wealth of a Londoner's daughter, while an elderly London justice and an atheistic courtier are purged of jealousy and lechery respectively.

In all of these Caroline plays, both the London landscape and the form of city comedy are purged of their rivalrous, amoral, and exploitative character. The plays re-establish, from the point of view of an urbanizing gentry, the romantic motifs of triumphant virtue and social harmony that had earlier supported the bourgeois ethos of such citizen comedies as *The Shoemaker's Holiday*. Their emphasis on the civilized virtues of the gentry do not simply reflect the changing moral temper of the Caroline court; they reflect as well the transformation of the court and its affiliated classes by a pattern of metropolitan development that urbanized the gentry even while it gentrified the city.

Part IV

The dissemination of urban culture

9   Metropolis: the creation of an august style

A "place for verse": poetry and metropolitan sensibility

In *Several Discourses by Way of Essays in Verse and Prose* (1668), Abraham Cowley celebrated the countryside as the "proper" domain of poetry. As for the city, Cowley observed,

> one might as well undertake to Dance in a Croud, as to make good Verses in the midst of Noise and Tumult.
>
> As well might Corn as Verse in Cities grow;
> In vain the thankless Glebe we plough and sow.
> Against th'unnatural Soil in vain we strive;
> 'Tis not a ground in which these Plants will thrive.
>
> It will bear nothing but Nettles or Thorns of Satyre, which grow most naturally in the worst Earth.[1]

What was to Cowley an infertile urban soil was to his contemporary Alexander Brome, writing from London to Charles Cotton, a polluted atmosphere equally inhospitable to lyric poetry:

> Alas! Sir, London is no place for verse,
> Ingenious harmlesse thoughts, polite and terse,
> Our Age admits not, we are wrap'd in smoke;
> And Sin, and business, which the muses choke.
> Those things in which true poesie takes pleasure,
> We here do want, tranquillity and leasure.[2]

Cowley and Brome here express the sort of anti-urban bias that led their contemporary Thomas Hobbes to claim that the urban genres of satire and comedy were tainted by the pollutions of the urban atmosphere.

---

[1] *Complete Works in Verse and Prose*, ed. A. B. Grosart (2 vols. London, 1881), 2: 321–322.
[2] "To C. C. Esquire," lines 27–32, in *Poems*, ed. Roman R. Dubinski (2 vols. University of Toronto Press, 1982), 2: 227f.

Assigning the "three sorts of poesie, heroique, scommatique, and pastorals" to "the three regions of mankinde, court, city, and country," and comparing these cultural environments with the three natural "regions of the world," Hobbes observed that the court and its genres cast "a lustre of influence upon the rest of men, resembling that of the heavens," while the country and its genres exhibit "a plainness, and (though dull) yet a nutritive faculty, in rural people, that endures a comparison with the earth they labour." By contrast, however, the urban genres of satire and comedy were in Hobbes' view marked by "an insincereness, inconstancy, and troublesome humour, of those that dwell in populous cities, like the mobility, blustering, and impurity of the aire."[3]

Hobbes' hierarchical system, as Harold Toliver points out,[4] is dominated by the courtly genres of epic and tragedy. It denies a specific social standing to lyric on the grounds that "sonets, epigrams, eclogues, and the like pieces ... are but essays, and parts of an entire poem." In contrast with Hobbes, however, Cowley and Brome take the measure of the city in precisely the lyric and essayistic genres Hobbes excludes from consideration. The very urbane manner in which they define limited possibilities for urban poetry paradoxically belies those limits and exemplifies what Hobbes' system is meant to deny – the possible location of a new poetic domain in the new social domain of Caroline metropolitan life.

A major creation of the Caroline period, this poetic domain was represented not so much by a genre as by a style – a manner of beholding the self and the world – involving a constellation of classically inspired lyric genres that included epigram, elegy, epistle, ode, and prose character.[5] Generally less indebted to the fictions of song than to those of speech and address, and exploiting the resources of plainness and point that Alistair Fowler associates with the expansive reach of the seventeenth-century epigram,[6] this style represented the establishment of a

---

[3] "Answer to Sir William Davenant's Preface Before *Gondibert*" (1650), in *Critical Essays of the Seventeenth Century*, ed. J. E. Spingarn (3 vols. Bloomington: Indiana University Press, 1957), 2: 54–56.

[4] *Lyric Provinces in the Renaissance* (Columbus: Ohio State University Press, 1985), p. 65.

[5] The last of these Richard Aldington describes as a "prose lyric," *A Book of "Characters"* (London: Routledge, 1924), p. 3. I am conscious of omitting from this consideration of Caroline sensibility those associated strains of erotic lyric – petrarchan and pastoral – that John Danby sees as the "snobbish vulgarization and ... sectional narrowing" of Elizabethan aristocratic literature at the hands of Beaumont and Fletcher; *Poets on Fortune's Hill: Studies in Sidney, Shakespeare, and Beaumont and Fletcher* (London: Faber and Faber, 1952), p. 157.

[6] *Kinds of Literature: An Introduction to the Theory of Genres and Modes* (Cambridge, Mass.: Harvard University Press, 1982), pp. 195–202.

new "place for verse" within metropolitan life; it cultivated, in ways more far-reaching and profound than Brome's casual terms might suggest, a "true poesie" of "tranquillity and leisure," an urbane discourse of "ingenious harmlesse thoughts, polite and terse."

In discovering ways "to be more intimate and informal, and to deal with sentiments previously expressed only in Latin,"[7] the urbanity of Jonson and his Caroline successors was an ethical and social innovation with far-reaching literary implications. Not just a "creation of the period from about 1595 to 1640" that became "the possession of the period from about 1640 to 1680,"[8] this poetic mode, through a process of retrospective canonization that well into the eighteenth century anthologized Jonson and other pioneers of the mode alongside contemporary practitioners, also contributed substantially to the displacement of the courtly and popular modes of the Renaissance by an "august" reconstruction of the literary order at once more narrowly classicized, more socially elite, and more thoroughly professionalized. Shading off in one direction towards Pope's *Windsor Forest* and in another toward his Horatian Epistles, the Caroline exploration of a new metropolitan domain thus marked the beginning of what became, for the next century, the aestheticized literary institution in terms of which Englishmen would interpret their society and express its history and destiny.

The innovations of the social mode reflect the emergence – from the configuration of the court, the country, and city – of a new element, "the Town," at the confluence of the former three in the West End of Jacobean and Early Caroline London.[9] Supported by the magnetism of London's land, money, and marriage markets, by its law terms, by the proximity of the court, and increasingly by the allure of the pleasures it offered, the development of the West End brought a gentrifying city together with an urbanizing gentry, transforming seventeenth-century London into what Thomas Fuller called "the inn-general of the gentry and nobility of this nation." With the development of new patterns of landholding and national administration and finance, London became the central hub in an expanding network of communications – a system of coaching roads that made it possible for whole families to journey to London while enclosed from the elements, a system of correspondence and ultimately of printed journals that kept rural landowners in weekly

---

[7] Ibid., p. 202.

[8] Earl Miner, *The Cavalier Mode from Jonson to Cotton* (Princeton University Press, 1971), p. 87. It is because of the very longevity of the mode, which both preceded the Civil War and survived it to become part of an "august" manner that I prefer the term Caroline to the more narrowly politicized term Cavalier.

[9] This is Martin Butler's formulation in *Theatre and Crisis, 1632–1642* (Cambridge University Press, 1984), p. 141.

touch with the capital, and above all the new stock of gentrified housing in London's West End.[10] The development of the New Exchange and St. Martin's Lane by the Earl of Salisbury (1606–10), of Drury Lane by the Earl of Clare, of Long Acre by the Third Earl of Bedford (1612–18) and of Covent Garden by the Fourth (1631ff.), of Leicester Fields (1631), and later of Lincoln's Inn Fields and Bloomsbury established architectural and residential norms which, like the literary culture of this domain, prevailed for more than a century. By the early and mid-seventeenth century, then, the area between London and Westminster, which had earlier sheltered the innovative yet still marginal youth-culture of the Inns of Court, became the permanent, fashionable center for England's elite.[11] By 1640, with a population of more than 40,000, the West End had become "the largest urban community in the realm outside of the City itself," the "only truly national and international center" of a landed society "whose elite had never previously shown much attraction to cities."[12]

The new attractions of London thus made it possible by 1620 for Sir William Cavendish to balance against all traditional obligations to maintain social order, hospitality, and armigerous discipline through rural residence the necessity of "the conversation, of discreet, able, and understanding men," which "must bee sought where it is, and that is in Cities, and Courts, where generally the most refined, and iudicious men, be likeliest to be found ... a man will get that by conversation, hee will never learne either by letters, or report."[13] Sir Richard Fanshawe observed that the rural gentry

> Leave the despised Fields to clownes,
> And come to save our selves as 'twere
> In walled Townes.

[10] Quoted in Lawrence Stone, "The Residential Development of the West End of London in the Seventeenth Century," in Barabara C. Malament, ed., *After the Reformation: Essays in Honor of J. H. Hexter* (Philadelphia: University of Pennsylvania Press, 1980), p. 388; on new forms of transport and communication, see pp. 177–180, and Stone's *The Crisis of the Aristocracy, 1558–1641* (Oxford: Clarendon Press, 1965), pp. 386–398.

[11] Stone, *Crisis*, pp. 359–362; M. J. Power, "The East and West in Early Modern London," in E. W. Ives, R. J. Knecht, and J. J. Scarisbrick, eds., *Wealth and Power in Tudor England: Essays Presented to S. T. Bindoff* (Totowa, N. J.: Rowman and Littlefield, 1975), pp. 199–223; M. J. Power, "The Social Topography of Restoration London," in Roger Finlay and A. L. Beier, eds., *London, 1500–1700: The Making of the Metropolis* (London: Longman, 1986), pp. 199–223; F. J. Fisher, "The Development of London as a Centre of Conspicuous Consumption in the Sixteenth and Seventeenth Centuries," in E. M. Carus-Wilson, ed., *Essays in Economic History* (3 vols. New York: St. Martin's Press, 1962), 2: 197–207.

[12] R. Malcolm Smuts, *Court Culture and the Origins of a Royalist Tradition in Early Stuart England* (Philadelphia: University of Pennsylvania Press, 1987), pp. 57, 65, 67.

[13] *Horae Subseciuae. Observations and Discourses* (1620), pp. 163, 168.

Hither we bring Wives, Babes, rich clothes
And gemms.[14]

In a poem significantly entitled "Metropolis," Dudley, the Third Lord North celebrates the new attraction of Caroline London,

Where the refined spirits of our Ile
Ingenious discourse communicate,
And hourly fresh delights participate,
Dull tedious time pleasure to beguile.
We all best love our like, London is the best,
The fairest, richest Town of all the rest,
In all this continent there is none such ...
London the firmament, where every Star
Of magnitude, of power and virtue moves:
London the School, and forum of all Arts:
London the Empory that all imparts,
That use requires, or our affection loves.[15]

Epitomized in the necessity and appeal of "conversation" ("We all best love our like"), the social, literary, and ethical innovations of the urbanizing gentry helped to create a new technology of "metropolitan" life. The significance of this technology is usefully illuminated by Georg Simmel's classic essay on the subject, "The Metropolis and Mental Life," which formulates the problem of metropolitan life in terms of "the claim of the individual to preserve the autonomy and individuality of his existence in the face of overwhelming social forces." The problem of what Simmel calls a "reciprocity" or "equation ... between the individual and the supraindividual contents of life" was crucial to the changing culture of early seventeenth-century London, marking precisely the point in the urbanizing process where new forms of metropolitan organization and new traits in its individualized subjects were emerging in mutual genesis.

The key to Simmel's concept of the metropolis is the exponential point in growth where a city ceases to be identical with its environs, where "in transcending this visible expanse ... any given city becomes the seat of cosmopolitanism," and where the

quantitative aspect of life is transformed directly into its qualitative traits of character ... Man does not end with the limits of his body or the area comprising his immediate activity. Rather is the range of the person constituted by the sum

---

[14] *Shorter Poems and Translations*, ed. N. W. Bawcutt (Liverpool University Press, 1964), p. 6. Martin Butler has assembled a wealth of testimony from contemporary letters and journals on the new metropolitan life, pp. 101–103.

[15] *A Forest Promiscuous of Several Seasons Productions* (London, 1659), pp. 17–18. An earlier version appeared as *A Forest of Varieties* (1645), and most of the material in both additions is dated by the author in the 1630s.

of effects emanating from him spatially and temporally. In the same way, a city consists of its total effects which extend beyond its immediate confines.

In projecting itself beyond the boundaries of the city, cosmopolitan freedom is not a freedom *from*, as the civic freedom within London's boundaries was a freedom from feudal servitude, but a freedom *for*, a freedom to project and define a self that must "be somehow expressed in the working out of a way of life."[16]

In discovering "ways to be more intimate and informal" against a background of increasingly massive and complex metropolitan life, the urbane social mode of Jonson and his many imitators worked out just such a cosmopolitan "way of life" by moving inwardly and selectively toward the privatized domains of self, friends, distinctive place and occasion. Yet paradoxically these domains liberated the very type of personality they defined and distinguished, transforming massive urban scale and quantity into ethical quality, and thereby enabling the metropolis to transcend its physical limits through the traits of character and style that disseminated its influence beyond its boundaries. In the Caroline social mode, as in its classical sources, "cosmopolitanism and selectivity" were "closely allied."[17] What finally marks this mode as a product of metropolitan life is its widespread dissemination in the anthologies and original works of the later seventeenth-century, where a generalized Horatian *vers de société* – defining itself in retrospect, and increasingly in opposition to both heroic and popular genres, as *the* exclusively "literary" domain – merely assumed as a discursive background what its originators labored to establish *in situ*, that culture and civilization seat themselves in urbane subjects who are "free" to pass the city's boundaries. The fact that by the 1690s such poetry on the good life could become an arena for debate between the two classes and parties that had emerged as contending forces in the nation's life is but a further reflection of the socio-political impact of the metropolitanizing process.

The complex dynamics of the new metropolitan ethos are perhaps best approached through the irritations Dudley North's residence in the capital produced. In a letter purporting to explain to a friend his decision to leave London, North assembles a variety of fairly typical complaints:

When the Citie had most of my affection, I conceived reason sufficient why a Countrey Gentleman might, as I often found, grow soon weary, and distasted; costly and ill lodging and diet, enforced neatness, importunate visits, perpetual cap, courtesie, and complements, ceremonious acquaintance, tedious and

---

[16] "The Metropolis and Mental Life," in Richard Sennett, ed., *Classic Essays on the Culture of Cities* (Englewood Cliffs, N.J.: Prentice-Hall, 1969), pp. 47–50.

[17] Katharine Eisamen Maus, *Ben Jonson and the Roman Frame of Mind* (Princeton University Press, 1984), p. 138.

chargeable business, pastime to seek, his wonted healthful exercise, Air and command turn'd to a sedentary and servile obedience, and a sooty aire, such as the thickest rined Vegetables rather pine than live in.[18]

Quite apart from the specific objections (which will be taken up below), the remarkable feature of the complaint is its general tone and tenor, i.e., its generality as such, but also the absence of any principled complaint against London's violation of the traditional moral or social order and, instead of this, its reliance on affect, its tendency to respond almost viscerally, with weariness, distaste, and irritation, to an environment which has become almost wholly sensational. The profound novelty is that in evoking sensation, taste, and sensibility in this fashion, the metropolis may be seen already to have produced a new kind of inhabitant.

Simmel might have diagnosed North's complaint in terms of the neurasthenic problem of sensory overload, "the intensification of nervous stimulation" that comes with the quantum leap from the discrete and enduring impressions of customary communal life to the "rapid crowding of changing images, the sharp discontinuity ... and the unexpectedness of onrushing impressions" in the metropolis (p. 48). "Sooty aire," a small irritant in North's list, is perhaps the most symptomatic of the new sensory responses, especially to odor and noise, that characterize seventeenth-century complaints against London. Thomas Wentworth, the Earl of Strafford, objected to the "smothering" air of London, and John Evelyn, in *Fumifugium* (1661), composed the first treatise on urban air pollution.[19] Cowley, like many of his contemporaries, objected to London's "Exhalations of Dirt and Smoak,"[20] while Davenant complained that the city was smother'd with sulph'rous fires ... / Of Sea-Cole Smoak."[21] Fanshawe inveighed against "The smoaky glory of the Towne," and even Milton's Satan approached the salubrious Eden "As one ... long in populous City pent, / Where Houses thick and Sewers annoy the Air" (*Paradise Lost*, 9.445–446).

Jonson's *Epicœne* (1609), which, untypically of the heteroglot plays of his great comic period, confined itself to the new circles of the exclusive

[18] *A Forest Promiscuous*, p. 65.   [19] For Wentworth, see Stone, *Crisis*, p. 393.

[20] Howell, *Epistolae Ho-Elianae*, ed. Oliphant Smeaton (3 vols. London: Dent, 1903), 3: 39; Cowley, *Several Discourses by Way of Essays*, in *Complete Works*, 2: 328.

[21] Song from *The First Days Entertainment at Rutland House* (1657), lines 1–4, in *The Shorter Poems and Songs from the Plays and Masques*, ed. A. M. Gibbs (Oxford: Clarendon Press, 1972), p. 244; cf. the "Mists of Sea-coale-smoake" in "The Quene, returning to London after a long absence," line 1, p. 47, and Edward Benlowes' objection to London's "thicker clouds of griping care, than smoke," *Theophila*, Canto XII, The Segregation, st. 6, in George Saintsbury, ed., *Minor Poets of the Caroline Period* (3 vols. Oxford: Clarendon Press, 1905), 1: 446.

West End *beau monde* and thus became a principal model for later Caroline and Restoration comedians, exploited the comic effects of the noise pollution also being noted by contemporaries. Credit here goes to Everard Guilpin's imitations of Martial 12.57 and Juvenal 3 on the noise of Rome,[22] but by the mid-seventeenth-century, the quest for "freedom from the City noise," from "the sad tumults of the maze,"[23] had become a commonplace. Evelyn, for example, noted that the town was "pestred with hackney-coaches and insolent carre-men, shops and taverns, noyse, and such a cloud of sea-coal, as if there be a resemblence of hell upon earth, it is in this volcano in a foggy day."[24] By the end of the century, London had proverbially acquired "such a noise, an air so smoky, / That to stun ye, this to choke ye."[25]

These new sensitivities to odor and noise were undoubtedly occasioned by the growing use of coal fuel, necessitated by London's exhaustion of wood supplies,[26] and by the increased use of vehicles, which Henry Peacham called "the Rattle Snakes of old England."[27] But they were also aroused, as sensitivities to London's fogs were said to have been aroused by Whistler's painting at a later date, by the Horatian *fumum...strepitumque romae* (*Odes* 3.29; cf. 3.6), the Martialian *transeuntis risus* (12.57) or the Juvenalian *magnis opibus dormitur in urbe* (*Satire III*). More profoundly, however, receptivity to the sensitivities of these Roman poets, which lies at the heart of Caroline urbanity, was not simply a result of imitation; rather, imitation was itself a symptom of the seventeenth-century formation of metropolitan character. The sensitivities of metro-

[22] Epigram 68 and Satire 5 in *Skialetheia* (1598), ed. D. Allen Carroll (Chapel Hill: University of North Carolina Press, 1974), pp. 56, 83; see also Jonson's Epigram 92, "The New Cry."

[23] Charles Cotton, "To My Friend, Mr. John Anderson, from the Country," *Poems*, ed. John Beresford (London, 1923), p. 113; Henry Vaughan, "To My Ingenious Friend, R. W.," in *The Works of Henry Vaughan*, ed. L. C. Martin (2nd edn. Oxford: Clarendon Press 1957), p. 33. Cf. George Daniel, Ode 31, in *Poems*, ed. A. B. Grosart (4 vols. London, 1868), 2: 71; Robert Fage, *St. Leonard's Hill* (1666), p. 7; Richard Lovelace, "To a Lady that Desired Me I Would Beare My Part with Her in a Song," *Poems of Richard Lovelace*, ed. C. H. Wilkinson (1930; rpt. Oxford: Clarendon Press, 1953), pp. 90–91.

[24] *A Character of England* (1651, 1659), in *The Miscellaneous Writings of John Evelyn*, ed. William Upcott (London: Henry Colburn, 1825), pp. 156–157.

[25] Motteux, *Love's a Jest* (1696), in *Seventeenth-Century Lyrics*, ed. Norman Ault (1928; rpt. New York: William Sloane, 1950), p. 469.

[26] The consumption of water-borne coal increased in London and the Thames valley from 12,000 tons in 1575–80 to 455,000 tons by 1690, in part because rising industrial demand and deforestation increased the price of wood fuel eight-fold between 1530 and 1630, while the price of coal only tripled. See U. J. Nef, *The Rise of the British Coal Industry* (2 vols. London: G. Routledge and Sons, 1932), 1: 156–215.

[27] Henry Peacham, *Coach and Sedan* (1636; rpt. London: Frederick Etchells and Hugh Macdonald, 1925), sig. B4.

politan character, in other words, were more deeply a function of new modes of association.

Over the theories of the College of Physicians, and in contrast to the Elizabethan pattern, Evelyn maintained, with other seventeenth-century contemporaries, that London's polluted air was not a prophylactic against but an occasion of disease.[28] Equipped with the latest sanitation technology, both the new housing developments of the West End and the pleasure gardens and alcoves that sprang up within and around them were advertised as being *at once* sanitary and socially select, as providing "pleasure and freshnes for the health and recreation of the Inhabitantes there about," but as being chiefly "fit for the habitation of gentlemen and men of ability."[29] The metaphorical connection of social stratification and salubrity is clear enough in Owen Felltham's reflection that "infection is sooner taken by breath than contaction ... We can converse with nothing, but will work upon us; and by the stealth of time, liken us to itself. The choice, therefore, of the company we keep, is one of the most weighty actions of our life."[30] The social underpinnings of Felltham's emphasis on associational choice and selectivity are elucidated by Simmel's contention that the metropolite's compensatory response to the overwhelming variety of fleeting contacts and commitments is the specialization of personality, the hyperdevelopment of intellection in a capacity for "objective" judgement, quick and instinctive choice and discrimination. For seventeenth-century London metropolites, such selectivity was an essential counterbalance to the strains of urban living. On the one hand, London society was, as Dudley North complained, artificial and ceremonious, an endless round of "enforced neatness, importunate visits, perpetual cap, courtesie, and complements, ceremonious acquantaince." On the other hand, such ceremony barely concealed the competitive nature of an environment that, according to Sir William Cavendish, placed a man "as it were in a throng, wanting elbow roome: there bee so many his equalls, and superiors, and above him in place and merit, that he is reckoned for number, not weight; one of the troope rather for shew, then use" (p. 156). One effect of this highly

[28] *Fumifugium: or The Inconvenience of the Aer and Smoak of London Dissipated* (1661), in *The Miscellaneous Writings of John Evelyn*, p. 224; cf. p. 228. See also Burton, *Anatomy of Melancholy* (1628), ed. Floyd Dell and Paul Jordan-Smith (New York: Tudor Publishing Company, 1927), pp. 86, 209, 413; Henry Vaughan, *The Praise and Happinesse of the Countrie-Life* (1651), in *Works*, p. 128; Cavendish, *Horae Subseciuae*, p. 151.

[29] Privy Council, recommending the development of Lincoln's Inn Fields, quoted in Norman G. Brett-James, *The Growth of Stuart London* (London: George Allen and Unwin, 1935), p. 154; builder of Covent Garden, quoted by Stone, "Residential Development," p. 198.

[30] "Of Assimilation," *Resolves*, ed. James Cumming (London, 1820), p. 137.

formalized yet intensely competitive environment was to produce the paradoxical solitude of metropolitan man: "'tis not Company makes Society, since in the midst of it a man may be in solitude without love. As the Latine Proverb is, *Magna Civitas, Magna Solitudo.* A great City is a great Wilderness."[31] With its breakdown of the traditional social order, the atomistic variety created by the city presented a new challenge to the power of moral and social discrimination. "There are no fewer forms of minds, than of bodies amongst us," Jonson noted, "The variety is incredible; and therefore we must search" (*Discoveries*, lines 833–836).

The discriminating search for distinction accounts for many characteristic concerns of seventeenth-century social verse – its concern with friendships and social virtues, with the good life and its pleasures, with the proper uses of leisure, with the proprieties of social occasion in place and time. Such is the fit between discriminating sociability and its environment in this poetry, that the two come fully into existence through reciprocal influence. The representation of environment, in other words, is a function of socialization; it emerges, as Bakhtin notes in the case of ancient epistolary writing, from a certain type of literary–social expression:

in this intimate and familiar atmosphere ... a new private sense of the self, suited to the drawing-room, began to emerge ... "Landscape" is born, that is, nature conceived as a horizon (what a man sees) and as the environment (the background, the setting) for a completely private, singular individual who does not react with it ... Nature enters the drawing-room world of private individuals only as picturesque "remnants," while they are taking a walk, or relaxing or glancing randomly at the surrounding view.[32]

Just so was the urban landscape, its challenges and pleasures, constructed as a lyrical domain within the intimate social mode of seventeenth-century verse. John Earle identified the appropriative force in the formation of social bonds when he observed that "acquaintance ... is the hoard, and friendship the pair chosen out of it; by which at last we begin to impropriate and inclose unto ourselves what before lay in common with others."[33] In the creation of exclusive haunts like Covent Garden, the formation of choice society became the decorous means of ap-

---

[31] William Ramsey, *The Gentleman's Companion* (1669, pub. 1672), pp. 102–103. Cf. Vaughan, "The Praise and Happinesse of the Countrie-Life," *Works*, pp. 133–134; Jonson, *Iactura vitae, Discoveries*, lines 68–73, in *The Complete Poems*, ed. George Parfitt (1975; rpt. New Haven: Yale University Press, 1982), p. 376.

[32] "Forms of Time and the Chronotope in the Novel," in *The Dialogic Imagination*, ed. Michael Holquist (Austin: University of Texas Press, 1981), pp. 143–144.

[33] *Microcosmography, Or a Piece of the World Discovered* (1629), ed. Philip Bliss (Albany: Joel Munsell, 1867), p. 122.

propriating and gentrifying the urban landscape. As Brome put it in *The Weeding of Covent Garden*, the West End development was a "new plantation" that would eventually be colonized "with the better sort"; a suburban frontier orginally occupied by underworld denizens, it would be "purged so every day" that it would become "a scene for virtue and nobility."[34]

The perfect poetic vehicle for the appropriation of the urban landscape and the cultivation of the metropolitan self was the social mode of Horace and his Stoic–Epicurean sources, especially as represented to the age through the poems of Jonson and his imitators. It is in fact doubtful whether the newly fashionable life of the West End – with its new patterns of residence and seasonal migration, its pastimes, parks, and pleasure gardens, its new social circles and clubs, where "men of the same Country, of Sussex-men, of Bedfordshire-men... appoint their meeting, and agree, and make rules"[35] – could have taken the shape it did without such ethical underpinnings. The Stoic idea that the basis for *oikeiosis* or affinity lies in reasonable likemindedness rather than passionate attachment, for example, stressed the same hyperdevelopment of intellection – the capacity for discriminating choice – that Simmel locates in the metropolitan self. Similarly, the ancient ideals of detachment and self-sufficiency paradoxically helped to "effect the distances" neccessary to metropolitan life, so that what appears directly as withdrawal or dissociation was "in reality only one of the elemental forms of socialization."[36]

Based on common virtue and distinction, this resocialization was a matter of choice and adoption rather than birth or heredity. It took literary shape in the public celebration of distinguished social virtues, commitments, and pleasures. The new society enshrined in Jonson's *Epigrammes* (1616) was thus an aristocracy liberated from status in the traditional sense of "strict degrees of rank, or title."[37] Modelling his own project on Jonson's in this panegyric respect, Herrick called the community of choice souls assembled in his epigrams the "City here of

---

[34] 1.2.20–30; 5.2.273–278, in Donald S. McClure, *A Critical Edition of Richard Brome's "The Weeding of Covent Garden" and "The Sparagus Garden"* (New York: Garland, 1980). See above, p. 476.   [35] John Selden, *Table-Talk* (1689), p. 43.

[36] Simmel, "The Metropolis and Mental Life," p. 53. Cf. Bruno Snell, *The Discovery of the Mind: The Greek Origins of European Thought* (New York: Harper and Row, 1960), p. 65, quoted in Michael O'Loughlin, *The Garlands of Repose: The Literary Celebration of Civic and Retired Leisure* (University of Chicago Press, 1978), p. 34. For a summary analysis of *oikeiosis* and other Roman ethical concepts as deployed by Jonson, see Maus, *Ben Jonson and the Roman Frame of Mind*, ch. 5, "Jonson and the Roman Social Ethos."

[37] "To All, to Whom I Write," *Complete Poems*, p. 37. The importance of both adoption and publication are stressed in Maus, *Ben Jonson and Roman Frame of Mind*, pp. 127, 136.

Heroes I have made."[38] Aware of the potential snobbery in his own version of this project, Jonson denied in his epistle to Drayton that his aim was merely "to rub / Haunch against haunch, or raise a rhyming club / About the town."[39] Yet Falkland's tribute to Jonson maintained that his proper milieu was the sophisticated arena of "The Academies, Courts, and Towns," and the company of "Digby, Carew, Killigrew, and Maine, / Godolphin, Waller, and that inspired Train."[40] Reaching in its commitments across what was in fact a variety of *milieux*, and addressing itself to aristocratic patrons, statesmen, lawyers, and divines as well as friends,[41] the social range of Jonson's poetry defined a new set of ethical possibilities for those who, like Dudley North, were "ambiguously constituted, balanced in disposition, betwixt... Countrey, Town, and Court; private, or publick course of life" (p. 140).

For poets writing in the new urbane mode, "the Town" presented itself as the chief arena for discriminating choices and distinguished displays. Donne's epistolary epigram to Everard Guilpin, for example, extolled the retirement of its addressee to Suffolk and lamented the doldrums of London's Long Vacation, when "pleasure's dearth our city doth possess." But the purpose of Guilpin's retirement was finally to garner up a store of wit to be retailed on his return to London:

> fill not like a bee
> Thy thighs with honey, but as plenteously
> As Russian merchants, thyself's whole vessel load,
> And then at winter retail it here abroad.
> Bless us with Suffolk's sweets; and as that is
> Thy garden, make thy hive and warehouse this.[42]

For Herrick, as for other members of the "Tribe of Ben," it was more specifically "those Lyrick Feasts, / Made at the Sun, / The Dog, and the triple Tunne," and the "great over-plus" of Jonson's wit that produced the treasury of wit, the "precious stock" of cultural inheritance over which the poet's spirit continued to preside.[43] Francis Beaumont's

[38] "To the most learned, wise, and Arch-Antiquary, Master John Selden," line 9, in *The Complete Poetry of Robert Herrick*, ed. J. Max Patrick (1963; rpt. New York: W. W. Norton, 1968), p. 194.

[39] "The Vision of Ben Jonson, on the Muses of his Friend M. Drayton," lines 7–9, in *Complete Poems*, p. 267.

[40] Dryden, *Miscellany Poems* (6 vols. London, 1717), 2 (i.e., *Sylvae*, 1685): 158–159.

[41] On this range of commitment, see Geoffrey Walton, *Metaphysical and Augustan : Studies in Tone and Sensibility in the Seventeenth Century* (London: Bowes and Bowes, 1955), p. 99, and Hugh Maclean, "The Social Function of Jonson's Verse," in *Ben Jonson and the Cavalier Poets* (New York: W. W. Norton, 1974), p. 506.

[42] *The Complete English Poems*, ed. A. J. Smith (1971; rpt. Harmondsworth: Penguin, 1986), p. 202.

[43] "An Ode for Him," lines 15–20, in *The Complete Poetry*, p. 381.

epistle to Jonson similarly recalled the lavish dispensing of wit in the "things we have seen / Done at the Mermaid ... when there hath been thrown / Wit able enough to justifie the town / For three daies past."[44]

Taking on an aura of distinction that would later canonize the social mode, Jonson's immediate circle was, by the 1630s, but the most central instance of a more pervasive development of a "Town" ethic. This ethical development was fostered by a new royal interest in the capital. Whereas the orders of James I against residence in London by nobles and gentlemen had in traditional terms lamented "the decay of Hospitalitie" and expressed moral indignation that "a more private and delicate life, after the manner of forreine Countreys, by living in Cities and Townes" should displace "the ancient and laudable custome of this Realme in housekeeping," those of Charles I tended rather more pragmatically to stress the impact on London itself through the outflow of capital for luxury goods and the general inconvenience of overpopulation.[45] There is in the Caroline orders nothing like James' insistence "euery one" should "liue in his owne place, some at Court, some in the Citie, some in the Countrey."[46] Instead, there is every indication that the purpose of the Caroline orders was not to reverse the urbanizing process but to rationalize it, so that the ideal of good local government was to be epitomized in the capital itself.[47] In his attempts to restrict and regulate London building, James had already expressed the ambition that as "the first emperor of Rome ... had found the city of Rome of brick, and left it of marble, so ... we ... mought be able to say in some proportion, that we had found our City and suburbs of London of sticks, and left them of brick."[48] The pursuit of this august aim was enhanced in the Caroline period by numerous measures "to reduce the sprawling anarchy of the

[44] "Mr. Francis Beaumont's Letter to Ben Iohnson, Written before he and Mr. Fletcher came to London, with two of the precedent comedies then not finished, which deferred their merry meetings at the Mermaid," in *Poems*, ed. Alexander Chalmers, *The Works of the English Poets* (21 vols. London, 1810), 6: 202.

[45] Proclamation of James I "requiring the Residencie of Noblemen, Gentlemen, Lieutenants, and Justices of Peace, upon their chiefe Mansions in the Countrey," December 9, 1615, in Paul L. Hughes and James F. Larkin, *Stuart Royal Proclamations* (2 vols. New Haven: Yale University Press, 1973), 1: 356; Proclamation of Charles I "commanding the Gentry to keepe their Residence at their Mansions in the Countrey," June 20, 1632, *Stuart Royal Proclamations*, 2: 351.

[46] Speech in Star Chamber, 20 June, 1616, in *The Political Works of James I*, ed. C. H. McIlwain (Cambridge University Press, 1908), 343–344; cf. the attack on "women that doe London loue so well" in James' "Elegie ... concerning his counsell for Ladies & gentlemen to departe the City of London," in *The Poems of James VI of Scotland*, ed. James Craigie (2 vols. Edinburgh: William Blackwood and Sons, 1955–58), 2: 178–181.

[47] Kevin Sharpe, "The Personal Rule of Charles I," in H. Tomlinson, ed., *Before the English Civil War: Essays on Early Stuart Politics and Government* (New York: St. Martin's Press, 1983), p. 62.

[48] Proclamation for Buildings, June 16, 1615, in *Stuart Royal Proclamations*, 1: 346.

Fig. 18 "English houses of the older and newer form intermixed with trees and afar off a prospect of the City of London and the River Thames." Inigo Jones, *Britannia Triumphans* (1637)

Fig. 19 "Magnificent buildings [and] in prospect ... the suburbs of a great city." Inigo Jones *Salmacida Spolia* (1639)

metropolis to order, calm, and decency" – by the establishment of a building commission, under the supervision of Inigo Jones, which oversaw the new residential developments, by the creation of traffic regulations, by schemes for the repair of London Bridge and St. Paul's and for the levelling and drainage of streets, and by attempts to bring the unregulated suburbs and liberties under metropolitan jurisdiction.[49] Just as short-term leaseholding arrangements with city developers profited the noble holders of urban land while providing a new aesthetic means of expressing aristocratic virtue in creating "such buildings" as were "the honour of nation,"[50] so these royal initiatives, while exploring for new sources of revenue in the absence of Parliaments, also helped to establish an imperial ideal of metropolitan grandeur.

By the 1630s both the theme of public works and the definition of a correspondingly metropolitan ethos had become central concerns of the court masque, as scenes of London, virtually non-existent in the Jacobean period, played an increasingly important role. Designed as "a Triumph in Albinopolis the chiefe City of Albion," Aurelian Townshend's 1631 *Albion's Triumph* climaxes in "a Landscipt, in which was a prospect of the Kings Pallace of Whitehall, and part of the Citie of London, seene a farre off." The scene demonstrates a new royal preoccupation – the beneficial arts and works of Peace, as "Temples and Townes by thy stay'd hand, / First learne to Rise, and then to Stand."[51] James Shirley's *The Triumph of Peace* (1633) depicts the gentrification of the capital through a backdrop of urban renewal, "a large street with sumptuous palaces, lodges, porticoes, and other noble pieces of architecture, with pleasant trees and grounds."[52] In Davenant's *Britannia Triumphans* (1637), the framework for celebrating "all good arts and sciences" is once again metropolitan renewal. The august ambition of the controversial New Incorporation of 1637–38, whereby the Crown attempted to bring the suburbs under a jurisdiction independent of the City, takes shape in a "Scene wherein were English houses of the old and newer forms, intermixt with trees, and afar off a prospect of the City of London and the river of Thames" (see Fig. 18). As the mixture of "old and newer," domestic and neoclassical, architecture in the scene suggests, England's new potential, depicted in a classical Palace of Fame and a final maritime prospect "terminating the sight in the horizon," is realized in

[49] Sharpe, "Personal Rule," p. 62.
[50] Parliamentary speech of 1657 defending the Earl of Bedford, the builder of Covent Garden, quoted in Stone, "Residential Development," p. 206.
[51] *Aurelian Townshend's Poems and Masques*, ed. E. K. Chambers (Oxford: Clarendon Press, 1912), pp. 57, 76, 72–73, 75.
[52] *Dramatic Works and Poems*, ed. Alexander Dyce (6 vols. 1833; rpt. New York: Russell and Russell, 1966), 6: 263, 267–271.

the imperial "Britanocles, and those that in this Isle / The old with modern virtues reconcile." These modern virtues constitute a new civilized ethos and prescribe "nobler exercise than what / The ancient knights' adventures taught."[53]

In Davenant's *Salmacida Spolia* (1640), the last court masque of Charles' reign, civilization triumphs over barbarism as celestial deities shed their influence on a happy metropolis represented – ironically enough in light of the King's flight from London two years later – in a scene (see Fig. 19) of

magnificent buildings composed of several selected pieces of architecture. In the furthest part was a bridge over a river, where many people, coaches, horses, and such like, were seen to pass to and fro. Beyond this on the shore were buildings in prospective, which shooting far from the eye showed on the suburbs of a great city.[54]

These distant suburban prospects, with their reformed and sanitized spaces, and their idealized neoclassicizing architecture, reflect the emergence at even the highest echelons of a new metropolitan ideal of distinction and detachment.

"Masters of truth": the good life and the circuit of legitimation

As it was developed along more intimate lines in the lyric domain of Jonson and later "gentlemen who wrote with ease," the appropriation of the metropolis for new ethical and poetic possibilities adopted a similarly distanced perspective. While it was modelled on many of the same classical sources, such as Horace and Martial, as the formal verse satire and epigrams of the 1590s, the social mode of seventeenth-century poets defined itself in pointed opposition to the the harsh and violent manner of the Inns of Court satirists. The liabilities of satire and the frustration of the satirist are, of course, perennial themes of the mode, and the Inns of Court satirists were themselves preoccupied with the self-defeating aspects of their project. Several of the satirists themselves, moreover, participated in the turn from satire. Donne, for example, abandoned the public concerns of satire for the more intimate manner of epistle, elegy, and lyric, and Hall turned from the harsh Juvenalian manner of his

[53] *Dramatic Works* (5 vols. Edinburgh: William Paterson, 1872), 2: 265, 267, 273, 276, 283. For the New Incorporation, see Brett-James, *The Growth of Stuart London*, pp. 228–244, and Valerie Pearl, *London and the Outbreak of the Puritan Revolution* (Oxford University Press, 1961), pp. 30–37.
[54] *Salmacida Spolia*, lines 92, 436–441, in *A Book of Masques*, pp. 349, 360.

Virgidemiae to the stylistic composure that, in his *Characters of Virtues and Vices* (1608), would initiate a major Caroline fashion. While the manner of scourging satire lingered as an aging fashion in such popular–professional hackwork as George Wither's *Abuses Stript and Whipt* (1613), Richard Brathwait's *Strappado for the Diuell* (1615), and John Taylor's *Superbiae Flagellum* (1621), the more intimate and composed works of Donne, Jonson, and Hall – their epistles, elegies, and characters – became the enabling examples for a generation of distinguished Caroline amateurs that included Carew, Herrick, Randolph, Habington, Suckling, and Earle.[55]

Jonson is the figure in whom the transition is most fully and creatively embodied.[56] In his turn from satire, Jonson adduces many of the traditional objections – the wicked are not reformed, the good need no reforming, etc. – but the more telling objection is revealed in a desperate moment of self-reflection by Crites, the satirist-persona of *Cynthia's Revels*:

> Oh, how despised and base a thing is man,
> If he strive not to erect his grovelling thoughts
> Above the strain of flesh! But how more cheap
> When even his best and understanding part,
> The crown and strength of all his faculties,
> Floats like a dead drowned body on the stream
> Of vulgar humour, mixed with the commonest dregs?
> I suffer for their guilt now, and my soul,
> Like one that looks on ill-affected eyes,
> Is hurt with mere intention on their follies.
> Why will I view them?[57]

Like Donne's satirist, who strove "Against the stream...upwards" (5.50) and was "almost/Consum'd in going" (3.107–108), Crites experiences the giddy stream-effect so common in Inns of Court satire, the satirist's experience of finding the very soul and ethical distinction he wishes to establish amid the stream of life swept powerfully along its surface. Through Crites Jonson recognizes in satire what John Earle sees in another context as the danger of being "carried away with all outwardnesses, shews, appearances, the stream."[58] Attempting to establish personal distinction by means of classic norms, but constantly

---

[55] The latter point is owed to Richard Helgerson, *Self-Crowned Laureates:* Spenser, Jonson, Milton and the Literary System (Berkeley: University of California Press, 1983), p. 110.

[56] See Robert C. Jones, "The Satirist's Retirement in Jonson's 'Apologeticall Dialogue,'" *ELH*, 34 (1967), 447–467. See also Richard C. Newton, "'Goe, quit 'hem all': Ben Jonson and Verse Satire," *SEL*, 16 (1976), 105–116.

[57] 1.5.30–40, in *The Complete Plays*, 2: 22.   [58] *Microcosmography*, p. 85.

pushed toward the connoisseurship of London's many shifting surfaces, the satirists perceived themselves, and were perceived by Jonson, as being distracted by the multiplying superficies of metropolitan life. This, as Simmel puts it, is a danger to the metropolitan "personality in that stimulations, interests, uses of time and consciousness are made available to it from all sides. They carry the person as if in a stream, and one hardly needs to swim for oneself" (p. 59).

The alternative for Jonson was a capacity for moral and aesthetic discrimination, a detachment and self-possession, that derived ultimately from such moral qualities as Stoic *autarkeia* (or self-sufficiency) and *apatheia* (or freedom from passion), as well as Epicurean *ataraxia* (or imperturbability).[59] In Jonson's hands the verse satirists' "snaphaunce quick distinction"[60] – itself a mark of hyperintellection, the capacity for sure and rapid choice, demanded by metropolitan life – was consequently answered by the measured inward turning of the Horatian *nil admirari* (*Epistles*, 1.6.1).

This modulation strikingly resembles the other essential quality that Simmel identifies with the formation of metropolitan character – the "*blasé* attitude." A blunting of sensibility and susceptibility that might appear at first sight to be inherently opposed to the capacity for sharp and ready discrimination, the *blasé* attitude, as Simmel describes it, is not in fact an ignorance of differences but, like the classical *apatheia* or *ataraxia*, a kind of willed insensitivity to them. The *blasé* attitude, in effect, prioritizes among evaluations, so that in less essential matters, "the meaning and differing values of things, and thereby the things themselves, are experienced as insubstantial" (pp. 51–52). Though the worst consequence of this detachment – registered in Simmel's view that "the self-preservation of certain personalities is bought at the price of devaluing the whole objective world" – sometimes manifested itself in later poets writing in the social mode, Jonson's own poetic *œuvre* represents an ongoing attempt to overcome wasteful vexations of spirit while maintaining an ethical engagement that can "meet the fire, the test, as martyrs would."[61]

Thus, in the "Epistle Answering to One that Asked be Sealed of the Tribe of Ben," Jonson excludes from his intimate associates the distracted, uncomposed, superficially discriminating but overly censorious souls who

[59] See O'Loughlin, *The Garlands of Repose*, p. 40.

[60] Marston, *The Scourge of Villainy*, 4.132, in *Poems*, ed. Arnold Davenport (Liverpool University Press, 1961).

[61] "An Epistle Answering to One that Asked to be Sealed of the Tribe of Ben," *Underwoods*, XLVII, line 3, in *The Complete Poems*, p. 191.

                    are received for the covy of wits;
                That censure all the town, and all the affairs,
                And know whose ignorance is more than theirs.   (lines 19–24)

But in dissociating himself from such men, Jonson also asserts a new
selfhood, a vessel of engaged, rational intelligence set on a course of
personal choice:

                Well, with my own frail pitcher, what to do
                I have decreed; keep it from waves, and press;
                Lest it be jostled, cracked, made naught, or less:
                Live to that point I will, for which I am man,
                And dwell as in my centre, as I can.   (lines 56–60)

It is precisely because he can dismiss agitated and censorious wits in a
blasé manner that Jonson is freed to "honour, love, embrace, and serve"
(line 71) those sealed of his tribe.[62] Because his writing defines a mode of
association, his rational acts of social and moral choice are also gestures
of urbane style and bearing. Jonson's *Leges Conviviales* for the Apollo
Room (in Brome's translation) thus construct sociability along discursive
lines:

                Let none but Guests or Clubbers come,
                Let Dunces, Fools, sad, sordid men keep home.
                Let learned, civil, merry men b'invited ...
                Let none of us be mute, or talk too much,
                On serious things or sacred let's not touch
                With sated heads and bellies ...
                              And let us see
                That all our jests without reflection be.[63]

Dudley North, who manifests the metropolitan complex in so many
other respects, had clearly grasped the link between sophisticated
character and anti-satiric style when he noted that

the world had long since been much better than it is, if writing would have
effected it ... Spectators and Censurers of lives and action, exercise a Trade as
easie as lazy, Scepticisme, Criticisme, and Satyrism seldome miscarry. It is as
familiar to carpe, as hard to write of the times and not to become Satyrical. (p. 78)

It is something like North's conviction, finally unavailable to Juvenal and
his Elizabethan imitators, that it *is* possible to "write of the times" in an
anti-satiric vein that justifies Jonson's lofty condemnation of "scurrility,

---

[62] Geoffrey Walton argues that "being made up of small groups is an important feature"
    of Jonson's poetic *milieu*; "one does not find this sense in English poetry after the
    Restoration," *Metaphysical and Augustan*, p. 38.
[63] *Poems*, 1: 341–342. Cf. Drayton, "The Sacrifice of Apollo," lines 8, 33–40, in *Odes.
    With Other Lyrick Poesies* (1619), *Works*, 2: 357–358. For a text and commentary on the
    leges, see C. H. Hereford and Percy and Evelyn Simpson, eds., *Works* (11 vols. Oxford:
    Clarendon Press, 1925–52), 8: 653–657, 11: 294–300.

and petulancy … petulant paper or scoffing verses." The same conviction motivates his cavalier dismissal of Inigo Jones as one whose "forehead is too narrow for my brand," and it explains his relegation of such poems as "A Satirical Shrub" and "A Little Shrub Growing By" to the *Underwoods*.[64]

The modulation of verse satire into epistle, elegy, and ode was thus a dimension of the search for the formal vehicle and ethical norms of an anti-satiric manner. Already anticipated in the dynamics of verse satire itself, this search began to yield results in early seventeenth-century verse.[65] Chapman, for example, gathered into *Petrarchs Seven Penetentiall Psalms* (1612) a number of epigrammatic reflections on the good life drawn from Virgil, Plutarch, and Epictetus. Sir John Beaumont's poems, published in 1629, were a virtually complete anthology, in translation and imitation, of all the Roman odes, elegies, epistles, and epigrams on which Caroline examinations of the good life typically drew. Drayton's *Odes. With Other Lyrick Poesies* (1619) and *Elegies upon Sundry Occasions* (1627) contained, outside of Jonson's *œuvre*, the most successful (and later, most frequently anthologized) experiments in modulation of the social voice. His epistle to Henry Reynolds, for example, persuasively defined the intimate and exclusive tone appropriate to the pursuit of the moral and aesthetic distinctions of the good life:

> My Dearely loved friend how oft haue we,
> In winter evenings (meaning to be free)
> To some well chosen place us'd us to retire;
> And there with moderate meate, and wine, and fire,
> Haue past the howres contentedly with chat,
> Now talk'd of this, and then discours'd of that.[66]

Drayton's exploration of what he called the "mixed kind" of the Horatian ode helped to establish the social elasticity of this form,[67] while his handling of elegy opened the possibility of softening satiric force into a milder and more subjective affect.[68]

---

[64] *Discoveries*, lines 335, 350; "To a Friend, an Epigram of Him," line 14; *Underwoods* XX, XXXI; on the significance of the last two poems for the place of satire in Jonson's *œuvre*, see Joseph Summers, *The Heirs of Donne and Jonson* (New York: Oxford University Press, 1970), pp. 22–23.

[65] See D. J. Palmer, "The Verse Epistle," in Malcolm Bradbury and David Palmer, eds., *Metaphysical Poetry* (1970; rpt. Bloomington, Indiana: Indiana University Press, 1971), pp. 73–100.　　　　[66] Lines 1–6, in *Works*, 3: 226.

[67] Preface to *Odes. With Other Lyrick Poesies*, *Works*, 2: 345. On the social elasticity and flexible style of the English "Horatian" ode, see Robert Shafer, *The English Ode to 1660. An Essay in Literary History* (Princeton University Press, 1918), pp. 31–34, 114.

[68] See, e.g., "To My Noble Friend Master William Browne, of the evill time," *Works*, 3: 209–212.

Above all, however, it was Jonson, beginning with the epigrams he called "the ripest of my studies," who most effectively transformed the earlier satiric manner into a newly resilient anti-satiric resource.[69] As Jonson declared in his "Epistle to Elizabeth, Countess of Rutland," his epigrams and other poems were social rituals, Orphic summonings wherein

> all, that have but done my muse the least grace,
> Shall thronging come, and boast the happy place
> They hold in my strange poems, which, as yet,
> Had not their form touched by an English wit.   (lines 79–82)

This appropriation of the epigram for socially celebratory purposes opened up for later poets a choice between the less fashionable and declining manner of the harsh, corrective quip and the more composed and sophisticated manner of distinctive choice and compliment, a manner that discriminated good from bad "not to change the bad," but "to show that one can discriminate between vice and virtue and that one will affirm the good."[70] Taking his motto – *tanquam explorator* – from Seneca's willingness "to cross over into the enemy's camp," Jonson displays a penchant for "Vexing rude subjects into comelinesse."[71] His celebrations of virtue dramatize as a matter of moral and social choice his aesthetic attempt to secure a new poetic territory in the very wasteland where earlier English satirists had lost themselves.

Combining "the classical ideal of exploration" with "the subsequent recovery of a flexible position from which new discovery can be made,"[72] Jonson's modulation of poetic praise and blame is thus the discursive vehicle for the social mobility and moral questing of a new kind of metropolitan man, one who redeems "the necessary dynamism of existence."[73] Because "the will to withdraw is opposed by the will to invade and acquire," the tropes of turn and circumference are integrated

---

[69] For contrasts between Jonson's poised epigrams and the salty work of his predecessors, "To My Book," and "To My Mere English Censurer"; cf. Wesley Trimpi, *Ben Jonson's Poems: A Study of the Plain Style* (Stanford University Press, 1962), pp. 167–176.

[70] Earl Miner, *The Cavalier Mode from Jonson to Cotton* (Princeton University Press, 1971), p. 273.

[71] "In the Memory of the Most Worthy Beniamin Johnson," line 56, in *The Plays and Poems of William Cartwright*, ed. G. Blakemore Evans (Madison: University of Wisconsin Press, 1951), p. 513. On Jonson's motto and Seneca's *Epistolae Morales*, 2.4–5, see Richard Peterson, *Imitation and Praise in the Poems of Ben Jonson* (New Haven: Yale University Press, 1981), pp. 9–10.

[72] Trimpi, *Ben Jonson's Poems*, p. 174.

[73] Thomas M. Greene, *The Light in Troy: Imitation and Discovery in Renaissance Poetry* (New Haven: Yale University Press, 1982), p. 277.

in Jonson's poetry with figures of stand and center.[74] Jonson's famous tributes to William Roe (*Epigrammes* 128) and to John Selden (*Underwoods* 14) play movement against stasis, circumference against center, thereby describing the route by which consciousness actively appropriates the world even while it closes off or completes the circle of the self and its elite company. Just as the cultured devotees of the good life can, as a loosely constituted and "open elite," disperse as individuals without breaking the spiritual circumference of the circle that actually becomes incarnate on the occasions when they meet, so the self-possession of each individual, which is the mark of his membership in the circle, enables him to explore in moral security, "To extract, and choose the best of all ... known."[75]

The interdependent circles of the self and its chosen society form the basis of Jonson's moral universe. If one decisive factor in his poetic definitions of the moral self is the dramatic haecceity with which he "performs" his acts of inclusion and exclusion, then another is the disciplinary force of his virtuous audience, which governs the very rhetorical terms in which he performs.[76] The root sense of "conviviality" nicely suggests the extent to which intimate association makes both the world and the self available to Jonson's consciousness. For Jonson, society makes life happy by giving expression to the self through the reflexive medium of performance; it simultaneously makes life good by enforcing the moral and artistic decorum that dictate the terms of the performance. In this respect, the neoclassical impulse of "pruning and selecting" in order to produce the best shared with Puritanism not only an ideal of refinement,[77] but a sense that "goodness of character," no longer so clearly linked to traditional status, required not only "the inner conviction of the individual but community accreditation, a validating social consensus."[78] It is the embodiment of Roman virtues, reflected in the very name of Sir Horace Vere, that actually enables Jonson, too, to become "a Horace, or a muse as free."[79]

---

[74] Ibid., p. 278; Peterson's criticism (p. 21), paraphrased here, of Greene's earlier essay on "Ben Jonson and the Centered Self," is largely answered by Greene's further treatment of Jonson in *The Light in Troy*.

[75] "To William Roe," line 3, *The Complete Poems*, p. 84.

[76] On Jonson's poems as performances, see Greene, *The Light in Troy*, pp. 281, 287–288; on the relation of virtuoso performance to lyric appropriation, and of the "open" social circle to an audience, see Toliver, *Lyric Provinces in the Renaissance*, pp. 71–74, 88–90.

[77] Patrick Crutwell, *The Shakespearian Moment and Its Place in the Poetry of the Seventeenth Century* (New York: Columbia University Press 1955), p. 220.

[78] Michael McKeon, *The Origins of the English Novel, 1600–1740* (Baltimore: Johns Hopkins University Press, 1987), p. 194. Cf. Maus, *Ben Jonson and the Roman Frame of Mind*, p. 142.

[79] "To Sir Horace Vere" (*Epigrammes* 91), line 4, in *The Complete Poetry*, p. 64.

The cumulative effect of the ritual inclusions and exlusions that shape the corporate *œuvre* of Jonson and his imitators is to define the aesthetic qualities, social ideals, and moral traits of the good life. The temptation to summarize the content of this life in the form of a list reflects the importance of the list or catalogue as a resource to the poets who defined and celebrated it. The two most imposing classical models for this technique, Horace's second epode and Martial's epigram to Julius Martial (10.47), were both translated by Jonson (*Underwoods* 85, Ungathered Verse, 125) and in fact became two of the most frequently translated poems in seventeenth-century England.[80]

As much aesthetic as moral exercises, these poems' archetypal celebrations of the good life in catalogue form perforce assume "a pertinence principle which is socially constituted and acquired" and which stylizes life by enabling the poet "to pick out and retain, from among the elements offered... all the stylistic traits – and only those – which, when relocated in the universe of stylistic possibilities, distinguish ...the elements selected."[81] The strong schematic resources of the epigram were especially well suited to the elaboration of such implicit "principles of pertinence." The epigram's paradigmatic selections of virtuous pleasures defined social norms akin to the ideals enforced in Jonson's *leges conviviales* and other poetic tavern-rules. Like those rules, the epigram's norms excluded even as they included, so that the appropriation of features of the good life by the poet and for his "equall friends" was simultaneously a decontextualizing or disentangling of these features from the complex particularity of their socio-economic setting.

Selectivity of this kind accords with the combined features of hyperintellection and *blasé* attitude, the "effecting of distances" in the act of choice, that Simmel identifies as the traits necessitated by the complexity of metropolitan life. Camden had already linked London's "breed of excellent and choice wits" to the capital's "superabundance of

---

[80] Horace's "Beatus ille ... " was translated by Francis Beaumont, Sir John Beaumont, Sir Richard Fanshawe, Thomas Randolph, Alexander Brome, Abraham Cowley, Thomas Creech, John Dryden, and Thomas Fletcher; Martial 10.47 was translated by Randolph, Cowley, Fanshawe, Mildmay Fane, Edward Sherburne, Owen Felltham, Robert Fletcher, John Ashmore, and John Wilson. The fortunes of Horace's *beatus ille*, and more broadly of the good life, are tracked through the seventeenth and eighteenth centuries in Maren-Sofie Røstvig, *The Happy Man: A Study in the Metamorphosis of a Classical Ideal* (2nd edn. 2 vols. New York: Humanities Press, 1962). Cf. David Norbrook, "Marvell's 'Horatian Ode' and the Politics of Genre," in Thomas Healy and Jonathan Sawday, eds., *Literature and the English Civil War* (Cambridge University Press, 1990), p. 151.

[81] Pierre Bourdieu, *Distinction: A Social Critique of the Judgement of Taste*, tr. Richard Nice (Cambridge, Mass.: Harvard University Press, 1984), p. 50.

all things which belong to the furniture or necessity of man's life." By the early seventeenth century, however, the amenities of London had expanded to include "witty, learned, noble and pleasant discourses all day ... variety of wits ... delicate wines and rare fruits, with excellent music and admirable voices, masques and plays, dancing and riding, diversity of games ... poems, histories and strange inventions of wit ... rich apparel, precious jewels ... royal buildings and rare architecture."[82] The development of fashionable life had made London, as Edward Waterhouse explains in *The Gentleman's Monitor* (1665),

> a Collection and Digest of all men and things, to all ends and accomplishments of life, Learned, Mechanique, Religious, Civil, in all Faculties, of all Nations, of all Ages, of all Humours, of all Sexes; There are the best Preachers, the best Physicians, the best Lawyers, the best Traders, the best Artsmen in the Nation to be had and met with; There are Commodities the best and most general for all purposes to be bought, for Food, Clothing, Medicine, Muniment, Thrift, Recreation, serious and pleasant; There are to be seen and obtained, Rich Wives, Spruce Mistresses, Pleasant Houses, Good Dyet, Rare Wines, Neat Servants, Fashionable Furniture, Pleasure and Profits the best of all sorts; there are Friends of all kinds, for all seasons and conditions; There is the best Exchange for Money, the best Market for Wares, the best Security for Wealth, the best Imployment for Children, the best Nursery for Wisdom and Conversation. (p. 295)

Not identical with this boosterish list, but overlapping at many significant points with it, the choice life that evolved in the new social mode was inseparable from the new techniques of self-fashioning and socialization made available by metropolitan life.

As is suggested by many of its common tropes – the halcyon calm amid the storm, the enclosed garden, the stars or fireside against the night, the coterie, the happy tavern, the sessions of wits, the choice anthology – the social mode shared with such new metropolitan phenomena as pleasure gardens, exclusive and enclosed squares, clubs, private indoor theaters, and the enclosed coach and sedan in a process of appropriation by interiorization. As much a "Collection and Digest of all men and all things" as the city itself, the poetic ideal of the good life resembled nothing so much as another new feature of early seventeenth-century life, the rise of private collecting and the formation of a rudimentary museum culture.[83] In the many poems they wrote on gardens, houses, paintings,

---

[82] Nicholas Breton, *The Court and the Country* (1618), quoted in Smuts, *Court Culture and the Origins of a Royalist Tradition in Early Stuart England*, p. 65.

[83] The three great international collections gathered by Charles I, the Earl of Arundel, and the Duke of Buckingham were but the most prestigious examples of a fashion that extended from such bibliophiles and connoisseurs as Sir Robert Cotton, Elias Ashmole, John Selden, Peter Lely, and John Tradescant to such compulsive squirrels as George Thomason and Samuel Pepys.

music, and collections, the poets who followed Jonson were extending Jonson's own search for ways to "showcase reality."[84] When Jonson's poetic voice commands Selden to "Stand forth my object,"[85] it declares its power to select and display distinction. As "*my* object," Selden becomes, like "*my* Roe" and countless other figures, a choice exhibit in Jonson's personal gallery of worthies. Like the choicest of the new art collections, which aestheticized the earlier phenomenon of the wonder-cabinet by selecting from the heterogeneity of artifacts "discrete, and exemplary" instances of stylistic distinction,[86] Jonson's gallery, in its overall display of decorum, becomes an appropriative device that enhances self-definition.

The afflatus of poems like "To Penshurst" and the epigram "Inviting a Friend to Supper" derives not only from the pleasures of choice or decontextualization, but also from the recombination of isolated traits, ideals, and qualities as a totally distinguished *ensemble*. This ensemble creates what Pierre Bourdieu has called "an interminable circuit of inter-legitimation," in which the "play of cultured allusions and analogies endlessly pointing to other analogies" creates "a complex web of factitious experiences, each answering and reinforcing all the others" (p. 53). In contrast to verse satire, where the loose, associational structure of metonymy had led the quest for distinction along a chain of social surfaces from which moral substance appeared to vanish, celebrations of the good life, built on inter-legitimating analogies, could achieve more resonantly metaphorical effects. In Jonson's epigram "Inviting a Friend to Supper," for example, it is the paradigmatic principle of selection, adapted to the schematic, serial frame of epigram, that enables the poet to build up from "a particular set of interfused pleasures" – the analogous, inter-legitimating virtues of the host, guest, food, books, wine, conversation, and company – the illusion of weight and substance to which he can finally give the name "liberty" (line 42).[87]

It is perhaps the fact that "analogy, functioning as a circular mode of thought, makes it possible to tour the whole area of art and luxury *without ever leaving it*" that accounts for what others have identified in Jonson as the ethical "combination of motion with fixity," or the "activity of reception" that reconciles "stability with mobility."[88] Possessing *chez lui* the virtues of the circle, the poet in effect never leaves it, even though

---

[84] Toliver, *Lyric Provinces in the Renaissance*, p. 100.

[85] "An Epistle to Master John Selden," line 29.

[86] Steven Mullaney, "The Rehearsal of Cultures," in *The Place of the Stage: License, Play, and Power in Renaissance England* (University of Chicago Press, 1988), p. 62.

[87] Greene, *The Light in Troy*, p. 282.

[88] Peterson, *Imitation and Praise in the Poems of Ben Jonson*, p. 25; Greene, *The Light in Troy*, p. 282.

he continues to fill his circle with "general knowledge; ... men, manners too."[89] In one particularly striking instance of this paradoxical stasis-in-motion, Jonson asks "When I run, / Ride, sail, am coached, know I how far I have gone, / And my mind's motion not?" Here Jonson links the phenomenon of sedentary travel with the new vehicle that perhaps epitomized the reciprocity between the bustling activity of the metropolis and the security of privatized domains. At the end of the sixteenth century, Stow had already remarked that "of late yeares the vse of coatches brought out of Germanie is taken vp, and made ... common" (1: 84). As a social insider at a later date, however, Sir William Cavendish clearly appreciated the strange combination of publicity and privacy that made it possible for socialites to attend "the most publique, and most received places of entertainment" and then to "*retire* to their Coach, and so prepare for another company."[90] Even more than the coach, the newly fashionable sedan – as its etymology suggests – was the ultimate in sedentary devices, providing the means of settling with total security into the habitable environment being carved out of the metropolis. Unlike the coach, which, as Henry Peacham noted, required that its owners pass briefly through public space when they exited, the sedan could be admitted directly "into a Ladies chamber, had to the fire, dried, rubb'd, and made cleane both within and without" without ever exposing its occupant.[91]

As this small example suggests, the paradoxical stability and mobility of the new metropolitan self was a function of inhabiting a "circuit of inter-legitimation." Built up within the structure and dynamics of individual poems, within Jonson's *œuvre*, within the larger body of poetry that *œuvre* enabled, and ultimately within the sphere of social relations it helped to shape, a metaphorical system of mutually reinforcing values yielded the ethical substance of a new way of life. In Sir John Suckling's summons of John Hales to London, the round of urban pleasures constitutes the circle within which these two companions achieve their social authenticity as "Masters of truth":

> come to Town; 'tis fit you show
> Your self abroad, that men may know
> (Whate'er some learned men have guest)
> That Oracles are not yet ceas't;
> There you shal find the wit, and wine
> Flowing alike, and both divine;
> Dishes, with names not known in books,

---

[89] "An Epistle to Master John Selden" (*Underwoods* 14), line 32, in *The Complete Poetry*, p. 148.   [90] *Horae Subseciuae*, p. 119; italics mine.
[91] *Coach and Sedan*, sigs. B3–B3v.

And lesse amongst the Colledge-Cooks,
With sauce so pregnant that you need
Not stay till hunger bids you feed.
The sweat of learned Jonson's brain,
And gentle Shakespear's eas'er strain,
A hackney-coach conveys you to,
In spite of all that rain can do:
And for your eighteen pence you sit
The Lord and Judge of all fresh wit.
News in one day as much w'have here
As serves all Windsor for a year...
Then think what Company's designed
To meet you here, men so refin'd
Their very common talk at boord,
Makes wise, or mad a young Court-Lord,
And makes him capable to be
Umpire in's Fathers Company.
Where no disputes for forc't defence
Of a man's person for his sence
Take up the time, all strive to be
Masters of truth, as victory.[92]

The irony of such cultural legitimation is that the gentrification of London was *overdetermined*, that the process by which the gentry appropriated London for their needs and purposes was also a process – essential in the transition to capitalism – by which the gentry were themselves urbanized. The urbane celebration of virtuous pleasure and cultured leisure defined a cosmopolitan freedom that had important market aspects. It would be crude but not entirely inaccurate to credit the Caroline social mode as the first consumerist literature. Insofar as it promoted "differentiation, refinement, and the enrichment" of the person, it participated in the process of "growing personal difference within the public" that Simmel identifies with metropolitan life. In celebrating the good life, Caroline writers transmuted the luxury pursuits of "the Town" – its specialized markets, services, entertainments, and pleasures – without entirely transcending them. One may say of these writers what Simmel says of other metropolitan elites: distinction may appear to be an attribute of the competitor, but it also marks him as a consumer, as the target of an ever-specializing market (in books, clothes, services, entertainment, etc.).

This overdetermined connection between the urban market and the elite showcase is apparent in the collateral development of the prose

[92] "[A Summons to Town]," lines 11–40, in *The Works of Sir John Suckling: The Non-Dramatic Works*, ed. Thomas Clayton (Oxford: Clarendon Press, 1971), pp. 70–71.

character, another genre of metropolitan sophistication that was said by a contemporary to be "written by the Best witts, the Best men learne from them."[93] As the favored contemporary terms "characterisme" or "charactery" suggest, the genre was understood as a form of activity, as a version of that "mastery... to discern, what every nature, every disposition will bear" that Jonson called *Ingeniorum discrimina*. Derived from "sundry passages in the world," the self-described "accurate and quick description"[94] of the character was, like the concentrated "point" of epigram, adapted to the increasing pace and scale of metropolitan life. "More Seneca than Cicero,"[95] its compressed and syncopated style could assume principles of pertinence without having to declare them. It "gives you the hint of a discourse, but discourses not," one contemporary explained. In the claim of another that it was "not much Satyricall nor criticall [but] only glances"[96] we can see the presence both of *blasé* attitudes and of a new pictorial connoisseurship that was transforming the urban landscape into a voluptuous domain for gratuitous voyeurism. The tendency of the character "to make more and more distinctions" by "subdividing" urban *topoi*[97] not only replicated the diversification accompanying the urbanizing process; it transformed that process, a disaster in the minds of traditional moralists, into an asset for cosmopolitans. Diversity, Richard Brathwait noted, was a resource "in these more refined times of ours," when "nothing but rarities (bee they ever so light) can afford delight."[98] In the search for ever more specialized types – button-makers, tooth-drawers, night-soil-men, and French lutenists – the older traditions of prose grotesquerie yielded to an alcove realism that interpreted the deforming of the body as a hyperspecialized adaptation to its specific urban place and function. Saltonstall's water-man, for example, was "like a piece of Hebrew, spelled backward... for he rows one way and looks another" (sig. D9v). The profession of Lenton's gentleman-usher was betrayed by "the smallness of his legs" (p. 85), and Earle's trumpeter was "the elephant with the great trunk" who makes "a storm perpetually in his cheeks, and his look is like his noise, blustering and tempestuous" (p. 82). Brathwait's rope-maker, weaving his way backwards, was "the Lobsters Executor, and gets his living contrary to all men" (sig. B4). Feeding off a diversifying process that would ultimately yield the Parisian *quatorzième* and the hunchback who rented

[93] Bodl. MS Add. A.301, quoted in Benjamin Boyce, *The Theophrastan Character in England to 1642* (Cambridge, Mass.: Harvard University Press, 1947), p. 186.
[94] John Stephens, *Satyricall Essayes. Characters and Others* (1615), t.p.; R. M. *Micrologia*, sig. A2.   [95] Richard Flecknoe, *Enigmaticall Characters*, p. 92.
[96] *Characterismi* (1631, 1636), rpt. in Leota Snider Willis, *Francis Lenton: Court Poet* (Philadelphia: University of Pennsylvania Press, 1931), pp. 57–58; *Micrologia*, sig. A2v.
[97] Boyce, *The Theophrastan Character*, p. 165.   [98] *Whimzies*, sigs. A5–A5v.

out his hump as a curbside writing-desk, the prose character marks a crucial stage in what Jacques LeGoff has called the "urbanization of folklore."[99] Like the local-color settings of Caroline comedy, or the collection of street cries into ballad medleys and of street peddlers on the backs of playing cards, the prose character helped to produce a "social picturesque," a "populist objectivism" that, working through "distant proximity," legitimized the burgeoning variety of urban classes and life-forms.[100]

In view of Bourdieu's argument that such aestheticized realism "is a basic element in the relationship of the petite bourgeoisie to the working or peasant classes and their traditions" (p. 58), it is not surprising to find in the essentially "genteel" form of the character a new "bourgeois" tendency to legitimize the process of urbanization by approving and exploiting the burgeoning variety of urban life-forms. Given the constant search for novelty, the technique of innovating by subdividing, and the "framing" of character in discrete time and place, character-writing quite naturally expanded, by sketching the pleasurable or disgusting "character" of particular and typical places, into the landscape of London itself, a city become such "a great World," Donald Lupton said, "there are ... many little worlds in Her."[101] Earle's sketches of such places as "A tavern," "A bowl alley," and "Paul's Walk" were thus followed by R. M.'s London sketches in *Micrologia. Characters or Essayes, of Persons, Trades, and Places, offred to the City and Country* (1629) and by Donald Lupton's twenty-four London vignettes in *London and the Countrey Carbonadoed and Quartered into Seuerall Characters* (1632), where the Caroline improvements to a city "always mending" transformed London into "a great Booke faire Printed, *Cum Priuilegio Regis*" (p. 8).

In other ways, too, the cultivation of genteel, urbane pleasures was overdetermined by nascent bourgeois influences. An important corollary of the aesthetic abstraction that rendered the good life in exclusionary spatial terms was an opposition between work and leisure that produced the temporal "occasion." Distinguishing "the tastes of freedom" from the "tastes of necessity,"[102] the importance of the temporal "occasion" was itself overdetermined, not only because the contrasts between work and leisure, necessity and liberty, originated in the reorganization of time

[99] Jacques LeGoff, "The Town as an Agent of Civilization, 1200–1500," in *The Fontana Economic History of Europe*, ed. Carlo M. Cipolla (Brighton: Harvester, 1976), 1: 75, 87–88.   [100] Bourdieu, *Distinction*, p. 58.
[101] *London and the Countrey Carbonadoed and Quartered into Seuerall Characters* (1632), rpt. in *Aungerville Society Reprints* (Edinburgh, 1881–82), p. 59.
[102] Bourdieu, *Distinction*, pp. 55–56.

by the urban bourgeoisie,[103] but also because the occasions when "the wits of the Town ... flocked together"[104] were explicitly understood in terms of the work of producing and accumulating "cultural capital." Herrick and Beaumont, among many others, celebrated the "great overplus," the "precious stock" of wit produced in Jonson's company at the Mermaid, while Donne argued that it was the purpose of wit to be displayed in the vast "hive and warehouse" of the metropolis. In their celebration of happy social occasions, poets established for themselves a privacy and liberty that set them apart from the stress and constraints of the city's tumultuous life. Sir Aston Cockayne's epistolary epigram to Francis Lenton, for example, recalled the privileged times

> when you and I
> Frequently kept together company
> With Master Lightwood, and my Noble Brother
> Sir Andrew Knyveton, and som few such other ...
> While (at the Fleece in Covent Garden) we
> Drank roundly Sack in Rosen Cans and free.[105]

Written just after Strafford's impeachment and execution, Vaughan's elegiacally modulated "A Rhapsodie" reflected on the agitated, plebeian world that lay just outside the Globe Tavern, in night-time London's streets:

> Should we goe now a wandring, we should meet
> With Catchpoles, whores, & Carts in ev'ry street:
> Now when each narrow lane, each nooke & Cave,
> Signe-posts, & shop-doors, pimp for ev'ry knave,
> When riotous sinfull plush, and tell-tale spurs
> Walk Fleet street, & the Strand, when the soft stirs
> Of bawdry, ruffled Silks, turne night to day;
> And the loud whip, and Coach scolds all the way;
> When lust of all sorts, each itchie bloud
> From the Tower-wharfe to Cymbelyne, and Lud,
> Hunts, for a Mate, and the tyr'd footman reeles
> 'Twixt chaire-men, torches, & the hackny wheels:
> Come, take the other dish ...

Turning its back on this tumultuous exterior world, the poem proposed to "drink deep," in order that with

[103] See, e.g., Jacques LeGoff, "Merchant's Time and Church's Time in the Middle Ages," in *Time, Work, and Culture in the Middle Ages*, tr. Arthur Goldhammer (University of Chicago Press, 1980), p. 35.

[104] Suckling, "The Wits [A Sessions of the Poets]," lines 5–6, in *Works*, p. 71.

[105] Habington, "To my noblest friend, Sir I. P. Knight," line 4, in *The Poems of William Habington*, ed. Kenneth Allott (London: University Press of Liverpool, 1948), pp. 83–84; Cockayne, "To my very good Friend Mr. Francis Lenton," in *Small Poems of Divers Sorts*, p. 168.

> mirth we may retyre
> Possessours of more soules, and nobler fire;
> And ... to higher matters flye.[106]

Not only in such expressive tavern-poems as Vaughan's, but in the countless occasional poems set in the gardens, walks, salons, music-rooms and other environs of the metropolis, London became the seat of a new type of inhabitation. The mark of this new sedentarism was the modulation, for the first time in the history of the language, of patriotic into personal sentiment, the investment of private emotion in the surroundings of the metropolis. Even Milton's early poems in the Jonsonian vein evince this possibility. "L'Allegro" and "Il Penseroso," for example, canvass the pleasures of London's theaters and of "Tower'd Cities ... / And the busy hum of men," while Milton's first Latin elegy to Charles Diodati describes how the young poet (in Cowper's trans-lation) visits

> or to smile or weep,
> The winding theatre's majestic sweep;
> The grave or gay colloquial scene recruits
> My spirits, spent in learning's long pursuits.
> Nor always city-pent, when spring calls me forth to roam,
> Expatiate in our proud suburban shades
> Of branching elm that never sun pervades.
> Here many a virgin troop I may descry,
> Like stars of mildest influence gliding by.[107]

A sentimental investment in the pleasures of London is similarly the basis of Herrick's jubilant anticipation of "His returne to London," where the poet reclaims his birthright in a well-connected City family:

> Ravisht in spirit, I come, nay more, I flie
> To thee, blest place of my Nativitie! ...
> I am a free-born Roman; suffer then,
> That I amongst you live a Citizen.
> London my home is: thou by hard fate sent
> Into a long and irksome banishment;
> Yet since cal'd back; henceforward let me be,
> O native countrey, repossest by thee![108]

Insofar as the sentiments attaching to place and occasion were exclusive as well as inclusive, they not only transformed praise into pleasurable

---

[106] "A Rhapsodie," lines 35–47, 63–68, in *Works*, pp. 10–12; on the political circum-stances and meaning of the poem, see F. E. Hutchinson, *Henry Vaughan: A Life and Interpretation* (Oxford: Clarendon Press, 1947), p. 43.

[107] *Latin and Italian Poems of Milton Translated in English Verse* (1808), pp. 9–13; cf. *Elegia Septima*, lines 51–54.

[108] "His Returne to London," lines 3–4, 11–16, in *The Complete Poetry*, pp. 416–417, 320.

sentiment; they also transformed satiric anger and indignation into various forms of disgust. As Bourdieu indicates, "tastes are perhaps first and foremost distates, disgusts provoked by horror or visceral intolerance ('sick-making') of the tastes of others" (p. 56). Because disgusts are typically directed at "the groups closest in social space" (p. 60), gentrified Londoners typically expressed the strongest distastes for those who failed to observe the distinctions between work and leisure – for those, on the one hand, who joined the unrelieved spectacle of vain courtiership (those just above) and for those, on the other hand, who subscribed to the unrelievedly pecuniary ethic of the merchant class (those just below). By "effecting distance" through disgust and *blasé* attitudes, Habington's epistle "To My Worthy Cousin Mr. E. C. In Praise of City Life, in the Long Vacation," thus takes imaginative possession of the city in the seasonal exodus of its most distasteful inhabitants:

> Now's the time alone
> To live here; when the City Dame is gone ...
> We beginne
> To live in silence, when the noyse oth' Bench
> Not deafens Westminster ...
>   And who were busie here,
> Are gone to sow sedition in the shire.
> The ayre by this is purg'd, and the Termes strife,
> Thus fled the City: we the civill life
> Lead happily.   (lines 17–19, 24–26, 29–33)

Thomas Randolph's splendid "Ode to Mr Anthony Stafford to Hasten Him into the Country," "effects distance" by wearing its disgust more openly; it demonstrates a masterly command of the Town's pleasures even while it marshals a vehement distaste for the vapid souls who affect them.[109]

At one extreme, where discourse verged off toward real demeanor, disgust could manifest itself demonstratively in acts of snobbery. A particular variety of the occasional poem is the celebration of offensive or anti-social highjinks. It is probably no accident that the Earl of Surrey, the first Englishman to translate, in Horace's second epode and Martial's epigram 10.47, the most central poems in later definitions of the good life, was also the first poet to memorialize a rowdy night in London – the drunken binge on which he smashed the windows of London citizens with a stone-bow. Simmel observes that in seeking the "qualitative differentiation" that will "attract the attention of the social circle," the

---

[109] Lines 1–16, 28–34, 36, in *The Poems and "Amyntas" of Thomas Randolph*, ed. John Jay Parry (New Haven: Yale University Press, 1917).

metropolite may be "tempted to adopt the most tendentious peculiarities, that is, the specifically metropolitan extravagances of mannerism,
caprice, and precociousness" (p. 57). Brathwait's description of the
seasonal descent of the gentry on the Town as an invasion of Myrmidons
is confirmed, for example, by Aubrey's revelation of the well-known
secret that while Suckling was "civill enough" when "in the country,"
the "Devil got into him when he came to Brentford." Jonson's tribute to
Falkland eschews "riots, at your feasts, / Orgies of drink";[110] yet his
longest epigram "On the Famous Voyage" is but the most famous of the
many seventeenth-century poems celebrating escapades of the most
deliberately outrageous, insulting, and sometimes violent kind.[111]

The relation of such discomposure to the *blasé* attitude that insulates
the self from the metropolis is perhaps broached in the contention of
Deleuze and Guattari that "catatonia" (withdrawal) and "affect"
(assertion) are the two principal nomadic resistances to the legal
uniformity of the state. The *blasé* attitude and the expressive flaunting of
disgust would thus appear to be – as they certainly became in the political
resistance of the "cavalier" social mode to Puritan legality in the
Commonwealth and Protectorate – extremes within a single complex
that "effects distances." The connection of these extremes is perhaps
most evident in the evolution of the witty, explicit, anti-idealistic erotic
elegy that, from Donne and Jonson onward, offered itself as another
means of representing the insusceptibility of the *blasé* self. Following
Ovid, Sir John Beaumont, Sir Thomas Overbury, and Sir Aston
Cockayne had all touted the diversions of metropolitan life as an erotic
remedy. These diversions are celebrated in Suckling's jaunty lyric of
"The careless Lover" and in the dubious connoisseurship of Lovelace's
"La Bella Bona Roba." Coarsened by the general dissemination of the
social mode, and perhaps encouraged by the increasingly irrelevant social
standing of such Restoration aristocrats as Sedley, Buckhurst and
Rochester, the "ideal" of erotic insusceptibility eventually came to
take the exceedingly discomposed form of post-coital drunken carouses
celebrated in Buckhurst's "Letter to Mr. George Etheridge,"
Etheridge's "Answer," and Alexander Radcliffe's *The Ramble: An Anti-
Heroick Poem* (1682).

---

[110] "To the Immortal Memory and Friendship of that Noble Pair, Sir Lucius Cary and Sir
H. Morison" (*Underwoods* 70), lines 103–104, *Complete Poetry*, p. 215.

[111] See, e.g. Francis Beaumont, "The Good Fellow"; Mennes and Smith, "Upon a
Surfeit Caught at Drinking Bad Sack at the George Taverne in Southwarke," and
"Upon Madame Chevreuze Swimming over the Thames"; Matthew Stevenson,
"Upon Some Gentlemen Rowing down the River"; "To My Honoured Friend. A
Gentleman that in a Frollick Would Needs Barb Mee"; Henry Bold, "The
Adventure"; Samuel Sheppard, "A Iourney to Totnam Court."

As Radcliffe's title suggests, one stylistic corollary of social disgust was the development of new kinds of ironic distance in mock-heroic and burlesque, mask-like poses which enabled poets to express condescension and scorn without sacrificing personal composure. Jonson's epigram "On the Famous Voyage" thus uses mock-heroic style to emphasize the moral distance between its gentlemen–heroes and their flaunting escapade in London's filthy underbelly. In a mock-praise of London attributed to Randolph, the gestures of encomium are inverted to burlesque the citizen ethic as narrow and illiberal, as they are as well in Suckling's "Ballad of a Wedding." Davenant's 1635 epistle to Endymion Porter, about "The Long Vacation in London, in Verse Burlesque, or Mock-Verse," is perhaps the first English poem to scorn the baser side of the metropolis in what Dryden later referred to as "the sort of Verse which is called *Burlesque*, consisting of Eight Syllables, or Four Feet":

> Now London's Chief, on Sadle new,
> Rides into Fair of Bartholomew:
> He twirles his Chain, and looketh big,
> As if to fright the Head of Pig,
> That gaping lies on greasy Stall,
> Till Female with great Belly call.[112]

Adapting this style to a lengthy description of London under the Protectorate, Richard Flecknoe defined the "Burlesque or Drolling Poem" as the verbal equivalent of "a Breughel, and (in his kinde), Callot" and associated it specifically with the spirit of refinement and distinction: "as nations grow more polite and witty, they fall upon this strain, it being the luxuriant branches of a flourishing language, and the very intention of it, beyond the accesse of vulgar wits."[113] Dryden would eventually scorn Flecknoe's burlesque as "stuff the town at last despis'd,"[114] but the mock-heroic tenor that made *MacFlecknoe* a model for Augustan satirists suggests one further respect in which the anti-satiric manner of Caroline social verse contributed to the formation of the Augustan sensibility – by identifying in the humorous manipulation of low style a paradoxically more "civilized" alternative to the *saeva indignatio* of earlier English satire. Unlike the hircine "satyre" of the

---

112 Lines 91–96, in *The Shorter Poems*, p. 128; cf. Dryden, *A Discourse Concerning the Original and Progress of Satire* (1693), in W. P. Ker, ed. *Essays of John Dryden* (2 vols. 1899; rpt. New York: Russell and Russell, 1961), 2: 105; see also Ruth Nevo, *The Dial of Virtue: A Study of Poems on Affairs of State in the Seventeenth Century* (Princeton University Press, 1963), p. 189.

113 *The Diarium or Journall* (1656), sigs. A3–A3v.

114 *The Art of Poetry, Written in French by the Sieur de Boileau, Made in English* (1683), line 81, in *The Poetical Works of John Dryden*, ed. George R. Noyes (1909; rpt. Cambridge, Mass.: Houghton Mifflin, 1950), p. 917.

Elizabethans, the mode of burlesque, in its manner of distanced disgust, insulated its practitioners from emotional distraction and social contamination; it was the mark of successful adaptation to the sedentary process.

"The vast vicissitude of forms": institution and dissemination of the social mode

By widening the sphere of metropolitan influence through the ethical transformation of the individual, the cultivation of urbane pleasures in the social mode finally contributed to the dissemination of a new political vision. In this vision, the spread of metropolitan influence expressed itself in London's growing domination of the political nation and its increasingly imperial ambitions. Although the representatives of London's merchant and craftsman classes continued to figure largely in the elite social mode as objects of derision and disgust, a softening of hostility toward – and redefinition of – the citizen-image extended the powers of inter-legitimation to include those inter-class rivals whose labors and virtues were perceived as contributing to the prosperity and imperial potential of the metropolis.[115] Increasingly, "merchants imitated the values, attitudes, and habits of the gentry" and "in return the gentry were exposed to the cosmopolitan ideas and behavior of urban society."[116] Indeed, as the gentry became increasingly urbanized, it contributed to a new form of imperial, august urbanism that in turn redefined the bourgeois ideals and practices of the merchant class. By the Restoration, Edward Waterhouse declared the social changes wrought by London irreversible, claiming that "as all sumptuary Lawes are vanisht by the mixture of gentry with the plebs in Corporations, so ought all grudge between the Country and the City Gentry to be cessated." Matthew Stevenson endorsed the social metamorphosis in which "The Court, and City, like those silken wormes, / Meet in the vast viccissitude

---

[115] Thus Cowley, for example, proudly claimed that "that Citie t'whom I owed before / ...A Father, gave me a Godfather too," "To His Very Much Honoured Godfather, Master A. B.," in *Complete Works*, 1 : 27. Even the ultra-royalist Crashaw could offer an extremely decent epitaph "Vpon Mr. Ashton, a Conformable Citizen" and protestant, "An Epitaph ...," in *The Poems, English, Latin, and Greek, of Richard Crashaw*, ed. L. C. Martin (Oxford: Clarendon Press, 1957), pp. 192–193. See also Herrick's poems "Upon Himself," "To His Kinsman, Sir Thomas Soame," and "To His Worthy Kinsman, Master Stephen Soame," in *The Complete Poetry*, pp. 230, 236, 265.

[116] Richard Grassby, "Social Mobility and Business Enterprise in Seventeenth-Century England," in Donald Pennington and Keith Thomas, eds., *Puritans and Revolutionaries: Essays in Seventeenth-Century History Presented to Christopher Hill* (Oxford: Clarendon Press, 1978), p. 381.

of Formes."[117] Though in origin a matter of ethics and aesthetics, the cultivation of urbanity contributed ultimately to a new social vision in which, as Rochester put it, "London is / Itself the nation, not metropolis."[118]

The appeal of this vision was reinforced by a process of institutionalization and dissemination that made the ideals of the Caroline social mode the basis for a national literature. Within a year of the King's flight from the capital, elegiac recollection was transforming the Stuart Peace and its artifacts into cultural icons.[119] In *London, King Charles His Augusta, or City Royal*, published under Davenant's name in 1648, London itself became a symbolic embodiment of the cultural refinement and social distinction that royalists saw as threatened by revolution. Beginning in 1646, when royalist delinquents were included in the newly enforced Elizabethan and Jacobean laws forbidding recusants to enter London without license, royalists were periodically subjected to banishment from the capital.[120] Personal deprivation of "the delight of conversation" thus frequently became the poetic occasion for gestures of cultural despair:

> Oh London! Center of all Mirth
>   Th'Epitome of English Earth;
> All Provinces are in the streets,
>   And Warwick-shire with Essex meets.
>
> Then Farewell Queen-Street, and the Fields,
>   And Garden that such pleasure yields,
> Oh who would such fair lodgings change,
>   To nestle in a plunder'd Grange.[121]

Although, as the revolutionary "Mansion house of liberty," the metropolis itself became inaccessible, a "frowning... step-dame" to royalists,[122] the institutionalization of metropolitan norms as ethical and

---

[117] *The Gentlemans Monitor* (1665), p. 71; *Poems: Or, a Miscellany of Sonnets, Satyrs, Drollery, Panegyricks, Elegies, &c* (1673), p. 73.

[118] "To His Sacred Majesty, on His Restoration in the Year 1660," lines 5–6, in *The Complete Poems of John Wilmot, Earl of Rochester*, ed. David M. Vieth (New Haven: Yale University Press, 1968), p. 155.

[119] See, e.g., Henry Glapthorne, *White-Hall. A Poem. Written 1642.* (1643), in *The Plays and Poems of Henry Glapthorne*, ed. John Pearson (2 vols. London, 1874), 2: 246–248.

[120] See Paul H. Hardacre, *The Royalists During the Puritan Revolution* (The Hague: Martinus Nijhoff, 1956), pp. 78–79, 130, 135.

[121] Letter of Percy Herbert, Lord Powis, cited in ibid., p. 79; "Of banishing the Ladies out of Town," in *Rump: Or an Exact Collection of the Choysest Poems and Songs Relating to the Late Times* (2 vols. London, 1662), 1: 240.

[122] Aston Cockayne, "To My Wife," in *Small Poems of Divers Sorts* (1658), pp. 188–189; cf. Brome, "Upon the Cavaleers departing out of London" (*Rump*, 1: 298) and "The Lamentation" (*Rump*, 1: 221), in *Poems*, 1: 95–96, 170–172; Lovelace, "A Mock-Song," *Poems*, pp. 154–155.

stylistic resources of human character ensured the possibility of their poetic reproduction. The canonical durability of metropolitan norms could thus offer an interregnum poet like Alexander Brome continuing possibilities for renewal:

> Why mayn't we hope for Restauration, when
> As ancient Poets Townes, the new raise men,
> The tale of Orpheus and Amphion be
> But solid truths with this Mythology?...
> A day will break, when we again may see
> Wits like themselves, club in an harmony.[123]

Built into the polite institution of English letters, the poetic interpretation of the interregnum years as a cultural hiatus or exile needs to be understood as expressing *more* than either crude partisanship or the simple survival of the values and outlook of the *ancien régime*. To the extent that the means of restoring or reproducing the social order were sustained, as a kind of mobile genetic potential, in the ethical and stylistic resources of a new type of character, they must be understood *also* as continuing a persistent vector of social change. In literature, as in other respects, "the dissemination of metropolitan styles and standards of dress, décor, and deportment was essential to the development of the more homogeneous culture of the eighteenth-century English ruling class."[124]

In the same way, neither the harshness of wartime conditions nor the exigencies of partisanship alone can explain the more deeply political nature of the conceptual and stylistic changes that accompanied the modulation of the Caroline good life into "cavalier" acerbity – the tendencies of anacreontic to slip toward coarse catches, of the virtuous pursuit of pleasure to become the libertine flaunting of gratification, of the selective inward turn to become the exclusionary "litany," of anti-satiric detachment to become mockery and burlesque, and of the cultivation of taste to become the display of disgust. Contributing alongside the political climate to this general coarsening was a more deeply institutional process, a process involving simultaneously both the dissemination downward of social values and ideals to a growing body of royalist supporters in the commercial and laboring status groups and the

---

[123] Lovelace, "On Sanazar's being honoured...," in *Poems*, p. 193; Brome, "To Colonel Lovelace on his Poems," lines 11–14, 19–20, in *Poems*, 1: 289. On the urbane use of Ovidian and Horatian motifs of cultural exile by royalist poets, see Graham Parry, "A Troubled Arcadia," in Thomas Healy and Jonathan Sawday, *Literature and the English Civil War* (Cambridge University Press, 1990), p. 43.

[124] Gary Stuart de Krey, *A Fractured Society: The Politics of London in the First Age of Party, 1688–1715* (Oxford: Clarendon Press, 1985), p. 2.

appropriation upwards of popular seriocomic techniques and genres into a single, dominant literary system.

During the passage of the seventeenth century, there is decreasing evidence of the provocative tensions that manifested themselves in the first explosion of urban literature in the Elizabethan period – the tensions, for example, between subversion and conformity in seriocomic prose, between the elite and popular, schematic and serial, inscriptional and oral impulses of the epigram, between correction and complaint, soul and surface in verse satire, between predatory intrigue and romance harmony in the private and public theaters. The raw and inchoate potential of these impulses persisted in a number of ways – through their incorporation as residua in the polite and innovative accomplishments of later urbane writers, through the continuing vitality of popular culture, public theater, and professional writing, and through the almost universal tendency of the newest elite practices and genres to pass into the hands of less able and less educated writers, among whom the resistances of popular tradition were stronger. Throughout the earlier seventeenth century, for example, collections of scourging satires and barbed but wayward epigrams continued to appear alongside their more fully modulated successors in the social mode; and similarly, many of the grotesque techniques of seriocomic prose survived in character-writing, especially as the newer mode was taken up by professionals like Brathwait and Lupton. But decreasingly did these heteroglot survivals threaten to deform or "give the lie" to the manner or vision of their more refined, domesticated, and monological alternatives. In most instances, rather, the older manner was incorporated as a way of reinforcing or "naturalizing" the new, whether in the play of praise and blame in the fundamentally anti-satiric manner of Jonson and his successors, in the adoption of popular romance techniques in the city comedies of Caroline playwrights, in the tendency of character-writing to extend the naturalizing techniques by which Dekker had begun to domesticate the pungent social vision of Greene and Nashe, in the assimilation of the most popular ballad-writers of the revolutionary period (Martin Parker, John Taylor, and John Crouch) to the royalist cause, or in the adaptation of popular crudity to the elite projects of burlesque and mock-heroic. The contribution of all these changes to the definition of a cohesive and dominating literary system is confirmed by a correspondingly more vigorous tendency to regard wholly unassimilable Elizabethan survivals as marginal, subliterary, or "out of style."

In its stabilizing capacity to orchestrate a repertoire of styles and modes in a way that the formerly dominant courtly manner had not, the dissemination of a generalized *vers de société* might be said to have successfully urbanized folklore and appropriated popular tradition. However, the overdetermination of the urbanizing process – the overlap of gentrification with commercial expansion – suggests that confluence and *rapprochement* more accurately describe this newly institutionalized combination of classical urbanity with bourgeois influence. The national literature did not become homogeneous, nor were its elements identical – a world of difference still separated Dryden's *Miscellanies* from Tom D'Urfey's *Wit and Mirth*, or Ned Ward's *London Spy* from Pope's *Dunciad*. But the general interorientation of various urbane *decora*, at least from within the institution, made this difference negotiable in ways that the differences between, say, *Astrophil and Stella* and Greene's cony-catching pamphlets, were not. As D'Urfey sang, "The Town may da-da-damn me for a Poet, but they si-si-sing my Songs for all that."

The phenomenon of "Interregnum" anthologies – generally known as "drolleries" – nicely illustrates both the institutional framework within which the social mode was disseminated and the social over-determination that enabled this framework to encompass such a variety of literary works. Begun by Richard Tottel in 1557, the great age of Elizabethan poetical miscellanies – with their songs, sonnets, and pastorals – ended with the publication of Davison's *A Poetical Rhapsody* in 1602. Such occasional collections as *Iusta Edouardo King Naufrago* (1638) and *Jonsonus Virbius* (1638) represent the only form in which poets were anthologized over the next forty years.[125] The first edition of *The Academy of Complements* in 1640, however, began a new wave of anthologizing that, counting issues and editions, produced forty "drolleries" alone in as many years.[126] As such titles as *Choyce Drollery* (1656), *Wit and Drollery* (1661), and *Merry Drollery* (1661) suggest, the drolleries share with the contemporaneous "droll" or privately performed facetious skit, a set of rubrics that include witty and convivial mockery, an affectation of frankness and "realism," and an air of exclusivity.[127] A few Elizabethan poems appeared in these anthologies, but the overwhelming favorites were poets in the newer social mode – Drayton (whose ground-breaking epistle to Henry Reynolds appeared frequently), Jonson, the Beaumonts, Carew, Suckling, Davenant,

[125] Shelagh Hunter, unpublished study of *The Miscellanies of Light Verse in the Commonwealth Period* (St Hilda's College, 1946–48).

[126] C. C. Smith, "The Seventeenth-Century Drolleries," *Harvard Library Bulletin*, 6 (1952), 40–51.

[127] According to Marchamont Nedham, the "right knack of living in the world" was a matter of being "*Ioco-Serio, Betwixt Earnest and Jest*, which the most learned in the languages of the suburbs have translated *drolling*," *Mercurius Politicus* (1657), cited in James Holstun, *A Rational Millennium: Puritan Utopias of Seventeenth-Century England and America* (Oxford University Press, 1987), p. 268.

Cowley, Habington, Cartwright and (in slightly later collections) Waller, Dryden, Etheridge, Behn, Sedley, and Wycherly. The tendency of the anthologies to canonize the social mode is perhaps epitomized by the 1672 publication of *The Poems of Ben Jonson Junior*.

Typically professing to be collected by "A Person of Quality" and to represent "the refined'st Witts of the Age," the collections were clearly inseparable from the larger ethical transformations associated with metropolitan life. Titles like *The Academy of Complements*, *Wits Interpreter* (1655), *The Marrow of Complements* (1655) and *The New Academy of Complements* (1671) reflect in small the considerable overlap in the drolleries between canonical collection, commonplace book, courtesy manual, and pocket dictionary; it is reflected more fully in the expansive title of *The Academy of Pleasure. Furnished with all Kinds of Complementall Letters, Discourses, and Dialogues; with Variety of New Songs, Sonets, and Witty Inventions. Teaching All Sorts of Men, Maids, Widows, &c. to Speak and Write Wittily, and to Bear Themselves Gracefull for the Obtaining of their Desired Ends: How to Discourse and Demean Themselves at Feasts and Merry-Meetings at Home and Abroad, in the Company of Friends or Strangers. How to Retort, Quibble, Jest, or Joke, and How to Return an Ingenious Answer upon any Occasion Whatsoever* (1656). The inclusion of commonplace phrases, exemplary letters, games, puzzles, rebuses and codebooks in many collections reflects a fundamental absorption with social codes; but unlike the earlier canting dictionaries, where the aim was to decode an unstable and menacing environment, the function of the drolleries was to *encode* sophistication and selectivity. The publication of drolleries peaked between 1653 and 1658, when approximately twenty collections or editions appeared, and when other new forms of metropolitan literature were appearing in John Crouch's night- and low-life newspapers, the *Mercurius Democraticus* (a "Perfect Nocturnall") (April, 1652–February, 1654) and *Mercurius Fumigosus, Or the Smoking Nocturnall* (June, 1654–October, 1655) and in James Howell's *Londonopolis* (1657). Increasingly tight censorship under the Protectorate may have forced many writers out of politics and into these London velleities, but the sudden increase in works dealing with the life of London also reflects a renewed interest in the metropolis at this point. The contributors and compilers of these new works were for the most part lacking the means to follow the court into exile and so had to subsist independently of its financial or cultural support.[128] Meanwhile, mercantilist policy and imperial ambitions were revived by the first

---

[128] See, e.g., Sir John Berkenhead's poem, "Staying in London after the Act for Banishment," in Henry Lawes, *Ayres and Dialogues* (1653), p. 34.

Anglo-Dutch war (1652–54), and several factors – a growing anti-Independent backlash in London, the gradual return of many royalists to the metropolis, the dismissal of the Rump and the creation of the Protectorate – all stirred the cautious hopes for a return to order. London *was one of the chief remaining monuments of this order, and insofar as* the Caroline mode was one of its continuing institutional embodiments, it is not surprising that the younger Town poets represented in the drolleries – Bold, Brome, Flecknoe, Jordan, Mennes, Smith, and Stevenson – gathered under its shadow, side-by-side with Jonson and his Caroline contemporaries. Having begun before the Interregnum, the new wave of social verse anthologies also survived it, continuing the process of institutionalization well into the Restoration in such collections as *Covent Garden Drollery* (1672), *Westminster Drollery* (1672), *Holborn Drollery* (1673), and *London Drollery or the Wits Academy* (1673).

There is surely a point in the later history of its dissemination when *vers de société* shaded off in various directions – toward songbook collections like *Vinculum Societatis, or the Tie of Good Company* (1687) in one direction, toward the poetic miscellanies of Dryden, Tate, Tonson, and Dennis in another, and toward the popular amusements of Ned Ward, Tom D'Urfey, and James Wright in yet another. But the precise points of divergence are difficult to locate, and in any case a systemic ethical and literary decorum affiliates all of these strands to a general framework of urbane expression.

The institutional function of this framework was perhaps broached in Pope's objection that "this modern Custom of appearing in Miscellanies is very useful to the Poets, who, like other Thieves, escape by getting into a Crowd, and herd together like *Banditti*, safe only in their Multitude."[129] As Pope's objection suggests, the collection and dissemination of a generalized *vers de société* helped to monopolize societal resources by monopolizing "the instruments for appropriation of those resources (writing, reading, and other decoding techniques)." In other words, the institutionalized norms of social verse could operate impersonally, supporting a "Crowd" or "Multitude" of incompetent poetic functionaries. They could, like the educational apparatus described in Bourdieu's analysis of "cultural capital," give "the same value to all holders of the same certificate," making it "possible to relate all qualification-holders ... to a single standard, thereby setting up a *single market* for all cultural capacities." As with attempts to reform or rationalize societal resources at the Restoration – whether in the attempt to rationalize a national

---

[129] Pope to Wycherly (May 20, 1709), in *The Correspondence of Alexander Pope*, ed. George Sherburn (5 vols. Oxford: Clarendon Press, 1956), 1:60.

language, to reform education, or to further stratify consumer goods[130]
– the transformation of the individualized and intimate acts of Caroline
poets into an objectified public institution helped to create a new "social
world which, containing within itself the principle of its own con-
tinuation," freed individual "agents from the endless work of creating or
restoring social relations."[131]

The outpouring of imperial and Golden Age motifs that greeted the
restoration of monarchy in 1660 may have adapted to the exigencies of
the moment a fund of classical ideals available to regimes throughout the
Renaissance period.[132] But much of the specific impetus behind this
vision (of "progress, refinement, and the peculiar beatitude of the
age")[133] lay rather in the institutional continuity of the metropolitan
social ideals and public works first developed in the earlier reign of
Charles I. Witnessing the revival of Town life under Charles II, Edward
Waterhouse recalled that it was "in the great years of Trade, from 1630,
to 1640" that "the great flocking to Town first appeared in request," and
Cowley, too, looked back in 1661 upon the earlier Caroline peace as
having consolidated a national destiny:

> all the riches of the globe beside
> Flow'd into thee, with every tide;
> When all that nature did thy soil deny,
> The growth was of thy fruitful industry;
> When all the proud and dreadful sea,
> And all his tributary streams,
> A constant tribute paid to thee;
> When all the liquid world was one extended Thames.[134]

Alongside the ethical and aesthetic changes that attended the development of Town life had come a new appreciation of the role of public
works in defining civilized ideals. Inigo Jones' restoration and remodel-
ling of St. Paul's, a fabric that represented both "Our nation's glory, and
our nation's crime," became a centerpiece of the renewal efforts in this
decade. In Waller's tribute "Upon his Majesties repairing of Paul's"
(1635), this public work of rebuilding was at once a preeminently
civilizing act and an assertion of national power:

[130] See Nicholas Jose, *Ideas of Restoration in English Literature, 1660–71* (Cambridge,
Mass.: Harvard University Press, 1984), pp. 18–19.
[131] Pierre Bourdieu, *Outline of a Theory of Practice*, tr. Richard Nice (Cambridge
University Press, 1977), pp. 187, 189.
[132] Jose, *Ideas of Restoration*, pp. 47, 49; cf. Frances Yates, *Astraea: The Imperial Theme
in the Sixteenth Century* (London: Routledge & Kegan Paul, 1975).
[133] Jose, *Ideas of Restoration*, p. 47.
[134] Waterhouse, *The Gentlemans Monitor*, pp. 169, 293; Cowley, *A Discourse Concerning
the Government of Oliver Cromwell* (1661), in *Complete Works in Verse and Prose*, 2: 296.

He, like Amphion, makes those quarries leap
Into fair figures from a confused heap;
For in his art of regiment is found
A power like that of harmony in sound.
    Those antique minstrels sure were Charles-like kings,
Cities their lutes, and subjects' hearts their strings...
    Glad, though amazed, are our neighbour kings,
To see such power employed in peaceful things;
They list not urge it to the dreadful field;
The task is easier to destroy than build.[135]

Manifesting royal power in an urban mode, the effect of such works is to inter-legitimate city and nation, bourgeois community and royal seat. The effect is one-sided, certainly, in Waller's baroque prospect on the "seat of empire" from *St James Park, as Lately Improved by His Majesty* (1661) or in the "fair view" of "The town, the river, and the fields" in Waller's poem *Upon her Majesty's New Buildings at Somerset House* (1665). But the inter-legitimizing effect is both more balanced and more potent in Cowley's celebration of the latter subject, where

Behold, in a long bending row,
How two joint Cities make one glorious Bow:
The Midst, the noblest place, possess'd by Me;
Best to be seen by all, and all O'ersee.
Which way soe'r I turn my joyful eye,
Here the great Court, there the rich Town, I spy;
On either side dwells Safety and Delight;
Wealth on the Left, and Power upon the Right.[136]

In Pope's *Windsor Forest* (1713), the rebuilding of Whitehall, burnt in 1698, provides a basically identical focus for the mutual reinforcement of aristocratic and bourgeois values:

Behold! Augusta's glittering spires increase,
And Temples rise, the beauteous Works of Peace.
I see, I see where two fair Cities bend
Their ample Bow, a new White-Hall ascend!
There mighty nations shall inquire their Doom,
The World's great Oracle in Times to come...
The Time shall come, when free as Seas or Wind
Unbounded Thames shall flow for all mankind,

---

[135] Lines 11–16, 61–64, in *Poems*, pp. 16–18. On public architecture as poetic motif, see Robert A. Aubin, *Topographical Poetry in XVIIIth Century England* (New York, 1936), pp. 351–358; Paul Fussell, *The Rhetorical World of Augustan Humanism: Ethics and Imagery from Swift to Burke* (London: Oxford University Press, 1965), ch. 8; Isobel Rivers, *The Poetry of Conservatism, 1600–1745: A Study of Poets and Public Affairs from Jonson to Pope* (Cambridge, Mass.: Rivers Press, 1973), p. 8.

[136] "On the Queen's Repairing Somerset House," in *Works in Verse and Prose*, 1: 164.

> Whole Nations enter with each swelling Tyde,
> And Seas but join the Regions they divide;
> Earth's distant Ends our Glory shall behold,
> And this new World launch forth to seek the Old.[137]

By the time it made its influence felt in the third draft and first published edition of Sir John Denham's *Cooper's Hill* in August, 1642, Waller's celebration of the repair of St. Paul's had transformed London into one of the three cultural symbols (along with Windsor Castle and St. Anne's hill) orchestrated in this topographical meditation:

> I first looke downe
> On Pauls, as men from thence upon the towne.
> Pauls, the late Theme of such a Muse, whose flight
> Hath bravely reacht and soar'd above my height:
> Now shalt thou stand, though Time, or Sword, or Fire,
> Or Zeale (more fierce than they) thy fall conspire,
> Secure, while thee the best of Poets sings,
> Preserv'd from ruine by the best of Kings.[138]

Beset by a "thicker cloud / Of businesse, then of smoake" (III. 28–29), the London of the 1642 published text is further vitiated by the contemporary political "plots" and "mischiefes" (III. 41, 44) that threatened the royalist cause at the outbreak of civil war. In keeping, however, with this version's royalist advocacy of political balance ("Happy when both to the same Center move; / When Kings give liberty and Subjects love," III. 317–318), the cultural achievement undertaken at St. Paul's ramifies in Denham's later treatment of the Thames, where the use of the river to signify the balance of good and evil fortune in earlier drafts gives way to a clearer vision of England's imperial destiny:

> So Thames to London doth at first present
> Those tributes, which the neighbouring countries sent;
> But at his second visit from the East,
> Spices he brings, and treasures from the West;
> Finds wealth where 'tis, and gives it where it wants,
> Cities in Desarts, woods in Cities plants,
> *Rounds the whole Globe, and with his flying towers*
> *Brings home to us, and makes both Indies ours*:
> So that to us no thing, no place is strange
> Whilst thy fair bosome is the worlds Exchange.　　(III. 209–218)

---

[137] Lines 377–380, in *The Poems of Alexander Pope*, ed. John Butt (New Haven: Yale University Press, 1963), p. 208.

[138] Lines 13–20 in "Draft III" of the poem in Brendan O Hehir, ed., *Expans'd Hieroglyphicks: A Critical Edition of Sir John Denham's Cooper's Hill* (Berkeley: University of California Press, 1969), p. 110. Citations incorporated into the text cite draft number in Roman numerals, followed by line number in arabic.

Balancing "East" and "West" by centering "both Indies" in London, the poem sets the imperialist course to be followed in later poems by both Denham and his many imitators. William Godolphin, for example, celebrated the Cromwellian maritime and colonial policies that "make our Isle the World's Exchange." Robert Fage anticipated Denham's further issue of *Cooper's Hill* as a Restoration artifact in 1668 by plagiarizing earlier versions in *St. Leonard's Hill* (1666):

> Look a far off, where the great City stands,
> Who by its riches all the world commands;
> And whose great Ships, bring Spices from the East
> To enrich our Land, and Ingots from the West.[139]

The reverberations that, from Dryden's *Annus Mirabilis* to Pope's *Windsor Forest* and beyond, extended the theme of imperial projection in *Cooper's Hill* demonstrate one major respect in which the metropolitan ethic and style of the early Caroline years transcended their place and time, contributing finally to the expansionist vision of the Restoration and eighteenth century.

Denham's rural prospect on "the happinesse of sweete retir'd content" of course represents another – the extension of ideals of civilized leisure into poetic fictions of retirement. By the mid-seventeenth century, the late-feudal (and residually nomadic) pattern of the royal progress, so successfully exploited by Elizabeth I, was tending toward a more regularized sedentary pattern of seasonal exurbation. Many poems of rural retirement continued to exhibit an anti-urban bias:

> Once how I doted on this jilting town.
> Thinking no heav'n was out of London known,
> Till I her beauties artificial found,
> Her pleasures but a short and giddy round ...
> Quite surfeited with joy I now retreat
> To the fresh air, a homely country seat,
> Good hours, books, harmless sports, and wholesome meat.
> And now at last I've chose my proper sphere,
> Where men are plain and rustic, but sincere.[140]

But as the increasingly urbane pleasures associated with retirement suggest, appreciations of rural life came more and more to represent but

---

[139] Godolphin's Latin poem, which first appeared in *Musarum Oxoniensium Elaiophoria* (1654) is quoted from the English of *State-Poems Continued From the time of O. Cromwel, to the Year 1697* (London, 1709), 1: 13–15, in O Hehir, pp. 284–288. Fage, *St. Leonards Hill. A Poem* (1666), p. 5.

[140] "The Town Life," lines 1–4, 9–13, in *Poems on Affairs of State: Augustan Political Verse, 1660–1714*, ed. George deForest Lord et al. (7 vols. New Haven: Yale University Press, 1963–1975), 4: 62–67; cf. Thomas Ravenscroft, "In Derision of a Country Life," in *The New Oxford Book of Seventeenth-Century Verse*, ed. Alistair Fowler (Oxford University Press, 1992), p. 738.

another dimension of a social and poetic universe held together by the metropolitan sensibility of tasteful choice. Country and city no longer exemplified conflicting moral absolutes but the different pleasures and advantages available to mobile sophisticates:

> Sir,
> I hate the Countries durt and manners, yet
> I love the silence; I embrace the wit
> And courtship, flowing here in a full tide.
> But loathe the expence, the vanity and pride.
> No place each way is happy.[141]

For many seventeenth-century poets, the boredom of rustication only underlined the fundamentally urbane motives for retirement. Complaining that "the Country now can be no longer born," Charles Hopkins' epistle to Anthony Hammond, for example, longs for the occasions

> When you, and Southerne, Moyle, and Congreve meet,
> The best good Men, with the best-natur'd Wit,
> Good Wine, good Company, the better Feast,
> And whene'er Wicherly is present, best.[142]

While Robert Gould's *Epistles from the Country* begin by jauntily declaring "Happy the Man that from the Town retires," they end with disillusionment at the cultural barrenness of rustic life:

> Ah Wretch! to this unhappy Clime confin'd;
> Lost to my Friends, and cut from Human kind...
> Depriv'd of London, then too little priz'd,
> Before I knew the Blessing I despis'd.
> For Towns, like Tallies, Man for Man does fit,
> And Wit does keenliest whet it self on Wit...

The metropolis thus finally inscribes itself within Gould's poems of retirement, beckoning as a mental *urbs in rus* with all the delights that

> adorn the Arts of Peace!
> What Shoals of People pour thro' ev'ry Street!
> In passing on, what Myriads must you meet!

---

[141] William Habington, "To My Noblest Friend, I. C. Esquire," lines 1–5, in *Poems*, p. 95. Cf. Cowley, *Several Discourses by Way of Essays in Verse and Prose*, in *Complete Works*, 2: 336.

[142] "To Mr Anthony Hammond Esq.; By Mr Charles Hopkins," in Dryden, *Miscellany Poems* (1684), 4: 23; cf. Sir Francis Fane, "To the Late Earl of Rochester, upon the Report of his Sickness in Town, Being Newly Recovered by his Lordships Sojourn in Country," in Nahum Tate, *Poems by Several Hands on Several Occasions* (1685), p. 13; Cotton, *Poems*, ed. John Buxton (Cambridge, Mass.: Harvard University Press, 1958), p. 263; Oldmixon, "The Country Wit," in *Poems on Several Occasions* (1696), p. 22.

> How gay! how richly clad where e'er you come!
> What gallant Youths and Beauties in their Bloom![143]

In Pope's "Epistle to Miss Blount, on her leaving the Town, after the Coronation" (1717), the far more accomplished balance between the "wholsom country air" and the vexation of being "still in town," is perhaps a better indication of the mobile but unified sensibility created by the metropolis.

Given the creation of this sensibility, it is not surprising that so many poems of retirement, like so many country houses themselves, reconstituted urban sophistication in rural outposts. Charles Cotton's estate at Beresford, for example, became a center of urbanity,

> Where now each à la mode Inhabitant,
> Himself and's Manners both do pay you rent,
> And 'bout your house (your Pallace) doth resort,
> And 'spite of Fate and War creates a Court.[144]

More deeply than by immediate political circumstance, however, the image of the countryside was transformed by the infrastructural features of metropolitan sedentarism: "This City sets in her Tryumphant Chair," Matthew Stevenson declared, "And all the Country, but her tenants are."[145] By the first half of the seventeenth-century, the decline of the provincial towns and outports caused by the growth of early Tudor London had begun to reverse itself, as the development of internal trade, driven by London, created a new "urban Renaissance." New patterns of distribution and migration doubled scheduled carrying services from the capital between 1637 and 1715. The "exchange of tastes, ideas, and mores" between London and the provinces "played a vital early role in stimulating and satisfying ... the burgeoning appetite of the gentry for an urban life style and culture."[146] The influence of the metropolis spread

---

[143] "To My Lord of Abingdon at his Country House" and "The Dream to Sir Charles Duncomb from the Country," in *The Works of Mr Robert Gould* (2 vols. London, 1709), 1: 125, 156–161.

[144] "The Triumphs of Philamore and Amoret. To the Noblest of our Youth and Best of Friends, Charles Cotton Esquire. Being at Berisford, at his House in Staffordshire. From London. A Poem," in *Poems*, pp. 170–171. For all his celebration of *The Wonders of the Peake*, Cotton was buried in the most fashionable quarter of the capital, St James' Picadilly. For other city-in-country poems, see Mildmay Fane, "To Sir John Wentworth, upon his Curiosities and Courteous entertainment at Summerly in Lovingland," *Otia Sacra* (1648), p. 153; Cotton, "To My Friend, Mr. John Anderson, From the Country," *Poems*, p. 110. See also James Turner, *The Politics of Landscape: Rural Scenery and Society in English Poetry, 1630–1660* (Oxford: Basil Blackwell, 1979), pp. 120–122.   [145] Stevenson, *Poems* (1673), p. 74.

[146] de Krey, *A Fractured Society*, p. 2; Peter Borsay, *The English Urban Renaissance: Culture and Society in the Provincial Town, 1660–1770* (Oxford: Clarendon Press, 1989), pp. 12, 22, 223; cf. Penelope Corfield, "Urban Development in England and

along the coaching towns of all the great thoroughfares, while the taste for London fashions and luxuries was distributed through regional centers to the countryside. Seasonal migration from the capital created fashionable spas like Tunbridge, where "all the good company that used to be in London ... adjourned." Provincial centers like York developed their own "in-town" seasons to which local gentry resorted "as to London, from every part of the country round." The burgeoning news and book trades reinforced the influence of the metropolis, while, with the rebuilding of post-fire London, a new urbanism was disseminated, by architectural pattern-books and engravings, throughout the nation. Northampton's new streets were as "large as most in London"; Liverpool was "London in miniature"; Temple Row Birmingham was "as ... elegent" as "Bedford Row"; Queen Square Bristol was "somewhat like Lincoln's Inn Fields" and Bristol's new Exchange was "in miniature the Change at London." By 1761, it could be claimed that England's "several great cities, and we might add many poor country towns, seem to be universally inspired with the ambition of becoming little Londons."[147]

The countryside itself had thus become, in Chetwood's translation of the fifteenth ode of Horace's second book, a poetic, achitectural, and recreational domain domesticated by the metropolis:

> Then this unwieldy Factious Town
> To such prodigious Bulk is grown,
> It on whole Counties stands, and now
> Land will be wanting for the Plow ...
>   If any Tree is to be seen,
>   'Tis Myrtle, Bays, and Ever-Green;
> Lime-trees, and Plane, for pleasure made,
> Which for their fruit bear only shade.[148]

Implicit in Chetwood, as in his Horatian source, are reserves of traditionalism seemingly unassimilated by the metropolitan ethic. Yet even these reserves of traditionalism, so potent in Jonson's "To Penshurst" and many later poems, were redeployed by the end of the century, when the poetic exploration of the countryside came to embrace the antagonisms of party, the conflicts between "the landed and the trading Interest"[149] that the growth of London had created. In Dryden's

Wales in the Sixteenth and Seventeenth Centuries," in Jonathan Barry, ed., *The Tudor and Stuart Town* (London: Longman, 1990), pp. 56–58; John Patten, *English Towns 1500–1700* (Folkstone: Dawson, 1978), p. 89.
[147] Borsay, *English Urban Renaissance*, pp. 141, 140, 164, 290, 287.
[148] Dryden, *Miscellany Poems*, 1: 102.
[149] *The Spectator*, No. 174, in Daniel McDonald, ed., *Selected Essays from "The Tatler," "The Spectator," and "The Guardian,"* (Indianapolis: Bobbs-Merrill, 1973), p. 336.

epistle "To My Honor'd Kinsman, John Driden," for example, the ethical and poetic inter-legitimation of countryside and metropolis, "rural and urban activities,"[150] enables the poet to fuse an evocation of the good life in retirement with a projective vision of the political nation. Though opposed in its fiscal conservatism to the speculation and militarism of the new "moneyed" interests, Dryden's "tory revisionism" adapts the traditional rural ideals of conservative husbandry in order to create, in a modified version of mercantilist expansion, the basis for a "factionless national interest":[151]

> Part must be left, a fund when foes invade;
> And part employ'd to roll the wat'ry trade...
> And he, when want requires, is truly wise,
> Who slights not foreign aids, nor overbuys,
> But on our native strength, in time of need, relies...
> Safe in ourselves, while on ourselves we stand,
> The sea is ours, and that defends the land.
> Be then our naval stores the nation's care,
> New ships to build, and batter'd to repair.

(lines 131–132, 137–139, 146–149)

The space traversed, in Dryden's poem, between the rural privacy of his kinsman and the mercantile basis of the nation's destiny, may be taken as a final measure of the expanding reach of the metropolis, the extension of its influence into the countryside and into the political imagination of the nation.

---

[150] Alan Roper, *Dryden's Poetic Kingdoms* (New York: Barnes and Noble, 1965), p. 125.
[151] Jay Arnold Levine, "John Dryden's Epistle to John Driden," in *Dryden's Mind and Art*, ed. Bruce King (Edinburgh: Oliver and Boyd, 1969), pp. 116, 119; see also Roper, *Dryden's Poetic Kingdoms*, p. 133.

10   In place of place: London and liberty in the Puritan Revolution

"To your tents, O Israel!": the city and the people

As wealth and population concentrated in seventeenth-century London, the cultural influence of the metropolis was expanded through a process of diffusion and dissemination. A corollary of growth within the city, in other words, was the transformation of the local into the cosmopolitan, of community into communication. This is evident not only in the emergence of an "august" literature of urbane sophistication and imperial tenor, but also in its apparent ideological opposite, the puritan, radical, and republican writings of the revolutionary period. A common goal in these revolutionary writings was not just the preservation of local liberties but a more universal "advancement of a communitive Happinesse, of equall concernment to others as to ourselves"; as William Walwyn, Londoner and Leveller, put it, "all men going in their separate ways ... whether publique or private" were "free to communicate in all Civill Offices of love and friendship, and cordially joyne with any, for a publique good."[1]

In the case of both cavalier privilege and puritan liberty, habits, ideals, and values deriving from the urban community, but hitherto delimited and defined by the city's boundaries, became the basis for more mobile and expansive projections of the city's influence. As at the Reformation, when the first substantial impact of London's commercial and demographic growth had combined with religious reform and royal absolutism to produce the sharply opposed utopian visions of advanced humanism and retrograde complaint, so at the Revolution, when the tensions held in balance by the Elizabethan–Jacobean neofeudal synthesis had erupted in rebellion and open warfare, the literary culture of

---

[1] *A Manifestation from Lieutenant Col. John Lilburne, Mr. William Walwyn, Mr. Thomas Prince, and Mr. Richard Overton* (1649), in William Haller and Godfrey Davies, eds., *The Leveller Tracts 1647–1653* (Columbia University Press, 1944), p. 277; William Walwyn, *The Vanitie of the Present Churches* (1649), in Jack R. McMichael and Barbara Taft, eds., *The Writings of William Walwyn* (Athens: University of Georgia Press, 1989), p. 351; hereafter cited as *Writings*.

London was polarized by the opposed utopian extremes of privilege and liberty. But in both cases, an expansive utopian pattern of dissemination and distribution emanated from a radical concentration of power at the metropolitan center – in keeping with the pattern of ubanization itself, which expanded through diversification and liberated through a regimen of increasingly specialized and differentiated functions.

The convergence of such opposite developments as cavalier privilege and puritan liberty is testimony to the underlying influence of the urbanizing process on the politics and culture of the period. The First Navigation Act (1651), promulgated under the puritan commonwealth of Oliver Cromwell, was confirmed by the Second (1660) under the restored monarchy of Charles II, just as the august civilization celebrated by such poets as Denham, Dryden, and Pope overlapped at its commercial, metropolitan center with the millennial vision of a global protestant empire imagined by many revolutionary puritans. The perception, by the later seventeenth century, that "the interest of Trade and Land are the same"[2] illustrates in yet another way the convergence of different points of view in the influence of the metropolis. Despite excessively harsh instances of reaction at the Restoration, a civil consensus on the limits of royal power, prerogative courts, and unparliamentary legislation and on the Bill of Rights (1688) was gradually reached by a society that had been as much transformed by the urbanizing process as by the Revolution itself. When they finally came, the Toleration Act (1688) and non-renewal of the Licensing Act (1695) were justified by the secular motives of commerce rather than by moral right.[3]

The ethical counterpart to the urbanizing process was a sense of liberation and empowerment that outstripped the limits of traditional institutions and forms of community. Between the "Town" ethic of polite, cavalier literature and the social vision of religious radicals there are many similarities – a reliance on a morally select community withdrawn from the larger physical one, a cultivation of personal integrity and liberty, and above all a potentially alienating sense of the ethical priority and privilege of the individual subject – a subject not confined by physical or social boundaries and possessing reserves that are supposed to be untouched by the very urbanizing process that actually creates them. In both cases, the ultimate in sedentarism, in being at home

[2] *Some Thoughts Concerning the Better Security of Our Trade and Navigation* (1695), p.4, quoted in Joyce Oldham Appleby, *Economic Thought and Ideology in Seventeenth-Century England* (Princeton University Press, 1978), p. 177.

[3] See Lawrence Stone, "The Results of the English Revolutions of the Seventeenth Century," and Christopher Hill, "A Bourgeois Revolution," both in J. G. A. Pocock, ed., *Three British Revolutions: 1641, 1688, 1776* (Princeton University Press, 1980), pp. 23–139.

in the urban environment, is the sense of liberation from it, the sense of no longer being tied to social or geographical "place." If Jonson, cultivating Roman urbanity could claim to be *chez lui* everywhere, or if Suckling and his interlocutor could style themselves the urbane "Masters of Truth," a political radical like Walwyn could maintain that while "for many yeers my books, and teachers were masters in a great measure of me," through free grace "I became master of what I heard, or read ... I became also, much more master of my affections."[4] Though it developed from different sources and by different routes, the revolutionary idea of Christian liberty converged with the secular cultivation of urbanity in creating personalities suited to the expanding influence of the metropolis. Like the creation of an "august" literary institution, the Puritan Revolution ultimately produced "secular models of social discipline."[5]

Among contemporary writers who traced the Revolution to socio-economic change, the republican James Harrington laid special stress on the ethical corollaries of such change. According to Harrington, Henry VIII's measures to curb the power of the feudal nobility transferred "a great part of the lands unto the hold and possession of the yeomanry, or middle people." Under the neofeudal arrangements of Tudor absolutism, the nobility "became courtiers, where ... their revenues were found wanting." These changes

brought with it the declining estate of the nobility so vast a prey unto the industry of the people, that the balance of the commonwealth was too apparently in the popular party to be unseen by the wise council of Parthenia [i.e., Elizabeth I] who, converting her reign through the perpetual love tricks that passed between her and her people into a kind of romance, wholly neglected the nobility. And by these degrees came the house of commons to raise that head, which hath been so high and formidable unto their princes ... Nor was there anything now wanting unto the destruction of the throne but that the people, not apt to see their own strength, should be put to feel it.[6]

For Harrington, a corollary of this change in the balance of wealth was a striking moral transformation:

For the balance, swaying from monarchical into popular, abateth the luxury of the nobility and, enriching the people, bringeth the government from a more private unto a more public interest, which, coming nearer, as hath been shown, unto justice and right reason, the people upon a like alteration is so far from such corruption of manners as should render them incapable of a commonwealth, that

---

[4] *Walwyns Just Defence* (1649), in *Writings*, p. 398.
[5] James Holstun, *A Rational Millennium: Puritan Utopias of Seventeenth-Century England and America* (New York: Oxford University Press, 1987), p. 24. See also Ernst Troeltsch, *The Social Teachings of the Christian Churches*, tr. Olive Wyon (2 vols. London: George Allen and Unwin, 1931), 2: 749.
[6] *The Commonwealth of Oceana* (1656), in *The Political Works of James Harrington*, ed. J. G. A. Pocock (Cambridge University Press, 1977), pp. 191–198.

of necessity they must thereby contract such a reformation of manners as will bear no other kind of government. (p. 202)

In Harrington's view, as the result of an historic change in the balance of wealth, the English people had morally outgrown their established governmental institutions. Insofar as Harrington's *Oceana* belongs to the "genre of historical utopias ... in which social forces supposedly operating at the time of writing are shown as reaching culmination and resolution in an ideal future," it is important to recognize that in the process of socio-economic and moral evolution leading to this future Harrington had included "the latter growth of this city [of London], and in that the declining of the balance unto the popularity."[7]

London's citizen class had of course long taken pride in the City's loyal contributions to the nation, and for many generations London had influenced both national policy and, through "action at a distance,"[8] the shape of government itself. But with the coming of the Revolution London became, in the eyes of contemporaries, a distinct power in the overt political transformation of the kingdom. Blaming London for "the whole course of this Rebellion, which it first bred and doth still nourish at her breasts," royalists commonly alleged that "all the miserie of warre, blood, and rapine which doe now overflow the Kingdom, come from no other fountaine than the Citie of London." It was "the proud, unthankefull, Schismaticall, Rebellious, Bloody City of London" that "broke downe the bounds ... dissolved Monarchy, inslaved the Lawes, and ruined their Countrey."[9] From the standpoint of radicals as well, London was the "first in opposition to oppression; the first leader and example towards freedom."[10] In 1642–43, the wealth of Londoners had supported the "fortifying of the whole Citie and the Suburbs of it, against their own peaceable and glorious Sovereign." The Parliamentary cause, Thomas Hobbes observed, was supported by "the great purses of the city of London." In the eyes of contemporaries, it accounted for the newly "visible influence they have in the publike government."[11] But so too did "the tumultuous Assemblies of unruly People, gathered from all parts of that potent but unquiet City, to awe the Parliament."[12]

Behind the rising of the populace lay not only grievances but the

---

[7] Pocock's Introduction, p. 74; Harrington, *The Art of Lawgiving* (1659), in *Political Works*, p. 607.

[8] Perry Anderson, *Lineages of the Absolutist State* (1974; rpt. London: Verso, 1979), pp. 39–40.

[9] *Lord Haue Mercy Upon Us: or a Plaine Discourse Declaring that the Plague of Warre ... Took its Beginning in and from the Citie of London* (August, 1643), pp. 3–4; *A Letter from Mercurius Civicus to Mercurius Rusticus* (August, 1643), p. 32.

[10] *Londons New Colours Displaid* (July 13, 1648), p. 1.

[11] Hobbes, *Behemoth*, ed. Ferdinand Tönnies (1889; rpt. London: Frank Cass, 1969), p. 2; *Lord Haue Mercy Upon Us*, pp. 8, 43.   [12] *Lord Haue Mercy Upon Us*, p. 6.

ferment of ideas which, welling up among the city's multitudinous migrants, laborers, tradesmen and sects, led Clarendon to describe the city as "the sink of all the ill humours of the kingdom," and prompted another writer to ask "whether like an over-growne Oyster," London did "not now stew in her owne pickle."[13] In 1648, the "People of London" were alleged to have spread this ferment by sending Leveller "Agents into every City, Town, and Parish ... of the Kingdome."

Rebellion was thus alleged to have spread in the manner of plague, following "the venting of Commodities from infected Cities to the rest of the Kingdom." The patterns of migration and trade, in so many ways crucial to the urbanizing process that expanded the influence of the metropolis, were seen as the means by which rebellion was disseminated "from our principal Citie, to which all sorts of people usually resorted, either for business or pleasure: and by that mean more easily diffused it selfe into all quarters of the Kingdome."[14] More striking, perhaps, than the expansive circulatory pattern of metropolitan influence was the qualitative moral transformation wrought at the heart of the system. One pamphlet depicted the "many disconsolate parents ... in the Country, that sent their Children hither to this Citty ... to bind them apprentices to Trades & Manufactures, hoping that hereafter ... they might live to see their sonnes Lord Mayor of London" but "now sit in mourning" over sons killed and maimed in the revolutionary cause.[15] John Lilburne was one of those sons. He "thought as a childe" and "did as a childe" until "my Father brought me to London, and bound me apprentice"; but in his manhood he argued that if citizens could "set the City of London right in the enjoyment of her priviledges: (being the Metropolis of England,) ... she may indeed be a true President to all the Citties and Corporations in the Kingdome, and a ballance to all the Tyrants, or Arbitrary-principl'd men in the same."[16]

The moment of the Revolution was in fact the point in the metropolitanizing process when quantitative growth yielded qualitative change, when the scale and intensity of urban growth, mobility, and

[13] Clarendon, *The History of the Rebellion and Civil Wars in England* (6 vols. Oxford: Clarendon Press, 1888), 1: 264; *Londons New Recorder* (September 30, 1647), s.sh. Cf. the testimony of George Masterson in *A Declaration of Some Proceedings of Lt. Col. John Lilburne* (January, 1648), in Haller and Davies, *Leveller Tracts*, p. 98; Thomas Edwards, *Gangraena* (February 26, 1646), p. 16. On Masterson's testimony, see Norah Carlin, "Leveller Organization in London," *Historical Journal*, 25 (1982), pp. 955–959.
[14] *Lord Haue Mercy Upon Us*, pp. 4–5.
[15] *A Letter from Mercurius Civicus to Mercurius Rusticus*, p. 28.
[16] *The Legall Fundamentall Liberties of the People of England* (June 8, 1649), in Haller and Davies, *Leveller Tracts*, pp. 403–404; *Englands Birth-Right Justified* (October, 1645), in William Haller, *Tracts on Liberty in the Puritan Revolution 1638–1647* (3 vols. New York: Columbia University Press, 1934), 3: 296. Hereafter cited as *Tracts on Liberty*.

diversification yielded intellectual and ethical changes with revolutionary implications. An enlarged sense of human liberties and capacities, not just the range of the market, were the result of expanding metropolitan influence. One indignant observer, commenting on this qualitative transformation, protested that "the monstrous growth of this one Citie hath brought a Consumption on all the rest: and whereas it attracted to it all the wealth, commodities, and pleasures of all places else, it payed them back in factious Principles and seditious Practices."[17]

A major source for the transformations that produced "the whole freedom of man ... in spiritual or civil liberty"[18] was the ideal of Christian liberty expounded by protestant radicals. "Moses and Aaron, Josuah and Gideon," one writer observed, "were not instruments of more glorious victories for Israel of old, then those deliverers whom God sent London, have been of late."[19] The Lutheran assertion that through faith in Christ all believers attain their birthright as God's people, kings, and priests became a basis for the theories of natural right, equality, and personal autonomy embodied, for example, in Richard Overton's claim that "every man" is "by nature ... a King, Priest, and Prophet in his own naturall circuit."[20] The main impetus for the expansion of Christian liberty came not, however, from the established Church, but rather from those excluded from the visibly emplaced state order, from the exiles, underground sects, and independent congregations that had in one way or another detached themselves from the official community.

With its large, diversifying population of refugees, migrants, and underprivileged laborers and craftsmen, London had become a haven and nursery of separatists.[21] By the early seventeenth century the illegal London conventicles of the Elizabethan period had given rise to such early independent congregations as the Henry Jacob church in Southwark (1616), its Baptist offshoots, and the followers of lay preachers like Praise-God Barebone and Richard Rogers.[22] Furthermore, in the early decades of the seventeenth century, an independent system of

[17] *Lord Haue Mercy Upon Us*, p. 43.

[18] Milton, *The Ready and Easy Way to Establish a Free Commonwealth* (2nd. edn. 1660), ed. Robert W. Ayers, in *The Complete Prose Works of John Milton* (8 vols. New Haven: Yale University Press, 1953–82), 7: 456. References to this edition are hereafter abbreviated as *CPW*.

[19] *A Moderate Reply to the City Remonstrance* (June 12, 1646), sig. D4v.

[20] Luther, *The Freedom of a Christian* (1520), tr. W. A. Lambert, in *Three Treatises* (1943; rpt. Philadelphia: Fortress Press, 1970), p. 289; Overton, *An Arrow Against All Tyrants* (1646), p. 289.

[21] See Geoffrey F. Nuttall, *Visible Saints: The Congregational Way, 1640–1660* (Oxford: Basil Blackwell, 1957), p. 5. See also Andrew Pettegree, *Foreign Protestant Communities in Sixteenth-Century London* (New York: Oxford University Press, 1986).

[22] See Murray Tolmie, *The Triumph of the Saints: The Separatist Churches of London, 1616–1649* (London: Cambridge University Press, 1977), chs. 1–4.

puritan lectureships grew up alongside the official parish ministries, placing radical preachers in London pulpits "over their Parochiall Ministers heads"[23] – Hugh Peter at St. Sepulchre's, Holborn, John Archer at All Hallows, Lombard Street and John Downham at St. Bartholomew, Exchange. At the same time, a number of puritan rectors, many of them supported after 1626 by the same committee of London merchants, lawyers, and clergymen who raised endowments for the lectureships, became incumbents of London parishes – William Gouge at St. Anne's, Blackfriars, Richard Stock at All Hallows, Bread Street (young Milton's parish), John Davenport and later John Goodwin at St. Stephen's, Coleman Street, John Stoughton and Edmund Calamy at St. Mary Aldermanbury, Henry Burton at St. Matthew, Friday Street, and Cornelius Burges at St. Magnus, London Bridge.[24] Continental poets seeking refuge from the Thirty Years' War lauded London as a haven of religious liberty, while Francis Quarles extolled the city as "A place of common refuge, and reliefe / To banisht Shepheards, and thir scatter'd Sheep."[25]

But the puritan subcommunities of London had been shaped by official persecution, and, to a large degree, it was from the experience of separation, wandering, and exile – into which so many London lecturers, ministers, and congregations were actually driven by the intensified Laudian persecution – that many of the ideals, principles, and advocates of religious Independency finally emerged.[26] From these exiles, from the semi-legal lectureships and gathered congregations of London, and from such returning American colonists as Hugh Peter, Roger Williams, and Hanserd Knollys,[27] men who "left their native soyle, and went into a vast and Howling wildernesse to the utmost parts of the world,"[28] came many of the new ideas – of covenant, popular consent, spiritual enlightenment,

---

[23] *Mercurius Civicus to Mercurius Rusticus*, p. 5.

[24] Valerie Pearl, *London and the Outbreak of the Puritan Revolution: City Government and National Politics, 1625–1643* (London: Oxford University Press, 1961), pp. 162–168; see also Paul Seaver, *The London Lectureships: The Politics of Religious Dissent, 1580–1662* (Stanford University Press, 1970), and, on the Feoffees of Impropriations, Raymond Phineas Stearns, *The Strenuous Puritan: Hugh Peter, 1598–1660* (Urbana: University of Illinois Press, 1954), pp. 37–40.

[25] *The Shepheardes Oracles* (1646), in A. B. Grosart, ed., *Complete Works in Verse and Prose* (3 vols. 1880; rpt. New York: AMS Press, 1967), 3: 206. For praise by refugees, see Jan Sictor, *Panegyricon Inaugurale* (1637), and Wenceslaus Clemens, *Trinobantiados Augustae sive Londini Libri VI* (Leyden, 1636).

[26] Tolmie, *The Triumph of the Saints*, p. 104; Tai Liu, *Puritan London: A Study of Religion and Society in the City Parishes* (Newark, Del.: University of Delaware Press, 1986), pp. 107–109.

[27] William L. Sachse, "The Migration of New Englanders to England, 1640–1660," *American Historical Review*, 53 (1948), 251–278.

[28] John Owen, *Of Communion with God* (1657), p. 170, quoted in Nuttall, *Visible Saints*, p. 68.

individual sufficiency and autonomy, religious toleration, and separation of Church and State – that gave a revolutionary impetus to the ideal of Christian liberty, transforming religious into political radicals and giving "temporal and concrete" form to the puritan millennium.[29] The Revolution in London was fomented by men who had ceased to identify with the community in the traditional sense.[30]

Not just the gospel, then, but the way it was adapted, under specific conditions, to the resocialization of individuals in an expanding metropolis, accounts for the revolutionary impact of religious ideas. The puritan lectureships and congregations appealed not primarily to the City's established elite but to "men newly come to the city, uneasy there, not yet urbane, not yet sharing the sophistication of the town-dweller or the courtier ... the congregational discipline taught them an urban style, provided new standards of order and a new routine, set them apart from the motley population of the expanding city and eventually produced a new self-confidence."[31] Such religious experience may have "helped them, through the transition, to become Londoners,"[32] but in a special sense: in setting them "apart from the ... population of the expanding city," it taught them to become a new kind of Londoners – Londoners whose identity was no longer linked to the local limits and body of the established community so much as to the centrifugal forces of diversification, mobility, and expansion of which that community was the center. Like these migrants, the returning congregational exiles, having lost many of "their social and institutional ties ... were free, in a sense, from all historical limitations in their search for truth."[33] The chief support for these groups came, moreover, not from the established leaders of the City's dominant Mediterranean and Eastern trading companies, but from the interlopers of the new American trades. The majority of these new men were not from London's traditional mercantile elite but from the city's middling ranks of retailers; they were "mostly born outside London and were, in many cases, the younger sons of gentry

---

[29] Liu, *Puritan London*, p. 61. On the analogies between religious and political liberty, covenant and contract, etc., see, e.g., A. S. P. Woodhouse, ed., *Puritanism and Liberty: Being the Army Debates (1647–49)*, Introduction, pp. 72–76, and Brian Manning, "Puritanism and Democracy, 1640–1642," in Donald Pennington and Keith Thomas, eds., *Puritans and Revolutionaries: Essays in Seventeenth-Century History Presented to Christopher Hill* (Oxford: Clarendon Press, 1978), pp. 140–156.

[30] *Mercurius Civicus to Mercurius Rusticus*, p. 4; cf. *Persecutio Undecima* (164*), p. 21.

[31] Michael Walzer, *The Revolution of the Saints* (Cambridge, Mass.: Harvard University Press, 1965), p. 243.

[32] Michael Walzer, "Puritanism as a Revolutionary Ideology," *History and Theory*, 3 (1963), p. 78.

[33] Liu, *Puritan London*, p. 43; cf. B. S. Capp, *The Fifth Monarchy Men* (Totowa, N.J.: Rowman and Littlefield, 1972), p. 97.

or prosperous yeomen"; many had been abroad and prospered in the new American colonies before returning to set up businesses in London.[34] As a result of these social circumstances, the political implications of Christian liberty were developed in tandem with a psychological disinvestment in the social and physical "place" of the established community. This disinvestment contributed, in turn, to the centrifugal effects of the urbanizing process.

It is therefore not surprising that the radical ideas of religious Independency overlapped at so many points with secular movements to enlarge and distribute liberties, franchises, and privileges that had hitherto accrued to "place" – movements by the guilds' yeomanry to challenge the exclusive liveries, by journeyman and specialist guilds for separate incorporation, by proponents of free trade to curb monopolies and patents, by colonial projectors and their tradesmen supporters to interlope in global commerce, by Levellers to expand the electoral franchise, sometimes through appeal to the customs of London, and by democratic movements to reform the Corporation of London by expanding the Common Hall franchise from liverymen to all free-holders and by freeing the popularly representative Common Council from the control of the oligarchic Court of Aldermen.[35] These movements have in common the attempt to claim new liberties and legitimize new modes of association by extrapolating or analogizing, as from a genetic potential, from previously localized and exclusive customary rights. Like much of the social complaint of the early Tudor period, these movements also had in common an attack upon the concentration of power in the metropolis, but with a crucial difference: despite rhetorical appeal to tropes of "restoration," the point of these revolutionary attacks was not to undo the power of London but to decentralize and distribute it.[36] The aim was no longer to return to an agrarian, pre-urban past, but to transform the socio-economic landscape of England in the image and likeness of London, to new-model the organic relation of subordinate parts to hierarchic whole through a rank-and-file of self-contained and self-sufficient units, each of which was all in all.[37] Implicit in such autonomy was the resocialization through which a new type of community inscribes itself within its members. The pursuit of a radical, distributive justice, in

---

[34] Robert Brenner, *Merchants and Revolution: Commercial Change, Political Conflict, and London's Overseas Traders, 1550–1653* (Princeton University Press, 1993), p. 114.

[35] The best survey of these movements remains Margaret James, *Social Problems and Policy During the Puritan Revolution* (London: Routledge, 1930), chs. 4–5.

[36] On the Independents as a party of "decentralization," see Gordon Yule, *The Independents in the English Civil War* (Cambridge University Press, 1958), p. 54.

[37] See, e.g., Milton, *The Reason of Church Government* (February, 1642), *CPW*, 1: 789; cf. *Paradise Lost*, Book 6.

other words, was conditioned by a radical concentration of power in new forms. The expansion and dissemination of liberties was linked to the expanding influence of the metropolis, just as demands for individual autonomy and for the toleration of difference were conditioned by a regimen of increasingly differentiated and specialized functions for a growing urban populace.

These paradoxes account for what was, in fact, the ambiguous and often conflicted position of London itself during the revolutionary period: "London," said one contemporary after Royalist "King and Kirk" mobs and bonfires had shaken the capital at the outset of the Second Civil War in 1648, "hath long been in dispute, what colours to hold forth, that should demonstrate, who they were for, and who they were against."[38] Behind the partisan divisions, power struggles, and shifting alliances within the city lay not only the overdetermined status of the early modern urban community – its paradoxically dependent and erosive effects on royal absolutism – but a crisis of identity during a revolutionary period of transition, a movement toward autonomy and freedom from the influence of locality that was nevertheless conditioned by an expansion of that very local influence. Playing center against periphery, place against placelessness, local custom against universalizing rationales, consolidation against growth, community against creative autonomy, the contradictions of the urbanizing process helped to shape the characteristic tensions in revolutionary thought and its legacy – tensions between reform and liberty, national covenant and apocalypse, holy state and separation, the common cause and the ineradicable particularism of the individual.

Among the alterations in the social taxonomy effected by the growth of London, the novel term that marks the revolutionary moment is "people." Like the "town," a term which reflects a metropolitan influence widened through new patterns of mobility and new phases of ethical development, the term "people" marks the point at which the metropolis extended its influence beyond its boundaries through the transformation and dissemination of a nuclear human potential. An elastic term that accumulated many different meanings, it nevertheless developed much of its revolutionary potential in the streets of London. In September, 1640, 10,000 London citizens prepared against the convening of the Long Parliament a petition of grievances against impositions and monopolies, religious innovations and unparliamentary rule.[39] On October 22 and November 1 crowds rioted against the

---

[38] *Londons New Colours Displaid* (July 13, 1848), p. 1.
[39] *CSPD*, 16/467/135; see Valerie Pearl, *London and the Outbreak of the Puritan Revolution*, pp. 174–175.

bishops' Court of High Commission.[40] In December, *The First and Large Petition of the City of London*, with 15,000 signatures, was presented to Parliament by a delegation of citizens; this "honour of our cheiff Citty," as Milton called it, was followed by similar "Root-and-Branch" petitions from throughout the country.[41]

Popular agitation, often on a massive scale, continued during 1641. Large and sometimes unruly crowds of several thousand demonstrators, organized by London's radical MPs, besieged Westminster Hall during consideration of the Root-and-Branch Bill and the proceedings against Strafford in the spring of 1641.[42] Within days of the presentation of the Grand Remonstrance in December, a petition "about three quarters of a yard in breadth and 24 yards in length" and "subscribed with the names of above 20,000" Londoners took exception to the Lord Mayor's attempt "to miscontrue the Citizens dutifull and loyall" agitation for reform, and it called for ending "the abuses crept into the ancient government of this City."[43] The polite and orderly presentation of this petition was followed by the largest and most violent disorders to date, the December 27–29 riots against bishops in the House of Lords and Royalist control of the Tower of London.[44] The effects of popular demonstration culminated on January 5, 1642, when Charles I rode into London to seek from a Parliamentary committee adjourned to the Guildhall the arrest of five MPs who had sought refuge in Colemanstreet ward. Threatened by the hostile crowds that mobbed his coach as he was leaving the city, Charles fled Whitehall on January 10, and on the next day the five members returned in a triumphant barge flotilla to Westminster.

Clarendon reported that when "the rude people flocked together, and cryed out, 'Privilege of Parliament! privilege of parliament!'", one demonstrator among those "pressing very near his own coach" shouted out "with a very loud voice, 'To your tents, O Israel!'" Another report claimed instead that "that seditious Pamphlet" of Clement Walker "*To Your Tents, O Israel*, was thrown either into, or very near his coach."[45]

---

[40] Keith Lindley, "London and Popular Freedom in the 1640s," in R. C. Richardson and G. M. Ridden, eds., *Freedom and the English Revolution: Essays in History and Literature* (Manchester University Press, 1986), pp. 118–119.

[41] *Animadversions, CPW* 1: 677; Tai Liu, *Discord in Zion: The Puritan Divines and the Puritan Revolution, 1640–1660* (The Hague: Martinus Nijhoff, 1973), p. 12.

[42] Brian Manning, *The English People and the English Revolution, 1640–1649* (London: Heinemann, 1976), pp. 5–18.

[43] *The Citizens of London's Humble Petition to ... the ... House in Parliament* (December 11, 1641), sigs. a4, a3–a3v.

[44] Manning, *The English People and the English Revolution*, pp. 74–80.

[45] Clarendon, *The History of the Rebellion* (6 vols. Oxford: Clarendon Press, 1888), 1: 154; *Mercurius Civicus to Mercurius Rusticus*, p. 17; see also *The Occasion of His Majesties Comming to Guild-hall, Somer's Tracts*, 4: 345–348. See also Ernest Sirluck, "'To Your

Whatever form it took, the invocation of Jeroboam's rebellion against Rehoboam and "the children of Israel which dwelt in the cities of Judah" (1 Kings 12: 16–17) epitomized the condition of a people whose new sense of moral enlargement and mobility had outgrown the limits of sedentarism. The text was a fitting description of the mobilization of a militarized urban populace, who, as Clarendon reported, "would frequently... convene themselves, by the sound of a bell or other token, in the fields, or some convenient place, and receive orders." In late October, 1642, as Royalist troops were marching toward London, the aristocratic leaders of the war party urged every Londoner to "shut up his shop,... arme himselfe, and arme his apprentizes, and come forth with boldnesse and with courage" to turn back the King's forces outside the city at Turnham Green. In the fevered spring of 1643, when another attack on London was expected, a proposal was floated to supplement the weekly assessments with a recruitment scheme that would have "16. or 18. Tents or boarded Houses... raised in Finsberry Field, or elsewhere." All "the Shops in London and the Suburbs, by strict command," would be "kept shut so that in the time of going forth into the Fields, men may have nothing to hinder them from appearing," and "all the Forces of what kind soever in the City and Suburbs" would be "drawn into the Field... and be divided to guard every tent."[46] Jeroboam's subsequent apostacy in settling down to his own form of carnal idolatry would later lay bare the limits of the revolution, the paradoxically sedentary origins and effects of popular liberation; but 1 Kings 12: 16 became a canonical rallying cry for the gathered congregations, for the claim of Milton and other political Independents "that the right of the people is more ancient than that of kings," and for the claims of Overton and the Levellers that "right Reason," as embodied in a contractual Agreement of the People, must take precedence over "All Formes of Lawes and Governments,"[47] and especially over the retrograde elements in the City of London.

The popular agitations of 1641–43 were paralleled by a "visible

Tents, O Israel': A Lost Pamphlet," *HLQ*, 19 (1955–56), 301–305, and Lindley, "London and Popular Freedom," pp. 113–114.

[46] Clarendon, *History of the Rebellion*, 1: 453; Speech of Lord Brooke, *Eight Speeches Spoken in Guildhall... Octob. 27, 1642*, pp. 18–19; *An Humble Proposal of Safety* (May 25, 1643), pp. 4, 7.

[47] Milton (who also struggles with Jeroboam's apostacy), *A Defence of the People of England* (1651)", *CPW*, 4.1: 405–406; Overton, *An Appeale From the Degenerate Representative Body... To the Body Represented* (July, 1647), t.p. (citing but misidentifying 1 Kings 12: 16 and 24), in Don M. Wolfe, ed., *Leveller Manifestoes of the Puritan Revolution* (New York: Thomas Nelson and Sons, 1944), pp. 155–157; cf. *The Baiting of the Great Bull of Bashan* (July, 1649), in Howard Erskine-Hill and Graham Storey, eds., *Revolutionary Prose of the English Civil War* (Cambridge University Press, 1983), p. 152.

alteration in the temper of the City,"[48] a revolution within the government of the City of London itself. The Common Council elections of December, 1641 returned a radical majority that held sway through the summer and autumn of 1643.[49] Out went "the grave, discreet, well-affected Citizens" – the magnates and oligarchs tied by financial interests and civic tradition to the court – and in came men "we did not thinke two yeares agoe to have met" in Guildhall, complained Sir Henry Garroway, a Royalist and former Lord Mayor.[50] Aided by the radical City MPs and the attrition and purging of a third of the Royalist-dominated Court of Aldermen, Parliamentary Puritans in the Common Council gave that popular representative body a new influence in City politics.[51] They successfully challenged the aldermanic and mayoral powers of veto and, by operating independently and through the use of popular agitation and petitions, placed the City Militia in the hands of a radical committee. Following the impeachment of the Royalist mayor Sir Richard Gurney (July, 1642), the radical MP and Levant Company trader Isaac Pennington was elected Lord Mayor over the heads of more senior candidates at a Common Hall. Under Pennington's radical leadership a system of weekly assessments in support of the Parliamentary forces was established, and, in the winter of 1642–43, a vast network of forts and trenches was flung up around the City in anticipation of a Royalist offensive. The fortifications were as much to prevent Royalist insurrection from within as to resist attack from without: the curbing of the City's radical leadership by the majority of London moderates and conservatives in the summer and autumn of 1643 was a first step toward the Presbyterian counter-revolution of 1646–47. But democratic change had produced a distinction between "City Collective" and "City Representative," dynamic people and static civic constitution, that would be invoked against attempts to restore the aldermanic veto in 1645, against the Presbyterian establishment in 1646–47, and by Levellers against Independents in 1649.[52] Just as important, a number of the most important London gathered congregations – among them those of Walter Craddock, Thomas Brooks, Henry Burton, Nathaniel Holmes, William

---

[48] Clarendon, *History of the Rebellion*, 1: 275.
[49] My summary relies heavily on Valerie Pearl, *London and the Outbreak of the Puritan Revolution*, esp. chs. 6–7.
[50] *Mercuricus Civicus to Mercuricus Rusticus*, p. 15; *A Speech Made by Alderman Garroway, at a Common Hall* (January 17, 1643), p. 3.
[51] For the view that Royalism was even less common in the aldermanry than Pearl suggests, see Austin Woolrych, "Court, Country, and City Revisited," *History*, 65 (1980), 236–245.
[52] See John Bellamie, *A Plea for the Commonalty of London* (1645), pp. 15–16; *A Moderate Reply to the City Remonstrance* (June 12, 1646), sig. B.

Carter, William Greenhill, William Bartlet, and John Briscoe – sprang up under the relaxed authority of the temorary radical coalition.[53] In these and other ways, the capacities of Londoners had been seen to outstrip their traditional environment. As, by an 18-mile fortified circuit, "Westminster, the Strand, and all the liberties thereof" were "taken under the custodies of London," this enlargement took visible form. "London was never truly London till now," said one observer, "for now she sits like a noble lady upon a royal throne, securing her encroaching pendicules under the wings of a motherly protection. Grand Cayro excepted, I have not seen a larger inveloped compasse within the whole universe."[54]

Strong men: revolution and moral growth

The expanded powers of the people were linked, in revolutionary thought, to the millennial doctrine of progressive enlightenment, through which moral and intellectual growth, resulting in enlarged or rediscovered capacities, liberated individuals from their dependence on the physical and institutional limits of place. "Within the compass of this age we now live in," Thomas Goodwin observed,

it hath been that the "kingdoms of the world" have become again "the kingdoms of Christ," Rev. xi.15, and the "temple opened," and "the ark of the testament," ... and all his riches have been broken up and searched into, and discovered to the eyes of all ... And, my brethren, these are the times.[55]

Under the influence of the millennial ideas of Brightman, Mede, Alsted, and others, a centrifugal turn was given to the centripetal apocalypticism embodied in the Tudor ideal of a Constantinian, Christian empire seated in the British throne.[56] Isaiah's prophecy of new heaven and new earth was now taken to mean not "that Christ shall come and reign personally ... but that Christ will ... have a glorious kingdom in the spirits of his people." Embodied in the saints' "knowledge of their spiritual liberty in Christ" and the "knowledge of their liberty from men," the "glory of this new heaven" was to consist "first in the abundance of knowledge.

[53] Liu, *Puritan London*, p. 111; Tolmie, *Triumph of the Saints*, pp. 94–95.
[54] William Lithgow, *The Present Surveigh of London and Englands State* (1643), in *Somers Tracts*, 4: 537, 541. On the fortifications, see Norman Brett-James, *The Growth of Stuart London* (London: George Allen and Unwin, 1935), ch. 11.
[55] *The Glory of the Gospel*, in *Works*, ed. John C. Miller (12 vols. Edinburgh: James Nichol, 1861), 4: 237.
[56] William Lamont, *Godly Rule: Politics and Religion, 1603–60* (New York: St Martin's Press, 1969), p. 95.

Isa 11.9: *The knowledge of God shall cover the face of the earth, as the waters cover the sea.*"[57] Daniel's prophecy of an apocalyptic fifth monarchy, characterized by a progressive enlightenment in which "many shall run to and fro, and knowledge shall be increased" (Dan. 12: 4), became a favored text among revolutionaries who saw a millenarian potential in the spiritual growth of a people who kept "*Zion* and *Ierusalem* ... in their eye and in their heart."[58] Lord Brooke argued that the spread of spiritual light among the people was such that "now to stint it, is to resist an enlightened, enflamed Multitude." A new intellectual ferment, Brooke maintained, led plebeian separatists to expect that revelation "should be yet still more and more accomplished every day, till knowledge cover the Earth, as Waters fill the sea."[59] The revolutionary sermon *A Glimpse of Syons Glory* (1641) found prophetic confirmation in the "voice of a great multitude" proclaiming that "the Lord God omnipotent reigneth" (Rev. 19: 6), that

the voice of Jesus Christ ... comes first from the multitude, the common people, ... before it is heard from any others ... The people at the first are more forward. In Neh iii.5, it is said that the nobles did not put to their necks, but it is said that the people blessed those that came to dwell at Jerusalem ... The Ark ... now ... is opened to all ... Before, what a little of the mystery of the Gospel and the righteousness of the faith were discovered! But this will grow brighter and brighter till that time, which is the great design of God for his glory to all eternity.[60]

William Sprigge put it more bluntly when he declared that magistracy puts "too effectual an obstruction in the way of truth, which comes not in always at the same end of town – not always by the learned and eminent in parts or power (John 7.48), but even by the people, oftentimes."[61]

Comparing the capacity for enlightenment "to growing things; small in the beginning and first appearance, but increasing by degrees unto glory and perfection,"[62] the doctrine of progressive enlightenment

---

[57] Thomas Collier, *A Discovery of the New Creation*, in Woodhouse, *Puritanism and Liberty*, pp. 390–391. Cf. Nathaniel Holmes, *The New World Discovered* (Parliamentary Sermon, 1641), pp. 7–8.

[58] Henry Wilkinson, *Babylons Ruine, Jerusalems Rising* (Parliamentary Sermon, October 25, 1643), p. 21; for the use of Daniel 12: 4 see, for example, Thomas Goodwin, *The Glory of the Gospel*, *Works*, 4: 247; Sprigge, *The Ancient Bounds*, in Woodhouse, *Puritanism and Liberty*, p. 259.

[59] *A Discourse Opening the Nature of Episcopacy* (1641), in Haller, *Tracts on Liberty*, 2: 139, 151, 160.

[60] *A Glimpse of Syons Glory* (1641), in Thomas Goodwin, *Works*, 12: 66–67, 76.

[61] *The Ancient Bounds* (June 10, 1645), in Woodhouse, *Puritanism and Liberty*, p. 255.

[62] John Owen, *A Vision of Unchangeable Free Mercy* (Parliamentary Sermon, 29 April, 1646), p. 1.

implied that institutions could be outgrown, that "that great mountaine (in your understanding) government," could be "but a molehill if you would handle it familiarly, and bee bold with it."[63] Milton, who shared the view that God had chosen "to dispense and deal out by degrees his beam," believed that "our hearts are now more capacious, our thoughts more erected to the search and expectation of greatest and exactest things."[64] The "pure, spiritual Comprehensive Christian," John Saltmarsh declared, "is one who grows with God from administration to administration, and so walks with God in all his removes and spiritual encreasings and flowing." Men are thus "disburdened of the legal terrours, fears, delusions, false conceptions, traditions under which they have lived as they grow up into truth."[65] To pass from the Old Testament servitude to New Testament sonship in Christ was, for Walter Craddock, to come of age: "they were under tutors and governors,... little children, as it were, in their coats, and we are grown strong, grown men to full age."[66] Milton agreed that through Christ's liberation from sin men were "educated from... elementary, childish, and servile discipline to the adult stature of a new creature, and to a manly freedom under the gospel, worthy of God's sons."[67]

For John Goodwin, the maturing of human potential also entailed an irreversible diversification: "Men are now grown more various in their opinions than before, and will be as easily persuaded to forsake their meat as to relinquish their tenets... Therefore there is not only a reason but also a necessity, of toleration."[68] Unidirectional in nature, the process of enlightenment was perceived as a process of widening comprehension, an enlargement in "the circumference of free understanding."[69] Consequently, no person who had tasted the "sweetnesse" of spiritual liberty could "without extreme discontent be brought back into another house of bondage."[70] He "who is arrived in the full age of a man," Walwyn maintained, was no longer "timerous" or "scrupulous," but able "to deale with every one in every age and condition, to shew them their

[63] Walwyn, *The Power of Love* (September, 1643), in Haller, *Tracts on Liberty*, 2: 276.
[64] *Areopagitica* (October, 1644), in *CPW*, 2: 566, 559. Cf. Henry Robinson, *Liberty of Conscience* (March, 1644), in Haller, *Tracts on Liberty*, 3: 165.
[65] *Sparkles of Glory* (May 27, 1647), pp. 316, 184.   [66] *Gospel Libertie* (1648), p. 18.
[67] *De Doctrina, CPW*, 6: 517.
[68] *Independency Gods Verity* (1647), in Woodhouse, *Puritanism and Liberty*, p. 186.
[69] Wilbur K. Jordan, *Men of Substance* (University of Chicago Press, 1942), p. 127. On the process of comprehension, see Liu, *Discord in Zion*, p. 48, and Ernest Sirluck's Introduction to *Areopagitica*, *CPW* 2: 181.
[70] Robinson, *Liberty of Conscience*, in Haller, *Tracts on Liberty*, 3: 121; cf. J. Goodwin, *M. S. to A. S.* (1644), p. 86.

vanity, ignorance and mistakings: and to point them out the path of vertue."[71]

Having "enfranchis'd, enlarg'd, and lifted up our apprehensions above themselves,"[72] the progress of popular enlightenment thus created a sense of gigantic potential. "Freedom," said Winstanley, "is the man that will turne the world upside downe."[73] The heroic Samson exemplified for many revolutionaries the way in which man "grows up to a noble strength and perfection."[74] As a "noble and puissant Nation rousing herself like a strong man after sleep, and shaking her invincible locks," revolutionary England approached the ideal commonwealth that Milton thought should be "but as one huge Christian personage, one mighty growth, and stature of an honest man, as big, and compact in virtue as in body."[75] The ethical equivalent of this giantism was what William Sprigge called

the universality of spirit in a wise man, whereby he takes a view, and enters into consideration of the whole universe. Like Socrates, who contained in his affection all human kind, he walketh through all as if they were near unto him; he seeth, like the sun with a settled and equal regard, the interchangeable courses of things; which is a livery of the Divinity, and a high privilege of a wise man, who is the image of God upon earth.[76]

Such moral expansiveness was incompatible with the customary limits of place or locality. "The most beautiful and greatest spirits," *The Ancient Bounds* maintained in paraphrasing the skeptical Pierre Charron, "are the more universal, as the more base and blunt are the more particular. Every man calleth that barbarous that agreeth not with his palate and custom; it seemeth that we have no other touch of truth and reason than the examples and the idea of the opinions and customs of that place or country where we live."[77] According to Marchamont Nedham, "custom and education" caused the moral retrogression whereby men "choose to live in those places and customs of government under which they have been bred" rather "than submit to better."[78] The rev-

---

[71] *A Still and Soft Voice from the Scriptures* (1647), in *Writings*, p. 265.

[72] *Areopagitica, CPW*, 2: 559.

[73] *A Watch-Word to the City of London and the Armie* (August 26, 1649), in George H. Sabine, ed., *The Works of Gerrard Winstanley* (Ithaca: Cornell University Press, 1941), p. 316.

[74] *Londons Liberties in Chains Discovered* (Oct.– Nov. 1646), p. 34; Milton, *The Reason of Church Government, CPW* 1: 858–859. For other appeals to the example of Samson, see Walwyn, *A Word in Season* (May 26, 1646), in *Writings*, p. 207, and Milton, *First Defense, CPW* 4.1: 402.

[75] *Areopagitica, CPW*, 2: 557–558, *Of Reformation, CPW*, 1: 572.

[76] *The Ancient Bounds*, in Woodhouse, *Puritanism and Liberty*, p. 261.

[77] Ibid., p. 261.

[78] *The Case of the Commonwealth of England, Stated* (May, 1650), p. 112.

olutionary resistance to place drew much of its force from religious Independents, who, like Milton, denied that God is "appointed and confin'd, where and out of what place these his chosen shall be first heard to speak...lest we should devote ourselves again to set places, and assemblies, and outward callings of men."[79] No man should believe, John Saltmarsh argued, "that God is only in a place, or Temple, or form of worship...since that time is come, that we do no longer worship in this Temple, nor at Ierusalem; but...in spirit and truth."[80]

The scandal of Independency, in its more extreme forms, was not the call for gathered congregations or religious toleration, but the outright denial "that Gods Salvation is also Nationall."[81] The basis for the denial was the distinction between the old and new covenants, the orders of law and grace. Whereas the Israelites "had a covenant to gather them up into a national way of worship, and were under the laws of an external pedagogy," Saltmarsh explained, "now...there is a fulness of spirit let out upon the Saints and people of God that gathers them up more closely, spiritually, and cordially."[82] God's ways with Israel were linked to the Promised Land, "but," asked Henry Robinson, "did God ever say to any Christian people as he did to Abraham, Gen. 7.18. I will give unto thee and thy seed thy neighbours Country?"[83] The license extended to Old Testament prophets was thus a prefiguration of the Christian temple of the "upright heart and pure," for "whereas it was not lawful by the national religion to sacrifice in any place than the temple, a prophet was his own temple, and might sacrifice where he would."[84]

The congregational ideal of a "free society or communion of visible Saints, embodyed and knit together by a voluntary consent," was thus a radical reinterpretation of the Old Testament idea of national covenant.[85] In dissociating Christians in the Word from Christians in baptism it dissociated them from the carnal, national Church and its parishes. "Christ travelled About the Holy Land," said John Sadler, Town Clerk of London under the Commonwealth, because "the time was coming, yea and Then come, when not only at That or other Mountains of the

---

[79] *Areopagitica*, CPW 2: 566.   [80] *Sparkles of Glory*, sig. A3v.
[81] Robinson, *Liberty of Conscience*, in Haller, *Tracts on Liberty*, 3: 143–144.
[82] *Smoke in the Temple*, p. 185.
[83] *Liberty of Conscience*, in Haller, *Tracts on Liberty*, 3: 144.
[84] Harrington, *Oceana*, in *Political Writings*, p. 186. Cf. John Goodwin, *Innocency and Truth Triumphing Together* (January, 1645), p. 16; Saltmarsh, *Sparkles of Glory*, sig. a2v; Roger Williams, *The Bloody Tenent of Persecution* (1644), in Woodhouse, *Puritanism and Liberty*, pp. 284–286.
[85] William Bartlet, *Ichnographia. Or a Model of the Primitive Congregational Way* (March 25, 1647), p. 30. For other definitions of the congregational covenant, see Goodwin, *Innocency and Truth*, p. 6; Saltmarsh, *Smoke in the Temple*, in Woodhouse, *Puritanism and Liberty*, p. 179.

Holy Land, but in All places, men should Worship God in Spirit and in Truth."[86] No longer hampered by the carnal limits of the parochial order, the gathered congregations enjoyed a new capacity for spiritual growth: "the members of this same societie," said John Goodwin, "grow up freely into it...They count themselves not perfect, but stand ready to receive further light."[87]

But herein lay a paradox, for insofar as it gathered "visible Saints" who "set our feet on earth among you,"[88] the new covenant of Independents remained continuous with the Old Testament legal covenant that was its origin; the truth continued to partake of its shadowy type, as the centrifugal pull away from the bondage of place was balanced against a centripetal millennium, in which "righteousness... shall be a town dweller."[89] Definitions of spiritual liberty were therefore often actually rooted in prior models of community, and defenses of diversity were typically tied to the process of diversification at the urban center of the social order. The "City compact (Ps. 122.3)" was thus among the common models for the congregational "free society or communion...embodyed and knit together by a voluntary consent."[90] London, with its quasi-democratic electoral system, its multiplying craft and trade associations, and its diversifying population and subcommunities, was frequently invoked as the model for new types of spiritual community. The right of "a single congregation...to an entireness of rule and government within itself," was likened, for example, to the "grants of Government and rule within themselves unto Towns and Corporations."[91] The rights of congregations to elect their officers were defended on the analogy that freemen "must be a corporation, before they can choose a Maior."[92] The right to religious assembly, of worshippers "to choose their own company, place and time," moreover, was likened to the rights of association among such urban subcommunities as

a body or college of physicians in a city, ... a corporation, society, or company of East India or Turkey merchants, or any other society or company in London; which companies may hold their courts, keep their records, hold disputations, and in manners concerning their society may dissent, divide, break into schisms and factions, sue and emplead each other at the law, yea, wholly break up and

[86] *Olbia. The New Iland Lately Discovered* (1660), p. 124.
[87] *A Paraenetick* (November 30, 1644), p. 13.
[88] *An Apologeticall Narration* (January, 1644), in Haller, *Tracts on Liberty*, 2: 391.
[89] Nathaniel Holmes, *The New World Discovered*, pp. 8–9.
[90] Bartlet, *Ichnographia*, pp. 32, 30.   [91] Goodwin, *M. S. to A. S.*, pp. 72–73.
[92] Thomas Hooker, *A Survey of the Summe of Church-Discipline* (1648), pt. i, p. 93; cf. pt. ii, p. 73.

dissolve into pieces or nothing, yet the peace of the city not be in the least measure impaired or disturbed.[93]

Religious congregations, John Goodwin argued, need be tied to the neighborhood parish no more than guilds or trading companies, whose mobile members "dwell scatteringly and promiscuously up and downe the Citie, with the greatest irregularitie of intermixture that lightlie can be, and without... inhabiting within one and the same parish; and yet without any complaint or incovenience."[94] Modelled, then, on other forms of diversification within the expanding metropolis, the ideal of religious Independency was that "persons dissenting in very sub-stantialls of their respective religions" might "lovingly and peaceably combine and live together... even in the same Citie, yea, in the same street or neighbour-hood" and be "mutually helpful and serviceable one to another."[95]

The analogy of sectarian liberty with civic subcommunities perforce assumed, as Roger Williams put it, that "the city was before them, and stands absolute and entire when such a corporation or society is taken down."[96] This helps to explain the peculiar contradictions of rev-olutionary thought, the tensions between order and liberty, custom and reason, consolidation and expansion that seemed to limit the possibilities of change at every phase of the Revolution. In one sense *critical* of the concentration of power, revolutionary thought was in another sense *apologetic* for it – a defense of the process of diversification by which an urbanizing social order was actually establishing itself.[97]

There is, for example, more than a grain of truth in Lilburne's claim, after the defeat of the Levellers, that his effort had been "a strong endeavour for the prosperity and flourishing estate of this renowned City, the Metropolis of England."[98] Like corporate analogies used in defense of religious congregations, the political rights advanced in Lilburne's version of the Leveller program were paradoxically derived both from custom and from reason, from an antecedent historical order and the rational order that superseded it. The "liberties, Trade, and

---

[93] John Cook, *What the Independents Would Have* (March, 1647), p. 2; Williams, *Bloody Tenent*, in Woodhouse, *Puritanism and Liberty*, p. 267.

[94] *Theomachia* (October, 1644), in Haller, *Tracts on Liberty*, 3: 37.

[95] John Goodwin, *Innocency and Truth Triumphing Together* (January, 1645), p. 54.

[96] *The Bloody Tenent*, in Woodhouse, *Puritanism and Liberty*, p. 267.

[97] For this distinction and for radical Independency as the embodiment of *critical* bourgeois thought (i.e. bourgeois thought in its rationalist rather than empiricist mode), see Andrew Milner, *John Milton and the English Revolution: A Study in the Sociology of Literature* (Totowa, N.J.: Barnes and Noble, 1981), chs. 2–3, and esp. p. 60.

[98] *The Picture of the Council of State* (2nd edn. October, 1649), in Haller and Davies, *The Leveller Tracts*, p. 238.

Freedom" of Londoners, Lilburne argued, were confirmed both by "the fundamentall Lawes and Constitutions of this Kingdome" and "by God, and the great Charter of Nature."[99] Thus, on the one hand, Lilburne could argue for a contractual Agreement of the People as the logical extension of customary rights being claimed "by a company of honest men, living in and about London ... that in the worst of times durst own our Liberties Freedomes."[100] On the other hand, insofar as it was an extension of customary liberties to their *rational* conclusion, Lilburne's formulations finally transcended those "ancient customes and practices of the Grandees of London" which were not "agreeable to the word of God, the Law of Nature, and sound Reason."[101] Movements for democratic form within the City government embodied similar paradoxes.[102] While a call for civic reform in 1650 reminded Londoners that servile precedents "cannot tye you in your generations from the claiming and assuming of your indubitable natural rights," a collection of such precedents from City charters was used in 1648 to exhort Londoners to extend their customary liberties to others, "to stand up like men, ... in assisting to the utmost your selves and your neighbours both in the City and Country, that you may be free from all tyranny."[103] Meant to undo the power of London, the "Hypocritical City" that gave "freedome to the rich," even Gerrard Winstanley's communist, agrarian utopia was to be founded through a national expansion of the City's electoral procedures, "for the peace of London is much preserved by removing their officers yearly."[104] In these and countless other cases, the new order that was to displace the old was in fact an expansion and intensification of it. As one Royalist complained "that ancient little Modell the City (not circumscribed now in the Lines of Communication) ... hath reduced and whitled that maine prop and post of our English Government (the Parliament) to lesse power and proportion then a Sheriffes white rod, or a Constables painted staffe."[105]

Not surprisingly, then, local and universal, center and periphery are dialectically related in revolutionary thought. Milton's *Areopagitica*, for example, defends the principle of free inquiry with a stirring appeal to the revolutionary transformation of London into a bastion of liberty:

[99] *Londons Liberties in Chains Discovered*, p. 40
[100] *Englands New Chains Discovered* (February 26, 1649), in Haller and Davies, *Leveller Tracts*, p. 168.   [101] *Londons Liberties in Chains*, p. 45.
[102] See, e.g., John Bellamie, *A Plea for the Commonalty of London*, p. 19.
[103] *Newes from Guildhall* (February 18, 1650), sig. B2v; *Londons Ancient Priviledges Unvailed*, s. sh.
[104] *A Watch-Word to the City of London and the Armie* (August 26, 1649), in *Political Writings*, pp. 335, 316; *The Law of Freedom* (1650), in Christopher Hill, ed., "*The Law of Freedom*" *and Other Writings* (Harmondsworth: Penguin, 1973), p. 321.
[105] *Londons New Recorder* (September 30, 1647), s. sh.

Behold now this vast City; a City of refuge, the mansion house of liberty, encompast and surrounded with his protection; the shoppe of warre hath not there more anvils and hammers waking, to fashion out the plates and instruments of armed Justice in defence of beleaguer'd Truth, then there be pens and heads there, sitting by their studious lamps, musing, searching, revolving new notions and idea's, wherewith to present, as with their homage and their fealty, the approaching Reformation: others as fast reading, trying all things, assenting to the force of reason and convincement.[106]

On the one hand, Milton's evocation of the revolutionary atmosphere in London partakes of the centripetal millennial fervor that led thousands of Londoners to erect the lines of communication – "the walls of Jerusalem," as one pamphlet called them.[107] But on the other hand, for Milton, the true manifestation of the city's power lies rather in the far-flung process of circulation and diversification that emanates from it. The true wonder is that as the center and engine of a revolutionary *process* the city should transcend its imposed physical limits:

when a City shall be as it were besieg'd and blockt about, her navigable river infested, inrodes and incursions round, defiance and battell oft rumor'd to be marching ev'n to her walls and suburb trenches, that then the people, or the greatest part, more then at other times, wholly tak'n up with the study of highest and most important matters to be reform'd, should be disputing, reasoning, reading, inventing, discoursing... is a lively presage of our happy successe and victory. (p. 557)

In celebrating "the earnest and zealous search after knowledge and understanding which God hath stirr'd up in this City" (p. 554), Milton shares with Thomas Goodwin the view that "this city (for aught I know) hath been the greatest mart for truth in this last age, of any part of the world, and Wisdom hath cried her wares here more then in any other place."[108] In both cases, the active search for truth runs in metaphoric tandem with the expansion of free trade, an extension to all of rights hitherto concentrated in the hands of London monopolists.

Arguments on behalf of unrestricted trade insisted that commerce was "the great link of humane society," the providential means by which civilization extended and elaborated itself globally; there could therefore be nothing "so advantageous and commendable in a Trade, as Community and Freedome," for "the more common and diffusive a good thing is, the better it is."[109] Milton's objection that "Truth and trade are

---

[106] *CPW*, 2: 553–554.
[107] *A True Declaration of the Great and Incomparable care of the Right Honourable Isaac Pennington* (April 27, 1643), p. 6.
[108] *The Glory of the Gospel, Works*, 4: 313; cf. p. 253.
[109] *A Discourse Consisting of Motives for the Enlargement and Freedome of Trade* (April 11, 1645), pp. 1, 3; cf. Edward Misselden, *Free Trade* (1622), p. 25.

not such wares to be monopoliz'd and traded in by tickets and statutes"
thus defends the "diffusive" good of unrestricted publication by analogy
to theories that extended to "every free-born subject" the "right to have
freedom to trade … to go out of the realm of England, and to come, and
abide, and to go through the Realm of England."[110] Among the active
proponents of these theories were the members of the interloping
colonial companies that were challenging the political control of London
by such established syndicates as the East India Company – the puritan
members of the Massachusetts Bay Company, for example, whose twin
goals were "the propagation of the Gospel of Jesus Christ and the
particular good of the several adventurers."[111] While noting that "the
support of Trade is the strength of this Island," Hugh Peter added that
"the West Indies and the East too offer themselves to our devotion." In
introducing a number of mercantilist and colonialist proposals to
Parliament, Thomas Chaloner explained how mercantile expansion
served both material and spiritual purposes, enriching England "with
gold, with pearls and gems," while enlightening and liberating native
populations "from Spanish yoke and Romes Idolatry."[112] The two-fold
dissemination of commerce and spiritual light prompted Thomas Hill's
observation that "Plato called Merchants, Planets, that wander from
City to City. You will never trade for Truth in good earnest, till you
express an inquisitive, active disposition, in the cause of Religion,
knocking at every doore, plying the Market, where you may purchase any
acquaintance with the truth."[113] For Thomas Goodwin, this active,
expansive search was a collaborative venture in a diversifying world:

"Many shall run to and fro, and knowledge shall be increased." That is, by doing
as merchants do, travelling from place to place, comparing one with another,
knowledge will be increased … Therefore exchange and truck with one another to
that end … The knowledge of any one man is imperfect, some have more skill in
one part, and some in another, and so in several ages several truths have been
delivered and revealed, Heb. 1.1, *polymeros*, by fragments and pieces, and

---

[110] Thomas Johnson, *A Plea for Free-Mens Liberties* (January, 1646), sigs. A2, AV. On
Milton's economic metaphors in the *Areopagitica*, and their connection to his sympathy
for the man "labouring his hardest labour" (2:562), see Michael Wilding, "Milton's
Areopagitica: Liberty for the Sects," in Thomas N. Corns, *The Literature of
Controversy* (London: Frank Cass, 1987), pp. 17–18.

[111] Pearl, *London and the Outbreak of the Puritan Revolution*, p. 169; see also Robert
Brenner, "The Civil War Politics of London's Merchant Community," *Past and
Present*, 58 (1973), 53–107, and James E. Farnell, "The Social and Intellectual Basis of
London's Role in the English Civil Wars," *Journal of Modern History*, 49: 4 (1977),
646, 653.

[112] Hugh Peter, *Mr. Peters Last Report of the English Wars*, p. 9; Thomas Chaloner,
prefatory poem to Thomas Gage, *A New Survey of the West Indies* (1648), sig. A7v. See
also Brenner, *Merchants and Revolution*, ch. 12.

[113] *The Trade of Truth Advanced* (Parliamentary sermon, August, 1642), p. 29.

therefore use the help of all... Let the market stand open, take heed how you prohibit any truth to be sold in your markets.[114]

For Milton and other revolutionaries, the "flowery crop of knowledge and new light sprung up and yet springing up daily in this City" was a function of increasing diversity and discursive exchange, of a productive "struggle of contrarieties."[115] A "free trading of truth," by eliminating "the tunaging and poundaging of all free spok'n truth," would bring Christian liberty to the maturity embodied in the Pauline exhortation to "prove all things."[116] If the waters of truth, Milton observed, "flow not in a perpetuall progression, they sick'n into a muddy pool of conformity and tradition" (2:543). The obverse to his celebration of "this vast City, ... the mansion house of liberty" was thus a resistance to the centripetal forms of millennialism, an anti-sedentary insistence on the centrifugal thrust of the revolutionary moment. London was a "house of refuge," but "he who thinks we are to pitch our tent here, and have attain'd the utmost prospect of reformation,... that man by this very opinion declares, that he is yet far short of Truth" (2:549). Such premature or infantile sedentarism, like that of the Presbyterians calling for censorship and limits on toleration, would be "but to translate the Palace Metropolitan from one kind of dominion into another" (2:541). Yet paradoxically – and whether or not Milton was bearing in mind the urban as well as ecclesiastical implications of the word – the true translation of "metropolitan" influence lay in the new form of sedentarism that Milton celebrates in the discovery of "onward things more remote" (2:550). In its centrifugal expansion of the urbanizing process, the anti-sedentary force of revolutionary thought appeared to dissolve the very center whose power it was actually consolidating.

This paradox helps to explain the resistances to revolution that emerged from within the various parties to the Revolution themselves, beginning with the Presbyterian reaction in the city of London. The radical London alliance had never fully curbed the power of Royalists on the elite aldermanic bench; the election of a Presbyterian conservative, John Gayre, as Lord Mayor in 1646 provoked Lilburne's contest with the "Prerogative men of London" in *Londons Liberties in Chains Discovered* (1646) and, according to Walwyn, marked the point at which "there broke forth here at London a spirit of persecution."[117] Numerous concerns buttressed resistance to the course of revolution in London:

[114] *The Glory of the Gospel*, in *Works*, 4:247–248.
[115] *Areopagitica, CPW*, 2:558; *The Reason of Church Government, CPW*, 1:795.
[116] *The Ancient Bounds*, in Woodhouse, *Puritanism and Liberty*, p. 58; *Areopagitica, CPW* 2:545, 514; cf. Robinson, *Liberty of Conscience*, in Haller, *Tracts on Liberty*, 2:157.
[117] *Walwyns Just Defence* (June–July, 1649), in *Writings*, p. 386.

deep-seated royalism among those members of the mercantile and civic elite whose financial interests had been tied to court patronage; a traditional deference to the neofeudal ethic of the merchant class; a resentment of interlopers in syndicated trade, of "new men" in government, and of increasingly defiant craftsmen and laborers; resentment also of the deleterious financial impact of the First Civil War, the weekly assessments, and the Excise; a profound anxiety over religious heterodoxy. A common factor in many of these concerns, however, was the perception that the centrifugal effects of the Revolution – the widening of liberties and of active participation in society – were eroding the integrity of the urban community, the inviolability of its local interests and franchises, its traditional communities and social organization. Much of the original impetus toward revolution in the city had arisen over royal encroachment on local interests through the exaction of Ship Money and other impositions, challenges to City and company charters, and the establishment of court patents and customs farms. Even during the radical rule of 1642–43, London's leaders tended to act in behalf of local interests – resistance to radicalization of the Militia, for example, came through opposition to recruitment in the unincorporated suburbs.[118] Not surprisingly, then, resistance to the course of revolution typically presented itself as a defense of the traditional idea of place.

A strong bulwark in this defense was the appeal, among Londoners, of the program for a Presbyterian system of classes and synod that would maintain a uniform national religion, a licensed clergy, and the established network of local parishes and vestries. By 1648, one third of the London parishes were indeed without ministers, and the Presbyterian propagandist John Vicars, in "A general Bill of Mortality of the Clergy of London," listed more more than eighty London parishes where incumbents had been challenged by religious radicals.[119] For Presbyterian adherents to the traditional parochial order, the heterodox doctrines and Church polity of Independents and separatists were kindling a "City-devouring fire"; they threatened, as one divine preached to the Lord Mayor and aldermen in 1644, to reduce the orderly community "to a chaos without forme and void."[120] Because the system of parishes and vestries was an integral component of the civic order, democratic movements within the City government were represented as

---

118 Pearl, *London and the Outbreak of the Puritan Revolution*, pp. 267–268.
119 Tolmie, *The Triumph of the Saints*, p. 117; John Vicars, *Persecutio Undecima. The Churches Eleventh Persecution ... More Particularly within the City of London* (November, 1648), pp. 44–48.
120 Edmund Calamy, *The Door of Truth Opened*, p. 4; Richard Vines, *The Impostures of Seducing Teachers Discovered* (1644), p. 2, both quoted in Liu, *Discord in Zion*, pp. 43–44.

attempts to "throw up all the enclosures of Order in the City of London."[121] The expansion of religious freedom was castigated as an attempt to "pluck up the hedge of the parish order," to "ruinate the wall, and pluck-up the Hedge or safe Fence" of religious harmony within the city.[122] As Richard Vines complained to the Lord Mayor and aldermen, the Independents and separatists were nomads and walkers "who will not endure to sit at the feet of a constant Godly ministry."[123]

But just as important was the perception among reformers themselves that the erosion of the established parochial order would retard the centripetal momentum towards the establishment of a millennial community.[124] Thus Thomas Hill attacked the centrifugal effects of gathered congregations by declaring that "to tolerate all religions, to make London an Amsterdam, ... is such an undermining of the Temple, that this would soon pull down Gods house here, but never build it up."[125] Baxter's critique of "the Independent way" was that it offered "no probable way of Concord; ... Their Building wanteth Cement." Horrified that in London "the Parishes ... are but like a dead Corps without Life," Baxter declared that "I would not be a member of a Church gathered out of any Parishes, in such a place as London: Cohabitation is ... the necessary Disposition of the Materials of the Church."[126] The admonition of Independents against those who cry "The Temple of the Lord, The Temple of the Lord," was sufficient proof, as Robert Baillie put it, that they "oppose the building of the Temple."[127]

Conservative London clergymen had several times petitioned the Westminster Assembly and Parliament against gathered congregations and separatism, and by the autumn of 1645 they were joined by a rising Presbyterian lay movement within the city. The counter-revolutionary campaign, as Walwyn explained, involved "bitter Invectives in Pulpits ... framing petitions for the easy and ignorant people, ... urging them

---

[121] Irenaeus Lysimachus, *Bellamius Enervatus* (May 2, 1645), p. 1; Philip Henry, *Diaries*, quoted in Nuttall, *Visible Saints*, p. 108; John Vicars, *The Schismatick Sifted* (June 22, 1646), p. 5.   [122] *The Pulpit Incendiary* (May 4, 1648),

[123] *The Impostures of Seducing Teachers* (April 23, 1644), quoted in William Haller, *Liberty and Reformation in the Puritan Revolution* (New York: Columbia University Press, 1955), p. 165.

[124] See Pearl, "London's Counter-Revolution," in G. E. Aylmer, ed., *The Interregnum: The Quest for Settlement* (London: Macmillan, 1972), pp. 31–33; Tolmie, *The Triumph of the Saints*, p. 116; Michael Mahoney, "Presbyterianism in the City of London, 1645–47," *Historical Journal*, 22 (1979), 93–114.

[125] *The Season for Englands Selfe-Reflection, and Advancing Temple-Work* (Parliamentary sermon, August 13, 1644), p. 34.

[126] *Reliquae Baxterianae*, 2: 14 and App. iii, pp. 59, 63, 62, quoted in Nuttall, *Visible Saints*, pp. 100, 108.

[127] John Owen, *A Vision of Gods Unchangeable Free Mercy* (April 29, 1646), p. 25; Baillie quoted in Sirluck's Introduction to *CPW* 2: 99.

upon the Common Councell, and obtruding them on the chusers of Common Councell men, at the Wardmote Elections."[128] Announcing that "this great City and the Ministers" would purge the "rude and undigested Chaos" besetting it, Thomas Edwards' enormously influential *Gangraena* (February, 1646) prepared the way for the presentation of the great "City Remonstrance," in which the official bodies of the Corporation announced their outrage at "the daily invectives against us from the Pulpit, ... the scurrilous and seditious Pamphlets daily broached against, and in the City: And the great contempt of ... the Ministers of the Gospel, who adhere to the Presbyteriall Government." Calling for the old social order of "Noblemen, Barons, Knights, Gentlemen, Citizens, Burgesses, Ministers of the Gospel" to "endeavour in their Severall Places and Callings," this "DIVELISH, WICKED, BLOODY, UN-CHRISTIAN, PAPISTICALL REMONSTRANCE of the Prerogative-men of London" (as Lilburne called it) staked its stand against the centrifugal effects of revolution in a staunch sedentarism, a belief that if men live in religious and civic unity "the Lord may delight to dwell in the middest of us."[129] In the view of Hugh Peter, the attempt of the City Remonstrance to make Parliament "speak pure London" was "parochial" or insular in the moral sense, the work of inward-looking citizens who "never lived beyond the view of the smoke of their own Chimnies, that measure States and kingdomes with their interests, by their private shopwards."[130]

As the rhetoric of its supporters suggests, this sedentarism, meant to reconsolidate power over the local community, paternalistically assumed the moral inadequacy of its individual members. Thomas Crawford, for example, asked Londoners who had withdrawn from the parochial order

why should you go abroad to buy, when you have food at home? God hath been gracious to this City; I may speak it without arrogance, it was hardly ever better provided for; the losse of the country hath been your gain: Why should you withdraw yourselves? The mothers milke is most naturall for the infant; the sheep that wanders most far from the flock is in most danger to the wolfe; change of diet is not wholesome for the body; is it for the soule? ... children that change their Masters, seldome become good scholars.[131]

[128] Burton, *Conformities Deformitie*, p. 16; Walwyn, *Tolleration Justified* (January 29, 1646), in *Writings*, pp. 156–157.
[129] Edwards, *Gangraena* (February 26, 1646), p. 4; *The Humble Remonstrance and Petition of the Lord Mayor, Aldermen, and Commons of the City of London in Common Councell Assembled* (May 26, 1646), pp. 7, 3; Lilburne, *Londons Liberties in Chains Discovered*, p. 36.
[130] *A Word for the Armie* (October 11, 1647), pp. 5–6. Second passage, without identification, is quoted in Pearl, "London's Counter-Revolution," p. 34.
[131] Crawford, *Haereseo-Machia*, pp. 36–37.

This was, in the view of Independents and separatists, to circumscribe human freedom – to "build up the walls of Babylon" – with what John Goodwin called an "invisible line, which surroundeth so much of the superficies of the earth as times of ignorance and superstition thought meet to appropriate and allow to their respective parishes."[132] Freedom from local order was justified by the new covenant of grace; it was no longer possible "to make a law for all England," or even one "that should be good for ... one Town that is for another," because when God gave "lawes in the Old Testament, there was but one nation, and a little nation, and the Gospel was not to remove from that nation, but the Gospel being now to be preached to all nations, he hath left a latitude to his people, that they may apply the Gospel, to all countries and nations."[133] In a satiric work of Walwyn, the heresiologist Thomas Edwards was made to recant his defense of a national Church and parochial order by admitting that

all places are indifferent, whether in the mountain or in the fields, or the water, in the ship, or on the shore, in the Synagogues Or, privat houses, in an upper or low-roome; all is one ... Not in Jerusalem nor in this mountaine, but in every place he that lifteth up pure hands is accepted. Wheresoever two or three are gathered together in my name (saith our Saviour) I will be in the middest of them.[134]

As Overton observed, Mr. Persecution had at last taken refuge "in a petitionary garb in the behalfe of the London Ministers," there to become an "enemy to all spirituall knowledge, a hinderer of its increase and growth."[135] Without a "compulsive Presbytery in the Church," he added, "a compulsive mastership, or Aristocraticall Government over the People could never long be maintained."[136]

Levellers like Overton, Lilburne, and Walwyn had long supported the toleration of diversity among the sects, but with the escalation of the London counter-revolution during the demobilization crisis of the spring of 1647 – which cowed many religious Independents – the Levellers began to lead and widen, both in London and in the Army, the movement for decentralization of power. It was among the Levellers and other radical groups of the Second Civil War that the centrifugal force of

[132] John Goodwin, *M. S. to A. S.*, p. 101; *Anapologesiates*, p. 185, quoted in Tolmie, *The Triumph of the Saints*, p. 100   [133] Walter Craddock, *Gospel Libertie*, p. 23.
[134] *A Prediction of Mr. Edwards His Conversion and Recantation* (11 August, 1646), in *Writings*, p. 233.
[135] Overton, *The Arraignment of Mr. Persecution* (April, 1645), in Haller, *Tracts on Liberty*, 3: 211–212, 234.
[136] *A Remonstrance of Many Thousand Citizens*, in Don M. Wolfe, *Leveller Manifestoes of the Puritan Revolution* (New York: T. Nelson and Sons, 1944), pp. 121–122.

the campaign for religious liberty was extended to the systematic attack on concentrated power in all forms, "the Antichristian interest, interwoven, and coupled together in civill, or spirituall things."[137] Lilburne, in *Englands Birth-Right Justified*, for example, linked together several forms of monopoly, all of which restricted a proper distribution of liberties: "the Patent ingrossing Preaching of the Word"; "The Patent of Merchant Adventurers, who have ingrossed into their hands the sole trade of all woollen commodities"; and a "third Monopoly... that insufferable, unjust, and tyrannical Monopoly of Printing."[138] Richard Overton's *Remonstrance of Many Thousand Citizens* (July 7, 1647), the first major document of the organized Leveller movement, placed its case against the unjust concentration of power squarely in opposition to the Presbyterian strategy for manipulating "the generality of the Citie of London," and to the "exhorbitancies in the Cities Government... against the Freedoms of the Commons," which had been reduced "to the same point they were at in Garrawayes time" (i.e., 1639–40).[139] Its grievances included not only "the exhorbitancies in the Cities Government," but also the "Synod in judgement... discountenancing all Separation, Anabaptists and Independents," restriction of the "Printing-presse to one onely, and that to the Presbytry," "the oppression of the Turky Company, and the Adventurers Company, and all other infringements of our Native Liberties," and the "trade of Judges and Lawyers" (pp. 121, 124, 125).

London's rulers, Walwyn argued (not incorrectly) were part of a conspiracy centered in the Presbyterian peace party in Parliament, "the sons of Zeruiah... that is to say, the Malignants, and Delinquents, the Lawyers (some few excepted), the Monopolizing merchants, the sons and servants of the Lords."[140] The petition was burned by order of Parliament on May 22.

As Parliamentary Independents were increasingly cowed by London mob support for the purge of radicals and for peace, a revolutionary counter-movement, linking the interests of the Army, Levellers, and separatists, and supported by disenfranchised popular elements in London, undertook a "memorable contest" against "the corrupt party then prevalent in both Houses and the city," making a case for the dissemination and distribution of liberties in all respects.[141] With the

---

[137] John Owen, *The Shaking and Translating of Earth and Heaven* (1649), p. 35.
[138] *Englands Birth-Right Justified*, in Haller, *Tracts on Liberty*, 3: 267–268.
[139] In Wolfe, *Leveller Manifestoes*, pp. 118, 121.
[140] *Gold Tried in the Fire* (June 14, 1647), in *Writings*, p. 279.
[141] Nedham, *The Case of the Commonwealth*, p. 97. See, in addition to Pearl, "London's Counter-Revolution," Ian Gentles, "The Struggle for London in the Second Civil War," *Historical Journal*, 26: 2 (1983), 277–305.

publication of Overton's *Appeale from the Degenerate Representative Body ... to ... the Free People ... and to All the Officers and Souldiers* (July 17, 1647), the conflict between the centripetal and centrifugal forces in the capital had come to a head. Overton's tract asserted on its title page that God's warning to "the children of Israel which dwelt in the cities of Judah" might "now be applyed to London." All liberties or privileges of "place," all "Orders or titles,... all Lawes, Customes, and manners amongst men must be subject to *give place* and yeeld... to *Popular safety,*" to which "all the Children of men have an equall title by Birth."[142] From the time in August, 1647, that the Army marched on the metropolis and was admitted to the City with the cooperation of the Southwark trained bands and their Leveller supporters, it was no longer the local custom of London (whose Presbyterian leaders were purged and jailed) that held the day, but the mobile body of the Army, "not a mere mercenary army ... but called forth ... to the defence of our own and the people's just rights and liberties."[143]

There subsequently grew up, among radicals, a whole mythology against the misbegotten, centripetal forms of sedentarism. Winstanley's account of the historical origins of property and oppression, for example, is a striking elaboration of "the incroaching usurpations of some great and mighty Nimrods in the world" that Lilburne had associated with the "Prerogative men of London." According to Winstanley, "the rise of kingly power" came about "first by policy, drawing the people from a common enjoyment of the earth and to the crafty art of buying and selling."[144] For the "true levellers" of Buckinghamshire, as well, the common treasury of the earth was parcelled out in a sedentary system of feudal "Charters, Pattents, and Corporations," all "devised onely to uphold the kings Tyranny." Through the incorporation of their communities

petty-tyrants ... domineer over the Inhabitants by vertue of their Patent, and enclose all,... and claime a Priviledge from their Charters and Patents that they scorn to be accountable to others, but to their Prerogative-masters; so that you see all tyranny shelters it self under the kings wings ... and untill those Corporations be thrown down, we can expect never any hope of freedome ... See how Londons Common-Counsell stir up their Hackneys with Petitions and Mutineys, for a Treaty with our conquered enemy, &c.[145]

---

[142] In Wolfe, *Leveller Manifestoes*, pp. 156, 178.
[143] *A Representation of the Army* (June 14, 1647), in Woodhouse, *Puritanism and Liberty*, p. 404.
[144] *The Law of Freedom*, in Hill, *The Law of Freedom and Other Writings*, pp. 309, 348–349.
[145] *Light Shining in Buckinghamshire* (December 5, 1648), in Sabine, *The Works of Gerrard Winstanley*, pp. 619–620; cf. pp. 616, 636.

Behind this myth of sedentarism lay the Biblical Cain, first tiller and encloser of the earth, the founder of the urban order who "builded a city, and called the name of the city, after the name of his son, Enoch" (Gen. 4: 17). According to Winstanley, the earth was a "common treasury of livelihood for the whole mankind in all his branches" until "one branch of mankind began to lift himself above another, as Cain lifted up himself, and killed his brother Abel."[146] From this initial division of the common treasury into property and "place" came the "kingly government... that makes the elder brother freeman in the earth, and the younger brethren slaves in the earth."[147] "Being a younger brother," Lilburne "was bound Apprentize in London," but he met with nothing but "discouragements" because of "the mysteries of Corporations and Monopolies, which are both sons of one father."[148] Winstanley, who associated the mark of Cain with the mark of Revelation 13: 16 ("no man might buy and sell save he had the mark of the Beast") proclaimed, "Thou City of London, I am one of thy sons by freedome ... but by thy cheating sons in the theeving art of buying and selling ... I was beaten out of both estate and trade, and forced ... to live a Countrey-life."[149] The whole "civilizing" process was nothing but "Cain killing Abel to this very day."[150]

The question asked at Putney – "whether the younger son have not as much right to the inheritance as the eldest?" – was a question about the distribution of rights, about the handing on of power from liverymen to freemen, aldermen to councillors, monopolists to tradesmen, Church authorities to believers. It was also, as the parallel with the older and newer covenants suggests, a question about movement from center to periphery, local to universal. "In all the Dispensations of God, *out to the World*," John Sadler observed, "the Elder ... must give place to the second. Even the first Covenant it self, must be rejected and disanulled ... in order to a Second, Better, and more Gracious."[151] Just as the new covenant, in which "the soul of man is his national Temple," extended the national to the universal, so the unrelenting Leveller campaign for an Agreement of the People was a search for a social covenant that would extend locally restricted liberties to all. To the charge that they "will Center no where," the Levellers answered that the "determinate and

---

[146] *A Watch-Word to the City of London and the Armie*, in Sabine, *Political Writings*, p. 323. Cf. Lilburne, *Londons Liberties in Chains*, p. 17.

[147] *The Law of Freedom*, in Hill, p. 307.

[148] Humphrey Brooke, *The Charity of Church-men* (1649); Lilburne, *Legall Fundamentall Liberties* (January 8, 1649), in Haller and Davies, *Leveller Tracts*, pp. 344, 436–440.

[149] *Watch-Word*, in Sabine, *Political Writings*, pp. 315, 335.

[150] Ibid., p. 323; on religious persecution and fraternal oppression, see Robinson, *Liberty of Conscience*, and Overton, *The Arraignment of Mr. Persecution*, in Haller, *Tracts on Liberty*, 3: 171, 220.   [151] *Olbia*, p. 87.

fixed center" lay in Agreement that formalized the liberties of all; to such an agreement, embodied not in place but in persons, Lilburne and his cohorts would devote "hand, heart, life and blood,...and there center."[152] To the charge that he sought to "have the City destroyed," Walwyn answered that he sought merely to become "master of my affections."[153] If there was justice in the charge that a Leveller Agreement would reduce "the Kingdome unto Atomes," it was because it would establish the "right, freedome, safety, and well-being of every particular man, woman, and child in England."[154]

The "advancement of a communitive Happinesse" through decentralization was a feature not only of the Leveller Agreement but of numerous utopias and utopian schemes in the revolutionary period. Gabriel Plattes' *Macaria* (1641), for example, demonstrated how "great Cities, which formerly devoured the fatnesse of the Kingdome, may...make a considerable retribution," through a system of colonies, commerce, and "High-wayes," which, extending "through the fruitfull Garden" of the realm are "as faire as the streets of a City." The system of distribution within Macaria is thus a model for dissemination, as "the Arts of Printing will so spread knowledge, that the common people, knowing their own rights and liberties, will not be governed by way of oppression; and so, by little and little, all Kingdomes will be like to Macaria."[155] Influenced by the schemes of Baconian science and Comenian Pansophism, but also by the developing communications network of the metropolis, a number of utopian plans emerged for the centralized distribution of knowledge, information, and culture. Samuel Hartlib, declaring that "Gods intention is, that his goodnesse and glory should not be concealed...but made common to all that can partake thereof," sought to advance "the liberty of publique communication of the best things" by proposing the establishment of an office "for the Addresse of Accommodations" in London, "the most Centrall place." By gathering and disseminating information among buyers and sellers, employers and employees, producers and consumers, the office would transform the one-way downward flow of information into "sociable encounters and communications" nationwide, in recognition of the fact that "Mutuall Communication in good things is the chief fruit of all Society."[156] By

---

[152] *The Picture of the Council of State*, in Haller and Davies, *Leveller Tracts*, pp. 210, 225.
[153] *Walwyns Just Defence*, in *Writings*, pp. 394, 398.
[154] *A Declaration of Some Proceedings, The Just Defense of John Lilburne* (August 23, 1653), in Haller and Davies, *Leveller Tracts*, pp. 104, 453.
[155] *A Description of the Famous Kingdome of Macaria* (1641), pp. 11, 5, 4, 23.
[156] *Considerations Tending to the Happy Accomplishment of Englands Reformation* (1647), in Charles Webster, ed., *Samuel Hartlib and the Advancement of Learning* (Cambridge University Press, 1970), pp. 107, 136, 128.

1650, the London merchant and libertarian Henry Robinson was operating a "Center of Intelligence" out of Threadneedle Street that made it possible for "any person, living in any part of England," to dispatch business "without his comming up to London."[157] By 1657, competition among "several Offices of the like nature," and the degeneration of expansive inquiry into a commercialized weekly national classified section, revealed the extent to which the centrifugal flow of information was in fact a function of the concentration of economic force in the capital.[158] Nevertheless, this centrifugal flow was linked in the minds of revolutionaries to the expansion of liberty.

Thus, in Winstanley's utopian *Law of Freedom*, postal officers "in the chief city" would gather and distribute to all quarters of the land information about "any secret in Nature, or new invention in any art or trade or in the tillage of the earth ... whereby the commonwealth may more flourish." Meanwhile, in recognition of the two-way, collaborative nature of discourse, "everyone who hath any experience, and is able to speak of any art or language," would be allowed to address the local assembly on "what he hath found out by his own industry and observation in trial." The justification of the scheme was that "when commonwealth's freedom is established, ... then wil *Knowledge cover the earth, as the waters cover the seas* (Isa. 11: 9)."[159] Even Milton proposed to "spread much more knowledge and civilitie" by having "one chief town or more" in every county "made cities" and having the local "nobilitie and gentry ... annexed to each citie."[160]

Linking center to periphery, the expansive circulatory network of the revolutionary utopias was part of the same metropolitanizing pattern that inspired the imperial visions of the Restoration establishment. Thomas Sprat, for example, proposed London as the logical seat for the expanding empire of scientific knowledge:

If we should search through all the world, for a perpetual habitation, wherein the Universal Philosophy might settle it selfe; there can be none found, which is comparable to London, of all the former, or present seats of Empire ... It is London alone, that enjoys most of the others advantages, without their inconveniences. It is the head of a mighty Empire, the greatest that ever commanded the Ocean: It is composed of Gentlemen, as well as Traders: It has a large intercourse with all the Earth: It is, as the Poets describe their House of Fame, a City, where all the noises and business of the World do meet.[161]

---

157 *The Office of Addresses and Encounters* (1650), p. 6.
158 See, e.g., Oliver Williams, *A Prohibition to All Persons who Have Set up Any Offices* (May 27, 1657), s.sh.; *The Office of Publick Advice* (May, 1657), s.sh.
159 *The Law of Freedom*, in Hill, ed., *The Law of Freedom and Other Writings*, pp. 346, 355, 347.   160 *CPW*, 7: 460.
161 *History of the Royal Society*, ed. Jackson I. Cope and Harold Whitmore Jones (1959; rpt. St. Louis: Washington University Press, 1966), pp. 86–88.

In Dryden's imperial vision too, a restored London, "opening, into larger parts," stands at the center of an expanding commercial and scientific empire that "makes one city of the universe."[162]

This convergence of revolutionary utopia and Restoration empire reflects the growing and pervasive influence of a metropolitan way of life; it demonstrates the extent to which expansive movements toward a periphery were conditioned by a consolidation of power at the center. God's mark on Cain was lest anyone should slay him, lest he should be a fugitive and vagabond in the earth; it made him the father of sedentary order in its fallen form. Even in revolutionary thought and rhetoric, change and centrifugal movement were conditioned by a necessary reversion to the sedentary, to the communal forms of the old covenant, to the ways of the elder brother. Early in the Revolution, Roger Williams had objected that the Independents had laid too much "at the feet of the civil magistrate,"[163] and he was proven right in 1647 when, with the Army's march on London and purge of City government, the imprisoned leaders of the Levellers were not released. On the eve of the Putney debates, the agitators and their Leveller allies could object that, despite the occupation of a recalcitrant London in August, nothing had been accomplished since the Solemn Engagement in June.[164]

The debates at Putney revealed the reason why: the pursuit of an "absolute natural right," Ireton argued, flew in the face of "civil right" based on established custom. It was only "a permanent fixed interest," a "local interest" – of "persons in whom all land lies, and those in corporations in whom all trading lies" – that could define the political nation. The limits of reform, in other words, were defined by an inveterate sedentarism opposed to freedom of movement:

I mean by permanent [and] local, that [it] is not able [to be removed] anywhere else. As, for instance, he that hath a freehold cannot be removed out of the kingdom; and so there's a [freeman of a] corporation, a place which hath the privilege of a market and Trading, which if you should allow to all places equally, I do not see how you would preserve any peace in the kingdom, and that is the reason why in the constitution we have but some few market towns.[165]

As it was put by the religious Independents and sectarians of London – who had always found their alliance with the Levellers difficult – "God hath built up a wall of seperation between the estates of man and

[162] *Annus Mirabilis*, lines 1180, 651, in *John Dryden*, ed. Keith Walker (Oxford University Press, 1987), pp. 69, 52.
[163] *The Bloody Tenent of Persecution*, in Woodhouse, *Puritanism and Liberty*, p. 287.
[164] *The Second Part of Englands New-Chaines Discovered* (March 24, 1649); *The Case of the Armie Truly Stated* (October, 1647), in Haller and Davies, *Leveller Tracts*, pp. 175, 66.
[165] Woodhouse, *Puritanism and Liberty*, pp. 54, 57.

man."[166] The apocalyptic prophecy that "the merchants of the earth shall weep and mourn" (Rev. 11: 12), the right-wing London Independent William Strong explained, did not mean that with the fall of spiritual Babylon "men shall merchandize no more," for "the world shall continue, and trading still shall be."[167] In Walwyn's view, the victorious Independents had merely "scumm'd the Parish Congregations of most of their wealthy and zealous members," and begun to "new-mould the City" with the Army's aid. "These men of Jerusalem," he added, "drest out to the people in the sacred shape of God's Time,... now ... rest themselves in the large and full enjoyment of the creature."[168] For the Independents and their Army allies, however, the "sacred shape of God's Time" was a gradualist continuum in which the civil order was to be reformed in a moderate, rational manner under the progressive enlightenment of grace. Among the Independent ideologues, there was a measure of consistency between opposition to the Levellers in 1647–49 and opposition to Fifth Monarchists in 1653. If, on the one hand, the Leveller program for broadened liberties threatened to dissolve the "permanent fixed interest" at the heart of the social order, on the other hand a Fifth Monarchist theocracy threatened to halt the possibility of historic change with the declaration of a premature apocalypse, "an imaginary Paradise ... never to have end."[169] Both programs failed to recognize, as William Strong had put it, that "the world shall continue" in an ongoing dialectic of order and change, a process integrating matter and spirit, regimentation and diversity, consolidation and expansion. The protection of this process, of "a seasonable Mean ... of Peace and Settlement," held forth the hope of "a durable continuance to succeeding ages."[170] Milton, likewise opposed to the premature "pretending to a fifth monarchie of the saints," argued in defense of the Protectorate that "those whose power lies in wisdom, experience, industry, and virtue ... however small their number," were best able to carry forward a progressive program of reform. As he had identified them three years earlier, these were the members of the "middle class, which produces the greatest number of men of good sense and knowledge of affairs."[171]

---

[166] *A Declaration by Congregationall Societies in, and About the City of London, as of Those Commonly Called Anabaptists, as Others* (November 22, 1647), p. 10.

[167] *Babylons utter ruine, the Saints Triumph* (August 29, 1649), in *XXXI Select Sermons* (1656), p.78.

[168] *The Vanitie of the Present Churches*, p. 316; *The Second Part of Englands New-Chaines Discovered*, and Humphrey Brooke, *The Charity of Church-Men* (May 28, 1649), in Haller and Davies, *Leveller Tracts*, pp. 179, 344.

[169] *A True State of the Case of the Commonwealth* (1654), pp. 3, 18.

[170] Ibid., p. 52.

[171] *Second Defense, CPW*, 4.1: 636, 673–679; *First Defense, CPW* 4.1: 471.

The expansive sense of human possibilities in revolutionary thought had always been in part conditioned by the centrifugal effects of the power concentrating in a new metropolitan order. In the event, the Independents and republicans, like the Levellers before them, were brought down with the support of Londoners who demanded settlement in the belief "that nothing but kingship can restore trade."[172] But the restored order that was promised, and to some extent the one that was eventually and fitfully delivered, had more in common with the revolutionary movement toward expansion, diversity, progress, and increase than with the ancient regime that had preceded it. And not least of the enduring legacies were the ethical innovations – a cosmopolitan disinvestment in the local and "parochial," a reliance on reason, autonomy, and self-discipline, a self-restraint in the face of diversity – that, by linking personal liberty dialectically to new patterns of social discipline, helped to consolidate the urbanizing process. Perhaps typical of the revolutionary force of these innovations is Walwyn's view that nothing "maintains love, unity and friendship in families; Societies, Citties, Countries, Authorities, Nations; so much as a condescension to the giving, and hearing, and debating of reason." The emergence, from the Puritan Revolution, of views like Walwyn's and others makes it possible to see how the historical development of sedentarism could give moral force to Burke's later claim that liberty is a function of ethical maturity:

Men are qualified for civil liberty in exact proportion to their own disposition to put moral chains on their own appetites...Society cannot exist unless a controlling power upon will and appetite be placed somewhere, and the less of it there is within, the more there is without.[173]

"The utmost prospect of reformation": personhood and place in *Paradise Lost*

The epic thesis of *Paradise Lost* embraces not only the "loss of Eden," but also its aftermath, "till one greater Man / Restore us, and regain the blissful Seat."[174] With its emphasis on restoration, Milton's thesis

---

[172] *The Ready and Easy Way, CPW*, 7: 462.

[173] Walwyn, *The Fountain of Slaunder Discovered* (May 30, 1649), in *Writings*, p. 372; Burke, *Letter to a Member of the National Assembly*, in *Works* (8 vols. London: G. Bell, 1884–93), 2: 555, quoted in Stone, "The Results of the English Revolutions of the Seventeenth Century," p. 96.

[174] Lines 4–5, in *Complete Poems and Major Prose*, ed. Merrit Y. Hughes (1957; rpt. Indianapolis: Bobbs Merrill, 1975), p. 211. Unless otherwise indicated, subsequent references are to this edition.

openly defies both the general rhetoric of Restoration panegyric[175] and that particular species which, in the aftermath of the Fire of London, associated the renovation of the city with the restored powers of the monarchy. The still-smouldering city, encomiasts proclaimed, would experience "by second Charles, a Second Rise"; "hatch'd by a kind Monarch's breath," London would "rise a fairer Phoenix after death." Charles would add the title of "London's Restorer, to Great Britain's King"; it was

> He that shall this City now restore,
> To greater glory than it had before.[176]

As they are hurried from the Garden, Adam and Eve behold

> all th'Eastern side...
> Of Paradise, so late their happy seat,
> Wav'd over by that flaming Brand, the Gate
> With dreadful Faces throng'd and fiery Arms. (12.641–644)

The "blissful seat" that will be restored is not the locality of Eden, the "happie Native seat" (6.226; cf. 4.247) of which Adam and Eve are the only remnant, but "Heav'n the seat of bliss" (6.273). Yet the manner of its restoration will also demonstrate an ultimate indifference to place: at the time when "God shall be All in All" (3.341), the Son will receive the saints

> into bliss,
> Whether in Heav'n or Earth, for then the Earth
> Shall all be Paradise, far happier place
> Than this of Eden, and far happier days. (12.462–465)

Like Deucalion and Pyrrha after the flood, Adam and Eve pray after the fall in an attempt "to restore / The race of mankind" (11.12–13); but it is the "greater Man," not they, who will regain the "blissful Seat." He will not, like Aeneas and his epic progeny, simply reconstruct a locale; rather, he will "Restore us," Adam's descendants.

In its refusal to identify the act of restoration with any locality,

---

[175] See Michael Wilding, *Dragon's Teeth* (Oxford: Clarendon Press, 1987), p. 226; David Quint, *Epic and Empire: Politics and Generic Form from Virgil to Milton* (Princeton University Press, 1993), pp. 268–281.

[176] Simon Ford, *The Conflagration of London, Poetically Delineated* (1667); *Londinenses Lachrymae* (1666); *Londons Resurrection* (1669); *The Citizens Joy* (1667), in Robert Arnold Aubin, ed., *London in Flames, London in Glory: Poems on the Fire and Rebuilding of London, 1666–1709* (New Brunswick: Rutgers University Press, 1943), pp. 13, 52, 137, 120.

Paradise Lost is thus also a daringly iconoclastic revision of the norms of epic *translatio*, a rejection of the myth-historical mode of narrative by which Virgil and his Renaissance imitators balanced the loss of Troy with its grander reincarnation in settlements and civilizations throughout Europe. In *Paradise Lost*, this heroic impulse toward sedentarism is associated principally with Satan and his fallen cohorts, who attempt to "repossess thir native seat" (1.634), to establish a simulacrum of their lost realm, a "nether Empire... / In emulation opposite to Heav'n" (2.296–298), and to extend this "Infernal Empire" by taking possession of "a spacious World" and making "this World, one Realm, one Continent / Of easy thorough-fare" (10.389–391, 467). Milton's well-known rejection of classical heroism is rooted in his conception of Christian liberty; no man should presume to "sing high praises of... famous cities unless he have in himself the experience and practice of all that is praiseworthy."[177] But the indifference to place in *Paradise Lost*, while reflecting these Miltonic priorities, owes much of its importance to the immediate context of revolutionary thought and thus to the matrix of metropolitan culture out of which that thought arose. A sense of liberation – or alienation – from the local and customary limits of the urban community was essential to the extension of metropolitan influence, to the expanding patterns of migration, national markets, colonial trade and world-wide commerce that were to mark London's ascendancy as the largest metropolis in Europe. And significantly, for Milton, as for others, the ethical innovation put in the place of place – in this case a mobile inner paradise of expanding personal powers and responsibilities – provided a substitute for those traditional forms of communal discipline which grew less effective in the face of an expanding, diversifying, and ever more mobile urban populace. In keeping with the paradox of metropolitan growth itself – whereby power is concentrated through its diffusion and dissemination – the anti-epic resistance to sedentarism in *Paradise Lost* paradoxically provides a way of becoming "to the place conform'd" (2.216). In its anti-sedentary program, *Paradise Lost* is thus truly a *translatio* of epic norms: it carries on the process of sedentarism by other means.

After the fall, Eden becomes "the Paradise of God" (11.104), and the expulsion comes as a necessary correction of both Adam's misprision that "the bitterness of death / Is past, and we shall live" (11.157–158) and Eve's Belial-like proposal, "Here let us live, though in fall'n state, content" (11.180). When Adam learns from Michael of his impending exile, he asks,

[177]   *Apology, CPW*, 3: 303.

In yonder nether World where shall I seek
His bright appearances, or footstep trace?

His question is a variation of the epic questor's – Aeneas', for example:

Whom should we follow? Or by what sea way
Dost thou direct us? Where may we settle now?[178]

Or, as Milton translated it from Commelin's *Rerum Britannicarum* (1587), Trojan Brutus' question to Diana:

tell
What Land, what Seat of rest thou bidst me seek,
What certain Seat, wher I may worship thee
For aye, with Temples vow'd, and Virgin quires.[179]

Michael's answer to Adam, in establishing the basis for Milton's rejection of epic norms, explains why Milton never produced his contemplated national epic:

Adam, thou know'st Heav'n his, and all the Earth,
Not this Rock only; his Omnipresence fills
Land, Sea, and Air, and every kind that lives,
Fomented by his virtual power and warm'd:
All th'Earth he gave thee to possess and rule,
No despicable gift; surmise not then
His presence to these narrow bounds confin'd
Of Paradise or *Eden*: this had been
Perhaps thy Capital Seat, from whence had spread
All generations, and had hither come
From all the ends of th'Earth, to celebrate
And reverence thee thir great Progenitor.
But this preeminence thou hast lost, brought down
To dwell on even ground now with thy Sons:
Yet doubt not but in Valley and in Plain
God is as here, and will be found alike
Present, and of his presence many a sign
Still following thee, still compassing thee round
With goodness and paternal Love, his Face
Express, and of his steps the track Divine.   (11.335–354)

If Eve's grief that she must "leave / Thee Native Soil" embodies the epic exile's lament,[180] Adam embodies the epic impulse to memorialize the lost homeland in monuments:

---

[178] *Aeneid*, 3.85–89, tr. Robert Fitzgerald (New York: Random House, 1983), p. 68.
[179] *The History of Britain*, *CPW*, 5.1: 14.
[180] Christopher Fitter, "'Native Soil': Exile Lament and Exile Consolation in *Paradise Lost*," *Milton Studies*, 20 (1984), 147–162.

> here I could frequent,
> With worship, place by place where he voutsaf'd
> Presence Divine, and to my Sons relate;...
> So many grateful Altars I would rear
> Of grassy Turf, and pile up every Stone
> Of lustre from the brook, in memory,
> Or monument to Ages.   (11.317–326)

But such impulses are inappropriate to a spirituality that will become interior and universal; as Michael later explains in his account of the Flood, even "this Mount / Of Paradise" will

> by might of Waves be mov'd
> Out of his place, push'd by the horned flood,
> With all his verdure spoil'd, and Trees adrift
> Down the great River to the op'ning Gulf,
> And there take root an Island salt and bare,
> The haunt of Seals and Orcs, and Sea-mews clang.
> To teach thee that God attributes to place
> No sanctity, if none be thither brought
> By men who there frequent, or therein dwell.   (11.830–838)

Like other Independents, who objected to carnal worship as a "way of fixing God, and his spirit," and who thought it "a kind of Idolatry, to conceive that God enters into outward things," Milton believed that a carnal ministry turned "the inward power and purity of the Gospel into the outward carnality of the law; evaporating and exhaling the internall worship into empty conformities, and gay shewes."[181] The "impertinent fabling" of martyrdoms, for example, replaced the doctrine of the apostles with the fanciful memorials that here a martyr

taught, here he stood, this was his stature, thus he went habited, and O happy this house that harbour'd him, and that cold stone whereon he rested, this Village wherein he wrought such a miracle, and that pavement bedew'd with the warme effusion of his last blood, that sprouted up in eternall Roses to crowne his Martyrdome.[182]

The fallen angels in the catalogue of Book 1 acquire their names through the idolatrous establishment of local shrines and temples. The localization of worship in carnal form enables them to "fix / Thir Seats long after next the Seat of God, / Thir Altars by his Altar" (1.382–385). Fixed in locality, altars and shrines may be "profaned" (1.390), "unfrequented" (1.433), "disparaged" and "displaced" (1.473), or "filled / With lust and violence" (1.495–496). Idolatry is parasitic upon

---

[181] Saltmarsh, *Sparkles of Glory*, sig. Av; *The Reason of Church Government*, *CPW*, 1:766.
[182] *Of Prelaticall Episcopacy*, *CPW*, 1:642, cited in connection with the same passage in *Paradise Lost* by Fitter, "'Native Soil': Exile Lament," p. 151.

the sacralization of space: Belial takes up residence "In temples and at altars ... / In courts and palaces he also reigns, / And in luxurious cities" (1.494–498).

The omnipresent deity and potentially omnisacred creation described by Michael are thus an antidote to the idolatrous impulses of sedentarism. With the dissolution of fixed and privileged locality goes the hierarchy of "place" or status: as Adam is disinherited of the locality that "had been / Perhaps thy Capital Seat" he is also divested of his "preeminence" as a "Progenitor" and "brought down to dwell on even ground now with thy Sons." In place of the sedentary seat there is now the "track Divine," the tracing and adoring of God's footsteps from afar (11.354, 329, 332). The mountaintop to which Michael leads Adam, however, adds a further dimension to the pilgrimage that takes the place of place:

> Ascend, I follow thee, safe Guide, the path
> Thou lead'st me ...
> So both ascend
> In the visions of God: It was a Hill
> Of Paradise the highest, from whose top
> The Hemisphere of Earth in clearest Ken
> Stretcht out to the amplest reach of prospect lay.   (11.371–380)

Ascending the path while in the visions of God, Adam and Michael ascend a path that *is* the visions of God. This path is also the hill ("It was a Hill") whose name is "the Visions of God," a version of the *visio pacis*, or Jerusalem, that St. Augustine contrasted to the *confusio* of Babylon.[183] Not just pilgrimage but vision takes the place of place, and locality becomes significant only for the larger prospects it unfolds.

Adam's prospect partakes of both Babylon and Jerusalem, just as his vantage point conflates the dangerous mountaintop "Whereon ... the Tempter set / Our Second Adam in the Wilderness" with both the Pisgah sight of Canaan by Moses (cf. especially 12.137–146 and Deut. 34: 1–4)[184] and with the Templar pinnacle that marks Christ's triumph over Satan in *Paradise Regained*. The prospect opens first upon the splendid but fallen future of a sedentary human order:

> His eye might there command wherever stood
> City of old or modern Fame, the Seat
> Of mightiest Empire, from the destin'd Walls
> Of *Cambalu*, seat of *Cathaian Can*,

[183] *Ennarationes in Psalmos, Patrologia Latina*, 36: 773, quoted in John R. Knott, *Milton's Pastoral Vision: An Approach to "Paradise Lost"* (University of Chicago Press, 1971), p. 163.
[184] See Jason P. Rosenblatt, "Adam's Pisgah Vision: *Paradise Lost*, Books XI and XII," *ELH*, 39 (1972), 66–86.

> ... nor could his eye not ken
> Th'Empire of *Negus* to his utmost Port
> *Eroco* and the less maritime Kings
> *Mombaza*, and *Quiloa*, and *Melind* ...
> On *Europe* thence, and where *Rome* was to sway
> The World: in Spirit perhaps he also saw
> Rich *Mexico*, the seat of *Montezume*,
> And *Cusco* in *Peru*, the richer seat
> Of *Atabalipa*, and yet unspoil'd
> *Guiana*, whose great City *Geryon's* Sons
> Call *El Dorado*.   (11.385–411)

Adam's first sight from the hilltop resembles Satan's first view of the world, as, like a scout, he

> Obtains the brow of some high-climbing Hill,
> Which to his eye discovers unaware
> The goodly prospect of some foreign land
> First seen, or some renown'd Metropolis
> With glistering Spires and Pinnacles adorn'd,
> Which now the Rising Sun gilds with his beams.   (3.546–551)

What Adam in fact sees is the afterimage of the infernal sedentarism that begins with "Th'ascending pile" (1.722) of Pandemonium in Book 1, a false settlement that arises "anon out of the earth a Fabric huge," the "high Capitol / Of Satan and his Peers" (1.710, 756–757). By the time of Satan's return in Book 10, this templar capitol has become the "City and proud seat / Of Lucifer," with multitudes "reduc't in careful Watch / Round thir Metropolis" (10.424, 438–439). From his high throne in this metropolis, Satan proclaims possession of his empire, "a spacious World" (10.467).

Modelled on the foundational themes of the *Aeneid*, and following up that poem's declaration of an *imperium sine fine*, both the building of Pandaemonium and its global afterimage from the Mount of Speculation epitomize an epic sedentarism that deeply attracted the younger Milton. Milton's sixth Prolusion, for example, had described his return from a vacation in "that city which is chief of all cities,"[185] while his first Latin elegy celebrated the sophisticated pleasures of "my native place," the "city which the Thames washes with its tidal waters" (lines 9–10). In "L'Allegro," these became the pleasures of "Tower'd Cities" and "the busy hum of men" (lines 117–118). Milton identified himself to his Italian mentors as *alumnus ille Londini Milto* ("Ad Salsillium," line 9), while his first greeting of his "native Language," already anticipating an epic culmination of his poetic career, concluded with an image of "Royal

[185] *CPW*, 1: 266.

Tower'd Thame" ("At a Vacation Exercise," lines 1, 100). His "Manso," similarly announcing plans for a British epic, also celebrated the place "where the silvery Thames with pure urns spreads her green locks wide in the swell of the ocean" (lines 32–33).

At the same time, however, Milton had also thanked his father for sparing him from the legal career of his younger brother and thus for leading him "away from the uproar of cities into these high retreats of delightful leisure" ("Ad Patrem," lines 74–75). And in the Attendant Spirit's distaste for "the smoke and stir of this dim spot" and for being "Confin'd and pester'd in this pinfold here" (*Comus*, lines 5, 7), Milton had anticipated the likeness of Satan's arriving in Paradise to an urbanite

> long in populous city pent,
> Where houses thick and Sewers annoy the Air,
> Forth issuing on a Summer's Morn   (9.445–447)

Areopagitica's celebration of "this vast city" as the "mansion house of liberty" distinguishes between these images of sedentarism by opposing the stagnancy of settlement to the unsettling dynamism of the city as a process of "musing, searching, revolving new notions and ideas." The glory of revolutionary London is that it refuses confinement and, despite being "besieged and blocked about," continues in its "disputing, reasoning, reading, inventing, discoursing." By contrast, the danger of sedentarism is that it leads us to "pitch our tent here," before we have "attained the utmost prospect of reformation."

In *Paradise Lost*, the movement toward this "utmost prospect" begins with the purging of Adam's sin-bleared eyesight, the erasure of the vision of the world's great seats with a distillation that pierces "Ev'n to the inmost seat of mental sight" (11.418). The "utmost prospect" from this "inmost seat" is, as commentators have noted, the faithful vision "of things not seen" in Hebrews 11, the text which provides the typological skeleton of Books 11–12.[186] But it is also the vision of those patriarchs who went out from the confinement of inherited places in search of "a city which hath foundations, whose builder and maker is God"; it is the vision of those who became "strangers and pilgrims," knowing that God "hath prepared for them a city" (11: 8, 10, 13, 16). Insofar as this mode of vision issues in an inner discipline – an Arminian confidence in individual human powers and responsibilities – it also resembles that

---

[186] See esp. Barbara Lewalski, "Structure and the Symbolism of Michael's Prophecy, *Paradise Lost*, Books XI–XII," *PQ*, 42 (1963), 25–35; William G. Madsen, *From Shadowy Types to Truth: Studies in Milton's Symbolism* (New Haven: Yale University Press, 1968), pp. 95–97; Joseph H. Summers, *The Muse's Method: An Introduction to "Paradise Lost"* (Cambridge, Mass.: Harvard University Press, 1970), p. 198.

pattern which, according to Socrates, is "laid up in heaven for him who wishes to contemplate it and so beholding it to build a city in himself."

The purging of Adam's eyesight thus marks the beginning of a purgation of epic sedentarism:

> His eyes he op'n'd, and beheld a field,
> Part arable and tilth, whereon were Sheaves
> New reapt, the other part sheep-walks and folds;
> I' th' midst an Altar as the Land-mark stood.   (11.429–432)

History begins, as Adam's desire to monumentalize had already predicted, at an altar, at the fixing of a sacred spot over the *mundus* or pit that marks the connection between heaven and earth.[187] Standing, in Milton's version, "I' th' midst" of the subjected plain, the altar also serves as the "Land-mark" dividing two economic and moral orders, the Georgic order of the plowman Cain and the pastoral order of the shepherd Abel, the order of metallurgy, digging, and striated space and the order of husbandry, wandering, and smooth, continuous space. Cain's fratricidal act marks the historical ascendancy of the former over the latter, and it originates the endemic violence and violation that underlie the later forms of sedentarism. "It is recorded of Cain," St Augustine reported, "that he built a city, but Abel, being a shepherd, built none."[188] It was the view of one of Milton's models for Books 11–12, Du Bartas, that the "strangers and pilgrims," the patriarchs, of Hebrews 11, were "Shepheards all."[189] The subsequent history that unfolds in *Paradise Lost* 11–12 is thus a continuing spiritual struggle against the appeal and danger of sedentarism.

The vision of the sons of Lamech and the sons of Seth, for example, links the poem's first act of settlement, in Hell, to the subsequent history of earthly civilization, and it therefore re-enacts the fall of man as itself a misbegotten and premature act of settlement. The opening image of "a spacious Plain, whereon / Were Tents of various hue" (11.556–557), evoking Hell's "Plain in many cells prepar'd" (1.700) establishes a well-known series of parallels between the building of Pandaemonium and the civilized achievements of the sons of Lamech, a descendant of Cain.[190] At

---

[187] Rabbinic legend held that Cain "endeavored ... to immortalize his name by means of monuments, and he became a builder of cities," Louis Ginzberg, *The Legends of the Jews* (6 vols. 1909, rpt. Philadelphia: Jewish Publication Society, n.d.), 1: 115. See also Ricardo J. Quinones, *The Changes of Cain* (Princeton University Press, 1991), ch. 1. On the *mundus*, see Joseph Rykwert, *The Idea of a Town: The Anthropology of Urban Form in Rome, Italy and the Ancient World* (London: Faber and Faber, 1976), p. 59.

[188] *The City of God*, 15.1, quoted in Knott, *Milton's Pastoral Vision*, p. 153; cf. Cowley, "God the first Garden made, and the first City, Cain," "The Garden," also quoted in Knott, p. 153.   [189] Quoted in Knott, *Milton's Pastoral Vision*, p. 157.

[190] On these parallels, see Stanley Fish, *Surprised by Sin* (Berkeley: University of California Press, 1967), pp. 296–300.

the core of these parallels is the nexus of excavation, metallurgy, and musical creation. Excavating the volcanic hill in Hell (a counterpart to the one on which Adam stands), the cohorts of Mammon commit the orginal violations that will henceforth connect the patterns of sedentarism with those of warfare and violence. As forward as pioneers who "trench a Field / Or cast a Rampart," they connect the military *castrum* with the civil *urbs*, performing at once a military maneuver and the sacred act of defining the *sulcus primigenius*, the furrow that will become the outline and walls of a city.[191] At the same time, as they ransack "the Center... with impious hands" and rifle "the bowels of thir mother Earth" (1.686–687), they commit the act of violation, of dividing and despoiling, that will henceforth be associated with the descendants of the plowman–city-builder Cain. The wondrous metallulgical creation of Pandaemonium by organ-like conveyances, and its rising "like an Exhalation" to "the sound / Of Dulcet Symphonies" (1.707–712), are re-enacted in the achievements of Lamech's sons, Jubal the musician–organist and Tubal-Cain the metallurgist. In both cases, the musical foundations of technology and city-building, based on the Orphic and Amphionic myths, implicate the arts and poetry as agencies of sedentarism (in an exactly contemporary instance, one poet had implicated himself by claiming that Peace "Shall Ride Triumphantly in Charles his Waine; / Then shall it's Harmony our Thebes advance, / And make rude Stones into a City Dance").[192]

To Adam's delight that in the happy scene of Lamech's sons "Nature seems fulfill'd in all her ends," Michael sardonically replies that

> studious they appear
> Of Arts that polish Life, Inventors rare,
> Unmindful of thir Maker, though his Spirit
> Taught them, but they his gifts acknowledg'd none.   (11.609–612)

This is a version of the poet's own warning in Book 1:

> And here let those
> Who boast in mortal things, and wond'ring tell
> Of *Babel*, and the works of *Memphian* Kings,
> Learn how thir greatest Monuments of Fame,
> And Strength and Art are easily outdone
> By Spirits reprobate.   (1.692–697)

Nimrod's Babel and Pharoah's Memphian splendors and cruelties will both become later versions of the sedentary bondage figured in Pandaemonium and on the plain where Lamech's sons pitch their tents.

---

[191] See Rykwert, *The Idea of a Town*, p. 65.
[192] *A Poem on the Burning of London*, in Aubin, *London in Flames*, p. 59.

In the latter instance, captivation by sedentary ways becomes, in fact, a re-configuration of the fall itself, as the descendants of Adam's third son, Seth,

> a different sort
> From the high neighboring Hills, which was thir Seat,
> Down to the Plain descended; by thir guise
> Just men they seem'd, and all thir study bent
> To worship God aright, and know his works
> Not hid, nor those things last which might preserve
> Freedom and Peace to men: they on the Plain
> Long had not walkt, when from the Tents behold
> A Bevy of fair Women, richly gay
> In gems and wanton dress.   (11.574–583)

Descending from their hilltop seat of vision, and entering the artful tents of the daughters of men, the sons forsake "Freedom and Peace" for settlement in a manner that both repeats Adam's seduction by Eve and anticipates the descent of Adam and Eve from Paradise to the "subjected Plain" (12.640) that opens onto history. The episode demonstrates the persistent impulse to a premature sedentarism, the fallen instinct – prefigured by the altar "I' th' midst" – "to tread / Paths indirect, or in the mid way faint" (11.631–632). Their apostasy will be repeated in the "foul idolatries" that lead the sons of Abraham into the Babylonian captivity.[193]

The outcome of this sedentary union is the hideous splendor of the giant race before the flood and the false grandeur of the tyrannical civilizations – such as Nimrod's – that follow it. Satan's settlement of Hell continues to resonate in these episodes – both in the maneuvers and councils of the giant race and in the Babylonians' excavation of

> The Plain, wherein a black bitmuninous gurge
> Boils out from under ground, the mouth of Hell;
> Of Brick, and of that stuff they cast to build
> A City and a Tow'r, whose top may reach to Heav'n.   (12.41–44)[194]

All such misbegotten foundations follow the precedent of Cain, who embarks on a futile search for Eden, for peace and security, by going "out from the presence of the Lord" and into a land, Nod, whose name means only "wandering" (Gen. 4: 16). Thus alienated from God, he seeks security of his own making, building himself a city and calling "the name of the city, after the name of his son, Enoch" (Gen. 4: 17). With this

[193] Raymond B. Waddington, "The Death of Adam: Vision and Voice in Books XI and XII of *Paradise Lost*," *MP*, 70 (1972), p. 10.
[194] See Steven Blakemore, "Pandaemonium and Babel: Architectural Hierarchy in *Paradise Lost*," *Milton Quarterly*, 20 (1986), 142–145.

name, which means "to initiate," Cain initiates his own opposing human creation, as if God's were nothing.[195] As with Cain, an infantile attachment to the visible security of place characterizes both those antediluvians who "practice how to live secure, / Worldly or dissolute, on what thir Lords / Shall leave them to enjoy" (11.802–804) and those postdiluvians who build to "get themselves a name, lest far disperst / In foreign Lands thir memory be lost" (12.45–46). If the one embodies Satan's impulse to "reign secure" (1.261) and Belial's counsel to remain "thus sitting" in "ignoble ease and peaceful sloth" (2.164, 227), the other embodies the anxieties of Belial, who fears being "swallow'd up and lost / In the wide womb of created night" (2. 149–150), of Adam, who would rear altars "in memory, / Or monument to Ages" (11.325–326), of the latter-day wolves who will "avail themselves of names, / Places and titles" (12.515–516), and of the Milton who in 1659 momentarily despaired that the failure to build "this goodly tower of a Commonwealth, which the English boasted" would transform the nation into modern Babylonians, who have "left no memorial of thir work behinde them remaining, but in the common laughter of *Europ*."[196] In each case, the sense of identity is bound to its setting, the limits of the latter curbing the expansion of the former.

The heroes who break free of this confinement are those individuals who, unlike those "just men" who abandoned their remote hilltop seat to enter the tents of the plain, dare "single to be just" and thus come to "walk with God / High in Salvation and the Climes of bliss" (11.703, 708–709). They deliver themselves from "the secured existence of any established order," and they are the vanguard of the poem's larger movement "from the specific ... to the more general, or from the local to the universal."[197] They are the pilgrims, sojourners, and separatists who, like Noah, "remov'd his Tents far off" (11.727), and, like Abraham, left "his Gods, his Friends, and native Soil" for "a land unknown" (12.129, 134). Their original exemplar is the angel Abdiel, seen at the end of Book 5 turning his back in scorn "On those proud Tow'rs to swift destruction doom'd" (5.907). With these figures come new modes of communication, in signs and revelation, and of community, in covenant, that mark the beginnings of liberation from the bondage of place. The sign of promise in the rainbow and the shift from vision to narration that mark the transition from Book 11 to Book 12 also mark a movement – first announced in God's exhortation to "intermix / My Cov'nant in the

---

[195] I take this reading of the Cain story from Jacques Ellul, *The Meaning of the City* (Grand Rapids: Eerdmans, 1970), pp. 3–8.   [196] *Ready and Easy Way, CPW*, 7: 423.

[197] John T. Shawcross, "*Paradise Lost* and the Theme of Exodus," *Milton Studies*, 2 (1970), pp. 8–9.

woman's seed renew'd" (11.115–116) – from the infantile fixity of externalized, sedentary order to the mobility of an inward and semic dispensation. The "peculiar Nation" of Abraham's Covenant establishes a new concept in the place of place, the concept of a culture set apart, "select / From all the rest" (12.111–112). It is not so much a different place as the absence of a place that sets such a culture apart. It is while wandering "in the wide Wilderness" that this nation's people will "found / Thir government" (12.224–225), "Ordain them Laws" (12.230), and form their identity; it is while Israel is under Roman rule that the "king Messiah" is born "Barr'd of his right" (12.359–360). At its core, then, this is not a national identity in the ordinary sense; it exists, through its Law and Scripture, only to be superseded, to nurture the seeds of the semic order that will outgrow or transcend it. The seed nurtured by Israel is finally meant for all. God will "raise / A mighty Nation ... so, that in his Seed / All Nations shall be blest" (12.124–126). Canaan shall exist "that all Nations of the Earth / Shall in his Seed be blessed" (12.147–148). With the coming of Christ, "Salvation shall be Preacht" not only "to the sons of Abraham's Loins," but "to the Sons / Of Abraham's faith wherever through the world; / So in his seed all Nations shall be blest" (12.447–450). In the final Pentecostal *coup* that makes further mockery of the diaspora at Babel, a process of dissemination that originates and centers in Israel extends itself to the world's outermost periphery: "the Spirit ... whom he sends / To evangelize the Nations ... shall them with wondrous gifts endue / To speak all Tongues" (12. 497–501) – all!

This is not a unitary "all." As predicted in the Israelites' preference to "Return them back to Egypt, choosing rather / Inglorious life with servitude" (12.219–220), the allure of the sedentary will continue, from those Israelites who twice fetishize and lose the Temple to those Christians who will unbuild God's "living Temples" by imposing "outward rites and specious forms" (12.526–527, 534). Liberty, expansion, and motion will belong rather to those who inhabit Scriptural places – "places of safety under the tuition of holy writ" – which are "written in the hearts of believers through the Holy Spirit, and will last until the end of the world."[198] The great exemplar in this regard is the Christ of *Paradise Regained*, a man who has "revolv'd / The Law and Prophets, searching what was writ" (1.159), so fully as to have become one with it and thus immune to all the vanities of worldly "place" set forth by Satan. It is, in fact, precisely Christ's strict adherence to all the places of the Law that, by fulfilling the Law, becomes the new Scriptural

---

[198] *Of Prelatical Episcopacy*, CPW, 1: 627; *De Doctrina*, CPW, 6: 521.

basis for the renewal of the covenant, for the further dissemination of his righteousness and liberty to all. His achievement, in other words, is to have become that Word that transforms local servitude into universal sonship:

> True Image of the Father, whether thron'd
> In the bosom of bliss, and light of light
> Conceiving, or remote from Heaven, enshrin'd
> In fleshly Tabernacle, and human form,
> Wand'ring the Wilderness, whatever place,
>   ... still expressing
> The Son of God.   (4.596–602)

So different, then, do the courses of World and Word come to seem[199] – the one tending always centripetally to the sedentary concentration of power in "place," the other moving always centrifugally toward the expansion and distribution of liberty – that the meanings of the one, as Adam's constant misprisions suggest, can scarcely be read in the other.[200] Milton's logic would have it that there are two entirely separate meanings to the commands to "possess and rule" (11.339), to "fill the Earth, / Subdue it, and throughout Dominion hold" (7.531–532). Milton is in fact at great pains to separate these meanings, as in Satan's exasperated complaint to *Paradise Regained*'s Christ, "What dost thou in this World? The Wilderness / For thee is fittest place" (4.372–373). But just as Milton's iconoclastic rejection of the norms of pagan epic ill conceals an underlying identification with them, so his anxiousness to separate World and Word, personhood and place, hints at the ways in which the centrifugal force of his argument for Christian liberty remains inseparable from a sedentary impulse to "possess and rule the earth." The moment that defines the beginning of a universal Christian liberty is after all the moment that Christ stands above "fair Jerusalem, / The holy City," perched on the "highest Pinnacle" of the Temple, above the Mercy-seat and the very spot on which, according to Jewish legend, Cain had slain Abel at the altar (*Paradise Regained*, 4.544–545, 549). The whole providential temper of the final books of *Paradise Lost*, moreover, is haunted by the shadow of millenarian aspirations, by the temptation to read the plot of history for covergences of Word and World.

One way to underline the paradoxical relations between sedentarism and liberty would be to note that the radical individualism – the alienated sense of liberty – espoused in *Paradise Lost* is a cultural function of the

---

[199] For the opposition of Word and World, see Georgia B. Christopher, *Milton and the Science of the Saints* (Princeton University Press, 1982), p. 187.
[200] On the instability of typology in the final books of *Paradise Lost*, see William Walker, "Typology and *Paradise Lost*, Books XI–XII," *Milton Studies*, 25 (1989), 245–264.

urbanizing process at a certain stage, just as, conversely, it could be argued that Milton's ethical innovations – an affected indifference to place and a correspondingly enhanced sense of personal powers and responsibilities – are adapted to the technical needs of that stage of urbanization. Milton's strenuous attempt to divorce the courses of World and Word in *Paradise Lost* needs to be balanced against his assertion that "the church might be called a commonwealth and the whole commonwealth a church."[201] In the *De Doctrina*, one of Milton's amanuenses emended "The faithful" to read "Those who are eager to do good works, in other words, believers."[202] It is certainly true that with the establishment of an Arminian inner paradise Michael hastens to make his own amendments, adding to Adam's grasping at the straw of strict obedience a host of activist virtues, barely in time for the descent of Adam and Eve to the "subjected Plain" and "thir place of rest":

> only add
> Deeds to thy knowledge answerable, add Faith,
> Add Virtue, Patience, Temperance, add Love,
> By name to come call'd Charity, the soul
> Of all the rest: then wilt thou not be loath
> To leave this Paradise, but shalt possess
> A paradise within thee, happier far.
> Let us descend now therefore from this top
> Of Speculation. (12.581–587)

What lies before Adam and Eve at the end of the poem is not the Word but the "World."

After the Restoration, nonconformists had even less reason than other Londoners to identify themselves too closely with the urban community. "The City Air," John Howe wrote in 1685, "was much better and more healthy to me formerly, than since; the Anger and Jealousys of such as I have never had a disposition to offend, have of late times occasioned Persons of my Circumstances very seldom to walk the Streets."[203] Milton would have called Howe a victim of "custom, and a World / Offended" (11.810–811). Yet for many, spiritual alienation from the community made it possible, as Thomas Gouge explained, to "follow your worldly business with a heavenly mind, as a citizen of heaven, and pilgrim on earth."[204] Membership in the spiritual Jerusalem, Thomas Vincent explained, was what kept nonconformists in plague-ridden

---

[201] Mary Ann Radzinowicz, *Toward Samson Agonistes: The Growth of Milton's Mind* (Princeton University Press, 1978), p. 151.

[202] *CPW*, 6: 448. Cited in Radzinowicz, *Toward Samson Agonistes*, p. 155.

[203] Quoted in N. H. Keeble, *The Literary Culture of Nonconformity in Later Seventeenth-Century England* (Leicester University Press, 1987), p. 188.

[204] Quoted in ibid., p. 221.

London when its regular clergy fled in fear, just as it was membership in
"an abiding city, which the fire cannot reach" that kept Londoners from
discouragement when their metropolis was razed to the ground.[205]
Paradoxically, the spiritual liberty claimed by nonconformists was
precisely what kept them tied, generation after generation, to their
commercial and manufacturing careers.

Of greater poetic interest, however, is the fact that the most strenuous
effort in *Paradise Lost* to separate personhood and place, self and setting,
is undertaken by the Original Sedentarist, Satan:

> The mind is its own place, and in itself
> Can make a Heav'n of Hell, a Hell of Heav'n.   (1.254–255)

Satan's belief is that the mind can transfigure reality, that it cannot "be
chang'd by Place or Time" (1.253); but the outcome of such a belief –
and the belief is essential to the outcome – is to turn transfiguration into
adaptation. To say that the consolations of exiled selfhood are many is
only to say that they are endlessly adaptive to settlement and reconciliation. The point, finally, of the great philosophers of cosmopolitanism – Horace, Plutarch, Seneca – is to be at home: "One's *Patria*
is wherever it is well with one," wrote Milton, paraphrasing Erasmus, to
Peter Heimbach in August, 1666.[206] The building of Pandaemonium is
strangely unannounced, prompted perhaps by Satan's suggestion that
"these thoughts / Full Counsel must mature," but following immediately upon his defiant declaration of autonomy and illimitability: "this
Infernal Pit shall never hold / Celestial Spirits in Bondage" (1.657–660).
The cry of autonomy, in other words, is the true prompting for the
building of the first city in Hell. Later, having brought the influence of
that city to the verge of Eden, Satan can declare that he bears in his
mobility and autonomy the mark of his sedentary origins: "myself am
Hell" (4.75). The connection between these two events is perhaps
clarified by the arguments of Belial and Mammon for settlement in Hell.
For Belial, it is precisely the desire to preserve the motility of
"intellectual being, / Those thoughts that wander through Eternity"
(2.146–148), that justifies the choice of becoming "to the place conform'd" (2.216). And for Mammon, the ideal of being "Free, and to
none accountable" is inseparable from the constricting choice to "live to
ourselves" (2.252–257). In both cases, the argument for liberty and

---

[205] *Gods Terrible Voice in the City* (1667, rpt. London: James Nisbet, 1831), pp. 49–50, 77;
   cf. "A Pulpit to be Let," in *Poems on Affairs of State: Augustan Satirical Verse,
   1660–1714*, ed. George deForest Lord (7 vols. New Haven: Yale University Press,
   1963), 1: 298–301.
[206] *CPW* 8: 4. The letter is cited by Fitter, "'Native Soil': Exile Lament," and by
   Radzinowicz, *Toward Samson Agonistes*, p. 114.

autonomy is shown to be linked inevitably and fallaciously, to a constrictive sedentarism.

No more in this case than in others more familiar are the projects of *Paradise Lost* meant to be equated with the Satanic. Milton's inner paradise is diametrically opposed to Satan's inner hell. But, as in those other cases, the resemblances are revealing. The adaptive nature of Satan's strategic separation of self and setting helps to reveal the adaptiveness in Milton's own; and it helps to clarify the ways in which Milton's concept of spiritual liberty was a product of and contribution to new forms of human community as they had developed in early modern London.

Index